Psychotherapy
and Managed Care

RELATED TITLES

Psychotherapy: Processes and Techniques
Christine Brems
ISBN: 0-205-27532-X

Counseling Strategies and Interventions, Fifth Edition
Sherry Cormier and Harold Hackney
ISBN: 0-205-29347-6

Gender and Sex in Counseling and Psychotherapy
Lucia Albino Gilbert and Murray Scher
ISBN: 0-205-28502-3

Theories and Strategies in Counseling and Psychotherapy, Fourth Edition
Burl E. Gilliland and Richard K. James
ISBN: 0-205-26832-3

Room for Change: Empowering Possibilities for Therapists and Clients
Evie McClintock
ISBN: 0-205-28438-8

Introduction to Psychotherapy: Common Clinical Wisdom, Second Edition
Randolph B. Pipes and Donna S. Davenport
ISBN: 0-205-29252-6

For more information or to purchase a book, please call
1-800-278-3525

Psychotherapy and Managed Care

Reconciling Research and Reality

Catherine Hartl Chambliss
Ursinus College

Allyn and Bacon

Boston • London • Toronto • Sydney • Tokyo • Singapore

Dedicated to Chris, Jason, Brett, and Amy:
You are amazing . . . thank you for understanding

Copyright © 2000 by Allyn & Bacon
A Pearson Education Company
Needham Heights, MA 02494

Internet: www.abacon.com

Library of Congress Cataloging-in-Publication Data

Chambliss, Catherine Hartl.
    Psychotherapy and managed care : reconciling research and reality
/ Catherine Hartl Chambliss.
        p.   cm.
    Includes bibliographical references and index.
    ISBN 0-205-27950-3
    1. Psychotherapy—Effect of managed care on.   2. Managed mental
health care.   I. Title.
    RC465.5.C43   1999   98-56528
    616.89'14—dc21   CIP

Printed in the United States of America

10   9   8   7   6   5   4   3   2   1   03   02   01   00   99

CONTENTS

PREFACE

Managed care has permanently altered delivery of behavioral healthcare. Consumers and providers alike are struggling to adjust to the new emphasis on demonstrable need, measurable outcome, and cost-effective provision of services. Reconciling the empirical treatment outcome literature with these new demands for accountability and efficiency is demanding, but possible. I hope to leave practitioners optimistic about their ability to help patients in meaningful ways, while abiding by the new rules of managed care. There are constraints, and they are sometimes quite frustrating, but the evidence suggests it is still possible to do high-quality clinical work while operating within a world undeniably preoccupied by the need for cost containment.

Keeping abreast of the ever changing managed care scene has been challenging for me and for most clinicians. I'm eager to use this book to help new clinicians anticipate and prepare for the new expectations of mental health practitioners and also to assist more experienced clinicians in adapting to the revolution underway.

Psychotherapy and Managed Care is a practical overview of the new way of thinking about psychotherapy being compelled by managed care and other market forces. Rather than presenting discrete, competing theoretical orientations, this text emphasizes the findings from the "common factors" research to urge an integrative approach to therapy. In addition to examining the common underpinnings of all helpful therapies, the book reviews the solution-focused approach and brief problem-solving methods. It also discusses the specific disorders where use of particular techniques has proved to be optimal. The book examines the detailed evidence supporting specific empirically supported treatments for particular disorders and stresses the need for measurable outcomes in all treatment. Rather than limit discussion to the dwindling outpatient treatment realm of the "worried well," *Psychotherapy and Managed Care* also includes an examination of treatment strategies that work with severe mental illnesses and other refractory problems.

Psychotherapy and Managed Care presents information that will help psychotherapists-in-training respond more constructively to changes in the mental health delivery system and to the evolution of managed behavioral healthcare. It examines the pros and cons of these revolutions and develops the rationale that the growing demand for greater accountability and efficiency will ultimately improve service delivery, if clinicians contribute to the process. The book reviews the increasing pressure managed care has placed on providers and details the strategies that have helped those who have been successful in meeting the new demands.

This text reflects recent upheavals in the clinical realm and explores problems confronting future psychologists, social workers, and psychiatrists. Dramatic changes in insurance coverage for psychotherapy have made it more important than ever for therapists to know how to apply cutting-edge research in their efforts to help patients. Simultaneously, more and more of the actual counseling of patients is being delegated to paraprofessional helpers (case managers, providers of "wraparound services," etc.). Understanding the research comparing the effectiveness of professional and paraprofessional helpers can facilitate more thoughtful delegation of clinical responsibilities.

Today's clinicians need a quick resource to familiarize themselves with the major issues facing psychotherapists. This book emphasizes the role of research in improving the therapeutic process and includes consideration of current clinical outcomes evaluation methods. As future consumers, as well as producers, of clinical outcome research, many of today's mental health students need an efficient summary of the five key bodies of psychological research most relevant to managed care practice: (1) general psychotherapy effectiveness, (2) common factors, (3) solution-focused interventions, (4) brief problem-solving techniques, and (5) empirically supported treatments for specific disorders.

The Book's Structure

Psychotherapy and Managed Care begins by acquainting the reader with the philosophy and history of managed care and how this perspective challenged prevailing approaches to psychotherapy. Next, in Section II, the pros and cons (both the hopes and the fears of those in the field) are reviewed. Section III provides practical information about how to meet the expectations of managed care organizations (MCOs). Since both "MCO" and "MBHO" (managed behavioral healthcare organization) are used interchangeably, the more mellifluous "MCO" is adopted throughout this text. Section IV reviews general psychotherapy outcome research; mastering the strengths and limitations of this literature is useful in justifying the practice of psychotherapy to managed care companies. Section V provides guidelines for using three general treatment strategies, based respectively on the common factors, solution-focused, and brief therapy literatures. Section VI reviews specialized psychotherapies for particular disorders, by summarizing the empirically supported treatment research. The final section's chapter explores future trends and innovative practice directions some enterprising clinicians are pursuing. A glossary provides details on managed care terminology, and convenient lists of the most current empirically supported psychotherapies and drug therapies are also appended.

In order to help readers evaluate managed care fairly, inaccurate nostalgia is challenged and criticisms of traditional practices are discussed. In addition, a review of treatment issues that are consistent with managed care objectives is presented, encouraging readers to look at therapy in ways that facilitate working more incisively. A summary of provider accommodation research is provided to help the reader better understand the specific characteristics associated with more successful coping.

A chapter reviews the research on general therapeutic factors, which supports reliance on these common or nonspecific mechanisms of change in the majority of cases. Additional chapters examine the premises underlying solution-focused treatment and brief problem-solving methods, to help the reader consider the benefits associated with the managed care imperative for these types of concise, goal-directed treatment. Finally, summaries of the best empirically validated treatments are provided, grouped by diagnosis. These will assist clinicians in making appropriate treatment choices in those cases in which more generic strategies (common factors, solution-focused techniques, and brief problem-solving methods) have failed. Use of these summaries will streamline the treatment planning process and facilitate productive utilization review by arming providers with appropriate justifications for their treatment intentions. The book also examines strategies for integrating treatment and outcome evaluation and for conducting interdisciplinary treatment.

Applying Research

The dramatic changes in insurance coverage for psychotherapy have made it more important than ever for therapists to know how to apply research findings in their efforts to help patients. This book emphasizes the role of research in improving the therapeutic process and includes consideration of current clinical outcomes evaluation methods.

This book reconciles managed care's insistence on efficiency and accountability with conclusions based on the scientific literature. Practical suggestions are offered for implementing a "speed sequence" that matches patients' needs with intensity and intrusiveness of service delivery. The book describes ways of providing the services that managed care companies seek and using research findings to support treatment decisions. It aims to help the reader understand the empirically supported treatments that have been established to be effective in addressing the most common psychiatric diagnoses. The reader will also learn about recent meta-analytic, naturalistic, and collaborative studies, which can help in responding to some of the most pressing psychotherapy questions of the day, including: How should managed behavioral healthcare evolve? When is third-party reimbursement appropriate? How "brief" can effective therapy be?

Intended Audience

This book is directed at a broad spectrum of clinicians-in-training, including counseling students, psychology students, social work students, addiction counselors, psychiatry residents, and even primary care residents (who increasingly will be serving as mental health liaisons). Established therapists and case managers who are interested in adapting more effectively to the changing demands on mental health professionals might also find the book helpful. Agencies and group practices may also find it useful as they try to motivate clinicians to respond more constructively to the frustrations associated with utilization review and other facets of managed care.

For teachers of introductory therapy courses (at either the graduate or advanced undergraduate level), *Psychotherapy and Managed Care* would serve well as a complement to a standard therapy text that reviews all the main traditional theoretical approaches. Given its thorough overview of psychotherapy outcome research, *Psychotherapy and Managed Care* could also be used as a main psychotherapy text in a more advanced psychotherapy or practice establishment course (especially given the growing pressure to acquaint students with the empirically supported treatment literature).

Distinguishing Features

Psychotherapy and Managed Care presents an optimistic view of the future of mental health work, while providing a balanced look at both sides of the managed care debate. Unlike books that portray managed care as either all good or all bad, this text sees managed care as part of an evolution that requires the cooperative participation of informed therapists. The demands for accountability and efficiency are here to stay; *Psychotherapy and Managed Care* is a tool that future clinicians can use to help them get up to speed.

Psychotherapy and Managed Care seeks to be persuasive and practical. It enables the reader to become acquainted quickly with the dominant issues surrounding managed care and see how these relate to longstanding debates in the field (e.g.: How do we ascertain which treatments work best, when, and delivered by whom? How do we define treatment goals? How do we diagnose without creating stigma? What constitutes medically necessary care?). It provides convenient access to an enormous amount of information that future clinicians need to communicate productively with managed care companies.

Psychotherapy and Managed Care urges tomorrow's clinicians to exercise caution in aligning themselves with some managed care companies. Managed care organizations are not all alike, and providers need to use their talents to help the companies that are more quality-conscious overcome those that use unethical practices to cut costs.

Market Review

Managed care is threatening the livelihoods of established private practitioners and is revolutionizing the work of agencies and group practices. This has created an enormous appetite for current information about managed care systems, and many authors have obliged. However, no other book is designed primarily to meet the needs of today's managed care providers-in-training.

This book examines how the psychotherapy enterprise is being reexamined as a result of various converging forces. Economic pressures, spurred by managed care and state and community funding cutbacks, are making therapists more accountable and efficiency-conscious. Challenges from the intellectual community (Dawes, 1994; Lambert & Bergin, 1994) are compelling a widespread reexamination of claims of therapeutic efficacy. This book systematically integrates research findings from five separate, extensive literatures: (1) general psychotherapy effectiveness, (2) common factors, (3) solution-focused interventions, (4) brief problem-solving techniques, and (5) empirically supported treatments for specific disorders. It reconciles the conclusions of this empirical research with the changes in clinical practice that managed care has made imperative.

Managed care has revolutionized the mental health workplace. Clinicians-in-training are demanding more information about the changing terrain, yet there are few balanced books that integrate the relevant theory and research with practical suggestions.

No longer complacent, teachers widely recognize the need to restructure their presentation of information about psychotherapy, but existing books continue to emphasize more traditional theories and therapeutic tactics. This book emphasizes the need to focus training on empirically supported treatment methods, which provide the efficient, measurable treatment outcomes that managed care companies demand. A clear, concise book examining these issues is badly needed.

This book succinctly reviews the crises confronting therapists and discusses some effective responses to them. *Psychotherapy and Managed Care* is intended to help future therapists/counselors cope with the demands of managed care in constructive, positive ways. By addressing some of the field's long-held, untested, and possibly indefensible assumptions about how therapy should operate, *Psychotherapy and Managed Care* urges critical thinking and change. The book emphasizes how increased accountability can spur the field's growth and improvement, if practitioners are helped to perceive it as a challenge rather than a threat.

The Book's Intent

I hope to help mainstream therapy instructors update the training they give their students, in order to prepare students for the new challenges they will be facing as a result of managed care. Having a coherent understanding of how recent therapy research findings relate to managed healthcare companies' requirements will help these new clinicians survive professionally, while offering the most responsive treatment to their patients.

I'm extraordinarily grateful to all of those who helped make this book possible, especially my colleagues at Ursinus College. Thank you to the following reviewers of the manuscript for their helpful comments: Harvey G. Gayer, Valdosta State University; Richard P. Halgin, University of Massachusetts, Amherst;

Lynne A. Kellner, Fitchburg State College; Kathleen P. Lawless, Ocean Mental Health Services, Inc., Toms River, New Jersey; and Max Molinaro, Catch, Inc., Philadelphia. *Psychotherapy and Managed Care* attempts to articulate the essence of new therapy directions in familiar language and to couch the contemporary movement in terms of many of the major classic debates within the field. Initially, when my search uncovered a few other books with similar ideas, I was distressed. However, upon reflection I concluded that these extant books validate many of my convictions about the direction that therapy needs to be moving in and may affirm the timeliness of this treatise.

Patients, Clients, Consumers?

Throughout this book the terms "patient" and "client" are used interchangeably, as they tend to be in the literature. "Patient" may carry more connotation of distress and a quest for relief (although the term unfortunately suggests a relatively passive supplicant), while "client" may seem more "businesslike" (but fails to convey the distress that leads people to seek mental health services).

Some psychotherapists prefer to use the term "client," believing it describes a more egalitarian helping relationship. However, the Latin root for the word *client* is "one who depends." The root of the word *patient* is "one who suffers," which often captures the current status of most individuals seeking psychotherapy. Given these origins, the term "client" might actually be viewed as more belittling, condescending, and demeaning. Of course, few people are acquainted with these roots, and so the current connotations are arguably more relevant to how individuals experience and react to these different labels.

Some critics of the practice of using the term "client" maintain that for them, "client" connotes too great an emphasis on the business aspect of the therapy relationship, because some associate the term with the work of accountants and the like (Wachtel, 1993). Others actually favor "client" in part because their view of therapy in some ways parallels the practice of law, insofar as it involves intermittent expert assistance with focused problem solving. As managed care systems defray the cost of medically necessary care, many centers and practices dependent on this funding find it more suitable to use the term "patient."

Addressing this matter empirically, by surveying individuals' preferences and assessing the differential psychological impact of these labels, might be useful in guiding clinicians' use of nomenclature. Unfortunately, little work has been done, and the findings of such studies are generally ephemeral, because of shifts in common associations to these terms. A small survey of prospective psychotherapy candidates found that a third preferred the term "client," another third favored "patient," while only 10% preferred "consumer" (Reynolds, Ogiba, & Chambliss, 1998). A survey of patients in a psychiatric hospital setting yielded similar results. Although "consumer" is for many the current term of choice, some "consumers" report finding it unnatural and even distasteful. For them, instead of suggesting an empowered, discerning purchaser of services, "consumer" con-jures up unflattering images of energy consumption—someone eating and devouring . . . taking in and using up rather than giving back and reciprocating. These are hardly desirable associations for individuals with severe mental illness, who are often already saddled with feelings of failing at keeping their relation-ships with others fair and mutual. By repeatedly shifting labels, are we really doing anyone a favor?

SECTION ONE

Psychotherapy in the Age of Managed Care

When this book was started several years ago, it was unclear how radically the advent of managed care would alter provision of mental health services in this country. New terms have come to dominate the field. Behavioral healthcare has supplanted mental health. Therapists are now providers. Patients are consumers. Shifts in jargon have been accompanied by changes in how service delivery is conceptualized and evaluated. In some respects the nature of psychotherapy has been altered substantially by managed care. Therapists are now more responsible for producing efficient, measurable outcomes and must actively balance the requirements of patients against those of managed care policies. In other ways the actual conduct of many therapists' sessions has changed only negligibly. Many psychotherapists have been offering brief, focused, conscientious treatment for years and have always strived to incorporate research-based innovations in their clinical work.

Newcomers to the field may be confused by the conflicting responses of psychotherapists to the incursion of managed care; some hail its potential to improve service quality (Austad, 1996; Hoyt, 1995b; Cummings, 1997), while others depict it as evil incarnate (Shore, 1996). This book attempts to take a balanced look at how managed care has brought longstanding fractures in the field to the surface. While no easy resolutions are possible, reliance on the scientific method offers a strategy for organizing our thinking about how to respond most constructively to this new era. Empirical findings can help to clarify how much things have really changed,

Parts of the Section opening and Chapter 19 were excerpted from articles by C. Chambliss originally appearing in *Perspectives: A Mental Health Magazine*, copyright © 1996–1998, Mental Health Net (http://www.cmhc.com/perspectives/). These are included with the permission of Mental Health Net.

how successful therapists are accommodating managed care, and which thera-peutic interventions are most likely to optimize treatment outcome. Reconciling the research literature with the demands of managed care provides a basis for an ethically satisfying approach to our patients. A Chinese proverb advises that it is best to live in changing times; those in our field certainly have this good fortune. Our challenge is to respond thoughtfully and productively to this dynamic period and to make the most of the energy our changing times generate.

Protests against Managed Care Practices

Recently a critical mass of disgruntled consumers and despairing clinicians seems to have developed. Their protests against some managed care practices have already resulted in legislation limiting the freedom of managed care companies in several states. The use of gag clauses and certain provider incentives has been judged inappropriate, and practices that threaten to violate client confidentiality have been challenged. Regulatory legislation constraining the utilization review process is being considered in several states.

Lawsuits have been filed against companies that have terminated providers without cause. Several organizations are beginning to collect outcome data on the differential performance of various managed care companies, to permit payors to make more informed decisions about the relative value of different plans before deciding which to join. The media are making consumers more aware of limi-tations in their healthcare coverage; more aware laypeople are becoming more actively involved in petitioning their employers to select companies on the basis of quality as well as cost.

Providers are viewing contracts with greater sophistication and suspicion and are more likely to insist on the removal of questionable contract clauses. Some professionals are withdrawing from panels they feel demand unethical practices. A variety of alternative methods for constraining mental healthcare costs while preserving service quality are being developed by dismayed providers.

If third-party payor fee for service created incentives to overtreat, unac-countable capitated managed care systems have created dangerous incentives to undertreat. These incentives must be counterbalanced by pressures to ensure that quality care is provided. Threats of litigation, regulatory reform, and annual con-tract renewals apply considerable counterpressure to the temptation to neglect consumers' needs. In theory, HMOs and managed care companies profit by reduc-ing need for healthcare services and are therefore strongly motivated to fund pre-ventive programs to help subscribers remain as healthy as possible. However, if managers' time frames are short because of mergers and the like, and as a result there is no accountability for the long-term health of subscribers, myopic shortcuts will be favored, even when in the long run they are not cost-effective.

Correcting this new delivery system will take time, and it is understandable why many of those currently being hurt are feeling extremely impatient. However, checks and balances are rapidly being instituted to prohibit unfair practices, more accurately inform the public about managed care products, and build in greater long-term accountability for subscribers' welfare. The grotesque care-denying and reimbursement-denying practices of a few disreputable managed care organizations (MCOs) have already spurred corrective action to deter future exploitation. This seems to be part of the expected evolutionary process that accompanies any major systems change. Those who have pushed the envelope too far, the deviant outliers, help us to clarify the appropriate boundaries, in light of the vying interests involved. All those with a stake—payors, consumers, and providers—are now struggling to create a more balanced, responsible way of accommodating their conflicting needs.

The Successes of Managed Care Companies

Meanwhile, despite widespread criticism and these varied efforts at reform, most MCOs continue to grow and prosper. Their profitability has attracted eager investors and nauseated skeptical critics. Managed care companies have succeeded in curtailing the growth in mental healthcare spending, much to the delight of employer payors.

Companies have found managed care plans to be an important cost-containment tool. Offering such coverage is so advantageous in some cases that companies create incentives to enroll employees in managed care plans. For example, the Boeing Company persuaded half its U.S. work force to drop traditional health insurance coverage in favor of a more restrictive managed care plan by offering workers $600 each if they would make the switch into an HMO and another $600 if they stay in the HMO for 2 years.

While some are critical of such manipulation of consumers, for many small businesses the less expensive managed care insurance option has permitted the retention of employee healthcare benefits. Many believe that without the managed care options many more employees would be uninsured. Government is following suit, rushing to use managed care to bring Medicare and Medicaid spending under control.

Some professionals view managed care as an impetus for greater professionalism among mental healthcare workers. The elimination of fee-for-service incentives to overtreat may be viewed as reducing the iatrogenic harms (damage born of the healing process) associated with unnecessary tests and treatments and has freed clinicians to serve a broader base of clients and encouraged therapists to learn to work more efficiently. The development of standard treatment protocols has enraged those who see manuals as destroying the delicate art of psychotherapy, while it has pleased those who have been wary of the widespread deployment of treatment methods with little if any scientifically established utility. The efforts of psychologists to organize the research on treatment outcome in order to develop practitioner-friendly presentations of information on empirically supported treatments (EST) represent what some clinicians feel the American Psychological Association should have been doing all along. The American Psychiatric Association has similarly responded to the expectations of managed care companies by encouraging its members to use more behavioral impairment criteria and more systematic approaches to treatment planning and outcomes assessment.

Not All Managed Care Companies Are Alike

Some of the rhetoric about managed care has probably presented complex issues too simply. The heterogeneity of MCOs has been obscured by those who cast managed care in monolithic terms. In fact, there are a range of companies, with widely divergent policies. The important task of distinguishing between those that have managed to maintain high-quality service delivery while containing costs and others that use unethical practices is often difficult for healthcare professionals, and all but impossible for payors and subscribers.

Not All Providers Are Alike, Either

It is similarly important not to overgeneralize about the responses of mental health providers to the incursion of managed care. While some professional groups have experienced managed care to be a considerable threat to the autonomy and profits they had previously enjoyed, other groups have found that managed care has expanded their practices and possibly improved the quality of service they are offering their clients.

While psychiatrists and doctoral psychologists have felt their power eroded by managed care, social workers and nondoctoral-level psychologists working in community agencies seem to find it easier to adapt to the new demands of this system. A survey of over a hundred managed care providers revealed that master's-level clinicians expressed less overall dissatisfaction with managed care systems than did doctoral-level providers (Chambliss et al., 1996; Scholl et al., 1996).

Accountability Is Here to Stay

You may have read that many people are already predicting the demise of managed care. Many therapists can't wait for managed care to die. They actively solicit horror stories about neglect, almost seeming to hope for mass suicides to demonstrate the evils of managed care. This might leave you thinking it would be wiser to just stand back and wait it out, rather than invest a lot of energy trying to develop the skills managed care companies are looking for. This is probably not the best response, however. While the present incarnation of managing behavioral healthcare costs is very unlikely to last forever, the shift to greater accountability and cost-consciousness will probably be permanent. The autonomy previously enjoyed by psychotherapists receiving third-party reimbursement is a thing of the past.

This means that it is very important for therapists to learn the new case management skills that MCOs expect from providers, including how to match patients' needs to different services within the new continuum of care, to provide parsimonious treatment that is both least restrictive and least intrusive, to use group service delivery methods whenever appropriate, to develop clear treatment plans with measurable outcomes, and to communicate effectively with utilization reviewers. Therapists must also master state-of-the-art technical eclecticism, learning how to provide common treatment factors expediently, to conduct solution-focused therapy, to offer brief problem-solving methods, and to select the most appropriate ESTs when diagnosis warrants this.

A Caveat: Managed Care Won't Affect Private-Pay Clients

Managed care is changing how we envision and conduct therapy, but not all clients we see will choose to use their MCO to obtain psychotherapy. Many individuals who are eligible for MCO-covered psychotherapy services choose to contract privately with a provider outside their system. Over 63% (according to one study by the National Center for Health Statistics) go outside their managed care system or pay out of their own pockets. Many of these clients cite confidentiality concerns as responsible for their decision to forego their healthcare benefit. Although entitled to prepaid or very low-cost sessions, they are aware that the MCOs require providers to share considerable information about a client's problems and response to treatment, and these clients are sometimes concerned that this information might fall into the wrong hands, particularly the hands of their employers. Although there is a small risk of this feared breach of confidentiality actually occurring, as employer–MCO relationships become stronger and better publicized, it is understandable why some employees would be uncomfortable sharing their innermost secrets with a therapist compelled to open records for frequent utilization reviews.

Many clients prefer self-pay, fee-for-service consultation, even when insurance would otherwise defray the cost, because confidentiality is assured, and it is clear that the therapist is working for them alone. Dual relationships (either to an agency or an MCO) can compromise the therapeutic relationship, and many clients are willing to pay in order to avoid that possibility. They frequently feel that an independent, fee-for-service practitioner is more certain to be their advocate, without any competing allegiances.

Other clients prefer the fee-for-service route because they have heard about the restrictiveness of MCO-paid therapy and don't want to risk their treatment being cut off abruptly. Some therapists are even trying to make a specialty out of offering "no records" psychotherapy, although failure to keep appropriate records is a violation of license in many states.

Given the increasing negative publicity about managed care, until the marketplace sorts out the good from the bad, patients will probably continue doing what they have long done in the field of mental illness: Those with the resources will dig into their pockets and discreetly pay for care themselves (Brink, 1998).

While not all of your clients will be managed care subscribers, the expectations of all clients will reflect the profession's growing systematization being compelled by managed care. Managed care is encouraging all therapists to evaluate their clinical work more critically and to make greater use of research in justifying treatment decisions.

While doing therapy may be less fun for some than it was in the past, it is still possible to do good work and to find that work personally satisfying. In fact, some therapists may well be doing better work than they did in the past. The chapters that follow will discuss the new opportunities for clinicians to deploy research findings, the new threats to professional satisfaction, and some ways to help you ward off burnout and achieve enduring clinical success.

CHAPTER

1 The End of Psychotherapy As It Was

Evolution or Revolution?

Being or becoming a psychotherapist today is more challenging than ever before. Today's market will not tolerate a complacent, business-as-usual stance. The current generation of psychotherapists is being compelled to reinvent therapy, in order to meet the changing needs of clients in a context of ever increasing accountability and pressure for speed. Newcomers are exhorted to assume responsibility for adroitly deploying cutting-edge treatments, while simultaneously curbing costs. Graduate training often fails to prepare new therapists for the practical challenges they face in trying to meet patients' needs adequately in no more than six sessions.

In addition to adapting to the new demands for measurable outcomes, flexible service delivery, and efficiency derived from the influence of MCOs, therapists must sort out a wide variety of discrepant etiological models and conflicting treatment theories and methods. Beyond this, increasingly psychotherapists are being expected to substantiate their therapeutic judgments by making justifying references to the appropriate scientific literature. Both experienced and newly trained therapists are being asked to defend their choice of interventions and their use of time in a brand-new way. Sometimes it certainly feels more like "revolution" than "evolution."

The luxury of conducting unstructured, open-ended treatment, during which the therapeutic process unfolded gradually with little pressure, and in which many difficult, risky choices could be postponed, is disappearing fast. The new therapeutic challenge is to help clients make the changes they need quickly.

The privacy and isolation of the therapeutic relationship are also being challenged. The old system assumed that all licensed therapists would manage each case optimally; insurance companies did not second-guess clinicians. With managed care that presumption has changed. Utilization reviewers evaluate therapists' treatment plans and monitor patients' progress in order to avoid paying for unnecessary services. In justifying clinical decisions, therapists must make use of research findings and treatment guidelines. The need for therapists to demonstrate clinical prowess to those outside the consulting room can be both a burden and an opportunity; greater visibility places pressure on providers, but it also permits fairer allocation of resources to those offering the highest-quality services.

In responding to this new reality, it can help to revisit certain traditional assumptions about therapy that may stand in our way. The imperatives associated with managed care (do more with fewer resources) can be viewed as either a panic-engendering threat or an inspiring challenge. This book attempts to make the case that this historic juncture represents an opportunity for the field of psychotherapy to become even more consumer-centered and to integrate decades of learning about the therapeutic process in ways that will ultimately enhance the quality of service we routinely provide.

To achieve this, we must focus more consistently on the outcomes therapy is intended to produce, especially as they are understood by our clients. Working within new fiscal constraints, we have no choice but to appraise how we configure the helping process, looking closely for inefficiencies and how they might be modified. This critical stance need not make us defensive; we should recognize this field's longstanding tradition of self-scrutiny and confrontive self-analysis and how these habits have prepared us to welcome opportunities for self-improvement. We must distill the best lessons we have learned about how to promote growth, and experiment with ways of doing these things even more expediently. Perhaps in a perfect world we would cover all bases and very slowly deliberate before making any suggestions about how a client might try living differently. In our current real world of practice, cutting corners is a necessity. We need to make informed choices about the right corners to cut. Increasingly we will be expected to make some snap decisions; we want to be prepared to make sound ones.

The evolving clinician needs to move beyond angry disappointment with the escalating expectations of the market, in order to seize new opportunities to reach a larger audience with therapy and preventive interventions and to participate in improving quality of care by helping to develop meaningful mechanisms for assessing therapeutic outcome. This book developed out of my students' and my efforts to adapt to the new market realities. As we analyzed changes in the field, we came to appreciate some of the benefits of this revolution.

For example, rapid improvement was almost always what clients had in mind when they came in for treatment, even before managed care developed. Managed care companies are forcing us to create more of what clients really want: efficient therapy. Although some survey data suggest that patients in long-term psychotherapy evaluate their experiences more positively than those in shorter treatment (Consumer Reports, 1995), selection factors limit the generalizability of this finding. The fact is that the majority of outpatients have always opted for brief treatment (Garfield, 1986b). Psychotherapy has usually been short-term, even when longer care would have been partially reimbursed, and many patients have always sought solutions in one visit. Despite all the protesting, the fact is that the mean number of sessions hasn't shifted much as a result of managed care, and the mode hasn't moved at all!

Some providers bemoan the loss of discretion. On the other hand, critics of the previous system argue that autonomy was frequently misused. Lack of accountability sometimes served as an excuse for clinicians to neglect the growing empirical literature specifying optimal treatment techniques; only a minority of practitioners stayed current with the research literature on psychotherapy (Dawes, 1994). Without a mechanism for objectively reviewing the progress of treatment the potential existed for therapists to drag out unproductive therapy, so long as they didn't recognize it as such and the patients were unassertive enough not to mention it.

Although the duration of psychotherapy has been reduced in some instances, MCOs' preference for outpatient treatment over inpatient care and their sympathy toward psychological interventions that prevent more-expensive-to-treat chronic physical maladies may offset any negative impact on providers by actually resulting in increased referrals for services. This can mean that, over time, participating psychotherapists may have access to a much broader range of clients. As a result, in the future a much wider range of individuals may be helped to employ psychological findings in order to enhance their satisfaction and productivity, thanks to the changes associated with managed care. In addition, managed care's surveillance and structure should reduce the iatrogenic harms of dependency-fostering, goal-less, protracted therapy. Accountability and outcome measurement are allies of those doing good work. The new attention to quality of service will provide tools that competent therapists can use to distinguish their systematic, methodical work and articulate their successes.

Working more incisively can be threatening for some clinicians schooled in conservative traditions, which often caution against rapid intervention because clients are viewed as very fragile. Perspectives that emphasize the deficits and pathology of clients form the basis for understandable alarm at managed care's stringent restrictions on length of treatment. This book examines strategies for assessing clients' resilience, in order to allow clinicians to make prudent choices about whom to treat with briefer modalities and when and how to challenge the MCOs about inappropriate requests for treatment brevity.

Although clients and insurers generally want us to do brief therapy, many therapists have been encouraged to think of the change process as a gradual unfolding that cannot be rushed. Certainly in some cases, clients resist change efforts and clearly seem to resent being hurried. But in these cases extended psychotherapy is only one option, and often an expensive one at that. An alternative in such cases that often works well is intermittent therapy sessions, timed to maximize treatment effect. Clients and therapists can jointly plan to have meetings at strategic junctures, times when the client may be more open to consider trying new ways of doing things. Taking advantage of these periodic episodes of greater receptivity can make treatment far more cost-effective.

Therapists need to form the habit of looking more flexibly at how we do our work. Many therapists long ago parted with the "1 hour weekly" standard model of outpatient treatment. Twice monthly sessions often give clients more time to experiment with recommended changes and to obtain feedback about the effectiveness of the changes they are making. As long as the client's memory is sufficient, the reduced continuity is not so serious a disadvantage as to outweigh the improved economy of such timing of sessions.

The "long-term analysis brought to closure with a methodically executed termination" model has also been challenged by many. Well-planned terminations rarely seem to go as therapists have tried to orchestrate them. Supervisees frequently voice discouragement when their textbook-style, technically unflawed therapy termination experiences are cut short by clients who abort the therapeutic mission early or seem to genuinely feel less of a need for an agonizing parting than do their therapists. The notion that a client who returns to therapy after leaving represents a treatment failure has been widely questioned in recent years. While this kind of "recidivism" may indicate a relapse and failure to establish the foundation for maintenance of therapeutic gains, it may also mean something very different. A patient's return may be a sign of highly successful therapy, which met the client's needs so well that the client is willing to return for a reexperiencing of the valued services when faced with another time of need.

In reviewing our timing of treatment with an open mind, we can learn from other helping professionals who have used outcome data to guide their methods of timing service delivery more optimally. For example, orthodontists for years waited until an adolescent's teeth were fairly mature before applying braces to realign problem mouths. An extended course of treatment during early adolescence was the norm, and it resulted in measurable oral improvement most of the time. However, outcome studies revealed that the short-term gains associated with this way of timing treatment were sometimes short-lived. While it was relatively easy to get adolescent teeth to yield to the pressure of urging appliances, they sometimes moved back into misaligned positions easily as well. A rethinking of their intervention strategy led many orthodontists to experiment with a new, two-phase method of treatment. A brief period of intervention earlier in a patient's life, followed by a second treatment phase after teeth matured, was associated with greater long-term improvement. Achieving these more lasting results was a bit less convenient for practitioners; their contact with a given client spans a longer period over all, and during the middle period, clients pay nothing while their records and the hassles associated with them remain open. However, this inconvenience was seen as justified, given the enhanced long-term effects. Our impact on clients is far harder to x-ray, but we need to make similar use of followup information to help us develop optimal methods of timing therapeutic sessions.

Few of us have been prepared to market our practices or agencies in maximally effective ways to MCOs. Responding to the new demand to demonstrate how our therapeutic work is anchored in the research literature is equally daunting. This book was written to help providers understand both the "good" and "bad" motivations behind managed healthcare organizations; develop a therapeutic style that conforms to new practice requirements; and learn the mechanics of becoming a favored, long-term preferred provider. It will also help you reconcile the demand to stay current with the literature and incorporate new research on standardized treatment methods with the practical need to individualize therapy and tailor interventions to the idiosyncratic features of the client.

We need to learn how to be systematic without being programmatic (Magakis & Chambliss, 1997b). All too often standardized, formulaic treatment fails to engage the client as a learner and therefore fails—period. "By-the-book" psychotherapy often does not work for an individual client. Clinicians need to learn to appreciate the magnitude of the new challenge we face: to offer individualized treatment that "reaches clients where they live" and quickly makes a lasting difference in their lives, while conforming to treatment standards derived from detailed professional journal methods sections. This book will help clinicians become current with the burgeoning literature without having to sacrifice sleep.

Reconciling Research and Managed Care Practice

Ordering the Chaos and Untying the Knots

The psychotherapy field remains quite primitive, even a century after Freud started things. Part of what has held up progress involves the discipline's frequent fixation on great historical figures. We think about theories in terms of their creators, often in the fossilized form in which they were originally presented. Hero worship, as well as purist allegiance to a particular school of thought, often stymies evolution and integration. Oddly enough, for decades the majority of clinicians have actually described themselves as "eclectics," skilled in drawing from a broad spectrum of clinical theories and techniques (Prochaska & Norcross, 1994). Yet, each generation of new clinicians is presented with an uncoordinated array of competing, often contradictory theories of therapy. New therapists are largely left to their own devices as they try to synthesize the myriad ambiguous directives of their training.

The psychotherapist umbrella falls over a large number of disparate professionals, including psychologists, psychiatrists, social workers, certified addiction counselors, marital therapists, sex therapists, hypnotists, and pastoral counselors. Training of these groups varies widely. Some practitioners emphasize the "science" of therapy, others the "art." Some focus on measurable outcomes and empirical data, others on their intuitive feel for what seems to help people. They use different rules of evidence in making decisions about how to help people, which impedes communication and resolution of differences. Some believe that accurate assessment and diagnosis are absolutely crucial, while others mistrust the diagnostic enterprise and see it as harmful and dehumanizing.

According to some estimates, roughly one-third of the client population experiences a significant enough deviation from normal brain functioning to warrant diagnosis and "medically necessary treatment." This group includes patients with schizophrenia, bipolar disorder, borderline personality disorder, anxiety disorders, severe depression, substance abuse disorders, eating disorders, and post-traumatic stress disorder.

Patients with psychophysiological problems might also be appropriately included in this "medical problem" group of clients. If left untreated, patients with these conditions are at risk of failing to function independently, because of debilitating mental or physical symptoms. They may become psychotically incapable of judging reality accurately (and therefore dangerous to themselves or others), or incapacitatingly anxious or depressed (and consequently impaired in their capacity for self-care), or they may develop life-threatening medical conditions related to chronic, poorly managed stress. Health insurance should probably cover the costs of treating these fairly well-defined, diagnosable conditions; they are arguably "health problems."

This leaves the remaining two-thirds of the population seeking psychotherapy, who many believe fall into a more ambiguous group. Some are experiencing severe, acute distress related to life stressors. Their temporary difficulties in adjusting to life changes can mimic the severity of some of the conditions in the group described previously. However, the problems of these individuals are usually expected to abate spontaneously with time and informal (cost-free) support measures. Providing professional psychotherapeutic services in these cases can often help restore the clients' comfort more quickly, but such service is not, strictly speaking, "medically necessary."

Other psychotherapy consumers are seeking ways of resolving chronic relationship difficulties at home or at work. Still others are looking to psychotherapy for help in filling a void in their lives and in resolving longstanding, nagging problems with milder anxiety and depression. Changes in insurance have reopened questions about casting members of this latter group in medical terms. "Problems in living" rather than "pathology" may be a more suitable metaphor in many of these cases. If this is true, then the use of limited healthcare dollars to defray the cost of therapy in these cases may become debatable.

Clinicians have made noble efforts to harmonize theories of childhood development, well-being and healthy functioning, abnormal behavior, and change, but vehement debate is still the rule in each of these research domains, so it is no surprise that integrative efforts to synthesize everything are still premature. It may be easier to develop and use techniques that can help people to change their way of functioning than to comprehend exactly why the techniques work. While therapists would like to have a thorough understanding of why each particular strategy works, often they must proceed pragmatically without complete knowledge.

The large-scale collaborative outcome studies, ambitious meta-analytic reviews, hundreds of rigorous experimental efficacy studies, and "common factors" findings collectively demonstrate how frequently clinicians' initial hunches about why a given technique works are probably inaccurate. This research shows fairly convincingly that nonspecific elements of the helping process account for most of the change we usually see in clients. The therapist's particular choice of treatment method often makes little difference to outcome. This suggests that, if we want to improve the treatment process, we should focus more attention on maximizing these nonspecific factors, rather than fighting endlessly over the relative merits of one discrete approach versus the next.

If all methods are associated with comparable relief, our task is to discover how to supply the common, universal effective ingredients of change most efficiently and most cost-effectively to as many people who need them as is possible. Decisions about optimal treatment should ideally include consideration of overall long-term costs and risks of medical side effects, destabilization of the informal support system, and social stigma. A trial of solution-focused treatment, designed to minimize disruptive psychotherapy side effects, is consistent with our obligation to minimize harm while facilitating relief. When such a focus on patients' strengths does not suffice, use of brief problem-solving methods often becomes the treatment of choice.

In some cases these generic helping methods are insufficient. Certain patients continue to combat disabling symptoms following brief, solution-focused, problem-solving therapy. In these cases, diagnosis can guide our selection of a specific empirically supported treatment method. Research evidence favoring particular forms of intervention in the case of specific disorders permits clinicians to offer state-of-the-art techniques to appropriate patients. Customizing these methods by accommodating individuals' learning styles can help to further optimize outcome.

Efficiency and Accountability: Really Nothing New!

In some ways, MCOs are helping us be the type of therapists our training always intended us to be. Most clinical training programs in the scientist-practitioner tradition have long encouraged reliance on established, empirically verified treatment methods. Clinicians were taught the common, nonspecific factors found across different types of treatment and were encouraged to incorporate these in their work. Therapists were trained to deliver proven effective treatments as efficiently as possible. They were taught assessment techniques to select optimal candidates for specific interventions, and they explored the challenges involved in obtaining unbiased estimates of the effectiveness of treatment. In courses and supervision, they learned how to be self-critical, wary of their own motives, and skeptical about self-flattering interpretations about patients' responses to treatment. Both training and licensing encourage practitioners to be accountable to high professional standards in providing the highest-quality, ethical services to their patients.

Neil Jacobson (1995) made a compelling plea for the orientation advocated by this text:

> Today our field faces the challenge of making sure that therapy promises nothing it can't deliver, and delivers the best, most honestly presented care of which the clinicians are capable. Therapists can no longer afford to ignore the scientific foundations of their profession; science is what presumably distinguishes therapists from the expanding cadre of self-proclaimed psychics, new-age healers, religious gurus, talk-show hosts and self-help book authors.
>
> Therapists must only treat clients who have given informed consent, and they are ethically mandated to stop treatment when it is apparent that it is not working. Psychotherapists are obligated to be familiar with the research literature on whatever disorders they are treating, to present to their clients the full range of treatment options along with the costs and benefits—based on currently available information—and to refrain from overselling the brand they happen to be providing. When outcome evidence is available, it should be presented. Clients should be given the

information they need to make informed choices before being asked to consent to treatment.

Managed care services are frequently criticized by psychotherapy advocates for denying coverage for adequate treatment. In fact, managed care providers are placing the burden of proof where it belongs—in the hands of psychotherapists. It is frustrating that we cannot justify long-term treatment, nor the hiring of M.D.'s or Ph.D.'s to provide services when master's- and bachelor's-level providers would, on the average, perform just as well. We may resent having to talk to care managers, request additional treatment sessions, and lower our fees, but the demands made by managed care bureaucrats follow from the psychotherapy research literature with a great deal more logic than do the criticisms directed at them by psychotherapy lobbyists.

Becoming a Practitioner-Scientist

Research Matters: Therapists as Practitioners of Science

Psychotherapy has long been anchored in psychological research. The application of the experimental method in clinical efficacy studies has permitted us to isolate causal factors responsible for therapeutic changes. Meta-analytic reviews of the treatment efficacy literature have synthesized vast literatures and presented the general conclusions in clear, readily grasped terms. Effectiveness and process research has also illuminated our understanding of the helping process. While it is true that therapists continually blend art and science in their work with clients, they generally strive to inform their work with current research findings whenever possible.

With managed care the pressure is on to maximize efficiency and demonstrate clinical efficacy. Both clients and payors want therapy to produce rapid change. To achieve outcomes efficiently, it is important to prevent unsupported theories from burdening your work and encumbering the therapeutic process. Distinguishing research-substantiated helping techniques from those based solely on anecdotal evidence can give your work a firmer foundation that will be easier to justify to treatment reviewers.

Putting the Scientist-Practitioner Model to the Test

The heightened accountability associated with managed care compels us to stay current with research on psychotherapy. Members of previous generations of therapists often learned one "school" of thought and practiced it for decades, frequently disregarding innovations in technique associated with other theoretical orientations. Consumers were often not sophisticated enough to realize that there might be more effective strategies for resolving their problems, so they generally accepted the treatment approach the provider chose to offer.

Incidentally, those who argue that managed care has denied clients an important freedom of choice often overlook the fact that few clients previously had much information about different providers and the services they offered. Few clients sought second opinions, and most stayed with their initial choice if they continued treatment. Freedom of choice is very desirable in the abstract but may have contributed negligibly to most consumers' quality of care. Curtailed choice may be a price worth paying for more consistently high-quality, research-supported, systematic therapy.

We Don't Know It All, So Anything Goes. Wrong!

We actually know a great deal about how to optimize clients' functioning. Mental health professionals should subject their techniques to the type of scientific scrutiny found in randomized controlled experiments. According to Dawes (1994), the less they use such scrutiny, the more confident they will become that they are doing good, even when they are not. A research orientation is essential because it is easy for people to trick themselves into believing that they have special insight into the sources of psychological distress and unusual talents for remedying these problems.

Generating plausible explanations for people's problems is easy; uncritical minds will accept any arbitrary explanation that is reasonably cogent. Relying on the patient's endorsement of a given explanation is problematic. Many contradictory versions of causation may all seem plausible enough to be accepted by the patient. The therapist's expert status increases the likelihood that any story the therapist fashions will be supported by a patient who is anxious to please and be helped. Patients' agreement with our formulations cannot be taken as evidence of their validity.

Regardless of how we spend our time with patients, their symptoms are likely to diminish over time as a result of regression effects. Given that patients begin treatment in a rare, improbable state of intense distress, as treatment progresses, usually their emotional state will moderate. It is an error to take this regression to the mean as proof of our effectiveness. Couple this with the effects of support from informal helpers, habituation, and changes in the environmental stressors that precipitated treatment in the first place, and it is understandable why the spontaneous remission rates found among patients assigned to wait-list control groups are so high. Without use of appropriate control groups, it is all too easy to ascribe this naturally occurring improvement to whatever treatment method was attempted. Because patients aren't eager to believe they wasted their time coming to treatment, they rarely ask themselves what therapy uniquely contributed to their recovery. To believe treatment was a waste of time is to believe they were foolish and wasteful; it may be self-protective to see therapy as having been a wise investment.

Therapists want their patients to feel better, and they want to be competent in helping others. All mental health practitioners are therefore subject to an overinflated belief in their own effectiveness, and they should constantly subject themselves to the discipline of testing their ideas empirically or reading about others' tests of them.

According to Dawes:

> It is possible to argue that since not much is known, evaluating psychological treatment should be equally vague and uncritical. A more justifiable argument is that the less we know, the more scrupulous and careful we should be in applying and monitoring what we do know. That requires a knowledge of scientific methodology and a demand that conclusions rise to the challenge "show me"—a minimal requirement of science. . . . [T]he very real need does not justify the pretense the "something" we might wish to do—often, really, anything—is necessarily valid or helpful, in the absence of evidence that it is in fact valid and helpful. (Dawes, 1994, p. 19)

Many foster the impression that psychotherapy treatment is all a matter of opinion or conjecture. It really isn't, but many practitioners treat it that way.

> The uncertainty of knowledge and its application in the mental health area means that responsible professionals should practice with a cautious, open, and questioning attitude. . . . Instead of relying on research-based knowledge in their practice, too many mental health professionals rely on trained clinical intuition. But there is ample evidence that such intuition does not work well in the mental health professions. (Dawes, 1994, p. 49)

Medicine has repeatedly witnessed the costs associated with failure to conduct objective, controlled evaluations of treatment methods. Unjustified claims about the effectiveness of lobotomies were challenged in the 1950s, revealing the tragedies that can result when assessment of treatment effects is based solely on the subjective, poorly defined criteria of the treating professional (Dawes, 1994). When the widespread practice of removing children's tonsils was subjected to scrutiny, physicians' judgments of the need for tonsillectomies were found to be extremely unreliable (Bakwin, 1945). This meant that many cases of surgery were not justifiable, given the mortality risks associated with the anesthesia used in the procedure. Experimental evaluation of internal mammary artery ligation for angina pectoris found this standard procedure no more effective than a placebo; the risks of surgery were clearly not worth taking (Roberts, Kewman, & Mercier, 1993).

Standards and Manuals Are Not All Bad

> In a field that prides itself on its mavericks and creative innovators, from Sigmund Freud to Milton Erickson, doing therapy without training is often viewed as an indication of a willingness to reject stultifying orthodoxies and break with outmoded clinical traditions. But the argument that individual clinicians need the autonomy to work intuitively can often become an excuse for not bothering to become thoroughly prepared and knowledgeable about what has already been developed. . . . If we take our accountability as professionals seriously, we can no longer afford to ignore the state of research on psychotherapy and its effectiveness. (F. Shapiro, 1995a, p. 49)

In 1967, Arnold Lazarus coined the term "technical eclecticism" to describe therapists whose clinical strategies are scientifically grounded, but whose tactics and interventions vary with the situation at hand. He distinguished this from the "subjective and wooly, fly-by-the-seat-of-your-pants eclecticism" frequently found in therapists' offices (Lazarus, 1997). He maintains that to be truly effective, therapists must balance flexibility and sensitivity to differing patient needs with evidence-based treatment planning and execution.

Incorporating the Relevant Research into Therapy

In this age of growing accountability, practitioners need to have an organized mastery of the research that informs their treatment decisions. Systematic application of empirically supported treatments (ESTs) is replacing intuitive clinical wisdom. Our thinking must increasingly emphasize the relevant practice research. To facilitate this, several of the chapters that follow will review some psychological research literatures, summarizing the conclusions that are most relevant to the managed care psychotherapist.

First the different types of psychotherapy outcomes research will be described and critiqued. The sometimes contradictory conclusions of large-scale meta-analytic studies will be reviewed. Limitations of current research paradigms will be examined, along with recommendations for enhancing the quality and utility of psychotherapy research in the future.

Next the research on common therapy factors (also called nonspecific or universal factors) will be summarized. The specific techniques we employ often matter less to outcome than client factors such as motivation and expectation of improvement. When time is short, maximizing the opportunity for these general components of the helping process to operate becomes especially important.

Following this the solution-focused approach will be outlined. This method emphasizes patients' strengths while minimizing the potential disruptive effects of therapy that pathologizes human experiences and requires patients to focus on negative events and symptoms.

An examination of the findings about brief therapy methods follows, along with a review of some of the generic tactics for efficient, cost-effective treatment. Common strategies to help enhance patients' problem-solving skills include such things as clear goal setting and monitoring.

Next, chapters review the main ESTs identified by members of the American Psychological Association (Division 12). While the Division 12 list is in no way exhaustive, it contains examples of the treatment approaches that have been assessed systematically and found to produce effects that justify their use over alternative methods of intervention. In justifying the need for additional sessions, reviewers ask providers for detailed treatment objectives, plans for intervening, and tools for assessing patient progress. The EST literature can be extremely helpful to clinicians looking for scientifically supported modes of intervention. These treatment methods are organized according to diagnostic categories, to make referencing these ESTs more convenient.

The Hierarchy of Treatment Restrictiveness and Intrusiveness

Using Least Restrictive and Intrusive Treatment Methods

The goal of managed care psychotherapy is to achieve the greatest good at the least cost. Although cost often refers to economic price, evaluation of the cost of therapy also includes consideration of its psychological price. Unnecessary, unproductive meetings with therapists do more than merely waste money. Overly extended psychotherapy can waste the patient's time, impair self-concept, reduce self-sufficiency, and sometimes compromise relationships with family and friends. In addition, some therapy techniques produce considerable distress for many patients. The pain these more intrusive methods cause must be justified in terms of both necessity and probable outcome. Several authors have explored the iatrogenic effects of psychotherapy and have concluded that it is erroneous to think of all therapeutic experiences as at worst benign (Carkhuff & Truax, 1966; Truax & Carkhuff, 1965, 1967; Dawes, 1994; F. Shapiro, 1995).

The common factors research supports the notion that there are many equally valid technical paths to psychological improvement. Given this, it would certainly seem to make sense to select the treatment methods that are least restrictive and least risky, if they are equally effective in addressing a particular clinical problem.

Least Restrictive Treatment

The evidence indicates that while psychotherapy of any variety appears to be generally superior to no psychotherapy, longer and more intensive forms of treatment do not consistently outperform their less expensive counterparts. Brief outpatient care appears to be equal in effectiveness to both time-unlimited outpatient care and inpatient care, and brief inpatient care appears to be equal in effectiveness to time-unlimited inpatient care (Bloom, 1992). Given these findings, a strong case can be made for insisting on the use of least restrictive forms of treatment.

Cummings (1988) has invoked the concept of the "least restrictive alternative" in the psychotherapy domain and has proposed the following Patient's Bill of Rights: "The patient is entitled to relief from pain, anxiety, and depression in the shortest time possible and with the least intrusive intervention" (1988, p. 312). These notions are quite consistent with some trends in managed behavioral healthcare. Avoidance of long-term inpatient stays both reduces costs and forces development of less restrictive alternative forms of care. Avoidance of long-term outpatient therapy and greater reliance on solution-focused methods when they suffice simultaneously save money and promote use of less intrusive methods of psychotherapy.

We can imagine a hierarchy describing different therapeutic methods in terms of their relative restrictiveness (their associated loss of personal freedom) and their relative intrusiveness or psychological risks. Intensively supervised inpatient treatment on a locked unit represents highly restrictive treatment; outpatient participation in a community group meeting would be a minimally restrictive form of care.

Moving Up the Treatment Intrusiveness Hierarchy

Supportive listening and encouragement are the least intrusive, generally least risky forms of helping. Solution-focused methods aimed at identifying patients' strengths and episodes of "exceptions" to their problems offer a somewhat more structured, but still very positive form of intervention. Brief, practical problem-solving approaches might represent the next step up the hierarchy. Specific ESTs requiring patients to systematically focus their attention on their deficits and distressing or maladaptive experiences, in order to help them develop more effective coping methods, are more intrusive still. Last on the hierarchy might be treatments involving use of medications with significant risks of undesirable side effects.

All of these forms of intervention can be clinically justified, but their appropriateness depends upon the needs of the patient. In some cases the least intrusive approach suffices; in others, symptoms will persist until a powerful psychotropic drug is used. As the common factors research suggests that most techniques work comparably well, why not first try an encouraging, narrowly directed approach that appeals to the client's common sense? Our first contact with a patient should be aimed at making the best use of the patient's heightened receptivity to change at the beginning of treatment. A systematic approach to psychotherapy escalates treatment on the basis of a conscientious rationale for so doing. Sometimes less is more.

Steps of the Speed Sequence

A Research-based, Rational Progression

1. Case management: Supportive listening and encouragement
2. Solution-focused therapy
3. Brief problem-solving therapy
4. ESTs selected on the basis of symptoms and diagnosis
5. Psychopharmacotherapy based on symptoms and diagnosis

1. *Case management: Supportive listening and encouragement.* Providing this type of attention and the hope of improvement has been repeatedly demonstrated to be very helpful to many psychotherapy candidates. Studies using credible attention placebo control groups have found that the mean effect size for this sort of nonspecific treatment is an impressive .42–.48 (Wampold, Mondin, Moody, Stich, Benson & Ahn, 1997; Lambert & Bergin, 1994; Lipsey & Wilson, 1993). If this approach is sufficient in a given case, terrific. If not, we need to move up the hierarchy and contemplate using additional methods.

2. *Solution-focused therapy.* Initial use of a solution-focused approach, which is highly pragmatic and positively slanted, often makes sense. This trial of solution-focused work, which redirects clients' consciousness to their strengths, can reduce many of the iatrogenic dangers associated with other therapeutic approaches.

3. *Brief problem-solving therapy.* If the problem persists, a brief approach emphasizing problem solving and concrete behavioral change is often sufficient.

4. *ESTs.* When these less intrusive methods prove inadequate, then it makes sense to move up the hierarchy and deploy the sometimes more intrusive ESTs. Patients' failure to respond to the more general treatment approaches can also inform our diagnoses. Those who continue to have disruptive symptoms after a brief experience of solution-focused and problem-solving therapy may be experiencing a more stubborn Axis I disorder warranting use of an appropriate EST.

If the patient continues to show negligible improvement after ESTs, revisiting the diagnostic decision is often necessary. Conceptualizing the problem differently may suggest use of a different EST or recommend use of psychopharmacotherapy. Alternatively, the patient may be insufficiently motivated to implement changes at the present time. If this is the case, postponing additional treatment for a period may be the most prudent thing to do. Rehashing the same ideas week after week may be a poor use of therapeutic resources.

Empirically Supported Treatments

Today's practitioner-scientist strives to offer the most appropriate, efficacious treatment available. The literature on empirically supported treatments, or "evidence-based treatments," is of great importance in advancing the quality of psychological care we offer. The efficacy (or RCT, for randomized controlled trials) literature details the specific treatment techniques that have proved to be helpful in treating those suffering from a particular presenting problem in controlled, randomized (sometimes even double-blinded), experimental studies. These studies also often describe the comparative advantages of one approach over another.

The EST literature can be an extremely valuable resource for clinicians looking for scientifically supported modes of intervention. This book's EST Section (VI) includes description of the diagnostically relevant outcome measures that have been used by researchers. These can also give clinicians clues about measures they may wish to begin incorporating in their own work.

Having a good grasp of what the profession defines as "state-of-the-art" treatment will help to make you more confident and less defensive in your discussions with both patients and reviewers. The sprawling clinical literature can be daunting. This is probably partly responsible for why so many practicing clinicians in the past have shirked their responsibility to stay abreast of the literature; it seemed an absolutely impossible expectation to fulfill! The EST Section attempts to distill the essence of the seventy or so studies identified by Division 12 of the American Psychological Association as exemplifying some of the best psychotherapy literature available.

Making Managed Care Work

Managing Rather Than Reacting to Managed Care

The mental health and substance abuse professions are about to experience their next evolutionary wave. In 1985, few understood or appreciated how remarkably healthcare delivery would change over the next 15 years. In the next decade we will experience even more dramatic changes in the design, delivery, and financing of psychotherapeutic services. There will be many casualties, but those who anticipate and appreciate these changes will thrive (Cummings, 1997).

Industry experts and informed providers agree that the way healthcare is delivered and managed will continue to change dramatically. There are strong differences of opinion about what will happen, and even stronger differences about what should happen. But everyone agrees that behavioral healthcare delivery will not remain the same.

In the new competitive behavioral healthcare marketplace the successful practitioners are those who adopt an informed, assertive, proactive approach to managed care. The winners will be those who deliver the highest-quality and most cost-effective care and provide clear, convincing evidence of the value of their services. Practitioners must become adept at effectively articulating the clinical rationale for their services. Using patient behavior to justify particular forms of treatment, with reference to clearly detailed impairments and severity ratings, can expedite the review process. Use of behavior-focused patient objectives generates useful data for articulating the patient's progress and the need for further care, measuring patient outcome, demonstrating the effectiveness of treatment provided, and documenting the clinical competence of the provider.

Building Commitment

If you are a relative newcomer to the field, your edge lies in your having fewer calcified preconceptions of what good therapy "must be." Less experienced therapists are often adapting better than their older counterparts!

Productivity is enhanced by a sense of commitment to one's work. Motivation is higher among employees and employers who have a strong sense of purpose and find their activities in the workplace meaningful. Kobasa (1979b) established the importance of a sense of commitment to good health. She found commitment to be a central aspect of hardiness or stress-resistance.

Our resilience in the face of stress is critical to our success in being therapists. In this type of work, we care deeply about outcomes we can only indirectly influence. We frequently find ourselves in the role of mediator, needing to balance the conflicting needs of different parties (parent and children, spouses, consumers and payors, etc.). Our ability to meet the inevitable frustrations that arise in providing behavioral healthcare is central to our professional effectiveness. A strong sense of commitment to delivering high-quality psychological services within a managed care environment is required for our success in this context.

Resolving Ambivalence

In order to develop an optimal sense of commitment to being successful within a managed care system, therapists need to resolve their ambivalence about the current revolution in behavioral healthcare. There are many voices in the field, and many offer scathing indictments of managed care. The vocal, emotional critics of managed care cannot be ignored; their protests are everywhere. Impassioned arguments against managed care attract media attention, and dire predictions about the crises brewing as a result of changes in behavioral healthcare delivery are impossible to avoid.

But there are other sides to this debate, often far less publicized. Building a sense of commitment requires a critical assessment of all the issues related to the evolution of managed behavioral healthcare, with due consideration to the sources of the various positions being offered. In order to help you develop a balanced view, the following chapters provide a brief review of the history of managed behavioral healthcare and examine many of the facets of the heated controversy that has developed around it.

2 The New Era of Psychotherapy

What Is Managed Care?

Managed care is becoming the main system for healthcare delivery in the United States, and all indications are that in one form or another, it is here to stay (K. Christensen, 1995; Cummings, 1997). Of the 180 million Americans with health insurance today, 75% are enrolled in plans with some type of managed mental health care coverage (Brink, 1998). This represents a fifteen-fold increase since 1984, when only 5% were enrolled in such plans.

There is so much being written about managed care that it can seem much more complicated than it actually is. This chapter will review the basic functions, methods, and mindset of managed care systems.

In a U.S. survey of 304 managed healthcare organizations, Levin, Glasser, and Jaffee (1988) found that 97% of the HMOs offered some type of mental health coverage in their basic benefit, 79% offered twenty sessions of outpatient care, and 67% offered some type of substance abuse benefits. The survey also found that over the 10-year period from 1976 to 1986, both mental health and drug and alcohol treatment benefits in managed healthcare organizations remained constant, with a median outpatient therapy benefit of twenty sessions per member per year and inpatient benefits of 30 days per member per year.

Aggressive marketing and strategic competitive pricing explain why more than 160 million Americans are enrolled in some form of organized health-delivery system—an HMO, managed care network, or preferred provider plan (Brink, 1998). Market penetration varies from locale to locale, but the trendline is clear. In many regions of the country the majority of those insured are part of managed care programs. For example, by 1996, 85% of the Minneapolis/St. Paul population was reported to belong to managed care (Gleick, 1996).

Managed healthcare has been variously defined. The lack of standard definitions for the various types of managed care arrangements (i.e., health maintenance organization [HMO], preferred provider organization [PPO], independent practice association [IPA], etc.) makes accurate comparisons difficult (Walworth, O'Donnell, Pearson, & Solem, 1987). Anderson and Fox (1987) describe the essence of managed healthcare as being attention to both healthcare delivery and healthcare costs, in an effort to combine cost savings and quality care.

The designation "managed care" encompasses a wide range of organizational forms, financing arrangements, and regulatory devices that vary in their impact on patient care. Mechanic et al. (1995) defined the broadest use of the term as "organizational arrangements that alter treatment decisions that would otherwise have been made by individual patients or providers." They then grouped these organizational arrangements into three broad categories, all of which appear in a variety of forms but have defining characteristics: prepaid health plans (HMOs), utilization management by third-party organizations, and high-cost case management.

HMOs have become one of the most common types of MCOs serving people with psychiatric disorders. The majority of HMOs provide some coverage for mental healthcare. However, most HMOs only cover an acute care mental health benefit and do not provide any coverage for the treatment of chronic mental illness in their standard plan for private enrollees. The enactment of parity legislation in 1997 prompted some carriers to expand provisions for severe mental illnesses, but this may still be seen as a neglected area of need.

Different Managed Care Delivery Systems

Managed care has been defined as "a set of techniques used by or on behalf of purchasers of health care benefits to manage health care costs, by influencing patient care decision making through case-by-case assessments of the appropriateness of care prior to its provision" (Institute of Medicine, 1989). The term "managed care," however, is commonly used more broadly to refer to various programs designed to control access to care, types of care delivered, or the amount/costs of care. The purposes of managed care under this broader definition include cost containment and allocation of resources, as well as monitoring and improving quality and/or outcomes of care. To date, cost containment and resource allocation have been most emphasized.

Preferred provider organizations (PPOs) are networks of providers that are usually organized by managed care companies or third-party carriers. PPOs reduce their fees to attract consumers, select panels of providers who are considered to be very competent and efficient in order to attract patients and lower costs, enter into contracts with large firms to help recruit providers who hope to expand their practice, and utilize review procedures to control costs and ensure quality (Wells, Hosek, & Marquis, 1992; Zwanziger & Auerbach, 1991; Altman & Frisman, 1987). These networks constitute one of the most rapidly growing, but least studied forms of managed care.

Group practice–style HMOs rely on capitation and other incentives to provider groups to control costs, and they offer predictable premiums to attract consumers (Luft, 1978). The group practice structure facilitates access to and more selective use of specialists, including mental health specialists, often through a primary care gatekeeper (Tischler, 1990). HMOs commonly also lower costs by relying on nonphysician providers and by employing less expensive procedures like brief treatment or group therapy.

Independent practice associations, another form of prepaid care, rely on capitation and more loosely connected individual and small group practices to produce some of the same efficiencies as group practice–style HMOs (Tarlov et al., 1989). Increasingly group practices may provide care under a variety of prepaid and managed fee-for-service contracts with different types of financing arrangements for different patients. Patients, in turn, may face different types of reimbursement rules (e.g., varying co-payment levels) for different providers, especially under "point of service" coverage (Hoy, Curtis, & Rice, 1991).

Larger group practices often conduct their own managed care monitoring activities, such as utilization and peer review, precertification, and practice profiling; this offers clinicians greater control over cost-reduction and clinical decisions (Astrachan & Astrachan, 1989). From the perspective of a contracting employer or insurer, in-house management may be less costly than contracts with independent/ managed care companies, although the latter may nevertheless be called upon to act as consultants for the in-house activities.

Medicare's prospective payment system (PPS) is a form of managed care that achieves cost containment through preset reimbursement amounts, either for a given hospital or for a given diagnosis-related group. In addition, cost containment is promoted through precertification procedures and concurrent review organizations (Jencks, Horgan, & Taube, 1987; Wells et al., 1993).

Independent managed care firms, including specialty managed mental health-care firms, reflect perhaps the largest degree of diversity because they do not represent any one system of healthcare delivery, but rather offer a variety of services to employers and third-party carriers. The free enterprise inherent in private sector managed care firms leads organizations to take pride in the uniqueness of the managed care methods each practices. Many of their procedures are considered proprietary, which can impede free flow of information and obstruct comparative efforts.

Appreciating the Variability among MCOs

Managed care has been becoming the backbone of health care delivery in the United States for over a decade (Sederer & St. Clair, 1989; Ellwood, 1988). Because of its relatively recent development, fairly little is known about its effects on access, quality, and outcomes (Tarlov et al., 1989; Dorwart, 1990), partly because the term "managed care" subsumes a very heterogeneous mix of systems of care.

One common error many people seem to be making currently involves treating managed care as if it were a homogenous monolith. In reality, heterogeneity reigns. Managed care refers to a vast array of organizations that have developed highly variable standards and procedures to meet the needs of payors.

For-Profit versus Nonprofit MCOs

For many the most important distinction between MCOs is for-profit versus nonprofit. The for-profit segment, which has grown more rapidly, trades shares publicly and is not governed by the rules of charitable organizations. The administrative costs, as a percentage of income, are usually much higher in a for-profit MCO, due to large CEO salaries, dividends, and cash reserves for acquisitions. With prices set by the market nearly equal across the for-profit and nonprofit programs, the for-profit MCOs must compensate elsewhere, which may mean cutting corners in delivering treatment.

Another important distinction involves the relationship an MCO has with its professional providers, in terms of both compensation and practice autonomy. All systems have financial incentives that influence practice behavior. Individual capitation and low job/income security have the potential to threaten patient care by encouraging undertreatment by the provider. The fee-for-service model avoids this, but it alternatively encourages overtreatment and has higher costs. The group capitation model reduces both of these somewhat, by providing job security and diffusing the losses a provider faces when giving care more restrictively.

History: Why Did Managed Care Emerge?

The History of Soaring Healthcare Costs

Until the late 1970s, healthcare delivery in the United States was shaped by two axioms: "The doctor knows best" and "We must spend whatever is needed." By the 1980s, there was growing recognition that the cost of this "deluxe care" had become prohibitive.

After World War II, when many employers started to offer health insurance as an employee benefit, healthcare costs began to climb steadily. Spending on healthcare has been growing faster than the economy, rising from 8% to 14% of gross domestic product from 1975 to the early 1990s (Sperry et al., 1996). Mental healthcare costs have grown even faster, doubling from $150 per employee to over $300 between 1987 and 1992.

In the 1950s, an average stay in an acute hospital required about 2 weeks of work for the median-income American family. In 1990, despite a lower likelihood of being hospitalized and a shorter length of stay, the same median-income family had to work more than 7 weeks to pay for one acute admission (Grant, 1994). In the 1950s, getting sick meant a loss of wages; in the 1990s, getting sick meant possibly facing the leading cause of personal financial catastrophe—medically induced bankruptcy (Barlett & Steele, 1992). In 1995, 41 million Americans lacked healthcare coverage, and the worrisome economic prediction is that by the year 2000, more than 20% of the population from ages 21–65 will be uninsured unless broad reform measures are undertaken (American Medical Association, 1995). Expectations are that the growing elderly population, increasingly expensive technological advances, expensive malpractice settlements, and mounting advertising expenses due to growing competition among healthcare providers will continue to propel healthcare costs even higher.

Historical Need for Managed Behavioral Healthcare

Although all healthcare costs have been disturbingly on the rise, spending for mental healthcare in particular skyrocketed in the 1980s. Employers faced a 50% increase in expenditures for psychiatric inpatient services between 1986 and 1990, yielding increases in insurance costs that threatened to make policies unaffordable for many small businesses. Some form of mental health cost containment was required. Most blamed for excessive spending were inappropriate hospitalization practices, especially with certain target populations such as adolescents and substance abusers. Suspected overutilization of unmonitored, long-term outpatient psychotherapy services also contributed to the urge for reform, although the actual contribution of these outpatient services to spiraling healthcare costs remains undetermined.

In an effort to limit mounting costs, many state legislatures licensed more mental health professionals, including social workers, nurses, and marriage and family counselors. Many insurance companies reimbursed these professionals, who offered a cheaper alternative to treatment than did doctoral-level psychologists and psychiatrists. Although this was intended to restrain costs, instead the expansion of the pool of providers was actually associated with an increasing demand for treatment, resulting in further cost increases.

For many years, corporations assumed a relatively passive attitude toward these rising costs and continued to rely on group indemnity insurance plans. However, as costs continued to escalate, corporations found themselves under increasing financial pressure, and as a result they began exploring ways to contain healthcare insurance costs.

The Evolution of Behavioral Managed Care

Mental Health Service "Carve Outs"

Most managed healthcare plans included behavioral health (or mental health) services (Levin, Glasser, & Jaffee, 1988). There was an increasing demand for managed care strategies for the delivery of mental health and substance abuse services. Mental health and substance abuse benefits were often specified and managed separately from general health benefits in employer-sponsored insurance (Hoy, Curtis, & Rice, 1991). Responsibility for oversight of mental health services has often been separated out, or "carved out," of health insurance plans and delegated to specialized managed behavioral healthcare firms.

Managed behavioral healthcare (MBH) started with a handful of external review companies that began overseeing the utilization of inpatient mental health benefits. These review companies gradually became dominant players in the healthcare marketplace, making up a managed behavioral care industry that generates yearly revenues in excess of $1.9 billion (Goodman, Brown, & Deitz, 1992).

Most managed care contracts initially provided only administrative services; the MCOs were not at financial risk if they overspent in authorizing care, and there was no direct financial incentive for them to restrict care severely. As time went on, MCOs began to develop contracts that placed the MCO at risk financially. Soon capitation became standard in MBH.

Capitation

With capitation, MCOs were compensated with a fixed monthly fee for each subscriber to the plan. Contracts that specify a preset "per head" (hence "capitation") payment discourage those holding contracts from providing services (tests and treatment) beyond a certain spending level. In some of these "carve-out" arrangements, MCOs contracted with provider groups to administer service delivery provided under a capitated contract, making the providers themselves "capitated." Capitation rewards MCOs and providers who offer efficient, effective treatment and those whose emphasis on prevention obviates the need for more expensive procedures and hospitalization.

With capitation, MCOs were required to provide adequate levels of care to patients for a fixed annual fee set by the payor. Money left over after paying for care and overhead expenses was the MCOs' profit. Case management and utilization review became more intensive with MCO capitation.

Utilization Review

MCOs generally subject all behavioral healthcare practices, inpatient and outpatient, to rigorous utilization review. To justify services, providers must show their scientific basis and demonstrated capacity to benefit consumers (clients and payors). Prepaid group practices primarily lower costs by reducing inpatient care. However, this is not always associated with increased outpatient care. They also lower costs by substituting costly outpatient services with less intensive and less expensive outpatient services. The use of utilization management generally saves the greatest amount of money by reducing length and frequency of hospitalizations; some research seems to indicate that it has only been effective in cases with groups that had previously experienced above-average expenditures for these services. Utilization review is believed by some to have the potential to improve the standards of appropriate treatment in areas where practice variations are large, by encouraging all providers to make use of more optimal forms of treatment.

Incentives for Delivering Appropriate Care

Balancing the factors that might encourage a capitated provider to undertreat are the professional duty to benefit and not harm patients, professional and personal integrity, and accountability for consumer satisfaction and peer respect. In order to secure annual contract renewals, MCOs must satisfy their corporate payors by offering a competitive price for behavioral healthcare and satisfying the needs of the consumers who subscribe to the plan. Consumers need to see services as contributing to desired clinical outcomes as they understand them (see earlier discussion of clients' goals). They typically expect prompt, responsive, individualized care that addresses their presenting problems and produces discernible change. Employers expect reduced absenteeism and increased work productivity as a result of their offering a mental healthcare benefit. Employer-sponsored health prevention and service programs, including employee assistance programs (EAPs), originated in attempts to improve work performance and job stability (Jerrel & Rightmyer, 1982). Additional, external forces that encourage a proper level of care include treatment guidelines, peer review, fear of malpractice litigation, patient feedback to payors, and legislated regulation.

The most financially successful MCOs were those capable of eliminating all unnecessary healthcare services and effective in compelling clinicians to choose the least expensive forms of healthcare delivery. These companies generously rewarded their executives and shareholders and still had resources left over to buy smaller companies and expand their territory.

When case management interrupted traditional indemnity reimbursement for mental health services, many clinicians felt besieged by the new demands of managed care. Time-consuming telephone tag, ever expanding required paperwork, and the need to justify both level and type of care choices made many providers regret the development of managed care.

On the other hand, corporate payors were thrilled by the success of managed care in reining in runaway behavioral healthcare spending. An illustration of how managing behavioral health can benefit payors is provided by the experience of IBM. When IBM adopted a managed mental healthcare contract, costs declined significantly from $97.9 million in 1992 to $59.2 million in 1993.

Meanwhile, capitation rates kept going lower and lower, under pressure from large corporations as well as from partnerships between corporations and insurers who were trying to drive down costs (Sperry et al., 1996). With many competing HMOs and carve-out firms in the field, behavioral healthcare had gradually become a commodity, with sales driven by price. Because there were few measures of care other than price, contracts generally went to those with the lowest bid, whether or not the services being provided were the best in terms of rate of patient improvement or long-term cost-effectiveness.

Enhancing Value through Better Outcomes Assessment

When price is the sole basis of competition, the pressure to decrease profits becomes relentless. Buyers seek the cheapest price, driving down the MCOs' profits. However, when MCOs compete on the basis of value, their profit margins are more protected. The corporate purchaser is then making a decision to buy on the basis of value, which does not necessarily push the MCOs' profits downward. For this reason, as managed care continues to evolve, it is to the advantage of competing MCOs to encourage corporate payors to attend more to value and cost-effectiveness, rather than focusing on price alone.

It is also advantageous for potential patients to demand attention to value and to urge their employers to consider more than price in evaluating different insurance contracts. Patients are no longer shielded from the escalating expenditures for healthcare by traditional indemnity insurance. They are becoming more informed healthcare shoppers and are expected to increasingly influence how care will be delivered.

Currently many companies are looking for ways to reduce costs while maintaining or improving the quality of care. However, determining the relative value of competing MCOs is not always easy. For example, time perspective influences estimates of value. An investment in current care that significantly reduces the need for future spending on care will seem very valuable if one adopts a broad time frame, although it may seem wasteful if one has only a short-term perspective. In assessing the value of behavioral healthcare, it is also important to recognize that value may mean different things to the patient, his or her family, the clinician, the employer, the community, the government, and the society at large. Each constituency uses different criteria in evaluating quality. When a family has a member who is suicidal, the fact that a treatment site is open 24 hours a day may be of enormous value. The employer may appreciate brief family interventions that allow the worker to refocus on the job as quickly as possible. The community may value effective treatment of substance abuse patients who might otherwise be involved in street crime.

More and more employers are looking for an effective approach to improving value and enhancing cost-effectiveness by monitoring outcomes in mental healthcare treatment (Sperry et al., 1996). Assessing outcomes offers MCOs a way to compete on the basis of quality as well as cost. However, finding accurate measurement tools to evaluate the effectiveness of treatment has proved to be extremely difficult.

Measurement is challenging because of the complicated mix of levels of care, types of care, and diagnoses that characterizes current behavioral healthcare. In many cases inpatient care has been replaced by different levels of care, ranging from residential; to full- and part-time day care; to regular outpatient sessions with a clinician and different types of care, including individual or group therapy, medication, or shock therapy. This can make measuring the cost-effectiveness of a particular treatment for a particular patient very challenging (see later section on outcomes assessment for additional information).

The Rapid Pace of Change

Although the growth of healthcare spending in the United States has recently slowed somewhat, spending is still rising. A 1998 report indicated that annual U.S. healthcare spending growth dropped to a record low 4.4% in 1996, but overall expenditure still managed to top the $1 trillion mark for the first time ever (Levit et al., 1998). Statisticians at the Health Care Financing Administration's (HCFA) Office of the Actuary reported that, after adjusted for inflation, overall spending growth dropped to just 1.9%, the lowest level in HCFA's 37-year history of record keeping. However, the proportion of the U.S. gross domestic product that Americans spent on healthcare in 1996, 13.6%, remained unchanged from that of the previous 4 years. Annual per capita spending on medical costs actually rose by $126 to $3,759 per person.

Most of the slowed inflation in health spending can be traced to curbs on private-sector spending; between 1975 and 1989, healthcare spending in both the private and public sector increased by nearly 12% each year. By 1996, the private sector had managed to reduce that annual increase to just 5.8% per annum, compared to 9.8% for public-sector expenditure (Levit et al., 1998). According to Levit et al., this suggests that managed care payment incentives and public program initiatives aimed at slowing healthcare spending growth have had a real impact on healthcare costs. The longstanding gap between the rate of inflation for healthcare expenditure and the general inflation rate continues to narrow. However, savings by private insurers and MCOs may not translate into savings for consumers, because premiums are now rising steeply after years of only modest increases.

Annual growth in Medicare spending has also decelerated, from 10.6% in 1995 to 8.1% in 1996. Some of that deceleration may be due to massive reductions in the annual growth of Medicare expenditure on home-based and nursing home care, which has fallen from nearly 60% in the early 1990s to 13%–14% in 1996. Other influential factors include recent legislation putting caps on Medicare payments to providers and government crackdowns on fraud and abuse. But the study also found that, despite cutbacks, Medicare spending grew at a rate 4.9% higher than that of the private sector. This has raised concerns among policy makers that Medicare is not as capable of controlling growth in spending as are private health insurers.

Some segments of the healthcare system showed greater cost reductions than others. Spending on hospitals and physicians was either stable or declined in 1996, although HCFA experts say bills for these two services still account for 54% of total spending. Expenditures for prescription drugs (9.2% annual growth), home healthcare (6.2%), and other personal healthcare services (9.4%) continued to rise during 1996 (Levit et al., 1998).

In many areas of the United States, the face of managed care is literally changing monthly. Mental health agencies and provider groups have been unable to plan even for the next 6 months with any assurance about the validity of their current assumptions about funding, city and state regulations, and which managed care companies will be dominant.

Despite this rapid state of flux, providers can prepare themselves by mastering certain essential skills. Although the specific details of managed care will certainly continue to evolve, general underlying principles of effective managed care practice will remain stable. The chapters that follow will help you master the basics necessary to work well within the developing behavioral healthcare system. No one is predicting a return to the times when third-party reimbursement was almost entirely at the discretion of the professional providing treatment. The need to learn how to work within a framework of greater accountability to payors, while remaining appropriately responsive to the needs of clients, will not go away!

The Goals of Managed Care

The primary goals of managed care are to control costs and increase treatment efficiency, availability, and quality. The dual objectives of cost reduction and enhanced clinical effectiveness create challenges for providers and MCOs alike.

The main goal of managed care is to limit unnecessary medical utilization while not withholding necessary and efficacious medical care. This goal is achieved by a care manager, who is responsible for treatment decisions about expensive diagnostic procedures, inpatient admission, or referral to specialists, or by a third party, who reviews such decisions and assesses their validity. These treatment decisions can be influenced by any one or all of the following: budget constraints, financial incentives for providers, and review of treatment plans against criteria defining appropriate care. These influences can alter the treatment practices of therapists in MCOs.

These managed care goals are typically accomplished in several ways. Therapists report to care managers or gatekeepers who, guided by managed care policies, restrict the therapists' treatment decisions and control referrals for specialty services. Financial incentives are used to influence providers to choose the least expensive mode of therapy. Care managers, upon reviewing medical records, have the right to deny therapists payment for any medical care they deem unnecessary. Managers, both implicitly and explicitly, ration certain services.

Participating in the Evolution

This industry is in a tremendous state of flux: The cast of characters changes regularly. While the profit motive may incline some companies to neglect clients and undertreat, counterbalancing this force is the MCOs' need to satisfy payors and maintain consumer satisfaction, as well as fear of malpractice litigation.

Vocal opponents of managed care have already organized effectively in several states, which are evaluating legislation that would give the government power to oversee managed care companies, credential utilization reviewers, regulate administrative costs, prohibit gag clauses, and the like. While many believe that additional reform is inevitable, few ever argued that the first generation of managed care companies were performing their duties perfectly.

While some insist that ethical psychotherapists have no option but to abstain from involvement in managed care, others feel the involvement of those with high integrity and professional standards is vital for the proper evolution of this system of managing care. Reasonable critics operating within the system will allow their voices to be integrated into the developing processes of managed care; their voices can help to curb inappropriate excesses. Those who turn their backs on managed care will not make it go away; it will simply fall into the hands of less proficient providers, who may lack the experience and/or judgment to rein in its inappropriate extremes.

This is not to say that appropriate legislative reform is unnecessary. This industry needs some regulating and mandates to disclose, if clients are to be appropriately informed about their benefits. During this period of transition, it seems important to recognize that any systematic shift toward greater constraints on reimbursed treatment would feel like an assault on established providers who had comfortably accommodated to the old system. While the current incarnation of managed care is few people's idea of ideal (those splendidly paid CEOs are probably the exception, of course), many believe the status quo is just a point on a trendline of difficult but necessary reform. This conceptualization argues for greater participation among those with the greatest experience in meeting the public's mental healthcare needs. The alternative would almost seem an abdication of professional responsibility.

The Hopes and Dreams: The Rationale for Managed Care

The most optimistic voices suggest that once the bugs are worked out, MBH will offer advantages to various constituencies. Consumers will benefit in several ways, because managed care is prompting much-needed reform in how their needs are met.

By compelling more up-to-date implementation of research findings, patients will receive more cutting-edge care. By making therapists more accountable, through capitation and utilization review, unproductive treatment will be more promptly revised. Managed care companies insist that providers offer high quality, timely treatment and have mechanisms for offering emergency care.

Greater use of brief and outpatient treatment may well reduce the iatrogenic harms associated with certain traditional psychotherapy practices. Use of impairment indices and symptom severity rather than traditional diagnoses permits more exact communication about the need for treatment and reduces the risk that global labels will limit patients.

By keeping costs down, use of brief, outpatient, group therapy methods and paraprofessional providers may ultimately increase access to psychological care and permit more individuals to benefit from services. Managed care may bring down the out-of-pocket costs and potentially reduce the stigma associated with obtaining mental healthcare.

The expanding continuum of care offers clinicians more options. More flexible treatment delivery, duration, and dosage can help clients by creating more opportunities for individualization of care.

Corporate and governmental payors will benefit from the cost-containment strategies that managed care is using to keep healthcare insurance costs down. Better-quality psychological care is also expected to improve workplace productivity. Both corporate and government payors should also benefit from the medical cost offset associated with effective psychological treatment; early treatment of psychological problems should prevent the development of some medical problems, reducing the need for some types of costly long-term health care, given

Fifteen Potential Advantages of MBH

1. Greater accountability may enhance treatment quality.
2. Capitation may inspire preventive approaches.
3. Utilization review may educate providers and raise standards.
4. Treatment guidelines may make optimal treatment standard.
5. Use of an impairment index may orient care to relevant behaviors.
6. Justification for services may reduce waste and harm.
7. Medical necessity criteria may curtail rambling therapy.
8. Greater use of community resources may improve care.
9. Brief, outpatient, group, and paraprofessional care save money.
10. Appropriate treatment may be more widely available.
11. Increased access may reduce stigma of help seeking.
12. Continuum of care includes flexible delivery, duration, and dosage.
13. Use of symptom severity analysis may compel the least intrusive care.
14. Attention to outcomes may reward the best therapists.
15. Data collection may improve knowledge about psychotherapy.

the association that exists between psychological stress and compromised immune system functioning.

Providers who embrace the opportunity to develop effective, innovative, financially sound methods of psychotherapeutic intervention can become highly successful under managed care. Those who collaborate with researchers in trying to find better, more relevant answers may make a lasting contribution to the field. The chance to work with a larger, more diverse group of consumers and to contribute to preventive programs that seek to reduce the incidence of serious psychological disorders will hopefully offset some of the lost opportunities to develop deep, long-term relationships with clients.

SECTION TWO

The Managed Care Maelstrom: The Battle, Protests, and Reforms

The sometimes malicious debate about managed behavioral healthcare continues to intensify in many regions of the country. Many providers are angry and eager to eliminate the profiteering "managed care middlemen" from behavioral healthcare. Defenders of managed care construe the angst associated with ever-shifting contracts, late payments, and malfunctioning data analysis programs as the inevitable growing pain associated with system development.

Seligman and Levant (1998) and others persuasively challenge MCOs' inappropriate use of research findings to justify cost-containment practices which reduce the quality of care. On the other hand, Cummings (1998) argues that managed care has been an unrecognized and unappreciated benefactor to practitioners; without it, he believes healthcare benefits would have priced themselves out of existence. Attempting to integrate both elements of this dialectic are voices like that of Monica Oss (1998), who writes about the need for balanced judgment in the evolution of our thinking about best practices.

Advocates for consumers and providers must acknowledge the constraints imposed by payors; the need to develop more cost-effective services predates today's MCOs. It is difficult to ascertain how many resources we should be devoting to behavioral healthcare; any answer to this question is arbitrary. As providers, if our expectations of insurance are excessive, "covered services" will always seem inadequate. As the joke goes, the question may not be whether the glass is half full or half empty, but whether the glass is too big.

3

A House Divided

How Managed Care Has Fractured the Field

The expansion of MCOs has set off an acrimonious battle within the helping professions. Providers who actively participate are often viewed as traitors by those who cast managed care in evil terms. Some particularly histrionic professionals have even gone so far as to liken the process to that of Nazi Germany and to describe those providers who collude with the "enemy" as immoral, unethical, and corrupt. They characterize the MCOs as paternalistic, dictatorial, and totalitarian.

Critics perceive those providers who cooperate with managed care to be "defeatists" because they are resigned to working within the system. On the other hand, these "defeatists" see themselves as "realists," eager to collaborate in evolving more fiscally accountable, efficacious treatment approaches. These providers frequently view the critics of managed care as myopic and nostalgic people who are thinly veiling their self-serving position with rhetoric about the quality of patient care. The critics' unwillingness to contribute to the evolution of managed care is seen as an abdication of professional responsibility.

The Despair: The Battle against MBH Problems

Managed care has its enemies (including many mental health professionals) and its enthusiasts. Critics have coined a variety of disparaging names that capture their distaste, including mangled care, mismanaged care, damaged care, managed neglect, discounted care, Shop-a-Doc, Gag Me with a Spoon Care, and managed chaos.

Managed care has inverted payment incentives, paying set fees that encourage therapists to make their profits by shortening treatments. Many therapists argue that the pressure to cut costs is restricting the type of treatment being offered and how long it can continue. Mental health professionals are increasingly disenchanted with managed care. Some argue that promises of innovative quality care have been subordinated to profits through cost containment and that the needs and concerns of patients and healthcare professionals are considered last, if at all.

Twelve Arguments from the Advocates of Managed Care

1. The old system of benefits was wasteful; healthcare costs spiraled out of control.
2. Greater financial accountability and emphasis on efficiency were needed. The fee-for-service system created an incentive to overtreat.
3. The old system was ultimately exclusionary because of its inefficiency. Forty million plus are uninsured now, presumably because of skyrocketing costs.
4. Long-term psychotherapy is unethical. Research has generally failed to support the superiority of lengthy outpatient treatment. Progress in therapy usually plateaus rapidly (Howard, Kopta, et al., 1986).
5. Unnecessary psychiatric hospitalization is unethical. Research has shown the iatrogenic harms of inpatient care.
6. Brief, solution-focused, cognitive therapy is highly effective and is far less expensive to dispense.
7. Most outpatient psychotherapy has always been short-term: it is what clients want.
8. Nondoctoral-level providers may be as effective in delivering services, and they're far cheaper.
9. The development of empirically supported treatment protocols will improve the standard of mental healthcare.
10. MCOs must manage delivery of care because the providers were derelict in policing themselves sufficiently. Sixty percent of the doctors admit they "game the system." They lie and break the rules, to be paid for uncovered services. They apparently feel "above the law" and therefore require close policing.
11. MCOs can conduct large-scale research to discern appropriate lengths of treatment for particular diagnoses and detect superior specialists by referencing comparative statistics.
12. MCOs can conduct large-scale consumer satisfaction research to attune services more effectively to clients' needs.

Twelve Arguments from the Opponents of Managed Care

1. MCOs maximize profit by neglecting patients' needs. Authorization of care is frequently denied; criteria keep shifting. The new incentives favor undertreatment.
2. Utilization review compromises the doctor–patient relationship. Untrained, overworked utilization reviewers impede quality care. Nondisclosure rules erode trust and are unethical. Utilization review violates confidentiality.
3. MCOs exploit naive providers who are willing to endure the burden of excessive case loads, underpayment for services, and excessive assumption of legal liability. MCOs thereby limit patients' choice and create discontinuity of care.
4. MCOs ration via inconvenience. Consumers are deterred from seeking specialists or second opinions by intimidating referral paperwork. Providers are punished for seeking authorization by having their time wasted. When they cave in and see the client without approval, they are never reimbursed for providing the treatment.

5. Consumers will gradually realize how their care has been compromised. MCOs have exploited consumers' trust in physicians by hiding changes in medical practice by keeping doctors quiet with gag clauses. Patients assumed nothing had changed when in fact the new reinforcement contingencies in a capitated healthcare practice reward physicians for keeping patients away. Capitated providers are paid per covered life, regardless of whether clients obtain treatment. While this could theoretically increase provision of high-quality preventive care, the frequent mergers that have dominated the field have fostered very short-term thinking.

6. Managed care CEOs are making extremely high salaries without being accountable for the long-term health consequences of their decisions, because buyouts are the rule and corporate longevity is rare.

7. MCOs represent wasteful, bureaucratic middlemen who provide no real valuable service, yet extract huge profits from the pool of money available for healthcare. Outpatient psychotherapy was not responsible for escalating mental healthcare costs. It is not cost-effective to manage outpatient care; the savings come from reducing expensive inpatient care.

8. MCOs rely excessively on the least-well-trained, least-expensive providers of care and psychotropic medications. Controlled studies raise questions about the efficacy of the antidepressants often favored by MCOs. A *Consumer Reports* study (1995) found that clients preferred long-term outpatient therapy, and least preferred care offered by marriage and family therapists.

9. MCOs have engaged in a sleight of hand. They have siphoned off the more healthy consumers (e.g., those who don't expect to need a specialist's services), which has exaggerated the savings attributed to the MCOs. They are dumping the costly care folks on the states and the prisons.

10. Sixty percent of doctors must "game the system" to protect their patients' welfare. Their manipulation of the criteria is a sign of their necessary and appropriate advocacy for patient rights.

11. In profiling providers, MCOs unjustifiably assume that providers who are outliers are offering inferior service, when their atypical conduct may in fact be attributable to an unusual case mix.

12. MCOs' outcome research often overemphasizes trivial indicators (e.g., the number of telephone rings before a staff member answers). Furthermore, its huge scale obscures negative outcomes. For example, if 95% of a 2 million–member sample is satisfied, is that sufficient, given that under 3% of the population have severe mental illness? The healthy individuals who don't need care may be delighted at lower premiums. The 100,000 consumers who are frustrated by denials of care they need become part of a statistically insignificant minority.

The perceived abuses of many managed care companies include compromised patient confidentiality, pressures to homogenize treatment, inefficient management from a distance, and profit margins well in excess of most businesses.

Objections emphasize the perception that managed care companies extract obscene profits from the healthcare system by denying needed care, unnecessarily threaten the autonomy of providers, and compromise patients' rights to informed consent and to confidentiality, through gag clauses, incentive systems, and close utilization review procedures. The following section reviews both the concerns about the adverse impact of managed care on patients and the problems that managed care has created for providers.

The Downside for Patients: Cost Cutting Compromises Care

Karon (1995) decries the cost-cutting methods that some feel have purged healthcare of its traditional commitment to quality. These have included neglect of prevention programs in high-risk populations, excessive reliance on medication rather than psychotherapy, substituting less expensive personnel as caregivers, and restricting the scope of behavioral health services actually provided. Karon maintains that, in some cases, quotas were established that dictated how many patients must be processed per hour.

Access to Care

Some critics believe that managed care companies wish they didn't have to make provisions for psychotherapy at all, and that they only do so because excluding it would interfere with recruitment. Critics maintain that the aim of most MCOs is to provide as little psychological care as possible, while seemingly providing adequate mental healthcare. According to Iglehart (1996), HMOs currently spend only 3% to 5% of their treatment budget on mental health, which many see as inadequate. Federal HMO guidelines focus on brief, crisis-oriented care (Talbott, 1981). It has been estimated that approximately 10% of those who seek mental healthcare cannot be managed within the usual HMO restrictions (Carr-Kaffashan, 1989).

There is widespread concern that managed care may be applied to the treatment of the mentally ill and substance abusers in ways that neglect the special needs of these populations. For example, there may be a failure to identify enrollees with severe mental illnesses, and therefore these individuals may receive less treatment. With capitated systems, financial incentives favor neglecting the care needs of chronically mentally ill patients. So long as failure to provide care does not result in blatant evidence of negligence (death or serious injury to self or others) that could form the basis for costly litigation, many capitated organizations will be financially rewarded for looking the other way and ignoring the misery and isolation of their severely mentally ill enrollees. Alternatively, organizations that respond conscientiously to the sprawling needs of these draining patients will be at serious financial risk. In competition with service-denying companies their contracts will probably not cover anything like the true costs of providing the necessary care required by the severely mentally ill. The "good guys" will lose and the callous will win, unless appropriate safeguards are put into place.

The mandated minimum coverage (twenty sessions per member per year and inpatient benefits of 20 days per member per year) has become the maximum benefit in many organizations. Clients often expect to receive full mental health benefits when they seek care, and they are frequently upset to discover barriers, such as co-payments, complicated screening methodologies, and treatment limitations. If the economic interests of managed health plans result in more obstacles than do traditional indemnity plans to accessing mental healthcare (e.g., mandatory physician referrals, long waiting lists, triage screening prior to therapist assignment, approval of therapy sessions in small numbers), then managed care is less advantageous for consumers (Richardson & Austad, 1991).

Increasingly policies' mental health benefits cover only crisis intervention and stabilization, not treatment. A subscriber might have coverage for up to twenty sessions of outpatient therapy and 20 days of inpatient treatment, but this only covers acute care and stabilization. Some providers have expressed concerns that such policies will create a serious bind when they conduct evaluations on individuals who have serious problems that could be treated effectively and efficiently (such as obsessive-compulsive disorder), but the client is not in a formal crisis. If the insurance company won't approve treatment and the client can't afford to pay out of pocket, some wonder what providers will do.

The insurance company's solution might be for providers to refer such clients to the local community mental health center, but many of these sites have few staff members who have training in treating certain specific disorders, and furthermore, as funding streams for community mental health centers shift, their ability to subsidize treatment is rapidly diminishing. This system creates an incentive for clients who want treatment to go into crisis, or for therapists who want to provide treatment to lie about the client's status. This highlights the importance of understanding the plan you're participating in and being sure that participating is ethical and legal, not simply financially viable.

Managed care has made the process of getting treatment more challenging for many patients. Brink (1998) found that, in many of the big systems, patients call a toll-free phone number and begin pouring out their problems to a stranger, who decides if a referral for psychotherapy is necessary. If getting into proper care is hard, staying in treatment can be next to impossible, given the stringent requirements for utilization review. Psychotherapy is often approved for three to five visits. Thereafter the patient or therapist must argue for each subsequent visit.

Another limitation of managed care is that subscribers in typical HMOs must choose their providers from those within the system instead of having free choice. In addition, most managed systems do not permit patients to consult a specialist directly but instead require that a client receive a referral from the primary healthcare provider to the specialist. This gatekeeping process reduces unnecessary and expensive visits to specialists, but can inconvenience consumers. If such practices are used in an organization with a small number of providers, other problems result, including long wait periods for appointments and assignment to nonpreferred providers. Especially for mental health services, few providers or areas of specialization may be available (Richardson & Austad, 1991).

Quality of Care

The financial motivation of managed care insurers sometimes undercuts and denies competent standards of practice provision of mental health services. Patients are more likely to get a drug treatment for a mental problem than ever before, even though some studies show psychotherapy is sometimes a better choice. Brink (1998) found that therapists themselves report that they are increasingly pressured by the managed care industry into prescribing drugs even when patients don't want them. Paul Ling, a Quincy, Massachusetts, psychologist and co-founder of the Advocates for Quality Care, says, "I have personally been told that if the patient does not get on an SSRI [selective serotonin reuptake inhibitor—the new class of antidepressants that included Prozac], they will not authorize any psychotherapy."

A June 1996 article in the *Arizona Republic* by Steve Wilson maintains that antidepressants are being overprescribed:

> Primary-care physicians, who have little or no psychiatric training, are delivering 65 percent of the psychiatric care in this country and doing it primarily with drugs. About 43 million prescriptions for anti-depressants were written in America in 1995. Sales of Prozac, Paxil and Zoloft were up 24, 35 and 45 percent, respectively, in 1995.

Wilson voices concern about the growing power of the drug companies over healthcare. Drug companies are spending lavishly to advertise prescription drugs such as Serzone and Effexor directly to consumers, encouraging them to believe their pills can cure whatever is bothering them. A 1998 Associated Press report indicated that in the past decade there had been a 20% increase in the share of doctor visits resulting in a prescription for psychotropic drugs. In terms of percentage of total psychotropic medications prescribed, antidepressant prescriptions grew from 30.4% to 45.2%.

Primary care physicians receive little if any training in psychotherapy and consequently rely heavily on medication management when confronted with psychological disorders. MCOs see this as very cost-effective, as they can limit the cost outlay for psychotherapy by treating primarily with medications. Primary care physicians are cutting costs by prescribing the majority of psychotropic medications and refraining from making referrals to specialists, despite the fact that psychiatrists may be more familiar with the complexities of using some of the newer medications and conducting symptom-focused pharmacotherapy.

Referrals for counseling to master's-level providers also have cost advantages, as these subdoctoral counselors tend to adhere more to the cookbook guidelines established by the MCOs and are reimbursed at a lower rate. One care manager stated off the record that MA/MSW-level providers "took direction better and didn't give us as much trouble." Several MCOs use paraprofessionals (BA or less) and nurses to do intake assessment, case management, and utilization review. Access to a doctoral-level professional is often only obtained after an appeal for review of a refusal to reimburse care on the grounds that it is "not medically necessary."

Although research has thus far failed to establish the superiority of highly trained professionals in providing structured psychotherapy, some studies have found that professionals perform better when treatment must be brief.

Confidentiality

The introduction of utilization review has prompted serious concerns about patient confidentiality. Since the earliest days of psychotherapy, confidentiality has been seen as one of the fundamentals of treatment, a prerequisite for giving patients the freedom to explore their innermost feelings and fantasies. Indeed, many therapists say, confidentiality is to therapy what a sterile field is to surgery—a basic requirement of good practice. But even as the use of therapy is expanding, with more kinds of professionals seeing more patients, the confidentiality of psychotherapy is being eroded by a wide variety of outside forces, including the spread of managed care, the computerization of medical records, and the use of therapists' notes and records in law enforcement.

In justifying care, providers are expected to share increasing amounts of information about patients' symptoms, treatment goals, planned interventions, and patients' responses to care. As consolidation continues and MCOs increase in size, enveloping smaller companies, the risk to confidentiality is increased. Patients' records are placed in a computer database, making care managers and other administrative personnel working in the MCO privy to unguarded information. Before managed care such files were considered privileged information and they were more closely safeguarded; in outpatient cases, therapists would often even challenge court orders attempting to access protected information. Now outpatient therapists are routinely expected to discuss cases over the phone with utilization reviewers. Therefore, some feel that the nature of the confidential therapeutic relationship has been dangerously uprooted by the advent of the MCO and the ubiquitous utilization review.

In interviews with providers and consumers, Brink (1998) found that the heavy dose of bureaucracy in managed care systems increases the fears of some mentally ill consumers who need help. The stigma attached to mental illness keeps many people silent about their problems. Professionals are united in the belief that for therapy to work, people must believe that their secrets will never leave the therapy room. But managed care's requirement that therapists prove that continued treatment is medically necessary gives people reason to worry about the HMO staff violating the sanctity of the treatment relationship. Ironically, the harder the therapist lobbies for more treatment for a patient, the more likely it is that increasingly personal details will be released to insurers.

Although many MCOs pride themselves on responding promptly to client calls, some practices may result in miscommunication that deters actual treatment. Some fault the current managed care intake interview process, because it subtly discourages clients from pursuing the treatment the clients initiate. Many of the patients interviewed do not return for treatment through the managed care company because they don't expect to get treatment. Some don't realize that the person conducting the intake interview was not the psychotherapist and that the discussion was not meant to be a therapeutic session. When clients don't feel the intake session helped, they quit. This is advantageous for the managed care company, but obviously a problem for consumers. Clearer communication with clients is needed, but the managed care companies that profit from clients' ignorance are unlikely to initiate these improvements without some external prodding.

Potential Conflicts of Interest

Questions have been raised about the ethical and practical soundness of current managed care systems because they pursue contradictory goals. Although the goals of managed care purport to be in the best interest of the patient, often they conflict with the financial interests of the MCO (Rodwin, 1995). MCOs have the following objectives: Reduce expenditures and the use of services, increase efficiency, eliminate unnecessary and potentially harmful treatments, provide better or more desirable treatments for patients, expand the range of services offered, and improve patients' quality of life.

These objectives can jeopardize the integrity of the therapist's decisions and cause divided loyalties because of competing obligations. For example, a care manager, in order to reduce expenditures and the use of services, may require a physician to use a less expensive and less effective treatment that the physician knows may be detrimental to the patient's quality of life. Increased efficiency and provider productivity may cause the patient to receive less individual attention. Conversely, the reduction of medical costs will benefit patients in that it will lower their premiums and perhaps ultimately make healthcare more widely available.

Informed consent, which requires physicians to explain to patients the choices available, the risks and benefits of any proposed treatment, and any alternatives, is being compromised because providers do not inform patients of their restricted clinical choices. Public policies need to be developed to mitigate these conflicts of interests.

Evidence of Medical Harm

In the medical realm a 1996 study reported in the *Journal of the American Medical Association* (*JAMA*) indicated that fee-for-service, private care benefits patients. The study looked at over 2,000 patients with high blood pressure, non–insulin-dependent diabetes, recent heart attack, and depression. Physical and mental health status was measured over 4 years. When recipients of care through PPOs were compared with those getting care in private offices on a fee-for-service (FFS) basis, researchers found the following:

Elders with decline in health: PPO = 54%; FFS = 28%.
Poor who improved in health: PPO = 22%; FFS = 57%.
Elderly and poor whose health declined: PPO = 68%; FFS = 27%.

Primary care physicians (PCPs) are under pressure to handle more and more matters they ordinarily would refer out. There are increasing data showing that PCPs often misdiagnose skin cancer, depression, and other conditions. An October 1996 *JAMA* study from the University of Pittsburgh showed that, when severity of illness was controlled for, intensive care unit use did not differ between managed and non–managed care patients. Possibly MCOs just look successful because they have skimmed off the cheaper-to-treat cases.

The Downside of Managed Care for Providers

The downside of managed care from the providers' perspective can be distilled into nine major objections:

1. Managed care companies interfere with the doctor–patient relationship in that they attempt to (and do successfully) dictate treatment.
2. Managed care companies demand sensitive information about patients in great detail, without statutory or any other credible assurances that confidentiality will be protected.
3. Managed care companies are making huge profits, made obscene by the fact that they are derived from money being diverted from patient care.
4. Managed care companies have reduced the healing arts to accounting, with an emphasis not on cost-effectiveness, but on profit.
5. Managed care companies have created a climate of fear in the professional community—fear of advocating for the care doctors believe their patients need.
6. Annual recredentialing fees and recredentialing assessments are thinly veiled profit-making schemes.
7. Clinical judgment and patient choice produce better outcomes than case management does.
8. Long-term therapy works more effectively for certain conditions and is worth the cost.
9. Licensed and experienced doctoral-level providers do a better job of diagnosis and therapy than do relatively untrained master's-level providers.

Autonomy

For providers the new increases in accountability for treatment outcome have been ironically accompanied by reduced control over how they provide their patients' treatment. The demand to be measurably efficacious is threatening to providers who feel they must surmount new hurdles to keep patients in treatment.

Mental healthcare professionals are experiencing frustration as their ability to dictate the necessary course of treatment for their patients is threatened by utilization reviewers who authorize services. These care managers assign patients to the least expensive appropriate treatment in the name of cost containment (Iglehart, 1996).

Managed behavioral care companies limit services by permitting patients to use only preferred panel providers who have been approved by the MCO. These providers consistently have their decisions reviewed and are monitored closely, especially in the treatment of chronic patients who pose a greater cost risk for the MCO. Mental healthcare providers thus feel their autonomy and incomes slipping away.

Ivan Miller (1996) has challenged the scientific validity of some of the research supporting managed care practices. Miller is vice-president of the National Coalition of Mental Health Professionals and Consumers, the nation's largest grass-roots anti–managed care organization.

In justifying the use of time limits in psychotherapy, MCOs have often referenced a group of research studies that purportedly prove the superiority of time-limited therapy (TLT) over clinically determined therapy (CDT). In the latter the length of treatment is more fluid, being determined by the client and therapist. Miller argues that design flaws in these studies have resulted in significant misinterpretation and misrepresentation of the empirical findings. For example, several studies lack comparison groups, and two others compare completed TLT cases to partially completed CDT cases. In one, Miller found that the researcher deleted statistics indicating that CDT might occasionally be superior to TLT.

Lester Luborsky's influential 1975 meta-analysis of several early studies favorably comparing TLT to CDT repeated a researcher's unjustified conclusion about the superiority of TLT. The error was compounded because inappropriately the researcher had reported three times on the same study.

Miller strongly believes that the claim that TLT is superior to CDT remains unproved. For problems such as phobias and depression, time-limited therapy is by and large effective for the average person (Cooper, 1997b), but there is no evidence that it is the only or best therapy. While Miller does not dispute that short-term therapy can be an appropriate clinical approach, he believes that decisions about treatment length should be based on clinical judgment, rather than predetermined on the basis of cost. Miller maintains that setting stringent limits on the number of sessions without regard to individual variables, such as patients' personalities or larger systemic influences, is ultimately unjustified by anything other than short-term profit concerns.

The Inefficiency of Outpatient Utilization Review

Psychotherapists have found the process of utilization review (UR) a cumbersome nuisance that frequently places them in an adversarial stance with the managed care company, feeling the need to fight for the opportunity to offer patients the treatment they require. Phone tag with utilization reviewers often delays approvals long enough that concerned providers go ahead and treat without authorization. This works to the MCOs' advantage, because they will then generally deny payment on the grounds that it was never authorized.

In opposing current UR practices, some clinicians have invoked the "Goldwater Rule," which refers to an ethical principle adopted by the American Psychiatric Association following many members' questionable responding to a magazine's poll of psychiatrists during Goldwater's presidential bid. The principle states that psychiatrists should not render opinions on the diagnosis of patients they have never met. Some believe this rule should be applied to reviewers, who not only comment upon or contradict diagnoses but also challenge treatment plans for patients they have never met. These critics believe that the insurance company consultant should see the patient in person and provide a written consultation to the therapist for the hospital chart. The report should meet all the standards of the clinical community and be contestable in court if adverse to the patient or supportive to charges brought against the therapist or hospital if the treatment is fraudulent. While "costly" compared with phone calls and the like, the presence of respected consultation might decrease the antagonism of therapists.

However, some companies that are trying to implement face-to-face evaluations are finding that many clinicians seem to feel even more threatened by these than by phone reviews. One supervisor for a major behavioral MCO commented:

> With utilization review at a distance, reviewers are not there to see the clinical picture. It feels like an infringement for clinicians and it makes it tricky for us because we never quite know if/when we're being "snowed." That is why our company has implemented a face-to-face evaluation program in which we send out our consultants to see the patients in person and make their own assessments. As far as antagonism from providers, I can tell you that while some facilities have agreed to allow our evaluator/consultants on their premises to provide this "service," there have not been a whole lot of providers lining up for this opportunity. Even at facilities where we have made agreements to do evaluations, many psychiatrists feel incredibly antagonized and do not see the opportunity to use it as a forum for engaging in a meaningful dialogue about what might be the best treatment for that patient.

Critics argue that outpatient UR can be a wasteful process that increases administrative costs dramatically. Most outpatient cases tend to be brief, anyway, so the savings associated with close monitoring may be negligible and more than offset by the costs of the utilization reviewers' salaries.

While UR has proved cost-effective with inpatient care, questions remain regarding its utility for outpatient care. Zach and Cohen (1993) maintain that utilization reviewers do not provide any added care and may actually increase administrative expenses as much as 20%. A study in the *New England Journal of Medicine* concluded that the administrative costs of UR could consume as much as 50% of total healthcare spending by the year 2030 (Schilling, 1993). Increasing assumption of UR responsibility by providers may remedy this inefficiency, if they can demonstrate an appropriate level of fiscal accountability.

Critics of outpatient UR argue that, as outpatient psychotherapy was not responsible for previous soaring healthcare costs, constraining it will not produce useful savings. Analyses of utilization patterns have shown that all or almost all of the increases in mental health and substance abuse treatment costs were due to the increased costs of inpatient care. Arguably, outpatient care kept people out of the hospital and actually saved money. Sixty to 70% of those hospitalized had bypassed outpatient care, thereby circumventing the outpatient gatekeeping function.

Many analysts believe that the real behavioral health savings lie in reducing inpatient care. Schilling (1993) states that 70%–80% of all mental health dollars presently are spent on inpatient care, even though about 50% of hospitalized patients could be cared for as effectively in less costly outpatient settings. German (1994) concurs, reporting that approximately 70% of mental health dollars in the United States were spent on inpatient care, despite a decade of clinical research demonstrating that outpatient treatment and in-home care can be as effective as inpatient psychiatric treatment. A 1996 BellSouth study has shown that mental health spending can be cut in half while increasing psychologist visits 99% and psychiatrist visits 226%, if you use outpatient and partial treatment rather than inpatient care. Therefore, employers are turning increasingly toward managed care systems to reduce unnecessary hospitalization.

Excessive Profit Taking and Administrative Overhead

Marvin Berman (1997) offers a very critical view of current trends in managed care, arguing that soaring profits for CEOs and stockholders have provided the funding for the large-scale mergers that now dominate the healthcare delivery system. For example, a 1996 survey reported a 7.7% jump in median hospital CEO pay, which eclipsed the 2.7% pay hike received by the average U.S. worker in the same period.

Managed care has not yet proved itself a cost-containing, efficiency-maximizing ideal. The extravagant profit taking of some MCO executives has understandably been unsettling for many. For example, the February 5, 1996, issue of *Time Magazine* included an article (p. 45) about the generally increasing compensation rates for all corporation CEOs. It notes that, compared to their peers in companies of comparable size and performance, the executives of managed healthcare companies are obtaining more than twice the compensation of their counterparts. An example given exemplifying this disparity was that of Daniel Crowley, CEO of Foundation Health Corporation, who averaged $6.1 million annually over the last 3 years. Crowley's compensation was reported to be 277% of that of his counterparts in other industries.

Despite their reputation for skyrocketing profits, recently there have been signs that some managed care companies are starting to experience less financial success. Some critics argue that this may be associated with the expansion of managed care to include subscribers from populations with higher rates of healthcare needs. The aged, poor, and chronically ill (groups with high mental health service needs) have until recently been underrepresented in many managed care or HMO systems, because most of these plans are directed to employed persons and their dependents, and therefore younger and healthier populations (Feldman, 1986). Critics argue that this selective enrollment may be responsible for much of the savings being attributed to managed care practices.

Some fear that in protecting profits during this more challenging period, many managed care companies will further jeopardize the welfare of consumers. The reality of limited resources may necessitate better coordination of healthcare delivery. Many oppose using managed care as a means of denying needed benefits or services in order to shift money to managerial and investor levels, under the guise of "cost control" and utilization management.

A February 1996 *American Journal of Public Health* report challenged the notion that managed care has pared wasteful administrative practices. This study showed ballooning numbers of healthcare managers (a 700% increase from 1968 to 1993), with an accompanying decline in the percentage of caregivers (from 51% to 43%). MCOs' administrative overhead is seen by some as astronomical; estimates run as high as 55%. Furthermore, the creative accounting some companies use to calculate overhead can obscure actual allocation of resources. The insurance companies consider everything they pay to the MCO as going for "patient care" (Miller, 1995). In addition, Cunningham (1995) cites an example of an HMO placing UR in the category of "patient care expenses." This is in addition to all of the administrative work that is done by the provider (still classified by the MCO as costs devoted to patient care). The result is that figures exaggerate the expenditures on services that actually benefit consumers.

Providers criticize MCO decisions to deny or limit treatment to people who have paid for coverage. Some perceive the desire to please stockholders as having overrun concerns for quality care. The interests of the patient should not be subordinated to the interests of the corporation, yet some contend this disgrace is pervasive.

The elimination of access to effective treatment methods by arbitrary administrative cost-containment decisions, moving patients to the lowest-cost providers without regard to the standards of care, and intrusions into the confidentiality of the psychotherapy relationship are serious problems cited by concerned providers. The pressure to move toward "capitation" contracts is also alarming to those who feel providers are unreasonably accepting increasing shares of the risk without commensurate advantages; they criticize state legislatures for permitting this to occur.

Ware, Lachicotte, Kirschner, Cortes, and Good (1998) conducted an ethnographic study focusing on clinician experiences of managed care at a mental health and substance abuse service of a community mental health center near Harvard. Their data suggest that for the practitioners they interviewed, "the threat lies in the prospect of being gradually, unknowingly, and unwillingly transformed from critics into proponents of managed care, and losing their particular moral vision of communitarian mental health in the process." Ware et al. describe how managed care evokes in clinicians a moral dilemma that transcends issues of professionalism.

The intent of managed care is to ensure that care is efficiently produced and that the limited resources of the community are wisely allocated. This was the original ideal of community healthcare. However, some argue that in recent years the community's interest has been supplanted by corporate interest. "One generation's socialism became the next's capitalism" (Starr, 1982). Psychotherapy has traditionally been practiced by professionals who see themselves as working in the general interest of the community. Many therapists feel deeply committed to a moral vision of mental healthcare, which is currently being disrupted by the pressures of managed care (Ware et al., 1998).

According to Martin Seligman, the survival of psychology as a profession and as a science is being jeopardized by managed care. In his words:

> As a profession, practitioners, particularly long-term therapists, are being forced out of the market by short-sighted health schemes, which often are run as much by greed as by concern for patient well-being. Those patients who need longer term treatment are routinely denied the full treatment they need and are routed to cheaper and briefer alternatives—which work much less well for them.
>
> As a science, government funding and the availability of academic jobs are in drastic decline. Scientists at the top of the feeding chain are in trouble, and you can imagine how desperate things are for the new Ph.D. Amplifying these troubles is the fact that practice and science—natural allies—don't get along at all well. Only when practice flourishes does science flourish, and only when science flourishes does practice flourish. (Seligman, 1995, p. 974)

Seligman and Levant (1998) attack MCOs' reliance on an inadequate scientific foundation.

> Being an experienced, highly trained doctoral-level psychologist and skilled in long term therapy has become a disadvantage, rather than an asset, in today's market. Is there empirical justification for cutting length of therapy and lowering the qualifications of mental health providers? We do not think so and conclude managed care organizations (MCOs) have seized upon inappropriate and inadequate data to rationalize their downsizing of mental health care.
>
> The conclusion from a review of both (the therapy efficacy and effectiveness) literatures: 1.) For some patients certain short term treatments are likely to work well and provide considerable benefit. 2.) For other patients long term therapy is necessary to produce substantial gains. And, 3.) Focused clinical effectiveness studies of the duration of therapy for different disorders and its cost–benefit ratio are urgently needed. Unfortunately, the current state of affairs allows MCOs to continue justifying predominantly brief therapy. They claim—citing only the efficacy literature and ignoring the effectiveness literature—that only brief therapy has been "empirically validated" and long term therapy has not . . .
>
> In our judgment the scholarly argument for less qualified providers is (also) seriously flawed. It wholly relies on studies where manuals are used, mild and uncomplicated clinical problems are diagnosed (by doctoral level providers), and duration of therapy is very brief and fixed. This is precisely where clinical judgment, experience, and education matters the least. . . . Effectiveness studies of level of education, qualifications, and experience of providers for different disorders, severity, comorbidity, and cost–benefit analysis are urgently needed.
>
> Some MCOs "justify" using less experienced and less well-trained providers even in complicated and severe cases. We believe patients are being deprived of adequately skilled treatment on a massive scale. Until this issue is resolved by

appropriate clinical effectiveness studies, public policy should err on the conservative side and provide highly qualified providers in all but the simplest cases. (p. 211)

Individual Providers Complain about Managed Care

. . . I'm now in over 100 panels. They have made my professional life a nightmare of applications, dreadfully conceived credentialing forms, inane telephone and paper reviews, arbitrary authorizations and per hour income reduction. But what are my choices? I ignored managed care for years and nearly went out of business. My income dropped 40% in just one year. I have seen very competent clinicians go under. If it were not for gaining admission to panels, I would now be out of business.

Our clientele cannot and will not pay us privately. It seems to me that it is indeed a reality that if one wants to stay in practice, one must deal with managed care.

The frustration associated with overly restrictive treatment protocols of one established MCO provider is clear from the following statement:

A managed care organization has taken over management of the mental health benefits for a local HMO which accounts for perhaps 20% of our referrals. The new MCO has come up with some "interesting" treatment protocols. For example, their care managers tell us they are only allowed to authorize up to four sessions for the treatment of Major Depression, four sessions for Dysthymic Disorder, six sessions for Obsessive–Compulsive Disorder, etc. They don't simply mean that after this number of sessions we need re-authorization. They mean that this number of sessions should be all we need and that to get additional sessions we have to get a "medical review" by one of their psychiatrists and then maybe a few more sessions will be authorized.

We do state-of-the-art short term treatment, but obviously the time frames they have in mind are absurd. We immediately took this up with the executives at the MCO and they promise that the policy will be changed. If not, we'll have to drop them too, because we don't feel we can ethically start treatment knowing that long before treatment is completed we'll face a choice between abandoning the client because they can't afford to pay out of pocket or accepting a fee lower than we can afford in order to allow the client to complete treatment. If we have to drop this plan, it will be a financial hardship, since they account for a significant portion (20%) of our referrals.

This highlights the importance of not becoming too reliant on one HMO or MCO, because when their policies change, providers can be hurt financially. It also illustrates the importance of protesting blatantly problematic guidelines, because the company in question did revise their policy a few months after the complaints were made.

A particular managed care company requires me to fill out a lengthy and intrusive form about the client and his/her personal and familial history with mental illness and prior counseling—which may or may not have anything to do with the presenting problem. In the past, I have told "customers" of this managed care company that if they wish to protest this procedure I will support them. (I usually fill out the required form and show it to them in advance. I try to keep the revelation of personal information to a minimum.) So far, no one has wished to protest this practice. My hypothesis, of course, is that clients feel helpless and/or reluctant to protest for fear of losing their coverage. But I do not pursue this directly in therapy because at that moment it seems to be more my issue than theirs. I feel reluctant to impose my agenda, even though it may involve a therapeutic issue for them. I focus more or less exclusively on the therapeutic issue without tying it directly to managed care or to their reluctance to object to managed care practices. Yet it is my perception that if these clients were emotionally healthy they would protest the practices. I think that some providers are handcuffed by their very ethical principles. They end up unable to assist clients in protesting managed care practices which are clearly unethical and not in clients' interests.

Managed care sometimes ends up benefitting from emotionally unhealthy attitudes of clients who fear retaliation, rejection, and minimization of their emotional status. This seems to operate against mental health patients much more insidiously than against medical/surgical patients.

MCO Insiders' Frustrations

An anonymous, disgruntled former managed care provider shared some insider experience that may be helpful to those deliberating about joining forces with MCOs.

While some of my colleagues were competent therapists, others were not. In fact, the Peter Principle was alive and well. In one instance, the utilization reviewer screamed down the hall, cursing about how stupid providers were because they kept asking for authorization to hospitalize clients. This reviewer had three answers for such requests: "No," "NO," and "Damn it, NO."

In another instance, it was discovered that our office manager had been referring clients to her husband, a local marriage and family therapist, and that there had been no checks or balances to prevent this from happening. Case reviews were often embarrassing assaults on the abilities of the providers. The lack of professionalism was sad. There was only one way to do therapy, and providers were often not given further referrals if they called to consult on a case or ask for more visits. These attitudes were expressed by employees who had graduated from a program supposedly providing them with systematic training in marriage and family therapy.

The treatment of in-house personnel was no better. We were expected to have over 30 bookable client-contact hours each week. That meant that if every slot was booked and everyone showed up, we could be expected to see over 30 families, complete hours of computer case notes, manage outside cases, act systemically to connect with other community resources, etc.

Another disgruntled provider also chose finally to abandon managed care. "I no longer see managed care cases as I feel that the oversight is far too destructive to the therapist/patient relationship to permit psychotherapy to occur on any meaningful level. And the breach of privacy and confidentiality is insurmountable."

Another "provider casualty" wrote:

> I'm giving up, after losing the managed care fight. As a psychologist who has been in private practice for about 10 years, I realized last night that it was almost time to pay another estimated tax payment. I will have to liquidate some of the resources that I thought I would live on when I retire.
>
> I think I am a good therapist. I have built a practice doing work that I am proud of. I read about how long term therapy was a thing of the past and thought, "So what?." I have done brief problem focused cognitive and behavioral therapy since the beginning.

Reform Efforts: Working toward a Better Balance

At this point there is a power struggle going on between major players in the healthcare arena who are struggling to contain costs and to maintain their piece of the trillion-dollar pie. Some of these players are HMOs, PPOs, employee assistance programs, managed care companies, hospitals, insurance companies, big business, government, consumer organizations, labor unions, provider organizations, etcetera. These different groups have competing, divergent, parallel, complementary, or similar interests and agendas, and, to complicate matters further, each are often owners (full or part), owned, or in partnership with each other.

There is a compelling need for therapists to interact with the major players in the healthcare drama. Some recent articles in the press suggest that the form that managed care takes is partially a function of the political situation in a given location, and there can be major differences in offerings and profit margins within the same company in different locations. It is imperative that providers be organized on a local level, as well as on the state and national level.

The most effective provider groups to date have included psychiatrists, psychologists, and social workers. Each of these professions has access to information about different parts of the healthcare system, and with cooperation and support they may effectively counteract the "divide and conquer" tactics sometimes practiced by managed care companies.

There are many potential allies who are invested in quality care for their constituency at a fair price, and these allies have considerable influence and are frequently receptive to provider-furnished information. Examples would be consumer advocacy groups, labor unions, EAPs who use managed care companies, state government agencies such as civil service bureaus that have the task of analyzing the performance of managed care companies and influencing which ones continue to offer services and which ones don't, the public health department, state and national legislators, and big business itself (they don't want striking workers or too many missed workdays). There are also allies in HMOs who are committed to providing quality care. The influence of some of these groups has been demonstrated in Rhode Island, as well as in the Ohio audit and findings regarding Medico Behavioral Care. In addition, impressive reforms have been made in many states through legislative action.

Strong efforts are underway to change perceived abuses of both patients and clinicians. People have organized efforts in Michigan and other states to address these problems. Since 1993, a group of Michigan providers has worked with employer groups, labor, insurance companies, HMOs, and other entities to preserve the right of subscribers to see the clinician of their choice and the right of providers to make independent clinical decisions. The Michigan group has defeated the efforts of MCOs to develop provider panels exclusively featuring master's-level therapists, and they continue to work to make changes that truly benefit the subscriber, not just the clinician.

Given the capitalistic model that shapes the way we conduct business in the United States, we probably should realize that third-party payees have always restricted funding for mental healthcare, even before formal "managed care" came to be. It is important to keep in mind that insurance companies are businesses. They pay for services that people use as part of their healthcare benefit. They try to do it in a way that yields a profit. In the long run, competition is good, because it provides for checks and balances and allows the consumer, in our case the subscriber, to receive a good product at a good price. It is our task as providers to make sure the subscriber will still be able to use our services in the future.

For years many providers have been committed to a number of principles: fighting on behalf of anyone who seeks our services, not acquiescing to any demands that violate the privacy of our clients, and not continuing to work with insurance or managed care companies that deny individuals the right to choose their own therapist or restrict the clinical decisions by the treating clinician. Generally such providers have been successful because they provide high-level clinical services and are well known by the employer groups that hire these MCOs to handle the mental health benefit. By adopting positions advocated by trusted providers and making them clear, employer groups have insisted on changes in policy by the managed care companies, protecting the subscriber's freedom of choice and the clinician's clinical autonomy.

Beneficial changes are coming about as a result of providers challenging managed care practices in their communities. In Michigan, for example, Options, which won the contract for State of Michigan employees, has now started a new program called CareFirst, in which they will no longer micro-manage the outpatient benefit, but rather will simply grant the whole benefit up front at the start of treatment. They have eliminated the need to seek reauthorization for further sessions and similar constraints. This seems to have come about because of many clinicians speaking out against the previous model, as well as their own internal realization that it was a ridiculous waste of money to micro-manage the benefit.

The way psychotherapists will have continued relevance and impact will be by delivering good clinical services, demonstrating their competence within our communities, being known to the business community where the decisions are made about the healthcare benefits for employees, and bringing about reforms in managed care that reestablish the rights of the subscriber/client and the professional autonomy of the clinician.

The big payors, the corporate employers who provide insurance for their workers, have started to take a closer look at the quality of services being offered by MCOs. Audits are revealing that managed care companies restrict spending on direct care in order to provide for high profits and administrative costs. In addition, courts and legislatures have grown increasingly uncomfortable with MCOs' focus on their own financial health over patient well-being. One of the most outspoken public opponents of MBH is Karen Shore, Ph.D., co-founder and president of the National Coalition of Mental Health Professionals and Consumers (Commack, New York). Many newspapers, magazines, and television programs have run stories highly critical of various managed care policies.

Powerful groups are critically appraising managed care practices. For example, The Institute of Medicine issued a report in 1997, calling on the federal government to monitor the quality of managed behavioral health plans. The National Alliance for the Mentally Ill, a patient advocacy group, issued a report card in September 1997 surveying nine of the country's largest mental health managed care companies—and flunking all of them. Among the findings were that some plans still prescribed Haldol, a decades-old drug with side effects including severe and irreversible tremors, for schizophrenia rather than newer, more expensive drugs like Clozipine and Rispordol.

The Backlash Has Begun

Public Protests

A July 1998 one-day strike of Kaiser mental health providers in Denver was prompted by concerns about quality of care. Protesters rallied and attempted to articulate their dissatisfactions with various managed care practices.

The May 1996 Nurses' March on Washington protested managed care's harm to patients, destruction of quality in our healthcare system, and de-professionalization of patient care. This demonstration illustrated the passion of some of managed care's most adamant opponents.

Karen Shore's address at the Nurses March (excerpted with her permission), maintained that:

> Managed care is literally killing people and destroying our medical and mental health care system. We will never regulate this industry adequately. We must move America beyond Managed Care and Managed Competition. Patients and clinicians have become powerless, dominated by greedy, dishonest, and uncaring corporate dictatorships that are taking billions of dollars out of the system at the cost of our citizens' lives and well-being and at the cost of our professions.
>
> . . . Let me say clearly: Managed care is immoral. Managed care deprives citizens of three basic rights: the right to choice, the right to privacy, and the right to

make their own treatment decisions. Clinicians and hospitals are chosen and re-tained if they make a profit for the managed care company, not because of their skill, training, or ethics. Managed care has also brought us an outrageous lack of privacy as detailed information about patients is put into the insurer's computers. This invasion into privacy humiliates and re-traumatizes mental health patients. Clinicians feel forced into betraying their own patients' needs for privacy.

Managed care's incentives and directives to undertreat are immoral. Drastic cuts in psychiatric hospital admissions, lengths of stay, and aftercare have brought an increase in re-hospitalizations, patient injuries and patient deaths due to suicide and the inability of the mentally ill to take care of themselves.

Managed care has destroyed psychotherapy and replaced it with a superficial model of crisis intervention, usually limiting therapy to about 3–12 sessions, regardless of the problem. Even children are being deprived of psychotherapy and forced to take medications because the insurer wants a quick fix. Money counts. People don't. Managed mental health care will never help us solve our problems with homelessness, psychosis, crime, suicide, teen pregnancy, child abuse, spouse abuse, and the many troubled children who grow up to be troubled adults who raise another generation of troubled children, because managed care does not want to spend the money and doesn't care about people.

Managed care is immoral because it hurts people most when they are vul-nerable. People must often fight for proper treatment at a time when they should be spending their energy on getting well or taking care of a sick loved one.

Managed care has demoralized clinicians who feel forced to be compliant with a system that puts the insurer's needs above the patient's needs. Patients can no longer be sure they can trust their clinicians' motives, and clinicians can't even be sure they can trust themselves.

Competition has not brought the highest quality at the lowest price. It has brought a search by the employer for the cheapest policy, and a search by the in-surer for the cheapest, least-trained clinicians who are expected to provide the least treatment possible.

We do not want a system of corporate dictatorship, and this industry will fight our attempts to regulate it sufficiently. We need a system in which our citizens have control over their own lives. We need a system in which clinicians are chosen because they are the best, most highly trained and most ethical they can be, not the "cheapest" and most compliant. We need a system based on compassion, not on the bottom line; and on freedom, not on authoritarian control over patients and clinicians. Whether we have a single payor or a multiple payor system, benefit designs must make the consumer cost-conscious so they can retain their freedom. Our idea for such a plan is called "Managed Cooperation." Medical Savings Accounts are another idea, and Congress should stop playing politics with it. Some states may wish to experiment with Single Payor plans. . . ."

Testimony before the House

Larry Gage's August 2, 1995, testimony before the House Ways and Means Health Subcommittee voiced serious concerns about managed care. Gage is president of the National Association of Public Hospitals.

The term "managed care" is now so ubiquitous that it dominates the field of vision in both the private and public sectors of the health industry. More than just a helpful tool, managed care has become a preoccupation—perhaps even an obsession—for private insurers, employers, and individuals, as well as for legislators and bureaucrats at every level of government. Yet it is an obsession that obscures the need for greater scrutiny of the managed care industry, in order to avoid potentially irreversible damage to the future viability, quality and ethical standards of health care providers, as well as to the good health of many millions of Americans.

. . . There are perhaps several ironies here. The first, of course, is that there is increasing evidence that managed care is not much more effective over time in holding down health costs than the fee for service system it is rapidly supplanting. A second irony is that the major underlying reasons for cost increases in the American health industry have little or nothing to do with either managed care or fee for service medicine. Rather, they depend on such factors as the large and ever-growing numbers of uninsured. . . . The third, and perhaps greatest, irony is that the steps which clearly could reduce health costs over time—prevention, wellness and public health services—are the last services added and the first ones on the chopping block when the primary goals are short term cost containment and profit-taking. . . .

Ultimately, of course, if "managed care" is seen only as a tool for cutting costs, the result will be a health system that is neither "managed" nor "care." We all know that there are more than a few dirty little secrets about the explosive growth in Medicaid managed care over the last several years. . . . [Many MCOs] devote their effort to enrolling mostly people who are young or healthy (or both), invest as creatively as possible the enormous cash flow generated by capitated payments, ratchet down payments to providers wherever they can, keep support staff to a minimum, erect subtle and not-so-subtle barriers to access, and pray no one needs a liver transplant before they can cut a deal to sell out.

Now it may sound from these statements that I am cynical—perhaps even that I oppose managed care. But nothing could be farther from the truth. . . . Done properly, managed care can result in genuine improvements in health status and expansion of access for some of our most vulnerable patient populations. It is just that, done poorly, implemented too rapidly, or for the wrong reasons, it could be a setback, not an improvement, both for patients and for entire communities.

We need only look at the TennCare Medicaid debacle to see some of the problems we face when cost becomes the only issue. With TennCare, the State of Tennessee dumped all Medicaid and many uninsured patients overnight onto ill-prepared managed care plans with inadequate provider networks, only to pay them premiums that were originally found to be 40% below acknowledged actuarial soundness.

Rapid Changes

Increased media coverage of the conflicts between managed care systems and providers and consumers is contributing to a variety of responses to address the inappropriate practices of some MCOs. Professionals and consumers are protesting, and the battles being waged will almost certainly compel some beneficial reform. Optimists believe that recent outcries for change will lead to greater scrutiny of managed care practices and create a window of opportunity for those interested in contributing to improvements.

With most of the country shifting to managed care, a backlash of criticism by doctors, nurses, consumers, and politicians is forcing health plans to abandon a range of cost-cutting practices that reward doctors and hospitals for limiting care. The majority of states have outlawed or curtailed methods that many HMOs have used to shorten some types of hospital stays, discipline physicians, or keep patients in the dark about the incentives and ground rules of managed care.

Fueled by horror stories of care denied and by physicians' rancor at losing their freedom to treat patients without second-guessing, hundreds of bills affecting managed care practices are being introduced in state legislatures each year, according to the National Conference of State Legislators. In Congress, members of both parties are also pushing managed care legislation.

Now that so many people have experience with managed care, the nation's attention appears to have shifted from concern about getting runaway costs under control to questions about whether managed care has gone too far.

Litigation and Legislative Reforms

The following sections describes some of the litigation and legislative reforms that have already started to temper some of the more problematic elements of managed care.

The Concept of Vicarious Liability

Managed care officials had formerly assumed that a federal statute would protect them against liability suits. The 1974 Employee Retirement Income Security Act (ERISA) was intended to provide a uniform body of law governing employee benefit plans. According to the statute, ERISA supersedes any and all state laws relating to any employee benefit plan (Rutkin and Garay, 1997). It thereby exempts employers who "self insure" their health benefit plans from state regulation, taxation, and control. Although this pre-emption is broad, it is subject to changing judicial interpretation (Wroten, 1997). A 1997 decision supported the concept of vicarious liability. MCOs that dictate treatment decisions that harm patients can be held financially accountable. This decision makes MCOs more accountable for the long-term consequences of their cost-cutting policies.

As many of the safeguards against MCO liability for malpractice are removed, these companies are going to become increasingly responsive to circumstances in which research findings clearly support providers' requests for additional treatment. While MCOs will continue to object to blanket insistence that brief therapy fails (when accumulating research convincingly argues otherwise), they have no choice but to respond to reliable findings about its inappropriateness in certain specified instances. Ignoring such evidence would create a window of opportunity for litigation that these companies definitely wish to avoid.

Verdict against HealthNet, and Other Court Cases

A $1 million plus verdict was entered in 1996 against HealthNet, California's second-largest HMO (after Kaiser) in favor of the family of a 34-year-old woman who died from breast cancer. The verdict, reached in arbitration, was based on breach of contract and the "intentional infliction of emotional stress." The patient developed a breast malignancy in 1992 and was treated properly with mastectomy and chemotherapy. By 1994, the cancer had spread, and her doctor recommended high-dose chemotherapy with bone marrow transplant. The patient was referred to the UCLA Medical Center, where it was decided that the patient was, indeed, a candidate for this treatment. However, the patient's insurer, HealthNet, denied authorization for the treatment, calling it "experimental and investigative," "not proven effective," and "not widely accepted."

In a similar vein but with a larger scope, a New York law firm has filed a class action lawsuit against Aetna, Cigna, and US Health Care for a group of patients and physicians. Because the HMOs use hindsighted practice guidelines instead of foresighted practice guidelines, they are seen as forcing the physicians to give high-cost, poor-quality healthcare.

Litigation has also occurred in the area of MBH. In 1996, the New Jersey Psychological Association (NJPA) announced that, along with seven psychologists, it had filed a complaint against MCC Behavioral Care, Inc. (MCC) in the Superior Court of New Jersey, Morris County. The NJPA and the psychologists filed this potentially precedent-setting complaint as a result of MCC's termination of the psychologists from its provider network "without cause." The complaint alleged that MCC substituted its judgment for that of the psychologists concerning the appropriateness of requested professional services for patients. The complaint further alleged that MCC improperly concluded that each of the psychologists overutilized the professional sessions available to their patients under the patients' health plans administered by MCC, and, as a result, MCC terminated the psychologists, designating them "not managed care compatible." The complaint also alleged that MCC took this action despite the fact that the health plans promised a certain number of sessions as part of their benefits package and the psychologists had not exceeded this number of sessions.

Legislative Reforms

In 1998, at least twenty-one states considered whether the medical director of a managed care plan can be sued for malpractice. This is significant, as 85% of U.S. employees now have managed care coverage compared to 50% 4 years ago. In 1996, sixteen states adopted laws nullifying gag clauses imposed by MCOs on their doctors. The state laws vary, but all protect the rights of doctors and patients to talk about all treatment options (including expensive ones!). A survey of state legislative activity reports that in 1997, twenty-four states passed new "gag clause" laws, fourteen states passed laws that allow direct access to specialists, fourteen states passed laws mandating minimum hospital stays for mastectomies, and twenty states passed laws mandating emergency room services. In 1998, nineteen states considered mental health parity legislation, fifteen legislatures considered bills on mandatory external grievance procedures for plan enrollees, ten states considered the "prudent layperson" standard for emergency room visits, and sixteen states considered bills that would impose quality standards on health plans ("Efforts to Rein in Managed Care Worry Blues Plans," 1998).

At the federal level, in 1996, the Department of Health and Human Services took steps to ensure quality care by placing certain limitations on physician incentive arrangements that could influence physicians' care decisions. "No patient should have to wonder if their doctor's decision is based on sound medicine or financial incentives," according to HHS Secretary Donna E. Shalala. "This regulation should help put Americans' minds at rest."

NCQA Regulations and Standards

The National Committee for Quality Assurance (NCQA) released the final version of the first national accreditation standards for managed behavioral healthcare organizations in 1997 (Voelker, 1997). The NCQA is an independent, nonprofit watchdog organization, dedicated to assessing and reporting on the quality of care delivered by the nation's MCOs.

"The new standards were spurred by the explosive growth during the 1980s of specialized managed care companies that contracted with health plans to provide mental and behavioral healthcare services. The NCQA estimates that more than 300 such organizations currently are serving about 100 million people in the United States" (Voelker, 1997, p. 366). The market for MBH is expected to grow as state governments increasingly cover Medicaid recipients' behavioral healthcare through managed care plans.

The NCQA hopes that implementation of the new accreditation standards will bring the following improvements:

1. Provide consumers, employers, public purchasers, and the MBH industry itself with a means of assessing the quality of managed behavioral health plans.
2. Make MBH organizations accountable for the quality of services their patients receive.
3. Stimulate effectiveness in behavioral healthcare services through integration with general medical care, prevention, and early intervention.

The last of NCQA's goals is especially good news for psychiatrists, who in recent years have become increasingly concerned that managed care trends are pushing primary care and psychiatry further apart (Voelker, 1997).

In an attempt to bring the specialties closer, in late 1995, the APA published the *Diagnostic and Statistical Manual of Mental Disorders, Fourth Edition—Primary Care Version* (*DSM-IV-PC*). As the first manual of mental disorders developed specifically for primary care physicians, the *DSM-IV-PC* points out that about 28% of adults experience a mental or addictive disorder. There are data suggesting that most generalists are very poor at recognizing very straightforward psychiatric diagnoses (Voelker, 1997).

In the new NCQA standards, psychopharmacology is an opportune area for collaboration. To earn accreditation, MBH organizations will have to work with medical care providers to reduce the inappropriate use of psychotropic drugs and adverse effects. This is important because the dangers of interactions are real but often not as obvious to nonpsychiatrists.

The NQCA regulations are viewed by some managed care company insiders as an unworkable burden. In fact, some believe that managed care is in the process of being destroyed by the very entities that created it. Large employers are now, as a result of the NCQA standards, imposing such stringent requirements on HMOs and MCOs that managed care as we all have known it may soon be a thing of the past.

While some providers and advocates for those seeking mental health services welcome this news, there are concerns that before the end arrives, providers will be swamped even more by unreasonable requests for documentation, not only of treatment, but of credentials and proof of treatment efficacy. Providers will be increasingly expected to provide explanations for every action a disgruntled patient may attribute to the provider, including accusations of "rudeness" ("I was simply confronting the patient with the consequences of their own actions"); not returning phone calls ("I tried to return calls but the patient said I should only call them at home between 6 and 7; when I did they weren't home and they had no voice mail"); and quality-of-care issues ("The patient states you talk too much or too little and as a consequence you are ineffective").

The NCQA is instructing managed care companies that they must follow up, in writing, on each and every complaint alleged by any patient, against any provider, to anybody, when it comes to the attention of the managed care company. As a consequence, providers will be even more inundated with paperwork, because the NCQA now mandates that patients, providers, and facilities must each be notified, in writing, within 2–3 days, of any authorizations made to you. Given how often providers and patients change their minds about what they need or want and for which family member, it seems likely that authorizations and changes will often cross and that paperwork will become ever more confusing.

The NCQA also requires that every authorization and other communication with the patient be accompanied by a statement indicating that the patient or the provider has the right to appeal a decision. Many patients will want to appeal, and providers too will want to appeal. Each of these appeals will require supporting documentation from providers and be followed by requests for additional information from the managed care company. Ultimately the sheer volume of documentation of every activity and action will bring managed care companies to their knees, but not before providers spend even more time documenting than treating. This is occurring because of the very legitimate complaints about managed care. Large employers have reduced costs to the bone and are now trying to improve quality by establishing standards that are intended to protect the consumer and the provider, but which will become a form of regulation of the profession by non-professionals who know little or nothing about psychotherapy.

Managed Care's Criticism of Its Critics

The managed care industry has attempted to dismiss the flurry of legislation and grass-roots protests, although trade groups have been lobbying furiously against many of the changes. The industry argues that these reform efforts are the product of "individuals with a vested interest in maintaining the old style of health care," according to Karen Ignagni, president of the American Association of Health Plans, a trade group based in Washington, DC.

Managed care officials have also complained for several years that the media are creating a "backlash" against HMOs through coverage that is biased and laden with emotional anecdotes that portray the industry as villains, the patients as victims. Citing opinion surveys that indicate that 75% or more of HMO members are "satisfied" with their health plans, the industry blames the media for focusing on what they say are a relatively few incidents involving unhappy customers.

The Kaiser Family Foundation conducted a study (Brodie, 1998) that challenges the industry's argument. The study by the nonprofit healthcare charity (not affiliated with the Kaiser Permanente HMO) systematically reviewed coverage in newspapers such as the *Wall Street Journal* and the *Los Angeles Times*, magazines such as *Time* and *BusinessWeek*, and the network evening news programs. It found that 64% of the stories in newspapers, magazines, and on TV from 1990 to 1997 were "neutral" in tone. During that period, 25% of stories were critical of managed care, while 11% praised it. The study also found that 75% of stories used no anecdotes at all, and only 5% used anecdotes with "high drama."

But the study also found that news coverage has grown decidedly more critical over time. In 1990, positive stories about managed care appeared twice as often as critical ones. By 1997, 28% of stories were critical, while only 4% were positive. Ignagni maintains that managed care critics selectively publicize alleged denials of service and failures of care, which are then amplified by the media and become the basis for hastily considered legislation enacted in the name of consumer protection.

4

Being Fair

Looking Critically at Our Nostalgia and Revisiting Assumptions about Therapy

Combatting Nostalgia for What Never Was

The more things change, the more they stay the same. Even before managed care most therapists practiced eclectic, brief therapy, often using intermittent contacts.

Although many decry the corrupting influence of managed care on psychotherapy, the facts suggest that it has not changed actual service delivery all that dramatically. Managed care's insistence that providers use techniques of proved efficacy, emphasize brief treatment, and schedule sessions on the basis of need rather than rigid expectations largely conforms to the standards many practitioners have long set for themselves.

For decades most therapists have regarded themselves as "eclectic" practitioners, rather than as adherents of a particular perspective (Garfield & Kurtz, 1977). The majority of psychotherapists choose techniques that serve them best, independent of their theoretical source. For some time, clinicians have been trained to stay open to innovation and to stay abreast of the clinical literature exploring novel treatment approaches. The field's responsiveness to the potential of eye movement desensitization and reprocessing (F. Shapiro, 1995) and other innovative techniques testifies to the commitment practitioners have to searching for the best solutions for their clients' problems. This flexible, pragmatic stance is consistent with managed care's emphasis on selecting optimal techniques for particular types of client problems.

Furthermore, the majority of outpatient clients have always pursued a fairly short course of treatment. Many come for a few sessions, leave, and return years later when they are confronting a new set of life challenges. Although this use of treatment did not conform to the expectations of many outpatient therapists whose training left them imagining a process that was structured quite differently, outpatients have had considerable power to define the parameters of treatment in terms of their needs. Despite the therapist's plans and intentions, clients who had obtained what they were looking for left. Casting such cases as "premature termination" or "dropouts" on the basis of the clinicians' ambitions for these individuals defines these cases as treatment failures. Viewed from a client-centered perspective, these cases may represent the best of what therapy can be: client-defined! The high rate of "no shows" in many outpatient treatment settings can be taken either as evidence of the pathology of the clients or as a sign of over-offered services.

The theoretically mandated managed care health benefits do not appear unreasonable when compared with national statistics on mental healthcare use (Richardson & Austad, 1991). Research has demonstrated that 50% of all mental health clients are improved in eight or fewer sessions, and 75% to 80% in twenty-six or fewer sessions (Carr-Kaffashan, 1989; Goodstein, 1986; Pallak, 1987). Moreover, the modal client stays in outpatient treatment for only one visit, with the average length of treatment being four to six visits regardless of the type of treatment or the setting (Budman, 1989; Phillips, 1988). The mental health service attrition curve developed by Phillips (1985) shows that only 50% of all clients return for the first therapy session after the intake interview, and a declining number continue in therapy, so that by the fifth or sixth session 70% of all clients have left therapy, and only a very small percentage of clients remain in treatment after the tenth session. This use pattern applies to all types of clients, whether treated with short-term or long-term therapy, regardless of the theoretical approach. Similar utilization statistics are found in HMOs (Richardson & Austad, 1991).

The standard treatment protocol under managed care does not deviate all that radically from what many clinicians have been doing for years. Managed care contracts that cover six annual sessions should meet the need of the vast majority of the clients we have traditionally been serving in outpatient venues. Perhaps our focus should be on trying to reform such limits in cases of severely mentally ill individuals, for whom such limited treatment is unconscionable, rather than on emphasizing the entitlement of the worried well.

Many clinicians have long been convinced of the value of flexibly spreading sessions over time (e.g., holding twenty meetings intermittently over the course of a year) rather than establishing rigid schedules and session limits. In several settings (including many college counseling centers) the majority of clients are seen intermittently (not on a standard weekly basis) at some point in their counseling. This frees up clinicians to do a reasonable amount of longer-term work, when that is indicated.

Revisiting Assumptions

Before rejecting managed care, it is important to resist the temptation to idealize the former system. Many of the assumptions underlying traditional psychotherapy practices have been challenged over the years. Few have been submitted to careful empirical validation. But, despite this, many practitioners continue to cling to them. The evolution of managed care is providing a valuable excuse for the field to revisit many of our premises.

More Isn't Always More

When we don't feel our clients have improved after six sessions, it is tempting to assume that more sessions are the answer. However, sometimes additional contacts don't produce any measurable advantage. As therapists, we don't have a magical way of helping people to change when they don't want to or aren't yet ready to put recommended changes into action.

When therapy works, it tends to work fairly quickly. Many clients experience some relief from their problems after just an initial interview (Howard, Kopta, et al., 1986). Prior to changes in reimbursement limits, it was reported that the majority of outpatient psychotherapy cases concluded after the first few sessions (Phillips, 1985). Regardless of the therapist's orientation or the practice setting, the average number of psychotherapy visits is four to eight. One-third to half of patients who come for psychotherapy conclude treatment with a single session. By the sixth session, only about 30% of those who started remain in treatment. Only 8% to 10% of patients continue therapy beyond ten to fifteen sessions. Well over 90% of outpatient care was found to be completed by the twenty-sixth session.

Studies assessing the relationship between the number of psychotherapy sessions and objective ratings of patient improvement at termination of therapy paint a picture of diminishing returns after the first couple of months of treatment. The data indicate that the highest rate of improvement occurs within the first 2 months of treatment. After twenty-six sessions the percent of clients showing improvement plateaus, suggesting little or no incremental gain associated with psychotherapy extended beyond that point. In an analysis of three decades of psychotherapy outcome research involving over 2,400 clients, Howard and his colleagues (1986) found that after 2 months of weekly therapy sessions, 50% of the clients were substantially improved. The improvement rates then significantly tapered off. After 6 months, 75% had improved; after a full year, 85% had improved (Howard, Kopta, et al., 1986). These authors conclude that "8 sessions is the median effective dose of individual therapy." Clearly the greatest improvement occurs during the early stages of psychotherapy. When the point of diminishing returns is reached, it is probably appropriate to assess whether additional commitment of resources is justified.

Time-limited cognitive-behavioral treatment and systematic desensitization compared favorably to psychodynamic, gestalt, client-centered, transactional therapy, and behavior modification in a comprehensive review of 475 outcome studies (Smith, Glass, & Miller, 1980). Short-term psychodynamic therapy and behavior therapy (systematic desensitization) produced comparable improvement (80% versus 48% in a wait-list control group) in a rigorous outcome study conducted at the Temple University Outpatient Clinic (Sloane et al., 1975). In this research "neurotic" patients matched for sex, age, and severity of problem were randomly assigned to treatment or control groups. Outcome was evaluated through psychological tests, reports from the clients' close associates, and interviews of the clients by blind, independent raters.

Is Traditional Psychotherapy Always Therapeutic?

Iatrogenic Risks of Long-Term Psychotherapy

The risks of traditional, long-term psychotherapy include dependence, negative focus, stigma, and relationship disruption. The research literature includes many findings that support the premise that briefer psychotherapy can often be preferable for clients. Extended treatment can produce counterproductive dependency. Long-term psychotherapy clients run the risk of coming to feel that their therapist's judgment is superior to their own. They often feel the need to run any decisions by their therapist for comment and evaluation prior to execution. Many therapists' conservative (litigaphobic?) tendencies can make clients more rather than less fearful of making changes.

The longer clients are in treatment, the more they succumb to negative labeling effects ("I must have a pretty serious psychological problem, or I wouldn't be in need of this lengthy treatment"). The more the therapist justifies long-term interventions by using diagnostic labels, the greater the risk of a self-fulfilling prophecy being created ("I must have abnormally high anxiety reactions or I wouldn't have been labeled as having generalized anxiety disorder . . . this makes me even more fearful for my future . . . which leaves me feeling anxious . . . so the label must be right . . .", etc.).

It seems that the longer clients are in psychotherapy, the greater the likelihood that those in their family and social circle will learn of it and make stereotyped assumptions about them. The resulting narrowed expectations that others have of them can affect clients' behavior and further reify their "pathology."

The need to reduce cognitive dissonance can compel clients to convince themselves of their need for continued treatment ("If I don't need continuing treatment, why am I going? I keep making and keeping appointments; therefore, I must need this in my life"). Therapists are often trusted to "know best" when it comes to assessing when treatment should be ended. Clients assume their therapist will call a halt to treatment when in the therapist's expert opinion it is no longer necessary, while therapists show respect for their clients by letting them be the judge of when treatment should end. This mutual abdication of responsibility for carefully assessing the incremental gains associated with additional sessions can prolong treatment significantly. Under fee-for-service systems of reimbursement there is often limited incentive for therapists to rush termination, so it frequently drags on, with diminishing returns.

The Negative Placebo Effect

Although placebos are generally thought of as having only helpful effects, research described by A. Shapiro and Shapiro (1997) suggests otherwise. In one controlled study (A. Shapiro et al. 1974), patients given placebos in the form of a drug tablet reported significantly more somatic side effects, whereas cognitive and affective side effects were reported by those given a psychotherapeutic-type placebo stimulus and by patients in the control condition. Placebo response was positive in 51% of patients receiving placebos (symptoms decreased; the patient felt better) negative in 12% (symptoms increased; the patient felt worse) and absent in 37% (there was no change); placebo-induced side effects (new unpleasant symptoms) occurred in 57% of the total sample (86% of negative placebo reactors, 63% of positive placebo reactors, and 40% of nonplacebo reactors) in other studies (A. Shapiro & Shapiro, 1984a, 1984b).

A phenomenon known as the "negative placebo effect" can occur when, despite additional treatment, the client experiences a plateau in symptoms (Storms & Nisbett, 1970; Chambliss & Murray, 1979a). Because they expect progress, when life does not improve during extended therapy, clients often conclude that they must really be seriously dysfunctional. When the benefits of treatment level off, rather than continuing "supportive" treatment when little additional movement is expected, it might be better to address the issue of unrealistic expectations (e.g., "No amount of therapy, however well executed and received, will make life perfect or painless!"). Otherwise, clients are likely to blame themselves for failing to maintain the rapid rate of change associated with the earlier phase of treatment.

Clients probably prefer brief treatment in part because it is more convenient and less stigmatizing. Apparently clients often have far more modest ambitions for psychotherapy than their therapists do. Although a 1995 *Consumer Reports* survey showing high consumer satisfaction with psychotherapy found clients most pleased by longer treatment, given this study's survey methods, it is difficult to distinguish between cause and effect. Perhaps those who found less engaging and effective therapists understandably dropped out quickly. This would have made it seem that longer therapy is better, when in fact the results merely mean that patients abort work with lousy therapists. Another possibility is that those who made a substantial investment of time in treatment may have needed to justify this investment by evaluating treatment more favorably. The positive association between treatment length and satisfaction may therefore have been at least partially artifactual. Selective attrition (those who weren't happy discontinued treatment earlier) and cognitive dissonance (the need to rationalize the decision to continue treatment longer by casting it in a more favorable light) may have accounted for the apparent superiority of longer treatment.

It is also possible that long-term, supportive treatment is actually often preferred by some clients. Unpressured psychotherapy, especially the nonconfrontive, nonjudgmental, unconditional positive regard–filled kind, should be quite reinforcing for many people, especially when insurance subsidies reduce or eliminate the financial burdens of extended treatment. Indulgent therapists who ally themselves with clients and support their externalizing and criticisms of others can be quite gratifying. Such surrogate friendship can be extremely comforting. Therapists who don't push or pressure the client to make changes are supporting the client's choice to maintain the status quo (which is often reasonable). However, this kind of one-sided supportive social interaction, however comforting and good it feels, may not be the kind of therapy that should be subsidized by third-party payees. It may be a luxury for some. Cheaper, more mutual, and less formal and artificial social options might be preferable for many.

High Fees

The tradition of charging high fees for psychotherapeutic services started long ago, with Freud's realization that clients frequently embrace inertia and are loath to change longstanding patterns of behavior or defense. In order to counterbalance this conservatism trend, he used hefty fees and the economic hardship they produced as a source of motivation for clients to overcome their resistance (Langs, 1973).

We charge clients a lot for their treatment in part to enhance their motivation to get better. From this perspective, third-party payments can undermine therapy. Removing the patient's economic stake in a prompt response to therapy defeats the process assumed to underlie the fee structure and thereby can interfere with the client's improvement. Some analysts therefore see therapists' acceptance of third-party payments as unethical. When there is little or no out-of-pocket expense, a sense of personal sacrifice may not be experienced in the therapy. However, the importance of such sacrifice to therapeutic effectiveness has been challenged by some. Mental health service user rates do not accelerate rapidly when financial obstacles are removed. Prepaid mental health clients appear to exhibit no higher utilization rates than fee-for-service adult consumers (Blackwell, Gutmann, & Gutmann, 1988).

Nonetheless, subsidized treatment requires delimitation if it meets powerful social needs of clients; many clients will not want to leave therapy if it is the easiest way they have to meet their needs for acceptance and belonging. Therapists must be encouraged to guard against promoting this expensive route to reassurance and social inclusion; peer support groups make far more sense in many of these cases.

Risks of Seeing Questionable "Experts"

Dawes (1994) details the risks of overly certain and "authoritative" psychotherapists who inadvertently overdetect instances of childhood trauma:

> "Knowing" within ten minutes from the way a client walks that she was an incest victim as a child can easily lead a psychologist to ask questions that suggest to her that she must have been a victim. This suggestion in turn can lead the client to reinterpret inaccurately recalled instances of benign behavior toward her as indicative of abuse, which can lead her to conclude that abuse occurred when it didn't. . . . That belief can lead the client to be alienated from her family and to adopt a stance of incompetence in the face of her own "recalled" trauma. The resulting distress reinforces the therapist's conclusion that the client has suffered greatly from her childhood trauma. . . . Responsible professionals should practice with a cautious, open, and questioning attitude.

Francine Shapiro (1995) writes that, in her eyes,

> One of the very disturbing parts of both the managed care and the "false/delayed" memory controversies is that we opened the door to the attacks ourselves by allowing abuses to remain unchallenged.... Some of the major abuses start with the words "The only way you can heal is...." Perhaps our clinical experience has led us to believe that there is only one way we can do therapy, but it is certainly not the only way a person can heal. We need to provide clients with choices regarding available therapies. Clinicians who believe that a necessary precursor to healing involves "detaching" the client from all social supports, or reliving all the pain of the trauma, or retrieving clear memories of old abuses need to make clients aware of other therapies that do not make the same demands. And we need to set sufficient standards of practice, preparation, and peer review before we claim any psychotherapeutic method we happen to be using is beneficial. (p. 49)

Shapiro (1995) continues, saying, "Some of us have not had sufficient sense of our own ability to harm just through the very power our clients invested in us. We have not realized that any method with the potential to heal also has the potential to hurt" (p. 49).

There is no explicit corollary to the Hippocratic oath's injunction against harming clients in the field of psychotherapy. While the literature includes some examination of the problem of iatrogenic effects of therapy, concern about the psychological risks associated with poorly conducted therapy has been minimal. Some of this neglect is probably due to the small effects many attribute to therapy; only highly influential procedures carry the potential for doing great inadvertent harm. According to this argument, marginally effective interventions must carry a proportionately low risk of damaging impact, so minimally influential psychotherapists must be relatively benign, even at their worst.

Yet, in many ways, therapy can backfire and exacerbate a client's problems. It can deepen feelings of despair, powerlessness, and self-derogation. By focusing the client's attention on the negative, by laying out a recommended set of options the client may fail to actualize, therapy has the risk of intensifying negative affect and self-loathing. The message that underlies some therapy is that it is necessary and valuable to dissect all the imperfections of one's life and emphasize the self and one's feelings about the self. Some patients assume that in order to function well they must reach a point where they "like themselves," yet they find it extremely hard to operationalize this objective in specific enough terms to make it possible for them to feel their goal has ever been accomplished. The whole concept of self-esteem is muddy to begin with. Couching the targets of therapy in terms of this amorphous variable becomes exceedingly problematic.

Random interval sampling research has revealed that people feel better when they are busily engrossed in activities. Dwelling on the self was generally associated with more negative affect. Therapeutic approaches that foster such introspection arguably make some clients worse.

Many therapists begin each meeting with well-intended queries about all that's gone wrong in the past week or two. They plumb for instances of mistakes, victimization, and malaise. When the innocent-sounding question "So how are things going?" is offered sympathetically accompanied by a sober, searching expression by someone who has in the past repeatedly reinforced discussion of pain, frustration, and failures, it orients clients to the negative. The implicit expectation of many therapies is disclosure of the dark side. Clients may understandably feel that they're therapeutic failures if they don't generate a long list of recent negative experiences that can serve as grist for the therapist's mill. Because the purpose of therapy is to improve one's understanding of one's personal problems, sharing an array of problems is a necessary starting point. But what is the price associated with this regular biased exploration that highlights the most negative aspects of one's experience? In a 1993 study, Janis observed that higher self-disclosure was actually associated with poorer outcome.

Avoiding Risks to Children

Lawrence Shapiro (1994) believes:

> Avoiding unnecessary disruption is especially important in the treatment of children. Therapy, in and of itself, is an intrusion into the child's life. One argument for using short-term therapy techniques is that children should be spending most of their time with family and friends in age-appropriate activities rather than spending it with a therapist. Consequently, any technique that disrupts the child's normal day-to-day life is an intrusion, but certain techniques used in short-term therapy are inherently more intrusive than others. The general premise of short-term therapy is to minimize the disruption of a child's life by treating the problem as efficiently as possible, and the same rule of minimal intrusiveness applies in selecting specific techniques.

However, use of an intrusive therapy is sometimes unavoidable because of the extreme or crisis nature of the problem.

Therapists often overlook how discomforting it can be to attend therapy. Cooper (1997e) discusses research by Cederborg challenging the fairness of some conventional family therapy practices. Swedish psychologist Ann-Christin Cederborg studied twenty-eight videotaped therapy sessions of seven different families, each with a child from 4 to 7 years old. Evaluating the amount and quality of the children's participation in therapy sessions, she found that young children seem to exist primarily as sources of diagnostic information for therapists and that family therapy often becomes marital therapy in the presence of the children. Rather than having "full membership" status in family therapy sessions, young children often have the participant status of "nonpersons."

Although this study used a small sample, the findings corroborate similar research on children's interactions in therapy. Cederborg asks, "If children are not talked to but rather talked about, one has to ask why they should be part of the process that, to a great extent, may be threatening for them" (quoted in Cooper, 1997e).

Farberman (1997) describes the increasing interest some therapists have in reducing iatrogenic risks. For example, best-selling author and clinician Mary Pipher believes that therapists must make a greater commitment to do no harm: "We are very fair and nonjudgmental to people in the therapy room but are not always so fair to people outside of the room."

While no family is perfect, many therapists believe that the worst thing some therapists do is turn people away from their families. "When therapists alienate people from their families, we don't begin to take up the slack. We don't invite people to Thanksgiving dinner and we don't pay their rent if they lose their jobs," Farberman writes, quoting Pipher.

Farberman supports Pipher's practice of spending part of every therapy session asking patients whether her advice makes sense to them. "Therapists don't get challenged as much as they should. Therapy itself is set up in such a way that one can become delusional about how wise one is. I think our field produces people with a greater sense of importance than they should probably have." Pipher (1996) argues that "a therapist is a consultant who helps people process life thoroughly. In terms of priorities for loyalty and attachment, therapists should come after family, friends and co-workers. We care about clients, but we are hired help."

Pipher sees psychotherapy as currently undergoing a paradigm shift, with the field moving from a focus on pathology to one based on patients' strengths, and emphasis moving from a narrow, individualized focus on family of origin to broader cultural regularities.

Harm to Families

Although Szapocznik, Rio, et al. (1989) found structural family therapy and individual psychodynamic child therapy to be equally effective, as a side effect of the psychodynamic therapy an undesirable deterioration of family functioning resulted. These authors concluded that, for individual therapy to be both successful and not deleterious to the young person's family, it needs to strategically target family interactions as part of the therapeutic process (Szapocznik, Kurtines, et al., 1990).

Campbell (1992) describes situations in which individual-oriented therapists put themselves in competition with the client's family, possibly even to the point of disparaging a client's parents or fostering defection from the family. Such patterns were reported by Balaban and Melchionda (1979) when they began to expand their program to include families. This kind of triangulation puts undue pressure on those clients who are closely tied to their families, and they frequently defect from treatment in order to get out of this bind (Stanton & Shadish, 1997).

The Psychological Price of Inpatient Care

Zusman (1967) has described the "social breakdown syndrome" associated with long-term institutional care. Isolation from one's home community causes social and independent living skills to atrophy, while often inadvertently reinforcing maladaptive behaviors. Although inpatient care can offer a helpful respite and provide a welcome sense of belonging, the artificiality of the sanctuary it provides inherently limits the opportunities it can create for useful, generalizable learning. The passive, compliant responses that are generally rewarded in the hospital may only be remotely related to the coping skills demanded in the community.

Do No Harm! Less Can Be More

Neil Jacobson (1995) argues that

> . . . therapy should never be interminable, as Freud once referred to psychoanalysis. Progress should be expected to occur in a timely manner, or alternatives should be discussed. Criteria for determining progress should be part of a dialogue initiated by the therapist and regularly assessed by both therapist and client. When therapy isn't working, the therapist has an ethical obligation to try something else—another form of therapy, a referral to another therapist, a psychotropic drug, a self-help book, meditation, yoga, gardening, exercise or something else. Alternatives to psychotherapy may often be the best solution when timely progress is not evident. (p. 39)

In summary, consideration of the risks of poorly conducted psychotherapy enjoins us to make a conscious effort to do no harm. Although we're familiar with thinking about the negative side effects of medications, we often overlook the risks associated with verbal psychotherapy methods. Diagnosis can help us select the most appropriate treatment strategy; it can also stigmatize the client and fix a negative identity that will be hard to shake. As providers, we need to avoid unnecessary pathologizing and use the least intrusive methods necessary.

The Previous System's Unfairness to Providers

Leveling the Playing Field: Long versus Brief Therapies

Managed care is frequently indicted on the grounds that its profit motive creates incentives to undertreat. While the risks of patient neglect are certainly real and measures need to be taken to create appropriate safeguards against this, a balanced consideration of this issue requires that we also look at how the profit motive operated in the previous system. One could argue that the selfishness of those who have an economic stake can contaminate any system and that perhaps the best we can do is to try to counteract excesses by building in accountability.

While with managed care, profits rise by providing fewer services, with fee-for-service systems, providers' profits rise through provision of more (even unneeded) services. The old system of largely unmonitored reimbursement created incentives to overtreat. This created an odd paradox. Some private practitioners were financially penalized for adhering to the principles they had been taught. Those who delivered efficient, appropriately targeted, state-of-the-art psychotherapy and achieved more rapid therapeutic outcomes required a steadier stream of patients in order to remain fiscally solvent than did clinicians who were less adroit, less incisive, and less focused on rapid problem resolution.

Although this efficient psychotherapy was exactly what many patients sought, because of the stigma associated with mental illness, satisfied psychotherapy customers didn't always pass the word to their friends and thereby produce abundant referrals. Efficient therapists didn't necessarily enjoy the rewards of their competence, because no one was watching, while therapists offering more unfocused treatment often found it easier to keep their schedules booked because each case lasted longer. Therapists catering to the long-term therapy crowd may actually have benefitted more from word-of-mouth marketing, because long-term psychotherapy becomes part of the patient's lifestyle and eventually comes to be seen as more normative, thereby reducing inhibition about discussing it publicly.

Those who allowed therapy to ramble on leisurely often profited. It was easier to maintain a full case load when the long-term approach to therapy offered patients a haven from any pressure to change and an adjunct to their proclivity to procrastinate. By defining the rehashing of issues as "working through," therapists could feel they were still doing a good job. Some took comfort in the notion that "clients move when they're ready," choosing to neglect the possibility that this might mean they shouldn't be obtaining expensive professional services until that time.

Others abdicated their professional responsibility to judge whether continuing treatment was necessary or likely to be fruitful, on the democratic grounds that "clients know best." They rationalized that they were empowering their clients by permitting them to control treatment decisions. In fact, broaching the topic of termination is difficult for most clients. Many assume that is the therapist's job and find it a challenge to communicate, "I no longer find it useful to spend time with you," because it seems impolite.

Managed care changed the professional arena. It in effect punished therapists who had been failing to live up to their training. In making them accountable to timely outcomes and requiring use of proved treatment strategies, managed care returned some to their earlier ambitions. By requiring conscientious, focused treatment from all therapists, managed care is leveling the playing field. Those who treat efficiently are being rewarded with more referrals. Longer therapy is only provided when an objective utilization reviewer deems it medically necessary, thereby eliminating the costly *folie à deux* that formerly occurred when both therapist and "worried well" client convinced themselves that the other believed that treatment was probably still needed. Ongoing encouragement and support can often be provided far less expensively through peer groups and other community resources; managed care encourages therapists to help their patients to develop these alternative ways of meeting their lifelong needs for social encouragement and respect.

Was Long-Term Therapy Unethical?

Austad (1996) argues that in many respects the former system for insurance reimbursement of psychotherapy costs was unfair and that, under certain circumstances, long-term therapy was unethical. Austad found that

. . . confidence and public trust in the authority of mental health professionals has clearly eroded. Discouraged, payors have begun to resent these professionals. Objective, measurable information about psychotherapy remains elusive. Reasonable questions are not getting reasonable answers. Mental health professionals appear to be a self-serving lot, especially those with the attitude that nonprofessionals should not question their judgment.

Payor suspicions that some providers are motivated by greed and act in their own best interests rather than their patients' have been confirmed. Unfortunately, as a result these suspicions have extended over the entire field of mental health. Some payors believe the health care system has become so unmanageable that the only way to deal with it is to find a consultant or institution to mediate between the forces involved in delivering care. (Austad, 1996, p. 179)

Limits on Reimbursed Therapy

Who should define need for treatment? When is third-party reimbursement appropriate? Who should pay for psychotherapy? While one might argue that everyone can benefit from psychotherapeutic interventions and education about their thoughts, beliefs, values, and feelings, this doesn't mean that health insurance should cover therapy for everyone. Definitions of medically necessary treatment are often heavily influenced by emotional, political, moral, and economic biases. Some providers have been shown to have very little compunction about defining someone as mentally ill, if so defining them will result in their obtaining insurance reimbursement for the therapists' services. Such biases also influence decisions about what constitutes appropriate treatment and the end-point of treatment.

Some argue for an abandonment of the medical model in many cases of psychotherapy. In these cases the use of health insurance to defray therapy costs is inappropriate. Perhaps what is needed is a recognition that psychotherapists often provide a human service rather than alleviating illness. In many ways the assistance therapists provide more closely parallels the work of lawyers than that of medical specialists; we serve as hired consultants to aid in the decision-making and problem-solving process (Magakis & Chambliss, 1997a). Therapists help clients consider the options they have and weigh the relative advantages and disadvantages associated with different courses of action. Therapists help them learn to choose the most beneficial alternative and to confront the challenges they face. It requires real contortion for this to be framed as ridding patients of pathology, but the field's clinical heritage often demands this. The medical metaphor is inappropriate to much of what psychotherapists do, and pathologizing takes its toll on clients; yet, its use lingers because it supposedly confers legitimacy to psychotherapy.

A more accurate framework for describing the nature of the service being provided would eliminate the need for clinicians to be dishonest in assigning diagnoses and enable insurance companies to monitor delivery of psychological services more meaningfully. Jettisoning the concept of psychopathology where it is not actually relevant may allow development of tighter, more rational criteria for medically needed services, which ultimately could reduce the cost of behavioral healthcare.

Some see the real purpose of MBH as being to figure out the boundary between mental illness, which employers are willing to cover as part of a medical benefit, and other mental health interventions, which are far too costly for employers to cover for their entire work force. While many companies struggle to draw this distinction reasonably and appropriately, other companies seem to exploit the confusion associated with this ambiguous dividing line and withhold contracted services in order to unfairly inflate their profit margins. Some providers seem to be attempting to recapture the past by resisting all varieties of managed care, presumably to return to the formerly broad markets that would protect providers' income and standards of living.

As these positions are taken, each side at times lies about the other, with managed care companies saying that providers are stealing from them and providing inappropriate open-ended care with no proof of effectiveness, and the other side declaring managed care to be intrinsically morally bankrupt, uncaring, and beyond redemption. Misrepresenting the other side is simpler than grappling with the tough matter of delineating appropriately reimbursable mental healthcare.

Who Knows Best What Clients Need?

Is Clinician-Determined Treatment Length Best?

Managing care is not new; clinicians have always managed their patients' care. But only recently have cost and detailed accountability become central to clinical decision making (Schreter, Sharfstein, & Schreter, 1994). Formerly therapists worked with patients in private and generally answered only to their patients and peers. Third-party payees rarely questioned the need for services, assuming that clinicians and patients were responsible judges of this.

In response to insurance payors' demands for cost containment, insurance companies revisited this assumption, challenging the appropriateness of clinician-determined length of treatment. Gatekeepers and utilization reviewers now sit in judgment of clinicians' work. Although some practitioners staunchly defend clinician-determined treatment length (Miller, 1996), the available research addressing its potential advantages to date is inconclusive. Although clinicians understandably resent the loss of their former autonomy, some therapists report that working within defined time limits actually seems to have had some positive effects on their work (Austad, Sherman, & Holstein, 1993).

Incorporation of progress measures and external review processes was based on concerns about clinicians' judgments and the potential for their being biased. Sperry et al. (1996) discuss a case in which outcome data were obviously discrepant with the therapist's general impression of therapy effectiveness. It highlights how prolonged use of ineffective methods can occur when external accountability is absent. Therapists who believe in particular methods may define effective treatment in terms of conformance to their model, despite the methods' failure to produce the effects the client is seeking (usually symptomatic improvement).

In this case the therapist stated that at discharge, the client "responded well to psychodynamic, insight-oriented therapy which focused on understanding her current [situation] in terms of childhood and adolescence." The client was seen as choosing to discontinue treatment (after twenty-four sessions) to pursue treatment elsewhere that would be completely reimbursed by insurance. In fact, outcome measures taken throughout treatment revealed that the client's condition had worsened significantly during the course of treatment. According to both self-report and therapist ratings, therapy had been far from successful. Yet, the therapist's perception of the psychodynamic process was favorable, and therapy would probably have been continued long term in the absence of external review or client initiative.

While this may be an isolated and unrepresentative example of clinician error, the fact is that we have no way of knowing how common such mistakes were prior to managed care. There have been few instances in which traditional, autonomous therapists have subjected their clinical work to such careful scrutiny in order to assess the veracity of their judgments. In the absence of more data it is impossible to refute definitively the allegations that clinicians' estimates of progress may have often been at odds with those of their patients.

Reynolds, Ogiba, and Chambliss (1998) found that therapist expectations often exceed client expectations in therapy. Clients generally aren't asking for a personality transformation. If therapists try to create such change, they probably will (should?) encounter resistance.

What Do Clients Want?

We should respect the individual autonomy of clients to determine what they wish to change and the form of help they desire. Symptoms as experienced by the individual should be the defining elements in setting treatment goals and assessing the quality of treatment outcome (Dawes, 1994).

Cummings (1988) encourages patients to retain the major responsibility for decision making in the therapeutic encounter:

> In making a therapeutic contract with the patient, we want to make clear that we are there to serve as a catalyst, but the patient is the one who will do the growing. This contract is stated: "I will never abandon you as long as you need me, and I will never ask you to do something until you are ready. In return for this I ask you to join me in a partnership to make me obsolete as soon as possible." (pp. 312–313)

In their book *Every Session Counts: Making the Most of Your Brief Therapy,* Preston, Varzos, and Liebert (1995) give consumers the following guidelines to use in evaluating the quality of care they are receiving: (1) informed consent of the patient, with ample information provided at the outset; (2) assurance of confidentiality; (3) careful assessment and treatment planning; (4) objective evaluation procedures (e.g., test, surveys, peer review by other professionals); and (5) research support for treatment procedures (literature references should be available if you ask).

Clients seek therapy for a variety of reasons: to change their perspective, their understanding, their decisions, their feelings, or their behavior (Reynolds, Ogiba, & Chambliss, 1998). Distinguishing among these different therapeutic agendas is important in streamlining the helping process.

Psychotherapy usually addresses five main client objectives. The first involves determining whether or not a given problem actually exists and whether its magnitude is sufficient to warrant special attention. Our society's open, relativistic discussions about the wide range of human experience fail to provide some people with a clear sense of what is appropriate. While some find this relieving and conclude that anything goes, others drift uneasily. Without clear boundaries, private fears can incubate. Casual use of diagnostic nomenclature fuels these self-doubts (My boss said my desk looked "compulsively" organized . . . is there something wrong with me?). Popularly publicized norms of self-reported sexual experience from questionable surveys invite disturbing comparisons. Televised portrayals of "dysfunctional families," which seem eerily familiar, prompt more questions. It can be hard to know whether "You're Okay." Many clients use therapy to compare their experiences with a yardstick of normality they assume the therapist possesses. They are interested in gauging how unusual or deviant their experience of distress is and reaching a decision about whether or not their life is enough of a mess to warrant changes. They may use therapy to measure the severity of their problems in living and to specify the serious stumbling blocks they are confronting.

Psychotherapy can also be used as a tool for fashioning an intellectually satisfying, cogent, plausible explanation for the circumstances of one's life. Clients often use therapy to address their need to understand and make sense of themselves and their relationships. Therapy offers a broad menu of explanatory options, and clients with this second agenda will usually be happiest when a therapist succeeds in creating a credible story of causation that simplifies complex and confusing phenomena in a way that restores the client's sense of control and optimism. It is best to say "usually," because some clients seem perversely drawn to very lengthy, elaborate, intricate, even counterintuitive tales of origin that seem to cast them as enduring victims. This is consistent with the observation that some clients seem to expect from therapy little beyond a compelling explanation for their pain. They evaluate therapy and their therapist very positively, despite the fact that their symptoms remain intact. Increasing the client's sense of having a grasp on a situation may be all a client seeks. Sometimes clients use this self-discovery process as a way of stalling change. It is often far less threatening to figure out why you're in the mess you're in than to change the mess. This is especially true if manipulating words and abstractions comes easily for a client. Creating a life story that expiates and serves defensive needs for self-flattery is reinforcing for many clients.

The third need that clients may present is deciding whether or not they should make changes. After clients make the determination that their life is a mess, they still must assess whether they want to do anything about it. Making the decision to change is frequently extremely difficult, because few life situations are clear cut; the status quo offers both advantages and disadvantages, and the future looms unseen and untested. Judging amorphous circumstances and evaluating unpredictable consequences is both intellectually and emotionally demanding. Change requires courage; yet, capricious, impulsive change is stupid. No wonder therapists often grow impatient with clients making this third use of treatment. The process can be time-consuming. It is also no wonder that many clients prefer to follow the quest for a cleaner autobiographical account, rather than to decide whether and when to jump. The decision to change requires an acceptance of personal responsibility many people prefer to shirk.

The fourth and fifth needs that drive clients to therapy involve assistance in implementing a decision to change. Many want to learn techniques for managing their feelings more constructively. They want to change their affective experiences, and are asking for expert guidance in so doing. The fifth need revolves around the desire to implement behavioral changes. Here clients seek specific suggestions about how to stop drinking, get along with their children, negotiate with their spouses, find a better job, etcetera. They approach the professional as an expert in living, employing their therapist to teach them skills that will make changing more efficient and effective. Historically therapists have been rather suspicious of clients who baldly ask for this kind of guidance. Such obvious dependence on others may trigger therapists' own counterdependent ambivalence about seeking help, or therapists may fear creating a "patient for life" if they indulge needs for gratification. Clients who seek direct advice are also sometimes denied answers on the grounds that fulfilling their requests would stymie their self-actualization. It is assumed that discovering answers on your own is empowering and fosters greater confidence and internal directedness. However, clients think our business involves giving advice. They believe our role is to consult with them and recommend appropriate plans of attack to use in their battle to make their lives more satisfying. We should hardly be surprised when clients look aghast when told that we don't offer "quick fixes." That's what they want. And in reality we now do have some of the technologies they crave. Although far from perfect, the behaviorists, cognitivists, and others have developed tools that can expedite change. These should be shared with clients who are eager to learn, and shared promptly (before their willingness to experiment passes). In these cases, clients should be given the type of brief problem-solving therapy their needs warrant.

Focus on the Consumer: Treating the Presenting Problem

It is vital to stay attuned to the client's desired objective throughout treatment, because this not only provides a yardstick for evaluating treatment efficacy, but also should frame the selection of therapeutic interventions. Clarity about what the client desires allows the therapist to circumvent much resistance. It can guide how every minute of the session is used and how therapists allocate their attention. It can shape how they phrase their comments, in order to make them maximally influential. The client's objectives should shape the process and outcome measures used to evaluate treatment efficacy.

The true measure of psychotherapy is not how well the therapist understands the client, but how well the client lives his or her life (Magakis & Chambliss, 1997b). Generating creative, clever, internally consistent, parsimonious explanations of the client's life is not the goal of treatment. Therapy should be directed at satisfying the client's need for a practical solution, rather than at satisfying the therapist's intellectual need for a psychological story that makes sense. Rather than using clients to support our theoretical world view (complete with interesting assumptions about the impact of early family dynamics) or refining a standard treatment approach that we'll pull out time and again, as therapists we should try to use all our energy to tailor what we do completely to each new client's individual needs (what the client needs to learn and how he or she learns best). Each case should be an adventure.

The starting point for therapy is the presenting problem, and in most cases that should also be the ending point (Magakis & Chambliss, 1997b). Patients know what's bothering them or what their problems are. They come for help, and the therapist should help them. This does not mean that their problems are unrelated to other issues; however, the patient should be the one to make the choice about whether these other issues need to be explored. It is patronizing and disempowering for therapists to assume they know what's best for the client.

Intermittent Treatment versus Termination

When the goals of psychotherapy are delimited in this way, our way of conceptualizing termination must change. The old assumption was that successful therapy was marked by an effective termination session that provided neat and tidy closure and finality. The diagnosed disorder had been successfully resolved, and treatment could end for good. Additional contact with patients following termination was often viewed as ill-advised, confusing, and countertherapeutic.

Perhaps we as therapists need to address the possibility that our old ways of conceiving termination were shaped by global and dichotomous thinking. Why did we assume that one episode of psychological treatment was the ideal and that variations on this represented technical errors? How realistic is it to think that all of a patient's problems stem from one isolated disorder, or to believe that once this discrete disorder has been treated there will be no future problems? In actuality, even when we can identify a specific disorder, it frequently changes over time (e.g., schizophrenia, obsessive-compulsive disorder), and treatment that helped at one point (behavioral or pharmacological) often is no longer useful.

Implementing new, delimited objectives in some ways makes it easier to initiate termination. By treating only the presenting problem, the therapist will know when treatment is complete. Clearly delineated, problem-focused treatment also means that it may be appropriate for successfully treated clients to return at a later date to work on a new problem.

A Caveat: Clients Don't Always Know Best

Although a case can certainly be built for making psychotherapy an entirely consumer-centered endeavor, there are some situations in which blindly accepting the patient's judgment might actually impair the quality of care. Obviously there are cases of egosyntonic pathology, when patients fail to recognize their real limitations and find their symptoms comfortable (even though they may create monstrous problems for those around them). Psychotic, delusional patients may not recognize their need to attend to reality more objectively. In such cases, clinicians would be abdicating their professional responsibility if they failed to insert their own agenda into the treatment plan.

Arguably clients can't always know what's best; after all, often their "knowing" is what is impaired. They have a narrowed view, with distortion and blinders making life seem overwhelmingly complicated and hopeless. Therapy aims at fostering a new conceptualization of the patient's predicament. The therapist facilitates the patient's taking a more objective view, and replacing their previous myopic perspective.

Patients are often ambivalent about their goals. Many seek treatment in part to clarify their confusing circumstances. This ambivalence complicates the process of defining treatment goals. For example, psychotherapists generally collaborate with clients in trying to help them behave more appropriately in the situations they confront. Therapy makes behavior more "normal", more "modal," to approximate optimal responding in all the varied situations of life. The paradox is that behaving more normally may not always be what clients really desire, deep down.

The reason for this is that when they behave more "ideally," our clients may feel that their personalities are vanishing; "normal" behavior is more scripted by the context than by the unique, special person. Adaptive behavior is not guided by rigid, inflexible traits; it derives from the situation, not from the character of the actor. If in fact what clients yearn for is acceptance of their unique selves and tolerance of their idiosyncratic flaws, learning how to act more optimally may leave their deepest yearnings unaddressed. If resistance to change is understood in these terms, it becomes somewhat less mysterious. Helping patients to develop alternative ways of expressing their uniqueness, which are less threatening and disruptive for others, can increase their willingness to abandon symptomatic ways of asserting their individuality.

Drawbacks of Emphasizing Consumer Satisfaction

While patient satisfaction is important, it is often not an accurate assessment of treatment outcomes (Sperry et al., 1996). Indeed, while a variety of studies have tried to show that greater satisfaction is associated with greater symptom reduction, these experiments have contained methodological flaws (Vuori, 1987). For example, by the time treatment ends, most patients have forgotten how sick they were at the beginning of therapy, so they don't really know how much they have improved. The healthier a patient is at the beginning of treatment, the more he thinks he has improved by the end of it and the more satisfied he is. But the patient's satisfaction may have little or no relationship to actual improvement. Other variables that may affect patient satisfaction include the amount of prior psychotherapy, the duration of the current problems, the perceived importance of treatment, and the patient's level of confidence that treatment will be successful.

Patient satisfaction has previously been found to be a poor measure of clinical improvement. For example, Attkisson and Zwick (1982) showed that symptom improvement explains only 10% of the variance in patient satisfaction. And, according to a study conducted by Compass Information Services (1995), the relationship between clinical improvement and reported satisfaction was not statistically significant, either for patients still in treatment or for those who had completed treatment.

Should We Always Treat the Presenting Problem?

While it certainly can be a mistake to dismiss the client's presenting problem as "superficial" and proceed with attempts to effect structural personality change, it is also an error to assume that always taking the client's initial goals at face value will lead to useful change.

As one of my colleagues once said, "If therapists could rely on their clients' statements of what the 'real' problem is and what they want to do about it, therapy could be done by 10-year-olds!" (thanks to Max Molinaro). Many believe that people often have a hard time divining what they really want from life and that clarifying confusion about goals and priorities is a central task of most therapy cases.

If inner conflicts about what one should want are common and distorting of self-knowledge (as Freud certainly was convinced), then, even if for the moment we ignore how social desirability can warp the external revelations about inner desires, therapists better not take clients' formulations at face value. Therapists need to come to their own independent conclusions about what is getting in the way of what clients say they want and how honest clients are being with themselves and the therapist about what it is they want.

Many clients initially attribute all their woes externally. New therapists often sit perplexed, thinking "How can I, sitting here meeting alone with this individual, be of help, given how the problem seems to lie with the bad spouse, bad kids, and bad job?" Sometimes clients are correct in their externalizing, although it is interesting how it often seems that the ones who would be most justified in blaming others are the ones who come in depressed with a general and global tendency to overpersonalize. But often the task of therapy is to redirect clients to a careful consideration of how, given the inevitable vicissitudes and frustrations of life, they can manage their reactions better.

When we believe a client cannot or chooses not to reveal his or her true agenda, traditional therapy assumed it was important to work toward more accurate self-understanding. The therapist's job was to work carefully to prepare clients for the truth about themselves, albeit frequently unflattering. Brief therapy challenges the assumption that this is necessary or even always desirable.

Discovering that one is cloaking real wishes in self-protective disguises is a delicious notion for some whose minds play comfortably with issues of ambiguity and relativity, but not all minds do. Some find the idea of unavoidable self-deception unsettling, threatening, and disturbing. It takes considerable psychological resources to handle certain insights, and not all clients with conditions in need of medically necessary psychotherapy have these resources.

A middle-age, traditional woman who had been married 40 years had fallen in love with another man and decided to leave her alcoholic husband but felt the need to insist the "new option" in her life in absolutely no way figured into her decision. Convincing her otherwise might have been incorrect (how could the therapist have known with certainty what was really causing what?), would have taken a lot of time, and might have actually created more problems.

One solution is to initially assume clients are the best judge of their ambitions and to start by working toward the goals they identify. Then, if it becomes apparent that a client is unwilling to do what both of you agree must be done to address the identified problem, it makes sense to point this out and to consider the possibility of an alternative agenda. The challenge for the brief therapist is to arrange for tasks that will rapidly betray such misdirection. Homework assignments are an important way of gauging whether the treatment is on track.

On one level, clients must determine their own therapy goals, but, on another level, part of our task as therapists is to help them make decisions about their objectives. Long-term therapy provided much more time for deliberation. Now we generally must make a working decision within the first contact. By the second session, we usually need to gather whatever information we can to help us reassess our initial formulation, making revisions when appropriate.

Making Referrals

In trying to make sense of behavior, there is a risk of engaging in circular reasoning. Invoking motivational explanations for behavior gives the appearance of explanation, without actually adding any new or useful information. To say someone produces original, creative works of art because the individual is "very creative" explains nothing. The motivation is defined by the very behavior it purports to explain. The motivational construct is actually mere description, posing as more.

Similarly, when therapy fails, therapists may be tempted to make a parallel error of circularity. "The client won't try what I suggested, so he's not sufficiently motivated. When he does what I suggest, it is because he's gotten motivated . . . as evidenced by his doing what I suggested."

Many therapists think they should be able to work with everyone, and they dismiss as "unmotivated" or "resistant" those clients who do not respond optimally to their treatment. In many of these cases, attributing treatment failure to internal characteristics of the client may protect the therapist's self-esteem at the expense of potential progress. Referring the case or consciously attempting a new strategy might be more appropriate than blaming the client's inadequacy.

How Can We Best Facilitate Change in Clients?

All therapists want to offer the best possible services to their clientele. Clinicians who rail against managed care resent the constraints it places on the conduct of psychotherapy, because they perceive those limits as compromising the quality of care they offer. Because managed care values empirical treatment outcome findings, conscientious therapists can use the research literature to foster constructive managed care policies. The clinical literature provides guidelines that are useful in developing tactics for promoting beneficial changes in patients as efficiently as possible. Several of the chapters that follow will explore how research can assist us in making choices about how to optimize treatment.

The common therapeutic factors that operate across all forms of intervention can be more systematically employed for greater effect. Solution-focused methods that emphasize patients' strengths can be used to build on existing competencies. Brief, problem-solving methods that emphasize specific behavioral changes can be

Summary of General Considerations about Psychotherapy

Managed Care Psychotherapy Is Not a Radical Departure
The more things change . . . the more they stay the same.

- Most therapists have been eclectic for some time.
- Most therapists have been brief therapists.
- Intermittent treatment isn't new either.

Traditional Long-Term Therapy Is Not Always Therapeutic
Iatrogenic Risks of Long-Term Psychotherapy

- Dependence
- Negative focus
- Stigma
- Relationship disruption
- Negative placebo effects

Five Common Client Therapy Agendas

1. Normalization
2. Analysis
3. Decision making
4. Feelings modification
5. Behavior skills

used to offer patients concrete suggestions about how to proceed, while communicating the expectation of rapid improvement. When particular diagnoses warrant this, specific ESTs can be used to facilitate rapid symptom resolution.

Equally important is avoiding the previously discussed risks of iatrogenic harm associated with psychotherapy. By keeping therapists accountable and focusing on rapid achievement of measurable outcomes, managed care reduces the risk that therapists may inadvertently facilitate their patients' procrastination by providing unfocused, rambling therapy that distracts them from their real need to make constructive life changes. In framing goals, it can be useful to remember that there is absolutely no scientific evidence that feeling good about oneself is a necessary condition for engaging in desirable behavior (Dawes, 1994).

5 Making Peace with Managed Care

Managed care is not some omnipotent, evil force that will destroy behavioral healthcare. It simply represents the current attempt to control healthcare benefits. In reality, psychotherapists have never had control of the flow of the healthcare dollar. With managed care the people who have this control are insisting on learning what they are getting for that dollar and are seeking less expensive means of providing necessary services. The resultant changes in providers' work have produced an angry backlash among some professionals who feel entitled to their former autonomy.

Although it is fashionable to demonize managed care and to view ourselves and the public as victims of the greed of MCOs and the corporations that hire them, this oversimplification may interfere with our capacity to perceive events accurately. Focusing on the acknowledged abuses of managed care may prevent us from accepting our own responsibility for failing to fashion better solutions to the crisis in the healthcare industry.

Did Psychotherapists Ask for It?

Healthcare costs have been running roughly one trillion dollars annually. These costs have quadrupled during the past 25 years; in 1996, medical costs represented 14% of the gross domestic product. Medicare is increasing at the rate of 10% a year, and mental health services have risen at the rate of 11.7% a year for the last 20 years. If healthcare costs had not been contained, some expected them to consume 100% of wage increases, represent 60% of the growth in the federal budget, and erode two-thirds of projected economic growth by the end of the millennium. These economic realities cannot be ignored. Clearly some changes in behavioral healthcare delivery were necessary. There is nothing ethical about maintaining policies that might drive the healthcare system to financial insolvency, forcing it to sacrifice essential services because of failure to limit discretionary services.

In recent decades, psychotherapists made great strides in marketing their services to the general population. The stigma associated with seeking treatment that existed strongly through the 1950s began to disappear, as the human potential movement and media popularized mental health professions, making it easier and more acceptable for people to seek mental health services. Inclusion of outpatient mental healthcare benefits became an enticing marketing tool for insurance companies interested in offering attractive benefits packages to employers.

With increasing numbers of people seeking psychotherapeutic services, the cost of a psychotherapy session increased from roughly $30 per 60-minute hour in 1970 to about $90 per 45-minute hour in 1990. During the 1980s it was very common to find professionals raising their hourly rates $5 annually. For years many insurance companies willingly paid these fees, because they could pass the cost increases on to the employers who were paying the premiums. In the late 1980s, employers contemplating ever rising benefits costs began to complain and seek efficiencies to reduce their burdens. Health insurance had become an entitlement many employees took for granted, but, as costs became more exorbitant, these benefits were excessively straining payor's budgets. Managed care developed in response to employer demands for a means to curb the growth in healthcare costs.

Wylie (1994) offers this summary:

> The therapeutic community has brought its current woes upon itself by its amazing failure to provide decent explanations, let alone a measure of cost and outcome accountability, for its treatment methods. . . . Psychotherapists have been held to almost no objectively measurable, external standards for deciding what is wrong with the client, what to do about it, how long it should take to do, when it should be considered done, and how anybody knows if it is done. (p. 30)

Managed care industry officials argue that someone needed to put the brakes on psychotherapy that could go on for months or years with no measurable improvement (Brink, 1988). An increasing body of knowledge shows that short-term, goal-oriented psychotherapy, rendered at significant times throughout life, can be very effective.

Perhaps if all licensed providers had held themselves more accountable and had worked harder to define, measure, and articulate outcomes, mental healthcare would not have become vulnerable to the cost-cutting excesses of some MCOs. Some professionals acknowledge that at least part of the criticism directed at practitioners is legitimate (Austad, 1996; N. Jacobson, 1995; Dawes, 1994). Too little energy was directed at monitoring outcomes; fee-for-service payment motivated some therapists to expand treatment objectives to fill the available compensated time, rather than to work efficiently toward delimited, specific treatment objectives. Diverting ourselves from this reality by battling big business, as if it were the cause of our woes, is naive, self-defeating, and misdirected.

The fact is that working with managed care is necessary in order to remain accessible to a growing percentage of the community. Many feel that it is inappropriate to deny your clinical services to an increasing percentage of the population because you don't like their insurance carrier. Providers work with MCOs because it allows the person seeking treatment to be seen; if the benefit runs out before treatment is completed, they usually work out a reduced fee that allows the person to continue treatment (Scholl et al., 1996). If providers are committed to making themselves available to the whole spectrum of the population, not just those who can pay cash or have a mental health benefit that doesn't frustrate them, they must develop means of working with managed care.

While MCOs are generally driven by the capitalist principle of optimizing profit, their success depends upon customer satisfaction. Managed care companies that misrepresent the quality of services they provide will eventually be supplanted by those offering more responsive services and value. Because managed care is new, it has been poorly understood by both payors and consumers. This has permitted some MCOs to foster false expectations about mental health benefits. Experience and education will jointly work to expose exploitative managed care companies; employees will complain, and contracts will not be renewed. This evolutionary process will help to refine a still primitive and obviously flawed industry.

Present incarnations of managed care are far from perfect; the system will undergo considerable reform as it evolves. However, it is no more inherently flawed than any previous method of managing and distributing healthcare resources. It is important to keep in mind that managed care is still in its infancy. The potential advantages of these new healthcare delivery systems, including improved integration of medical and psychological services, more extensive provision of services, and greater delivery of preventive services, are not all immediately realizable. The balanced interplay between corporate innovation, consumer feedback, payor demands, provider input, and legislative reform that we are beginning to witness will optimally permit the evolution of fairer, cost-effective systems with appropriate safeguards to ensure both quality and confidentiality.

Current consumers are the testing ground for these new means of curbing healthcare spending; they have every right to resent having the role of guinea pig foisted upon them. However, feedback from consumers and providers and development of appropriate regulatory legislation are integral to the development of managed care. Rather than angrily fighting the managed care approach at this point in its immature development, it might be wiser for providers to try to see the profit-taking excesses of some short-sighted companies as cases of impulsive adolescence. We may need to muster faith that market and legislative forces will redirect policies and compel corrections where necessary. Checks and balances need to operate on most new industries to make them function optimally; what is occurring with managed care is an inevitable mid-course correction. Inflammatory media reports probably help to spur the process along, although at times they present a rather biased, unrepresentative picture that may exaggerate the defects of managed care systems.

It is easy to get the sense that the majority of psychotherapy professionals are struggling mightily with this transition, and that most are kicking and screaming in protest. While there is no question that MBH has some very vocal, articulate, and thoughtful critics, in order to get a balanced view of things, it is important to remember who is authoring much of what is being written. Probably a disproportionate number of those writing about managed care are likely to be critics of it, because they are less likely to be busy preferred providers. The voices of the most successful providers are also sometimes silenced by the threat of peer rejection.

Vehement critics view MCOs as evil; describing successful negotiations with such a presumed nemesis leaves the managed care–friendly practitioner looking like a participant in satanic collusion. Many have been accused of "being in managed care company pockets" for suggesting constructive ways of responding to the challenges our profession is confronting. Those who try to accommodate are defined as part of the problem.

It seems that some of the most scathing indictments of managed care are crafted by those who can afford to withdraw from the present clinical realm and its pressures, often because their careers are already established and they don't need to cooperate. Those with academic positions and part-time private practices are sometimes in a position to stay fee-for-service, conduct traditional lengthy treatment with a few clients, and take the "high road" and oppose the changes mandated by managed care. Unfortunately, the training some of these academics are providing upcoming psychologists and psychiatrists reflects the mentors' biases and lack of familiarity with today's mental healthcare marketplace. This leaves many new professionals ill-prepared for their work. Most positions being filled today go to those whose values are compatible with managed care. The reality is that most clinical settings now require the ability to work within the managed care framework. In the clinical world, opponents of brief, solution-focused, cognitive-behavioral therapy approaches are being gradually purged. The clinicians who remain will have realistic expectations of what is expected of them and will accept the growing preoccupation with measurable clinical outcomes. They will resist the notion that what we do is too magical, elusive, and special to be monitored (by us or anyone else) and that effective helping generally requires limitless therapy contacts.

Weighing the Pros and Cons: Better Research Needed

At present a cloud of uncertainty hangs over MBH. The quality of care patients receive, treatment outcomes, and patient satisfaction have not been adequately addressed in most assessment studies of MCOs. While cost containment and profitability have been touted time and again in studies, what mental health behavioral healthcare is based upon—the health and lives of the patients—have often appeared to be ignored. Cost savings obtained at the expense of quality become a liability, not an asset.

Three Key Issues

Future research on the impact of managed care on the use, quality, and cost of mental health services needs to address three central issues:

1. What can we expect of the typical managed care plan covering mental health and substance abuse?

2. What potential is offered by the best and most effective versions of managed care?
3. What risks are associated with less careful applications of managed care?

Iglehart (1996) points out that so much change has taken place recently in the treatment of mental disorders and substance abuse because of the growth of for-profit companies providing MBH that we have outstripped our ability to collect comprehensive data upon which to base our decisions. The relationship between mental healthcare providers and managed healthcare organizations has developed uneasily in this climate of uncertainty, rumor, and innuendo.

Iglehart's report states that there has traditionally been less coverage for mental health and substance abuse in private insurance, because of the uncertainties often associated with their diagnosis and treatment. Also, private insurance companies have traditionally preferred inpatient care, which led providers in the same direction.

The role of managed care is to control costs by limiting the use of services. This causes concern that there may not be enough coverage for the severely and persistently mentally ill. The emergence of MBH is seen in part as a reaction to abuses in private psychiatric hospitals. Managed care companies operate by using reviewers to authorize services, and they often place providers in some degree of financial risk. The performance of these groups is controversial with providers because it often directly interferes with treatment decisions. They have grown in number rapidly, however, because payors are satisfied with them because they reduce costs.

Currently MCOs are primarily measured by how well they reduce costs and on process-related measures, such as how quickly they answer patients' calls. There is a growing awareness of the shortage of information about their impact on the availability of care or on patient outcomes. The proliferation of managed care has been so rapid and recent that existing research has been primitive, generally only examining basic variables such as utilization patterns, consumer satisfaction, and quantity of care. Staunch critics complain that the quality of care is jeopardized when treatment is forced to conform to the parameters of managed care. However, given the absence of empirical research, these objections are based largely on conjecture.

Most conclude that MBH has realized significant cost savings and that it has also had a significant impact on the role of providers; however, there is little information about patient outcomes. Iglehart (1996) and others have expressed concerns about the possibility that MBH may stifle development of new drugs and treatments and that the chronically mentally ill will not be well enough served. David Mechanic et al. (1995) assessed the management of mental health and substance abuse services and concluded that managed care is being applied to the treatment of these problems in ways that are not sensitive to the special characteristics that distinguish these conditions from other health needs. It is easy to find anecdotal examples of both outstanding and distressing managed care practices. This makes it difficult to assess with any certainty the general consequences of managed care.

Many professionals believe that a broader array of outcome measures must be used, including ones that take into account the burdens of untreated mental illness on families and neighborhoods (including the physical and mental health of caregivers and the social costs of community living for people with mental illness). Only a comprehensive evaluation of how managed care affects outcomes will permit confident assessment of its potential for achieving efficiency while protecting or enhancing quality. To prevent expansion of practices that compromise quality of care, many individuals advocate more independent studies, including those undertaken by a watchdog group, as opposed to mental healthcare providers and MCOs. Better research is sorely needed to develop a more complete picture of managed care effects and its success in actualizing its potential for achieving efficiency while enhancing the quality of service delivery.

Difficulties in Accurately Assessing Managed Care

Although for years the critics of managed care have actively contacted therapists to solicit horror stories illustrating the human tragedies arising from managed care companies' denial of psychological services, they have been unable to prove that restrictions on psychological services are doing great damage.

Granted, building a compelling case against managed care is difficult because many of those receiving inadequate psychological care may be reluctant or unable to come forward. However, if the changes in behavioral healthcare delivery associated with managed care were responsible for the great harms the critics claim, some clear evidence of greater suicide or self-injury or family abuse among those covered by managed care plans should be accumulating. Thus far such has not been the case. Instead, the most obvious casualties of managed care are some therapists, many of whom are taking active steps to make career changes (Chambliss et al., 1996).

In evaluating MBH it is important not to overgeneralize findings from the medical and surgical areas. Managed healthcare has restricted access to both diagnostic tests and medical specialists. In the medical/surgical realm the specific efficacy of particular treatments for particular disorders has often been consistently demonstrated. There are many medical problems for which we have highly effective, specific treatments. Furthermore, unlike the case in the psychotherapy realm, many of these medical problems have a low rate of spontaneous remission and respond minimally to supportive placebo alternatives, and our diagnostic tests permit fairly accurate prediction of patients' need for specific forms of intervention and the likely prognosis if treatment is withheld. The conservative "wait-and-see" approach seems less appropriate in many of these cases than it does in the behavioral healthcare realm. Therefore, the accumulating evidence showing more negative medical health outcomes among patients belonging to more miserly managed care plans is not necessarily always generalizable to the behavioral healthcare domain.

While there are some anecdotal examples of both outstanding and distressing managed care practices, few well-controlled studies exist. This makes it difficult to assess with any certainty the general consequences of managed care.

On the one hand, therapists' desire to protect their clients may lead us to underestimate the true casualties of MBH. For example, *60 Minutes*, *Nightline*, and other exposé-style programs periodically solicit managed care horror stories from mental health clinicians. These requests highlight the ethical bind that "managed care" puts psychotherapists in. Aggrieved clients may come to the clinician's mind, but they are not obvious "horror stories" (perhaps no one died), and so there is a reluctance to come forward. More importantly, clinicians often quite rightly feel reluctant to place a client in this exposed position, seeing it as an imposition that might add to the stress the client has already experienced at the hands of managed care. Being labeled a "managed care tragedy" would rarely be psychologically helpful for the patient.

On the other hand, haphazardly compiled negative anecdotes build a shaky case against managed care, because even in many of the horror story cases presented by critics of managed mental healthcare, documentation of lasting harm associated with short-term psychological treatment has been absent. Although in these cases the clinicians felt outraged that treatment was limited by utilization reviewers, often no followup data are provided showing that these frugal UR decisions were actually damaging.

Furthermore, establishing a causal connection between denial of care and negative psychological outcome is impossible in most cases. Lazarus (1995) challenges the assumption that managed care is at fault in all unsuccessful cases linked to these plans, because the base rate of negative outcomes must be considered in evaluating the contribution that any healthcare delivery system makes to patient outcomes. Lazarus reviewed four cases of client suicide associated with HMO provider networks and concluded that, despite the fatal outcomes, the treatment in each case conformed to or exceeded professional standards (he used the American Psychiatric Association *1989 Guidelines for Psychiatrists* in his analysis). Families of the deceased patients were not reportedly dissatisfied with their HMOs, and no malpractice litigation was initiated in these cases. Obviously, however, the researchers were not able to interview the patients.

Lazarus argues that the quality of psychiatric care is not solely the product of the delivery system (HMO); the caregiver plays a large role in dictating the quality of mental healthcare. Maligning managed care on the basis of anecdotal evidence is possibly alarmist. It may be unfair to overlook the efforts at enhancing prevention and quality management that HMOs have initiated (Goldfield, 1991).

The Positive Impact of Managed Behavioral Healthcare

Educating Providers and Improving Services

A study by Craig and Patterson (1981) showed that managed care often enhances the productivity of psychiatrists. Other studies indicate there is often better-quality service in HMOs than in traditional community fee-for-services practices (Lurie et al., 1992; Ware et al., 1986).

Managed care companies have devoted substantial resources to trying to improve the service delivery of providers while containing costs. These companies give clinicians extensive written materials, with frequent updates reflecting new research findings. Long-distance educational opportunities are offered via the Internet and through scheduled conference calls to large networks of providers.

Achieving improved quality of care requires changing provider and patient behavior in usual care settings. Changing provider behavior is a relatively new field of study, but one in which there has been particular activity is depression in primary care. Some studies attempted to improve detection of depression by providing feedback to providers based on screening for depressive symptoms of disorder. Some studies of screening have found positive effects, while others have found either no effect or a negative effect (Schade, Jones & Wittlin, 1998). Short screening instruments with well-selected questions appear to perform as well as more elaborate ones, leading many to favor brief measures. Collaborative efforts between psychiatry and primary care such as training programs to improve diagnostic accuracy have been shown to affect interviewing behavior and reduce costs of care.

Saving Employers Money

Managed care has reduced mental healthcare costs by restricting use of hospitalization, making use of less-expensive therapists, limiting the number of reimbursed outpatient sessions, insisting on measurable outcomes, and stringently defining medical necessity. Reducing access to mental healthcare services has made MCOs many enemies, but employers were relieved to have this monster tamed. Employers had never intended to cover the cost of psychotherapy for those who were not suffering from mental illness, yet many who had been accessing the treatment system did not meet stringent definitions of mental illness.

Reducing Outpatients' Expenses.   Prior to managed care the vast majority of Americans had insurance policies without mental health coverage or with coverage that was extremely costly to the patient. The typical mental health benefit allowed for 30 days of inpatient care and 20 days of psychotherapy, usually with relatively high co-payments (Brink, 1998). Hospitals acted accordingly; treatment was often designed to reflect insurance limits, rather than being research-driven.

Linda M. Richardson and Carol Shaw Austad (1991) have argued that although the mental health benefits typically found in managed care plans have been severely criticized by some for their limited coverage, when examined closely, they do not differ greatly from the coverage offered by traditional indemnity plans. Actual out-of-pocket expenses for psychotherapy are often less with managed care than with traditional indemnity plans. A traditional group insurance indemnity plan such as Blue Cross/Blue Shield usually covers only 50% of the costs of outpatient psychotherapy up to a limit of from $600 to $2,000 per year, depending on the plan (Zimet, 1989). For psychotherapy for 20 weeks a year (the typical managed care benefit) at a rate of $100 per session, the client with a traditional insurance plan would have to pay $1,000 out of pocket (Zimet, 1989), whereas the managed care member would typically pay a small co-payment for twenty sessions. HMOs were found to charge a mean co-payment of $15 per visit for outpatient mental healthcare, and this co-payment was charged only after an average of five visits (Levin, Glasser, & Jaffee, 1988). Prepaid systems can be attractive, especially to younger people who may appreciate the generous outpatient benefits (Flinn, McMahon, & Collins, 1987).

Competition forces all providers to pay attention to what buyers want. Despite many doctors' notions that medicine is special, apparently many buyers are willing to take less than top of the line for a lower price.

Improving Cost-Effectiveness.   An example of the potential for improved cost-effectiveness can be drawn from the corporate giant IBM. IBM's experience in developing a collaboration with its managed care vendor and an independent mental health advisory board was quite successful. The program reduced utilization rates by 7% over a 2-year period (Battagliola, 1994).

According to data provided, as of the end of 1992, approximately 19,000 members and/or their dependents had telephoned for assistance. Of that number, 2,100 went to case management, 1,000 of whom were referred to alternative treatment settings instead of inpatient hospital facilities. This program utilized 22,000 providers and 1,300 facilities and programs. Two years before the program commenced, IBM's costs for mental health programs totaled $105.5 million a year. Disbursements of $98 million yearly were recorded during the first 2 years of the new program. Further evidence of cost containment for 1994 shows mental health program disbursements totaling $49 million. Acute inpatient care was reduced by 50% and length of stay was reduced from 29 to 14.86 days. As a result, alternative care costs rose from zero to $22.9 million. The cost of outpatient services was unchanged. From 1989 to 1992, utilization costs decreased at a rate of 14.8% to 10.5%.

This example suggests that the combination of an impartial advisory board working with an MCO and a corporation is cost-effective. Additionally the advisory board can monitor providers and ultimately can service beneficiaries with a higher-quality health plan. However, this study (Battagliola, 1994) failed to include measures of client or provider satisfaction.

More Extensive Service Delivery

Good managed care systems provide mental health services to subscribers who otherwise would not receive treatment. Bittker (1985) found that per capita use of outpatient HMO mental health services was better than twice the rate for fee-for-service systems. Lange et al. (1988) note that HMOs have expanded the client base for outpatient psychotherapy; therapy is no longer exclusively a resource for the privileged minority.

An Ally to Behaviorists

Managed care can be an unexpected ally to therapists who are already behaviorally inclined. Increasingly, in defining medical necessity, companies are emphasizing behavioral description over diagnostic groups. Implicit in this shift is a recognition of heterogeneity within diagnostic classifications and an appreciation of the day-to-day behavioral variability of people falling within a given category. Those diagnosed with severe mental illnesses have their "good days," even their "good months." Tying treatment decisions to specific recent behaviors rather than to general expectations based on diagnostic stereotypes can communicate more positive expectations about the potential for constructive change in clients.

A history of problem behavior is somewhat less likely than a serious diagnosis to doom someone to the unquestioning conclusion that additional costly treatment will inevitably be needed. There is greater recognition that people can change and that, in addition to stable traits of the client, fluctuations in the situation may account for symptom exacerbations. As a result, more efforts are made to alter the context in which a client lives, for instance by developing more social supports.

The scientific literature suggests that, in addition to avoiding unnecessary diagnosis, and using interactional models of causal attribution, we can often help more by doing less. Increasingly therapists are embracing the notion that once may be enough in some cases.

Facilitating Objectivity

Practitioner-scientists recognize their value as objective, impartial observers. Consistent with this, it seems reasonable for us to moderate our closeness with clients, using the therapeutic alliance to bring about the timely end of the therapeutic relationship, rather than to offer the intimacy and rapport of therapy as a surrogate for real mutual friendships. Managed care probably reduces the development of countertherapeutic dependency and inappropriate savior fantasies, by encouraging focus on specific, narrow problems. The use of treatment plans and outcomes measures helps us stay on track to maintain the objectivity we need to avoid bias and our own burnout.

Preserving Confidentiality

The restricted observance of confidentiality associated with the managed care review process is disturbing for many clinicians. However, the use of informed consent can reduce the risks to the client's privacy, as can first previewing with the patient any information to be shared with a reviewer. While some therapists balk at such disclosure, it sometimes changes the therapeutic relationship in ways that can be beneficial. Sharing information about treatment goals, methods, interim progress, troubling behaviors, and the rationale for continuing treatment can make therapy a far more collaborative process. It can clarify misinterpretations and provide the clinician with a far more accurate understanding of the patient.

Innovation: Reducing Emergency Room Visits

Desires to reduce expensive inpatient treatment have spurred research on innovative ways of responding to crises related to mental disorders (Sabin, 1998). One study was conducted under the auspices of the Department of Psychiatry of New York Medical College. Their Comprehensive Psychiatric Emergency Program is made up of a mobile crisis team, an emergency room with two extended observation beds, two satellite programs in other parts of the county, and a crisis residence. The program's goal is to treat patients in the least restrictive and most cost-effective way. Experience has shown that use of the mobile team to treat crisis patients in their homes results in fewer admissions than treatment of patients who present at the ER. (Only 30% of the patients seen by the team require admission.) The teams consist of two mental health professionals (usually one psychiatrist and a clinical social worker, RN, or Ph.D). Patients whose evaluation indicates no need for admission are seen by the clinical social worker, who arranges outpatient followup or admission to the crisis residence. Patients may stay in the residence for up to 5 days. The mobile team provides treatment and referral services for these patients.

Preventive Research

Managed care may foster preventive research. For example, a national HMO sponsored a large research project to explore the advantages and disadvantages of the use of generic medications. The results showed that while the generic drugs were cheaper initially, they were associated with higher residual costs tied to emergency room and extra office visits, so that over all they were less cost-effective than brand-name drugs. This is an example of how MCOs, with their substantial resources for comprehensive outcome research, may benefit deployment of existing healthcare technologies. Their structure makes them responsible to all facets of care, which may ultimately help the healthcare system function more holistically and could result in better healthcare decision making.

NCQA, which accredits MCOs, has standards on prevention that address screening, education, and implementation of prevention projects. Some MCOs are developing a "disease management" approach, which focuses on early identification and intervention. For example, both Medco and Managed Health Network, Inc. have programs for depression using nurse or pharmacist phone contacts to increase medication compliance and to determine the need for further treatment (Rudd, 1998). The 1998 report indicated that Accordant Health Services' disease management program reduced average hospital length of stay and admissions by more than 50%, by emphasizing patient education, monitoring, and prompt crisis intervention.

Improving Care for the Severely Mentally Ill

Many anti–managed care professionals focus on those cases in which MCOs blithely disregard the severely mentally ill. However, while some companies may behave with a blatant lack of regard for the pain and suffering of the truly mentally ill, others are working hard to develop more efficient and effective means of providing services to this population. Traditional inpatient methods for treating substance abuse, borderline personality disorder, schizophrenia, depression, and bipolar disorder have been far from optimal. Outcome studies reveal disturbingly high relapse rates for all of these serious problems. If not confronted, these high treatment failure rates merely serve to perpetuate the status quo, by guaranteeing a steady flow of returning clientele.

Research evaluations of inpatient psychiatric treatment indicate that inpatient care of severely ill psychiatric patients is generally no more effective than any of a variety of alternative outpatient treatment programs. Kiesler (1982) has reviewed all ten published experimental studies he was able to locate that randomly assigned patients to either inpatient care or to some outpatient alternative. These studies included an impressive array of outcome measures, including psychiatric status, subsequent employment, school performance, and independent living arrangement. Kiesler concluded:

> For the vast majority of patients now being assigned to inpatient units in mental institutions, care of at least equal impact could be otherwise provided. There is not an instance in this array of studies in which hospitalization had any positive impact on the average patient which exceeded that of the alternative care investigated in the study. In almost every case, the alternative care had more positive outcomes. (1982, pp. 367–368)

Caffey, Galbrecht, and Klett (1971) contrasted three inpatient programs in fourteen different Veterans Administration hospitals to which 201 schizophrenic men were randomly assigned. The programs were (1) standard hospital care, (2) standard hospital care followed by a 1-year outpatient aftercare program, and (3) an accelerated 21-day hospital program followed by 1 year of outpatient aftercare. In spite of the fact that length of hospitalization in the standard care groups was three times as long as in the accelerated care group, there were remarkably few differences among the groups during the 1-year followup period. All three groups improved during their hospitalizations. While the patients in the longer hospitalization groups were less symptomatic at the time of discharge than were the patients in the short hospitalization group, these differences were no longer in evidence either 6 months or 12 months after discharge. Rehospitalization rates did not differ significantly among the three groups during the year following discharge, nor did the level and nature of community adjustment.

Glick, Hargreaves, and Goldfield (1974) and Hargreaves et al.(1977) have reported findings from a study in which outcomes were compared for two groups of schizophrenics hospitalized at Langley Porter Neuropsychiatric Institute in San Francisco. The study randomly assigned 141 patients to either short-term (21- to 28-day) treatment oriented around crisis resolution and symptom relief or to long-term (90- to 120-day) treatment that emphasized psychotherapy and major rehabilitative measures. Long-term patients did not function better in the community than short-term patients did.

The iatrogenic costs associated with long-term hospitalization have been well documented (see Zusman, 1967, for a discussion of social breakdown syndrome). The grinding demoralization that results from repeated experiences with unsuccessful brief hospitalizations is evident in talking to relapsed patients. Better means of addressing the needs of the severely and persistently mentally ill (and their families) must be developed. The critical eye that managed care brings to the mental health delivery system threatens those with a heavy investment in the status quo, but it offers an opportunity to those who are eager for better solutions. In this era of scarce resources, we are being challenged to consider new treatment options. Our research has established that for patients with many chronic mental illnesses expensive psychotherapy contact with professionals is not measurably more beneficial than time spent with paraprofessional helpers (Berman & Norton, 1985; Christensen & Jacobson, 1994; Durlak, 1979; Hattie, Sharpley, & Rogers, 1984).

Given that underscoring the need for medication compliance figures so prominently in the care of those with severe mental illness, therapists need to engineer more cost-effective ways of providing education about the value of psychotropic medications and eliminating the barriers to compliance. Intensive case management has proved superior to traditional forms of treatment delivery in many states. Providing for ways to reduce case manager burnout and attrition will help this approach succeed in the long term.

Constructive Strategies for Improving Managed Care

Using Accountability: Rating Managed Care Companies

Even fans of MCOs concede that there are some bad apples in the barrel. Eager to maximize profit, and aware of the typical limited lifespan of today's MCO, some companies have blithely ignored the needs of subscribers and instituted review hurdles that are so inconvenient for providers that they often give up and provide services that will not be reimbursed. Because avoiding authorization of services increases profits, in the short run, MCOs that excessively deny services or postpone reviews are at an advantage. To counter this inequity, professionals are starting to coordinate their efforts to identify these problem MCOs.

This can be a powerfully effective strategy because MCOs compete furiously with one another for subscribers. As health plans merge and employers switch medical coverage to cut costs or improve services, HMOs and MCOs face an ongoing problem of how to retain members. Throughout the industry, managed care plans have averaged a 15% annual turnover in membership.

Systematic rating of managed care companies can help to protect both providers and consumers. Employers could not easily justify buying a plan rated inferior, even if it were a bargain. A rating system reflecting both provider and consumer satisfaction would be advantageous for responsible MCOs that have balanced their concerns for profits and providing quality services. It is quite apparent that the best companies are currently jeopardized by those that unscrupulously cut too many corners.

There is a pressing need to inform and educate the public about their employers' choices in mental health coverage. "Sorry, this plan does not cover marriage counseling." "Your child has ADD? Treatment for that is not covered by the company policy." "You were told you could continue counseling after your five EAP visits? You can, but not with the same counselor."

Of the over 160 million people covered by managed care plans, most have little understanding of their coverage limits or restrictions on the privacy of their records. "I have twenty visits" is something frequently heard from those who have attempted to do some research. The truth is, in many cases, subscribers have five visits, followed by a telephone review of therapeutic issues, symptoms, progress, strengths, and weaknesses, and then a random reviewer with no particular credentials will decide how many more sessions will be authorized, typically doled out two or three at a time. Because that reviewer's performance evaluation will be based on how well costs were contained, it is easy to speculate about the potential for biased judgment.

Managed Care May Not Affect Outpatient Utilization Rates

Some predict that outpatient UR is on the way out (Peck, 1997). It is estimated that for the past two decades behavioral healthcare's share of total spending has remained constant, between 12% to 14%. Outpatient utilization has also been stable, and studies by the Rand Corporation (Manning, 1986) and others seem to indicate that this usage tends to be relatively independent of the generosity of the benefit package.

Some of the research done on therapy utilization suggests that clients avail themselves of services at a fairly constant rate, regardless of the administrative structure of the helping agency. There is little evidence that setting limits on the number of sessions reduces the average number of sessions per client in general outpatient populations.

In one 4-year investigation at a university counseling center, 1,614 clients presented at intake. Eight hundred of these completed a first session. By session two, there were 700 clients left; by session three, there were 600 remaining. Only 464 clients remained after a fifth session, and only 170 clients had a tenth session. The mean number of sessions was 4.44 and the standard deviation was 5.56. (Interestingly, 87 of the clients had more than fourteen sessions.)

When the study was extended to a sample drawn from a Japanese university, there were 1,281 clients at a first session, 557 at a second meeting, 320 at a third visit, and only 179 at a fifth meeting. Sixty-three clients had more than fourteen sessions; the overall mean for the population was approximately four. Counseling centers in the 1995 survey averaged five and a half sessions per client (Gallagher-Thompson & Steffen, 1994).

What many conclude from such investigations is that the duration of therapy seems to be as much determined by clients as by therapists and that the attendance patterns of clients are relatively stable across settings and administrative arrangements. A large number of clients attend a few sessions, the average number of visits tends to be from five to eight, and a small percentage of individuals (5%–10%) get longer-term help.

Most of the recent increase in behavioral healthcare spending was attributable to hospitalization expenses, which account for between 70% and 85% of the mental health dollar. On the outpatient side the top 10% of users of outpatient treatment account for more than 50% of outpatient costs. The heavy costs of hospitalization clearly must be contained by creative alternatives and careful management, but several studies have demonstrated that if outpatient visits are limited to twenty a year, as they are in many benefit packages, it is not cost-effective to do additional UR and micro-management. Benefit design (amount of co-pays, deductibles, etc.) is increasingly believed to be all that is necessary to control outpatient costs.

Critics of UR conducted by nonproviders argue that it threatens care and causes provider morale to plummet. Zach and Cohen (1993) point out that nonprovider utilization reviewers don't provide any added care and may actually increase administrative expenses as much as 20% by some estimates. In contrast, some argue that UR conducted internally, by providers, improves care, reduces costs, and is less of a threat to provider morale. As more provider groups enter into capitated contracts directly with payors, the practice of internal UR will increase dramatically.

The Possible End of Micro-Management

Many MCOs are beginning to recognize that money is not saved by outpatient reviews. Lynn Johnson (1995) wrote that

> ... the medical director of a large insurance company privately admitted to me that they do not have any evidence they can save money by reviewing outpatient cases. He conceded that they do it because their competitors do it and the companies they insure think it is a good idea. It has become obvious there is little justification for outpatient reviews, especially the intrusive ones that occur after two or three visits.

While some MCOs are abandoning intensive outpatient reviews, others plan to use them to ensure increasing quality of care. In these cases the review process is presented as a total quality assurance mechanism. Many experts predict a reduction in intrusive reviews, such as those taking place after only three visits. In exchange for less oversight, clinicians will be expected to demonstrate that they generally follow acceptable treatment protocols and use an outcome-based approach.

In a recent conversation a managed care executive confided that she felt little benefit was gained by close outpatient UR, and that she would prefer to be in the business only of profiling providers and developing an expanding database of information that would be a valuable business asset. This may be a coming trend in MBH. Clearly both UR and provider profiling are labor-intensive, high-cost activities for the MCO. However, the latter can be done with computers and clerks more credibly than the former and as a result is potentially more profitable for the managed care company.

Some MCOs have begun to recognize this. For example, Options (a managed care company that insures a segment of State of Michigan employees) now only requires an automated telephone call that establishes the eligibility of a self-referred employee and requests an estimate of the number of sessions needed, with automatic authorization granted and no requirement of information on the client being sent out of the therapist's office. Therapists who fall too far on the extremes may be subject to case management at a later date. It will be of great interest to see how this plays out.

Developing a Balanced Perspective: Resolving Ambivalence

The conclusions that many therapists have drawn after considering all of the issues in the preceding review are far from straightforward. Many have decided that managed care is neither all bad nor all good. A balanced view of the various arguments leaves some feeling cautiously optimistic, and these therapists are most likely to find working in a managed care context comfortable and successful.

These providers have concluded that with managed care the potential exists to develop a more responsive means of providing behavioral healthcare for a large percentage of the population that needs it. They believe that the disadvantageous press for treatment of shorter duration is offset by a greater focus on consumer satisfaction and improved access to prompt, timely, competent care. Paring down the treatment process by eliminating waste can liberate resources that can be used to reach a larger segment of the population. Preventive approaches save money while reducing unnecessary suffering and anguish.

For those who are most optimistic, managed care can be seen as offering an unprecedented opportunity for progress in the behavioral healthcare field. The emphasis on measuring outcomes, making providers more accountable, and anchoring treatment decisions in the research literature has the potential to improve the quality of care quite dramatically. Managed care invites us to challenge traditional assumptions about diagnosis, treatment, professional training, and disciplinary divisions. By focusing on the needs of the consumer rather than the conventions of particular schools of therapy or groups of professionals, managed care can help to dissolve fractious barriers to improved understanding.

Managed care companies are threatening those who profited from the status quo, but these organizations are asking some reasonable questions. For example, do we know that less trained counselors can't be as helpful with this type of client? Do we know that weekly sessions are more helpful for this problem than more spaced sessions? Do we know that resolving issues from the past will improve current functioning? Do we know that seeing a professional therapist will do more good than harm in this case?

Simultaneously the risks inherent in managed care delivery systems should not be overlooked. The potential for abuse certainly exists, and the record suggests that some have exploited the system and taken unreasonable profits. Until more sensitive measures of quality of care are developed and until mechanisms for making all parties appropriately accountable are in place, surveillance and exposure of unethical practices must be continued. But optimists see this as part of the expected swinging of the pendulum and anticipate corrections in the systems as the evolution of managed care proceeds.

Coping with the Ambiguity: Achieving Commitment

Regardless of their ambivalence about managed mental healthcare, psychotherapists in clinical practice are expected to find it difficult to survive financially if they choose not to participate in such systems, because the majority of the American population probably will obtain their future healthcare through some form of managed healthcare organization. Adaptation to today's changing health service delivery systems requires that clinicians test their traditional assumptions about mental healthcare, including clinical and administrative practices.

Psychotherapists and counselors are facing unprecedented challenges. The demands for increased accountability and efficiency in treatment can prompt either growth or defensiveness. Therapists can respond to the challenges currently facing them as threats or as opportunities to improve therapy by resolving some longstanding controversies and ambiguities in the field. This may be seen as a time for constructive integration of knowledge about the helping process. At this juncture, territorial infighting among clinicians from different theoretical schools will probably not be in the best interest of our clients. Better would be an emphasis on the common ground shared by most therapists and a response to insurers and regulators based on our common interest in our profession and our clients.

Psychotherapists can no longer afford the luxury of their old amorphous, preparadigmatic approach to their science, with its encouragement of endless, unresolvable (and deliciously fun) debate. Vying theoretical models all offer partially satisfactory means of capturing complex, multidetermined psychosocial reality. This smorgasbord of models and metaphors is collectively useful in increasing our grasp of the challenging world we seek to understand. Therapists do not expect simplicity. Yet to outside eyes these competing theoretical models imply a lack of expertise. If there is no consensual, bedrock understanding, what do therapists really know? It seems to those outside the fold that psychotherapists can't agree on anything and that they don't know what they're doing. The survival and growth of the helping professions depends upon correcting this widespread misunderstanding.

Managed care providers are insisting that therapists demonstrate their competence and effectiveness, or they will stop paying. This demands that mental health professionals identify and articulate the consensus that exists among themselves. Psychotherapists must learn to speak more with a common voice, in order to provide an accurate picture to outsiders of what they actually do know and can provide their clients. This book represents one small contribution to this process of clarification. By examining the common ground and identifying some useful tools for separating the "wholly ambiguous" from the "more or less certain" notions in the discipline, fractious infighting can be reduced. Therapists need to specify their common assumptions and approaches with greater precision, or they risk being dismissed by others.

By articulating shared assumptions and highlighting common approaches to helping clients, clinicians can make the therapeutic process both more accessible and more acceptable to outsiders. After all, almost 50 years of outcome research supports the idea that psychotherapists' effectiveness is principally due to the common, nonspecific elements of various treatment strategies, rather than to any specific feature found in one specialized, narrow technique (Garfield, 1995). This fact should help therapists coalesce and work collaboratively to bring their talents to a larger proportion of those they have the potential to assist. Infighting just contributes to the erroneous external perception that psychotherapists lack a real knowledge base. By focusing on strengths and emphasizing more the vast areas of agreement, therapists may be able to squelch the myth that "shrinks" have outlived their usefulness. In reality, with greater transiency and social complexity, psychotherapists are more necessary than ever!

Finding Positive Potential in Perceived Negatives of Managed Behavioral Healthcare

The Impetus for Managed Care

1. Very lengthy treatments were considered to be "needed" protocols, even though they may have (financially and egotistically) benefitted the providers much more so than the clients.
2. Hugely increasing insurance costs threatened to bankrupt employers and government payors.
3. Greater efficiency was a way to achieve the cost containment that would prevent limiting utilization of behavioral healthcare services to all but the very rich.

Some Advantages of Managed Care for Psychotherapy Professionals

- Satisfaction of achieving positive outcomes with short-term therapy.
- Data collection by MCOs that can guide and explain treatment, sparing individual practitioners from doing ongoing, time-consuming research.
- Opportunities to assess patient outcomes more clearly.
- Satisfaction of working with a broader spectrum of consumers.
- Satisfaction of positively affecting more lives through the provision of briefer therapy.

The New Accountability

Managed care, with its more critical, demanding eye on treatment, is creating a quiet revolution among psychotherapists. Accountability was limited before. Records were largely confidential. Independent practitioners were shielded from any systematic form of monitoring or external review. The therapist's judgment was the final arbiter of care. The fact that the therapist had a considerable financial stake in extending treatment was of concern to some, but until managed care became the norm, few saw this as an important conflict of interest.

In the absence of explicit criteria delineating what forms of psychotherapy were candidates for reimbursement, providers with the right professional credentials were given free license to call whatever they felt to be a suitable form of intervention "therapy." So long as a reasonably appropriate diagnosis could be found, insurers assumed the care being billed for was reasonable, justified, necessary, and efficacious. No one really measured outcomes, other than the client and the provider. They did so in isolation, with a variety of factors making them far from objective evaluators of treatment success. Clients wanted to feel their time and energy were being well spent, and they didn't want to be labeled as treatment failures. Professionals certainly had a stake in seeing their services as valuable.

Therapists often colluded with clients who were using therapy as a strategy to stall making frightening changes in their lives. Labeling unfocused, rambling personal discourse "therapy" was an abuse of a poorly monitored system. Yet this was fairly common. Clients often found talking about making changes, deliberating the pros and cons associated with various proposed courses of action, far easier than actually making changes. This type of "therapy" was of mutual benefit to both therapist and client. If the government or insurance companies were willing to foot part of the bill for these egocentric explorations, all the better. Clients were entitled. But the money was coming from somewhere. It was coming from taxes or increasing insurance premiums being paid by everyone. And eventually tolerance for inflation of mental health care costs ran out.

Benefits of Providing Managed Care

In a sense, managed care asks us as practitioners to fulfill the mandate of our training: to develop and use rigorous measures of our clinical effectiveness, to incorporate the most recent research findings in our therapeutic arsenal, and to work as expediently as possible to assist clients who seek our help. Many MCOs are viewed with disdain because they encroach on our professional autonomy, robbing us of the freedom to practice in total independence. However, an argument can be made that the dizzying rate of new developments in the field precludes anyone from staying appropriately current without some institutional support. It is redundant for thousands of independent practitioners to make time to read, analyze, and synthesize the thousands of books and articles about psychotherapy written annually. The electronic era compounds the problem of information explosion. While it makes it much easier to produce contributions to the scientific literature, it does not greatly aid in the process of assimilation and accommodation; these remain largely individual, time-consuming processes. Managed care companies can afford to pay professionals to synthesize the current literature and then share it efficiently with their colleagues. Providing technical assistance and education to providers can improve psychotherapists' skills. Many MCOs have been criticized for over-burdening providers with reference guides, revised manuals, newsletters, and similar materials (Anonymous, 1995). However, in fact, receiving these tools is an advantage for practitioners who wish to stay "cutting-edge" without spending all their time at the computer terminal.

Although many providers balk at the UR process, it is not terribly different from the longstanding tradition of clinical supervision. Granted, licensed professionals define themselves as beyond the need for supervision, but most acknowledge the value of periodic consultation on difficult cases. As managed care develops and reviewers with appropriate training are recruited, the UR process could become something clinicians view as an adjunct to treatment. Quality UR can be a valuable mechanism for improving service delivery rather than an unwanted obstacle.

Managed care is forcing therapists to articulate what they do with clients with greater care. Amorphous descriptions of the helping process are being supplanted by clearer, more consciously thought-out descriptions of specific, effective interventions. This process of clarification can be threatening and frustrating. It asks therapists to examine critically what they do and why. The evaluation apprehension that results is certainly understandable. However, being encouraged to examine our work and assumptions more closely can also make us better therapists. It is arduous to approach our clinical work scientifically, repeatedly looking for cause-and-effect relationships and trying to consciously experiment with more incisive techniques. But continuous improvement requires that therapists stay students of this science and remain skeptical of anyone who argues that things are about as good as they will ever get—psychotherapy has tremendous room for improvement!

Managed care demands greater precision from us as professionals. Before managed care, terms such as "medical necessity" were used in broad, ambiguous ways. Managed care is forcing therapists to evaluate carefully the models they use to define the care they deem medically necessary.

Another benefit of managed care, as discussed previously, involves the promotion of interdisciplinary collaboration. Managed care has the potential to draw the helping professions together, although at the moment this seems to be occurring largely as a result of their shared contempt for managed care. In the future, however, participation in managed care networks may foster greater interdisciplinary communication, to the benefit of clients.

Defending Treatment Standards

Kleinman (1998) argues:

> It is all too easy to point to the potentially dark side of treatment standards and regulations without acknowledging their positive contribution. After all, in the absence of standards, practitioners are licensed to treat according to their own therapeutic

biases and remunerative preferences. The results are all too familiar, i.e., unwarranted surgery, endless psychotherapy, therapeutic fads, and so forth. There is a genuine dilemma between useful and flexible standards that protect the public and rigid regimentation on the basis of received wisdom that locks both care giver and patient into an iron cage of orthodoxy. This dilemma is sharper now for all professionals, not just psychiatry. And the problem almost certainly will become worse, because of a broad societal movement toward ever more elaborately refined standards. (p. 28)

Reconciling Ourselves to the World of Managed Care

Whining is probably a waste. Bemoaning the fact that managed care won't accommodate traditional long-term psychotherapy, which is premised on the assumption that "real change" only occurs slowly, won't make managed care go away. Given that, it seems far better for clinicians to respond constructively to the challenges ahead.

Reframing the new demands placed upon us can promote a more positive response. Although it is easy to feel threatened when anybody suggests we must do things differently, and a defensive rush to protect the status quo can easily result, the truth is that accumulating evidence from within our own discipline has been challenging us to look more critically at how we engage in the helping process.

Outcome research has generally failed to demonstrate the superiority of any one distinctive mode of treatment, yet enormous amounts of professional energy continue to be invested in championing one treatment modality over another. Understanding the literature on common factors or on nonspecific treatment variables can help us reduce this wasteful preoccupation with competing techniques. If we challenge the notion that any particular psychotherapy theory is absolutely "right" and the others "wrong," then we are free to examine critically a host of assumptions about what good therapy requires and when corners can be cut without compromising the quality of care. Managed care companies demand efficiency and accountability, but they are also looking for value.

It is in the MCO's best interest to work with providers who share their vision of optimal outcome. They prefer clinicians who are sympathetic to their need to contain costs. Establishing a record of providing streamlined, "no frills," "no waste" treatment will develop trust. When you encounter a case that demands more lengthy contact with you, your request for reimbursement of additional sessions is much more likely to be honored if this trust has been previously established. A survey of MCO providers found that therapists who had longer records of providing effective brief treatment when given MCO referrals reported greater satisfaction with the MCO's responses to reimbursement extension requests.

Risks of an Adversarial Stance

Delivery of healthcare has never been entirely fair, nor is it likely to be in the future. More healthcare is available to those who can afford it. Some find this unacceptable, but that doesn't necessarily convince the majority to make the sacrifices an alternative would require.

What alarms many people at this juncture is the risk of inflammatory presentation of the facts, which can promote dichotomous thinking. To evolve better solutions, we need to remain our most mature selves, mindful of the whole picture. If we fail, and cast the roles simplistically, we'll end up in an endless quagmire of legal battles that will absorb all the savings associated with this painful process and then some. To save 10% of healthcare costs, we'll spend 30% on litigation costs. Transferring these healthcare dollars to attorneys would be a shame. Only mutual problem solving will avoid this.

In considering insurers' reimbursement criteria, it is tempting to cast this problem in adversarial terms—"bad" insurers withholding care versus "good" patients being victimized. Some media reports challenge the appropriateness of insurers' decisions to withhold reimbursement. The reality is that these are tough calls; the term "rationing" incites, but the fact is that rational lines must be drawn. Escalating healthcare costs eventually would have made healthcare insurance unaffordable for almost everyone.

Insurance is no gift from unseen benefactors; it is our collective way of sharing risk. While we might all desire the most comprehensive, cautious, ample, and generous care for everyone, the truth is there are trade-offs we seem unwilling to make. Insurers and MCOs have stepped in to make the necessary but difficult choices that providers weren't always making very well. For the most part their process has included an appeals mechanism and some collaboration with providers. While imperfect, thus far this seems to be the best mechanism we have for addressing the unavoidable healthcare dilemma of defining the standard of care as a society that we are willing and equipped to pay for collectively.

Enjoying Your Work

Some mental health professionals have become discouraged. A survey reported in the November 1997 *New Republic* found that one in five mental health professionals was planning to make a career change. Interpreting this figure is difficult in the absence of a comparison sample of other professionals, but 20% does seem to be a high rate of defection from the ranks.

The new challenge is to find satisfaction in clinical work, despite the injunction to focus less on addressing the question of "why" people are the way they are. This section examines alternative paths to career satisfaction (e.g., helping *more* people, although doing it in less depth). Some emphasize taking pleasure in preventing small problems from festering. Others appreciate the chance to help larger numbers of individuals by working in a briefer format and by using group methods to reach more than one patient at a time.

Some managed care therapists find advantages in intervening less intrusively and less disruptively. Long-term psychodynamic therapy often created substantial dependency on therapists, which was sometimes disempowering for patients. Believing too confidently that the therapist knows best reduces patients' confidence in their own judgment. We all know of cases of people in therapy who feel the need to run every life decision by their therapist. By reinforcing inappropriate reassurance seeking, therapy can actually have a negative effect on patients' outside relationships.

Most of us are also familiar with the tendency of patients in longer therapy to idealize and romanticize their therapists. Although a reeducative therapeutic interpersonal relationship is intended to generalize to real, extratherapy relationships, we all know of cases in which transfer of social skills and affection failed to occur. Some patients become mired in unresolved transferences, whether or not their therapists acknowledge this. This problem of mismanaged transference is tragically illustrated by situations in which ex-patients have stalked their therapists. Sadly, this experience is one many therapists report having shared (Chambliss, 1996).

Many people who become therapists do so because they enjoy promoting and sharing the special type of closeness and sense of personal discovery that many clients find in longer-term therapy. Many therapists delight in figuring out the many complex factors that contribute to an individual's problems and behavior and enjoy sharing their insights with clients to help them fashion a more complete understanding of why they are the way they are.

Brief therapy and the elimination of being paid for longer-term treatment of more intractable problems threatens to eliminate or sharply attenuate these pleasures of therapy for many therapists. While research may show that the majority of therapy customers don't want or need this kind of therapy, some therapists will miss the satisfactions associated with more traditional, longer-term therapy.

It can be helpful to remember that long-term cases were always rare. Finding some self-pay cases or doing a little pro bono work can be useful if you want a few long-term cases to balance your work.

Accountability helps keep us all honest. We know better than anyone else how rationalization can taint our evaluation of our work. External review and requirements to remain focused on measurable outcomes may be inconvenient, but they prevent us from playing defensive, self-protective games in considering our effectiveness.

Managed care may create opportunities for touching more lives and doing better work, thanks to the coaxing of greater accountability. Accountability is a double-edged sword. No one likes to be policed, and we prefer to be trusted to do our jobs without oversight. However, simultaneously our performance is often improved by appropriate reinforcement contingencies and judicious evaluation. A more accountable system is often fairer and has the potential to reward more ideal provision of services.

Medicalized Psychotherapy versus Growth Counseling

Some therapists feel so deeply about long-term exploration of life issues that they have arranged their practices to avoid managed care and the constraints it imposes. Others preserve some time in their practices for longer-term fee-for-service self-pay work, while spending most of their time in managed care settings. Therapists who want to help people with leisurely "personal growth" will still find a market for this type of service, but in the future they will probably be wise not to expect health insurance to reimburse for these services. The challenge for such practitioners is to market their services appropriately, so that consumers can understand why such counseling is worth what it will cost them out of pocket. Use of group treatment modalities and small-group educative approaches can be another way of providing psychological services directed at enhancing functioning, rather than addressing medical necessity, to people in a way they will find affordable.

A Concern: Will Disgruntled Therapists Provide Worse Care?

The finding that working under managed care seems to accelerate burnout among many providers is of considerable concern (Austad, Sherman, & Holstein, 1993; Ware et al., 1998). Historically there has been widespread acceptance of the notion that attending to the psychological needs of caregivers can have a beneficial impact on the quality of care they provide to others. As we struggle to deliver quality mental healthcare within a tightening budget, attending to the reactions of providers is not frivolous, if adverse responses are linked to compromised care.

Because the greatest portion of mental healthcare dollar savings stem from sustained reductions in hospitalizations, a study showing how reduced therapist sensitivity is associated with increased inpatient admissions is worth noting. This research suggests a way in which we could win the battle but lose the war on cost containment, if we are short-sighted and neglect the long-term impact of forcing increased productivity on therapists.

The Segal et al.(1995) study on the effects of quality of care on the outcomes in county general hospital psychiatric emergency services found evidence of a link between therapist sensitivity and hospital admission. In psychiatric emergency services evaluation the main question is whether or not the patient should be retained for inpatient care. These researchers found that an interpersonally sensitive approach to the patient was associated with both improved functioning and release from acute care.

Conscientious Streamlining: Cutting the Right Corners

Ethical care management requires that in any conflict of interest the patient comes first. Providers are expected to advocate for the patient's best interest, while remaining mindful of the objectives of the MCO.

> The transition from the individual perspective to the population-based perspective has been difficult for many clinicians who have not had a broad public health, community mental health, or managed care background. This shift is all the more difficult because patients and the courts ultimately hold clinicians responsible for treatment outcome. One solution is for clinicians to position themselves as their patients' advocates within the system of care. (Schreter, 1997, p. 656)

Many construe the obligation to advocate for the patient's needs to be a cornerstone of ethical care management.

Simultaneously clinicians must remember that patient advocacy is not synonymous with simplistically declaring war on all managed care practices. Competent advocacy is realistic rather than idealistic. It demands flexibility and creative treatment planning. Skillful representation of patients in the utilization management process is as important as the willingness to appeal when all else fails. Clinicians and managers have long recognized that the most skillful advocates are also the most successful.

Some advocate the following rule of thumb: If you wouldn't want to see it in the newspaper, don't do it. Conversely, if you couldn't, in good conscience, explain to a reporter why it wasn't done, figure out how to get it done (Schreter, 1997).

Managed Care: Friend or Foe?

Professional psychology and psychiatry conferences, journal articles, and web sites are filled with angry criticism of managed care. Many argue that managed care compromises clients' welfare and that vast profits for MCOs are coming at the expense of healthcare consumers and exploited providers.

While the current system clearly falls short of perfection, the key question seems to be whether behavioral healthcare management represents a beginning step in the right direction. If it does, then the professional community should find ways of enhancing its effectiveness, rather than setting up an adversarial stalemate that can hamper communication and collaboration.

The managed care movement emphasizes cost containment and efficient provision of services. The better MCOs have also made the concept of value central; they promote the consumer-centered provision of cost-effective services. In order to achieve their objective of enhancing the quality of services provided, MCOs also emphasize accountability. Therapists are expected to demonstrate their effectiveness through outcome assessment.

It is hard to argue with the goal of cost containment. Prior to managed care, spiraling indemnity plan costs were threatening to bankrupt employers and government payors. The largely unmonitored fee-for-service approach to providing mental healthcare to insured clients was very rewarding to therapists who provided lengthy, expensive sessions to every insured individual who contacted the therapist about the possibility of treatment. Without incentives to be judicious about client selection and with no demand for objective monitoring of client progress, it is easy to understand why many practitioners were comfortable defining everyone who thought they might benefit from therapy as "needing" therapy (on the basis of the longstanding tradition of using subjective, personal distress criteria for the selection of outpatients). It is also easy to understand how therapy often spanned periods of years and years; indemnity plans often made doing long-term therapy extremely lucrative. Without an external demand for use of objective outcome measures, therapists understandably relied upon their own expert opinions and clients' self-reports in assessing whether clients were moving in a desirable direction during the course of treatment—despite the fact that all these experts had studied how personal gain and demand characteristics can greatly bias and distort judgments in such situations.

As matters grew worse, employers were in a bind. Their options were to close down and lay off employees or drop coverage entirely wherever possible. Managed care was a reasonable response to the imperative for cost containment. Greater efficiency was a necessity. The use of increased accountability to bring about this efficiency was threatening, but legitimate. It is reasonable to expect psychotherapy and counseling professionals to articulate the results of treatment more clearly for consumers and to measure the effectiveness of what they actually do in practice. The extant outcome literature is valuable; however, it often reports only the average effects of atypical versions of standardized treatments provided to limited client samples by atypical providers in unusual settings. The generalizability of such findings is therefore often questionable. Extrapolating to the individual case from normative data has always been anathema; introductory psychology courses still teach that the many exceptions to the rule (variability) make such extrapolation misleading and dangerous. So it is incumbent on practitioners to develop ways of collecting outcome data that are relevant to their specific modes of practice. The MCOs have been attempting to do this in the absence of better techniques. They certainly aren't doing it perfectly yet, but their objective of enabling therapists to assess the outcomes associated with particular interactions with clients will help therapists to understand the actual impact of their services much more clearly. Therapists probably should adopt this mission to measure what therapy does more completely and relevantly.

The debate seems to be frequently sidetracked by complaints about some CEOs who have made millions of dollars by providing the cost-containment services corporations so desperately sought. Many argue that MCOs are a problem because their administrators have profited excessively from restrictions on care and limited payments to providers. It is helpful to keep in mind that the rapid evolution that is occurring in healthcare will probably remedy much of this problem in relatively short order. Corporations and governments are already realizing that for-profit MCOs may be unnecessary middlemen: Increasingly they are directly contracting with providers and eliminating the need for the MCO administrative level. As payors join directly with providers and large, capitated group practices develop, many expect a higher percentage of healthcare resources to go directly into service delivery, rather than to MCO profits. Some herald the fact that, as this evolution progresses, MCO executives won't be skimming so much off the top. The fact that this temporary, arbitrary element of the current managed care process is a problem should not keep us from taking an open-minded look at how managed care might eventually develop into a form that serves consumers better than the previous system.

SECTION THREE

Preparing for the New Demands of Managed Care

Understanding the expectations of MCOs will make your work as a provider more satisfying and far less frustrating. The following section summarizes the priorities of these companies and will help you learn how to think like a care reviewer. The goal of managed care systems is to meet the circumscribed needs of consumers as efficiently and effectively as possible, while maintaining high levels of client satisfaction. MCOs therefore seek and reward therapists who can provide competent, customized, cost-conscious care. Using research-grounded treatments, offering minimally restrictive and intrusive forms of intervention, and articulating your success through routine use of objective outcome measures will all help to establish your reputation as outstanding provider.

6 What Managed Care Expects from Providers

What do managed care companies want? What does managed care expect from behavioral healthcare providers? Becoming a successful managed behavioral healthcare provider can seem to be an overwhelming challenge, fraught with ambivalence. Adopting the requisite therapeutic framework will enable you to work more effectively in a managed care context. Understanding what these companies value and expect can also help you decide whether this type of work would be right for you. This chapter explores the answers to questions about what managed care expects in light of the experiences of successful managed care providers.

The wildly varying utilization and quality control practices subsumed by the label "managed care" make it difficult to generalize about the new rules and requirements governing effective practice. Managed care companies present providers with a constantly shifting patchwork of practices and standards generated by individuals with different underlying motivations. However, there are some regularities across all MCOs that offer useful guidance to those preparing themselves to work as clinicians under managed care. This chapter will explore some of the expectations that operate consistently across different MCOs.

Alongside discussion of these new expectations is commentary about common stumbling blocks that make it difficult for many therapists to adjust to the world of managed care. Many providers complain that there is a conflict between the way therapists have been trained to approach therapy and the demands of managed healthcare. Therapists need to resolve these conflicts in order to survive in the managed healthcare field.

The Managed Care Mindset

The directions in healthcare management have changed, chiefly because of the much more intense focus on accountability for efficiency and value. Efficiency equals the rate of return from the investment of time and resources. In healthcare, value equals outcomes/cost, where "outcomes" is the sum of clinical and satisfaction outcomes, less the costs associated with adverse outcomes. Although the field has only started to measure these variables with any precision, and much controversy about appropriate measurement is likely to persist, it is useful to adopt this perspective in evaluating proposed services for patients.

$$\text{value} = \frac{\text{desired outcomes} - \text{adverse outcomes}}{\text{cost}}$$

In saturated, mature managed care markets, healthcare delivery systems have had to address both the numerator and the denominator, because of competition for contracts. It is often considerably easier, especially for managers with short-term horizons, who are also accountable to investors and who move around a lot in their careers, to concentrate on the denominator. If nothing else, it is easily measured. However, the future belongs to those who can balance both quality and cost.

Research by Austad, Sherman, and Holstein (1993) on a large sample of psychologists, psychiatrists, and social workers showed that effective MCO and HMO psychotherapists tend to shed long-term psychodynamic orientations and to use more eclectic and nontraditional problem-solving short-term therapy models. Competencies in brief therapy, crisis management, and treatment planning were important clinical priorities, despite the fact that the majority of respondents (60.7%) felt they had not been adequately prepared for this type of work in graduate school. These researchers recommended that MCO and HMO policies should favor selection of clinical staff whose values are compatible with the philosophy, structure, and needs of the HMO.

No matter where you go, or what the organization's mission statement, if you are going to be both effective and satisfied, you need to be able to understand the worlds of both administrators and clinicians. You must span the boundaries of both roles and see the complete picture. In addition, you want to help guide your fellow clinicians to contribute actively to the process of developing, implementing, measuring against, and improving on treatment and utilization guidelines.

The concepts underlying MBH are derived from the need to provide quality care while continually curbing costs. Criteria for treatment direction, duration, dosage, and delivery have been developed with these joint ambitions in mind.

Care Management Expectations

Providing services to enrollees according to their specific benefit plans, including a schedule of benefit exclusions, is central to viable care management. Without such limitations there would be no way for MCOs to predict or control service delivery, which would make appropriate pricing impossible. Working within the constraints of particular policies may be unfamiliar, but it must be mastered.

A policyholder's medical benefit package represents an agreement by the insurer to treat certain medical conditions with specific treatment alternatives under a given set of conditions in exchange for a fixed dollar premium. It is not an entitlement to whatever treatment interventions the patient or clinician feels might

Ten Key Concepts Underlying Managed Behavioral Healthcare

Several concepts emphasized by MCOs are likely to shape the practice of all insurance-reimbursed psychotherapy in the future. The following list summarizes ten key care management expectations and treatment preferences of MBH organizations:

1. Provide services to enrollees according to their specific benefit plans, including a schedule of benefit exclusions:
   - Delimit care to services covered by the benefit plan.
   - Delimit care according to chain of causality.
2. Aim treatment at restoring baseline level of functioning.
3. Delimit care according to medical necessity:
   - Use the *DSM-IV* nomenclature and behavioral indicators of medical necessity (e.g., dangerousness to self or others).
4. Provide services at the appropriate level of restrictiveness, intrusiveness, and intensity.
   - Provide brief, outpatient care whenever possible.
5. Coordinate care using various mental health resources.
   - Facilitate the case management process.
   - Refer to community-based service alternatives.
   - Provide smooth transitions across levels of care.
   - Reduce fragmentation along the continuum of care.
   - Avoid duplication of services or inefficiencies.
6. Select treatment interventions according to research.
   - Apply the common factors findings.
   - Apply solution-focused findings.
   - Apply brief therapy findings.
   - Apply empirical findings about specific treatments.
   - Select methods strategically based on time limits.
   - Provide brief, problem-oriented, goal-focused treatment.
7. Use an accountable treatment process that demonstrates quality.
   - Develop concrete, realistic, written treatment plans with measurable goals and measure treatment outcomes.
   - Organize patient care around standardized treatment guidelines and preferred practices, to ensure that care is consistently delivered, is evaluated by objective standards, and is based on clinical signs and symptoms.
8. Use less expensive treatment settings and methods whenever appropriate.
   - Use outpatient services whenever possible.
   - Use inpatient services to manage crises and stabilize, basing length of stay on clinical need, as opposed to rigid programmatic expectations.
   - Use group and self-help treatment modalities.
   - Use paraprofessional and peer helpers.
   - Offer couples and family systems interventions.
   - Employ pharmacotherapy to the appropriate level for your discipline.
9. Know and use preventive strategies to reduce future costs.

(continued)

Ten Key Concepts Underlying Managed Behavioral Healthcare   Continued

10. Collaborate in the mutual effort to optimize treatment quality while containing costs.
    - Attempt to maximize patient satisfaction.
    - Facilitate patients' acceptance of limited care.
    - Accept fiscal accountability, through capitation or incentive structures.
    - Accept ongoing evaluation of providers' performance.
    - Conform to administrative procedures in documenting care.

---

potentially be reasonable. For example, most health insurance policies do not reimburse for academic testing, even though most child and adolescent clinicians view academic testing as an essential part of the evaluation process of an academically underachieving student. Clinicians should understand each patient's benefit plan and organize treatment within its limitations. Doing so requires conscious inclusion of informal helping avenues. Clinicians contribute to their patients' health and welfare when they direct them to the school or community for uncovered services, just as they help their patients when they personally provide services that are covered under the patients' medical benefit.

Typical mental health conditions covered under managed care tend to be those that require an *immediate* intervention:

- *Emergency care* for patients who may be dangerous to themselves or others
- *Acute care* for short-term life crises
- *Marital or family conflict*, especially if abuse is involved
- *Brief solution-focused problem solving*
- *Assessment and referral for chronic mental illness* (screening for long-term therapy)

With a client's medical benefit package in mind, the provider's expected role is to:

1. Limit treatment objectives and scope of treatment.
2. Limit duration and depth of treatment.
3. Provide a seamless continuum of care.

Delimiting care according to a chain of causality can be challenging for providers, but managed care companies expect this. Our aim in managed care treatment is restoring the patient's baseline level of functioning, rather than promoting self-actualization. After justifying the patient's need for treatment in terms of medical necessity, providers are expected to resist the temptation to broaden the scope of treatment to include non–medically necessary objectives. Providers need to constrain the care they provide so that it addresses the justifying condition and goes no further.

What you are treating now must be related to the initial referral question. You may identify several relevant factors that operate in a given case, but you are expected to confine treatment to issues related specifically to the preliminary presenting diagnosis. If someone initially presents with panic attacks, it is inappropriate to extend treatment beyond those interventions needed to deal with that problem and to end up doing unrelated counseling, such as marital therapy, even though the individual might arguably be in need of marital counseling. This can be especially important in dealing realistically with personality disorders in the managed care context.

Therapists often see one delimited problem a patient presents as symptomatic of other more general problems in the patient's life. Managed healthcare requires a narrowing of emphasis on the presenting problem, to the exclusion of other ancillary problems. Both HMOs and MCOs contract to ameliorate specific psychiatric symptoms, rather than to defray the cost of counseling aimed at fostering personal growth and expanded consciousness. Instead of succumbing to the temptation to overtreat, aim treatment at returning patients to their best previous or premorbid level of functioning. It is important to resist the temptation to pursue more lofty goals than contracts stipulate.

Managed care expects providers to delimit care according to medical necessity and to use the *Diagnostic and Statistical Manual of Mental Disorders* (*DSM-IV*) nomenclature and behavioral indicators of medical necessity (e.g., dangerousness to self or others). The concept of medical necessity emerged in the 1980s when payors and their agents turned to UR of each treatment decision in an effort to contain costs (Kuder & Kuntz, 1996). Determining medical and psychological necessity involved an effort to standardize and eventually publicize the criteria by which payors commit to paying for services and decide on the level of care at which these services should be delivered. Providers need to organize their treatment plans around these published criteria if they hope to maximize services and reimbursement.

It is increasingly incumbent on providers to demonstrate the appropriateness of providing services in each particular case. Increasingly we are asked to justify our decision to intervene in terms of medical necessity. While in some instances we can point to physical risks that psychotherapy will reduce, more often we must couch medical necessity in terms of how the presenting problem is impairing the client's ability to perform some necessary major life function (work, family, or social). Medically necessary mental healthcare is defined in terms of a comparison of the client's capacity to function in a healthy manner with and without treatment.

Behavioral indicators of medical necessity (e.g., dangerousness to self or others) are also increasingly being emphasized in making treatment authorization decisions. In recent years, MCOs have been moving away from a diagnosis-based system of reimbursement. Instead, their priority is risk management, and accordingly their decisions about when to extend outpatient treatment beyond the stipulated minimum are based on evidence of client dangerousness. Suicidal and homicidal evidence counts heavily, as do behaviors that could escalate and result in the need for costly inpatient stays in psychiatric hospitals. *Behavior matters more than diagnosis.*

This does not mean the diagnostic system has become obsolete, but rather that we must make different use of the system than we did in the past. The *DSM-IV* describes the modal symptoms and behavioral risks associated with various disorders. In discussing utilization with MCO representatives, we need to translate diagnostic categories into behavioral terms relevant to the criteria being used by the MCO. What is important is how symptomatic behavior is immediately being manifested in ways that pose hazards. Someone with a longstanding eating disorder may or may not be in jeopardy. Reviewers want to understand the current level of threat and want treatment described in terms of how it will address the immediate needs of the client. Managed care contracts cover services that effectively reduce psychiatric symptoms; curing the underlying disorder is not the objective, per se.

Because many individuals who seek therapy are best described as having problems in living, rather than formal disorders, many candidates for therapy fail to meet the diagnostic criteria required for reimbursement of services. This often presents ethical dilemmas for the therapist. Survey data suggest that many providers have exaggerated the seriousness of clients' conditions in order to satisfy insurance criteria (Scholl et al., 1996). This frequent practice has the real risk of compromising trust between reviewers and providers, making mutual collaboration that much less likely. You need to resist the temptation to manipulate diagnoses.

Limiting the duration and depth of treatment without compromising the quality of care requires managed care providers to "work smarter." Clinicians must understand the impact of time limits on care, because brief interventions are favored at every level of care. Although the fact is that psychological interventions have always been short-term (Garfield, 1986a), in modern behavioral practice they must be short-term by design, rather than by default (Budman & Gurman, 1988).

In many respects, behavioral healthcare is coming to resemble the practice of primary care medicine. Typically patients come for help with acute problems or acute exacerbations of chronic problems. Treatment is concluded when the presenting symptoms are resolved. Although each individual episode may be short term, the treatment relationship may endure over a long period of intermittent treatment, managed care contracts permitting. Emphasis will continue to be on providing services at the appropriate level of restrictiveness and intrusiveness, using brief outpatient care to the greatest extent possible.

Managed care offers patients the greatest advantages when a seamless continuum of care is provided. Such a continuum recognizes the shifting needs of consumers and is designed to flexibly accommodate these changing requirements most cost-effectively. Using a wide variety of traditional and nontraditional mental health resources can meet patients' needs while holding costs down. Providing group treatment, encouraging use of self-help strategies, and using paraprofessional and peer helpers can all reduce spending, while ensuring that patients have the support and guidance they need.

Referring patients to community-based service alternatives when more costly alternatives are unavailable is also common with managed care. Providing smooth transitions across different levels of care and reducing fragmentation along the continuum of care are important for patient satisfaction. Many of the disorders we are trying to address are stress-responsive problems, and adding to patients' confusion by failing to coordinate different elements of their care will typically exacerbate symptoms, possibly increasing need for care. Coordinating care with primary and other healthcare providers can help us achieve the goal of providing more holistic, integrated solutions for patients' problems.

Managed care companies rely on case management to ensure appropriateness of care and avoid duplication of services or inefficiencies in service delivery. They make use of a variety of mental health professionals in addition to psychiatrists, and they try to integrate community resources into their client's care.

Behavioral interventions are increasingly delivered by nonphysician clinicians and treatment teams (Burk, Summit, & Yager, 1992). Effective care requires coordinating these different providers and the services they offer. Collaboration is especially important for patients with psychiatric and substance use disorders and those with psychological factors affecting physical conditions.

Closer coordination of disparate healthcare services should amplify the "medical offset" (Borus et al., 1985; Cummings, 1996), because patients who have been treated well for mental health and substance abuse problems should require less expensive medical surgical care. Groth-Marnat and Edkins (1996) reviewed the work of professional psychologists in general healthcare settings and demonstrated the financial efficacy of direct psychological treatment interventions.

Currently 20% of patients consume 80% of the mental healthcare dollars (D. Patterson, 1994). Case management represents an attempt to focus particular attention on high-cost, high-risk patients. Providers often view case management as a time-consuming and unnecessary burden, but it is becoming increasingly important as we struggle to allocate scarce resources more efficiently and humanely. Care managers contribute to the treatment process when they link providers, integrate treatment plans, and make systematic use of resources (Schreter, 1997).

Facilitating the case management process by nurturing good relationships with other members of the treatment team will both help the patient and improve your overall clinical effectiveness. In the past, communication problems often resulted in redundancies and duplication of services at best and countertherapeutic sabotaging at worst. Managed care demands that providers have the maturity to work collaboratively to find the optimal solutions for patients and resist the tendency to join patients in disparaging other "inferior" helpers, even though it can fuel a therapist's ego to see him- or herself as "the only one who really understands, the only one who knows, the only one who can help."

Continuous quality improvement programs can assist you in ensuring that consumers' needs are being promptly and appropriately addressed. These programs attempt to improve quality by identifying indicators that are routinely monitored. These indicators often focus on the five dimensions of high-quality healthcare:

- availability
- accessibility
- acceptability
- accountability
- appropriateness

Incorporating ongoing means of assessing your success in satisfying these criteria can assist your organization in detecting problems that can be remedied. Routine assessment of these indicators helps orient staff to important aspects of their work and motivates them to provide more patient-centered services.

Availability and accessibility indicators include the number of telephone callers who hang up before their call is answered, the length of delay before the initial appointment, and the user-friendliness of the benefit design. Patient satisfaction surveys and comparison of treatment protocols against standards are indicators of acceptability. Accountability and appropriateness can be demonstrated by outcomes data, utilization patterns, and actual cost savings for the payor. Organizing clinical and management services with the goal of continuous quality improvement will foster steady improvement in the nature of care your organization provides its patients.

Many mental health providers are unaware of the amount of behavioral healthcare delivered through employee assistance programs (EAPs) (Masi & Caplan, 1992). When EAP counselors refer a patient to outside providers for ongoing work, they may continue to serve as the patient's advocate in the workplace. Effective collaboration between mental health providers and the EAP can prolong employment, enhance performance, and improve the employee's functioning in the home setting. Working effectively with EAPs can enhance your success in being a managed care provider.

Costs of workers' disability compensation run roughly $70 billion annually, including those for medical care for injured workers, payments to employees during periods of short-term disability, and compensation to employees for permanently disabling conditions (Schreter, 1997). Presently employees' healthcare insurance and disability insurance are separate products, but many experts anticipate a future integration of these benefits. This integration will alter the role of clinicians, as they will increasingly be asked to help reduce the incidence and impact of job-related illness and facilitate employees' return to productive work. Understanding disability, workers' compensation, and other workplace issues can also make you more effective in providing managed care psychotherapy.

Treatment preferences for those who conduct psychotherapy should be to manage care ethically, optimizing rather than maximizing care. In doing so, the successful provider will:

- Adopt empirically justified methods.
- Provide accountable treatment of demonstrable quality.
- Favor cost-effective settings and methods.

Managed care expects therapists to use empirically justified treatment methods. Applying psychotherapy research findings conscientiously will help you to provide the cutting-edge, high-quality care that the best MCOs prefer.

Behavioral group practices and MCOs are accumulating vast amounts of data about treatment and outcome. Analysis of this information will reveal which treatments are most effective for which clinical problems and diagnoses in the hands of which providers. Clinicians must be willing to abandon less effective treatments and familiar theoretical positions in the face of persuasive, scientifically valid evidence.

Managed care providers are encouraged to provide services with a goal of optimal, rather than maximal, care. Overtreatment is recognized as wasteful and frequently countertherapeutic. The primary aim of managed mental healthcare is restoring the client's baseline level of functioning as efficiently as possible, disrupting the natural support system as little as possible.

To satisfy MCOs we must conceptually distinguish between supportive, conversational contact and directive, focused therapy. The former conversational activity can often be provided through less expensive avenues (including peer support groups and the informal support network of the client's family and friends). Although we as clinicians may pride ourselves in our knack for skillful encounters with clients in need of conversational support, a large body of research has failed to show the superiority of trained, experienced clinicians over untrained paraprofessionals in providing conversational counseling (Dawes, 1994).

On the other hand, this same research also demonstrates that the professionals are best at doing brief therapy (Berman & Norton, 1985). Apparently our training as clinicians makes us uniquely valuable in helping people make changes efficiently. It seems reasonable that MCOs should wish to use our services because of this special competence. Although we may enjoy conversational therapy and perceive a widely experienced need for this type of social interaction in our increasingly alienating society, extended conversational therapy is not the treatment of choice in the eyes of MCOs, and if it were, we trained clinicians would be less valuable to them, because we have yet to prove that our supportive conversational services are better than those available less expensively through alternative sources.

Working Responsibly to Pare Treatment

The nature of psychotherapy is changing drastically as a result of the growth of managed care. Many of the formerly dominant conversational therapeutic approaches are being used with an increasingly narrow segment of the population, and delivery of these less directive methods is increasingly constricted by managed care policies. Understanding the revised and expanded expectations of therapists associated with managed care can help you succeed and prosper. Adopting the required mindset will expedite your work and facilitate more effective collaboration with MCO representatives.

Working effectively within the system demands that we take responsibility for making the most prudent choices about length of treatment. We must not perseverate and keep clients who are not responding to our methods in ineffective treatment. We must recognize the difference between desirable and necessary treatment. And we must make use of our expertise where it makes the greatest difference, delegating forms of helping that can be provided less expensively by others to others. We need to learn to make more optimal use of the limited resources that will be at our disposal, and this requires adopting a new perspective.

Working for and with MCOs dramatically alters the nature of psychotherapy and the role of the therapist. Managed care providers need to be part lawyer, case manager, businessperson, referring agency, personnel manager, disciplinarian, and negotiator. Therapy will no longer be the simple expedient of sitting down with a client and discussing the client's problems, keeping notes, and collecting fees.

Increasingly providers are expected to justify their choice of interventions in terms of the research literature on empirically supported forms of psychotherapy. Treatment protocols and plans need to demonstrate the link between the presenting problem and the selected intervention strategies. The techniques being provided must be appropriate to the needs of the client and be reasonable given the demands for time-limited therapy.

Selecting treatment interventions according to the research literature can seem daunting at first. One way of demystifying the process is outlined at the end of this chapter. It is called the Speed Sequence. This strategy uses the findings from four research domains to help clinicians pare treatment by finding the least intrusive and intensive but sufficient type of intervention. The common factors findings emphasize how the majority of treatment success seems to derive from aspects of the patient and the generic helping relationship, rather than from any specific intervention technique a therapist may offer. Given this, it is sensible to try to elicit these universal agents of improvement as quickly and as inexpensively as possible. The solution-focused findings suggest that highlighting patients' strengths and competencies in therapy, rather than their weaknesses and dysfunctions, may result in faster recovery. When these techniques suffice, they offer a low-cost, low-risk form of intervention that has much to recommend it. The brief therapy findings highlight the advantages associated with focusing therapeutic work on clear, measurable goals and avoiding communications that implicitly convey the expectation that therapy must be arduous and prolonged in order to be useful.

The efficacy research on specific treatments developed to address particular diagnoses can be valuable in providing efficient solutions for those plagued with stubborn symptoms that fail to yield to more general types of therapy. The empirical literature on specific forms of psychological treatment permits you to use your patient's diagnosis as a basis for choosing highly specific interventions proved to be effective in similar cases.

Therapists who use a narrow theory to guide their therapy will run into difficulties, as their approaches will often fail to meet the requirement that providers avail themselves of what the literature has established to be the most efficacious form of treatment for a particular disorder. Providers are expected to be eclectic and scientifically grounded and to work independently of their allegiance to a particular school of thought. Managed care companies generally expect providers to have a mastery of short-term, focused therapy; diagnostic evaluation skills; and capacity for collegial interaction among psychiatrists, psychologists, and social workers (Lazarus, 1995). Don't be limited by a narrow theoretical orientation!

Accountable Treatment

Providing an accountable treatment process of demonstrable quality requires that providers develop concrete, realistic, written treatment plans with measurable goals and that they actively and objectively measure treatment outcomes. Organizing patient care around standardized treatment guidelines or protocols can help to ensure that care is consistently delivered, is evaluated by objective standards, and is based on clinical signs and symptoms.

Psychotherapy is increasingly assessed in terms of the impact patients experience and report on various outcome and satisfaction measures. Visible outcomes are a requirement of managed care; reviewers seek to quantify the changes in patients that accompany therapy, no longer trusting clinicians' self-appraisal of their work. Providers who demonstrate the effectiveness of the MCO by meeting their clients' mental health needs promptly and efficaciously will be favored. Provider profiling aims to describe each clinician in terms of their effectiveness in resolving particular types of client problems.

As a result of managed care there is growing interest in treatment outcomes and client satisfaction. As competition among MCOs grows and companies increasingly market themselves in terms of quality and "value added," consumer satisfaction is expected to become a major priority. Your providing consumer-centered, respectful care that meshes with the desires and values of the client will be prized. Retention of payors is in the MCOs' best financial interest, so they are highly motivated to keep those they insure content. Articulating the value of the care you provide both to patients and to their families is in your best interest, because this will ultimately perpetuate the MCO's contract to provide services to this payor.

Most patients seem to want the short-term treatment that managed care promotes. This may be because long-term therapy may have costs beyond the financial, such as iatrogenic harm to the patient's self-concept and the natural support system.

The MCO focus on consumer satisfaction provides an important check on unbridled greed. In a 1998 survey examining why organizations choose to contract with a particular HMO, 283 corporate executives were asked their major reason for selecting and evaluating an HMO. Access and geographic coverage topped the list, followed by member patient satisfaction (Land, 1998).

The Heart of Managed Care: Focused Treatment Planning

Treatment Targets

Managed care therapists are asked to identify target symptoms and develop a treatment focus. The treatment focus may reflect patients' chief complaints and life experiences (Strupp & Binder, 1984; Budman, 1992; Davanloo, 1978; Malan, 1976;

Gustafson, 1984), their internal thought processes (Beck, Rush, et al., 1979), their interpersonal relationships (Klerman et al. 1984), or their search for solutions (De Shazer, 1988a).

These targeted symptoms and treatment foci should be translated into treatment goals. Therapists will need to avoid "rambling" therapy by developing definitive goals early on that will direct therapy, rather than letting goals and concerns evolve naturally as part of an extended therapeutic process.

A clear, defensible treatment plan is the crux of good MBH. Treatment plans should be designed to achieve specified behavioral goals. Most clinical work with the patient should be intentionally directed at these specific goals. An episode of care is complete when the goals have been achieved, even if additional issues might be addressed in a longer treatment.

Therapists need to focus on observable and measurable changes in the client's life, and to emphasize getting the client to make discrete changes rather than processing emotional issues or exploring a variety of concerns. Methods for measuring changes in presenting problems are needed to demonstrate treatment efficacy.

Therapy increasingly resembles energetic corporate brainstorming sessions, in which solutions to problems are mutually generated and the patient is encouraged to experiment with various changes after the session. The thoughtful, digressive discussions of broad life concerns and a mutual search for understanding and insight into the causal factors that shaped the client's life are activities that are generally not considered part of the treatment services covered in managed care. These mainstays of long-term therapy may have value (the 1995 *Consumer Reports* study shows that clients find these pursuits helpful), but they go beyond what MCOs contract to do.

In the interest of speed, therapists need to make quick assessments of the client's problems and talk in practical, everyday terms that the client understands to get to the heart of the problem. Problems can no longer be couched in vague, clinical terms or veiled in intimidating jargon. Reviewers demand clear specification of problems, including reference to particular client behaviors. The general diagnosis matters less than the current specific manifestations of the diagnosis.

Although there are many different forms of managed care, they share an insistence on the development of a clear and focused treatment plan. The fact that brief treatments will be used for most patients challenges clinicians to design treatment plans that offer the patient the greatest return for time and resources invested. Realistic plans are aimed at returning the patient to adequate health and functioning, rather than curing underlying disorders and other conditions. Patients should be encouraged to take pride in even modest changes and should be reassured that continued growth is expected to occur outside of treatment. In providing brief care, leaving the door open for intermittent treatment can be useful; patients may be invited to return for additional work on the current issues if that proves necessary in the future.

Until recently a clinician's training and theoretical bias dictated his or her treatment plan (Schreter, 1997). Payors find this method of treatment choice too random and unreliable. In an effort to standardize care, professional groups, including the American Psychological Association and the American Psychiatric Association, are developing treatment guidelines and descriptions of preferred practices. Increasingly attention to scientific data and outcome studies will improve the quality of guidelines that can help to direct optimal, efficient care.

Utilization of standardized treatment guidelines or protocols is valued, in order to ensure that care is consistently delivered, is evaluated by objective standards, and is based on clinical signs and symptoms. Use of *DSM-IV* nomenclature, and written treatment plans with clear, measurable goals are also emphasized by most managed care companies. The process of developing psychotherapy standards of care is still in its infancy. The sketches of treatment protocols presented in the chapters that follow are based on work that future research will elaborate far more fully.

Providers need to articulate how they will handle cases of depression, anxiety, post-traumatic stress disorder, and marital and chemical dependency issues and to demonstrate the efficacy of the interventions they use. Designing justifiable treatment plans for various *DSM-IV* diagnoses can increase your effectiveness in working with MCOs. Familiarity with the outcomes literature described in chapters that follow will help considerably in developing empirically based treatment plans.

Managed behavioral health care is reshaping clinical practices by focusing on the goals of efficacy and efficiency. Norman Winegar (1992) maintains that increased productivity and standardization of products and services will be two inevitable outcomes of this focus, along with new clinical service marketing strategies, increased oversight of treatment plans and service delivery, better accountability for effectiveness and client satisfaction and increased services within a coordinated network of healthcare professionals and facilities.

Curbing Costs

Using less expensive treatment settings and methods whenever appropriate is central to MBH. Outpatient strategies are decidedly favored over more expensive inpatient treatment. Managed mental healthcare organizations have a strong preference for outpatient-based treatments, whenever they are clinically appropriate, because of their desire to reduce exorbitant hospitalization expenses. In authorizing outpatient care, they emphasize brief, solution-focused counseling approaches, aimed at restoring function as expediently as possible. Managed care companies are also interested in providers with skills in crisis management and stabilization, in order to stave off the need for inpatient care for those with severe mental illnesses.

Responses to the needs of the severely and persistently mentally ill and of the substance abusing population are different with managed care delivery systems than with traditional systems. Managed care companies use inpatient treatment sparingly, primarily for assessment and stabilization, with the length of stay based on objectively measured clinical need, as opposed to being programmatically driven (e.g., providing all substance abusers the same 30-day inpatient program). In the old days, when the typical mental health benefit allowed for 30 days of inpatient care, hospitals acted accordingly; treatment was often designed to reflect insurance limits, rather than being research-driven. Managed care rejects this practice and insists on a clinically defensible rationale for inpatient care. Managed care also encourages use of variable length of stay substance abuse inpatient treatment or detoxification services (Schreter, 1997). Many MCOs make use of intensive outpatient programs for the treatment of substance abuse.

Services are typically provided to enrollees according to a schedule of benefit exclusions, which unfortunately many enrollees fail to comprehend fully until they find themselves faced with the need for uncovered services. This can put providers in a challenging situation, because while in an ideal world they might hope for all services to be covered, if they sympathize with the patient and criticize the MCO, this might increase patients' dissatisfaction and threaten the MCO contract. Providers must balance their need to advocate for patients' interests with a realistic appraisal of sufficient care. Managed care often directly involves providers in fiscal accountability through capitation or incentive structures. In these cases, providers must starkly balance their own financial stake in minimizing costly treatment with their ethical obligation to provide necessary care.

Hospital care is now used for stabilization and patient safety. Full-day hospital care is limited to patients who are so dangerous to themselves or others or so unable to care for themselves that they can be treated only in the most highly structured and supervised settings (Schreter, 1997). In many inpatient units the average length of stay is only 5 days for all psychiatric admissions. Variations on the 24-hour day, including 23-hour observation beds and 3-day crisis beds, are emerging across the country. Patients are discharged to lower levels of care or back into the community as soon as they can tolerate discharge without danger.

Because inpatient services are increasingly used to manage crises and stabilize patients, discharge planning commences as soon as patients are capable of handling the demands of less complete supervision, even though they may at that point be far from "well." Partial hospital programs, intensive outpatient programs, and supervised community living arrangements permit patients to enjoy less restrictive treatment settings while they pursue their gradual return to baseline functioning.

As more policies restrict behavioral health coverage to crisis intervention and stabilization, rather than treatment, it is increasingly incumbent on providers to incorporate plans for community referral into their treatment. Dwindling resources at the community mental health level force us to make more creative use of peer support programs and educational mechanisms for helping clients address their social and behavioral problems.

Subscribers to these more highly delimited policies often have coverage for up to twenty sessions of outpatient therapy and 20 days of inpatient treatment, but this only covers crisis care and stabilization. Additional sessions beyond the initial evaluation would be authorized only if the individual was in crisis or if additional treatment would be needed to forestall a crisis.

Length of stay is increasingly based on the patient's immediate, objective, behavioral problem, as opposed to being determined by diagnosis or vague therapeutic aspirations (e.g., development of insight). Variable lengths of stay in both psychiatric and substance abuse inpatient treatment have become the norm. Rather than filling beds with candidates for rigid 30-day treatment programs, providers must constantly monitor the daily progress of their patients in order to determine whether continued inpatient care is medically justified. This creates more of a monitoring and paperwork burden, but it also probably improves the patients' quality of care, because therapists must stay on top of all their inpatient cases and know each person's current status.

Cost-consciousness compels therapists to be more open and flexible in their choice of treatment modalities. When dealing with many populations of patients, group treatments frequently offer various advantages (Donovan, Bennett, & McElroy, 1981; Budman, 1992). Educationally oriented, time-limited groups can be used for stress management and skill building with patients who suffer from less severe disorders. Groups can also be designed to focus on specific issues common to members, including parenting, anxiety, depression, bereavement, and eating disorders. Open-ended long-term groups, as well as intensive outpatient and medication management programs, are often helpful for patients with chronic, recurrent, and characterological disorders.

As the focus of behavioral health interventions is on facilitating efficient change, inclusion of members of the patient's natural support system can frequently be advantageous. Many clinicians have found family systems interventions helpful in maximizing the change process in brief treatments (Bergman, 1985; de Shazer, 1982; de Shazer & Molnar, 1984). Generally, if more than one person is involved in the problem, it can be useful to bring all of them into the office. Including family members usually increases the therapist's understanding of both the problem and potential resources for its solution. Improved communication increases the likelihood of effective collaborative problem solving and reduces family members' suspicions that therapists are colluding unfairly with the patient and blaming others unreasonably for the patient's problems.

Therapists will need to rely more on the natural, informal sources of social support in the client's life and the client's own resources in therapy. Rather than providing a setting where the client will work out all of his or her problems, the therapist will be more of a director of change and a consultant to the client, placing greater responsibility on the client to work independently or along with friends and family. The tendency to see psychological problems as requiring extensive help that can be exclusively provided by highly trained experts can be an obstacle to developing cost-effective forms of helping. It can be counterproductive to denigrate informal helpers.

Employing pharmacotherapy yourself or working closely with a physician who can prescribe psychotropic medications can expedite treatment. Appropriate use of psychotropic medications can provide symptomatic relief and enhance the impact of other treatment interventions for responsive patients. Confronted by the demand for efficiency, clinicians should maximize their ability to use psychotropic medications in their treatment planning. Clinicians who are not physicians must be able to recognize the indications for pharmacotherapy. Psychiatrists must be prepared to integrate their medication management into treatments provided by others.

Knowing how to use preventive strategies to reduce future costs distinguishes the most forward-looking managed care providers. Investing responsibly in preventive measures will have the greatest impact on future behavioral healthcare costs.

Capitation creates incentives for providers to institute preventive programs to reduce the development of disorders that are costly to treat. Preventive strategies are expected to assume a more prominent role in healthcare due to an increasing focus on populations instead of individual patients. This public health perspective encourages screening programs to identify patients at risk and those in the early stages of disorders, in order to stave off costly aggravation of problems. This orientation also promotes treatments that reduce the negative impact of health conditions.

The National Committee for Quality Assurance (1996) has identified several populations as targets for preventive interventions: children from abusive families, adolescents with high-risk sexual behavior, and adults who abuse substances or who have mood disorders. The development of cost-effective prevention programs requires thoughtful consideration of a variety of factors that affect the value of such efforts. The savings from prevention are a function of the cost of preventive services, their rate of success, the false positive rate in identifying the target service recipients (resulting in individuals receiving unnecessary preventive services), and the false negative rate (resulting in missed cases whose problems will not be prevented and will later emerge, demanding treatment).

One intangible benefit of prevention programs is the avoidance of suffering associated with the development of a potentially preventable condition. This needs to be balanced against possible deleterious consequences of receiving unnecessary preventive services, given the unavoidability of false positives; this cost is another intangible.

The greatest savings from preventive programs occur when the at-risk group can be accurately identified (few false positives and false negatives) and services can be provided during a brief critical period, which obviates the need for later, long-term care. Early intervention programs for children with pervasive developmental disorder represent a case in which early intensive treatment generally produces sizable savings over the long term.

Partnering with Managed Care Companies

Partnering with managed care companies requires empathizing with them and viewing problems from both their perspective and your own. Many providers complain about a sense of competing loyalties: to the MCO, to their traditional way of doing psychotherapy, and to their patients' best interests.

Therapy through managed care involves a three-way contract among therapist, client, and managed healthcare company. The goals of all three are not always aligned with each other, and the therapist often needs to negotiate the therapy contract within this atmosphere of conflicting goals. Doing so in an ethically responsible, balanced way requires considerable skill. Providers serve as representatives of the managed care company, and they should share the organization's philosophy and feel comfortable being committed to the success of the organization. However, this loyalty to the managed care company can compete with a desire to serve as an advocate for the client.

It can be destructive to align with the client against the MCO by suggesting that the client should be entitled to a wider variety of benefits that have not been forthcoming. Therapists' anger can endanger their work. Hostility can be displaced onto weak patients, and therapists can unwittingly collude with antisocial patients by aligning against the authority. Understanding such risks can facilitate more constructive responses.

It seems far more appropriate for providers to adopt the position that the managed care company's contract can legally restrict the availability of services, that the mature response of clients to these restrictions is to become as informed as possible about them in advance, and to operate as constructively as possible within these reality-based boundaries. It is generally unhelpful to promote the client's rage, which is often based on unreasonable expectations and the immature, illogical reasoning that there should be no restrictions on care now because at one point their employer or they could afford coverage that was more inclusive.

You will be more effective in working in the managed care era if you engage in what some refer to as "point of service" utilization management. This involves talking with clients in such a way that they participate in the decision-making process and assume increasing responsibility for considering cost-containment. Clinicians need to "sell" the value of less resource-intensive, but equally effective, options for diagnosis and treatment. As professionals, we have just recently become aware of the importance of seeking cost-effective ways of doing business. Our clients need to move from a position of entitlement to one of partnership, and to do that they require our guidance.

Collaborating in a mutual effort to optimize treatment quality while containing costs requires sympathy to MCO objectives. Their survival depends upon contract renewals. Attempting to maximize patient satisfaction and facilitating patients' acceptance of limited care will help the MCO stay in the payor's good graces, which improves the MCO's chances of renewal. While assisting negligent, irresponsible MCOs is undesirable, helping the better MCOs to thrive in the competitive marketplace can ultimately improve the quality of care and of work for providers.

Poynter (1994) argues that

> . . . we need to work with the system of managed care, not against it. And we need to find a way to fit in. If there is a change that we see to be necessary for effectiveness, we can become productive voices for that change. If we do run up against difficulties with managed care, we need to take a positive, proactive—but not angry—position. (p. 7)

Accepting fiscal accountability, through capitation or incentive structures that reward choice of the least expensive but still adequate form of treatment, is new for many behavioral healthcare providers. Accepting discounted fee arrangements with preferred providers has become a common way for providers to ensure a steady stream of referrals. Your net will be less per case, but by working with a large and secure case load, your overall earnings will be far more stable.

Managed care companies also conduct ongoing evaluation of providers' performance. Provider profiling is used to determine the relative effectiveness of different clinicians in meeting the objectives of the MCO (efficient, cost-effective delivery of high-quality treatment). Although most of us recoil with apprehension at the prospect of having our work closely monitored, it is helpful to remember that profiling will identify top performers and permit them to be rewarded. If you are a conscientious, hard-working therapist eager to improve your skills, provider profiling may ultimately prove to be an ally. In fact, some MCOs are considering doing away with UR in cases of providers previously identified as exemplary by profiling procedures.

One problem with provider profiling is that crude methods can systematically disadvantage those clinicians who work with more difficult, treatment-resistant patients. We would expect a clinician working exclusively with mildly depressed, college-educated patients to obtain higher average patient success and satisfaction scores than one working only with patients with borderline personality disorder. A fair system includes means of weighting the outcome measures for providers' case loads according to their proportion of difficult cases. Understanding the medical information systems used by your company and working to make them clinician-friendly and meaningful are important. Trying to get the population case mix adjusted to allow for a fair profiling system is important. Without this, clinicians working with more treatment-resistant patients will be systematically disadvantaged by the monitoring process. We must show other clinicians and administrators how performance can be improved by judicial use of appropriate outcomes measures, and we must be prepared for debate when biased measurement methods distort conclusions drawn about providers. In addition to contributing to the development of meaningful provider profiling methods, conforming to administrative procedures in documenting care will also make you more "managed care–friendly."

Tactics for Participating in the Evolution

To participate positively in the evolution of MBH, it is important to adopt a collaborative stance. In reviewing the requirements of MCOs regarding treatment direction, duration, dosage, and delivery, it is good to remember that much extant research supports the behavioral healthcare trends that managed care is promoting. Chapters that follow will summarize psychotherapy outcome research findings that generally support the advisability of using focused, brief therapy methods. The research also supports the use of group methods, peer support, and self-help techniques, as well as the work of paraprofessionals. In practically every case in which the literature has compared traditional practices with more cost-effective innovations, researchers have failed to prove that traditional psychotherapy delivery practices are measurably superior. This may be because our measurements have been invalid or insufficiently sensitive. Or it may be because traditional prejudices and assumptions have been wrong.

Until we have other findings, probably the wisest course is to be cautious about defending unsubstantiated notions about ideal therapy methods, delivery styles, and training regimes. It probably makes sense to remain open to new ways of thinking about meeting the pressing needs of consumers in a way that will be economically sustainable in the long run.

Need for Ongoing Innovation and Rethinking

Established MCOs and HMOs are feeling considerable pressure to hold down costs in a fiercely competitive market. We must look for new strategies for creating the future, because they will become increasingly necessary. Unfortunately very few healthcare systems are thinking seriously about where they need to be in 10 or 15 years. This is regrettable, because we are in a transitional, unstable period right now, and long-term planning would be very desirable.

The following comments are excerpted from a 1993 newsletter produced by Human Affairs / Aetna:

> Part of working with a managed care company like ours is understanding the philosophy behind the treatment methods it supports, which can be placed on a continuum. The best available research evidence appears to support the superior efficacy of treatments characterized . . . as progressive.

Comparing Regressive and Progressive Therapy

Goals

Regressive:	Vague and ambitious
	Described as personality change or growth
Progressive:	Specific and measurable
	Focus on resolution

Assumptions about How Change Occurs

Regressive:	Therapeutic relationship
	Expressions of emotion
Progressive:	Positive action on part of patient

Assumptions of Dose/Benefit

Regressive:	More is better
	Brief treatment as "bandage"
Progressive:	Creates gains in early sessions
	Intermittent treatment as good as continuous

Expectations of Patients

Regressive:	Emotional relationship with therapist
	Commitment to long duration of therapy

Progressive: Working relationship based on mutual trust
                Commitment to work outside of treatment to reduce frequency
                and duration of treatment

Therapist Behaviors

Regressive: Express emotional support
                Interpretation

Progressive: Express confidence in patient's abilities
                Teach and coach new skills/behavior

It is clear from the preceding comments and comparisons that MCOs expect providers to be willing to challenge various long-held assumptions about psychotherapy. They prefer clinicians they deem to be "progressive." These companies have reviewed the literature and have found research supporting their vision of therapy. They want creative, flexible therapists with a solid mastery of brief problem-solving and solution-focused therapy methods, coupled with an awareness of the need to curb treatment costs. Allies of managed care are interested in developing new, conscientious ways of streamlining the provision of behavioral healthcare, rather than bemoaning changes in reimbursement criteria. Cummings (1995) describes seven paradigm shifts in the way psychotherapy is viewed, by comparing the traditional dyadic model (DM) with the newer managed care catalyst model (CM):

1. **DM**: Few clients are seen, but for lengthy courses of treatment. **CM**: Many clients are seen, for brief episodes of treatment.
2. **DM**: Treatment is continuous, often weekly or more often. **CM**: Treatment is brief and intermittent throughout the life cycle.
3. **DM**: The therapist is the vehicle for change; the aim is a cure in some form. **CM**: The therapist is a catalyst for the client's change, emphasis is on restoring a drive to grow.
4. **DM**: Therapy is the most important event in the client's life. **CM**: Therapy is an artificial situation, and significant changes occur and continue to occur long after therapy has been interrupted.
5. **DM**: Therapy continues until healing occurs and the client is terminated as "cured" to some degree. **CM**: Therapy is the catalyst for growth outside of therapy, and formal treatment is often interrupted. Clients can return for periodic boosts as needed throughout the life cycle.
6. **DM**: Individual and group psychotherapy in the office are the main modalities by which healing takes place. **CM**: Every healing resource in the community is mobilized.
7. **DM**: Fee-for-service is the economic base for practice. **CM**: Prospective reimbursement or capitation frees the therapist to provide for the client's needs.

Cummings (1995) has also identified five changes in professional psychology compelled by managed care:

1. The increasing formation into group practices
2. Acquiring a growing arsenal of time-effective treatment techniques and strategies
3. A fundamental redefinition of the helping role
4. The ability to demonstrate efficiency and effectiveness through outcomes research in one's group practice
5. Regaining autonomy by qualifying as prime (retrained) providers

New Ways of Thinking about Psychotherapy and Treatment Goals

Treatment can be aimed at any of the following: behavioral improvement, recovery, remission, or cure. While lasting cures are desirable, managed behavioral care is more oriented to enhancing functioning as efficiently as possible. The priority is not treating "illnesses," but reducing symptoms. Our primary objective is to increase how much patients engage in useful behaviors. For some an appropriate focus is helping them learn to manage their illnesses more effectively, rather than trying to remove their disorders. Sometimes, rather than treating disorders, we are helping people to work with what they've got and to maximize their independent functioning. Rather than fixing brains, we are often most interested in helping patients learn how to use their brains to better advantage. Returning patients to adequate health and functioning is the prime directive, rather than curing their underlying disorders. What clinicians refer to as "structural change" (change in the basic psychic structures) and "character change" are no longer reimbursable under most insurance benefit packages.

CHAPTER

7   Joining Managed Care

Coping Constructively with New Constraints: Provider Accommodation Research

Do HMOs Help Clients But Hurt Therapists?

Critics of managed care assert that the quality of mental health treatment is at risk because traditionally trained psychotherapists must adapt their practice styles, and making these accommodations can be very challenging. Given the paucity of empirical data on providers' accommodations to managed care, it is difficult to estimate with certainty what the general response of practitioners has been to the changes in their field.

Austad, Sherman, and Holstein (1993) conducted a study to see how a particular HMO has affected the practice styles of 294 psychologists, psychiatrists, and social workers. Subjects had an average of 5.4 years of HMO experience and 6.7 years of prior experience; the mean age was 42.5 years. The majority stated that they "happened into" the HMO and had little knowledge of managed care prior to employment. A large part of the typical workday consisted of direct client contact, averaging over 5.1 "back to back" psychotherapy sessions. The mean number of hours per day spent conducting individual psychotherapy was 5.7, which was slightly more than the number of hours they believed it was possible to perform at a level of maximum effectiveness (mean = 5.2).

Ten-point scale ratings of the level of therapy effectiveness increased significantly after working in the HMO (mean = 7.6) compared to when they first started (mean = 6.6). Ratings of the quality of care personally rendered did not change significantly. The data indicated that HMO therapists believed that the quality of mental healthcare at the HMO was higher than what is offered in the community.

However, the ratings of the following declined significantly over time: overall work conditions, clinical load, professional fulfillment, job satisfaction, and enjoyment of work. Therapists looked forward to client cancellations more so then when beginning at the HMO. The average number of years they believed it was possible for a therapist to work at the HMO was 26.3 years on a part-time basis but only 11.8 years on a full-time basis. The HMO therapists reported that their actual salary was significantly lower than what they thought they ought to be receiving.

134

Almost half of the subjects reported that their biggest stressor was the number of patients to be "managed." When dormant patients increasingly became active, therapists felt forced to work with fewer resources and less time.

As far as psychotherapy and practice style, the majority of therapists believed that working at the HMO had influenced how they practiced. Only 9.8% believed that their practice style was not influenced by working at the HMO. The most important characteristic of a good HMO therapist, according to 68.2% of the subjects, was "competence in short-term therapies"; 60.7% reported that they were not adequately prepared in graduate school for this type of work. Austad, Sherman, and Holstein concluded:

> At the time of staff selection, consideration should be given to whether or not the therapist possesses the values and models of therapy that are compatible with the philosophy, structure, and needs of the HMO. The more closely matched in values, and the more short term and eclectically-oriented the therapist, the easier it may be to accommodate to the HMO style of practice.

Experience Desensitizes Fears

A 1996 study by Karg-Bray, Norcross, and Prochaska surveyed 1,000 randomly selected clinical psychologist members of the American Psychological Association. Of the 487 who responded, three-quarters participated in at least one managed care health program, and they predicted that 50% of their case loads will consist of managed care patients by 1997. The psychologists with the least managed care experience cited the most disadvantages, while those who had been seeing managed care clients for the longest period of time voiced the fewest dissatisfactions. Those who had never seen a managed care client ("precontemplators," who had declined to accept such clients) were consistently found to be most likely to express many disadvantages and few advantages of managed care.

A survey examining psychiatrists' and psychologists' attitudes toward managed care (Scholl et al., 1996) found consistent signs of dissatisfaction. Most found UR rarely helpful and felt it had an adverse effect on patient care. Almost all had had patients who terminated treatment prematurely due to denial of sessions; 71% exaggerated patients' symptoms to obtain authorization for additional sessions. Most respondents viewed reviewers as insufficiently qualified and felt they should be certified. Nearly half viewed the appeal process as inefficient, although very few had experienced a reduction in referrals following an appeal. All of the respondents believed they were at least somewhat effective in providing short-term therapy; 41% saw general provision of short-term therapy as somewhat to extremely effective for most patients. A similar investigation of 15,918 practicing licensed psychologists (Phelps, Eisman, & Kohout, 1998) found that four out of five participants reported negative effects of managed care on their practices; ethical and economic concerns predominated.

A survey of 200 master's- and doctoral-level providers drawn from a variety of treatment settings explored differences in their reactions to managed care (Pinto et al., 1996). Consistent with the Scholl et al. findings, most respondents reported having had problems with the review process, voiced concerns about confidentiality, and had experienced negative economic ramifications they attributed to managed care. Overall managed care dissatisfaction was associated with the total number of clients seen weekly, but not specifically with the number of managed care clients seen weekly.

Dissatisfaction was greater among doctoral-level providers than those with less training and among private practitioners. Managed care companies' preference for the "one-stop shopping" offered by interdisciplinary group practices and agencies, as well as their preference for less expensive providers, has placed the solo practitioner at a serious disadvantage. Larger practices and organizations probably find the oft criticized paperwork burdens of managed care easier to absorb.

Of all the professional groups assessed in the Pinto et al. study, those with master's degrees in social work and psychology seemed to be experiencing the easiest adjustment to managed care. These groups had more part-time clinicians, which other researchers have found to be more compatible with the expectations of managed care (Austad & Hoyt, 1992). In addition, they had experienced less decline in hourly rate, whereas doctoral-level providers had frequently encountered far more drastic fee reductions (e.g., 60% in some cases). Training differences may also have contributed to the social workers' and counselors' greater ability to tolerate the intrusion of managed care policies. Doctoral-level private practice providers were formerly the most advantaged by mental health benefit systems; perhaps their sense of loss is understandably greater.

A 1996 survey conducted by *The National Psychologist* (Saeman, 1996) found that most of the respondents described their experiences with managed care as unfavorable; only 1% said it has been very favorable. While some might attribute their dissatisfaction to loss of income, in fact the sample showed an increase in mean income between 1990 and 1995, from $73,893 to $86,163. However, most were working additional hours in order to keep pace with inflation and to retain previous income levels. In the managed care era, it appears that providing psychotherapy services can still be lucrative for professionals, but managed care is demanding that clinicians work harder than they had previously.

Thirty-five percent of the psychologist respondents said they have given some thought to leaving the profession; 15% had given it a lot of consideration. The majority (82%) responded that they are somewhat or very concerned about continuing to practice psychotherapy. The majority of the respondents in this survey were private practitioners; only 26% were salaried employees. Roughly half (53%) said their practices were about the same as they had been in 1990.

When this survey was repeated in 1998, *The National Psychologist* reported that average earnings of psychologists had decreased about 15%, dropping back to $73,850 (Saeman, 1998). Most of those interviewed blamed lower hourly fees paid by MCOs. Declines from $85 per therapy hour to $50–$65 have become common, closing the previous reimbursement gap between psychologists, social workers, and counselors.

Payments to Providers: Who Is Prospering?

Much of the complaining about managed care heard in professional circles revolves around reductions in reimbursement rates. Conducting psychotherapy has become significantly less lucrative for many providers, especially if the focus is on hourly fees (Scholl et al., 1996).

A national survey (Cooper, 1997a) revealed the following managed care hourly payment rates for different professional groups: psychiatrists, $85; psychologists, $75; professional counselors, $61; social workers, $60; and marriage and family therapists, $58. In contrast, in the fee-for-service market, psychiatrists command $105; psychologists $92, marriage and family therapists $75, social workers $74, and professional counselors $67. The percentage of income from managed care (as opposed to direct pay and other third-party payments) dropped slightly from 1995 to 1996 (31% to 29%). The average number of sessions per psychotherapy client actually rose slightly in 1996. Marriage and family therapists showed the greatest increase, from sixteen sessions to twenty, followed by professional counselors (sixteen to nineteen), and psychologists. Only psychiatrists showed a drop in the average number of sessions (twenty-four to twenty), which may account for their drop in income and may result from an increasing reliance on medications and decreasing emphasis on psychotherapy.

The Secrets of Successful Adjustment

Successful private practitioners have become more consumer-centered and service-oriented. They stand by the merits of long-term therapy when it is appropriate but acknowledge the benefits of brief treatment. They are developing psychoeducational models of intervention that are cost-effective and time-limited. They are working to become more adept at using brief therapy and are attempting to place their work in an empirical context that permits them to evaluate their impact more scientifically. They use a disciplined approach to treatment that emphasizes mutual development of goals with clients, consistent application of a selected therapy approach, incorporation of appropriate extratherapy experiences to enhance learning and generalization, and use of regular feedback in order to correct the steering of therapy.

Joining Managed Care

Richardson and Austad (1991) describe a variety of ways that clinicians can participate in managed healthcare. Providers may interact with various types of managed care systems, including HMOs, IPAs, and PPOs. HMOs provide specified health services using a restricted group of providers usually at a discounted rate, sometimes with a small percentage of fees withheld until year's end. The incentive for providers is the promise of increased volume of clients. IPAs allow consumers to choose independent practice providers but hold back a portion of the fees from the providers, who may be reimbursed either on a fee-for-service basis or on a capitated basis (Cummings & Duhl, 1987; Flinn, McMahon, & Collins, 1987; Gurevitz, 1984); "capitation" refers to a fixed monthly or annual payment according to the number of persons covered by the managed care plan; payment is unrelated to the amount of service provided. Health maintenance organizations and, to a lesser extent, PPOs have built-in incentives to use less costly and presumably less-well-trained mental health professionals (Richardson & Austad, 1991).

Clinicians' financial arrangements with different types of managed care systems vary. In a staff HMO, clinicians are salaried. Group HMOs may compensate mental health professionals using either salaried, fee-for-service, or capitated systems. Providers in PPOs and IPAs are typically reimbursed on a fee-for-service or capitated basis (Richardson & Austad, 1991).

In staff model HMOs, clinicians are employed full time or part time by the HMO. Group model HMOs usually function similarly, but some employees (usually physicians) also own an interest in the HMO. Two well-known examples of these types of HMOs are Community Health Care Plan in New Haven, Connecticut, which is a staff model HMO, and Kaiser Permanente in California, which is a group model HMO.

Some perceive there to be multiple advantages to the provider of being on staff in an HMO. According to Richardson and Austad (1991) the benefits include:

> A steady clientele, stable salary, often excellent benefits, the opportunity to practice in an interdisciplinary setting, involvement in the total healthcare of the client with the goals of integrating and coordinating services, a predictable work schedule, availability of colleagues, minimal involvement with fee collection, a wide range of clients and problems, the possibility of implementing programs for target persons or problems (or both), and the opportunity to use a wide variety of clinical skills. Disadvantages to this arrangement include restrictions on the amount and type of mental healthcare that can be provided, participation in on-call service, strong emphasis on short-term treatment for all types of problems, heavy case loads and little time for reading or reflection, limited involvement with clients, little or no control over numbers or types of clients seen, divided loyalty between client and HMO, concern over quality of care, and restricted focus of treatment. (p. 55)

In contractual managed care arrangements, clinicians operate as independent agents rather than as employees. Patients are encouraged to use the contracted providers because of their reduced fees and small or nonexistent co-payments. Solo practitioners or members of a group practice are considered "preferred" because they agree to reduce fees and to adhere to policies of the MCO (De Lissovoy et al., 1987). Contractors may have little voice in the MCO's decision making and little or no choice in selection of types of cases with which to work. Clinicians assume some financial risk if paid on a capitated basis (Richardson & Austad, 1991).

Evaluating MCO Contracts

Richardson and Austad (1991, p. 58) offer the following evaluation criteria for those considering whether or not to join a managed care system:

1. What are the ethical practices of the organization, and is there a demonstrated commitment to provide high-quality services to all clientele?
2. How financially stable is the organization providing the managed care?
3. What has been the staff or contractor turnover rate? (The state insurance board may be able to provide some of this information.)
4. What are the covered mental health benefits, and how are they presented to members?
5. How are chronic illness and specialized needs handled?
6. What roles do quality assurance and utilization review play in the system?
7. Are the quality of the interdisciplinary relationships primarily cooperative or conflictual?

In evaluating contractual arrangements, Richardson and Austad (1991) suggest the following considerations:

1. Organizationally, does the contracting group have a positive attitude toward providing managed care services, or is such care viewed as second class? Some settings (and providers) are simply ill suited to managed mental healthcare because of their philosophy of treatment or personality and probably should not participate.
2. Is there willingness to accept lower fees in return for a potentially larger volume of clients?
3. Clinically and administratively, is the group competent to work with a wide variety of types of people and problems over which clinicians may have little choice or control?
4. Who is responsible for crisis and emergency care and for hospitalization?

Cultivating Relationships with MCOs

Poynter (1994) feels strongly that it is in providers' best interests to accommodate the expectations of managed care companies. He believes that it is wise for providers to take active steps to establish themselves as preferred providers, especially with MCOs that are experiencing an expansion phase, during which they are eager to add providers to their lists.

First, Poynter urges acceptance of managed care. "This means accepting on a personal level that you are willing to work with this new behavioral health care delivery mechanism. What is required here is a global acceptance of the concept in principle, not an acceptance of every managed care company's policies" (Poynter, 1994, p. 11).

Next, he advises practitioners to develop both a global and in-depth knowledge of the managed care industry to understand trends, needs, and opportunities. Finally, he encourages providers to "develop a service, skill, or practice quality that could help a managed care company enhance its marketplace competitive position. Package the service, skill, or practice quality in such a way that you can communicate its advantages to the managed care company—especially to the MCO's marketing team."

Poynter has found that

> ... typically, psychotherapists discover new MCOs when those organizations notify providers that current patients are now covered under a new insurance contract. However, that notification occurs only after the MCO has been chosen by an employer and has begun to service the new contract. The notification period can be more than one year after the provider-contracting phase has been completed! (Poynter, 1994, p.15)

This is problematic, because in most cases, when an MCO develops its regional provider network, it oversubscribes the network. MCOs contract with far more psychotherapists than they anticipate ever needing in order to genuinely service the employer contracts they may obtain in the future. This is advantageous from a marketing perspective.

> All other things being equal, an employer might be much more interested in a bid from an MCO that has a contracted provider network of 1,000 local therapists than one that has a provider network of 500 local therapists—even when a network of only 250 therapists would be more than sufficient to fully service the contract. (Poynter, 1994, p. 16)

Because provider networks are often substantially oversubscribed during the expansion phase, providers who discover an MCO during its notification phase are usually unable to get into the network.

If you wish to market your practice to MCOs, you must develop ways of discovering new or expanding MCOs when those organizations are in their provider contracting phase for your geographic area. This is the first step of an ongoing process that will continue as part of your long-term marketing strategy. Once you have found and contracted with an initial group of expansion-phase MCOs, you should continue that process with additional companies (Poynter, 1994). The MCOs that hold contracts with employers in your area keep those contracts for only a relatively short period, usually about 2 years. At the end of the initial contract period, they are renegotiated. Employees who are locked into a contract that allows them to see you under a particular managed care company may become locked into different preferred provider networks if their present MCO is displaced in favor of a different one when the corporate contract comes up for renewal. By following a continuing program to discover new MCOs when they expand to your area, you can contract with all of the potential managed care players in your area and increase the odds of being a preferred provider for any MCO that wins the contract renewal of your area's employers (Poynter, 1994).

Poynter urges would-be managed care providers to learn to "talk the talk and walk the walk." By their very nature, insurance companies tend to be conservative, and managed care companies are often subsidiaries of insurance companies. Therapists who want to make a good business impression with MCOs should probably dress conservatively and be familiar with managed care business terminology (use the *Wall Street Journal* to orient yourself to business vocabulary).

Although there is no magic formula for approaching people, it is obviously helpful to show interest and consideration and to present yourself as a potential resource. In approaching any MCO staff, we need to ask "What can I do to help you?" rather than assertively present our own needs. It makes sense to ask how we would want to be approached. Don't assume that all the people you interact with are comfortable and confident. Help them become comfortable and confident by being attentive and supportive, rather than competitive and threatening. This may seem obvious, but often when we are trying to impress others, we become pre-occupied with our own performance and are insensitive to how presenting ourselves in a positive light may make others feel inferior. As providers, we are seeking to build a reputation of consistency and stability. Demonstrating this in all of our interactions with managed care colleagues can be very helpful.

A Triage Mentality: Evolving Criteria for Outpatient Treatment

When medical resources are scarce relative to demand, as in times of war, health professionals have long made use of a triage approach that quickly screens cases in order to determine treatment priorities. A similar screening strategy can help you make more optimal use of your clinical resources, given the limits imposed by managed care. A small segment of mental health service utilizers, and not necessarily the sickest ones, account for the overwhelming majority of mental health services and costs (Kroll, 1993). Making appropriate choices about how to handle these challenging cases is vital.

Clients usually access mental healthcare in managed care systems by referral from their primary care physician. They are assessed by telephone or in person to determine their eligibility and appropriateness for care. The gatekeeping approach is intended to prevent unnecessary and thus wasteful care, although this system assumes that primary care providers are qualified to assess mental health needs. Triage or screening interviews may be conducted by designated personnel, typically registered nurses, who determine whether mental healthcare is needed and, if so, to whom the referral will be made.

Once a case has been assigned to a clinician and therapy has begun, treatment is usually reviewed periodically by a UR committee. Typically this review involves paper scrutiny, although occasionally it requires the clinician to make an oral presentation. Feedback is then provided to the clinician about the adequacy of the progress of the case. In practice, various barriers to further treatment may be imposed, such as an upper limit placed on the number of additional treatment sessions. Treatment may not be allowed to continue until this review process occurs and reauthorization of care is granted. In other instances the clinician has a session or two automatically granted beyond the review point to allow time for the review to occur.

Reviewers and referral sources may also have incentives to curtail or severely limit services because their careers may be affected. Not without controversy, some managed care systems provide financial incentives to their primary care personnel and reviewers for not referring clients to specialists.

Whether you're working in a capitated or fee-for-service system, if there are constraints on the number of sessions you can provide clients, and concomitant measures of treatment outcome are being employed, it is vital for you to have a system for selecting those cases where you have the greatest likelihood of creating improvement and avoiding those cases where your treatment methods are most likely to be unproductive.

With capitation, you don't dare risk squandering time where it does no good. Cases with extremely poor prognoses need to be prevented from happening in the first place or when this is impossible, less costly forms of client maintenance or management must be developed. Your most expensive clinical services should not be devoted to cases with minimal probability of gain, lest you reduce the overall "value-added" of the system.

With a managed care system, because it is incumbent on you to demonstrate the positive impact of your services on the clients you serve, it is important to offer only appropriate treatment in each case. Cases with poor prognoses, given available treatment modalities, will deflate your overall efficacy indicators and possibly have a negative impact on future referrals.

Screening clients is not something new. Outpatient clinicians who could afford to have always preferred to work with clients carrying certain diagnoses more so than with others. "Ideal" therapy candidates were "YAVIS," an acronym for young, attractive, verbal, intelligent, and successful. (The obvious question is: Why would such a person need therapy?) Such clients have always been sought because they were more rewarding to work with in therapy; they changed, improved, and left happy. Whatever treatment model was used, these clients tended to get better and thereby flattered their therapists.

But what's needed now is a new type of screening. This screening is based partially on an assessment of how much the client truly needs our services (thereby excluding many of the old YAVIS group from care that will be reimbursed) and partially on an assessment of how much the client is likely to gain from our particular mode of treatment. Both of these factors need to be considered in order to make the best choices about outpatient care.

Need Is Not Enough

Many prospective clients need services that are not currently available. At the moment there is no foolproof way of resolving the problem of substance abuse; studies estimate a relapse rate of over 90% following the best of currently available treatment. Dissociative identity disorder and borderline personality disorder are increasingly diagnosed but remain tenaciously frustrating to treat effectively.

While promising treatment approaches are being developed for these vexing problems, no method on the horizon offers a reliable fast fix. For example, in cases of both dissociative identity disorder and borderline personality disorder, when a precipitating traumatic event plays a role, new treatments such as eye movement desensitization and reprocessing (EMDR) have been used efficiently to produce some improvement (F. Shapiro,1995b). However, while EMDR increases the client's comfort level and reduces unwanted intrusive emotion-stirring ideation, EMDR does not quickly resolve the interpersonal struggles of most dissociative identity disorder and borderline personality disorder patients. Cognitive approaches have been applied to both populations in recent years with some success (Layden et al., 1995), but even most advocates of these methods acknowledge that treatment is still likely to be very protracted in these cases. In reviewing the psychotherapy outcome data, Kroll (1993) states that the effectiveness of treatment for borderline personality disorder has not been demonstrated; roughly 50% of these patients drop out of treatment within 6 months, and 50% of those successfully being treated terminate against their clinician's advice.

Recognizing the limits of our current treatment methods can help us avoid the expense of inappropriate assignment of clients to treatment modalities that are likely to be ineffective. The old unrestrained fee-for-service method of reimbursement in some ways rewarded us for taking on frustrating cases with poor prognoses and cases our techniques were ill equipped to treat; even when long-term treatment was ineffective, we were paid. Some clinicians formed practices with a stable backbone of borderline personality disorder patients who never changed much but kept coming for years.

Some defend this use of clinical time on the basis that these patients had clear need of services. It would be hard to argue otherwise; these borderline patients were distraught, lonely people with crisis-filled lives, quite obviously in need of social continuity. The question, however, is whether weekly individual meetings with an expensive psychotherapist are the most efficient way to meet this need for support. Increasingly MCOs are challenging us to demonstrate the value-added associated with treating such clients over an extended period of time.

"Pick your battles," we often admonish parents we see in family counseling; similarly, we should probably select our own clinical battles with increasing care. Focusing our energies on those cases where we can do the greatest good, as efficiently as possible, is increasingly important.

Evaluating Candidates for Therapy

Before seeing a client for therapy, the therapist will need to make a determination about whether insured therapy is warranted. Two areas need to be evaluated. First, are there any medical problems that may be the source of the client's problems? Second, does the client abuse substances? In the first case, working with a physician may be necessary before proceeding further. In the latter case the MCO may demand referral for (1) detoxification, (2) outpatient or inpatient rehabilitation, and (3) peer group support like Alcoholics Anonymous (AA). However, if psychotherapy is allowed, it will generally be short-term, terminating as soon as clients can continue on their own in an AA-type group. Often in these cases, therapists will find themselves working with the employer, because often these referrals are made at the request of the employer. Following through with treatment referrals becomes a condition of employment for the clients; successful outcomes are linked to the clients' keeping their job. Recognizing when such special contingencies are operating is important for therapists wishing to maximize motivation for efficient change.

Traditional outpatient "therapy proper" is only one of five MBH options. Many times, therapists deal with family issues, often involving behavioral problems with children. In these cases therapists train parents as therapeutic agents, serving in a consultant role. In other cases involving couples issues therapists function as mediators, either negotiating differences or making decisions about staying together. In a third type of situation, therapists work with severely mentally ill patients requiring medication. Here the focus is often on education aimed at fostering medication adherence. In a fourth type of case, therapists address the problems of unstable yet functioning individuals. These patients often pose risk management challenges and are frequently candidates for long-term care. These patients create problems for MCOs. They are often difficult to treat, and their care can be prohibitively expensive. They have been known to bankrupt clinics. These patients require effective case management more so than conventional outpatient therapy. With these patients, therapy must often be explicitly task-oriented and quite directive. Finally, a fifth group of cases includes situations in which patients are candidates for more traditional outpatient individual psychotherapy. In such cases, managed care therapy is pragmatic, problem-solving, and time-limited.

Legal and Contractual Issues

Managed care psychotherapists need to appreciate how various legal issues can affect therapy. These include contractual issues with MCOs and also with employers. There is often an agreement between an MCO and an employer that may require clients to be in therapy as a condition of their employment. The therapist may thus be part of a disciplinary process and in effect be reporting to the employer about the client's progress and compliance with disciplinary conditions. The implications of such a role for the helping relationship can be quite profound. Clear communication about reporting plans, externally mandated therapeutic objectives, and the therapist's role are vital in such cases.

In addition, the therapist will often be involved in a three-way negotiation involving (1) what the therapist desires for the client in terms of sessions, (2) what the client desires, and (3) what the MCO allows. Liability issues will arise about premature discharge of a client when the MCO will not allow the client to continue in therapy, even on a nonpaying basis. Further, many MCOs may not want the therapist to reveal to the client the limitations placed on the therapist by the MCO. This can put the therapist in the awkward and potentially unethical position of withholding information about optimal treatment or actively misleading clients about their progress and readiness for termination.

One way of reducing this likelihood is to frame clear, measurable, short-term therapeutic objectives in the very first contact. This communicates the intent of therapy in explicit and certain terms and clarifies the scope of treatment. At the end of the allotted treatment period, if specific behavioral goals have been achieved, the therapist's task of presenting termination as appropriate should be easy and straightforward: Our job is done. By narrowly defining the expectations of therapy from the outset, the therapist has not been deceitful in conveying the idea that therapy was completed, even if on some level a possibility exists that additional contact with the therapist could confer additional advantages to the client's well-being. According to managed care's definition of therapy, all was a success.

In cases in which specific outlined behavioral goals have not been met, two main options exist. If these unmet goals relate to dangerous outcomes (e.g., the client has been showing an escalating pattern of suicidal behavior), the clinician must critically appraise the impact of the interventions used to date. If there is evidence of progress, the clinician has a basis for requesting a treatment extension. This may be granted by the managed care utilization reviewer on the grounds that successful outpatient therapy would be less costly than inpatient alternatives. If evidence of progress is lacking, the clinician may decide that this treatment modality is unlikely ever to transform the problem significantly and may choose to work with the care manager to develop a more appropriate treatment alternative.

When unmet goals are less serious, terminating treatment early in order to stay within managed care guidelines can actually offer some therapeutic advantages. The therapist can highlight any partial progress the client has made and provide review materials for the client's future application of methods of change the client has found to be most helpful. Frequently this type of self-administered followup treatment can help clients continue to work toward their ultimate objectives. Clients who are trying to put changes into effect across the various relationships in their lives will require a lengthy period of experimentation and practice before they feel entirely comfortable with their new way of responding to events. However, contact with an expensive professional may not be vital during this protracted period of practice. Helping clients to plan the particular people in their natural support network to whom they will turn for feedback and support during this period of extended learning and generalization can fill many of the same needs formerly met by long-term therapists. A client who is learning to be more assertive with others in order to stave off panic experiences may benefit from reassurance that it is normal to encounter occasional situations that "throw you" and create a reversion to timidity, and that these episodes are an expected, temporary part of the lifelong learning process and not a sign that all gains have been lost. Extending therapy sessions too long can create the faulty expectation that the client will eventually reach a point of perfection, when all will always go smoothly and according to plan, and treatment continues to be necessary until that point is reached. Help clients to recognize that many times, if they can achieve their behavioral objective 75% of the time, they are doing about as well as everybody else! Ending treatment on that note is not fraudulent overselling; it is pretty realistic. If there is no partial progress to highlight, structured termination can provide an opportunity to reflect on the therapist's and client's shared frustration and to do some troubleshooting to evaluate an alternative set of steps the client may wish to try independently.

There are myriad reasons for a client's failure to progress during brief therapy. There may be ambivalence about making changes because of secondary gain factors. Rather than treat this as a mysterious secret, a therapist can bring this issue to the surface in a constructive way, by showing respect for the client's difficult decision ("You want to move and make these changes, because doing so would offer these advantages, but at the same time part of you is reluctant to make these changes because you would have to give up X, Y, and Z, which are understandable to want"). This honest clarification of the client's quandary may be the most appropriate outcome of therapy in some cases. Longer therapy may not be better when clients may be deeply undecided about the direction they wish their life to take. Clients may find it helpful to discuss the pros and cons associated with different paths, but that type of conversational deliberation often does not require the professional services of a therapist.

Failure to progress may be due to inappropriate choice of treatment interventions. Discussing what has worked and what has not worked for the client can allow the therapist to make some new recommendations that may match the client's needs and abilities more appropriately. The pressure to achieve change as efficiently as possible can force us to detect unsuccessful approaches quickly and change course accordingly. It also forces us to become proficient at making clients feel comfortable with us. Putting clients at ease as quickly as possible is imperative, given the fact that they don't have the luxury of a drawn-out warming-up period.

Although it is admittedly frustrating to terminate a case before goals have been reached, it is important for therapists to acknowledge that they have limits and that sometimes extending treatment would produce little additional gain. For most clients the greatest rate of change in psychotherapy comes early on, when expectations of self and therapist tend to be highest. If we focus on the value we are adding to all of our clients' lives, it may make sense for us to put most of our professional energy into these opportunities for greatest growth, rather than to persist in cases in which clients may not yet be ready to change or are unable to profit from the techniques we have available.

Therapists need to engage in strategic risk-management practices. These involve taking special precautions in cases in which suicide, harm to others, and/or hospitalization are issues. Child abuse cases also require delicate handling, including those in which adult clients report earlier experiences of abuse. Increasingly courts demand expert opinions and severely punish errors in judgment and failure to report.

Providing the New Continuum of Care

The stringent efforts of MCOs have reduced the use of inpatient care, thereby substantially lowering costs. In many cases, inpatient care has been replaced by a complicated matrix of treatments, including different levels of care, ranging from

The New Continuum of Care

1. Community support and self-help groups
2. Outpatient treatment using the common factors
3. Outpatient solution-focused treatment methods
4. Outpatient ESTs for specific diagnoses
5. Intensive individual case management
6. Partial hospital programs using ESTs
7. Intensive outpatient programs using ESTs
8. Acute inpatient care using ESTs

Ten Managed Care Treatment Strategies

1. Greater use of groups
2. Greater use of self-help methods
3. Greater use of paraprofessionals
4. Use of common therapy factors in mobilizing change
5. Use of solution-focused treatment
6. Use of brief therapy methods
7. Use of empirically supported psychotherapy methods
8. Use of psychopharmacotherapy when appropriate
9. Use of specific, concrete behavioral goal statements
10. Use of objective measures of outcome

residential; to full- and part-time day care; to regular outpatient sessions with a clinician and different types of care, such as individual or group therapy, medication, or electroshock therapy. Working within the new continuum of care requires doing what's needed, optimally, and demonstrating this. The optimal treatment—from both the MCO's and the client's perspective—will be the treatment that is least restrictive, least intrusive, and least artificial and disruptive.

Duration, Dosage, and Delivery Decisions: Triage Today

Two fundamental principles shape modern behavioral healthcare practice: the principle of population-based care and the principle of parsimony (Schreter, 1997). The population-based perspective insists that clinicians shepherd limited resources to provide the greatest good for the larger society. Most seasoned clinicians were trained to respond to every patient's needs with the most intensive, comprehensive treatment available, without considering cost. In contrast, population-based practice holds the clinician responsible for all patients in the broader population, not just those currently seeking treatment. This public health view expands the clinician's responsibility to include patients who have not yet appeared for treatment and those who will present only after successful case finding, as well as those in need of preventive interventions. The principle of parsimony maintains that each patient should receive the least intensive, least expensive treatment at the lowest level of care that will permit a return to health and function. Although this principle is controversial and has not yet been the subject of comprehensive public debate, it is already operational in all managed care settings.

Effective managed care providers offer services at the appropriate level of intrusiveness, restrictiveness, and intensity at the appropriate level of care. In order to fulfill the new expectations of managed care, clinicians are working to develop a more seamless continuum of care, consisting of an array of services that exist between the 24-hour inpatient day and the 50-minute outpatient session (Schreter, 1997). These services include intensive outpatient programs, home care, mobile crisis teams, hospital diversion programs, foster care, residential care, and partial hospital programs. The practice of discharging patients "quicker and sicker" is possible because of the development of these lower-level services.

In addition, effective providers must increase their helping arsenal to include resources that exist in the community. Patients and their families have long used the phrase "continuum of care" to refer to these sources of help that begin where the formal medical continuum ends. These resources include consumer support groups, rehabilitation programs, vocational training programs, low-income and group housing, and sheltered living situations. Community-sponsored parenting and stress management seminars, bereavement groups, twelve-step programs for substance abuse or eating disorders, and couples workshops sponsored by religious organizations are among the many community-based service alternatives.

Clinicians working in managed care and community settings recognize that these services can contribute to growth and change for patients in treatment and can provide opportunities to continue the change process after face-to-face sessions have been concluded (Schreter & Budman, 1997). Clinicians must become more familiar with the various informal and formal services that exist over the emerging expanded continuum of care and more experienced at easing transitions as patients move from higher and lower levels. Escorting patients and providing appropriate preparatory information can facilitate patients' coping and reduce the need for more costly services. Providers also must be willing to innovate and develop lower levels of care or services that are currently lacking in their communities.

Level-of-Care Decision Making

Level-of-care decisions are involved implicitly whenever providers design treatment plans to meet patients' needs. Historically service providers' decisions about level of care have been idiosyncratic, resulting in a wide variability of services provided to patients with similar needs (Weed, 1991). Increasing the predictability of level-of-care decisions through the use of decision support tools can help both service providers and program planners, particularly under managed care (Newman & Tejeda, 1996).

Support tools for level-of-care decisions can facilitate appropriate and equitable allocation of services based on patients' clinical needs, enhancing client–treatment matching. Development of decision support tools for specific clinical populations can also guide the creation of service or benefit packages required for managed care (Feldman, 1992). Standards for making decisions about the appropriate level of care can support concurrent review decisions and quality assurance under managed care systems that otherwise may create incentives for restricting services (Burns et al., 1989; Schlesinger, 1989; Koyanagi et al., 1992).

At present, few tools exist for guiding level-of-care decisions for mental health outpatient clients. In some studies, cluster analysis has been used to first identify case mix group characteristics in a population or sample (Bartsch et al., 1995; Uehara, Smukler, & Newman, 1994). Level-of-care placement criteria and service programs are then designed for these "discovered" case mix groups. Cluster-analytic level-of-care models generate relatively homogeneous case mix groups, but this method can be insensitive to differences among clients that are clinically but not statistically meaningful (Srebnik, Uehara, & Smukler, 1998). Validating level-of-care decision-support models using past service utilization is insufficient, because it further institutionalizes system inadequacies, such as lack of funding and inflexible funding streams, that restrict service providers from making service decisions based on clinical need.

Srebnik, Uehara, and Smukler (1998) found that level-of-care placements based on a decision support tool they developed showed strong interrater reliability. Their tool used an a priori clinical framework for identifying case mix groups and an algorithm for level-of-care placements, to model complex clinical decision making closely while retaining many of the same strengths as cluster-based approaches. Concurrent validity was demonstrated by significant relationships in the expected direction between level of care and psychiatric hospitalizations, arrests, residential moves, homeless periods, residential independence, lack of work activity, medication noncompliance, and functioning as measured by the Global Assessment of Functioning Scale. There are plans to further refine such decision support tools by incorporating the impact of social supports, collateral services, current mental health services, and motivation for services.

Delivery Methods and Manpower

Group Treatment Methods

Both time-limited and long-term ongoing groups are expected to play an increasingly significant role in healthcare delivery over the next decade (MacKenzie, 1997). There is empirical evidence that for the two most common forms of psychological disturbance, anxiety disorder and depression, group treatment may sometimes be more effective than individual therapy. In a meta-analysis of treatments for agoraphobia, Trull, Nietzel, and Main (1988) found that better outcomes were associated with group therapy than with individual therapy. Brown and

Lewinsohn (1984) compared the progress of those taking a Coping with Depression (CWD) group course to those in a wait list control group, receiving individual tutoring based on the CWD course, or receiving minimal phone contact. All three active treatments produced significant improvements. However, those taking the CWD course still showed substantial improvements at post-treatment followups. The results showed little difference between group and individual CWD treatment. The results indicated that the CWD course format is a viable and cost-effective treatment approach for depressed outpatients.

Managed care has been credited with promoting a veritable renaissance and proliferation of innovative group therapies, especially various forms of short-term and crisis groups (Hoyt, 1995b). Such groups are often the treatment of choice for patients seeking mental health services, if patients are properly selected and groups are appropriately planned. Group therapy is an important part of managed care psychotherapy because of its clinical utility, not simply because of cost-effectiveness; there is no real cost conservation without treatment efficacy (Kaplan, 1989). Goldman (1988) and Shadle and Christianson (1988) found that more than 70% of HMO mental health patients receive individual psychotherapy, with group therapy alone being utilized in less than 15% of cases (the others are treated with combined modalities, such as individual plus marital or family therapy). Higher percentages of managed care patients are treated in groups where organized and supported group programs are available. Roller, Schnell, and Welsch (1982) estimate that 27% of the overall visits to Group Health Cooperative of Puget Sound were for group therapy; Budman and Bennett (1983) estimate that approximately 25% to 30% of treatment at their site is done in groups; Hoyt (1995) reports that at Kaiser-Hayward approximately 25% of post-intake patients are seen in group formats.

Klein (1985) summarized the goals of short-term groups:

> (1) the amelioration of distress (i.e., the reduction of symptomatic discomfort); (2) prompt re-establishment of the patient's previous emotional equilibrium; (3) promoting efficient use of the patient's resources (e.g., increasing the patient's sense of control or mastery, emphasizing adaptation, or providing cognitive restructuring, aiding behavioral change, self-help, and social effectiveness); (4) developing the patient's understanding of his current disturbance and increasing coping skills for the future. (p. 312)

Many forms of group therapy reflect the managed care emphasis on problem solving, crisis intervention preparedness, clear definition of patient and therapist responsibilities, flexible and creative use of time, interdisciplinary cooperative treatments, use of multiple formats and modalities, intermittent treatment throughout the life cycle, and quality assurance and UR procedures (MacKenzie, 1994). Developmental groups designed to aid life cycle "passages" have included a young adults (emancipation) group, a new parents group, a separation-divorce group, a bereavement group, and an older adults group. Hoyt (1995) describes success with time-limited groups for anger management, assertiveness training, phobia and panic management, chronic pain, and chemical dependency. Others report effective use of psychoeducational groups for new parents, for couples' communication skills, and for persons coping with physical illness (Lonergan, 1981; Rosenbaum, 1983). Groups for chronically mentally ill patients and medication groups provide patients with the destigmatizing experience of universality; promote education, support, and problem solving; and relieve clinicians of some of the tedium of repetitive individual work (Folkers & Steefel, 1991).

Crisis intervention groups provide quick intervention while someone is acutely distressed following a specific stress event, in order to support reconstitution of coping skills (Hoyt, 1995). Emotional ventilation, normalization, and group support are basic therapeutic elements. In crisis groups, therapists work actively to promote problem solving, counter regression, and provide a "safety net," if necessary, while additional treatment planning is done and put into action. Groups can also be developed with a prophylactic function, to help potentially traumatized persons after a specific event (critical incident debriefing sessions).

As we explore ways of helping our clients expand their natural support networks and form connections with others, it makes sense to make greater use of group therapy methods. Group treatment offers the opportunity to participate in a mutual helping capacity; the consumer is both giver and receiver of help. This can be empowering and can increase perceived self-efficacy (Chambliss, 1988). Group therapy experiences provide practice in pivotal interpersonal skills such as active listening, being assertive, maintaining confidences, and negotiating solutions when conflicts arise. These abilities directly generalize to the client's natural support system. This, coupled with the reduced intensity of intimate connection with the therapist, facilitates the "weaning" process as therapy draws to a close.

Group therapy may seem a more "natural" and familiar way to learn coping skills than individual therapy, because it resembles a grouping of "learners" similar to what we experienced in school. As a result, there may be less resistance and less negative stigma associated with using group than individual treatment modalities. Group treatment may be less disruptive of the client's ongoing outside relationships with family and friends, who might view the intense alliance that often develops between a client and an individual therapist as a threat or competition. These responses can undermine treatment and the ongoing relationships, by triangulating the client, so reducing this risk is of real value.

Community Resources

Years ago, George Miller (1969) expressed his dream of increasing public access to useful psychological findings:

> Our responsibility is less to assume the role of experts and try to apply psychology ourselves than to give it away to the people who really need it. (p. 1071)

> . . . I can imagine nothing we could do that would be more relevant to human welfare, and nothing that could pose a greater challenge to the next generation of psychologists, than to discover how best to give psychology away. (p. 1074)

Population-based behavioral healthcare will make it increasingly advantageous for us to actualize Miller's vision of deploying psychology for the greatest good.

Increasing our use of helping resources within the client's natural support system not only reduces the economic costs of care; it also reduces the stigma associated with receiving assistance. Therapy offers clients immensely reassuring validation; informal friendly encounters within the community can offer a similar service for free and without altering the recipient's social identity. While it is true that the stigma associated with defining oneself as a "patient" varies across cultural groups, and in some being a patient may actually have cachet, generally this identity is experienced negatively.

Support Groups, Peer Helping, and Self-Help Groups

Consistent with the recognition of the competence of paraprofessional providers (Dawes, 1994), research has shown peer helpers and support groups to have the potential to offer consumers considerable assistance. In recent years, use of peer mediators and peer counselors has offered many high schools a cost-effective means of addressing the psychological concerns of the student body (O'Connor, Helverson, & Chambliss, 1995; Kristel, Fielding, & Chambliss, 1997; Kristel, Young, & Chambliss, 1997; Young, Kristel, & Chambliss, 1997).

There are an estimated 750,000 self-help groups in the United States (American Psychiatric Association, 1989b), with roughly 7 million adult members (Jacobs & Goodman, 1989). This involvement is expected to continue to increase for various reasons, including cost. Managed care systems encourage providers to incorporate thoughtful referral to these groups as part of the treatment process.

Research on the efficacy of self-help groups is limited. Much of the available research has been flawed by failure to compare the outcome of self-help groups with other treatment or control conditions. Grimsmo, Helgesen, and Borchgrevink (1981) reported on the outcome of self-help groups for weight reduction. Lieberman (1986) summarized research on the sobriety of AA members. Other studies have compared the outcome of self-help groups with nonrandomized control conditions. Lieberman (1986) compared the outcomes of participants in THEOS, a self-help group for widows and widowers, with those of bereaved spouses who chose not to participate in THEOS and others who elected psychotherapy. Galanter (1988) compared participants in Recovery, Inc., a self-help program for people with psychiatric problems, with control subjects in the community. Only a few studies have compared self-help conditions with randomized control conditions. Levitz and Stunkard (1974) compared subjects who were randomly assigned to several different treatment programs, one of which was TOPS (Take Off Pounds Sensibly), a self-help organization for the obese. Jason et al. (1987) investigated whether self-help discussion groups developed at the worksite augmented a smoking cessation program. All of these investigations except for the study by Levitz and Stunkard (1974) found evidence of positive outcomes for participants in self-help groups.

Self-Help Techniques

Approximately 2,000 self-help books are published in the United States annually (Doheny, 1988), covering a variety of problems including psychiatric difficulties such as anxiety and depression. Starker (1988) found that most practicing psychologists prescribe self-help books to their clients and find these books helpful.

Self-help treatments have been predominantly applied to circumscribed problems, such as addictive behaviors and habit control. Although the research on self-administered treatments (self-help books, inspirational tapes, meditation, adult education courses) and peer support groups is not definitive, the studies completed so far show no clear advantage for clinical work with a therapist over a self-administered treatment (Jacobson, 1995). When peer support groups have been examined rigorously (e.g., the treatment of obesity), they generally seem to perform as well as psychotherapy conducted by a professional.

A number of studies have examined the effectiveness of self-help books and audiotapes when used alone or with minimal therapist contact. Scogin et al. (1990) conducted a meta-analysis on forty of these studies that compared self-administered treatment with a control condition such as no treatment or therapist-administered treatment. The studies in this review addressed five general problem areas: (1) habit control, such as smoking, alcohol, and weight problems; (2) depression and anxiety; (3) phobias; (4) skill training, such as parent training and study skills; and (5) an "other" category that included sleep, sex, and memory problems. Their results indicated that self-administered treatments were more effective than no treatment, and the differences between self-administered and therapist-administered treatments were insignificant. Many of the studies considered by Scogin et al. involved rather circumscribed problems that may be particularly suitable to educational and information-based interventions. It would therefore be an error to conclude from this study that self-administered treatments are uniformly as effective as therapist-administered treatments across all disorders.

Gould and Clum (1993) examined a different but overlapping set of forty self-help treatment studies that used no-treatment, wait-list, or placebo control comparisons. Their meta-analysis found that self-help treatments showed overall effect sizes comparable to those reported for psychotherapy in the literature. An examination of twelve studies that compared self-help and therapist conditions revealed no differences between the two. Gould and Clum concluded that self-help treatments were more effective with skills deficits and problems such as fears and depression than with habit problems, such as smoking, drinking, and overeating.

A meta-analysis of eleven outcome studies of various kinds of brief dynamic therapy (Crits-Christoph, 1992) found that individual dynamic therapy was only slightly superior to self-help groups. Beutler et al. (1991) compared professional therapists with a combination of self-administered materials and paraprofessional counselors to treat depression. This study also attempted to predict which patients would respond best to which treatments. Sixty-three patients diagnosed with major depressive disorder were randomly assigned to (1) group cognitive therapy;

(2) group-focused, expressive psychotherapy; or (3) supportive, self-directed therapy (clients were given a reading list of ten popular self-help books and provided weekly, supportive telephone contacts). The cognitive and expressive therapies were administered by Ph.D. psychologists with 5 or more years of experience. The supportive, self-directed psychotherapy was administered by advanced graduate students. At post-treatment and at 3-month followup there were no differences between conditions on independent psychiatric evaluations or on self-report symptom measures. They also found significant differential response to treatment. Supportive, self-directed therapy was more effective than the authoritarian treatments (cognitive therapy and focused, expressive psychotherapy) with high-resistant (defensive) patients. The authoritative treatments were more effective than supportive, self-directed therapy with low-resistant patients. Supportive, self-directed therapy was more effective than cognitive therapy for internalizing patients, while cognitive therapy was more effective than supportive, self-directed therapy for externalizing patients. Focused, expressive psychotherapy was not differentially effective across levels of patient internalization and externalization.

Hester et al. (1990) showed that AA and traditional counseling have similar effects over all. However, clients who prior to treatment saw alcoholism as a disease were more abstinent following AA, and those who prior to treatment viewed alcoholism as an addictive, bad habit did better with traditional counseling. Congruence between clients' views and treatment rationale was also associated with greater maintenance of therapeutic gains in studies investigating weight loss and smoking cessation methods conducted by Chambliss and Murray (1979a, 1979b).

In the future, self-administered treatment programs are expected to involve increasing use of video and computer technology as well as audio recordings and reading materials. Computerized treatments have been used successfully for obesity (Burnett, Taylor, & Agras, 1985), phobias (Ghosh, Marks & Carr, 1988), and depression (Selmi et al., 1990). Selmi et al. randomly assigned thirty-six depressed patients to one of three conditions: (1) therapist-administered cognitive-behavioral therapy, (2) computer-administered cognitive-behavioral therapy, and (3) a waiting-list control. The therapist-administered and computer-administered cognitive-behavioral conditions followed a similar format and content agenda. After treatment and a 2-month followup, both treatment groups improved significantly more than control subjects on a variety of dependent measures but did not differ from each other. Efforts are underway to improve the quality of the exploding arsenal of psychological services being provided via the Internet (Morse et al., 1998).

The current evidence suggests that self-administered treatments generally achieve outcomes comparable to those of therapist-administered treatments. Facilitating self-care when appropriate can help providers maintain consumers' health inexpensively.

Paraprofessionals and Rookies

Much to the chagrin of the M.D.s, Ph.D.s, and Psy.D.s, the research literature has generally failed to support the supremacy of trained doctoral-level professionals in providing helpful guidance to those in dire psychological need (Berman & Norton, 1985; A. Christensen & Jacobson, 1994; Durlak, 1979; Dawes, 1994; Smith, Glass, & Miller, 1980; D. Stein & Lambert, 1984; Strupp & Hadley, 1979; Trull, Nietzel, & Main, 1988). Although some criticize imperfections in this research, it appears that no one has succeeded in offering empirical findings refuting the converging studies indicating modest effects of clinical training.

In *House of Cards*, Robyn Dawes argues that:

> Psychotherapy works. The magnitude of its positive effects is greater than the magnitude of many physical treatments, deleterious lifestyles, and changes in those lifestyles. Those who believe they have problems are encouraged to try it, especially if they have been unable to change their behavior by simply "willing" a change. There is no reason, however, to seek out a highly paid, experienced therapist with a lot of credentials. If verbal therapy is sought, paraprofessionals are equally effective, especially empathetic ones. If the problems appear to require behavioral modification, as do phobias and lack of impulse control, a paraprofessional who understands behavioral principles is as effective as a highly credentialed professional. (Dawes, 1994, p. 73)

Dawes maintains that untrained helpers are often as effective in providing supportive counseling as those with advanced degrees. While training confers advantages in some cases of extreme pathology, is associated with greater adherence to ethical standards, and can increase a helper's incisiveness (thereby shortening the length of treatment and the client's suffering), in mild cases it may be appropriate to make greater use of less expensive paraprofessional helpers.

Paraprofessionals can be of tremendous value in helping consumers, even those with severe mental illnesses (Chambliss, 1988). Increasing reliance on bachelor-level case managers has helped reduce the length and number of inpatient stays for many severely mentally ill patients; these paraprofessionals frequently dominate the partial hospital programs that are gradually supplanting long-term hospital care for all but a small minority of the severely mentally ill.

The idea of using paraprofessionals threatens some traditional therapists who were heavily invested in the old indemnity system. But now that capitation is becoming the rule, the game has changed. In order to survive, group practices and mental health centers must implement efficiencies wherever possible. We are responsible for meeting the psychological needs of those for whom we hold contracts. As a clinician, it will behoove you to make creative use of nontraditional methods of ensuring that your patients receive the support they need. Recognize that you need not be the one providing all of that support. Some of your work can be done indirectly, by establishing connections with community resources (including appropriate adult education courses, peer support groups, etc.). Using paraprofessionals as allies to help you reach a larger number of patients often makes good sense.

For decades there has been a gradual trend to make greater use of nonprofessionals, trained and supervised by professionals, as therapeutic agents. Early reviews of this approach concluded that nonprofessional personnel can function as effective counselors and contribute to client improvement (Brown, 1974).

Nagel, Cimbolic, and Newlin (1988) showed that volunteer counselors, both elderly and adolescent, were effective therapeutic agents in helping to alleviate depression in the elderly. Compared with the no-treatment control subjects, the elderly who received regular visits from a volunteer counselor showed significantly less depression. Elderly and adolescent counselors were comparable in helping skills and in therapeutic outcomes. No differences were found between the empathy-trained volunteers and those receiving a general orientation. This may be because all workshops promoted enthusiasm, which might have heightened the effectiveness of all the volunteers.

In a study examining the effects of group assertive training on black adolescent aggression, Huey and Rank (1984) found no differences between counselor-led and peer-led assertive training groups. Both assertive groups scored significantly lower in classroom aggression than the no-treatment control group, and both assertive training groups were significantly different from both discussion groups. Responses to a client questionnaire revealed no significant differences between the groups in terms of level of clients' satisfaction with their group experience. This study illustrates that assertive skills can be taught to aggressive adolescents effectively by both professional and supervised peer counselors. It also supports other findings documenting the acceptance of peer counselors by adolescents.

Engelkes and Roberts (1970) investigated the effect of different levels of academic training on the job performance of rehabilitation counselors. Both measures (supervisors' global ratings and client reports of satisfaction) gave no indication that training improves the rehabilitation counselor's effectiveness on the job.

Because the evidence argues that the professional degree may not be a guarantee of competence (Dawes, 1994) and that many people without training are adept at providing the support many patients need, it is appropriate for us to develop ways of making more optimal use of paraprofessionals and volunteers. Finding ways to build the strengths of paraprofessionals and reduce their risk of burnout can help make a capitated practice function in the black.

Experience Is Less Important If Therapists Use EST

Research supports the notion that newcomers to behavioral healthcare can do as well as their more experienced counterparts if they master the proved techniques. After surveying the research literature evaluating the performance of clinicians who employed a broad variety of techniques, Garb (1989) concluded that professional clinicians make somewhat better judgments than do nonprofessionals, but he found that this can easily be explained in terms of differences in such characteristics as intelligence and the fact that practitioners who have learned to use valid techniques employ them better than those who haven't learned to use them. He found that, once the rudiments of the techniques have been mastered, their accuracy does not increase with additional experience in using them. The accuracy of the judgment of professional psychologists and other mental health workers is limited by the accuracy of the techniques they employ.

This increasing emphasis on adherence to empirically supported techniques (ESTs) may reverse a disturbing trend that some have observed.

> The quality of the training of clinical psychologists, a major group of therapists studied, has deteriorated rapidly in the past several years. That might not mean much, given that training and credentials don't predict therapeutic effectiveness; but along with the decreased quality of training has come an explosion in numbers that assures that there will be more poor therapists around in the 1990s than previously. A greater concern is that many new ideas and therapies have been initiated that are at best characterized as ideologically based or faddish. There are therefore more therapists who base their practice on such ideologies and fads. (Dawes, 1994, pp. 73–74)

Using Research to Improve Psychotherapy: Cutting Corners with Savvy

According to Lynn Johnson (1995),

> . . . an accountable therapist must be aware of current research and be a sophisticated consumer of that information. Retreating into a "know nothingism" in which research is discounted as any useful source of knowledge would mean abandoning any pretense that psychotherapy can be a profession. And while common wisdom holds that published research is frequently characterized by trivial results produced by academics desperate for tenure, for the alert reader there is a good deal of very useful information to be harvested. (pp. 23–24)

Limits of Continuing Education and Clinical Experience

Johnson (1995) argues that too often therapists learn about new developments in the field only through continuing education programs. Most therapists attend only workshops that appeal to their own theoretical stance, so there may be few opportunities to really learn something new. In addition, in many continuing education workshops material is presented on the basis of "clinical experience" rather than controlled experimental evidence.

> The presenster speaks *ex cathedra*, saying, "This is the way it is." The content often implies the presenter has unique understanding that makes his or her theory more potent than others. This is quite frustrating for one who has read the literature and knows that the general thrust of research has not confirmed those pronouncements. In saying this, there is no intention to point an accusing finger at any single theory. This phenomenon is present in presentations ranging from object relations to strategic, solution-focused, and Ericksonian perspectives. The cognitive therapists are a refreshing exception; their workshops tend to be well-founded in research findings. But unfortunately this is not generally the case. Therapists simply must become

more aware of what their own literature says, and not accept pronouncements based on what the presenter's clinical experience may be. (Johnson, 1995, p. 24)

The problem with clinical experience is that history reveals it to be notoriously unreliable. Therapists are very poor evaluators of their own theories and techniques and often do not know whether they are accurately attending to true causal factors. George Washington apparently died of medical treatment that was both state-of-the-art and based on sound clinical experience; he was bled four times (Flexner, 1984).

> There is some scientific knowledge about some mental disorders and types of distress and how to alleviate them. When psychiatrists and psychologists base their practice on this knowledge, they generally perform a valuable service to their clients. All too often, however, mental health practitioners base their practice on what they believe to be an "intuitive understanding" of their clients' problems, . . . gained "from experience." But when they practice on this intuitive basis, they perform at best as well as minimally trained people who lack their credentials, and at worst as licensed, expensive (if inadvertent) frauds. (Dawes, 1994, p. 106)

Recognizing the limits of clinical judgment creates a dilemma, because the current research foundation fails to provide therapists with guidance on a moment-to-moment basis. We often have no choice but to rely on our clinical experience. However, the literature can give us some general direction and help, and, to the extent that it does so, we should take heed.

Reading the Literature

It is hardly a foregone conclusion that all trained professionals will devote the time and energy necessary to stay current with the burgeoning clinical literature. If the past is predictive of the future, we should expect many therapists to renege somewhat on their scientific obligations.

Dawes (1994) reported a communication from the American Psychological Association publication board on February 14, 1991, stating that only approximately 30% of APA members (researchers and practitioners) subscribe to one or more of its scientific journals. This particular method of estimating practitioners' currency with the literature is no longer appropriate, because, subsequent to this data collection, APA raised dues to automatically include a journal subscription with membership. While we might optimistically hope that many practitioners avail themselves of library journals, few clinics and private practices boast large collections. Others have also indicted practitioners for failing to incorporate research findings into their clinical work (N. Jacobson, 1995).

Integrating Research and Practice

Clement (1996) argues that we need an immediate integration of research and practice in clinical psychology in order to survive in the current economic climate.

As consumers of behavioral health services become more sophisticated, more proof of competence will be required of providers. Specifically, providers will need to identify the best-known procedures, and they will need to demonstrate a proficiency in administering these procedures. The researcher-practitioner should use new computer software to facilitate data gathering related to the diagnostic process, treatment planning, client compliance, and evaluation of treatment outcome. Practitioners who use such a database for self-evaluation will hold a competitive advantage over those who do not.

Clement maintains that in designing effective treatment plans, practitioners should (1) use empirically validated treatments, (2) keep track of treatment settings and designed agents of change associated with treatment strategies, (3) generate clear goals expressible in measurable terms in collaboration with the client, (4) use the best available treatment manual, (5) keep records about the frequency and duration of treatment, and (6) specify criteria for termination at the beginning of therapy.

On the other hand, Fensterheim and Raw (1996) argue that clinical research and practice are two distinct fields and that an explicit deintegration is the best solution to the current conflict of interest between them. Noting differences in the perspectives that researchers and practitioners adopt, they perceive integration as problematic.

Nezu (1996) has encouraged what he refers to as "pragmatic compromise." In a market flooded with a variety of mental health vendors and limited subsidy dollars, consumers will increasingly seek information about the quality, cost, and efficiency of care. Nezu argues that if psychologists continue their internecine warfare over the question of whether and how to integrate research and practice, other professionals will provide treatment based on empirically validated protocols developed by research-oriented psychologists. In the collaborative scenario Nezu envisions, practitioners would identify constructs that they repeatedly experience in therapy, but for which no known method of measurement exists. Researchers would develop tests for these constructs, and test publishers would sell them to private practitioners. All the major players would profit.

Utilizing Therapy Outcome and Process Research

Far more so than was previously the case, your future in successfully delivering behavioral healthcare depends upon your ability to utilize the knowledge gained from several decades of psychotherapy research.

Generally the research is consistent with the possibility of providing effective therapy within a managed care framework. Despite the complaints of the angry and fearful providers who equate managed care with unfettered profiteering and unbridled greed, a dispassionate review of the outcome literature suggests that it should be possible to integrate current concerns about cost containment without seriously sacrificing the quality of psychological care.

While additional corrective steps may need to be taken to halt the transfer of savings effected by streamlining the therapy process to the pockets of a few temporary healthcare participants at the executive level, it is reassuring to note that some of this compensatory process is already well underway. Mastering the research will help you to contribute to this necessary correction.

Differences between Medical and Behavioral Managed Care

Providing efficient, cost-effective psychotherapy requires a recognition of spontaneous improvement rates, placebo effectiveness, our limited ability to predict individual patients' reactions to treatment, and the risks of iatrogenic harm associated with psychological treatment. Research has consistently revealed a high rate of spontaneous remission for many psychological problems. The outcome literature provides overwhelmingly convincing evidence that many patients respond quite positively to the minimal support and encouragement associated with attention placebo control conditions (A. Shapiro & Shapiro, 1997). Our current ability to predict particular clients' responses to specific treatment approaches is very limited (Wampold, 1997). We are not able to determine accurately at the outset which patients will require more intensive and intrusive forms of helping.

Although we generally think of psychotherapy as fairly benign, for decades we have been aware of research findings indicating its potential to cause harm in some cases. Iatrogenic damage has been conceptualized in a variety of ways: social breakdown syndrome, excessive dependency on therapists, negative focus, suggested memories, disruptions of the family system, etcetera. These risks seem to be greater when more intrusive, intensive, and long-term forms of therapy are used. Given these factors, it seems appropriate to proceed conservatively in offering psychological forms of treatment, in order to assess whether the least intrusive and least expensive methods will be sufficient. Starting with the most minimal level of intervention initially, monitoring progress, and escalating efforts only when the need for additional services is apparent seems to be a sound strategy for empirically matching patients' true needs to level of care. Interestingly the so-called "rationing" of care methods that characterizes many managed care protocols conforms fairly closely to this model. Very brief forms of focused, supportive, solution-oriented outpatient treatment are offered promptly to those in need. Approval of more lengthy, intensive, and intrusive interventions requires clinical justification and behavioral evidence of medical necessity.

When providing managed care, there is pressure from the first contact with the patient to promote rapid improvement and to facilitate maintenance of therapeutic gains to prevent relapse. There is rarely time for an extensive diagnostic workup and history, and still less time to experiment unsystematically with a variety of possible treatment approaches, so it is helpful to be prepared to apply knowledge from the empirical literature about general truths and base rates.

Even though much of this research was conducted during a different era, it still supplies valuable answers. Although times have changed, the results remain relevant for a variety of reasons. First, prior to managed care, when autonomous clinicians' judgments theoretically determined the length and pace of treatment, in practice the patients were in control of treatment duration. Long-term therapy was never the norm; most clients met with their therapist seven or eight times total, and many stopped after a single session (Garfield, 1986). Second, most treatment efficacy studies, which form the basis of the EST literature, were conducted by using time-limited versions of different therapies, provided by supervised therapists using treatment manuals to guide their work. This is parallel to how much therapy is delivered under managed care. The findings from such studies are therefore readily generalizable to today's healthcare scenario.

Key Areas of Psychotherapy Research

Four large bodies of research are important to master in responding to the current managed care environment. These areas of inquiry (common factors, solution-focused therapy, brief problem-solving therapy, and ESTS) will be briefly summarized here and presented in greater detail in chapters that follow.

First, the research on the *common factors* underlying treatment effectiveness provides an appreciation of the elements that cut across the different schools of therapy and promote patient improvement in nonspecific ways. Studies have consistently found that a variety of different interventions produce more or less the same therapeutic outcome. The research elucidating what these theoretically dissimilar methods have in common tells us much about the key mechanisms underlying change and how to facilitate these processes.

Second, work on *solution-focused approaches* to patients has demonstrated a way that often helps to circumvent the need for lengthy treatment by efficiently mobilizing the patient's strengths. Conservative therapists who want to minimize the risks of iatrogenic harm frequently use a trial of solution-focused therapy before assuming that more is necessary. Learning how to use focused methods can often assist patients in reaching their goals with minimal disruption to their lives and ongoing relationships.

Third, research on *brief treatment* has yielded several findings of relevance to managed care. Garfield's research indicates that the modal experience of psychotherapy has always been brief. Other studies suggest the rate of change quickly plateaus, which indicates that patients benefit progressively less from treatment as it lengthens. Other studies indicate that single-session therapy often has a positive impact on patients. Collectively this research challenges the assumption of superiority of long-term psychotherapy and suggests that therapists have been making meaningful use of brief treatment (whether intentional or not) for decades. In addition, several general practices have been shown to help facilitate efficient change in patients. Applying these practices can help you to promote the type of rapid recovery that managed care values.

Fourth, research on *ESTs* illuminates techniques that have proved to be treatments of choice in helping patients challenged by specific disorders. Although most of the EST literature assumes that, in matching patients and treatment, clinicians would use diagnoses to organize their thinking, these same methods can also be conveniently applied by those who think more in terms of symptoms or symptom clusters.

These four extensive literatures will be reviewed in some detail in the chapters that follow. These summaries will help you to see how anchoring treatment decisions in the knowledge of the discipline can enhance the quality of the care you provide, while obliging the demands of the current marketplace confronting behavioral healthcare providers.

Using a Research-Based, Rational Progression

Managed care compels providers to provide a rational progression of care, monitoring patients' responses throughout the process. In order to reduce unproductive meandering, it is useful to incorporate research findings in the clinical decision-making process. The following "speed sequence" presents a strategy for systematically employing the least intrusive forms of psychotherapeutic intervention necessary for progress in a given case. Application of research forms the basis of the speed sequence. This way of thinking about how to structure treatment expedites change while reducing wasteful, unnecessary clinical practices.

1. Applying common factors findings entails using the patient's heightened motivation at the outset of treatment as an impetus for rapid change. The common factors literature also suggests that formulating clear, individualized, consensual goals facilitates change, regardless of the specific type of treatment being provided. Such goals support and encourage the patient, and they also make the patient more explicitly accountable for making behavioral, affective, or life changes. Selecting managed care–appropriate treatment goals that fit the patient's objectives can help to align the therapist's and the patient's motivation to enhance treatment effectiveness.

2. Applying solution-focused findings involves using a trial of solution-focused treatment to highlight and enlist patients' current strengths. This strategy reduces the iatrogenic risks of pathology-focused therapy. It also can foster efficient change by building upon existing successes and encouraging patients to learn from the episodes that represent exceptions to their periods of difficulty.

Most patients, even the most severely mentally ill, experience fluctuations in their symptoms. This means that some of the time, and in many cases much of the time, their functioning is adequate and potentially satisfying. Consideration of the strengths that patients bring to treatment permits a trial of a solution-focused therapy in most cases.

3. Applying brief therapy findings entails developing specific, clear, measurable, behavioral, active, achievable treatment goals. These permit a clearly discerned outcome and avoid discursive treatment. Communicating the expectation that change can take place immediately, rather than first requiring a lengthy process of personal exploration, can assist patients in benefitting from brief therapy.

Certain practices can expedite treatment by clearly communicating expectations to patients. The research on brief and single-session treatment can keep us alert to the possibility of rapid change early on in treatment. The finding that the rate of change plateaus fairly quickly in most types of psychotherapy can also encourage us to make conscientious use of our window of opportunity at the beginning of therapy.

4. Applying empirical findings about specific treatment methods involves using diagnosis to permit selection of the most appropriate symptom-focused treatment, using the literature on ESTs as a guide. Using symptom-focused pharmacotherapy when appropriate can also help to optimize outcomes efficiently.

CHAPTER

8 Justifying Care as Medically Necessary

Conflict about mental health insurance coverage is rampant. Evaluating the appropriateness of treatments for reimbursement is enormously challenging for MCOs, and utilization reviewers' decisions are often at odds with those of providers. Can the proposed intervention reasonably be anticipated to achieve the intended result? Could a less costly intervention achieve a comparable result? These questions are compelling accelerated outcomes research, but they frequently leave us frustrated, given the presently limited empirical evidence about treatment effectiveness. Managed care review has become increasingly cumbersome and time-consuming for practitioners. Understanding the process is an integral part of most clinicians' ability to provide effective care. Often, without suitable and suitably expressed justification, authorization to treat will be denied, and care cannot be provided.

Given the requirements of utilization management, clinicians need to learn systematic ways to articulate and document their thought processes as they plan treatment. Unless practitioners can specify clearly what they are doing for their patients and also convincingly explain why it is necessary, MCOs are going to be increasingly unwilling to pay for their services.

In justifying care, providers must understand what managed care utilization reviewers need to know, and they must have a means of communicating clinical information that meets this need.

> As consultants to practitioners, healthcare organizations, and patients who are appealing reimbursement denials from various managed care companies, we continue to be impressed that more than half of these denials result from inadequate communication of the reasons for treatment and the clinical rationale for the specific services requested. Often, although the recommended care was clinically appropriate, the practitioner failed to communicate "why." When practitioners can approach the review process as a request for clarity of thought, rather than a threat of nonpayment, they may well be able to respond artfully and more effectually to reviewers as colleagues and not as menacing strangers. (Goodman, Brown, & Deitz, 1992, p. 22)

Reviewers need to know why particular treatment decisions have been made. Practitioners are expected to provide their rationale for the recommended treatment and to offer convincing clinical evidence that supports the treatment decision, often referred to as "articulating the process of care."

Utilization review can feel intrusive, because it challenges both practitioners' authority and their traditional right to operate in private. Managed care review examines the clinician's clinical rationale for the treatment decision. Mental health professionals who are trained to ask questions to explain the thinking, motives, and behavior of others are now being asked to explain their own thinking and motives in treating their patients (Goodman, Brown, & Deitz, 1992).

Working with Utilization Reviewers

While UR can seem an impudence to experienced practitioners who have enjoyed considerable autonomy in the past, it can also be viewed as a means of moving the psychotherapy professions forward. Given the overwhelming amount of treatment research being generated today, it is unrealistic to expect busy practitioners to keep up with all of it. The UR process provides one mechanism for ensuring that treatments being offered reflect the most recent standards of care. Widely used UR guidelines are not written by academics in a vacuum. They are written by real clinicians and are modified frequently by users' groups. When you disagree with them, in justifying your deviations it is important to offer arguments with clinical and scientific merit.

The most effective reviews focus on indicators of quality, including a competent assessment and diagnosis, a clear and fairly precise treatment focus, and a rational relationship between the treatment focus and what happens in therapy. Interventions should be closely related to the treatment goals, the goals should be accomplished in a reasonable amount of time, and the therapist should begin to space out sessions as the goals are met. Treatment ends once goals are accomplished. Patients are encouraged to be independent and active, and patients with chronic personality disorders are placed in group therapy or community support groups.

Rather than completing a comprehensive mental status assessment and history, it is often more important to conduct a more focused assessment of whether the patient is dangerous to self or others and whether there is a drug or alcohol problem. A *DSM-IV* diagnosis, including all five axes, is appreciated by reviewers, but some of that information can come from questionnaires administered outside of the session. While traditionally psychotherapy interventions have only been weakly related to the diagnosis, the development of treatment protocols is bringing treatment and disorder into close alignment. Clinicians are expected to develop treatment plans that follow specific treatment protocols for particular disorders. Once therapy is underway, it is important to assess interim changes. There needs to be some clear indication that the patient is making acceptable progress.

Ten Tips for Expediting Utilization Reviews

If you are trying to deal with a utilization reviewer, it can be helpful to keep the following suggestions in mind. They are based on a recognition that efforts to forge an alliance with managed care representatives is usually in the provider's best interest.

1. *Know the specific details of the client's insurance coverage.* Contact the managed care company representative and discuss your findings and your treatment plan with the reviewer early in the treatment process. Discuss what will be the most mutually convenient way that you can keep the reviewer informed about the case. Most managed care companies will provide means of assessing the client's progress, but agreeing upon a plan for making phone or e-mail contacts with the reviewer (e.g., Is it alright to leave messages? How will receipt of messages be confirmed? Can written authorization be sent electronically to reduce wasteful phone tag?) can save you headaches down the road.

2. *Think like a reviewer.* In trying to think like a reviewer, consider the following dimensions for assessing the quality of patient care:
   - Is the care *appropriate* (necessary) for the condition?
   - Is the provider *competent* to provide that care?
   - Is the care *effective*?
   - Is the care *cost-efficient*?
   - Is the care *accessible and timely*?
   - Is the care *coordinated over time*?
   - Is the care *safe*?
   - Is the patient *satisfied*?

   Try to be flexible and ask yourself whether you are requesting something out of habit. If the utilization reviewer is requesting a shorter length of stay or a different site of treatment, see if you can look at the matter through the reviewer's eyes and understand his or her reasoning.

3. *Learn the criteria* for admission, continued stay, and the various other levels of treatment (partial hospitalization, outpatient care, etc.) for the various conditions you treat. Learn them as well as you would if you were a reviewer. Learn what kind of documentation they use to make their decisions. If you have a chance to review or consult with reviewers, seize it.

4. *Give the reviewer the benefit of a doubt.* Assume that the reviewer really does have the patient's interests in mind. They generally believe that less-intrusive, short-term treatment in the least restrictive setting works best, and they have research to support their position. They also recognize that the money being spent is the patient's money (it is part of the compensation package provided by the patient's employer). It is important to follow through and provide the particular services you say the patient really needs. Just as you remember your reviewers, they remember you and keep notes of discussions about care.

5. *Don't confuse a life-threatening diagnosis with a life-threatening patient status.* Bulimia is life-threatening, but a particular patient may not currently have a life-threatening status. Document the current facts to show that the patient's present condition warrants the treatment you're planning now.

6. *Failure of outpatient treatment is often necessary before inpatient treatment will be approved.* Documenting patient behavior that shows this failure (rather than therapist feelings, accurate as they may be) is what reviewers look for.

7. *If you believe the utilization reviewer's determination is not medically sound, keep on discussing it.* Try to find out why you are disagreeing. Often, when there is a disagreement, it is due to a communication problem. Ask to see the utilization reviewer's "utilization guidelines." This can improve communication and may result in authorization.

8. *Rely on empirical data in your case notes.* "The patient reports binge/purging twice since yesterday morning," rather than "The patient is getting worse and needs an inpatient stay."

9. *Make sure your case management shows consistency.* Diagnosis, need for treatment (client's current status), intensity of treatment planned, and intensity of treatment delivered should all relate clearly to one another. Exaggerating the need for treatment, when coupled with routine scheduling of appointments, stands out baldly. A life-and-death client condition calls for urgent action from the therapist; why would weekly meetings be calmly scheduled?

10. In some cases, *you may need to initiate a formal appeal of a reviewer's decision.* Your patient may have to do this, but you can help by knowing the procedure. Insurance companies have higher-powered professionals to review denials and appealed claims. Overturned denials typically result from clearer documentation of the need for delivery of treatment.

    Although some MCOs have reputations for responding to clinicians who appeal with punitive measures such as denial of subsequent referrals, the limited empirical evidence available (Scholl et al., 1996) suggests that the majority of managed care providers do not report having had such experience. You may need to speak with the reviewer's supervisor or the medical director of the company. Newly implemented NCQA standards are expected to facilitate the appeals process in companies that formerly made it unwieldy. Familiarizing yourself with these regulations will help you use them to your advantage (available by contacting NCQA in Washington, D.C.).

Other indicators of quality include how soon the patient can be seen after calling for an appointment and whether the therapist has some kind of 24-hour coverage for handling emergencies. Most see the latency between the first phone call and the first available appointment as an appropriate indicator of quality. Johnson (1995) argues that

> . . . a patient should have a right to be seen within a few days of calling, or a week at most. A large EAP conducted an in-house study and found that the sooner the client was seen, the fewer sessions were needed for a satisfactory conclusion. Someone seen within 24 hours was much more likely to be satisfied with two or three visits. (p. 121)

Medical Necessity: Defining Insurance-Covered Problems

Insurance coverage is authorized on the basis of demonstrated need and established treatment efficacy, rather than clients' preference. If individual therapy is preferred but produces little change when compared with group treatment, the latter will be favored. What is this client suffering from? Is it a form of major depression or is it life . . . being divorced, jobless, and middle-aged that makes him feel lonely and angry? Should this case be cast in the framework of illness, patient, doctor, treatment, health insurance coverage? What kinds of mental suffering create legitimate claims for help from others through insurance?

"Medical necessity" for psychotherapy means that a condition, for example, depression, is severe enough to interfere significantly with daily functioning, that documentation shows that other interventions have not worked, and that therefore psychological treatment is necessary. Treatment for the purposes of support is not defined as medical necessity and will usually be rejected by managed care reviewers.

Sabin and Daniels (1994) studied difficult insurance coverage decisions brought to them by mental health clinicians and reviewers in a managed care setting, an HMO serving a half million members in the New England region of the United States. The authors interviewed the personnel involved, eliciting the individuals' views, varying key aspects, and examining effects of their reasoning. What surfaced was a common theme of disagreement between what the authors labeled the "hardliner" and the "expansive" views of medical necessity. The authors believe that this is indicative of a deeper moral conflict concerning the targets of intervention and the goals of treatment.

Challenges in Determining Medical Necessity

Sabin and Daniels (1994) identify three key challenges in assessing medical necessity: distinguishing treatment from enhancement, determining clients' responsibility for characterological problems, and addressing ambiguous clinical situations. While virtually all clients seeking reimbursed psychotherapy suffer various degrees of subjective unhappiness in their lives, many believe that unless a diagnosable illness is responsible for this unhappiness, insurance coverage should be denied. In general, when the *DSM-IV* can be used to justify a diagnosis, at least partial coverage is provided. If not, the cost for care generally becomes the responsibility of the individual client. Paradoxically, if the client's problems are expressed as somatic symptoms and presented to an internist, insurance typically covers medical investigation and treatment, which is often both less effective and costlier than psychotherapy.

In some cases, when arguments for the determination of medical necessity could go either way, the evaluator's estimate of the clients' willingness to try to change problematic elements of their behavior may be influential. Clients who show evidence of a "good attitude" and willingness to take responsibility for trying to improve themselves are sometimes seen as more "deserving" of treatment than those who externalize and blame others for their characterological problems (Sabin & Daniels, 1994). Decisions about whether to cast longstanding adjustment problems as nonreimbursable V-codes (e.g., interpersonal problem) versus reimbursable Axis I problems (e.g., presumptive atypical depression) are often subtly shaped by moral judgments. The appropriateness of this is subject to debate. A case could be made that because a client's willingness to accept responsibility frequently influences treatment motivation and outcome, it is appropriate to include estimates of these factors in making determinations about reimbursement. Alternatively it can be argued that medical necessity relates to etiology, not to prognosis, and therefore these factors should be irrelevant.

Insurers of mental healthcare are concerned about the unavoidable moral hazard created by any program that, in protecting against specified dangers, creates an incentive for the insured to falsely claim benefits. Mental health insurance inadvertently rewards those who are insured for claiming illness with the attention, solace, and care provided by psychotherapy, hospitalization, and the sick role, which can increase the insurer's claim liability. Many mental health professionals also understand the risks associated with overascribing diagnostic labels (Scheff, 1975) and seek to avoid iatrogenic harm by discouraging the overmedicalizing of normal "life problems." Moral hazard is a special problem for mental health insurance because judgments about medical necessity in mental health are less precise than in other areas of medicine. Several factors contribute to this ambiguity and consequently increase insurance company risks: Many symptoms are a part of everyday distress (making it difficult to distinguish where on the continuum actual pathology exists), diagnosis is often unreliable and uncertain (Perry, 1992), some forms of psychological treatment overlap with nonprofessional modes of providing support (leading some to label psychotherapy "rent-a-friend"), and demand for service increases with coverage (Manning et al., 1989).

Potential Models for Determining Medical Necessity

Sabin and Daniels (1994) have outlined three models for determining medical necessity: the "normal function," "capability," and "welfare" models. While each model defines the ultimate goal of psychiatric care as helping the client come as close to equal opportunity in life as possible, each differs in its answer to the question "Equal opportunity to do what?"

The normal function model requests healthcare to address disadvantages to individuals caused by disease or disability, in order to free all to be normal competitors. This model seeks to maintain or restore function, or compensate for restricted opportunity and loss of function, caused by disease and disability. It provides coverage only for those conditions listed in *DSM-IV.*

The capability model prescribes a broader healthcare role, holding that healthcare should seek to rectify inequalities arising out of the random distribution of personal capabilities. Those whose diminished capabilities place them at relative disadvantage should receive treatment, regardless of the cause of those deficient capabilities. This model makes functional disadvantage the basis for insurance coverage; any impairment in functioning justifies treatment, independent of an underlying "disorder."

The welfare model supports coverage of all those who suffer because of attitudes or behavior patterns they did not choose to develop and are not able to independently revise. With present distress as its basis, it provides for expansive coverage.

Sabin and Daniels (1994) predict rationing as the guiding force in mental health practice in the future and affirm how crucial the criteria used to make medical necessity determinations will be. They believe that only the normal function model is fair and workable, leading to results that society can afford. They recommend that the first three to six sessions with clients be designated for evaluation, so that those in need of care who fall outside of the medical necessity guidelines (those lacking a defined disorder) can be directed to appropriate alternatives (fee-for-service therapy or informal helping services offered in the community). Those with a defined disorder can be guided to appropriate treatment as covered by insurance.

Using Diagnoses Most Constructively

The Arbitrariness of *DSM-IV*

At the heart of the *DSM* is the conceptual definition of what constitutes a mental disorder, based largely on the proposal of Spitzer and Endicott (1978). The current *DSM-IV* definition includes the notion of dysfunction within the individual, as well as distress, disability, and disadvantage. Recently the validity of the *DSM* and Spitzer and Endicott definitions has been challenged, on both conceptual and logical grounds (e.g., Wakefield, 1993).

It is unsettling, but important, to realize that the psychiatric diagnostic system we now use is largely the result of so much historical accident. Anecdotally shared clinical phenomena seemed to be reasonably grouped together, so categories were created on the basis of early etiological hunches. Rhetoric defending these arbitrary groupings developed over time and was used to indoctrinate newcomers to the field, thereby narrowing their vision and fostering the impression that the system was somehow appropriately premised. The bottom line is that the *DSM-IV* is more a product of professionals' personality styles and their political factions than of rational, data-guided inquiry.

One result is that frequently people carrying very different diagnoses need to learn the very same things in therapy. Although described with disparate clinical labels, they may struggle with the same problem in getting their brains to do what they want them to do. The "depressed" client can't stop thinking about negative possibilities occurring; she needs to learn some new ways of controlling negative thinking. The "paranoid" client can't stop thinking about negative possibilities occurring; he needs to learn some new ways of controlling negative thinking. The "obsessive-compulsive" client can't stop thinking about negative possibilities occurring; she needs to learn some new ways of controlling negative thinking. The "agoraphobic" client . . . you get the picture. . . . The content of their repetitive, disruptive rumination may vary, but these patients share a common underlying need for assistance in learning how to direct their consciousness more constructively. Often these clients can be helped with many of the same interventions, even though they carry different diagnoses.

It can be misleading to think of current diagnostic categories as homogeneous in terms of the problems and needs they define clients as having. There is great overlap across diagnostic categories. While diagnoses can give us valuable information about obstacles we might encounter in trying to teach a particular client a skill, and clues about more efficient ways to build a given competency, we need to be careful not to miss the fact that many differently labeled people confront us with similar underlying deficits. We should take pains to focus on identifying the most central underdeveloped talent and helping build that competency, even if it is not particularly rare, exotic, or diagnosis-specific.

Criticisms of Diagnosis

Paula Caplan, a psychologist and former consultant to the *DSM*, has indicted the diagnostic system on the grounds that scientific methods and evidence are commonly disregarded as the handbook is developed and revised. She challenges the mental health establishment's creation of potentially damaging interpretations and labels that can have a devastating impact on an individual's life. At present, diagnostic categories are not always linked cleanly to preferred treatment strategies. A given intervention, whether it be verbal or pharmacologic, often effectively treats clients carrying very different diagnoses. Simultaneously, treatments are not uniformly successful for all of those sharing a given diagnosis. A diagnostic system organized on the basis of discrete behavioral and/or brain functions might map more systematically onto relevant treatment approaches. Several professionals have been proposing such a revision in diagnostic thinking for some time.

Thomas Szasz (1974) and Jeffrey Masson (1988) regard psychiatric diagnoses as socially constructed categories that derogate behavior or people we don't like. The arbitrariness of these labels is highlighted by occasions when political changes have resulted in dramatic shifts in the taxonomy, such as the American Psychiatric Association vote to exclude homosexuality from the new diagnostic roster in 1973. The same behavior can lead to the label "antisocial personality" if the patient is a male and "histrionic" if the patient is female (Hamilton, Rothbart, & Dawes, 1986).

The development of new, functional diagnostic categories would be one way to reduce the problem of within-group variability on dimensions that relate directly to the influence of particular therapeutic interventions. Our current classification system is partially an artifact of history and political compromise. In recent years, many have voiced concerns that we may soon reach the day when it will have outlived its usefulness and require drastic revision.

Diagnosis Is Not Always Relevant or Helpful

Most people seeking outpatient psychotherapy don't have actual, diagnosed "clinical" problems. An estimated 60% of those coming to the healthcare setting have no formal psychiatric disorder or at most a mild disorder (Quirk et al., 1995). Because the stringently diagnosable are relatively few in number, many clinicians have stretched diagnostic criteria to accommodate cases the categories were not originally intended to include (Novack et al.,1989; Scholl et al., 1996). There has been confusion about when psychotherapy is medically necessary and when it is more of a life-enhancing luxury. Attempts to justify reimbursement for all psychotherapy, independent of its necessity, is partially responsible for the growing behavioral healthcare costs that compelled payors to explore managed care in the first place.

We need to develop more carefully considered criteria for distinguishing between those patients whose care should be covered by insurance and those whose care shouldn't. Ultimately we might wish to argue that even the cases of "luxury" therapy should be covered, because it is cost-effective to help clients improve their management of stress because doing so is linked with improved immunological competence and consequently saves healthcare dollars down the line. However, in drawing the distinction at this point in time, our focus should probably be more on the issue of immediate necessity.

Managed care companies often define needed care in terms of their bottom line. If a given treatment can prevent the need for more exorbitantly expensive treatments (especially hospitalization), it is a sound investment. Treatment authorization is based more and more on such criteria and less and less on diagnostic ones (probably in part because of the limited predictive utility of the diagnostic system).

Confusing the Pathological and Nonpathological

Most people seeking therapy want help with practical, everyday problems in living (Magakis & Chambliss, 1997a). Those meeting the criteria for Axis I (*DSM-IV*) diagnoses are fairly rare, yet in the past, therapy and reimbursement systems often blurred the distinction between readily diagnosable clientele and their more modal brethren. This has contributed to confusion about how to define necessary treatment and what constitutes reasonably reimbursable care. It has also fostered some inappropriate clinical generalizing from the truly psychopathological population to the less dysfunctional group.

Clarifying these distinctions can assist us in determining when psychotherapy should be subsidized through increasingly scarce insurance resources. It can also prevent the overpathologizing of relatively "normal" individuals, which can result from failure to recognize the fact that many people without measurable disorders find outpatient psychotherapy very valuable. In drawing this distinction between "medicalized psychotherapy of patients" and "growth-oriented counseling of clients," managed care offers reimbursement to fewer of our traditional private practice clients. These "self-pay" clients now need to be convinced that the services clinicians are offering them justify the associated sacrifices. Freud would be happy; these people should be that much more motivated to take the work of therapy seriously! In the long run the stigma associated with seeking this type of counseling may be reduced, leaving more people comfortable seeking out psychological services.

Many of today's mental health policymakers draw a distinction between the consumers they describe as severely mentally ill (the "SMI") and the "worried well." The majority of those seeking private practice outpatient therapy fall into the latter category, yet our treatment and labeling practices do not always communicate this. There are often incentives for pathologizing many of these cases, which can counterproductively distort our responses to clients. We need to consider these risks carefully if we are to improve the quality of our work.

Matching Treatment to Specific Needs

The crucial distinction that needs to be drawn here is the one between those patients who can learn to operate successfully within their current defenses and those who must engage in the lengthy, terrifying battle of modifying their long-standing defensive strategies. Relatively easy experimenting with new behaviors and cognitions may be all that is necessary to improve the lives of those within the former group, whereas painful, doubt-engendering, pride-endangering work may be necessary for those in the latter group.

"Psychoeducation" may be a better term than "psychotherapy" for what therapists are doing with clients in the former group (Magakis & Chambliss, 1997a). The term "therapy" implies the existence of a pathological process and a need for healing, and arguably neither exists for many outpatients seeking the help of therapists. On the other hand, these clients do want to make changes, and they want to learn; education describes the process better than therapy, which conveys a more negative judgment about the person's current state/manner of being/behavior. (It is far less stigmatizing to be an inexperienced or yet-to-be-enlightened student than to be a pathologically aberrant and deviant patient.)

The Exclusion of the Worried Well from the *DSM*

Most of the "worried well" have more trouble with common practical matters than they do with true mental illness. They are usually hoping to make rather modest behavioral changes, to find more rewarding ways of sustaining relationships, to develop better ways of handling stress, and so on. However, our diagnostic nomenclature often fails to reflect this reality and in fact sometimes suggests otherwise.

The aim of the successive revisions of the *DSM* was to reduce the embarrassingly low reliability and validity of the previous diagnostic system used by psychiatrists, psychologists, and social workers. A major change involved the elimination of the pejorative term "neurosis," which was viewed as being too vague, theoretically contaminated, and overly inclusive. No completely comparable category was created to describe many of those formerly seen as neurotic. The problem became where to put these "garden variety," mildly overanxious, mildly depressed, and mildly overwhelmed individuals (the worried well) who then, as now, made up the majority of outpatient case loads. Many of the traditional models of psychotherapy (including the psychoanalytic, client-centered, gestalt, and rational-emotive) were originally developed to help such people and generally work best when used with these subclinical cases.

Ironically, making the diagnostic categories more precise and empirical excluded a large number of the individuals our psychological treatment methods were primarily designed to help. Many clients who formerly would have fit into the neurotic subcategories and been considered mildly psychopathological were now either left out or located on the V-code fringes of the revised labeling system (Magakis & Chambliss, 1997b). While this was advantageous in that it originally restricted the use of stigmatizing diagnostic nomenclature to the small minority of cases in which it was more justifiable, it created an awkward situation for many clinicians.

The Private Practice Paradox

In many respects the patients our methods most help are technically not really patients. The new, cleaner, clearer, tighter diagnostic categories exclude the majority of outpatients most likely to benefit from conventional outpatient psychotherapy. With the exception of the V-code categories, most private practice outpatient clinicians rarely encounter cases that strictly conform to the current diagnostic criteria. Here's the resulting predicament: As helping professionals we are forced to twist our work to accommodate a system it doesn't really fit. The current diagnostic system often fails to embrace the majority of clients we as clinicians seek to treat; our clients don't really belong in any of the delimited, clinical categories. However, pressure from third-party payees to cast clients' problems in pathological terms (in order to justify insurance reimbursement) demands application of diagnoses. The result: rampant diagnostic inflation.

Insurance Fraud and Deception.   Research has shown that some clients learn how insurance decisions are made and then "game the system" to obtain the desired benefits (Morreim, 1991). Likewise, in a survey by Novack et al.(1989), 68% of (responding) physicians were willing to deceive third-party payors if they believed coverage criteria were unfair.

With the spread of managed care and increasingly stringent UR criteria there have been increasing practitioner reports of suicide potential, imminent hospitalization, dangerousness to others, and similar extremes (Anonymous, 1995). Why are there more reports of such extremes than we have ever seen before? Some question whether these are bona fide evaluations of risk or exaggerations designed to extend treatment time, sometimes referred to as "up-coding."

The Problem of Diagnostic Inflation.   The problems associated with diagnostic inflation are twofold. First, exaggerated labeling of clients with only mild difficulties distorts the meaning of the clinical categories and reduces the amount of useful information conveyed by diagnostic labels when they are used appropriately (for the small number of clients who actually exhibit severe, debilitating symptoms that warrant clinical diagnoses). Second, and in some ways more seriously, erroneous diagnosing reifies abnormality. A diagnosis tells clients that they are no longer normal. Being diagnosed thereby transforms their experience, by framing it as exceptional, deviant, and "sick." We should not overlook the long-documented costs of unnecessary diagnostic labeling. Extensive research has demonstrated how psychiatric labels often serve as self-fulfilling prophecies, inadvertently promoting the very symptomatic behaviors they are intended to describe. We know that diagnoses can be psychologically and socially harmful. Yet they are often overused because the system makes it expedient to do so.

Today's Uneasy Compromise

For over 30 years, mental health professionals have been awkwardly straddling a divide. On the one hand, in recent decades, therapists have made increasing use of the psychiatric diagnoses, which are based largely on a medical model that assumes that patients can be grouped meaningfully on the basis of their pathology. On the other hand, during this same period, many therapists have actively sought to relabel "patients" as "clients," in order to avoid the stigmatizing effects of negative labels and to communicate an emphasis on strengths rather than on symptoms. Use of V codes and mild Axis I diagnoses (especially adjustment disorder) seemed to offer a workable compromise for many clinicians in this latter group, who were uncomfortable with the disadvantages associated with use of the medical model, but who simultaneously desired to have their work paid for through insurance.

Managed care seeks to restrict covered services to those that are medically necessary. Many policies only cover treatment for Axis I diagnoses, and use of the adjustment disorder category (which by definition includes cases expected to spontaneously remit, given adequate passage of time) is viewed with increasing suspicion. As a result, many managed care providers are now making more liberal use of the "anxiety disorder, not otherwise specified" and depression diagnoses to justify their services. Patients are not always fully informed about the risks of this, including how this might later compromise their eligibility for disability insurance.

Until the diagnostic system is improved, some clinicians will feel forced to be expedient. In order to make clients eligible for care their insurance will cover, these clinicians use diagnostic labels very inclusively. In doing so, they should recognize the dangers of diagnostic inflation and remember how inadequately the current diagnostic framework describes the majority of their private outpatients. While it may be necessary to accommodate to diagnostic requirements and find a label that at least partially captures the client's circumstance, it is important to keep the labels from misleading your clinical work. The factors emphasized within the diagnostic categories are not necessarily those most germane to a person's functioning. The diagnosis will often fail to direct you to the most salient features in need of change in the client's life. Goal setting should be more client-driven than diagnosis-based. Furthermore, clinical categories can narrow your vision and foster a tendency to stereotype. Don't miss the client for the label, nor allow the label to occlude your view of the whole, individual person.

A Solution: Behavior Over Diagnosis

One way of resolving these diagnostic problems is to use behavioral rather than diagnostic criteria in determining coverage. Increasingly this is what is happening in behavioral healthcare. Managed care is interested in having therapy address the behavioral needs of patients, rather than the diagnosis the patient carries. Diagnosis is an abstraction that may correlate with the treatment needs of an individual patient, but the diagnosis alone does not define the need for treatment, nor does it in isolation justify a particular level of care or intervention strategy. This is of particular concern in cases of SMI patients, whose therapists were formerly granted carte blanche. Carrying a serious diagnosis in and of itself now means little. The current level of behavioral impairment and symptom severity are emphasized in making decisions about appropriate care.

For the worried well, framing treatment as a brief response to a temporary crisis provides a way of providing prompt, timely service without having to burden the individual with a negative, critical diagnosis that implies a serious, stable defect. Acute care often helps with minimal risk of harm.

Impairment Ratings and Severity Ratings

The American Psychiatric Association advocates the use of the term "impairments" to provide a clear way of thinking about the features of patients that provide justification for service delivery. The APA offers a behavior-based treatment terminology, not intended to compete with *DSM-IV* nomenclature (APA, 1994).

Conversations with quality management consultants, third-party payors, and MCOs confirm the need for clear, objective, behavioral descriptions of psychiatric patients and the care they receive. The posture of the payors appears to be this: If the clinical necessity and outcomes of mental healthcare services are too elusive to measure, then they may well be too elusive to pay for (J. Brown, 1995).

The following guidelines were offered by the APA (1994):

Impairment Severity Ratings
Severity 4:   Imminently Dangerous
Severity 3:   Severely Incapacitating
Severity 2:   Destabilizing
Severity 1:   Distressing
Severity 0:   Absent or Nonpathological

A severity 4 describes an impairment that is *imminently dangerous* because either it is predictably destructive to oneself or others or totally interferes with the ability to care for oneself in any way. Behavioral examples include

- Active suicide threats or behavior
- Active violent or destructive behavior
- Active life-endangering runaway behavior or risk
- Total inability (> 90%) to perform self-care skills

A severity 3 defines an impairment that is *severely incapacitating* either because it is a potential and likely danger to oneself or others or because it severely compromises the ability to care for oneself. Behavioral examples include

- Recent suicide behavior, threat, or current active ideation with a plan
- Recent violent or destructive behavior or current active ideation with a plan
- Recent endangering runaway behavior or current active ideation with a plan
- Severely compromised (61%–90%) ability to care for daily personal, family, financial, or employment-/school-related matters.

A severity 2 defines an impairment that is *destabilizing* and, as a result, either markedly compromises (30%–60%) independent, vocational, or community functioning or inhibits the effectiveness of the treatment or the family-social support systems for "repairing" the patient's impairment.

A severity 1 defines an impairment that is *distressing* and, as a result, either compromises (< 30%) independent, vocational, community, or school- or work-related functioning or, although absent at the present time, has a predictable likelihood of occurrence or recurrence without treatment.

A severity 0 defines an impairment that is either *absent* (the impairment that has been completely "repaired") or, if present, is *nonpathological*. The 0 rating is actually an important marker for tracking the patient's progress in treatment.

The Problems of Jargon and Paperwork

One major problem of dealing with utilization reviewers is that review criteria are still idiosyncratic and considered proprietary by the MCO. Criteria tend to be written by administrators who are not involved in providing direct patient care; some of their measures of quality may not be meaningful in actual practice. Reviewers tend to focus on features of care that are most easily measured, regardless of whether they matter most to clinical outcome.

Goodman, Brown, and Deitz (1996) discuss their frustration in trying to fashion a systematic response to managed care reviewers:

Based on extended discussion with the largest nationally based managed care corporations (and other insurers) it is clear that while companies have virtually the same treatment plan information requirements, in the absence of national managed care review standards for systematically obtaining and assessing this information, and without a standardized language (or terminology) and format of recording mental health treatment (from which the necessary data could possibly be retrieved), this information is requested in as many different ways as there are reviewers and review organizations. (p. 115)

"What is your treatment plan?"

"What is the patient's treatment plan?"

"What are the patient's goals and objectives?"

"What are your goals?"

While providing consultation to a number of providers who were appealing reimbursement denial decisions from several different managed care entities, we uncovered an astonishing fact about these commonplace terms; consensus about the definition and intended use of these treatment catchwords is conspicuously absent. When we tried to obtain some clarification by asking for definitions of these terms, none of the practitioners or any of the managed care reviewers gave the same answers. Even different reviewers within one MCO had different conceptions about these terms. . . . The more practitioners and managed care reviewers we asked about these stock phrases, the more numerous and varied were the answers. Yet, access to treatment for the patients hinged on the practitioners' response to questions using this very vocabulary. A survey of 156 licensed clinical mental health professionals and managed care reviewers found less than 70% consensus on statements which could be classified as treatment goals, patient objectives, or interventions. Their practitioner and reviewer groups had comparable difficulty in correctly classifying these statements. (pp. 111–112)

As a result, practitioners often find managed care reviews quite perplexing and irritating. Presenting arguments for the clinical necessity of a patient's treatment is complicated by the ambiguity in the terminology.

Making matters worse, companies organize their documentation differently. The lack of consensus in how treatment plans are formatted creates a confusing paperwork labyrinth. Although federal guidelines exist, they change regularly, further contributing to the confusion. The latest mental health manual issued by the Joint Commission on Accreditation of Healthcare Organizations (1994/1995) refers to an "individualized" treatment plan, rather than the former "multidisciplinary treatment plan." Federal guidelines describe the plan as "the prescribed treatment, treatment given, and long- and short-term goals" ("Medicare Program," 1984, pp. 315–316); Standard TX 1.8 requires the plan to state "specific goals" and "specific objectives" and specify "settings, services, or programs necessary to meet the individual's needs and goals." Changing accreditation standards continue to force revisions of treatment plan documents. The current focus is more on the patient; instead of asking practitioners, "How are you managing the patient?" the question is now, "How is the patient managing?"

Psychiatric patient problems are often described in terms of problem lists: attention-seeking behavior, sexual abuse issues, resistance to treatment, poor ego boundaries, poor peer choices, overly demanding and dependent behavior, and poor impulse control. These types of terms fail to document why the patient needed treatment, why the various treatment services prescribed were necessary, and why a particular treatment setting was required to implement them.

Reviewers want to know how treatment decisions are made and what the clinical rationale is for each of them. Reviewers want to know why that treatment is necessary, why a particular treatment setting or frequency of service is required, and why alternative treatments are not considered appropriate. Lengthy problem lists and a multiplicity of treatment interventions do not adequately convey this information. (Goodman, Brown, & Deitz, 1996, p. 21)

Research on the Cost-Effectiveness of Psychotherapy

Both medical cost offset research and workplace productivity research provide a basis for arguing that timely provision of psychotherapy is cost-effective for insurers. Familiarity with this research can facilitate your advocacy for quality psychological care.

Medical Cost Offset Research

In justifying additional treatment sessions to managed care reviewers, it can be useful to help them understand the medical cost offset associated with psychotherapy. Money spent on psychotherapy often results in net savings in healthcare spending. Research has shown that for every dollar spent on psychotherapy, overall healthcare costs are reduced by between $4 and $5. Virtually every study done shows the same outcome: *Psychotherapy lowers healthcare costs* (Groth-Marnat & Edkins, 1996).

The American Psychological Association and Blue Cross/Blue Shield of Massachusetts began collaborating in 1996 on a landmark study to assess the benefits of integrating psychological services into medical treatment plans for women diagnosed with breast cancer (Sleek, 1995). In addition to documenting improved psychological well-being, the study is expected to quantify the association between psychological treatment and improved physical health outcomes. Russell Newman argues that "by incorporating psychological services into the plan, we can expect to see healthier behaviors, improved health outcomes and a reduction in overall health costs" (p. 2). Newman cites actuarial data showing a $5 savings in healthcare costs for every dollar spent on psychological services.

This type of investigation is based on the notion that nonspecific behavioral therapies may improve immunological functioning and thereby reduce the risk, morbidity, and mortality of infection, heart attacks, autoimmune disorders, and cancer (Temoshok et al., 1985; Eli et al., 1992; Lee et al., 1992; Waxler-Morrison, Hislop, & Mears, 1992; Fawzy et al., 1993; Gellert, Maxwell, & Siegel, 1993; Spiegel, 1993; Stein et al., 1993). Research has demonstrated that nonspecific psychological interventions improve mood, coping, and other psychosocial factors, as well as compliance with medical management. In some studies these factors are reported to prolong survival in cancer patients. Psychological treatments may reduce the reaction to distress and decrease depression, combat demoralization and hopelessness, and promote health-enhancing behavior. These changes may have a favorable effect on illness (Beecher, 1959a; 1959b; A. Shapiro & Shapiro, 1984b; Frank & Frank, 1991). Increase in survival rates, therefore, may be related primarily to psychosocial intervening variables such as compliance with medical management, improved diet, increased exercise and sleep, reduced substance abuse, increased assertiveness with physicians about treatment, and enhanced ability to cope with illness (House, Landis, & Umberson, 1988; Cohen, Tyrrell, & Smith, 1991; Williams et al., 1991; Perry et al., 1992; Frasure-Smith et al., 1993; Horwitz & Horwitz, 1993; Perry & Fishman, 1993; Spiegel, 1993; Stein et al., 1993).

The mechanism by which psychological factors and psychological therapies may affect physical illness and disease remains elusive. It has been proposed that psychological factors such as depression or stress can impair immune function, cause or cure illness, and delay or hasten death. For example, those suffering from depression-related insomnia have been found to have lower than normal levels of natural killer cells, immune system cells that fight tumor and virally infected cells. These interrelationships fall within the province of psychoimmunology, the discipline that explores the interaction of psychological, immunological, and brain relationships. Although critics question whether changes in immune parameters have any clinical use or relevance (Evans et al., 1989; Darko et al., 1991; Stein et al., 1991; Perry et al., 1992; Stein, 1992; Perry, 1994), others believe that appropriate application of these findings can produce beneficial health effects (Pennebaker, Kiecolt-Glaser, & Glaser, 1988; Rodin & Langer, 1976).

Workplace Productivity Research

The "cost" of illness goes far beyond the compensation of therapists. Untreated psychological problems are extremely costly from a social and personal point of view. Unresolved conflicts, interpersonal deficits, and maladaptive thinking compromise workers' ability to collaborate effectively. These "neurotic" issues are not only found among the "worried well"; they also affect many people with severe mental illnesses, such as schizophrenia and bipolar disorder. When used in isolation, medication rarely resolves these comorbid problems, so they continue to interfere with workplace performance.

Psychotherapy can eliminate wasteful obstacles to productivity and thereby yield indirect social and economic benefits for patients. When is treatment cost-effective from the patient's point of view? Treatment may allow patients to complete their education rather than flunk out; or avoid expensive divorce for neurotic reasons; or be more efficient in their work due to less conflict, avoidance, or denial; or to resolve conflicts that have prevented moving up in their profession; or to finally find a loving and gratifying relationship with another human.

A growing body of research shows that emotional chaos often puts a severe strain on organizations. Many organizations operate with a constant level of distortion, but because it has become familiar, its insidious effects are often difficult to notice. Accumulation of stress can compromise workers' ability to perform at high levels.

A 1998 report in the *Medical Tribune of the Internist and Cardiologist* estimates that sleeplessness accounts for between $92.5 billion and $107.6 billion in medical and decreased productivity costs annually in the United States. According to a national survey conducted by the Employee Assistance Professional Association (EAPA), 71% of employee assistance professionals rank clinical depression as the top problem in the workplace, and nearly all (97%) agree that it causes a reduction in workplace productivity. In the United States, on average, one million employees per day are absent from work due to stress.

Case studies have shown that workers who learned and practiced techniques for reducing mental and emotional stress experienced more physical energy and mental clarity and felt happier and more peaceful. They also experienced less depression, anxiety, and anger, as well as less fatigue, sleeplessness, tension, body aches, and indigestion (Cryer, 1998).

There is a need to evaluate more thoroughly the impact of psychotherapy on work productivity, care for family, marital satisfaction, and school performance (Krupnick & Pincus, 1992). To facilitate this, Frisch and his colleagues (1992) have validated a Quality of Life Inventory to assess the impact of psychotherapy on an individual's overall life satisfaction.

Work is at the very core of contemporary life for most people, providing financial security, personal identity, and an opportunity to make a meaningful contribution to community life. For individuals with severe mental illness, however, work has been a difficult and often unattainable goal (NAMI Advocate, 1998).

According to the National Alliance for the Mentally Ill, there are three million working-age adults with severe mental illness, of whom 70% to 90% are unemployed. The great majority of people with a serious mental illness want to work. Recent surveys report that approximately 70% of those with significant psychiatric problems rank work as an important goal for themselves. Innovative rehabilitation programs, which help people with the most serious mental illnesses, are placing more than 50% of their clients into paid employment. A number of innovative programs that move clients into "real jobs for real pay" as quickly as possible and then provide extensive supports for them either on the job or off the job, are reporting considerable success. An in-depth analysis of supported employment outcomes, for instance, found 52% of people still working after a year. Intensive case management, individual placement, and support produce significant increases in wages, hours worked, work tenure, and career advancement.

Although job loss continues to be a problem, those individuals with severe mental illness who are working can be helped to stay on the job if they receive the additional psychological supports they need. The reasons for job loss vary widely. In one study, only 12% of people who left their jobs said they resigned because they didn't want to work, and only 15% had to leave for medical reasons unrelated to their mental health. The others who became unemployed faced a variety of problems (e.g., layoffs, problems with co-workers or supervisors, and mental health symptoms) that led to diminished work capacities. Many of these problems might have been resolved without job loss if more effective ongoing support had been available.

9 Individualizing Treatment

Applying Knowledge about Specific Groups of Consumers

Managed care is developing more effective ways of addressing the needs of special populations. With managed care's insistence on brief treatment, those with characterological problems and substance abuse problems are often more challenging to help.

Personality Disorders

Patients with personality disorders are capable of creating havoc in managed care settings, much as they can and do in all other settings (Schreter, 1997). Their clinical needs are often the most difficult to address with the short-term interventions favored by managed care.

Clinicians and patients often argue that what is needed in the treatment of these patients is more extensive and intensive service delivery, including more frequent outpatient visits, more inpatient days, and a wider range of services over a longer period of time. On the other hand, care managers often react to these patients as if their crises and pathology are intentional, manipulative efforts at taxing the system and its resources. No evidence offers clear support for either one of these perspectives (Schreter, 1997).

To deal effectively with patients who have personality disorders, clinicians and managers must improve their ability to identify these difficult patients and develop consistent treatment approaches, including continuous treatments that sufficiently address their needs. The delivery system must provide for easy entry and reentry to prevent brief crises from escalating or resulting in unnecessary long-term hospital stays.

In these cases it is especially important for treatment plans to be reviewed on a case-by-case and episode-by-episode basis. These plans should include less traditional interventions when appropriate. For example, the clinician should consider group instead of individual treatments, community-based and self-help programs in place of mental health services, and cognitive-behavioral interventions rather than treatments based on ego psychology or object relations (Schreter, 1997).

Substance Abuse

It is important to differentiate substance abuse from mental health problems before beginning treatment. All initial evaluations should include a history of alcohol and drug abuse that is extensive enough to rule it out as a problem requiring treatment. Brief episodic treatments carry the increased risk that substance use disorders will go undetected and untreated, unless clinicians intentionally address these problems. Diagnosis of a substance use disorder should be an automatic indicator for referral for treatment for that disorder alone or as part of an integrated treatment to address concurrent psychiatric and substance abuse problems.

Sleep Disturbances

Sleep disturbances can profoundly affect functioning and response to treatment and are likely to play a major role in depression and disorders associated with decreased emotional control. Sleep research has shown four stages of sleep, ranging from light sleep to deep sleep. There are two principal types of sleep: (1) REM (rapid eye movement) sleep and (2) non-REM sleep. During REM periods the brain is highly active; this is the time when most dreaming occurs. REM periods become longer as the night progresses. Non-REM sleep includes four stages; stages 3 and 4 involve a particular type of brain wave activity referred to as delta sleep (or deep sleep). Most stage 3 and 4 sleep occurs during the first half of the night.

Preston (1997) points out that

> . . . experimental studies have shown dramatically that reducing the amount of deep sleep has significant consequences. After only two nights of sleep deprivation (participants were selectively deprived of stages 3 and 4) volunteer subjects experience the following:
>
> A. Significant daytime fatigue
> B. Difficulties with thinking (e.g., poor concentration, impaired memory, etc.)
> C. Decreased emotional controls
>   Changes in emotional functioning include the following:
> D. Irritability
> E. Lowered frustration tolerance, and
> F. Decreased ability to control or inhibit the expression of emotions in general.
>   (p. 95)

These characteristics closely resemble the symptoms we find in many patients. Helping them learn how to obtain more effective sleep can make a big difference in how they feel and function. Stabilizing the circadian (24-hour cycle) rhythm also fosters more productive sleep. Preston describes three activities that have been shown to be helpful in bringing this about:

> A. Establish regular bedtimes and times for awakening. The circadian rhythm organizes itself around highly regular patterns of exposure to light and dark, and this is best achieved by maintaining a regular sleep schedule.

B. Regular exposure to early morning bright light can also stabilize the circadian rhythm. This is best done for at least one hour upon awakening and with exposure to very bright light (2500 lux or above); this can be accomplished by exposure to outside light or the use of a commercially available light box.

C. A program of regular, aerobic exercise has many benefits (e.g., improved physical health, increases in serotonin, enhanced physical pain tolerance, etc.). Exercise has also been shown to increase the amount of time spent in deep sleep. (Preston, 1997, p. 98)

A number of substances can interfere with sleep; the most common are alcohol and caffeine. Helping patients appreciate the impact of these substances on the brain frequently expedites their progress. Alcohol, in moderate to heavy amounts, causes sedation and may help people to fall asleep. When stressed, many people turn to alcohol to numb emotional pain and to help them fall asleep. Unfortunately this solution usually backfires. A few hours after alcohol is ingested, some of the metabolic by-products of alcohol begin to affect the brain, actually causing arousal. As a result, many people who abuse alcohol report middle-of-the-night awakenings. The ensuing disrupted sleep often exacerbates the difficulties that prompted the use of alcohol to fall asleep in the first place (depression or stress). Therefore, it is wise to insist that all alcohol-abusing patients get treatment for substance abuse.

It is also widely known that caffeine can interfere with sleep and produce emotional dyscontrol; it is especially associated with insomnia. Although many people avoid the use of caffeine late in the day when bothered by insomnia, many patients do not know that caffeine can also cause an increase in middle-of-the-night awakenings and a decrease in the total amount of deep sleep (APA, 1994). This can occur even in the absence of initial insomnia, so many patients who consume a lot of caffeine may be compromising the quality of their sleep without even realizing it.

It is therefore important to take a caffeine history on all patients. Generally for patients ingesting over 250 mg of caffeine per day (regardless of the time of day ingested) there is some likelihood of its affecting sleep (Preston, 1997). In those taking 500 mg or more per day, caffeine is highly likely to cause a sleep disturbance. Many patients get into the habit of drinking large amounts of caffeine, especially when they are under stress. Caffeine reduces fatigue and provides some transient mood elevation. However, in the long run, it further compromises the person's ability to maintain emotional stability. Encouraging clients to eliminate caffeine often makes a big difference. The key to reducing caffeine use is to have the client cut back gradually, over a period of 3 to 4 weeks (Preston, 1997). Abrupt discontinuation often results in withdrawal symptoms (headache, jitteriness, anxiety, and insomnia).

Caring for Traditionally Underserved Groups

As managed care extends into the public sector and Medicare, it is becoming more important to develop programs for treating patients from traditionally underserved groups, including children and adolescents, elderly persons, and the disabled population. When assuming responsibility for populations of patients, providers must be able to address the needs of all patients, including all age groups and diagnoses. Failure to address these needs adequately results in unnecessary suffering and eventual increased societal costs.

"A positive consequence of the management of mental health services has been the emergence of clinical innovation, especially for special populations and patients with special needs. Innovative programs such as home care, hospital diversion services, community-based nonhospital respite facilities, and creative outpatient approaches are increasingly valued because they are efficient" (Schreter, 1997, p. 655). Clinical programs should be designed to accommodate the needs of the particular target population. For example, groups with a high incidence of AIDS or severe and persistent illness require different clinical programs than do populations with high levels of physical abuse or substance abuse.

Tailoring Treatment

"Tailoring" refers to specific ways of customizing treatment approaches to "fit" the unique needs, cognitive and emotional styles, and treatment expectations of the patient. An important literature on how different treatments interact with aptitude differences among patients is beginning to emerge (Beutler et al., 1991). From the clinician's point of view, it is useful to go beyond diagnosis to additional patient characteristics that indicate whether a given treatment is likely to be helpful. Unfortunately, robust patient-treatment matching findings have yet to be definitively specified.

> People being treated need individualized therapies. If we are saying that everyone responds to stress differently because of past experiences, then as therapists we need to be flexible and allow each person to focus on the part of therapy that works best for them. There is no one-size-fits-all . . . study upon study has shown that simple relaxation does not work in many people. (Carpi, 1996, p. 35)

Treatments delivered in combination can have an additive, and sometimes synergistic, effect. For example, in major depression, medication is more effective in remitting vegetative symptoms, while psychotherapy is better at improving interpersonal relations and cognitive symptoms (Frances, Clarkin, & Perry, 1984). Furthermore, the additive effect of medication and psychotherapy has been established for both major depression (Rush & Hollon, 1991) and agoraphobia (Greist & Jefferson, 1992).

While "combined treatment" refers to combining different modalities of treatment (e.g., individual and group, marital and family therapy, day treatment and inpatient), either concurrently or sequentially, integrative or tailoring treatment is different (Sperry et al., 1996). Integrative treatment is the blending of various treatment approaches (e.g., psychodynamic, cognitive, behavioral, interpersonal, and medication). For example, clinical investigators have recently advocated integrative treatment for borderline personality disorder (Linehan et al., 1993). The specific type of cognitive-behavior therapy developed by Linehan, dialectical behavior therapy, is an integration of various cognitive-behavioral intervention strategies and Zen practice (Heard & Linehan, 1994). Stone (1993) prescribes blending psychoanalytic, behavioral, cognitive, and medication interventions in the treatment of the borderline patient.

Tailoring to the Diagnosis

In quickly acquainting ourselves with new patients, diagnoses can help us think efficiently about the obstacles they are facing. For example, schizophrenia is a handicap that produces predictable challenges; we can expect people carrying this diagnosis to be up against certain modal obstacles in their attempts to live a satisfying, independent life. Obsessive-compulsive disorder can also be viewed as a handicap that challenges patients in predictable ways. Diagnoses can help us understand the patient much more quickly than we might otherwise. However, as there is so much heterogeneity within a given diagnostic group, it is imperative that we check the accuracy of our assumptions. The particular patient we are meeting may not conform to the stereotype. Although the problems presented may be congruent with the diagnostic criteria, he or she may be experiencing their disorder unconventionally and may not be bothered by the challenges most people so diagnosed find troublesome. If our mistaken assumptions are not corrected, they are likely to prevent effective treatment and may aggravate the patient's demoralization and sense of alienation.

Individualizing Treatment Plan Thinking

A foreign-born psychiatric resident made a treatment team erupt in laughter one morning by trying to ascertain what had precipitated the client's presentation. In faltering English he inquired, "How brought you to this hospital?" and the patient responded, "I came by car." During the conference that followed the physician was quick to attribute the patient's answer to the concrete thinking that is characteristic of schizophrenia; the rest of us in the room blamed the poorly worded question.

But he was right about trying to learn about the client's understanding of the situation and the client's expectations of treatment. What brings the client to treatment? Independent of their diagnoses, clients come to treatment wanting various things, and, complicating things further, their objectives may shift over time. In conjunction with using treatment guidelines, assessing the clients intentions can help us make more appropriate choices about which interventions to offer, because the clients' readiness to use a particular treatment strategy depends heavily upon whether or not it is congruent with their expectations of treatment (Chambliss & Murray, 1979b).

As mentioned earlier, it can be useful to conceive of therapy as addressing a combination of five principal client needs. The first involves helping the client to discern if a serious problem really exists and whether its magnitude is sufficient to warrant therapeutic attention. Psychotherapy can also be used as a means for developing an intellectually satisfying, cogent explanation for the circumstances of one's life. Clients may use therapy to make sense of themselves and their relationships in the context of their personal history. The third need that clients frequently present to outpatient therapists involves deciding upon changes they wish to make. Change is intimidating, and clients often need help in committing to it. The fourth need is for assistance in managing feelings more effectively. Others are most interested in getting specific suggestions about how to build behavioral skills. They may wish to overcome debilitating speaking anxiety, learn how to reduce premature ejaculation, be comfortable driving again after a panic episode in a car, inform their children about a decision to divorce, reduce self-defeating procrastination at work, cope with chronic pain, reduce their performance of compulsive rituals, etcetera.

Clients approach the professional therapist as an expert in living and assume their therapist has mastered some strategies that will make changing more efficient and pleasant. While diagnosis is important in organizing our thinking about how to proceed with therapy, staying attuned to the client's personal agenda is often even more important.

Facilitating Learning about Life

Why do clients need our help in learning coping skills? Clients often reach for our help when they are encountering an array of novel demands. They may have recently been abandoned by a spouse, diagnosed with a serious illness, laid off at work, or disturbed by their child's arrest. They are prompted to seek our help with a new situation about which they have limited information. Their inexperience leaves them receptive to any wisdom about similar circumstances we might have to offer. A broad array of life experiences, extensive reading, and a highly developed capacity for empathy equip therapists to respond to these situations. More systematic organization of available information about important life transitions can assist therapists in helping in cases where their own direct experience and knowledge is limited. Use of the Internet can facilitate therapists' ability to draw upon state-of-the-art information about rarely encountered predicaments. When the client's needs outstrip the therapist's capacity to provide answers, making referrals to other providers with greater experience with a particular type of personal problem can also often be appropriate.

Detecting Obstacles to Learning

As therapists we seek to educate clients about how to make more successful and satisfying use of their talents. While their problems and symptoms alert us to their need for help, and diagnosis can help us conceptualize how they may tend to function maladaptively, the crux of therapy lies in moving beyond their failures and focusing more on their potential to succeed. They've been learning about how to adapt to life's demands every day of their lives. In brief therapy, we have only a short time to contribute to this lifelong process. How can we make a difference in so short a time? Therapists can have a profound impact by discerning the key obstacles to their previous learning and establishing conditions that remove at least some of those obstacles.

For instance, do they typically overexternalize? If so, this can prevent them from benefitting from the educational message offered by life experiences. If they are biased to always blame others or outside forces for unpleasant outcomes, they will fail to inspect their own behavior for how it contributes to their frustrations. Do they typically overinternalize? This can be equally problematic, because of the debilitating effects of the depression it can foster.

Do they mistrust others and fail to ask for help? Do they withdraw when in pain or ashamed, allowing a downward spiral of uncorrected self-reproach? Do they seek out others' opinions too much, endlessly reaffirming their own lack of confidence? Do they habitually act before they think? Do they dwell to excess, passively retreating from risk? Do they delay gratification endlessly, never making sufficient room in their lives for pleasure and the spontaneous? Do they fail to make appropriate plans and interim sacrifices to build what they truly desire?

Symptomatic extremes can be viewed as hindrances to efficient learning. While it is desirable to reduce all symptoms, those responsible for repetitive maladaptive responding are the most valuable to change.

Finding the right balance between the different poles of these continua is the universal challenge in life. As therapists, we can sometimes help others learn how to expedite this learning process. If nothing else, we can help them find a place to begin.

Another goal of therapy is to help patients develop their own capacity for self-observation. We seek to help them to take appropriate responsibility for the events of their lives. We want to encourage their appropriate use of the support and reassurance others can offer. We want them to develop a more accurate picture of themselves and their behavior, both privately and in relation to others.

Achieving a better balance between the polarities described by Erik Erikson is another way of thinking about the general goals of therapy:

1. Trust versus mistrust
2. Autonomy versus shame and doubt
3. Initiative versus guilt
4. Competence versus inferiority
5. Identity versus role diffusion
6. Intimacy versus isolation
7. Generativity versus stagnation
8. Integrity versus despair

Although brief therapy precludes an exhaustive examination of these tensions, it can challenge extremist thinking. Communicating the value of balance can help to reduce clients' tendencies to think dichotomously. It can also be consistent with the need in brief therapy to leave many issues examined incompletely.

The achievement of balance is a lifelong endeavor; therapy can't be expected to continue until closure is achieved. Instead, therapy can be viewed as starting a process of enhanced reflection and problem solving that will outlast the formal helping relationship for many, many decades.

Customizing by Ego Control

A growing body of work has emerged linking personality attributes to patterns of psychopathology (S. Huey & Weisz, 1997). Researchers conceptualize psychopathology in children and adolescents in terms of two factors, internalizing and externalizing, derived from principal components analyses of the Child Behavior Checklist (Achenbach & Edelbrock, 1991). The internalizing factor includes such problems as anxiety, depression, and social withdrawal. The externalizing factor includes aggression, hyperactivity, and related problems of acting out.

In the personality literature, ego-undercontrolled individuals are described as spontaneous, emotionally expressive, and focused on the immediate gratification of their desires. Ego-overcontrolled individuals are relatively constrained and inhibited and minimally expressive of their emotions and impulses (Block & Kremen, 1996; Block & Block, 1980). Ego-resilient individuals are resourceful in adapting to novel situations, while ego-brittle individuals exhibit little adaptive flexibility in novel or stressful situations (Block & Block, 1980). Ego undercontrol has been found to be important in predicting externalizing problems, while both ego brittleness and ego undercontrol made equal contributions in predicting internalizing problems (S. Huey & Weisz, 1997).

These personality dimensions may influence how effective various interventions are in helping a child work through his or her problems. Several common therapies emphasize teaching strategies of self-control to hyperactive and aggressive children (Karoly, 1981; Kendall & Braswell, 1993; Meichenbaum, 1979), suggesting a recognition of the role of poor impulse control in treating externalizing problems.

Sex and Race Differences

Women are twice as vulnerable as men to disabling depression and anxiety, and men are five times as vulnerable as women to alcoholism and antisocial personality disorder (Robins & Regier, 1991). African Americans report nearly as much happiness as European Americans and are actually slightly less vulnerable to depression (Diener et al., 1993; Robins & Regier, 1991; Stock et al., 1985). While demographic generalizations such as these don't apply in every case, findings about group differences can help guide therapeutic inquiry.

Accommodating Cultural Differences

If we look at the person in whom the "illness" occurs, as Sir William Osler recommended to physicians, we find that, to understand our patients, we need to know of their culture, their childhood, their current community, and their whole life cycle. To make optimal choices, we must ask, "What will happen to this child if we ignore the symptoms now?"

S. Sue (1995) notes that in the past two decades, psychology and the mental health disciplines have engaged in a great deal of self-criticism over the effectiveness of psychotherapeutic services for ethnic minority groups. The criticisms have focused on prejudicial and discriminatory practices affecting ethnic clients and inaccessibility or unavailability of services. These criticisms have prompted studies examining ethnic or racial differences in the utilization of services, premature termination rates, client preferences for therapists, therapist prejudice, diagnosis and assessment, treatment strategies, and the process and outcome of treatment. Sue and other investigators have advocated changes in the way psychotherapy is conducted with different cultural groups, arguing that therapy is often ineffective with ethnic minorities.

One of the most frequent criticisms of psychotherapy with ethnic minority clients is the lack of bilingual and bicultural therapists who can communicate and can understand the values, life-styles, and backgrounds of these clients. Sue et al. (1976) found that Asian Americans were more likely than Whites to believe that mental illness is caused by organic or bodily factors and that mental health is enhanced by will power and the avoidance of morbid thinking. Problems in therapist–client mismatches in culture or language have been investigated for Native Americans (Attneave, 1985; Trimble & La Fromboise, 1985), Asian Americans (Leong, 1986; D. Sue & Sue, 1985), Blacks (Jenkins, 1985; Snowden, 1982), and Hispanics (Acosta, 1984; Casas, 1985; Munoz, 1982). Cultural differences in conceptualizations of mental health have important implications for psychotherapy. Clients may behave in accordance with cultural beliefs and values, but therapists may interpret the behavior in terms of pathology.

Another difficulty is that some therapists may hold stereotypes that may distort their work with ethnic minority clients, and ethnic clients may have similar biases concerning the therapist. These biases generally reflect the changing nature of race or ethnic relations in our society, making them somewhat difficult to specify. The mental health profession has not been immune to the forces of racism in society; racism may be reflected in diagnosis, assessment, and treatment (Clark, 1972). Griffith and Jones (1978) state that findings about the effects of race in psychotherapy "can do no more than capture a particular phase in time; they are by no means immutable and, in fact, are likely to change in important ways with the continued evolvement of the sociocultural context" (p. 228). Many contend that ethnic minority clients have a more difficult time than White clients in achieving good outcomes from treatment because of ethnic mismatches and therapist biases in treatment.

Substantial controversy exists regarding whether or not ethnic individuals are shortchanged by psychotherapy with a racially dissimilar therapist. Despite the strongly held opinions about the problems ethnic clients encounter in receiving effective services, empirical evidence has failed to consistently demonstrate differential outcomes for ethnic and White clients (S. Sue, 1995).

Comparative research has offered only partial support for the value of indigenous therapists, that is, workers similar to clients in background, lifestyle, and general personal and demographic characteristics. The only controlled evidence for the effectiveness of indigenous therapists has involved college students (C. Brown & Myers, 1975; Elliott & Denney, 1975; Fremouw & Harmatz, 1975; Karlsruher, 1976; Lamb & Clack, 1974; Lindstrom, Balch, & Reese, 1976; Murry, 1972; Russell & Wise, 1976; Ryan, Krall, & Hodges, 1976; T. Wolff, 1969; Zultowski & Catron, 1976; Zunker & Brown, 1966).

No one knows how prevalent race effects are in therapy as it is actually practiced. Atkinson (1985) points out that analogue and survey studies attempting to assess counselor prejudice and stereotyping directly have generally failed to establish the existence of these traits. Studies examining counseling process variables have produced an almost even split between those finding and those not finding an effect attributable to race or ethnicity. Archival documentation of differential treatment based on race or ethnicity is strong enough to warrant concern by the profession and continued monitoring by researchers; however, outcome research has failed to demonstrate that clients are better served by same-race or -ethnicity counselor-client pairings. The research in this area is so fraught with design limitations, however, particularly with respect to outcome criteria, that definitive conclusions are impossible (Atkinson, 1985).

The only real consensus among investigators has been on the state of the research. Not enough research has been conducted, and published research suffers from methodological and conceptual limitations (S. Sue, 1995).

Indigenous Therapists

The indigenous therapist (one native to a given minority community) has often been cited as the treatment agent of choice for low-income and minority group clients who have not received a fair distribution of services from professionals in the past. Many believe that indigenous therapists can establish rapport and identification with previously underserved populations, making them more effective than other professionals. S. Sue (1995) argues that "ideally, clients should have freedom of choice in the selection of therapists, and should have access to therapists of their choosing (e.g., feminist therapists, gay therapists, or psychologists rather than psychiatrists). This is particularly true in our society, which is pluralistic and which values freedom and individualism." However, at present there is a serious shortage of ethnic therapists to meet the demands of ethnic populations (Casas, 1985). This shortage is particularly acute for clients who want a bilingual, bicultural therapist.

There are no experimental data to support the superiority of indigenous therapists. In fact, data from two analogue and attitude studies indicate that Mexican American clients perceive White professionals to be as trustworthy, understanding, and helpful as indigenous therapists (Acosta & Sheehan, 1976; Andrade & Burstein, 1973). The comparative effectiveness of indigenous and professional helpers working with noncollege populations awaits further empirical documentation.

In attempting to match therapists and clients optimally, it is important to remember that ethnicity and race are not the only variables that mediate psychotherapy effectiveness. In fact, the inconsistency of research findings suggests that these factors may contribute only weakly to outcome. Matching therapists and clients on ethnicity may be counterproductive if in so doing we "unmatch" them on more important variables. Although ethnic groups exhibit cultural differences, considerable individual differences exist within groups. As S. Sue (1995) has pointed out,

> . . . ethnic matches can result in cultural mismatches if therapists and clients from the same ethnic group show markedly different values (a highly acculturated Chinese American therapist working with a Chinese immigrant holding traditional Chinese values). Conversely, ethnic mismatches do not necessarily imply cultural mismatches, because therapists and clients from different ethnic groups may share similar values, life-styles, and experiences. (p. 306)

Ideally our goal is to enrich convergence (commonalities) and divergence (pluralism) and to reduce conflict. The therapy encounter may serve to accomplish these goals. S. Sue (1995) maintains that

> . . . therapists and clients who match ethnically and culturally may relate well to one another and share experiences and perspectives. However, matches may not be conducive to transcending cultural biases and limitations. In mismatches, the advantage is that clients and therapists can learn about cultural diversity and confront conflicts. Problems can occur when cultural differences cannot be surmounted, and the capacity to communicate is limited. . . . Ethnicity is only one factor, embedded in many others, that shape therapy outcomes. . . . The meanings of ethnicity are more important to study than ethnicity itself, because they are more likely to influence therapy outcomes. (p. 307)

Cross-cultural Perspectives

In discussing the importance of cultural issues, Castillo (1998) maintains that

> Some of the information that has been found to be most important in spurring a move beyond the boundaries of disease-centered psychiatry has come from cross-cultural studies of mental illness. For example, the finding that the duration of schizophrenia is shorter, the course more benign, and the outcome better in non-industrialized societies than in industrialized societies has caused many researchers to reassess their conceptions of schizophrenia. . . . These cross-cultural findings on schizophrenia are contrary to expectations if schizophrenia is conceptualized as a genetically based, incurable brain disease. (p. 1)

The traditional biomedical paradigm in psychiatry is now being extended to include the neurobiology of adaptation and learning. This theoretical expansion emphasizes the effects of neuronal changes in the brain resulting from treatment, as well as the effects of individual and cultural learning on the brain. For example, it has been discovered that individual learning and memory storage change the neuronal structure of the brain (Kandel & Hawkins, 1992). Because culture determines many aspects of learning, cultural learning also has a biological basis in the brain and, therefore, in mental disorders. Thus, it is possible to conceptualize a biological basis for cultural differences in mental disorders.

> Neuroscience research has made it clear that life experiences program and reprogram the highly flexible human brain. The implications of this are that looking for exclusively genetic explanations for normal or abnormal behavior of any given individual is inappropriate. The great adaptability of the human brain in response to its environment makes it far more likely that an individual's behavior will be based on learning and psychosocial adaptation rather than on genetic inheritance. (Castillo, 1998, p. 2).

We are increasingly appreciating that the etiology, symptoms, course, and outcome of mental disorders are far more shaped by cultural context than previously imagined. It is clear that mental disorders need to be defined in a holistic manner that includes the interactions of the patient's sociocultural environment and the effects of diagnosis and treatment on the patient's brain. All of these factors combine and interact to yield the particular experience of illness found in a patient. The likelihood of culture-based differences in brain functioning creates a need for a client-centered, rather than a disease-centered approach. Treatment is increasingly based on a recognition of the effects of neural changes in the brain resulting from psychotropic medications, psychotherapy, internalization of cultural meanings, a person's habitual patterns of thought, and the effects of social stress on the mind-brain.

Fabrega (1998) argues for the integration of a cultural perspective even in our increasingly neurophysiological accounts of abnormal functioning:

> The drift of biomedical psychiatry is toward neurobiological explanations of psychopathology. Thus, the cognitive changes of schizophrenia are attributed to deficits in attention regulation and information processing. These in turn result from impairments of the mesolimbic system. The neurovegetative changes of depression and menopause are attributed to changes in subcortical neuroendocrine systems. Pushed to its extreme, this is the position of biological reductionism. To a relativist, it is also a form of cultural determinism and offers incomplete explanations. One who endorses a contemporary relativistic (not a determinist) perspective will explain part of such "physiological behavior" as a result of alterations in the experience of personhood (or selfhood). In other words, just as one may hold that neurobiological changes are fundamental features of psychopathology and/or psychiatric illness, one can hold that an altered phenomenology of the self in the context of prevailing cultural conventions is also fundamental. For example, schizophrenic "psychopathology" reflects an alteration of the ability of the self to orient symbolically in its culturally created and structured world . . . ; neurovegetative symptoms of depression flow from the altered meanings life now has for the altered "depressed" self . . . ; the "menopause" picture devolves from changes in self-perception of women due to failure to conceive, given the cultural conventions of their society about women and social worth or

Summary of Strategies for Helping Special Populations

Personality Disorders
1. Identify patients with characterological features.
2. Develop consistent, continuous treatment approaches.
3. Allow for easy entry and reentry to avoid escalations.
4. Use individualized, episode-by-episode reviews.
5. Use nontraditional programs (community and self-help).

Substance Abuse
1. Assess problematic sleep patterns and substance use choices.
2. Educate patients about the role of sleep in functioning.
3. Educate about effects of alcohol and caffeine on sleep; use relevant ESTs.
4. Help patients stabilize their circadian rhythm by:
   - Maintaining regular bedtimes and times for awakening
   - Being exposed to early morning bright light
   - Engaging in aerobic exercise

Caring for Traditionally Underserved Groups (Children, Adolescents, the Elderly, and Disabled Persons)
1. Develop special preventive and educational programs.
2. Develop innovative programs:
   - Home care
   - Hospital diversion services
   - Community-based nonhospital respite facilities
   - Specialized outpatient groups

---

purpose. . . . Even basic neuropsychological changes should be construed in bio-cultural terms; that is, as involving brain mechanisms and processes that reflect an enculturation in which native symbolic rules and schemata shape interpretations of reality, including conceptualizations of the self. . . . Suffice it to say that one who endorses a cultural relativistic, in contrast to a rigidly universalistic, position acknowledges the importance of neurobiological phenomena, but sees the basic ground of psychopathology as consisting of both cultural/symbolic and biological/neurological phenomena. Attempts to establish the "essential" basis or "real nature" of a disorder are judged as theoretically flawed. (Fabrega, 1998, p. 15)

SECTION FOUR

Justifying Psychotherapy to Managed Care

Providers must assume primary responsibility for communicating the value of the therapeutic services they have to offer. Therapists are the experts in evaluating the quality of care, and they have an important role in educating both consumers and payors about why psychological services are worth the investment. In providing a rationale for psychotherapy, providers must address the ambitions of both clients and payors. Consumers want to feel and function better as quickly as possible. Employers want to reduce obstacles to productivity, while curbing the cost of medical benefits.

Over the years, researchers have compiled a vast literature on the beneficial impact of psychotherapy. This section is designed to help you to interpret this sometimes ambiguous research. Mastering this information will enhance your ability to persuade others that psychotherapy merits funding, despite the ongoing debates within the field. In fact, a review of the literature may leave you convinced that the reason so much controversy exists among practitioners relates to this field's preoccupation with self-scrutiny, accountability to consumers, and application of high professional standards. If quality were less of an obsession, there probably would be less vehement arguing.

A Review of Relevant Psychotherapy Outcome Research

Arming yourself with relevant psychotherapy outcome research findings can be extremely valuable in working with MCOs. In approving treatment, reviewers want evidence showing that what you propose to do will work. The research literature generally supports the effectiveness of psychotherapy, but there is ongoing controversy about the merits of specific versus nonspecific treatment factors. Managed care will insist on the use of the least expensive procedure unless you can demonstrate the need for something else. Having a good grasp of the research literature, including its limitations, will help you to convince reviewers that you are offering appropriate care. Debates about managed care reimbursement policies will continue to include reference to this literature and its inconsistencies. For that reason, familiarity with the major findings from these studies will be helpful to your work as a practitioner and advocate for optimal behavioral healthcare (Shadish, Navarro, et al., 1997). The following section reviews the general literature examining the effectiveness of psychotherapy.

The History of Outcomes Research

Psychotherapy research has changed considerably since Hans Eysenck's 1952 publication of a paper seriously challenging the efficacy of psychotherapy. His claim that psychotherapy was no more beneficial than waiting for spontaneous remission received wide attention and stimulated the development of more rigorous psychotherapy outcomes research. For some 40 years the major focus of such research was to document unequivocally that psychotherapy works (Sperry et al., 1996). These efforts have been summarized in several statistical reviews (e.g., Lipsey & Wilson, 1993; D. Shapiro & Shapiro, 1982; Smith, Glass, & Miller, 1980) of the hundreds of outcomes studies that have been completed during this period. The verdict: Psychotherapy works. Research shows that psychotherapy is generally helpful to those who seek it.

In a historical analysis of psychotherapy efficacy research covering four decades, Stubbs and Bozarth (1994) describe an evolutionary process in which the utility of psychotherapy itself was first questioned, followed by a period in which core conditions for effective psychotherapy were investigated. This period was concurrent with a trend that studied both positive and negative effects of psychotherapy. In the late 1970s and early 1980s another trend was identified that questioned the sufficiency of core conditions for therapeutic change. The current emphasis is on identifying specific techniques for treating specific disorders; however, as you will see, not everyone endorses this.

Outcomes Studies

There are three main types of psychotherapy outcome studies. The first are effectiveness studies, which use correlational survey methods to assess therapy in vivo. The second are efficacy studies, which use controlled, experimental methods to assess treatment effects, either with individuals suffering from conditions analogous to actual clinical disorders (analogue studies) or with actual patients. The third type of research involves the use of meta-analyses, which summarize the results of multiple individual studies.

Effectiveness Studies: Naturalistic Research

The effectiveness literature provides evidence of the impact of psychotherapy approaches in natural settings. These studies typically involve less rigorous control than do efficacy studies, but they offer some advantages in terms of generalizability, because the clients are not prescreened for comorbid conditions. For this reason, their response to treatment may more closely resemble that of actual clients who seek our services.

One of the best examples of an effectiveness study is the *Consumer Reports* (1995) study, which assessed therapy as it is conducted by practicing psychotherapists. The *Consumer Reports* survey of therapy yielded qualitative conclusions paralleling those from other types of investigations, but did so with a sample of patients that was arguably more clinically representative. This study surveyed 180,000 readers, of whom about 7,000 responded to questions about mental health problems they experienced and how they dealt with those problems. Four thousand of the readers who responded to the survey had sought help from a mental health provider or family doctor for psychological problems or had joined a self-help group. Of those who responded, most sought therapy for marital or sexual problems, frequent low moods, child problems, job stress, grief, and alcohol or drug problems.

According to the study,

> People who went to their family doctor for help tended to do well, but those who went to mental health specialists did much better. Psychotherapy alone did as well as psychotherapy with medication, such as prozac or xanax. Those who took drugs felt side effects. Further, the survey revealed that those who stayed in therapy longer improved more. People who went to self help groups were very satisfied and felt they got better. Finally, the survey revealed the same progress whether clients saw a social worker, psychologist, or psychiatrist. Those who consulted a

marriage counselor felt the least helped. . . . One reason for the low scores for marriage counselors may be that working with a broken couple is very difficult. Also, almost anyone can become a marriage counselor with little or no training. Many people seemed more comfortable taking their problems to their family doctors, but the data suggests that they would do better with mental health specialists. Treatment with family doctors tended to be shorter and drugs were more likely to be prescribed. Clients who did seek help from their doctor tended to be less distressed yet only half were satisfied with their treatment.

Overall, the study showed that therapy works. Forty-four percent of people whose emotional state was very poor at the start of treatment said they now felt good. Consumer Reports suggests that people "shop" for their therapist, checking experience, and qualifications, as well as looking for personal chemistry in beginning sessions. (Consumer Reports, 1995, p. 739)

The results of this survey converge with results from previous therapy meta-analyses and generally support the effectiveness of therapy. This study's great strength is its evaluation of therapy as it is actually practiced. Its results support the generalizability of other therapy outcomes research studies. Seligman consulted with *Consumer Reports* in developing the survey, seeing it as a useful adjunct to efficacy studies. Its large sample size, clinical representativeness, and use of multiple measures of improvement (specific improvement, satisfaction, and global improvement) make it exceptional. Its most obvious weakness is that the study was a survey rather than an experiment, leading to significant ambiguity in causal inference. Other limitations include the fact that all survey respondents were of a particular group who actively returned surveys; the absence of control groups; reliance on patients' self-report; inadequate outcome measures; and its retrospective, nonrandom nature (Seligman, 1995). Seligman argues that the ideal study would improve upon the *Consumer Reports* study methods by (1) including all the different ways that success of psychotherapy could be operationalized (fewer symptoms, return to "normal," and better compared to no therapy) and (2) using a prospective approach that involves administering the survey to a large sample group both before and after treatment.

Efficacy Studies: Randomized Clinical Trials

Efficacy studies explore specific treatment effects by using experimental methods. The randomized controlled trial (RCT) has been the most favored model for outcomes research in psychotherapy. By contrasting a group of patients receiving some kind of therapy to a comparison group under well-controlled conditions, the RCT permits us to draw causal conclusions. Ideally RCTs evaluate the efficacy of therapy techniques by applying them to a group of patients whose improvement can be compared with that of a control group of similar patients assigned to an attention placebo condition eliciting similar expectancies of improvement. The RCT is more useful than other designs in addressing questions about the sufficiency of an intervention to produce desired changes: "Can this treatment produce this desirable effect in this type of patient?"

These experimental studies are often emphasized by researchers more than the naturalistic effectiveness studies because of the belief that systematic knowledge about the efficacy of psychological interventions is almost entirely dependent on research conducted within the experimental or quasi-experimental framework (Lipsey & Wilson, 1993).

Well-conducted efficacy studies can lead to widely accepted ESTs. ESTs (formerly referred to by Division 12 as "empirically validated treatments" or EVTs) consist of a list of evidence-based treatments, derived from those studies recommended by Division 12 of the American Psychological Association in their report on empirically supported psychological treatments (Chambless et al., 1996; Task Force on Promotion and Dissemination of Psychological Procedure, 1995). The original listing was recently expanded to include fifty-seven treatments that had withstood the test of careful empirical scrutiny.

In response to external pressures, Division 12 of the American Psychological Association proclaimed that "if clinical psychology is to survive in this heyday of biological psychiatry, APA must act to emphasize the strength of what we have to offer—a variety of psychotherapies of proven efficacy" (Task Force on Promotion and Dissemination of Psychological Procedures, 1995, p. 21). Accordingly, criteria were developed to identify empirically validated treatments; these criteria refer exclusively to studies that assess outcome rather than to process, theory, or psychological mechanisms of change, elevating the importance of "winners" (Wampold, Mondin, Moody, Stich, et al., 1997).

The Division of Clinical Psychology published a report on effective psychotherapies written by the Task Force on Promotion and Dissemination of Psychological Procedures (Chambless et al., 1993). Eighteen specific treatment interventions were cited from a total of thirty-three studies deemed worthy enough to claim the title "empirically validated interventions." The treatments were reviewed and documented based upon the recommendations of peers rather than a thorough review of the literature. Barber (1994) has pointed out that only 5.8% of a sample of outcomes studies of all major journals between 1980 and 1988 have used a comprehensive method to examine treatment methodology.

The intention of the task force was to identify all treatments for which there is empirical support, not just a small set (Task Force on Promotion and Dissemination of Psychological Procedures, 1995). The 1998 draft of the task force report lists twenty-one well-established treatments and thirty-six probably efficacious treatments. Thus, the empirical validation strategy, rather than weakening support for psychotherapy, has provided some support for at least fifty-seven specific psychotherapies for specific problems! Moreover, studies that only compared a psychotherapy with a no-treatment control, and therefore did not document that the unique ingredients were responsible for efficacy, were considered by the task force and included in the "probably efficacious" category.

Future Work with ESTs.   Not a single controlled study with adequate statistical power exists on standardized family or psychodynamic therapies for such common problems as social phobia, obsessive-compulsive disorder, major depression (nongeriatric sample), generalized anxiety disorder, agoraphobia, panic disorder, or borderline personality disorder; even cognitive-behavioral treatments of these disorders have modest success (Crits-Christoph, 1997). The need for standardizing and testing both existing and new treatments is obviously important. The need to develop and experimentally test new treatments that might enhance the effectiveness of existing treatments leaves an important ongoing role for the clinical trial methodology in psychotherapy research.

It would be consistent with findings of comparable effectiveness across ESTs to encourage therapists to select from among the ESTs the ones that seem most appropriate to individual clients. It is expected that managed care reviewers will increasingly expect familiarity with these methods and the relevant studies. Brief summaries of EST studies can be found in chapters that follow.

Limits of Single Studies. Individual efficacy studies are limited in their ability to provide definitive answers about particular therapeutic approaches because of their inevitable imperfections. For example, when it was found that insight-oriented marital therapy (IOMT) resulted in dramatically fewer divorces than did behavioral marital therapy (BMT) 4 years after therapy (3% and 38%, respectively) (Snyder, Wills, & Grady-Fletcher, 1991), Jacobson (1991) argued that IOMT had an unfair advantage: "It seems obvious that the IOMT therapists were relying heavily on the nonspecific clinically sensitive interventions allowed in the IOMT manual but not mentioned in the BMT manual. . . . To me, the . . . data suggest that *in this study* BMT was practiced with insufficient attention to nonspecifics" (p. 143).

Even the most expensive and thoroughly conducted clinical trial ever conducted (the 1989 NIMH Treatment of Depression Collaborative Research Program) could not avoid claims that a treatment was presented at a disadvantage for some reason (Elkin, Gibbons, et al., 1996; Jacobson & Hollon, 1996a, 1996b; D. Klein, 1996). Because every study has some flaws and because any single study that shows the superiority of a treatment could be due to a Type I error (involving rejection of the null hypothesis when it in fact is true), statements about relative efficacy of treatments based on the results of a single study are generally regarded as unjustified (Wampold, Mondin, Moody, Stich, et al., 1997).

Meta-Analyses

Meta-analyses provide a means of integrating and interpreting a large number of separate studies addressing the same question. Meta-analysis frames research integration as a research exercise in its own right. Eligible studies are viewed as a population to be systematically sampled and surveyed. Individual study results and characteristics are then abstracted, quantified, coded, and assembled into a database that is statistically analyzed much like any other quantitative survey data (Lipsey & Wilson, 1993).

Meta-analysis is a sophisticated statistical methodology that can parsimoniously summarize the results of many studies. Although complicated to use, it has been heralded by some as the sine qua non for future analyses of cumulative studies (Schmidt 1992; Nowak 1994). Meta-analyses determine the average difference in each study between the experimental and control groups on some outcome measure and then summarize these various estimates of "effect size." Effect size is a standardized, statistical measure of the magnitude of the difference between the experimental and the control group in controlled clinical trials.

Meta-analysis is based on an aggregation of estimates of the magnitude of treatment effects irrespective of whether, individually, they are statistically significant. Statistical tests are then applied to the aggregate results, for example, the mean and variance of the distribution of study level effect sizes (Hedges & Olkin, 1985; Hunter & Schmidt, 1990). The aggregation of samples inherent in meta-analysis greatly increases statistical power and decreases Type II error (failure to reject the null hypothesis when it is false). In cases in which the null hypothesis is false (i.e., treatment is effective) and individual studies use modest sample sizes (e.g., under 500), therefore, the conclusions of meta-analysis can diverge markedly from those of conventional reviews.

Meta-analysis is limited by the nature of the primary studies to which it is applied. Those studies too often report only crude comparisons between incompletely specified treatment packages and control conditions with little attention to potential interactions with client characteristics, the range of outcome variables, or temporal factors (Lipsey, 1988; Lipsey et al., 1985). Some maintain that meta-analyses are generally flawed because they summarize a diverse collection of studies using different measures, different treatments, different diagnostic procedures, and different therapists. In aggregating various studies of different methodological rigor without any systematic weighting system, meta-analyses risk being misleading. On the other hand, studies that use arbitrary weighting systems or that select among available dependent measures may end up with conclusions that are not truly representative.

The limitations of many extant meta-analyses cited by D. Shapiro and Shapiro (1982) include a predominance of studies assessing behavioral treatment, often using nonclinical analogues; the analyzed studies' use of recruited student volunteers and few clinically referred patients; and the use of the results from dissertations, published studies (more likely to contain positive rather than negative findings), and meta-analytic studies that are unrepresentative of clinical practice situations (thus limiting their generalizability to everyday practice).

Meta-Analysis Interpretation.   Although their beauty lies in their potential to simplify complex collection of studies, meta-analyses themselves are often far from simple to understand. Meta-analytic studies can be challenging to interpret, as many people are unfamiliar with the "effect size" statistic. Effect size is typically computed as $(M_t - M_c)/s$, where M_t is the treatment group mean, M_c is the control group mean, and s is the pooled standard deviation or, sometimes, the control group standard deviation. As Lipsey and Wilson (1993) have noted, "Treatment effect estimates [expressed] in standard deviation units have very little intuitive or practical meaning" (p. 1198). Assessing the clinical meaningfulness of an effect requires consideration of the context in which the treatment is being applied.

The meaning of psychotherapy effect sizes becomes clearer if they are compared with those of other types of treatment. According to Lipsey and Wilson (1993),

> In life-or-death medical situations, even a modest effect represents a significant contribution. Metaanalyses of medical outcome studies show that the mean effect size on mortality of coronary bypass surgery is .15 standard deviations. The mean effect size of chemotherapy for breast cancer is .10 standard deviations. The range of effect sizes for these treatments falls well below the overall mean effect size for psychotherapy (.58). When medical outcomes other than mortality are considered, effect sizes range from .24 to .80, quite similar to the range of effect sizes found for psychological treatments. (pp. 1198–1199)

In assessing meta-analytic estimates of the effects of psychological treatment, statistically modest values should not be dismissed. Comparable numerical values are judged to be beneficial and valuable in the medical domain. (See Table 10.1.)

TABLE 10.1 Selected Meta-Analyses of Medical Treatment Judged Effective (adapted from Lipsey and Wilson, 1993)

Outcome Variable	Mean Effect Size or Effect Size Range
Medical	
Mortality	
Aortocoronary bypass surgery*	0.15
AZT for AIDS*	0.47
Cyclosporine in organ transplants*	0.30
Chemotherapy for breast cancer*	0.08 to 0.11
Intravenous streptokinase for myocardial infarction*	0.08
Other Outcomes	
By-pass surgery; effects on angina*	0.80
Dipyridamole; effects on angina*	0.24
Drug treatment for arthritis; various outcomes*	0.45 to 0.77
Cyclosporine; effects on organ rejection*	0.39
Anticoagulants; effects on thromboembolism rates*	0.30
Psychological	
Drug treatment for behavioral disorders; behavioral and cognitive outcomes*	0.28 to 0.74
Electroconvulsive therapy; effects on depression*	0.80
Drug treatment for hyperactivity; cognitive, behavioral and social outcomes*	0.47 to 0.96
Neuroleptic drugs for dementia; effects on agitation*	0.37
Hypertensive drug therapy; effects on quality of life*	0.11 to 0.28

*For specific reference, see Lipsey and Wilson, 1993.

Several major meta-analytic reviews of efficacy studies will be described next, as examples of ways to interpret and utilize this kind of outcomes research.

Smith and Glass.   Smith and Glass (1977) summarized the results of 375 studies using meta-analytic methods and concluded that psychotherapy is very effective. They found that someone chosen at random from the experimental group after therapy had a two-to-one chance of scoring better than someone assigned to a control group. This effect is stronger than the findings for most medical procedures (Dawes, 1994). Smith and Glass also found that therapists' credentials (Ph.D., M.D., or no advanced degree) were unrelated to therapeutic effectiveness. Type of therapy was also unrelated to outcome, although behavioral methods appeared to be somewhat more effective for circumscribed behavioral problems. They also found that length of therapy was unrelated to treatment success.

Some critics argued that the Smith and Glass study was limited by its inclusion of heterogeneous, ill-defined studies, some of which failed to fully randomize subject assignment across experimental and control conditions. However, when Landman and Dawes (1982) reanalyzed the subset of the original Smith and Glass (1977) studies meeting more stringent methodological criteria, their conclusions closely paralleled the original findings.

Prioleau, Murdock, and Brody.   The Smith, Glass, and Miller (1980) conclusion that psychotherapy is more effective than control conditions was further challenged by a study conducted by Prioleau, Murdock, and Brody (1983). Critical of nonbehavioral psychotherapy methods, they focused on psychotherapy efficacy studies employing active placebo conditions, rather than mere wait-list controls. In order to be included in their meta-analysis, studies had to compare the experiences of those receiving a placebo treatment (not a wait-list control group) with those randomly assigned to a psychotherapy treatment other than behavior therapy. Psychotherapy treatments included all methods requiring the therapist to "engage in a process of exploration and clarification of the emotional experiences of the patient," with an accompanying "attempt to foster and develop an emotional relationship between the therapist and the patient."

In a reanalysis of a subset of the original Smith and Glass (1977) studies, including only those using real patients (psychiatric inpatients and outpatients), Prioleau, Murdock, and Brody found no evidence that the benefits of nonbehavioral psychotherapy are greater than those of placebo treatment. The effect size for the thirty-two studies that met their criteria was similar for patients treated with psychotherapy and those treated with placebo.

Thirty-six readers responded to the Prioleau, Murdock, and Brody paper. Their papers reflect current controversies about how to study psychotherapy; about the need for controls (including placebo controls); about the use of meta-analysis; and about whether psychotherapy is effective, is more effective than placebo, or is itself a placebo. One-third of the responders believed that the effectiveness of psychotherapy was supported by the Smith, Glass, and Miller meta-analysis, one-third believed that psychotherapy was ineffective or placebic, while the remainder were noncommittal.

None of the studies examined used individually tailored measures of outcome in which one specifies at the start of treatment the kind of changes that would indicate therapeutic progress for each patient. Use of such measures might provide a more sensitive test of the contribution of psychotherapeutic interventions above and beyond the placebo effect. Delineating specific behavioral treatment objectives may be an important way to surpass mere placebo effects. Such research would also permit us to determine which types of problems are amenable to psychotherapy and which are not.

Lipsey and Wilson.   Lipsey and Wilson (1993) conducted a very ambitious, integrative meta-analysis that summarized the findings of 302 meta-analyses of psychological and educational treatment, and in so doing they gave us a fairly comprehensive view of the efficacy literature. The most striking thing about their findings is the consistency of positive effects seen across the many meta-analyses.

The section of the Lipsey and Wilson study that specifically addressed psychotherapy involved summaries of therapy meta-analyses including data from hundreds of therapy outcome studies. The average mean effect size for these psychological studies was .58, which is considerably larger than the mean effect size of many widely used, "validated" medical interventions.

Lipsey and Wilson concluded that well-developed psychological and behavioral treatments generally have meaningful positive effects on the intended outcome variables. Placebo effects were found to account for only a portion of the generally positive effects of treatment. Because the Lipsey and Wilson analysis was based on existing meta-analyses, only those forms of psychotherapy that have attracted sufficient research interest could be specifically assessed; excluded therapeutic approaches may or may not show comparable levels of efficacy. The magnitude of effect size estimates that meta-analysis yields for psychological treatments seem sufficiently large to support the claim that such treatment is generally efficacious in practical as well as statistical terms. (See Table 10.2.)

Other Studies.   Crits-Christoph (1992) conducted a meta-analysis that concluded that brief dynamic therapy was more effective than placement on a waiting list, slightly superior to nonpsychiatric treatment (various types of active placebo control, such as self-help groups, clinical management, drug counseling, and low-contact treatment), and about equal to other psychotherapies and medication; that is, the various psychotherapies did not differ in effectivenesss.

In a meta-analysis comparing Albert Ellis's rational-emotive therapy (RET) with other therapies, on the basis of twenty-eight studies, Engels et al. found RET to be superior to placebo and no treatment but equally effective as variants such as RET bibliotherapy; RET classroom education; RET role-playing exercises with or without homework; rational role reversal with or without rational-emotive imagery; and

TABLE 10.2   Mean Effect Sizes for Different Categories of Treatment
(adapted from Lipsey & Wilson, 1993)

Category	Effect Size	N
General Psychotherapy	0.76	
Cognitive Behavioral Psychotherapy	0.63	
Family and Marital Interventions	0.59	
Health-Related Treatments	0.57	
Treatment Programs for Offenders	0.36	
General Psychotherapy		
Psychotherapy; all outcomes (Smith, Glass & Miller, 1980)[a]	0.85	475
Psychotherapy with adults; all outcomes (Shapiro & Shapiro, 1982,1983)	0.93	143
Psychotherapy vs. placebo controls; all outcomes (Piroleau, Murdock, & Brody, 1983)	0.42	32
Psychotherapy (random assignment studies with good controls); all outcomes (Landman & Dawes, 1982)	0.78	42
Psychotherapy; self-concept outcomes (Cook, 1988)[a]	0.37	34
Psychotherapy (individual); all outcomes (Tillitski, 1990)	1.16	9
Psychotherapy (group); all outcomes (Tillitski, 1990)	1.31	9
Psychotherapy with children; all outcomes (Casey & Berman, 1985)[a]	0.71	64
Psychotherapy with children and adolescents; all outcomes (Weisz, Weiss, Alicke, & Klotz, 1987)	0.79	108
Psychotherapy with adult neurotic patients; all outcomes (Nicholson & Berman, 1983)	0.68	67
Psychotherapy for neuroses, phobias & emotional-somatic complaints; all outcomes (G. Andrews & Harvey, 1981)	0.72	81
Psychotherapy for the treatment of depression; all outcomes (L.A. Robinson, Berman, & Neimeyer, 1990)	0.72	58
Psychotherapy for neurotic depression; all outcomes (Prince Henry Hospital, 1983)	0.65	10
Psychotherapy for unipolar depression in adults; all outcomes (Steinbrueck, Maxwell, & Howard, 1983)	1.22	16
Psychotherapy vs. drug therapy for the treatment of bulimia; all outcomes (Laessle, Zoettl, & Pride, 1987)	0.95	23
Psychotherapy for bulimia; all outcomes (Bryan, 1989)[a]	0.92	31
Client-centered therapy, transactional analysis, and non-directive therapy; all outcomes (Champney & Schulz, 1983)	0.25	18
Mental health specialists vs. general medical practitioners; all outcomes (Balestrieri, Williams, & Wilkinson, 1988)	0.22	11
Cognitive Behavioral/Behavior Modification		
Cognitive behavioral therapies vs. nonspecific factors controls; all outcomes (Barker, Funk & Houston, 1988)	0.67	17
Cognitive therapy for anxiety disorders; all outcomes (Berman, Miller, & Massman, 1985)	0.73	25
Cognitive therapy, modification of covert self-statements of adult patients; all outcomes (Dush, Hirt, & Schroeder, 1983)[a]	0.66	69
Cognitive therapy with nonpsychotic patients with clinic complaints; all outcomes (Miller & Berman, 1983)	0.77	48
Cognitive behavior therapy with adult populations; all outcomes (Polder, 1986)	0.69	53
Cognitive behavioral therapy; effect on trait anxiety and neuroticism (Jorm, 1989)	0.53	63
Cognitive behavioral therapy (paradoxical interventions); all outcomes (Shoham-Salomon & Rosenthal, 1987)	0.89	10

TABLE 10.2 Continued

Category	Effect Size	N
Cognitive behavioral therapy (paradoxical interventions); all outcomes (Hampton, 1988)[a]	0.15	29
Cognitive behavioral therapy (paradoxical interventions); all outcomes (Hill, 1987)[a]	0.99	15
Cognitive therapy for depression; Beck Depression Inventory outcomes (Dobson, 1989)	0.99	28
Cognitive and behavioral treatments of depression and phobic anxiety; all outcomes (Eifert & Craill, 1989)	0.83	36
Cognitive behavioral therapy with children; modification of self-statements (Dush, Hirt, & Schroeder, 1989)	0.37	48
Cognitive behavioral modification strategies with children; educationally relevant behavioral outcomes (Duzinski, 1987)[a]	0.47	45
Cognitive behavioral therapy with dysfunctional children; all outcomes (Durlak, Fuhrman, & Lampman, 1991)[a]	0.53	64
Cognitive therapy and systematic desensitization for public speaking anxiety; all outcomes (Allen, Hunter, & Donohue, 1989)	0.52	97
Systematic desensitization; all outcomes (Berman, Miller, & Massman, 1985)	0.62	25
Training children in use of verbal self-instructions to control their behavior in non-training situations; all outcomes (Rock, 1986)[a]	0.51	47
Behavior therapy vs. placebo controls; all outcomes (Bowers & Clum, 1988)	0.55	69
Behavioral self-management, social skills training, cognitive-behavioral therapy, and biofeedback/relaxation training with problem children; clinically relevant outcomes (Wyma, 1990)	0.61	43
Behavioral treatment (biofeedback) for Raynaud's disease; all outcomes (Montross, 1990)	1.06	18
Behavioral treatment (progressive relaxation therapy); all outcomes (Paterson, 1988)[a]	0.34	71
Behavioral treatment with spouse involvement in treatment of agoraphobia; effect on symptoms (Dewey & Hunsley, 1990)	0.10	6
Behavioral therapy and tricyclic medication in the treatment of obsessive-compulsive disorder; all outcomes (Christensen, Hadzi-Pavlovic, Andrews, & Mattick, 1987)	1.02	27

Family/Marital Interventions

Category	Effect Size	N
Family therapy; all outcomes (Hazelrigg, Cooper, & Borduin, 1987)	0.36	20
Family therapy (conjoint); all outcomes (Markus, Lange, & Pettigrew, 1990)	0.57	19
Family therapy for child identified problems; all outcomes (Montgomery, 1991)	0.61	43
Family and marital therapies; behavioral outcomes (Shadish, 1992)[a]	0.70	58
Behavioral marital therapy; all outcomes (Hahlweg & Markman, 1988)	0.95	17
Behavioral premarital intervention studies; all outcomes (Hahlweg & Markman, 1988)	0.79	7
Parent effectiveness training; all outcomes (B. Cedar & Levant, 1990; R. B. Cedar, 1986)[a]	0.33	26
Marriage/family enrichment programs for nonclinical couples and families; all outcomes (Giblin, Sprenkle, Sheehan, 1985)[a]	0.44	85
Minnesota Couple Communication Program (communication skills); immediate outcomes (Wampler, 1983)[a]	0.52	20

Health Related Psychological or Educational Treatment
Educational/Counseling for Medical Patients

Category	Effect Size	N
Educational or psychological interventions with adult hospitalized elective surgery patients; effects on patient well-being (Devine, 1984; Devine & Cook, 1983)[a]	0.46	105

(continued)

TABLE 10.2 Continued

Category	Effect Size	N
Preoperative instruction of adults scheduled for surgery; effects on postoperative outcome (Hathaway, 1985)	0.44	68
Special preoperative preparation of children for surgery vs. routine nursing care; effects on anxiety (Howell, 1985)[a]	0.40	23
Psychological preparation of children for medical procedures; all outcomes (Saile, Burgmeier, & Schmidt, 1988)	0.44	75
Patient education for people with a chronic disease or medical problem; effects on compliance and health (Mazzuca, 1982)[a]	0.52	27
Psychological support for patients facing surgery or recovering from heart attacks; effects on anxiety, cooperation, and recovery (Mumford, Schlesinger, & Glass, 1982)[a]	0.49	34
Programs to increase compliance with medical treatment regimens; all outcomes (Posavac, Sinacore, Brotherton, Helford, & Turpin, 1985)	0.47	58
Patient education about treatment regimens, preventive behavior, self-care, etc.; all outcomes (Posavac, 1980)	0.74	23
Biofeedback/Relaxation/Medication Training for Clinical Symptoms		
Biofeedback and relaxation training for migraine and tension headaches; improvement scores (Blanchard, Andrasik, Ahles, Teders, & O'Keefe, 1980)	0.63	35
Meditation and relaxation techniques; effect on blood pressure (Kuchera, 1987)	0.93	26
Relaxation training for clinical (medical) symptoms; all outcomes (Hyman, Feldman, Harris, Levin, & Malloy, 1989)[a]	0.52	48
Tobacco Smoking Cessation/Reduction Programs		
Smoking cessation/reduction programs; effects on abstinence (Feehan, 1984)	0.64	97
Smoking cessation/reduction programs (physician delivered); effect on quit rates (Dotson, 1990)[a]	0.34	8
Smoking cessation/reduction programs (worksite); effect on quit rates (Fisher, 1990)[a]	0.21	20
Psychological Treatments for Pain		
Music therapy in medicine to reduce pain; effect on pain reduction (Standley, 1986)[a]	0.98	29
Pain management interventions with children; behavioral, self-report and physiologic outcomes (Broome, Lillis, & Smith, 1989)[a]	0.39	30
Non-medical psychologically based treatment of chronic pain; all outcomes (Malone, Strube, & Scogin, 1989)	1.10	48
Cognitive coping strategies for the treatment of pain; effects on pain perception (Fernandez & Turk, 1989)	0.51	47
Multidisciplinary treatments for chronic back pain; all outcomes (Flor, Fydrich, & Turk, 1992)	1.25	65
Other Health Related Psychological or Educational Treatment		
Psychosocial preventive care for the elderly; all outcomes (Wilson, Simson, & McCaughey, 1983)	0.45	8

TABLE 10.2 Continued

Category	Effect Size	N
Adolescent pregnancy education programs; all outcomes (Iverson & Levy, 1982)	0.35	14
Prenatal childbirth class for adults; all outcomes (Jones 1983)[a]	0.34	58
Training of new mothers about sensory/perceptual capabilities of newborns; effects on maternal-infant interaction (Turely, 1984)[a]	0.44	20
Behavioral treatment for obesity; effects of weight loss (O'Flynn, 1983)	1.06	80
Behavioral management of obesity for couples; effects on weight loss (Black, Gleser, & Kooyers, 1990)	0.33	12
The Feingold diet (free of food additives) for children; effects on hyperactivity (Kavale & Forness, 1983)	0.02	23
Treatment for stuttering; all outcomes (G. Andrews, Guitar, & Howie, 1980)	1.30	42
Stress management programs; all outcomes (Nicholson, Duncan, Hawkins, Belcastro, & Gold, 1988)	0.75	18
Stress coping interventions; all outcomes (Cannella, 1988)[a]	0.46	94
Psychological treatment of Type A Behavior; effects on risk for coronary artery heart disease (Nunes, Frank, & Kornfeld, 1987)	0.61	10
Subjective well-being interventions among elderly; subjective well being outcomes (Okun, Olding, & Cohn, 1990)[a]	0.42	31
Exercise interventions for depression; effects on depression (North, 1989)[a]	0.54	77
Educational interventions for diabetic adults; knowledge, metabolic control, self-care and psychological outcomes (Brown, 1990)[a]	0.43	82
Death education; attitude and affective outcomes (Durlak & Reisenberg, 1991)	0.28	47
Treatment Programs for Offenders		
Treatment programs for juvenile delinquents; delinquency outcomes (Lipsey, 1992)[a]	0.17	397
Treatment programs for juvenile delinquents; all outcomes (Gottschalk, Davidson, Gensheimer, & Mayer, 1987a)	0.48	91
Treatment programs for adjudicated delinquents in residential/institutional settings; all outcomes (Garrett, 1985a, 1985b)	0.37	111
Treatment programs for juvenile delinquents (random assignment studies); delinquency outcomes (Kaufman, 1985)	0.25	20
Social learning treatment programs for juvenile delinquents; all outcomes (Mayer, Gensheimer, Davidson, & Gottschalk, 1986)	0.77	39
Diversion programs for juvenile delinquents; all outcomes (Gensheimer, Mayer, Gottschalk, & Davidson, 1986)	0.40	44
Behavioral treatment approaches for juvenile delinquents; long-term outcomes (Gottschalk, Davidson, & Mayer, 1987b)	0.40	25
Treatment programs for juvenile offenders; all outcomes (Whitehead & Lab, 1989)	0.27	50
Treatment programs for adult and juvenile offenders; all outcomes (Andrews et al., 1990)	0.20	80
Correctional treatment with adults; all outcomes (Losel & Koferl, 1989)	0.25	16

Citations are found in Lipsey and Wilson, 1993.

RET combined with systematic desensitization, client-centered behavior therapy, eclectic dynamic therapy, vocational training, and psychodynamic therapy.

Shadish, Montgomery, et al. (1993) published a meta-analysis of 163 randomized trials comparing the outcomes of therapy provided by practitioners of different therapeutic orientations; the types of therapy included family and marital therapies and individual therapies. The essence of the results was that marital and family therapies were mildly positive compared to controls, but were not significantly different from each other, nor did they show significant differences when compared with individual therapies. Orientations within therapies were not different from each other, except that humanistic therapies were less effective.

D. Shapiro and Shapiro (1982) presented meta-analytic findings based on 143 outcome studies in which two or more treatment groups were compared with a control group. They concluded that active treatments were superior to minimal placebo treatments and that the effects of different treatment methods were not impressively different from each other, except that the results of behavioral and cognitive methods were modest, while the results for dynamic and humanistic treatments were poor.

Kazdin's (1991) review of meta-analytic studies of child and adolescent treatment concluded that individual treatment techniques have not been found to differ from each other, consistent with the findings of Weisz, Weiss, and Donenberg (1992).

Since Smith and Glass's (1977) pioneering meta-analysis of psychotherapy research, literally hundreds of meta-analyses have been conducted in different treatment research areas. Although much of this work has been rather crude and certainly is not above criticism (Eysenck, 1994), there can be no doubt that meta-analysis has become an increasingly accepted technique (T. Cook et al., 1992; Durlak & Lipsey, 1991; Glass, McGaw, & Smith, 1981; Hedges & Olkin, 1985; Hunter & Schmidt, 1990; Rosenthal, 1991b).

Clearly, numerous quantitative, meta-analytic reviews of therapy outcome studies have convincingly concluded that those who receive therapy have better outcomes than those who do not receive therapy. Such analyses are frequently referenced in debates about whether therapy is sufficiently effective to merit insurance reimbursement (e.g., Depression Guideline Panel, 1993). Mastering these findings can make you more effective in justifying insurance reimbursement for psychological services.

Debates about Psychotherapy Outcomes Research

For many years there has been ongoing debate about the evaluation of clinical practice. One debate concerns the relevance of research and the difficulties therapists encounter in trying to apply findings in actual clinical settings. Another longstanding controversy focuses on the advisability of trying to prove the effects of specific interventions. This chapter concludes with an overview of questions related to the generalizability issue. The next chapter explores findings related to the specificity debate.

The Relevance of Research: Generalization Problems

Lynn Johnson (1995) complains that

> . . . many academic departments are full of professors who have never been in a full-time clinical practice since their internships. They are brilliant and thoughtful persons who were unusually productive of research and moved directly into the teaching arena after graduation. So sometimes the research is cleverly and thoughtfully designed, but not relevant to the questions of the practitioner. The practicing clinician often has a notion about research that suggests all articles have titles like, "Visual tracking of Identical Bosnian Schizophrenic Twins."

Practitioners and academicians need to do a better job of communicating with one another.

Howard et al. (1997) criticized the adequacy of RCTs as a means of establishing the relative efficacy of psychotherapies. Howard and his associates (e.g., Howard, Krause, & Orlinsky, 1986; Howard et al., 1997) have argued that there are flaws in clinical trials due to such factors as randomization problems, attrition, interactions with unknown causal variables, choice of dependent variables, and limited external validity. "Simply put, RCTs may reflect very little about the reality of psychotherapy practice where patients and clinicians are concerned about whether this treatment, conducted in this manner, is producing the desired effect" (Howard et al., 1997, p. 224).

Clinical Representativeness of Meta-Analyses

Few meta-analyses have systematically addressed the generalizability issue, and those that have yield a contradictory picture. Smith, Glass, and Miller (1980) found that effect sizes from therapy studies conducted in university settings ($d = 1.04$) were greater than in those conducted in typical clinical settings (e.g., mental health centers, $d = .47$; other clinic or outpatient facilities, $d = .79$).

In a review of four meta-analyses of more than 12,000 subjects who participated in more than 200 controlled studies, Weisz, Weiss, and Donenberg (1992) concluded that, over all, children and adolescents benefitted from treatment. However, benefit was associated more with the treatment of recruited subjects for focal problems by specially trained therapists with small caseloads, as well as with other features not representative of typical clinical treatment. Clinical studies of referred patients treated in clinics for more general psychopathology did not show significant therapeutics effects. The Weisz, Weiss, and Donenberg review of six clinically representative studies of child and adolescent therapies found that the studies using more representative treatment of referred clients in clinics showed more modest effects. They concluded that most clinic studies have not shown significant effects.

Twenty Problems That Limit Reliance on Outcomes Research

1. In research therapy, participants (often college students) are recruited by the researcher, while in practice patients initiate their own treatment.
2. The informed consent procedures required in research may introduce doubts about the treatment that have no direct parallel in real-world settings.
3. The process of random assignment to treatments does not represent the process through which patients choose and persevere in treatment.
4. Extraneous confounds are a problem in many outcome studies, despite randomization procedures, because of limited sample sizes.
5. Selective attrition is a particularly vexing, common source of confounding in outcome studies.
6. The use of credible, active placebos in double-blind studies is ideal, but rare.
7. In studies, patients are often homogenous in terms of many personal characteristics, compared with the heterogenous variety of clients treated in clinic therapy.
8. In research, treatment is often directed at one focal problem, compared with the blend of problems typically addressed in actual practice.
9. While in research, patients are prescreened for one pure diagnosis, in real therapy, patients are not prescreened for coexisting problems and excluded if they fail to be ideal candidates for treatment.
10. Research therapy focuses on previously defined outcomes (usually specific symptom reduction), while real therapy emphasizes more global, patient-determined objectives.
11. In research the therapist is usually instructed to use only the treatment method under study, while actual practitioners rarely are constrained by a single theory.
12. In studies a treatment manual is often used and treatment implementation is monitored, but this has been quite rare in actual practice.
13. Actual therapy is not usually of a predetermined, fixed duration and format (even with managed care, changes in plan are possible); it is expected to be self-correcting.
14. Individual therapist effects are confounded with treatment effects, because although patients may be randomly assigned to treatment conditions, therapists rarely are.
15. Use of inexperienced therapists plagues many studies.
16. In research, therapists are often recently trained in the specific procedure under study.
17. Measurement problems abound. Regression effects may produce overestimates of treatment effectiveness, while use of unreliable measures may underestimate effect sizes.
18. Patient and therapist expectations may taint assessment. Treatments with clearer demand characteristics may appear superior if measures transparently assess types of changes the therapist has been explicitly advocating in treatment.
19. Research often focuses on statistical rather than "real-world," clinical significance; favored treatments may yield only trivial outcome advantages.
20. Clinicians must extrapolate from normative studies to their individual work with individual therapy cases, yet variability makes this a questionable practice.

Several investigators, including D. Shapiro and Shapiro (1982), Steinbrueck, Maxwell, and Howard (1983), and Wittmann and Matt (1986) found no statistically significant differences between laboratory and clinical settings. D. Stein and Lambert (1995) obtained inconclusive results when comparing studies using experienced versus inexperienced therapists.

In contrast, G. Andrews and Harvey (1981) reported superior effect sizes for stuttering treatments delivered in both outpatient ($d = .76$) and inpatient settings ($d = 1.00$), than for those delivered in university settings ($d = .67$). Shadish, Navarro, et al. (1997) selectively reviewed fifty-six outcome studies whose conditions most closely mimicked those of actual practice. Their findings suggest that clients who receive therapy under clinical conditions do better than those who do not receive therapy and that effect sizes for clinic therapy are generally comparable to those yielded by past meta-analyses.

Meta-analytic studies demonstrate that many psychotherapies are clearly better than no treatment or a variety of different controls. However, questions remain about the specificity of treatment effects and the magnitude of treatment benefits in actual clinical settings.

The irony associated with trying to apply psychotherapy research is that the "best" controlled research is often the least representative of actual practice. Some argue that, in using experimental procedures, nonreferred subjects, specially trained therapists with small case loads, and other features that may not resemble conventional therapy, "research therapy" yields results that are not applicable to psychotherapy as it is usually practiced (Weisz, Weiss, & Donenberg, 1992). However, others have provided empirical evidence that the findings about the effectiveness of psychotherapy obtained in more naturalistic ways generally parallel those obtained in the large meta-analyses (Shadish, Navarro, et al., 1997; Seligman, 1995). While it is appropriate to be familiar with the potential limitations on generalizability, it is also reassuring to consider the data suggesting that the research findings probably do have some general relevance for actual practice.

Clearly not everyone has complete faith in the ability of efficacy research to define standards of care for all psychotherapists. Those who believe that the debate over the types of intervention that need to be developed is simply an empirical issue requiring more research will need to pay careful attention to the standards of that research and the adequacy of our traditional research paradigms as evaluations of meaningful outcomes (Scotti et al., 1991).

Many believe that the therapy outcome literature needs new, randomized experiments designed to be more clinically representative (Shadish, Navarro, et al., 1997). Future studies should have random assignment, low attrition, a reliable and valid posttest, and a pretest to factor out effects of attrition. They should arguably avoid patient selection processes beyond those minimally necessary to meet ethical obligations (e.g., discerning suicidal patients) and treatment monitoring, in order to maximize similarity to actual clinical practice. Unfortunately, random sampling of patients, treatments, and settings is rarely feasible in therapy outcome research. High-quality quasi-experiments (Shadish & Ragsdale, 1996), and single-case designs can also help to illuminate the effects of therapy.

The proper agenda for the next generation of treatment efficacy research, for both primary and meta-analytic studies, is investigation of which treatment variants are most effective; the mediating causal processes through which they work; and the characteristics of recipients, providers, and settings that most influence their results. Such a research agenda is justified by the well-established conclusion that psychological treatment can be, and generally is, effective. The questions of interest are no longer whether it works, but how it works and how it can be made to work better.

11 Squaring Off: The Specificity Debate

Specific Techniques versus Common or Placebo Factors

Wolberg (1977) estimated the number of distinct psychotherapies to be 200 in 1977. In 1980 the number had grown to more than 250 (Herink, 1980; Parloff, 1980). The total number of different psychotherapies that have been described in history probably exceeds 1,000, according to D. Shapiro and Shapiro (1997). The number of practitioners has increased over time as well. The spectrum includes psychiatrists, psychologists, social workers, counselors, paraprofessionals, and an expanding assortment of other mental health professionals and nonprofessionals holding various degrees (M.D., Ph.D., Ed.D., Psy.D., M.S.W., B.A., high school diploma, and assorted certificates attesting to competence).

D. Shapiro and Shapiro (1997) write that

The number of psychiatrists in the United States increased from about 7,000 in 1965 to about 42,000 in 1994, an increase of 600 percent. More patients are treated by about 50,000 clinical psychologists, who are exceeded by more than 100,000 social workers and more than 50,000 other mental health professionals, all competing with an uncountable number of assorted and ill-defined lay and quack therapists. . . . Psychotherapy is big business, with more than 250,000 psychotherapists in the United States; almost 80 million visits to the psychotherapists, accounting for $4.2 billion in fees . . . ; and 2.5 million children receiving treatment at an annual cost of $1.5 billion. . . . With the estimate that fewer than 100,000 psychotherapists will be needed in the coming health reform era . . . , psychotherapy is in crisis. (p. 103)

The proliferation of psychotherapeutic schools suggests that the treatments provided by all types of psychotherapists may work to some extent, not because of the theories or therapeutic procedures but because of underlying, unspecified or not clearly determined nonspecific effects—or what we now subsume under the rubric of placebo effects. Clinical and research psychiatrists, psychologists, psychoanalysts, and others have extensively discussed the nonspecific effects of psychotherapy, and most leading clinical researchers have concluded that nonspecific effects strongly outweigh specific effects. With more than 600 studies of psychotherapy today . . . , and 230 studies of techniques for therapy with children . . . , many controlled to one extent or another, there is no conclusion as to what specifically works in psychotherapy. An inescapable speculation is that psychotherapy has become this century's major placebo. (p. 105)

Common Factors and Placebo Effects

Those who emphasize the importance of common factors suggest that the strongly positive effects found in meta-analyses of studies of psychological treatment (e.g., Lipsey & Wilson, 1993) are not actually due to the specific efficacy of the treatments provided, but rather due to shared, common factors provided across all treatments. The superior treatment group performance that is reflected in meta-analysis effect sizes may result from some sort of placebo effect experienced by the treatment group. It may be that those common elements of treatment that are not usually present for control groups (e.g., receiving attention, encouragement, and building positive expectations) have fairly universal positive effects that show up in meta-analysis, even when the distinct elements of the treatments provided are ineffectual.

Numerous studies since the 1950s have in essence failed to disconfirm the view that various forms of psychotherapy do not show greater effectiveness than spontaneous remission or placebo treatment (Eysenck, 1994). Treatment effects estimated relative to placebo controls are smaller, on average, than those estimated relative to no-treatment control conditions.

However, it is important to note that when placebo comparisons are used, treatment effects do not disappear entirely. "The distribution of effects relative to placebo still falls largely in the positive range (90% are greater than 0.20) and thus shows evidence of 'value added' by treatment beyond that attained with administration of placebos" (Lipsey & Wilson, 1993, p. 1196).

The indication from the Lipsey and Wilson (1993) meta-analyses is that positive treatment effect sizes cannot be accounted for entirely by generalized placebo effects; indeed, such effects were found to be rather modest. While there are probably some generalized placebo effects that contribute to the overall effects of psychological treatment, their magnitude does not seem sufficient to account fully for those overall effects. (See Table 11.1.)

In psychological treatment, unlike medical treatment, it is conceptually difficult to distinguish placebo effects from the treatment with which they are associated. In medical treatments a relatively clear separation is possible between the nature of surgical or pharmaceutical intervention and the accompanying patient morale, expectations, and social interaction. In contrast, psychological treatment is often presumed to work through just those mechanisms of social interaction, expectations, and attitude change that probably constitute the key elements of the placebo effect (Lipsey & Wilson, 1993). As Wilkins (1986) has argued, placebo effects may be constituent parts of psychological treatment, not artifacts to be separated out in any assessment of that treatment.

> It seems likely that some of the positive results of psychological treatment stem from generalized placebo effects rather than the specific effects of the treatment delivered. However, whether one views placebo effects as artifacts that inflate treatment results or an intrinsic component of psychological treatment, their magnitude appears to be too modest to account for more than a portion of the generally positive effect of such treatment. (Lipsey & Wilson, 1993, p. 1197)

TABLE 11.1 Comparison of Effect Sizes Based on Studies
with Different Control Conditions

	Effect Size		
Control Condition	M	SD	N
No treatment control	0.67	0.44	30
Placebo treatment control	0.48	0.26	30

Data from the Lipsey and Wilson (1993, p. 1196) meta-analyses that
provided a breakout for this construct were included in this table. From
M. Lipsey and D. Wilson (1993), "The Efficacy of Psychological, Educational, and Behavioral Treatment," *American Psychologist, 48* (12).
Copyright © 1993 by the American Psychological Association. Reprinted
with permission.

Failures to Prove Treatment Specificity

Do the specifics of what we say and do as therapists matter? In 1936, Rosenzweig
argued that common factors accounted largely for the efficacy of psychotherapy
and used the conclusion of the Dodo bird from *Alice in Wonderland* (Carroll,
1962/1865) to emphasize his point: "At last the Dodo said, 'Everybody has won,
and all must have prizes'" (p. 412). Later, Luborsky, Singer, and Luborsky (1975)
reviewed the psychotherapy outcome literature, found that the psychotherapies
assessed were generally similar in terms of their outcomes, and proclaimed that
the Dodo bird was correct. Their argument was that all psychotherapies worked to
some extent for some patients. They stated that "what we do not know is whether
there are psychotherapies which produce significantly better results and whether
certain psychotherapies are especially well suited to certain patients" (Luborsky,
Singer, & Luborsky, 1976, p. 3) and suggested that more adequate research methodologies were needed.

While the efficacy of psychotherapy is typically established in clinical trials
by comparing a treatment with a waiting-list control, a placebo control, or an alternative treatment, relative efficacy is established by comparing two treatments that
are intended to be therapeutic (Wampold et al., 1997). Many individual studies
indicate that various effective forms of therapy often fail to show specific effects
when these methods are systematically compared with other established therapies.
Failure to observe significant differences in treatment outcome across widely
different treatments challenges the specificity of psychotherapy techniques and
supports the impression that common underlying factors account for much of the
effectiveness of all therapists.

One early study compared twenty-three patients treated twice weekly for a
maximum of twenty sessions by experienced Adlerian psychoanalytic and Rogerian
client-centered psychotherapists (Shlien et al., 1962). All of the patients improved,
without significant differences between therapies. Jerome Frank and colleagues

(1959) compared the treatment of three individual groups of fifty-four outpatients with psychoneurosis and personality disorder who were treated by three second- and third-year psychiatric residents for 6 months. One group was treated with 1-hour weekly individual psychotherapy, another with $1\frac{1}{2}$-hour weekly group therapy, and the third with $\frac{1}{2}$-hour visits every 2 weeks as a minimal-contact control. Discomfort scores significantly decreased for all three groups, but there were no differences among groups at 6-month evaluation, and discomfort scores continued to decrease at subsequent 1- and 5-year evaluations in each group. Measures of social effectiveness improved for all groups, but at 6-month evaluation the improvement was greater for patients in group psychotherapy; there was continued improvement at 1- and 5-year evaluations for all groups, and there were no significant differences among the three groups when they were evaluated after 5 years.

In an impressive comparative study of psychotherapy (Sloane et al., 1975; Sloane & Staples, 1984), ninety-four outpatients with anxiety neurosis and personality disorders were treated by experienced therapists for 4 months with psychoanalytically oriented or behavior therapy, and the members of a control group were given an initial assessment, assigned to a waiting list, and called every few weeks. The severity of target symptoms improved significantly for all three groups, but more so for the two treatment groups, which, however, were not significantly different from each other. At followup evaluations 1 and 2 years later, all three groups showed improvement, but did not differ significantly in the extent of this improvement.

The specificity of cognitive-behavioral treatment for panic disorder was compared with a control treatment (Shear et al., 1994). Cognitive-behavioral treatment included prescribed techniques targeting each component of the panic reaction (e.g., breath retraining, progressive muscle relaxation). The control treatment focused attention on frightening symptoms, life problems, and stress. Forty-five patients were treated for fifteen weekly sessions by psychotherapists who had 2 years' experience using cognitive-behavioral treatment and were supervised by a more experienced cognitive-behavioral therapist, and sessions were rated for adherence to the two treatments. Post-treatment and 6-month followup evaluations revealed a high rate of panic remission and equally significant improvement in both treatment groups.

The NIMH Depression Treatment Study

The standards of care in mental health have traditionally been much less clearly delineated than those in other areas of healthcare. While there has been a great deal of psychotherapy outcomes research, few large-scale studies examining the relative merits of various treatments for specific disorders have been conducted. One exception is the National Institute of Mental Health (NIMH) Treatment of Depression Collaborative Research Program (TDCRP) (e.g., Elkin et al., 1989), which compared three forms of treatment for depression.

This classic, federally funded, multisite investigation examined the mode-specific effects of cognitive-behavioral therapy, interpersonal psychotherapy, and antidepressant medication with supportive management on depressive symptomatology. None of the therapies produced outcomes consistent with their theoretical origins, and each of the modules produced essentially the same results.

In this large-scale attempt to clarify the differential effectiveness of several treatments for depression the most frequently used pharmacotherapy for depression, imipramine hydrochloride with clinical management, served as a reference condition, because imipramine's efficacy with depressed patients is considered to be well established (Kessler, 1978). The project also compared two of the most commonly used types of psychotherapy, interpersonal psychotherapy (IPT) and cognitive behavior therapy (CBT). A control group receiving a pill placebo and clinical management was used for comparative purposes.

Over all, patients in all the treatment groups showed a significant reduction in depressive symptoms, as well as an improvement in functioning over the course of treatment. Without regard to the initial severity of the illness, there was no evidence of greater effectiveness of one of the psychotherapies as compared with the other and no evidence that either of the psychological therapies was significantly less effective than the standard reference treatment of imipramine. Superior recovery rates were found for both interpersonal psychotherapy and imipramine with case management relative to placebo with case management.

The magnitude of differences in mean scores across the four treatment conditions was not large. The imipramine-CM group did the best upon termination, and the placebo-CM control group did the worst. The two psychotherapies fell in between, but closer to the imipramine group. In comparing group differences, analyses of covariance were conducted to reduce the unwanted effects of marital status on the dependent variables. Very few statistically significant differences emerged across the groups. Over all the dependent measures there was only limited evidence of the specific effectiveness of IPT and no evidence of the specific effectiveness of CBT when compared with the placebo-CM condition. The general lack of significant difference between the psychotherapies and the placebo-CM group seemed to be due to the very good performance of the placebo-CM condition. This is in contrast to the general finding of relatively poor performance of delayed treatment and waiting-list controls often used in other outcome studies.

The NIMH TDCRP placebo-CM group members were seen once a week for 20 to 30 minutes by an experienced psychiatrist who administered the placebo medication, reviewed symptoms, and offered support and encouragement. This combination of minimal supportive therapy and expectations regarding the medication, along with the generally supportive treatment environment, apparently enabled many patients to achieve a significant reduction in depressive symptoms and improvement in general functioning.

Meta-Analytic Estimates of Specificity

Researchers have also used meta-analytic methods to empirically examine the Dodo bird effect. Several meta-analyses have compared types of treatments by classifying the various treatments studied into categories (e.g., behavioral, cognitive-behavioral, and psychodynamic) and then comparing the effect sizes produced by pairwise comparisons of the classes (e.g., Robinson, Berman, & Neimeyer, 1990; D. Shapiro & Shapiro, 1982; Smith & Glass, 1977).

Smith and Glass's (1977) initial review of almost 400 psychotherapy outcome studies was the first attempt to meta-analytically test whether any particular type of therapy was better than another. For each study, they calculated the effect size of the psychotherapy vis-à-vis a control group. They reported that the average outcome study "showed a .68 standard deviation superiority of the treated group over the control group" (Smith & Glass, 1977, p. 756). They then aggregated these effect sizes within categories of therapies (e.g., Adlerian, systematic desensitization), to compare the relative size of the resultant effects, and found small differences among the categories. Roughly 10% of the variance in effect sizes was due to category. However, after combining into summary classes and equating the classes for differences in studies, they found that their summary results were consistent with the Dodo bird effect: "Despite volumes devoted to the theoretical differences among different schools of psychotherapy, the results of research demonstrate negligible differences in the effects produced by different therapy types" (p. 760).

Smith and Glass were the first meta-analytic researchers to report nonexistent to small differences among psychotherapies. Their conclusions were challenged vociferously (e.g., Eysenck, 1978; Rachman & Wilson, 1980; Glass & Kliegl, 1983). However, subsequent meta-analysts returned with conclusions substantially consistent with Smith and Glass's (e.g., Grissom, 1996; Robinson, Berman, & Neimeyer, 1990; D. Shapiro & Shapiro, 1982). But even then, increased emphasis on conducting clinical trials comparing psychotherapies showed a persistent belief that true differences must be discovered (Goldfried & Wolfe, 1996).

Rachman and Wilson (1980) reviewed the outcomes of psychoanalytic treatment, Rogerian psychotherapy, psychotherapy with psychotic patients, behavior therapy, and CBT and concluded: "Modest evidence now supports the claim that psychotherapy is capable of producing some beneficial changes, but the negative results still outnumber the positive findings, and both of these are exceeded by reports that are beyond interpretation" (p. 259). They were favorably impressed by the data on behavior therapy outcomes and the promise of cognitive methods: "There are well-established methods for reducing anxieties and fears . . . good progress has been made in . . . dealing with obsessions and compulsions, and significant advances have been made in dealing with some sexual dysfunctions" (p. 261).

Stiles, Shapiro, and Elliot (1986) argued that the psychotherapy outcome data still "appear to support the conclusion that outcomes of diverse therapies are generally similar. . . . The lack of differential effectiveness contrasted with evident technical diversity; that is, outcome equivalence contrasted with content nonequivalence" (p. 165).

On the basis of the Smith and Glass and other meta-analyses and reviews that examined the relative efficacy of psychotherapies, Lambert and Bergin (1994) concluded:

There is a strong trend toward no difference between techniques in amount of change produced, which is counterbalanced by indications that, under some circumstances, cognitive and behavioral methods are superior even though they do not generally differ in efficacy between themselves. An examination of selected exemplary studies allows us to further explore this matter. Research carried out with the intent of contrasting two or more bonafide treatments show surprisingly small differences between the outcomes for patients who undergo a treatment that is fully intended to be therapeutic. (p. 158)

Inclusion of Bona Fide Psychotherapies Only

Most meta-analyses of direct comparisons of psychotherapies have included treatments that may not have been intended to be therapeutic. Wampold, Mondin, Moody, Stich, et al. (1997) use the term "bona fide psychotherapies" to refer to those that are delivered by trained therapists, are based on psychological principles, and are offered to the psychotherapy community as viable treatments (e.g., through professional books or manuals) or contained specified components.

When only those cases that could be considered to represent bona fide treatments were compared, D. Shapiro and Shapiro (1982) found only two significant differences out of thirteen treatment comparisons; Shadish, Montgomery, et al. (1993) found one out of ten; and Robinson, Berman, and Neimeyer (1990) found four out of six.

Wampold, Mondin, Moody, Stich, et al. (1997) conducted a selective meta-analysis restricted to consideration of 114 studies that directly compared two or more bona fide psychotherapies. The "Dodo bird hypothesis" states that when treatments intended to be therapeutic are compared, the true difference between all such treatments is zero. The results of the Wampold meta-analysis suggest that the efficacy of bona fide treatments are comparable, although not necessarily interchangeable. (See Table 11.2.)

TABLE 11.2 Summary of Effect Sizes Produced by Meta-Analyses of Psychotherapy Outcomes

Comparison	Size of Effect
Psychotherapy vs. no treatment	.82
Psychotherapy vs. placebo	.48
Placebo vs. no treatment	.42
Differences between bona fide psychotherapies	.00 < ES < .21

From B. Wampold, G. Mondin, M. Moody, F. Stich, K. Benson, and H. Ahn (1997), "A Meta-Analysis of Outcome Studies Comparing Bona Fide Psychotherapies," *Psychological Bulletin, 122.* Copyright © 1997 by the American Psychological Association. Reprinted with permission. Effect sizes for the first three comparisons were derived by Lambert and Bergin (1994) from extant meta-analyses.

Some criticize Wampold for aggregating the effect sizes across outcome measures, arguing that some measures are of more importance than others and that aggregation tends to level responses across different treatments. Another problem related to aggregation is that researchers may have included dependent variables that were not expected to be sensitive to the treatment without making this explicit. Wampold treated targeted and secondary variables identically. Crits-Christoph (1997) points out that "if one treatment is superior to another on the primary presenting problems, but equal to the other treatment on other outcomes, the first treatment remains clinically more important, yet this difference is obscured through averaging of outcome measures" (p. 216). Avoiding this problem in the future will require that researchers clearly identify central outcome variables.

Others have indicted the Wampold study on grounds of unrepresentativeness. About 35% of the 114 articles used undergraduates (almost always solicited) as participants, rather than more representative samples of patients (Crits-Christoph, 1997). In addition, roughly 69% of the articles involved comparisons of cognitive and behavioral treatments for anxiety problems.

> The lack of differences between cognitive and behavioral treatments in particular does not mean that other types of noncognitive or nonbehavioral treatments would fare equally well with patients having anxiety problems. There are only four studies on psychodynamic therapy, three studies of child or adolescent treatment, and zero studies of family therapy in the meta-analysis. To the extent that distorted cognitions about the consequences of taking some action (e.g., belief that one would lose control, die, be ridiculed) are involved in anxiety, both cognitive (i.e., using verbal methods to convince a patient of the irrationality of their beliefs, thereby encouraging them to try something new) and behavioral (exposure treatment that demonstrates that the feared outcome does not happen) techniques might be effective ways of changing patients' chronic expectations and beliefs and thereby reduce their anxiety. (Crits-Christoph, 1997, p. 217)

Various methodological factors have been found to shape observed relationships between treatment approach and outcome. For instance, Shadish and Sweeney (1991) found that measurement reactivity, specificity, and manipulability, as well as number of participants and setting, moderated the association between treatment technique and effect size. They also found that treatment standardization and behavioral-dependent variables mediated the relationship between therapeutic orientation and effect size. Even if we consider only studies that contain direct comparisons of different psychotherapies, a few confounds remain, such as expertise of therapist and allegiance of researcher (Robinson, Berman, & Neimeyer, 1990). If allegiance to a particular treatment increases the efficacy of this treatment or decreases the efficacy of the treatment with which it is compared, then allegiance should tend to increase the size of the difference in treatment efficacy. Other possible confounds include treatment duration, skill of therapist, and nonrandom assignment.

However, despite various criticisms, the results of Wampold's study show fairly convincingly that the treatments that have interested researchers do not produce even weak evidence of differential effectiveness. All bona fide, psychologically grounded therapies appear to be comparably helpful (Wampold, Mondin, Moody, Stich, et al., 1997). However, the critical question may not be whether or not all bona fide therapies are similarly helpful, but rather whether treatments are interchangeable for particular diagnoses. The Wampold meta-analysis does not support the contention that treatments are interchangeable. Although the meta-analysts found negligible differences between bona fide psychotherapies (based on established psychological principles and use of an established manual or practiced by those with at least a master's degree), they did not find that all treatments work equally well for all problems.

There are about 250 types of therapy and 300 disorders (Goldfried & Wolfe, 1996). Some therapies are specific to disorders (e.g., exposure treatments for phobias), whereas others are more appropriate for a wide variety of disorders (e.g., cognitive therapies). Conversely, some disorders are amenable to many treatments (e.g., depression), whereas others may not be (e.g., obsessive-compulsive disorder). Consequently, it would be unwarranted to conclude from this study that all therapies are equally effective with all disorders.

The failure of the Wampold meta-analysis, the NIMH TDCRP, and other studies to find evidence of significant outcome differences across treatments raises some interesting questions about this way of establishing a given treatment's superiority. Perhaps all therapists, regardless of the theory they start with, are working to achieve the same desired outcome. If we only compare methods at the endpoint, when these different paths have converged, we should expect few differences (assuming all approaches have been given sufficient time to evolve workable solutions to clients' problems).

One especially exciting series of studies explored the common neurophysiological effects of radically different treatments for obsessive-compulsive disorder (Baxter et al., 1990, 1992). PET scans revealed similar changes in the caudate nucleus and other brain structures in OCD patients treated with either behavioral exposure therapy or a selective serotonin reuptake inhibitor (Prozac).

Apparently the same therapeutic ends can be achieved through a variety of means. Outcome may not be the best way of meaningfully differentiating among treatment approaches. Efficiency, provider prerequisites (training, personality qualities, etc.), and client comfort during treatment (both medication and psychotherapy have side effects, some quite unpleasant) may be more appropriate ways of comparing different treatment approaches, if in fact all are fairly identical in terms of their ability to achieve the desired outcome.

Often the existing comparative research looks at the impact of different treatments on groups of clients with heterogeneous problems and symptom manifestations (Lambert, Shapiro, & Bergin, 1986). This makes it difficult to use these studies to justify the choice of a particular intervention in a specific case. Even when studies focus on particular diagnoses, individual differences among clients carrying a given label are rarely explored, in order to assess treatment by patient personality characteristic effects (Blatt et al., 1995). This failure to investigate personality variation among similarly diagnosed patients precludes our detecting ways in which individual differences (e.g., in perfectionism) may mediate treatment impact.

Opposition to the EST Approach

Identifying treatments that are empirically validated has been linked to the survival of applied psychology, given advances in biological psychiatry (Task Force on Promotion, 1995). The goal of the empirical validation movement is to identify a small set of treatments that satisfy criteria, which are based on the assumption that the unique ingredients of the treatment are responsible for the efficacy of the treatment (Wampold, 1997). Unfortunately, Wampold, Mondin, Moody, Stich, et al. (1997) argue that the empirical validation strategy actually weakens support for psychotherapy as a mental health treatment rather than strengthens it. D. Klein (1996), an advocate of psychopharmacological treatments, summed up the issue succinctly: "The bottom line is that if the Food and Drug Administration (FDA) was responsible for the evaluation of psychotherapy, then no current psychotherapy would be approvable, whereas particular medications are clearly approvable" (p. 84). The basis of this bold statement is that the FDA requires that the efficacy of active ingredients of any medication be established. Klein argued cogently that CBT for depression is contraindicated because (1) CBT has not been shown to be more effective than placebo conditions; (2) various psychotherapies do not differ in terms of efficacy; and (3) CBT did not appear to be effective with those patients for whom it was indicated, denigrating the importance of the active ingredients in CBT. (See Jacobson et al., 1996, for the results that failed to validate the active ingredients of CBT.) Klein (1996) concluded, in an attempt to damn psychotherapy, that

> [The results of the NIMH study and other studies] are inexplicable on the basis of the therapeutic action theories propounded by the creators of IPT [interpersonal psychotherapy] and CBT. However they are entirely compatible with the hypothesis . . . that psychotherapies are not doing anything specific; rather, they are nonspecifically beneficial to the final common pathway of demoralization, to the degree that they are effective at all. (p. 82)

However, if we are drawing parallels to medicine, we should remember that there we don't consider a treatment invalid if another is equally effective (e.g., Tylenol, aspirin, ibuprofen for pain relief; different antibiotics; different antidepressant medications). There are many medical interventions that produce equivalent results in the treatment of an illness.

Wampold (1997) argues that Klein's (1996) criticism is painful only if one accepts the necessity of validating psychotherapy based on active ingredients. If one gives up the belief that psychotherapy treatments are analogous to medications and places faith in the scientific evidence that psychotherapy in general is extremely efficacious (Lambert & Bergin, 1994) but that relative differences are minimal, research in psychotherapy would differ considerably from the present focus on clinical trials. Why is it that researchers persist in attempts to find treatment differences, when they know that these effects are small in comparison to other effects, such as therapist effects (Crits-Christoph et al., 1991; Crits-Christoph & Mintz, 1991) or effects of treatment versus no-treatment comparisons (Lambert

& Bergin, 1994)? Common factors seem to be most important. However, the EST proponents are interested primarily in helping clinicians select the most appropriate treatments given particular disorders.

Some conclude that all psychotherapies are equally effective, so there is no need to focus on those with empirical efficacy data in particular. The Task Force on Promotion and Dissemination of Psychological Procedures answers this criticism by stating that current research has "led to more interpretable findings, with some treatments being superior to others depending on the disorder." Both the criticism and the Task Force reply represent the extremes of the argument clearly described by Norcross (1995). On the one hand, there is the "Dodo bird verdict" that all psychotherapies produce equivalent outcomes. On the other hand, there are those who subscribe to the "exclusivity myth"—a single psychotherapy is best for certain treatment outcomes. As Norcross eloquently states, "Different psychotherapies can and have specific effects, if you look with sufficient power in the right places. But specific effects do not translate into exclusive ownership" (p. 500).

The naysayers camp has a relatively easy job. Variability is on their side, because it inflates the chances of failures to find significant differences across treatments. We don't know everything, so there's no point in trying to match method and patient more specifically.

The EST camp has a more formidable task. Variability is their enemy. Recognizing the multidetermined nature of treatment outcomes, they labor to try to control for as many factors as they can in trying to demonstrate the unique effects of one particular type of intervention. To the extent they can build control into their designs, they're doomed to endure the criticism that their research lacks external validity: "We can't generalize from your rarefied study because in actual practice we can't prescreen our patients." To the extent their designs lack control and target heterogeneous populations, standard deviations climb and treatment effects appear equivalent.

When Specifics Matter

In certain cases, research has shown that some methods work better than others. Crits-Christoph (1997) examined the studies sampled in the Wampold et al. meta-analysis and found a trend among studies showing that CBT was superior to other types of therapy. He maintained that the Wampold meta-analysis may have obscured important exceptions to the general equivalence of psychotherapeutic efficacy. However, Wampold et al. argue that Crits-Christoph failed to aggregate all studies containing a cognitive-behavioral treatment and looked selectively at dependent measures.

Crits-Christoph (1997) maintains that differences between therapies are only expected for treatments of severe disorders: "With mild conditions, the nonspecific effects of treatments . . . are likely to be powerful enough in themselves to affect . . . outcomes, leaving little room for the specific factors to play much of a role" (p. 217). In a reanalysis of the Wampold et al. data, only 50 of the original 277 effects met the criteria of *DSM-IV* diagnosis and assessment at termination. Review of these showed results similar to the original analysis, although some of the studies showed greater effects.

There are cases in the literature of studies pointing to the advantages of specific interventions in working with particular presenting problems. For example, research by Foa, Rothbaum, et al. (1991) supported the use of CBT rather than a strict supportive, solution-focused approach in cases of rape. Apparently deflecting women from discussing their recent rape in counseling is less therapeutic than giving them cognitive problem-solving tools for restoring their sense of safety and competence.

Gallagher-Thompson and Steffen (1994) found that CBT was most effective for treating caregivers with depression who had been giving care for long periods of time, whereas psychodynamic therapy was most effective for treating those caregivers with depression who had been giving care for shorter periods of time. Mavissakalian et al. (1983) found that at termination paradoxical intention was far superior to self-statement training in the treatment of agoraphobia (although this superiority was not present at followup).

According to Crits-Christoph (1997), RCTs offer evidence of specific therapy effects. Some of their placebo conditions adequately control for common ingredients in psychotherapy. The effects of psychotherapies that are superior to such placebo groups are due to specific ingredients, and this then validates the therapy.

Although there aren't many studies demonstrating superiority of a psychotherapy to a pill placebo (Power, Simpson, et al., 1990), few of these studies have been performed. However, an increasing number of studies have documented the superiority of a psychotherapy to a control condition for nonspecific aspects of psychotherapy. Examples of replicated evidence for specific effects (i.e., superiority to comparison conditions that control for nonspecific elements) include cognitive therapy for panic disorder, cognitive therapy for depression, exposure therapy for agoraphobia, exposure and response prevention for obsessive-compulsive disorder, and CBT for generalized anxiety disorder (see review by DeRubeis & Crits-Christoph, 1998).

Applying Empirical Research: Using a Research-Based Rational Progression

Although at first this complex, contradictory literature may seem overwhelming, there may be useful ways to reconcile the various positions held by different researchers and practitioners. Some "nonspecific effects" people argue that it is unnecessary to apply particular techniques, because on average all techniques are similarly effective. Various empirical findings seem to lend credence to their position. To the extent that their position is true, it makes sense to follow the "hierarchy of intrusiveness," to start with the simplest, least expensive, least risky interventions (perhaps supportive, solution-focused therapy). The effectiveness of this approach can be assessed rapidly, usually after one or two sessions. If there is

Summary of the Psychotherapy Debate: Specific Techniques versus Common/Nonspecific Factors

Specific Therapies Have Specific Effects:

Internecine warfare among competing theories: Each claims superiority

Efficacy studies (RCTs)

Empirically supported treatment studies (APA, Division 12 list)

Most therapists identify themselves as "eclectic," attempting to use the best treatment for the particular patient they see (Prochaska & Norcross, 1983)

Nonspecific Factors Are More Important than Specific Factors:

Treatment of Depression Collaborative Research Program (TDCRP, 1989)

Meta-Analyses of Bona Fide Psychotherapy (Wampold, Mondin, Moody, Stich, et al., 1997)

Placebo Control Studies: Non-Behavioral Psychotherapy (Priolieu, Murdock, & Brody, 1983)

Placebo Controlled Studies of Antidepressants (Fisher & Greenberg, 1997)

PET Scans Show Same Brain Effects of Prozac and Behavior Tx (Baxter et al., 1990)

Common Factors Research (Lambert, 1992a, 1992b; Lambert & Bergin, 1994; Garfield, 1998)

---

insufficient improvement, the clinician is justified in progressing through more intrusive, specific methods.

In behavioral treatment, application of the least intrusive hierarchy has long been an accepted standard of practice (Turnbull, 1981; Scotti et al., 1991). According to this standard, the use of more aversive procedures can be justified only on the basis of the severity of the problem behavior and documentation of the failure of less intrusive methods. Although we are generally unaccustomed to thinking about specific forms of treatment such as systematic desensitization, cognitive restructuring, response prevention, EMDR, and assertiveness training as "aversive" procedures (they certainly aren't as bad as contingent electric shock), all require patients to endure considerable discomfort and to focus temporarily on experiences they would prefer to avoid. While deploying such methods when severity of diagnosis or previous treatment failure warrants is clearly justified and ethical, it might make sense to try a less stressful method initially.

While diagnosis is helpful in treatment planning, it remains insufficient because the diagnostic groups are not homogeneous with respect to all the factors that influence response to particular treatment regimes. Variability among people carrying a given diagnosis remains great, despite attempts to tighten behavioral criteria. Diagnosis does not correlate with all the variables that are relevant to attempts to optimize the match between patient and treatment. Some depressed patients will profit more from IPT, others from CBT. Until we discern the markers for this differential responsivity, clinicians must adopt an experimental mindset and remain flexible in selecting treatment tactics.

Therapists can use diagnosis to select an initial EST method (in cases of diagnostic ambiguity, after a solution-focused approach has failed). Presenting the approach constructively and confidently can enhance patient expectancy of improvement. Allowing for a potentially necessary shift of gears is also a good idea. "There are a variety of effective methods that we can use to try to help you achieve your goals. The approach we'll be using is called _____, and it is based on the following rationale. . . ."

During use of this EST the therapist should carefully monitor the patient's idiosyncratic responses. (For example, while relaxation training is generally experienced as pleasant and constructive, a percentage of patients report untoward effects and elevated anxiety. This is usually evident right away, if appropriate inquiries are made.) If there are signs of a poor match, the therapist can switch gears and offer another approach.

General Psychotherapy Strategies

Although the efficacy literature supports the use of very specific interventions in the treatment of certain disorders, other research has compellingly demonstrated the importance of general factors in psychotherapy. This section will familiarize you with three broad strategies for dealing with a wide variety of clients, based on the common factors, solution-focused therapy, and brief therapy literatures. Familiarity with these concepts will help you to mobilize healing, maximize strengths, and minimize consumers' disruptive dependence on formal helping.

Providing responsive, research-supported, reasonably priced care seems more feasible if we emphasize the findings about the role of clients' strengths and motivation in producing change. Collectively, the common factors, solution-focused, and brief therapy studies demonstrate the power of the consumer to shape outcomes. As therapists, we can set the stage, but the act is theirs.

CHAPTER

12 Psychotherapy Based on Common Factors

Common/Nonspecific/Universal Therapy Elements

The Common Factors Challenge

For decades, many clinical researchers have argued that all therapy effects stem from four factors (Garfield, 1995; Lambert, 1992): therapeutic technique, expectancy and placebo, therapeutic relationship, and client factors. The previous chapter examined how studies have generally failed to demonstrate treatment technique specificity. Luborsky, Singer, and Luborsky (1975) found that the particular school of therapy often seems to be immaterial; rather, psychotherapy works for reasons other than those theoretically postulated. Various meta-analytic reviews have confirmed that the theories clinicians hold do not seem to have any relationship to their therapy outcomes; instead, positive outcomes seem mainly attributable to other, common factors (see Bergin & Lambert, 1978; Meltzoff & Kornreich, 1970; D. Shapiro & Shapiro, 1982; Sloane et al., 1975; Smith & Glass, 1977; Smith, Glass, & Miller, 1980).

Some maintain that cognitive and behavioral approaches seem somewhat superior (Eysenck, 1993), but this could be an artifact of these methods' use of more specific and easily measured outcomes. When more general measures of functioning are considered, different approaches demonstrate comparable effect sizes (Steenbarger, 1994; Elliott, Stiles, & Shapiro, 1993).

These converging results indicate that the technical features of a particular approach account for only a small fraction of therapy's influence. Roughly 15% of clients' improvement is attributable to the specific theoretical orientation or intervention strategies of the therapist (Lambert, 1992). This is equivalent to the expectancy (or so-called placebo) effects. Common relationship factors account for 30%, or twice as much as technique, and extratherapeutic factors, such as client characteristics and fortuitous incidents in the patient's life, account for 40%.

The irony is that the bulk of psychotherapy research has been directed at examining these technical differences. Most therapy rhetoric champions one theory and its associated interventions, and most outcome studies pit standardized delivery of one set of techniques against another technique's standardized delivery. Despite the ongoing search for specific effects, large-scale meta-analyses have failed to find a "winner" among the vying techniques. Everything helps about the same, despite the enormously different rationales and contradictory premises of the various therapeutic techniques.

This implies that often, when therapy helps, it may not be helping for the reasons we think it is. Quite possibly clients aren't experiencing therapy as we imagine they are. We think they hear us clearly; maybe they don't. This could be part of why our predictions about their differential responses to varying techniques are inaccurate. They may not be assimilating much of what we intend to be communicating. Because therapy is about learning, we should recognize the limits of many learners. From the vast literature on educational outcomes, we know that human learning proceeds slowly and erratically and that distortion and inattention frequently garble the educator's message (we consider a 75% accurate grasp of conveyed material to be "C" or average work). In therapy our clients are generally emotionally distressed, which is known to interfere with information processing, so should we expect highly efficient learning? Furthermore, many of our theories provide a basis for imagining that clients have prior experiences that have distorted the way they habitually extract information from their environment. We should probably expect our clients to be even less accurate in taking in what we have to share than an average student would be. No wonder the specifics of the lessons being taught contribute modestly to therapy outcome.

It is also possible that *some* of our clients do experience therapy in the ways we intend, but that many others do not. Diagnostic and personality differences across clients may make the learning rate in therapy highly variable. In outcome studies that pool data from clients who "heard" the proffered wisdom as intended with data from those whose minds were really elsewhere much of the time, we lose the opportunity to evaluate the effectiveness of given techniques when they are actually "received" properly. Methodological changes in outcome studies, including taking measures of clients' phenomenological experiences throughout the treatment process and using them as covariates in assessing therapeutic impact, could partially address this problem. As clinicians, it would seem to be advisable for us to try to stay tuned in to our clients and what they are experiencing during our encounters. Person-centered clinicians have always advocated the need for this (Rogers, 1970), but it is relevant to all therapeutic approaches, because without attentive listening we can never be confident our messages (directive or nondirective) are getting across to clients in the ways that we intend.

If Technique Is Immaterial, What Should We Learn?

If therapeutic technique lags behind the other three factors in accounting for therapy outcomes, where should our training focus be? Does the common factors research mean that what we do doesn't make that much of a difference? Should we relax and simply "hang out" with our clients? Should we become much more methodical and systematic about how we promote positive expectancy and helpful relationship characteristics? Should we focus on the client factors and learn to respond with greater precision to different client needs?

The common factors research findings are inconsistent with an excessive reliance on a narrow application of empirically validated methods. The trend favoring greater specification of treatment technique is at odds with the conclusion of many studies highlighting the importance of patient and relationship factors over technical factors in influencing treatment outcome. If the generic components of therapy are the most influential, it might seem counterproductive to invest increasing amounts of time justifying particular technical choices through reference to the research literature. However, this trend favoring use of empirically corroborated practice guidelines seems to be unlikely to reverse.

Given this increasing pressure on clinicians to provide standard treatments of established effectiveness for a given disorder, there is a risk that psychotherapists will become even more inappropriately focused on rigid application of specific techniques. If we don't guard against this, the requirement that treatments be selected on the basis of their support in the research literature may foster less individualized and customized client care.

Researchers design studies to minimize error variance. In assessing a given treatment, they try to distill the essence of that approach and train therapists to provide that treatment as consistently as possible. Research therapists are discouraged from straying from the treatment protocol, in order to guarantee a common treatment experience for all participants. The researchers' inability to allow for much customization and creative application of a given technique may attenuate its efficacy.

This may partially explain why differences in technique fail to materialize in many outcomes studies: The standardized version of a technique may be less efficacious than an individualized presentation of that technique. If therapist spontaneity and innovation are helpful in engaging clients as learners and in communicating caring and maximizing the placebo effect, the research literature's exclusion of these things may systematically underestimate the impact of psychotherapy. Sterile, standard treatment, especially when provided by inexperienced, constrained, evaluation-apprehensive clinicians, may not be representative of the best counseling that occurs.

The standardized version of any treatment often bears little resemblance to what happens outside of a research context. In generalizing from the research setting to hospitals and community practices, we should exercise some caution. Techniques that work in analogue studies with subclinical populations may operate quite differently in the field. Techniques that work when presented in the context of a highly credible research institution may not always seem so impressive when disassociated from a formal study protocol. If we fail to duplicate the outcome measures used by the researchers, we may reduce the power of the techniques that may have stemmed from the seriousness of purpose conveyed by the elaborate measurement process used in the research study. "By-the-book" psychotherapy often fails, in part because counselors can't replicate all components of the original therapeutic milieu.

Employing standardized treatment techniques can also fail if in so doing our focus is on an abstract set of directions, rather than on the idiosyncratic individual before us. If we allow ourselves to become too program-centered, we may miss the client. Following the latest instructions for treating a borderline client, based on recent outcome data, may have miserable results if we get so lost in duplicating the standard method described by the experimenters that we fail to pay attention to our client's wandering attention. Keeping clients engaged may make a bigger difference in whether or not they learn and change than the specific things we have them think or do. The nontechnical components of therapeutic style seem to make a bigger difference than technique.

Client and Therapist Factors Contribute the Most

The complex interplay between client and therapist qualities shapes treatment outcome more powerfully than specific interventions. There are enormous differences between therapists (Luborsky et al., 1985). Some are quite good, and some things therapists do are "psychonoxious" or harmful to patients. Therapists can help or hurt—5%–10% of patients deteriorate in psychotherapy (Lambert, Shapiro, & Bergin, 1986; Ogles, Lambert, & Sawyer, 1995), and to the extent we can develop process and outcome measures that address these effects, we can improve our profession and help therapists develop less harmful and more and more helpful approaches.

With the development of ESTs there is accumulating evidence of the differential effectiveness of certain techniques for certain delimited disorders. Many agree that the intense focus on specific problems is yielding some promising results. However, the evidence consistently demonstrates that rigid application of particular theoretical models of psychotherapy has not produced advantages in designing treatments. Rather, it appears that there are many useful ways to achieve particular outcomes, and that it is the sharp focus on the problem, rather than the theory from which the interventions are derived, that is the operative agent (L. Johnson, 1995).

As Duncan (1997) points out, 30 years' of research evidence makes it clear that the similarities rather than the differences between models account for most of the change that clients experience across therapies. What emerges from examining these similarities is a group of common factors that cut across models.

The greatest support for emphasizing common factors comes from studies that originally set out to demonstrate the unique effects of one particular approach or another and instead found that all models work equally well. The body of this work indirectly but unequivocally demonstrates the importance of a set of core factors common to all methods that really account for therapy's positive outcome, regardless of what the model's theoreticians believe. Unfortunately, these factors do not, in themselves, have the ideological allure that initially draws many practitioners to a given model.

Four factors, each central to all forms of therapy despite theoretical orientation, mode (e.g., individual, group, marriage, family), or dosage (frequency and number of sessions) underlie the effectiveness of therapy (Duncan & Moynihan, 1994; Duncan, Solovey, & Rusk, 1992; Frank & Frank, 1991; Lambert, 1992). These factors are: the client, the therapeutic relationship, expectancy and placebo effects, and therapeutic technique.

Client Factors

The client is the single most potent determinant of treatment outcome, contributing an impressive 40% to outcome. The quality of clients' participation in treatment and their perceptions of the therapist and what the therapist is doing determine whether any type of treatment will work. In fact, the totality of who clients are (their strengths and resources, the duration of their complaints, their social supports, the environments in which they live, even fortuitous events that weave in and out of their lives) matters more in shaping therapeutic success than anything therapists might do. The impact of their contribution when compared to other factors serves as a powerful reminder that whatever the theory, model, or nature of the therapeutic relationship, however renowned the therapist or impressive the procedure, no change is likely to occur without the client's engagement.

The research on self-help approaches discussed earlier corroborates this point. In the treatment of anxiety and depression (the two most common mental health complaints), self-help approaches work about as well as treatments conducted by therapists. These findings highlight the fact that the most influential contributor to change is the client—not the therapy, not the technique, not the therapist, but the client.

Therapeutic Relationship Effects

Lambert (1992a, 1992b) estimates that the therapeutic relationship contributes roughly 30% to outcome in psychotherapy, making it a far more important factor than either expectancy or therapeutic technique. Clients who are motivated and connected with the therapist in a shared pursuit profit the most from therapy. Their participation largely results from the alliance that they establish with the helping professional. Studies indicate that the consumer's level of participation in therapy is the single most important determinant of outcome. In addition, several studies have found that clients' ratings of the therapeutic alliance, rather than the therapists' perceptions of it, are most highly correlated with treatment outcome.

Many studies have explored the importance of core relational processes operating across treatments (Imber & Evanczuk, 1990). Much of this work assumes that all participants in the therapeutic process, therapists *and* patients, are active, vital contributors to its outcome.

In a study assessing the differential impact of several types of therapy on patients with major depressive disorder, Beutler et al. (1991) found that the interaction of the coping style of clients and treatment effects was much greater than the main effects. Similarly, Kopta et al. (1994) found an interaction between symptom type and outcome. As McCullough et al. (1991) conclude, therapist interventions and patient responses are best studied in the context of the other. The quality of this interpersonal context is seen by Strupp (1995) as "the sine qua non in all forms of psychotherapy."

A characteristic of an optimal therapeutic relationship is focus; focus distinguishes brief, effective psychotherapy from counseling that is neither brief nor effective. In a good therapeutic relationship the patient strongly believes that therapy is doing what he or she wants it to do. The patient and therapist have consensus about the goals of therapy. Managed care therapists must understand how to co-create and manage a useful focus and how to communicate that to reviewers.

Other core processes found in the literature include the meeting of expectations (Silverman & Beech, 1979), capacity of the therapist to relate (Najavits & Strupp, 1994), the working alliance (Horvath & Symonds, 1991), and the therapeutic bond. According to a review by Luborsky et al. (1988), outcome correlates with alliance or relationship at approximately the .50 level.

A positive alliance seems to develop most reliably when the therapist is empathic, genuine, and respectful. These are the relationship factors that humanistic psychotherapist Carl Rogers considered to be the "core conditions" of effective psychotherapy.

In a series of studies on the conditions that promoted constructive personality change in both psychiatric inpatients and college counseling center clients, Truax and Carkhuff (1964, 1965, 1967) found that a sensitive and accurate attempt at therapeutic understanding of the client was very facilitative. This is an empathic response to the clients' being, which clients perceive as meaning they have been understood. Truax and Carkhuff found that nonpossessive warmth and counselor genuineness were variables that also promoted client growth. The rationale for the effectiveness of these ingredients is stated by the investigators as follows:

> The greater the degree of the therapist's accurate empathic understanding of the client, the greater the degree to which the therapist shows unconditional or nonpossessive warmth or integration of the therapist within the relationship, and the more intense and intimate the therapist in the relationship, the greater will be the degree of the client's interpersonal exploration and the greater will be the consequent extent of positive behavior change. (Truax and Carkhuff, 1964, p. 861)

If these ingredients are present in the relationship, clients may feel more free to be themselves and face their problems (Brammer, Abrego, & Shostrom, 1993). Truax and Mitchell (1971) reviewed research on various therapist qualities and concluded that counselors who are accurately empathic, genuine, and nonpossessively warm in attitude tend to be effective with a wide variety of clients regardless of their training or theoretical orientation. They also found that clients receiving low levels of facilitative conditions deteriorated.

Empathy has long been understood to be a primary determinant of therapeutic outcome. Retrospective accounts by former clients typically describe relationship qualities such as support and understanding as being the most helpful factors in successful therapy (Cross, Sheehan, & Kahn, 1982). However, in a study examining the outcomes of professionals and paraprofessionals working with children, Karlsruher (1976) unexpectedly found that ratings of therapist-offered empathy, warmth, and genuineness were negatively related to positive client change. In a more recent review of the literature, Gelso and Carter (1985) maintain that "the conditions originally specified by Rogers are neither necessary nor sufficient, although it seems clear that such conditions are facilitative" (p. 220). They also suggest that client deterioration is not related in a "clear, linear way" to low counselor facilitativeness, but rather to a complex constellation of therapist and client relationship variables. Gelso and Carter point out that much of the research based on Rogers's theories has looked at therapist variables and has ignored the two-way interaction that the therapeutic relationship involves.

Recent research indicates that strong alliances are most likely to be formed when clients perceive the therapist as warm, trustworthy, nonjudgmental, and empathic. Therapists' own evaluations of their success in creating this kind of therapeutic environment for the client are insufficient. Each client seems to experience the core conditions differently, so sensitivity to individual difference among patients is very important. The most helpful alliances tend to develop when the therapists establish a therapeutic environment that matches the client's definition of empathy, genuineness, and respect.

Expectancy and Placebo Effects

As a factor determining outcome, the impact of specific technique is equivalent to that of nonspecific placebo or expectancy factors. Seeking help from a formal caregiver increases hope and positive expectation of improvement. "He cures most successfully in whom the people have the most confidence," said Galen, the Greek physician, in the second century. Symptom relief with placebo is on average identical with that from 4 months of psychotherapy (Frank, 1978).

> The collaboration between therapist and client creates an experience of hope and optimistic possibility that many clients prize whether or not their specific presenting problems disappear. Not only does the process of being in such a relationship feel good to many clients, it may also have outcome benefits that have thus far eluded easy measurement. Even when the outcomes are not clinically significant, many clients are satisfied, and feel they have derived great benefit from the experience. They may not resolve their problem with one therapist, enter therapy with another, still not resolve the original issue, but nonetheless feel satisfied with both experiences of therapy! For many people, the process of treatment itself seems to provide some subtle but significant and meaningful benefits that have so far eclipsed our effort to measure or even define them. The power of the therapeutic alliance and the availability of a person who, at the very least, is present and caring should never be underestimated. (Jacobson, 1995, p. 39)

D. Shapiro and Shapiro (1997) argue that although the placebo effect is frequently disparaged, it is a powerful part of all healing. The history of medicine is largely the history of placebos: When subjected to scientific scrutiny, the overwhelming majority of treatments have turned out to derive their benefits from the placebo effect. Although medical treatments undergo rigorous testing to prove their effectiveness, many experts estimate that as few as 20% of the treatments routinely used by physicians today have actually been proved to be effective (W. Brown, 1997).

A placebo can be thought of as the components of care that have no specific, active therapeutic value for the condition being treated, but that nonetheless produce improvement. Some documented placebo effects in medicine have been very striking. For example, in the 1950s, many patients with angina pectoris (chest pain caused by insufficient blood supply to the heart) underwent a standard internal mammary artery ligation, a surgical procedure believed at the time to increase the heart's blood supply. The results were very encouraging: Up to 90% of the surgical patients experienced symptom relief. In an experimental evaluation of this procedure, those patients receiving the standard surgical procedure were compared with those randomly assigned to a placebo control group, who received only "sham" surgery. The sham surgery patients received a chest incision, in order to produce comparable expectancy of improvement (a credible placebo control), but none of their arteries were rerouted. With the standard surgery, 76% of patients improved; with the sham (placebo) surgery, 100% improved. These results demonstrated that the apparent benefits of the internal mammary artery ligation were actually attributable to the placebo effect (Roberts, Kewman, & Mercier, 1993).

Although some are appalled by the use of sham surgery in the preceding investigation, it is important to consider what might have happened if surgeons had never submitted the then standard method to experimental test. Without the realization that this procedure was not contributing anything specific to improvement, presumably surgeons would have continued to use this technique (with the attendant mortality risks associated with any heart surgery) rather than improving cardiac treatment methods.

It has been estimated that across various afflictions, including pain, high blood pressure, rheumatoid arthritis, asthma, and coughs, about 30% to 40% of patients experience significant relief with placebos alone. In some cases an astonishing 60% to 70% of patients will improve from placebos.

Double-blind clinical trials show that about half of patients with depression or anxiety obtain significant relief with placebo treatment (Fisher & Greenberg, 1997). In mild depression, placebo pills are almost as effective as antidepressants; about 60% to 70% of mildly depressed patients recover with antidepressant medication, 30% to 70% with placebos. The less severe the depression, the more likely it is to improve with placebo treatment. In severe depression, placebo treatment seems to be less effective than antidepressant drugs and electroconvulsive therapy (ECT); about 20% to 30% of severely depressed people recover with placebo treatment, whereas 60% to 70% recover with antidepressants and 80% to 90% with ECT. However, some attribute this to differential credibility in the active treatment and the placebo conditions (R. Greenberg et al., 1992). Comparisons between placebos and various types of psychotherapy for depression, including interpersonal therapy, behavior therapy, and cognitive therapy, have consistently shown that placebos are as effective as any of the psychotherapies, at least on measures of short-term improvement. A study reported in the *European Journal of Psychiatry* showed that people with schizophrenia who take placebo pills are less likely to relapse than those who receive no treatment.

Placebos may work in part by reducing the distress of the illness, so it comes as little surprise that placebo treatment seems most effective for afflictions in which distress directly affects the symptoms. In certain forms of depression and anxiety, for example, distress defines the illness, and placebos are remarkably effective. Pain often improves with placebo treatment, as do asthma and moderate high blood pressure; in these conditions, distress is one of the symptoms or contributes directly to the symptoms (W. Brown, 1997).

Frank (1961, 1978) has long argued that powerful placebo factors underscore much of the power of psychotherapy. The degree to which a client benefits from psychological treatment is a product of multiple factors, including clients' expectancies for therapeutic outcome (Safren, Heimberg, & Juster, 1997). From a clinical perspective, the data suggest that early detection of low expectancies for treatment outcome should be a priority. Low expectancies for treatment outcome should become a specific focus of attention early on, and this approach should be most seriously considered for severely or chronically impaired clients (Safren, Heimberg, & Juster, 1997).

The elicitation of hopeful optimism is greatly influenced by the therapist's attitude toward the client during the opening moments of therapy. Pessimistic attitudes conveyed to the client through an emphasis on negative symptoms, underlying psychopathological processes, or tales of the difficult road ahead are likely to work against the placebo effect. In contrast, an emphasis on strengths, possibilities, and the message that therapy can work will probably enhance placebo reactions and help to counteract demoralization, mobilize hope, and promote improvement.

Therapeutic Technique

During sessions, therapists ask questions, listen and reflect, dispense reassurance, challenge and confront, provide information and clarification, offer explanations, reframe and interpret, make suggestions, self-disclose, present exercises, and assign homework tasks. The specific content of the interchanges with patients often varies considerably as a function of the therapist's orientation. However, independent of the model being employed, most treatments share a common feature. In one way or another, they seek to prepare clients to take some form of action to help themselves. Across all types of therapy, therapists expect their patients to do something different in the future, whether the emphasis is on the development of new understandings, new freedom to experience emotions, new capacity to confront one's most feared situations, new willingness to take risks, or adoption of new patterns of interpersonal behavior.

As noted previously, Lambert estimates that the therapist's specific technique contributes only 15% to the impact of psychotherapy (Lambert, 1992). While this may be troubling to advocates of particular schools of therapy who take pride in their uniquely accurate conceptualization of the optimal treatment process, the data are unequivocal: Patients are largely unimpressed by their therapist's particular technique.

> Patients don't appreciate techniques and they don't regard them as necessary. They hardly ever mention a specific technical intervention the therapist made. I'd encourage therapists to realize that their phenomenological world regarding the experience of therapy is quite different from that of their patients. The nontechnical aspects are the ones patients mention. Also, when objective judges listen to tapes of therapy, the nontechnical aspects are the things that correlate with outcome more than any technical intervention. (Lambert, 1992)

Although many seem to mystify the process of therapy, often commonsense interventions are of real value. In fact, sometimes therapists may become so focused on certain technical approaches that they may inadvertently sacrifice their effectiveness. For example, in accounting for the superior results of insight-oriented marital therapy (IOMT) when compared with behavioral therapy, Jacobson (1991) argued that it was due to the IOMT therapists' heavy reliance on nonspecific clinically sensitive interventions allowed in their manual but not mentioned in the behavioral manual. When a particular treatment method proscribes use of nonspecific, commonsense strategies, it may yield poorer outcomes. It appears that flexibility is necessary to maximize clinical effectiveness.

Obfuscating, mystifying theories and jargon aside, the empirical data suggest that successful psychotherapy should be construed as a rather simple, straightforward business, distinguishable from other helpful experiences in life only by the explicit, formal contract to be helpful that exists between a therapist and client. Although clinical work may frequently be frustrating, that does not mean that the factors contributing to successful psychotherapy are necessarily terribly complicated. The previously discussed literature indicating the effectiveness of minimally trained and paraprofessional psychotherapists attests to the fact that the skills necessary for providing effective psychotherapy may be relatively easy to master, at least for some types of people (Dawes, 1994; Lambert & Bergin, 1994; Stein & Lambert, 1984).

Therapeutic Conditions: What Constitutes Quality Treatment?

The improvement a patient experiences following psychological treatment is due to multiple factors, some specific to the techniques employed by the therapist and others that are common to a wide variety of intervention strategies (Frank, 1973; Frank & Frank, 1993; Kazdin, 1992; Kazdin & Wilcoxon, 1976; Strupp, 1989). These shared, nonspecific, or universal sources of influence are often referred to as the common factors underlying psychotherapy.

Jerome Frank (1961) posited that a core group of factors was responsible for the relatively uniform outcomes of different treatment models. Frank (1978) identified four features shared by all psychotherapies: a person in distress, an expert, an explanation for the condition, and a healing ritual. Frank believes these features reverse demoralization and promote the expectation of recovery. The decision to seek treatment restores some sense of control. The symbols and rituals of healing offer reassurance. The prognosis, when favorable, reduces fear and uncertainty and, even when unfavorable, reduces the distress of uncertainty. A credible treatment mobilizes hope and creates the expectation of improvement. Studies by Strupp and Hadley have empirically supported many of Frank's ideas.

According to Howard, Krause, et al. (1997), some investigators have argued that it is not vital or even relevant to justify psychotherapy by demonstrating that different therapies contain unique active ingredients as medications are purported to. Lambert and Bergin (1994) have emphasized that common factors should not be interpreted as inert factors and have listed thirty common factors existing across therapies. Klein (1996) also described some of these factors: "A strong, knowledgeable, professional ally who therapeutically provides the patient with emotional support, usable coping skills, and success experiences and helps reframe life experiences so as to heighten self-esteem" (p. 82).

There is evidence that the more successful indigenous healers in the non-Western world may possess personalities that inspire confidence and respect for their personal power, while demonstrating empathy for the client's experience (Kleinman, 1988; Frank & Frank, 1991; A. Shapiro & Shapiro, 1997). In North America, research on psychotherapists has identified the tendency of effective therapists to have warm, supportive personalities (Truax & Carkhuff, 1962; Luborsky, Singer, & Luborsky, 1985).

How Is Therapy Distinctive from Other Helping?

What do we provide our patients that others in their lives usually don't? What makes the therapy relationship distinctive? Therapists strive to provide their patients with (1) objective cognitive reactions and (2) objective emotional reactions. The former includes information to help clarify patients' inner experiences and offer a reasonable explanation for what they are currently experiencing. In this way therapy provides two extremely important reassuring meta-messages: (1) This isn't worse than it is; (2) This uncomfortable state is probably temporary. Our objective emotional reactions, even to patients' extremism, are often very different from what other people in their lives provide. Our empathic and nonjudgmental reactions to patients' reports of even extreme emotional states and bizarre ideation convey two additional reassuring meta-messages: (1) You're not alone; (2) You're not bad.

Patients entering therapy are making a choice to deal with their problems rather than simply feeling overwhelmed by them. The therapist is an objective outsider with little investment in perpetuating the patient's previous coping strategies.

Therapy may interrupt the patient's self-defeating cycle. Starting therapy initiates a process of seeking changes in one's environment and lifestyle and taking risks and trying new things.

Another way of thinking about how common factors operate in psychotherapy emphasizes three processes. First, patients come to therapy with a subjectively experienced need that is sufficiently high to justify their taking the active, often threatening step of seeking help from a mental health professional. This suggests that, at the beginning of treatment, those seeking help on their own are generally highly motivated to change. The therapeutic setting establishes an expectation of improvement, and placebo factors may begin to operate. Although the mechanisms underlying placebo reactions are unknown, we assume placebos produce symptomatic improvement by reducing anxiety that inhibits usual coping and reestablishment of psychic and physical equilibrium. Those close to the patient who know about their beginning treatment are also affected; their expectations of improvement rise, possibly facilitating the patient's making changes.

Second, all forms of psychotherapy require at least some minimal disclosure to a therapist. Unless the therapist actively interferes with this process (for instance, by saying things that make it clear that he or she is on an entirely different wavelength), having someone listen to our self-disclosures usually leaves us feeling understood and more accepted. Most people find this intrinsically reinforcing. We might speculate that years of evolution have shaped our brains to take pleasure in social connection and to find its opposite intensely disturbing. Alienation and social disconnection threatened our ancestors' survival. Early humans who reacted to isolation with feelings of subjective distress and who were motivated by anxiety to correct the problem by rejoining the group had a significantly better chance of transmitting their DNA to the next generation. As a result, human brains may remain "suckers" for the experience of interpersonal acceptance.

The interesting thing about this is that if being accepted activates pleasurable feelings, even if the main source of our problems is not being addressed, this process may at least temporarily distract us from our specific problems. Feeling better, we may react to events more optimistically, which might unleash more effective coping efforts and willingness to take risks in other unrelated areas. What starts as a positive social interaction may have pervasive indirect effects.

Third, treatment requires patients to develop some sort of a goal or objective. Even in nondirective therapy there is an implicit goal that at least the client will attend scheduled meetings punctually. Having goals of any kind makes patients accountable. If any of their goals are achieved, their success can contribute to increased feelings of perceived self-efficacy. Doing anything right can help "remoralize" a discouraged patient. Compensatory self-improvement has long been a technique intentionally used by some existential therapists. Just being a reasonably good patient (following through on the obligation to show up or call to cancel, talking during meetings, etc.) may provide a sense of competence that helps patients to begin to think of themselves as capable of succeeding in other endeavors. This conceptualization parallels that of Weinberger (1995), who outlines four common features of psychotherapy: expectations, confronting problems, mastery, and attribution.

Therapists' Personalities Shape Treatment

Clinical training is designed to maximize the counselor's effectiveness in helping others. While many students expect training to equip them with a new, exotic arsenal of techniques that mysteriously yields client change, counseling trainees soon discover that the basis for most of their future helping activities lies in their personalities and the interpersonal skills they've been developing over the course of their life times. Accordingly, therapeutic practices vary widely.

Different therapists are comfortable with different approaches, because some are more consistent with their general personal style. The therapist's own confidence in and ease in delivering a technique is central to its effective use; therefore, therapists tend to have greater success with helping strategies that are consonant with their natural interpersonal style. The plurality of helping techniques parallels the plurality of therapist personalities. The fact that experienced therapists understandably advocate the techniques that they like best and that work best for them can complicate training if the student expects to be able to adopt the experienced clinician's approach wholesale. There is no one best therapy. Clients bring divergent needs and goals to therapy. Therapists' personalities mediate the impact of a particular technique.

Effective therapists are skillful at increasing patient motivation for change (Meichenbaum & Turk, 1987). In fact, Patterson and Chamberlain (1992) suggest that the therapist is the strongest contributor to resistance to change in patients. Successful treatments facilitate change in patients. Many of those changes occur outside of sessions and are then reported to the therapist, discussed, and reinforced, in order to promote additional change. The use of homework assignments is common to most eclectic or integrative approaches. In today's briefer therapy, patients can benefit by developing relapse prevention skills.

Common Factors in Treatment of Depression

Probably the most impressive study supporting an emphasis on exploring the common factors underlying apparently disparate therapies is the previously discussed NIMH TDCRP (e.g., Elkin, Shea, et al., 1989), which compared three forms of treatment for depression, IPT, CBT, and imipramine plus clinical management (IM-CM), and a placebo control plus clinical management (PLA-CM). The primary analysis of the data showed comparable effectiveness for all three treatment approaches. Nor were hypothesized treatment-specific differences found when the outcome measures were analyzed individually (Imber et al., 1990). These findings seem to support the notion that nonspecific treatment effects should be our greatest concern and that it is unproductive to continue research efforts to discern treatment-specific effects (Butler & Strupp, 1986). Some contend this may be especially true in the case of short-term therapies (Blatt et al., 1995).

Our priority should be facilitating the operation of the common therapeutic factors as quickly as possible, without a preoccupation with a particular theoretical school. We should not be bound by particular schools of therapy or become bogged down with specific arrays of interventions. Different therapeutic approaches should be viewed through this lens: Given that your opportunity to make a difference in a client's life will be increasingly limited, how can you have the most profound impact in the shortest amount of time? What is your most effective set of tools to mobilize the client's expectation of improvement and motivation to make changes? Most clinicians have functioned as eclectic technical experimenters for quite some time; the managed care imperative may have increased the pressure, but it hasn't radically altered the trajectory for most practitioners.

Using Common Factors in Individualizing Treatment

The literature tells us that common factors account for much of the change associated with psychotherapy. In most cases, features of the patient matter more in determining outcome than the specific theory we apply or interventions we employ. These common factors findings alert us to the importance of nonspecific dimensions of treatment.

How can we help patients feel that they are respected? How might we listen for and validate evidence of their strengths and resourcefulness? What questions can we ask to highlight areas of competence, past successes, or unrecognized resources? How can we best align our agenda with that of our patients? How can we clarify their objectives? How can we draw on the strengths, resources, and worldview of our patients in order to help them achieve their goals? To what extent can we make use of the clients' environment and existing support networks? How can we build on the spontaneous changes that clients experience outside of therapy?

Maintaining the patient's own momentum can be achieved by tailoring your approach to the distinctive particulars of each case. What patients want and how they understand their problem and its possible solutions, as well as the way patients use language to create their story about their problem are important initial foci. Clarifying the changes patients seek to make is one of the most crucial aspects of any treatment.

Spotting the potential limitations of some goals is also important. For example, many patients with substance abuse problems will readily declare in the first session that a clear, measurable goal of their treatment will be not drinking or doing drugs. We don't want to shake their resolve by challenging matters at this point, but the fact is that most abusers actually want considerably more than simply to stop using substances. What they really desire is to feel comfortable (not anxious, not bored, not empty) without using drugs. Achieving this will generally require that they make many additional behavioral changes. They will need to learn how to do new things, not just omit old self-destructive behaviors. Since "doing" is usually easier that "not doing" (to illustrate: Think about a purple bear. Now, don't think about a purple bear. Which was easier?), it is often helpful to develop some concrete steps these patients can take to fill their lives with new satisfying alternatives to drugs.

Listening carefully to clients for clues about their idiosyncratic experience can yield important clues about what changes they want and how we can help them make these changes. Rushing prematurely to conceptualizations about their "illness" and generalizations about people who carry this particular diagnosis may distract us from the most relevant information. Therapy stereotypes can be misleading and waste time.

Our first task is to think creatively about what this person seeking our assistance values and what seems to be the obstacle interfering with success. Helping patients to organize what they want from treatment is critically important. Developing measurable goals sets the change process in motion.

One troublesome thing about managed care is that it constrains the types of goals patients may address in reimbursed treatment. Although a patient may truly want to explore the childhood origins of his or her style of relating to others, this may not constitute an appropriate treatment objective. Managed care is aimed at restoring "normal" functional capacity rather than providing opportunities for growth and enrichment. Priority is placed on keeping people out of inpatient settings and teaching them to make optimal use of free, informal community resources to help them meet their psychological needs. Less formal treatment is better, so long as it doesn't produce a later need for more expensive forms of care.

The only caveat to this is that managed care is responsive to payors, who in turn are responsive to employees who consume the behavioral health services. Consumer satisfaction is taken quite seriously, which reduces the risk of companies' neglecting patients' needs and pocketing all the money that would otherwise have gone to care.

The problem is that consumer satisfaction offers a very imperfect means of correction. First, many dissatisfied consumers are reluctant or unable to come forward and complain. Second, many are insufficiently informed about what constitutes high-quality care and are therefore ill equipped to judge whether or not the services they received were appropriate. As a provider, you'll want to both provide high-quality care and help patients understand its value. This way you will be ethically providing care and surviving the managed care expectation that you keep the customer happy.

Some older models of therapy would have maintained that this is generally an impossibility. If clients are seeking unrealistic gratification in therapy, and to satisfy their unreasonableness would be countertherapeutic, then no therapist could simultaneously treat well and keep patients satisfied. Disparaging portrayals of regressed patients have been largely supplanted by different, more positive conceptualizations that support the feasibility of the managed care imperative. If patients are viewed as generally reasonable consumers of care, then with a proper approach, they can learn to recognize good care and will tend to be satisfied by the interventions that in fact are helpful to them.

But there are clients who require confrontation and challenging, and there are times when therapy is highly frustrating for the patient. How can we maintain high levels of patient satisfaction in the face of these inevitabilities? This remains a challenge.

Summary of Common Factors

Lambert (1992) and others have identified four common factors that underlie the effectiveness of therapy:

1. *Therapeutic technique.* Consistent with most research on treatment specificity, Lambert estimates that the therapist's particular technique contributes only 15% to the impact of psychotherapy.

2. *Client factors.* The client is the single most potent determinant of treatment outcome, contributing an impressive 40% to outcome. The quality of clients' participation in treatment, their perceptions of the therapist and what the therapist is doing, and their strengths and weaknesses determine whether any type of treatment will work.

3. *Therapeutic relationship.* Lambert estimates that the therapeutic relationship contributes roughly 30% to outcome in psychotherapy. Luborsky, Crits-Christoph, et al. (1988) found outcome correlates with alliance at approximately the .50 level. Other researchers have emphasized the capacity of the therapist to relate (Najavits & Strupp, 1994), the working alliance (Horvath & Symonds, 1991), and the therapeutic bond (Saunders, Howard, & Orlinsky, 1989). A positive alliance seems to develop most reliably when the therapist is empathic, genuine, and respectful.

   The therapeutic relationship offers an objectivity rarely found in other relationships. It provides both (1) objective cognitive reactions and (2) objective emotional reactions. Therapy provides four reassuring meta-messages: (1) This isn't worse than it is. (2) This uncomfortable state is probably temporary. (3) You're not alone. (4) You're not bad.

4. *Expectancy and placebo.* As a factor in outcome, the impact of specific technique is equivalent to that of nonspecific or common factors (the placebo effect). Frank (1978) identified four features shared by all psychotherapies: a person in distress, an expert, an explanation for the condition, and a healing ritual. Frank believes these features reverse demoralization and promote the expectation of recovery. Conveying the message that therapy will help promotes placebo reactions and permits clients to recognize their strengths once again. As you will see, these notions are highly consistent with the solution-focused approach described in the next chapter.

CHAPTER

13 Solution-Focused Treatment Methods

Working Backward and Building on Clients' Strengths

For many years, I've been doing therapy in a way that wasn't entirely consistent with the training I'd received in graduate school or the theoretical models of helping I use in teaching students. Despite this, the approach often seemed quite helpful.

Rather than focus initially on diagnosis and deficits, I often use client-centered tactics to try to help me become as clear as possible about the client's desired end-point: What exactly do they want to be different at the end of this treatment? What do they want there to be more of? Less of? Next I try to generate ideas about the practical steps the client can take in order to reach that goal. Rather than spend a lot of time exploring why things aren't totally as desired, we're working to find possible concrete solutions. In doing this, whenever possible, I rely heavily upon elements of the solution that seem readily within grasp, because they are already aspects of the client's repertoire.

Identifying times and situations when things are already going well, when the clients' experience already approximates their desired endstate, provides some of the clearest clues about how they might proceed most expediently to achieve their goals. Building upon what is already working well for them often offers the most rapid path to improvement.

I was uncomfortable with the fact that my way of working didn't seem to conform entirely to empirically substantiated methods. As it was heavily dependent upon some Rogerian ideas, I felt somewhat grounded in that orientation, but in practice much of what I was doing was rather directive. It prodded clients to take a different look at their experience and to adopt a less problem-centered focus in thinking about themselves and their relationships. I remained uneasy with my "theoretical homelessness" until several years ago, when I started to write about the approach I was using and discovered that it closely paralleled what others had increasingly been referring to as "solution-focused" therapy. In reading about other therapists' experiences with solution-focused methods, it became clear to me that many clinicians, working quite independently, had developed a similar strategy for helping their patients. Apparently many had the same qualms about the negative focus of many psychotherapy approaches and had developed similar tactics to help them minimize or circumvent these dangers.

Why Managed Care Favors
Solution-Focused Therapy

Many MCOs are encouraging behavioral healthcare providers to make use of solution-focused psychotherapy techniques. For example, in September 1997 a Cigna/MCC representative urged providers to be solution-focused, to emphasize the individual's strengths rather than pathology, and to utilize very short-term (six or fewer sessions) outpatient treatment duration. Such policies are prompting greater consideration of whether solution-focused therapy is appropriate or effective for all patients.

Because the solution-focused approach was "born" relatively recently, in practitioners' offices, it has received little empirical investigation. Despite this, it has become a favored approach among many MCOs. Part of why this has occurred has to do with how solution-focused therapists frame therapy. Implicit in this approach is the optimistic message that the clients are not all that far from where they want to be, and that moderate revision of existing strategies may be all that is necessary for them to become more satisfied with themselves and their lives. Building on the "exceptions" to the problem that already exist gives treatment a jump start.

This hopeful, encouraging stance is consistent with the managed care emphasis on brief, narrowly focused treatment; managed care does not want to frame the therapeutic endeavor as a lengthy, laborious, and mysterious process of digging up hitherto obscured, painful past events and hidden symbolic meanings. Managed care companies want to keep treatment as short and sweet as possible. But it also may be in the best interests of patients to have them pause and reflect on how the glass of their life is at least half full. It strengthens clients' confidence to be reminded that they're not doing everything wrong. If effective psychotherapy engages clients' willingness to experiment with new strategies for obtaining satisfaction, an optimistic, solution-focused stance can be facilitative because it usually increases clients' willingness to take some risks. It encourages clients to feel that they are at least in some ways already on the right path; this can build motivation by making the journey seem much less daunting. The collaborative, solution-focused approach communicates respect for the client. It is more egalitarian than some other treatment methods, which reduces the risks of disempowering dependency on the therapist. The therapist adopts a consultant-like stance, which can help clients to feel less stigmatized by the need to seek help. Kreilkamp (1989) agrees that it is often beneficial to present therapy as a consultation service. He views consultation as more user-friendly and approachable in our culture, where we are very open to soliciting opinions from our attorney, accountant, and broker without the dependency-related issues of being a psychotherapy patient.

The solution-focused approach's emphasis on practical problem solving is valued by MCOs, where commonly requests for services relate to needs in the here and now and are based on specific events that occur as part of the normal life cycle (Cummings, 1988). Accordingly, the least intrusive, most accessible avenues for receiving help are desired.

Solution-Focused Concepts

Clinical and theoretical work by de Shazer and his colleagues initially yielded the solution-focused model of family therapy (de Shazer, 1988a, 1988b; de Shazer et al., 1986; O'Hanlon & Weiner-Davis, 1989). This model is illustrated by the modal question posed to families during their first session of brief family therapy: "Suppose that one night, while you were asleep, there was a miracle and this problem was solved. How would you know? What would be different?" (de Shazer, 1988, p. 5).

In solution-focused therapy, less time is spent exploring the presenting problem, while more time is spent in looking for exceptions to the problem, or times when the problem does not occur. Exceptions can be identified by asking patients to track during the week what happens in their daily life that they want to continue happening (de Shazer & Molnar, 1984). During the next session the patient will often report having done something different or having had something different happen. According to de Shazer: "Solutions to problems are frequently missed because they often look like mere preliminaries; we end up searching for explanations believing that without explanation a solution is irrational, not recognizing that the solution itself is its own best explanation" (1988a, p. 10).

Chevalier summarized what she sees as the basic premises of solution-focused therapy in her book *On the Client's Path: A Manual for the Practice of Solution-Focused Therapy* (1995, p. 19):

1. Therapy is a setting where clients feel safe and their options are honored.
2. As clients set their goals and work toward them, their strengths are identified and highlighted.
3. Change is anticipated, talked about, watched for, and expected.
4. The client charts the course and the therapist gets on board as an assistant in that endeavor. . . . Clients are in charge.

Weiner-Davis (1990) identified the following four theoretical principles of this approach:

1. "Social reality is 'co-created' versus reality being simply an objective and external construct." Accordingly, therapeutic relationships should alter the patient's perception of reality in adaptive ways.
2. "Cooperation is inevitable; resistance is not a useful concept." Interpersonal behavior is not absolutely one extreme of acquiescence or opposition, but rather a mix that can be selectively highlighted for therapeutic gain.
3. "Change is inevitable; rapid resolution of complaints is probable." One of the few truisms in life is that nothing remains indefinitely static. Human existence involves the presence of gradual and precipitous problem-solving shifts that may serve as foundations from which each of us develops new adaptive behavior.
4. "Small change is all that is necessary; a change in one part of the system effects change in other parts of the system." Dramatic modifications in behavior are not necessary to create adaptive momentum, because the social-interpersonal context supports, encourages, and maintains adaptive change.

Assumptions of Solution-Focused Therapy

The solution-focused approach is both goal-oriented and consumer-oriented. In solution-focused therapy the therapist's role is to facilitate conversations that enable patients to get what they want. This consumer model assumes that patients want what they say they want, that they are motivated toward the goal, and that the therapist's job is to cooperate with their endeavor. It assumes that people usually show therapists how they think change takes place with regard to their goal and that it is efficient for therapists to cooperate with their views. Patients' beliefs about change, about the problem, and about the hypothetical solution fit recursively with their actions.

The solution-focused approach assumes that what we presuppose even by asking a question already influences the direction of response and the further direction of the therapeutic conversation. An emphasis is placed on reducing iatrogenic harm by avoiding questioning that establishes a negative, passive, less hopeful mindset. More constructive ways of framing issues include the following:

1. Rather than asking about symptoms through queries such as "So, what seems to be the problem? What's wrong?" solution-focused therapists are more likely to emphasize, "What is your goal in coming here?"
2. Rather than exploring the underlying sources of clients' symptoms or their situational antecedents, solution-focused work looks for exceptions. "When doesn't the problem happen? Are there times when you are already where you want to be with this? Is this happening somewhat already, some of the time? When?"
3. Rather than focusing on vague abstractions, solution-focused therapists try to help clients think concretely and specifically about their goals. Visualizing their hypothetical solution provides clients with ideas about behaviors to be tried and anchors treatment in measurable goals. "If the problem were solved, what would you be doing differently?"

Walter and Peller (1994, p.11) describe twelve assumptions that underlie their solution-focused approach:

1. Advantages of a Positive Focus
   Assumption: Focusing on the positive, on the solution, and on the future facilitates change in the desired direction. Therefore, focus on solution-oriented talk rather than on problem-oriented talk.

2. Exceptions Suggest Solutions
   Assumption: Exceptions to *every* problem can be created by therapist and patient, which can be used to build solutions.

3. Nothing Is Always the Same
   Assumption: Change is occurring all the time.

4. Small Change Is Generative
   Assumption: Small changing leads to larger changing.

5. Cooperation Is Inevitable
   Assumption: Patients are always cooperating. They are showing us how they think change takes place. As we understand their thinking and act accordingly, cooperation is inevitable.

6. People Are Resourceful
   Assumption: People have all they need to solve their problems.

7. Meaning and Experience Are Interactionally Constructed
   Assumption: . . . Meaning is the world or medium in which we live. We inform meaning onto our experience and it is our experience at the same time. Meaning is not imposed from without or determined from outside of ourselves. We inform our world through interaction.

8. Recursiveness
   Assumption: Actions and descriptions are circular.

9. Meaning Is in the Response
   Assumption: The meaning of the message is the response you receive. . . .

10. The Patient Is the Expert
    Assumption: Therapy is a goal- or solution-focused endeavor, with the patient as expert.

11. Unity
    Assumption: Any change in how patients describe a goal (solution) and/or what they do affects future interactions with all others involved.

12. Treatment Group Membership
    Assumption: The members in a treatment group are those who share a goal and state their desire to do something about making it happen.

Positive Therapist Expectations

"As therapists, clearly we have a duty. First, to achieve clarity in ourselves; and then to look for every sign of clarity in others and to implement them and reinforce them in whatever is sane in them" (Bateson, 1972, p. 487). Therapists' own expectations can significantly affect patients' progress. If we understand and interact with our patients in terms of their permanent, pervasive, personal pathology, we will inadvertently grant them little room to improve. On the other hand, if we challenge this emphasis on stable, global, internal causes for problems and recognize patients' potential and current strengths, improvement will be more likely.

It can be helpful to avoid psychological constructs that impede change. For example, thinking about patients' negative experiences in terms of stable personality constructs and diagnosis can block change because it implies stability. Alternatively, seeing them as "having a bad day" paves the way for improvement. Haley (1976) observed:

To label a child as "delinquent" . . . or to label an adult as an "alcoholic" or a "schizophrenic," means that one is participating in the creation of a problem in such a way that change is made more difficult. A therapist who describes a family situation as characterized by "a dominating mother and a passive father," or "a symbiotic relationship between mother and daughter," has created problems, although the therapist might think he is merely identifying the problems put before him. The way in which one labels a human dilemma can crystallize a problem and make it chronic. (p. 76)

Solution-focused therapists emphasize the aspects of patients' situations that seem most changeable. They recognize that promoting small, positive changes may have surprisingly broad effects in other areas. When behaviorists first started targeting symptoms, despite the psychodynamicists' predictions of symptom substitution, they unexpectedly found that making specific behavioral changes was often associated with global changes in self-concept and interpersonal relationships (Paul, 1966; Kazdin & Wilcoxon, 1976). The solution-focused therapist's job is to promote, identify, and amplify change.

Hudson O'Hanlon and Weiner-Davis (1989), in their book *In Search of Solutions: A New Direction in Psychotherapy* make the case that, ironically, change is constant.

> If you assume change is constant, you will behave as if change were inevitable. Through verbal and nonverbal means clients will be given the impression that it would be surprising if the presenting complaint were to persist. Physicists tell us that all is flux; atoms and molecules are constantly moving and rearranging themselves in the physical universe. Biologists tell us that we create new cells in our bodies constantly, so that eventually we have an almost totally new set of cells in our bodies. We see the universe as one of change. In fact, we think that people's situations are changing all the time. Their *views* of the situations are what remain the same when they report that nothing has changed. (p. 35)

A mother and teenage daughter seen at Weiner-Davis's agency were asked to report on a homework assignment they had been given during the first session. The task was designed to reduce the number of arguments between them. The daughter began describing in great detail an argument that had occurred during the week. Mother added her impressions of the altercation. Ten minutes into this discussion the therapist interrupted them by asking, "By the way, how was the rest of the week?" Mother's demeanor changed abruptly. "Oh," she said, "She was a perfect angel! Aside from that one argument she was great."

O'Hanlon and Weiner-Davis reflect that, had the therapist allowed this pair to discuss their fight, they would have done so for most of the session and would probably have left the session focused on the difficulties in their relationship, despite the fact that the vast majority of the week had gone exceedingly well. Luckily their solution-focused therapist chose instead to devote the remainder of the session to exploring what contributed to their having a relatively peaceful week.

Often a petty disagreement on the way to therapy distracts a couple in marital therapy and causes them to overlook the fact that they've been getting along much better lately. The therapist sees two angry individuals walking through the door, makes erroneous assumptions about their progress, and becomes discouraged.

The therapist's reaction in turn fosters a negative focus for the couple. If, instead, the therapist assures clients that their fight will be discussed after checking on the homework (providing an opportunity to report on the week's positive events), the positive feelings arising from this discussion may create quite a different context in which to later rehash the disagreement, if this is even necessary at that point. O'Hanlon and Weiner-Davis (1989) observe:

> As therapists we help to create a particular reality by the questions we ask and the topics we choose to focus upon, as well as those we choose to ignore. In the smorgasbord of information supplied to us by our clients, we think it important to focus on what seems to be working, however small, to label it as worthwhile, and to work toward amplifying it. (p. 37)

Recognizing Both Individual and System Strengths

Avoid adopting a blaming stance—it's not all Mom's or Dad's fault. Contextual family therapists have long stressed the importance of "multidirected partiality," which is a cumbersome term referring to the need for therapists to support all the elements of clients' potential support systems (Boszormenyi-Nagy & Krasner, 1986). Although it is tempting, when we sit alone with a client in pain, to align ourselves with the client and to construe the others in his or her life as mean-spirited, evil nemeses thwarting the client at every turn, the fact is we often are only hearing things from one biased side.

While it can be temporarily satisfying for clients to find a therapist who agrees that they are innocent victims, characterizing relationships in one-sided ways often leaves clients angry and alienated, often from those who have the greatest potential to care about their welfare (family and friends). The contextual approach strives to make the best use of all the potentially beneficial resources in clients' social contexts and therefore eschews simple-minded blaming that closes the door on future relationship possibilities.

For example, instead of pinning the blame on a "bad mother," a contextually oriented therapist might help the client begin to understand the forces influencing the mother's decisions in caregiving. Instead of focusing on the mother's failure to provide the nurturance that was "needed" early on, such a therapist might explore what the mother offered that was helpful, what blocked the mother's ability to do even better, and whether the mother might still wish for a chance to do more. The notion that all parents are limited, imperfect human beings who struggle to do the best they can at the time provides a helpful way of thinking about even a disastrous childhood. This perspective can help build the client's capacity for empathy, forgiveness, and negotiation of greater fairness in the future. A young mother, who at age 16 had sadly little to give to a young child who may have overwhelmed her patience, may have matured into a far more capable and generous parent by age 40. The now adult children may be helped immensely by therapy that doesn't foreclose on the possibility of their redeeming a formerly unsatisfying and unworkable relationship with a parent.

One especially articulate client affirmed my faith in certain solution-focused and contextual principles in explaining her rather remarkable turnaround after years of therapy for schizoaffective and borderline personality disorder.

> I've been in a lot of hospitals and this was the first place where the staff didn't blame my mother for my problems. Because of that, she kept visiting, and now our relationship is better than it's ever been.
>
> Diagnostic labels change how you look at yourself. It's hard to have much hope when they say you are "custodial," even though they never told me exactly what that meant. When therapists just look at your inadequacies, you start feeling less responsible for what you do, because what's the point.
>
> Now I'm spending more time thinking about my good days, and all the times I handle stress well, without thinking about hurting myself or others. I realize that most of the time, I actually do pretty well. That gives me more confidence, and makes me want to take better care of myself. I see that I'm already part of the way there.

Another client came to me complaining of bedtime enuresis. He had been unsuccessfully in therapy for 5 years with a psychodynamicist, who had apparently attributed the wetting to unresolved hostility toward male authority figures. For half a decade this client had met weekly with his therapist, discussing his unconscious anger at his father. After each session he would find himself so upset with the week's revelations about denied rage that, to calm himself down, he'd stop at a bar on the way home and have several drinks. When he'd finally get home, fairly drunk, he fell into bed, slept, and inevitably had an accident. He took his tendency to wet the bed the nights after therapy sessions as evidence corroborating his therapist's interpretation of the problem. His father must be the cause of the problem, because talking about him seemed to result in wetting.

He seemed totally unprepared for my musing that the real culprit might be all that alcohol before bed. It seemed plausible that his aftersession imbibing might have been making him less aware of the physical sensations associated with a full bladder while he slept. He stopped to think, and then he acknowledged that virtually all of his enuretic episodes followed nights of heavy drinking. For instance, when he was sick with a bad cold or the flu, he would not drink alcohol and would stay dry. Part of why his enuresis had become such an obstacle to his relationships with women was that he almost always had the problem when he slept with a woman. However, he also always drank very heavily when with women, to quell his anxiety about possibly wetting.

Rather than emphasize the familial derivation of his problem, we focused our energy on thinking about the exceptions and what they might offer to the development of solutions. Obviously it made sense to experiment with using alcohol differently. This was successful.

Before ending our work, I also gave the client some information about the use of a bell and pad, in case he ever needed to attune his body even more sensitively to the urge to urinate by using classical conditioning methods to augment his response to stimuli. He contacted me roughly a year later to get information he needed to file his taxes, and he reported that his problem had not recurred.

Given the lack of experimental controls here, I cannot know for sure whether recasting his problem in different terms was responsible for his apparent improvement. In fact, if I wanted to be very skeptical, I might even question the validity of his self-report and wonder if he was simply telling me he was no longer wetting in order to make us both feel good. But this admittedly anecdotal evidence is consistent with the notion that there may be some merit in avoiding blaming attributions for problems that can be understood in a variety of ways. In explaining our patients' experiences, we are often working in the dark. We have no way of definitively proving what caused what. The reasons we offer should probably be regarded as "best guesses." Given this, it seems prudent for us to be rather modest and to select the arbitrary story that offers the best promise for facilitating improvement with the least risk of harm.

Identifying Healthy Exceptions: What's Working?

Preoccupation with pathology can often impede clients' progress. We can become so focused on detailing what clients fail to do in their lives and pointing out the ineffectiveness of their unsuccessful strategies that they become demoralized. Often we approach cases with a narrow mindset about "normal" functioning. We look for deviations from a presumed standard of normality and match the abnormal characteristics we find with a list of symptoms in the diagnostic manual. Next we share our insights about how the client's responding is deficient ("I've noticed that in these types of situations you tend to . . . , which doesn't seem to work very well") and make (gentle, tentatively offered) recommendations about what we see as preferable responses ("I wonder if it would help if you tried to . . . the next time this happens?"). By pinpointing faulty responses and suggesting better alternatives, we feel we've made some helpful advance in the client's self-understanding and have set the stage for corrective learning. When clients experiment with the new behaviors we have encouraged, we reinforce them and take pleasure in having made a difference. However, very often clients never try the experiment. They don't make the recommended changes, and now, thanks to our pointing it out and giving it a name, they feel even worse about their defective way of doing things. They may even be able to accurately identify each time they make the error in question, and they feel compelled to report it to us guiltily in the next session ("She started talking about that and, like I always seem to do, I just . . ."). The result can be a demoralized client, who feels increasingly paralyzed and inadequate.

Some clients are adaptable and eager to try new ways of responding, but many seem to be inertial and prone to habitual modes of doing things. Identifying which of the clients' longstanding habitual ways of responding serve them well and working to maximize their use can be a quicker way to promote improved functioning. Even the most severely pathological client responds in healthy ways much of the time. Just as we encourage parents to "catch their children being good" in order to enhance the effectiveness of their nurturing, as therapists we need to emphasize the vast portions of our clients' behavioral repertoires that are adaptive and constructive.

This reorientation from "what's not working" to "what's working" is fundamental to the solution-focused approach to therapy. A similar shift in emphasis occurred in neuropsychology not too long ago. In doing a neuropsychological assessment, clinicians in the 1970s took great pains to try to specify exactly which portions of neuronal tissue were no longer able to function; pinpointing the locus and extent of damage was a major objective of the neuropsychological evaluation. As CAT scanners and later MRI equipment became more affordable and widespread, the pressure on neuropsychologists to focus on specifying pathology and clarifying diagnosis diminished. Many found it far more useful to now focus on the functions and competencies that remained, rather than those that had been permanently lost to brain damage. In helping someone with brain damage, it is clear that you must work with the remaining functional areas of the brain and learn how to corral them in order to compensate for missing functions that were formerly performed by the now destroyed areas. Rehabilitation involves making better use of what still works. Because neurons don't regenerate, specifying the areas that have been damaged in great detail may help us describe cases and understand the source of the limits on clients' functioning, but it doesn't offer a solution to their problems. Helping clients make optimal use of what they have left seems to be the only route to improvement.

Clients without brain damage may have fewer limits to new learning, but it is still often efficient to focus on what has already been learned. Using what is already there to better effect is often easier and more efficient.

Solution-Focused Methods

In solution-oriented therapy, emphasis is placed on the varied ways that therapists can help patients find their own solutions. Some of the communication techniques suggested by O'Hanlon (1993) include:

1. Acknowledging the person's point of view to develop rapport
2. Creating an expectation for change with solution-oriented language
3. Identifying the first signs that will indicate movement toward the therapeutic goal
4. Casting doubt on suggestions or actions that close the possibilities for finding a solution
5. Listening for things that support change for the better
6. Reinforcing the understanding that change will occur in small steps
7. Reinforcing other people's competence and skills to help with the patient's problem

Starting Sessions

Solution-focused therapists often begin sessions with comments such as: "I am very sorry to hear how things are going. Can you tell me what about this you would like to change or in what ways you would like to be handling things differently?" This

Five Basic Steps of Solution-Focused Therapy

1. *Define focal goals:* What is your goal in coming here? What would you most like to change about this? How will you know whether this change has occurred? If a miracle happened, and this problem were solved, what would you be doing differently? Can you begin doing these things now?
2. *Elicit exceptions to the problem:* When are you already doing some of what you want? When doesn't the problem happen?
3. *Describe the easier contexts:* What makes these times different? What do you do differently? How do you think differently? How are you seen by others at these times? Do they respond to you differently because you are acting differently at these times?
4. *Build upon exceptions:* Can you increase the number of times you do these constructive things? Can you act these ways more often or in new situations?
5. *Maintaining the exceptions:* How will you keep this up? How can you let others know that you are keeping this up?

kind of questioning supports the patient's feelings and poses a goal-oriented query that invites the patient to state the goal in terms of changing or an action response. For example, the patient might say, "Well, I want to be able to leave the hospital, and I know to do that I need to stop cutting whenever I get upset about something." This method focuses on defining clearly operationalized goals with the patient. In group therapy, articulating individuals' goals enables more constructive mutual support among members throughout the week.

Next the solution-focused method explores times when patients have already behaved in line with their objectives. These "exceptions" highlight the individuals' capacity to achieve their goals and the strengths that already exist within. Reducing the perceived difficulty of making a change increases the probability of the patients' making enduring and maintainable progress.

Solution-focused therapy also encourages patients to visualize adaptive alternatives and to think specifically and concretely about how they would prefer to be living. Therapists make use of what is referred to as the "hypothetical solution frame" to clarify patients' goals: "If a miracle happened, and the problem were solved, what would you be doing differently?" This is an adaptation of Erickson's crystal ball technique (Erickson, 1954). This powerful technique requires the patient to create a vivid image of a future with the problem solved or absent, and then to look backward at the present from this new future perspective, in order to identify strategies that were used to reach a solution.

Assuming and Maintaining Rapport

Walter and Peller (1994) make the working assumption that they have rapport with clients from the moment of contact. To save time in therapy, they do not assume that they have to do something exceptional to establish a relationship. To help the patient feel understood and supported, many solution-focused therapists use empathic and reflective listening techniques, restating what the patient said, with the same affect and tone. This is consistent with Rogers's client-centered approach (1951) and Bandler and Grinder's work (1975, 1979), which stresses the notion of pacing and matching the client's information processing style.

To Bandler and Grinder (1975, 1979), gaining rapport entails matching the dominant representational system of the patient. If patients tend to speak in visual terms, the therapist should match this by using visual terms. If patients use auditory terms, the therapist should emphasize auditory terms. Finally, if patients speak in kinesthetic or feelings terms, then the therapist should reciprocate. Bandler and Grinder maintain that emphasizing the same information-processing modalities the patient uses mobilizes rapport, although some challenge this belief. According to Bandler and Grinder (1979), therapists should flexibly accommodate their patients' styles by consciously striving to match their way of processing information.

The founders of the Brief Therapy Model of the Mental Research Institute (Paul Watzlawick, John Weakland, Richard Fisch, and Lynn Segal) stress the importance of initially supporting a patient's position to the establishment of rapport (Fisch, Weakland, & Segal, 1982). This is accomplished by reflecting and validating the patient's world view and initial conceptualization of the problem.

Various models recognize that differences among patients can influence the establishment of a therapeutic relationship. By being attuned to these variations, we can individualize treatment in a way that fosters rapid establishment of a productive relationship. Building a sense of rapport goes more quickly when we try to match the patient's unique way of thinking and feeling.

Defining Goals

The following types of questions can be useful in moving from wishes or complaints toward a statement of a goal or problem:

> "I am very sorry to hear how things are going. Can you tell me what about this you would like to change or in what ways you would like to be handling things differently?" This question supports the patient's feelings and asks a goal-oriented question in which she or he is invited to state the goal in terms of changing or an action response.

> "I am sorry to hear how badly things have been going. Can you tell me what about this I can help you with?" This question invites a specific statement about how you, as therapist, can be instrumental.

> "I am very sorry to hear how badly things have been going. Can you tell me again what you would like as a result of coming here?" This question sympathizes with what the patient has said and further restates the goal-oriented question.

> "This may sound like a strange question given all that is going on, but how is this a problem for you?" This question does not have the advantage of ori-

enting a patient to a positive statement, but sometimes the question can be useful in obtaining a delimited problem statement. A focal problem statement implies something can be done.

John Walter and Jane Peller (1994) offer the following guidelines for developing well-defined goals (p. 60):

Criteria	Key Words	Sample Question
In the positive	"Instead"	"What will you be doing instead?"
In a process form	"How"	"How will you be doing this?"
In the here and now	"On track"	"As you leave here today, and you're on track, what will you be doing differently or saying differently to yourself?"
As specific as possible	"Specifically"	"How specifically will you be doing this?"
In the patient's control	"You"	What will you be doing when that happens?
In the patient's language	Use the patient's expressions	For example, "So you'll bring it up and talk it out, the next time she bums you out."

Spacing Sessions

Many of us who have been trained in traditional therapy models are accustomed to scheduling one or more sessions regularly every week. Solution-focused therapists schedule each session on its own merit, based on:

- Time needed for the performance of some homework task.
- Promotion of confidence in the solution—time permits setbacks to be seen in perspective.
- Promotion of independence from therapy—weaning promotes confidence.
- The patient's responsibility for therapy—negotiate timing with the patient.

Applying Techniques to Challenging Patients

The solution-focused approach has been hailed as an efficient way of responding to the needs of outpatients, but it also can be incorporated into the treatment of more severely compromised inpatients. Although relatively few investigations of the effects of this method on inpatient populations have been conducted to date and there have been few assessments of solution-focused treatment administered in group format, some preliminary evidence has been encouraging. Oxman and

Chambliss (1998) targeted a group of sixteen high-risk patients with a recent history (during the past year) of violent responding within an inpatient psychiatric treatment setting. A solution-focused treatment approach was used in conducting two ongoing weekly therapy groups, each with seven or eight patient members usually in attendance.

Patients were encouraged to reflect upon occasions when they successfully resolved problems with internal tension and frustration without using violent strategies. Focus during the group meetings was on factors that contributed to why these episodes were "nonproblem" exceptions. As patients adopted this positive perspective, they were encouraged to think specifically about constructive behaviors and situational elements they might try to duplicate in future challenging situations.

During a 2-month period following a month of the solution-focused emphasis a modest behavioral improvement on some of the outcome measures was observed. The rate of self-injurious and assaultive behavioral episodes went down, although the number of requests for PRNs increased somewhat. This may have been because during group meetings the decision to ask for a calmative was presented as a form of positive coping preferable to acting out. While in some populations this would be viewed quite negatively—and such an increased use of medication always needs to be viewed with caution and monitored closely—in this highly compromised inpatient group, appropriate requests for PRNs were seen as adaptive.

De Shazer (1982) has offered a decision tree for influencing patterns of client cooperation.

1. If a client is willing to follow suggestions, and indeed wants them, then give straightforward direction.
2. If a client prefers to exercise autonomy and wants to modify tasks, then give tasks that include optional behaviors.
3. If a client resists direction, then generalize, offer broad perspectives, use defensiveness-limiting frames of reference. Each option seeks to match personality style and diagnosis with the client's need for expeditious, helpful direction.

Learning to Be Solution-Focused

Walter and Peller (1994) offer the following suggestions for those beginning to incorporate aspects of this approach:

> We suggest to those who may be learning this approach that . . . they suspend beliefs while trying this on. Later, after attaining some facility with this way of working, they can decide how much they want to incorporate in their work. We experienced both a gain and a loss as we began working this way . . . a loss as we realized that we were giving up that very emotionally close relationship with our patients we experienced using long-term models. We also found that the satisfaction of seeing people making concrete changes in a short period of time more than made up for our feelings of sadness. (p. 35)

Criticism of the Solution-Focused Approach

It would not be fair to omit consideration of objections to the solution-focused approach. While it may seem to be an intuitively appealing way to work with clients, at present there has been no rigorous experimental investigation of its efficacy.

L. Johnson (1995) has expressed concerns about uncritical endorsement of the solution-focused approach:

> Solution-focused techniques form a well-defined system that is very popular among clinicians. At workshops, the solution-focused approach seems very well received, and it would appear to be more easily applied than some other, more complex approaches. Unfortunately, there is little actual research on the topic, and our profession has a history of becoming enthusiastic about approaches that show no advantage over a well-designed attention placebo (i.e., a research design in which the control group is not simply ignored but is given an equivalent amount of therapeutic-appearing attention from the researcher). Is this because the techniques have been developed and expounded outside of the academic settings, so that the graduate schools are often unaware of even the existence of the skills, let alone having an idea of how to evaluate them? (p. 25)

Similar objections have been voiced by Jacobson (1995), who writes

> . . . it is all the more disappointing that family therapy is so guilty of making unsubstantiated claims of success. "This works, trust me!" has become the standard of proof on the family therapy workshop circuit, and the popularity of various approaches becomes a question of who is most persuasive, whose teaching tapes are most pristine, or even whose name is best known. The claims of astoundingly high success in an astoundingly few number of sessions made by some solution-focused therapists are particularly disturbing. Despite the assertion that these success rates are substantiated by research findings, nothing cited in the literature could conceivably be thought of as empirically valid clinical research. (p. 40)

> . . . False prophets are easy to recognize and need to be exposed. They expect you to trust their clinical judgment, while showing no signs of humility or doubts about the wisdom of what they are proselytizing. They show an indifference to independent tests of their ideas and sidestep the issue of research evidence. We have to ask our plenary speakers, theorists and workshop leaders questions such as, "How do you know this works?" We have to pin down 90-percent success claims with questions like, "How did you measure success?" "Was the *measurement* process independent of the *therapy* process, to ensure that it was not contaminated by the client's desire to make the therapist feel good? (p. 38)

Solution-focused therapists must rise to the challenge of building an empirical knowledge base, in order to gain greater scientific respectability. But even though this approach has yet to be fully embraced by the academic research community, because MCOs insist that therapists incorporate these methods into their repertoires, it probably makes sense to master the basics of the solution-focused method.

14 Brief Problem-Solving Methods

Integrating Outcomes Assessment and Treatment

Psychotherapists have failed to demonstrate convincingly that the benefits of long-term therapy are commensurate with its higher costs (Kroll, 1993). Comparative studies of brief and unlimited therapies show essentially no differences in results (Howard, Kopta, et al., 1986; Koss & Butcher, 1986). Smith, Glass, and Miller (1980) conducted a meta-analytic investigation of nearly five hundred outcome studies and found psychotherapy to be effective with an average of seventeen sessions. Another meta-analytic study found psychotherapy to be effective following a mean of roughly seven sessions (D. Shapiro & Shapiro, 1982). Approximately half of all clients are measurably improved after eight sessions and three-quarters after twenty-nine sessions (Howard, Kopta, et al., 1986). Most clients experience almost immediate improvement after beginning psychotherapy. Given the failure to find evidence that long-term therapy produces more changes than does short-term therapy (Butcher & Koss, 1978; Koss, Butcher, & Strupp, 1986; Luborsky, Singer, & Luborsky, 1975; Meltzoff & Kornreich, 1970), it seems reasonable to speculate that most change in psychotherapy occurs relatively quickly, within the period of time usually considered to be brief treatment. Additional changes sometimes may occur in longer-term treatments, and there may be different criteria for assessing these changes, but there may also be diminishing returns as one approaches a psycho-therapeutic asymptote. This was recognized by Appelbaum (1975), a psychoanalyst impressed by his experiences with brief therapy, who noted that even if long-term treatment were to produce some added gains, it would be questionable whether these gains would justify the added expenditure of time and money. Appelbaum applied "Parkinson's Law" to psychotherapy: Work often expands or contracts to fill the time available for it.

Although more naturalistic studies have yielded conclusions that differ some-what from those of controlled studies that use random assignment of clients to various treatment conditions, critics can discount claims of the superiority of longer therapy based on these studies on the grounds that self-selection and cognitive dissonance offer competing explanations for why those who stayed in therapy longer rated it as better. Research indicates that there is no significant difference in terms of outcome between what is labeled "brief" and what is labeled "traditional" therapy. The available data suggest that brief therapy achieves roughly the same results as traditional approaches. In addition, the research clearly indicates that most therapy is of relatively short duration and always has been, regardless of the treatment model employed. The average client in any type of psychotherapy only attends five or six sessions. The research also indicates that a single session is the modal number of sessions for all clients in therapy, regardless of the treatment model being employed. (See Chapter 4.)

The main advantage of doing brief therapy may lie in the therapist's having more accurate expectations, as most psychotherapy is and has always been "brief." The empirical evidence indicates that only a minority of patients who started psychotherapy stayed very long, even in the "good old days" before managed care, so we can surmise that often therapists were caught unaware. Therapists expecting a lengthy opportunity for the therapy process to unfold gradually, who waited patiently to collect comprehensive information before intervening, probably never got to the active treatment stage with many patients they saw. Most patients came for sessions for less than 2 months, and many came only once. Rather than become frustrated that patients don't seem to oblige traditional therapists' expectations about the duration of treatment, perhaps it makes more sense to ask, "What do patients really want from treatment?" Many who self-limited their treatment were very content with their therapy experience and credited it with having made a meaningful difference in their lives. If a brief encounter is often helpful, then it may be optimal to expect this in most cases and to develop methods accordingly, even if it is insufficient for the flowering of an interpretable transference.

Another advantage of brief focal psychotherapy is the pressure it puts on both patient and therapist to work actively and to maintain high treatment expectations (Markowitz, 1996). Brief therapy results in a great saving of available clinical time, enabling therapists to reach a larger segment of the population needing treatment.

Single-Session Treatment: Once May Be Enough!

Single-session psychotherapy episodes have always been common, although deemphasized and dismissed as "incomplete" by many clinicians. About half of the patients who come to a clinic do not come back again at that time (Phillips, 1985). Similar findings have been reported for a variety of treatment settings (Bloom, 1975; Ewalt, 1973; Fiester & Rudestam, 1975; Hoffman & Remmel, 1975; G. Jacobson et al., 1965; Kogan, 1957a, 1957b, 1957c; Littlepage et al., 1976; Reed, Myers, & Scheidemandel, 1972; Spoerl, 1975; Sue, Allen, & Conway, 1978; Talmon, 1990). Single-session episodes of care seem almost as common in university mental health facilities as in community agencies (Dorosin, Gibbs, & Kaplan, 1976; Glasscote & Fishman, 1973; Sarvis, Dewees, & Johnson, 1959; Speers, 1962).

Studies support the conclusion that a single interview can have significant therapeutic impact. Talmon (1990) reported that more than three-quarters of 200 patients whom he had previously seen only once reported that they were improved or much improved. Based on this observation, Talmon, along with two colleagues, attempted to conduct single-session psychotherapy with sixty randomly assigned adults who appeared for noncrisis routine intake appointments. The three therapists differed substantially in their general approaches to psychotherapy, and the patients were a very heterogeneous group in terms of severity of presenting complaint, race, ethnic background, age, and education. Between 3 and 12 months later, fifty-eight of the sixty patients were reached by telephone for a followup interview conducted by someone other than the patient's therapist.

Of the fifty-eight patients who were contacted, thirty-four (58%) were, in fact, seen only once. That is, in these cases, patient and therapist mutually agreed that no additional appointments were necessary. Of the thirty-four patients seen only once, 88% reported that they were either improved or much improved, which is comparable to the twenty-four patients seen more than once. Myriad authors report successful single sessions (Chick et al., 1988; Chapman & Huygens, 1988; Edwards et al., 1977; Getz, Fujita, & Allen, 1975; Malan et al., 1975; Zweben, Pearlman, & Li, 1988).

Hoffman and Remmel (1975) maintain that "treatment begins in the first interview, and the majority of work, in fact, may often be accomplished at that time. There are occasions when the client feels better after one session, and if this happens, the therapist need not feel like a failure for not involving him in continued treatment" (1975, p. 262).

According to Sifneos (1979), "At times . . . the therapeutic impact of the evaluation or of the first interview is such that there is no need for further psychotherapy because in reality the patient's problem is actually being solved" (p. 70). Barten (1971) felt that "There is a tendency to overlook the fact that a single interview can have beneficial therapeutic consequences . . . even when further interviews are available, they may not be needed" (p. 17).

Many Common Problems Suitable for Brief Treatment

A needs assessment survey funded by the National Institute on Drug Abuse (Sperry et al., 1996) showed that nearly half of 8,000 employees tested in thirty-five organizations were shown to be experiencing behavioral problems. Results indicated that 21% of the employees were experiencing high stress, 18% met the criteria for high anxiety, and roughly 12% were found to be problem drinkers. These highly prevalent problems are generally very suitable for brief treatment methods.

In outpatient work the majority of clients present therapists with problems involving depression, anxiety, or a mix of both. In assessing the appropriateness of MCOs' insistence on use of brief therapy modalities, it is therefore appropriate to focus specifically on the brief therapy track record in treating depression and anxiety and other common conditions.

The limited available evidence suggests that, contrary to intuition, brief psychotherapies often effectively treat chronic mood disorder. In understanding why protracted psychotherapy often fails to ameliorate chronic depression, Markowitz (1992) provides findings suggesting that longer-term therapists, discouraged by the fatalistic pessimism and nagging chronicity of dysthymic patients, may unwittingly collude with the dysthymia by setting lower psychotherapeutic goals, resulting in slower progress. Some believe that therapeutic optimism, a medical model of mood disorder that accommodates use of antidepressant medication when appropriate, a here-and-now focus on current issues, and the leverage of time-limited therapy may all help to resolve these patients' dysthymic pattern of responding.

Miller and Hester (1986) reported similar findings for the treatment of alcoholism. Intensity of professional treatment (inpatient versus outpatient) and length of treatment were unrelated to outcome. Nothing worked any better than a minimal treatment involving detoxification and 1 hour of counseling.

The *Consumer Reports* study (1995) suggests that many outpatients prefer longer-term treatment, but this may not be optimal for them. Anxious clients often find it reassuring to establish an ongoing relationship with a trusted therapist whom they can count on to help them appraise threatening situations more appropriately. The long-term therapist may serve as teacher, cheerleader, and debriefing session moderator. The alliance that develops over time may increase the therapist's ability to influence the client's choices in lasting ways, and the therapist's availability to provide helpful feedback during the working-through process may help the client to consolidate gains. Extended contact may permit early detection of ineffective attempts at change, which may give the client a second opportunity to obtain suggestions about how to work toward the treatment goal.

However, for various reasons, long-term treatment may not always be best for anxious patients, even if they seem to prefer it. One drawback is that long-term therapy invites clients to make the following attributional error: "My therapist solved my problem." Clients who credit their success to their therapist are often less likely to maintain therapeutic gains long term (Chambliss & Murray, 1979a, 1979b). Brief therapy reduces this risk by emphasizing from the outset that the therapist's role is that of facilitator; there is no doubt that the client is the central agent of change. The relationship is seen as of secondary importance to the efficient achievement of behavioral progress. Consequently the relationship is less likely to be credited with victory. The client becomes less dependent on recommendations and feedback from the therapist and may have an easier time generalizing lessons learned during the course of treatment. Long-term therapy can create the expectancy that eventually things will become so much easier that it will be obvious that the therapeutic relationship can be discontinued. Clients often assume that the therapist is carefully monitoring their readiness for therapy to end. When the therapist continues to schedule meetings, it is assumed that the client has yet to reach some objective criterion of accomplishment. Because anxious clients are likely to continue to experience some residual anxiety at times for the rest of their lives, as long-term treatment progresses beyond the period of active intervention, the clients can turn to recent bouts of fleeting discomfort as justifying their need for continued treatment. These experiences can be taken to mean that the client is not yet ready to "go solo." Unfortunately this can undermine the client's general sense of self-efficacy (Chambliss & Murray, 1979b).

Reframing can be advantageous here. A constructive way of interpreting anxious episodes is to see them as an inevitable outcropping of a life fully embraced and well lived. If you didn't care, you wouldn't be anxious. If you weren't trying challenging things, you wouldn't be anxious. Perhaps those with exquisitely sensitive nervous systems (whether as a result of genetic predisposition or early traumatizing experiences) feel life more intensely and more passionately. Their ongoing life challenge is to manage this full experience of life.

Brief therapists often openly acknowledge that some situations may always be challenging for the anxious client, perhaps because of autonomic or central nervous system characteristics. The goal of brief treatment is to establish basic skills that the client will need to perfect over many repeated trials, in order to gradually help the client to feel more comfortable in various challenging situations. Brief therapists avoid establishing the expectation that the patient will eventually reach a time when everything will be so totally effortless that termination will indisputably be appropriate. Some would argue that this prepares anxious clients more appropriately for their post-treatment experience.

Several outcome studies demonstrating the effectiveness of brief cognitive-behavioral methods in treating anxiety problems lend support to the view that a historical focus is unnecessary in treating these problems. Clients can change their cognition, behaviors, and affective experiences without an extended review of the past events that may or may not have played a causal role in shaping their tendencies to feel anxious and to respond avoidantly. Brief therapy reduces or omits the search for causes, in favor of a present focus on more appropriate responding. Rather than reviewing previous failures, brief treatment often builds upon strategies that the client has already found effective in trying to manage anxiety.

Being Brief: How-To Tips for Streamlining

The Therapist's Goals

Treatment time is being shortened, challenging us to reinvent our methods. Intermittent therapeutic contacts and directive, behavioral approaches to helping, coupled with expanded use of extra-office measures including homework and book-, video-, and audiotape-assisted home learning, and more systematic use of community resources and support groups, can help us continue to function despite the constraints of managed care.

When therapy is brief by design, the therapist accepts responsibility for helping to move therapy along, making sure that time is used wisely and is not wasted. The very brevity of the treatment creates a compelling focus on compliance with therapist directives; on overt, verifiable behavior; and on attention to change.

Good managed care therapists emphasize treatment brevity and are heavily results-oriented. They prepare patients for brief therapy and interview with the goal of identifying the patient's strengths and adaptive capacities and finding the way or opening for the patient to access and utilize his or her abilities. They strive to be parsimonious while promoting continuing growth and the possibility of later return to therapy should it be indicated (Hoyt, 1995a). These therapists value the contributions of natural helpers who can be utilized in groups and family therapy.

As Hoyt (1995) puts it:

> The goal of the HMO therapist is to become unnecessary quickly and to help the patient get "unstuck" and then to move on. Dramatic and profound changes can occur rapidly, to be sure, but the HMO therapist does not usually conceptualize the treatment in terms of a "definitive restructuring of character." The medical model of "cure" becomes less useful than an approach toward growth, problem solving, and enhanced coping skills. The good HMO therapist knows both that a great deal can be accomplished at once and that with some assistance people can do a lot on their own. There are also a multiplicity of ways to do and get therapy: for example, in addition to individual, group, family, and marital therapy, many people benefit enormously from psychoeducational approaches such as parenting classes, stress reduction workshops, and recommended readings. (p. 33)

Basic Steps of Brief Therapy

The goals of the brief therapist are well served by following twelve basic steps:

1. Avoid counterproductive psychopathologizing.
2. Focus on well-defined specific, measurable outcomes.
3. Evaluate risk factors and contraindications for brief therapy.
4. Begin the change process in the first session.
5. Foster encouraging cognitions, especially by reframing.
6. Develop concrete, behavioral assignments.
7. Use supplemental sources of information.
8. Teach problem-solving skills.
9. Schedule flexibly.
10. Permit single-session therapy to unfold.
11. Build natural sources of support in the community.
12. Stop before the end.

These steps are discussed in detail in the following subsections.

Eschewing Pathology. The first step is to avoid counterproductive psychopathologizing. The pursuit of a perfectionistic "cure" through the persistent probing of pathology will need to shift, if one is to work in a "time-sensitive" manner (Budman & Gurman, 1988), to a pragmatic and parsimonious promotion of patients' strengths regarding the presenting problem.

Milton Erickson was renowned for his unconventional, rapid therapeutic approach. Although the limited number of controlled investigations of his methods compels caution in adopting his techniques, many clinicians have found elements of his strategies to be very helpful. Erickson's approach to brief therapy was designed to help patients find nonsymptomatic ways of dealing with relationships; symptoms can be viewed as less useful strategies that patients have come to rely on to manage their relationships with others. Fisch (1982) has noted that Erickson eschewed conventional ideas about pathology. He did not view patients' problems as exceptional or unusual. Rather, Erickson dealt with patients as if they were perfectly normal and resilient, simply struggling, as we all are, with the human condition. From this point of view, concepts such as symptoms, defenses, or mental illness made no sense. Not only did he deal with patients as if they were perfectly competent; he did so with all of his patients, rather than with only some of them.

Measurable Outcomes.   It is important to focus on well-defined specific, measurable patient outcomes. This will also help in integrating outcomes assessment and treatment. Rapid change can be promoted through the articulation of specific, measurable goals and the use of concrete, structured exercises to achieve those goals. These help to clarify the client's situation, restore a sense of control, make the client accountable for change, and provide a measurable yardstick for assessing treatment effectiveness. Behavioral assignments harness the client's motivation to change and give the client a framework for describing the progress being made ("I initiated two conversations with my difficult boss this week.") Integrating outcome measures in the treatment process makes both the therapist and the patient more explicitly accountable. Reviewers expect therapists to use clear goals both to keep treatment on track and to define its endpoint.

During the first session, collaborate with the patient to define a treatment focus, consisting usually of one specific, achievable, measurable goal. Develop a bare bones plan of action that can be communicated clearly to both the patient and a reviewer. This treatment plan should address the specific focal problems that patients present. Target one or two limited problems at a time. Think in terms of the goals they express: What is getting in the way of their success? What concrete behaviors need to be addressed?

The goal formulation process can be used to communicate empathy. Most patients want to experience change. Helping them change efficiently therefore shows that you understand them. "Sharing their pain" when they are ready to move may actually express a less empathic grasp of their experience than directing their growth. If you are earnestly invested in trying to help them move their lives in the directions they desire, that caring will show that you understand their healthy impulse to find a better way. Empathizing with that impulse may be more productive than empathizing with their experience of distress.

Emmons (1986) found that having goals, making progress toward goals, and feeling freedom from conflict among one's goals were all predictors of subjective well-being. Happiness grows less from the passive experience of desirable circumstances than from active involvement in valued activities and progress toward one's goals (Diener & Larsen, 1993).

Risk Factors and Contraindications. The skillful brief therapist will evaluate risk factors and contraindications for brief therapy. (Later sections in this chapter will discuss the specifics of risk factors in terms of both children and adults.) Assess for any issues of danger to self or others; these must receive immediate attention. Be familiar with laws about the duty to warn and involuntary commitment in your state, and know the relevant agencies you might contact if necessary.

Engaging the Patient in Change. Engage the patient in the change process during the first session. Try to be enthusiastic, imaginative, funny, and memorable as you generate a list of potential solutions to the presenting problem. Help the patient find a delimited focus and begin to take control: Create a preliminary plan of action and begin to execute it. For example:

A. Engage in compensatory empowering actions: Exercise. Write. Talk. Practice relaxation exercises. Do something.
B. Write down my obsessive or hostile thoughts.
C. Make an appointment to worry. Schedule obsessing at a convenient time.

Work with the patient to decide the best place to start experimenting with changes. Often this decision-making process requires patients to clarify their values as they face choices between competing desirable ends. For instance, a perfectionistic depressed spouse may detest the idea of divorce but find the failings of his or her spouse unbearable. A married couple may want more time and energy for intimacy but may also desire a picture-perfect home and garden. Choices may need to be made; often accepting the inevitable need for compromise and trade-offs helps to resolve a problem.

Cognitive Reframing. Foster encouraging cognitions; reframing challenging situations is often very helpful. Generally people come to therapy because their current understanding of the problem(s) they are facing fail to provide them with useful clues about how to proceed. As a result, they feel overwhelmed, helpless, and hopeless. Brief therapy must help patients see their problem as potentially manageable and their distress as temporary. Although the situation they face is a challenging one, it will not go on forever. Helping patients change their frames, or viewpoints, modifies the meaning of the concrete situations they face. Reframing helps patients to react to the same situations differently, often making them less of a problem. According to de Shazer (1982):

> The effects of reframing are confirmed by the appearance of a new set of beliefs, or perceptions, and behavior modifications that can be described as a logical consequence of the shift in perception. . . . The result is that patients can look at things from a different angle. Once they "see things differently," they can behave differently. (p. 25)

Reframing is often considered a type of paradoxical intervention. Reframing involves changing the patient's conceptual view of a situation by placing it in another "frame" that fits the "facts" of the situation equally well or even better and thereby changes its entire meaning (Watzlawick et al., 1974). Empirical examinations have found reframing to be an effective strategy for reducing negative affect (Kraft, Clairborn, & Dowd, 1985). For example, when a client was overwhelmed by stress at work, reframing seemed to make all the difference. Her work in an overbooked urology office left her charged with the task of mollifying a roomful of ambivalent men awaiting vasectomies. Nightly she'd collapse in exhaustion and pain, filled with a sense of utter failure. While attributing more of her experience to the situation and avoiding personalizing was helpful, still more transforming was a simple reframe. She was instructed to look forward to the next especially busy workday, because the "bad days" would provide the best opportunities to put the new coping techniques she was developing to the test. Rather than fearfully awaiting the next "killer" day, she was encouraged to hope it would come soon. During the week that followed, she reported significantly reduced tension at work, although she said she was a bit frustrated because she wasn't having any of the "truly bad" days she was looking for. After a few weeks without the eagerly awaited "extraordinarily horrible" day, she said she was feeling better and no longer felt the need for treatment. While several nonspecific factors were operating in this case, each of which is probably in part responsible for the client's improvement, it is interesting to consider how the therapy process and its way of reframing difficult circumstances (e.g., as perfect opportunities to put new skills into practice) help clients adopt a more benign view of their life situations. Making a friend out of a miserable situation can make a big difference, and therapy often helps clients do just that.

Another client was overwhelmed by the need to locate a university teaching job near her husband's new position. The market was daunting, and she was facing a separation of several months because she had decided not to surrender her current tenured position until some other option was in hand. After discussion made clear that her decision to keep her tenured position was firm, the therapist chose to facilitate a perspective change. The marital separation would produce benefits as well as costs. After 10 years of marriage, weekend reunions were rekindling passion. Rather than taking one another for granted, this couple was enraptured and appreciative of one another's presence. As a weekday "single mom" the client was enjoying the rarely discussed pleasures of uncontested parenting: Her decisions did not need to be defended, and her children were not trying to circumvent unpopular edicts. The grueling job search, rather than a needless waste of time, could be seen as a marvelously disciplined way to lay the ground for an extensive professional network that would serve her well in years to come. These reconceptualizations shifted her perspective, and she reported dramatically improved affect. Therapy changes the eye of the beholder, helping clients make peace with the formerly intolerable. When circumstances can't or shouldn't be changed, expedient therapy often focuses on attitudes.

Often clients feel helpless or that they have little control over their actions. We as therapists need to arrange for their control of much they view as uncontrollable and involuntary. In these cases, paradoxical approaches are quite useful for helping the client demonstrate self-control. Paradoxical directives involve telling the client to continue performing the symptomatic behavior, which is often called "symptom prescription." When the directive is accompanied by instructions to schedule performance of the prescribed symptom, this is called "symptom scheduling." There is evidence for the effectiveness of paradoxical techniques in cases in which clients' symptoms appear to be produced by mental control attempts gone awry (Shoham & Rohrbaugh, 1997; Shoham-Salomon & Rosenthal, 1987). Research has shown that paradoxical interventions are often more effective than other types of interventions in treating various conditions, including depression, insomnia, and procrastination.

Some forms of psychopathology seem to be responsive to therapy that has the curious aim of encouraging people to stop treating themselves. This may work because when clients are advised to create their symptoms or are otherwise encouraged to rescind or reverse their habitual mental control activities, a reduction in deep activation may occur (Wegner & Smart, 1997). Deep activation represents a recent reconceptualization of unconscious influences. When deep activation becomes chronic, it can yield symptoms ranging from intrusive thoughts and emotional upsets to behaviors that express the deeply activated thoughts either directly or indirectly. Paradoxical therapies may work because they target deep activation quite directly.

Another cognitive strategy useful in doing brief therapy involves affirming clients' past choices. In a sense, life is always about choices. The need to choose between alternatives forms the basis for internal conflict. Intrapsychic conflict is what started the whole therapeutic enterprise, with Freud's consideration of how people's ability to try simultaneously to reach two contradictory goals gives rise to much maladaptive behavior and subjective distress.

People crave the sense that they have chosen well in their lives. This desire to feel good about one's choices goes well beyond wanting to have one's intelligence affirmed or one's skill as a decision maker validated. For most people it is simply unbearable to believe that you have wasted your only life. When clients sit before us, crying with a sense of deep regret about the path they have chosen to take, as therapists we can guide them through their existential malaise by offering a new perspective. We can point out ways in which they are exaggerating the negative aspects of the alternative they actualized, and highlight positive aspects that they in their self-torturing are unable to see.

For example, when a woman was extremely depressed by the realization that with her youngest child's fifth birthday she was no longer able to define herself as the mother of young children, it became clear that fueling her despair were unresolved issues about her decision to work outside the home while her children were very young. The child's fifth birthday finalized her choice; with only school-age children, she could never be a stay-at-home mother of preschoolers. When it was pointed out to her that, despite her work, she had in fact spent considerable time with her children when they were young, her attitude toward the whole matter shifted abruptly. She calculated the percentage of time she had in fact been a devoted, attentive mother and realized how she had allowed abstractions ("absent working mother" vs. "nurturant stay-at-home mom") to cloud her view. Suddenly her choices seemed acceptable and even advantageous, and her depression consequently lifted.

By reframing, we can dramatically alter clients' interpretations of their choices and thereby transform their sense of themselves. If we can help them feel the choices they have made were reasonable and in some ways desirable, clients will feel successful, competent, and as if their life has the meaning they need it to have. Doing isn't everything; developing conviction that you have shaped a good life for yourself is critical to satisfaction.

Often recognizing the temporary nature of crisis episodes can help reduce the catastrophizing that otherwise aggravates problems within individuals and families. Teaching patients how to catch and alter their global, extreme thinking when they face a difficult situation can also be very useful.

For some patients excessive self-blame may be preferable to feeling less than omnipotent. Taking less control may be difficult, but ultimately helpful. Learning how to depersonalize is challenging for many patients. For example, following the loss of a beloved alcoholic father, it seemed helpful to ask: "But what would have probably happened if you had tried to hospitalize him again against his wishes? He resisted treatment in the past and probably would have fought it this time. He would have become suspicious and angry toward you. Instead, you offered him respect. You tried to find compromises that acknowledged his preferences. This probably helped him to choose life as long as he did."

In addition to challenging cognitive distortions, it can be of value for patients to learn to enjoy the ironies of life. For example, while many employees feel powerless in the face of employers, many employers feel nearly as powerless in the face of their employees. This realization, combined with appropriate self-effacing disclosure on the part of the therapist, can make it easier for patients to begin to see themselves as equal adults in relationships with authority figures.

Behavioral "Homework" Assignments.   Developing specific, concrete, behavioral assignments often facilitates change more effectively than abstract discussions do. Often simple, straightforward, practical, behavioral interventions can be helpful, even with people whose problems initially seem very complicated and chronic. Having patients monitor both useful and problem behaviors can increase their sense of control and facilitate beneficial changes. Give homework assignments that are clear. Communicate the expectation that most of the work of the therapy occurs between sessions.

Using the active, directive techniques of strategic therapists such as Milton Erickson and Jay Haley can often make brief treatment more effective. Haley believed that a therapist should:

... identify solvable problems, set goals, design interventions to achieve those goals, examine the responses he receives to correct his approach, and ultimately examine the outcome of his therapy to see if it has been effective. ... Strategic therapy is not a particular approach or theory but a name for those types of therapy where the therapist takes responsibility for directly influencing people. (Haley, 1973, p. 17)

It is often useful to help patients recognize how their choices about sleep, alcohol use, and caffeine use can profoundly affect their functioning. Preston (1997) points out that neurobiological destabilization commonly occurs in psychiatric disorders. Brief therapists can provide information about sleep and sleep cycles, point out the need for deep sleep and how this has an impact on emotional functioning, and then introduce issues of substance use and exercise. Encourage patients to take action to change these habits. This provides a direct way to regain at least some control over their brain functioning and to enhance their ability for self-control. These are direct, concrete actions that allow patients to get more out of brief therapy.

Supplemental Information Sources. Using supplemental sources of information can be a cost-effective way to enhance the impact of psychotherapy. Rather than use scarce time during sessions to provide extensive education to patients about psychological phenomena, incorporate use of the Internet, handouts, audiotapes, videotapes, and books in your treatment.

Problem-Solving Skills. Teaching problem-solving skills, rather than solving all the problems, makes more efficient use of a therapist's time. Focus on equipping patients with skills they can use in relationships outside of sessions to support one another more effectively and to negotiate mutually tolerable compromises. "If I give you a fish, you can eat a meal. If I teach you how to fish, you can feed yourself forever." Don't use therapy sessions to mediate each and every conflict issue couples present. Help establish social supports outside therapy for both individuals and families, which will ease the transition out of therapy and help to maintain treatment gains.

Flexible Scheduling. Avoid rigid scheduling. The convention of meeting with all psychotherapy patients for hour-long sessions (or 50 minutes) on a weekly basis developed in part for the convenience of practitioners. Scheduling is simplified when patients can be accommodated with a more or less fixed slot of time each week. Freud often worked much more intensively with his patients, but scheduling variable numbers of weekly contacts can be confusing, and most outpatients find it cumbersome to meet with a therapist more than once a week. Adherence to rigid treatment timing is often viewed as therapeutic. The need to wait a full week between sessions can be rationalized on the grounds that it helps patients develop skills in functioning independently and delaying immediate gratification. It is interesting to note how often patients scheduled in this way mention the fact that things consistently seem to be going better the closer their next session approaches. This experience teaches them that they can ride out rough periods successfully on their own.

L. Johnson (1995) points out that

> . . . time-sensitive therapists do not automatically plan to see patients in one week. The main benefit of scheduling people at one-week intervals is to simplify the therapist's schedule, which is then more predictable. If we reverse our priorities, we will schedule the next session based on the patient's status. Suppose a patient has a strong commitment to work hard ("customer") and there is a clear and potentially useful homework assignment at the end of that session. It makes no sense to have the patient return in one week. Since the therapy has a homework slant, it makes more sense to schedule a return in two or three weeks.
>
> Subsequent sessions should be scheduled so as to communicate values and processes to the therapy relationship, not as a default process to fill the therapist's schedule. The therapist must even decide what the meaning is if the patient is given the same time every week, as opposed to being seen weekly but at different times in the day. The patient who is seen the same day every week is invited to think of the relationship with the therapist as a regular part of his life, to which he is to become accustomed. Conversely, a patient seen at different hours during the day, but still on a weekly basis, might be invited to think of the therapy as a temporary state, to which she will not become accustomed.
>
> When the patient hasn't done the homework, but has no real explanation, consider changing the schedule of appointments. The next session can be postponed indefinitely, with the statement that the client needs to think about whether this is a good time for him to be in therapy. Perhaps the therapist is pushing too hard and needs to back off. Perhaps outside distractions are keeping the patient from concentrating on treatment.
>
> Such a move is likely to surprise the client, since the expectation from childhood is, when I resist something, a parental figure will try to motivate me. When the therapist backs off rapidly and encourages more caution and less involvement, it has had a remarkable effect. The patient generally finds his motivation increasing as a result of the therapist's backing off. It is really quite possible that the patient is not ready for therapy at that time. The paradoxical message contains a powerful truth: Therapy takes energy and resources, and so one should not enter therapy without first counting the costs to determine whether one has the resources to complete the tasks. (p. 132)

Similarly, in determining the session length, L. Johnson (1995) emphasizes the need for flexibility:

> Sessions last 45 to 50 minutes strictly for the convenience of the therapist and the reimbursement systems. In a rational world, some sessions might last an hour, others two hours, and others ten minutes. In fact, it might be that hypnosis-oriented treatment and exposure-based treatment of PTSD ought to last at least 90 minutes to two hours. Conversely, many problems can be dealt with in much less time than 50 minutes. There is certainly no rational reason to rigidly cling to a 50-minute hour. Some therapists may be quite capable of doing effective interventions in 20 or 40 minutes, and they should be encouraged to do so.

The tendency to start therapy with one or two exhaustive intake sessions was based on the assumption that therapy was a slow and gradual process that typically lasted many months and sometimes many years. Leisurely history taking at intake made sense given these expectations; there would be plenty of time to use this meticulously compiled information.

The psychodynamic tradition assumes that meaningful change requires insight into the unconscious sources of current dysfunctional behavior. As secondary gain is emphasized, patients are expected to be ambivalent about surrendering symptoms. This tradition developed slow-paced therapeutic methods because it assumed the inevitability of resistance to change; uncomfortable realizations about immature, infantile wishes distorting the adult patient's ability to make reasonable and rational decisions are only embraced when interpretations are offered gradually and sensitively. Patients who do not return are assumed to be "treatment failures" because of lack of readiness or capacity to tolerate the anxiety associated with confronting threatening material. Patients who end treatment after only a handful of sessions are "premature terminators" who are assumed to be unwilling or unable to do the hard work of real therapy.

These ideas colored many clinicians' work, even those who did not endorse a psychodynamic orientation. When patients ended psychotherapy early on, many therapists were loath to call to inquire about the reasons for this decision, either because they desired to avoid putting the patient in the awkward position of having to reject the therapist or because they wanted to avoid their own vulnerability in such an encounter. Few considered the possibility that the patients who came only once or twice actually often represented success stories.

As Lazarus and Fay (1990) wrote:

> Some long-term therapy is not only inefficient (taking longer than necessary because it was insufficiently focused or precise), but even detrimental because of the reinforcement of pathological self-concepts. One of the great advantages of the short-term focus is that if the therapy doesn't work, it will be apparent much sooner. . . . In this regard, to paraphrase an old saying, effective treatment depends far less on the hours you put in, than on what you put into those hours. . . . We also believe that there are three major impediments to the development and clinical implementation of rapidly effective therapies: (1) the lack of a sufficiently broad technical armamentarium—largely the result of factionalism within our profession; (2) ignorance of, or inadequate attention to, the biological aspects of "psychological" problems; and (3) the concept of resistance and its elaboration, particularly the notion that the locus of resistance is within the patient. (pp. 39–41)

Lazarus and Fay advocate using a systematic schema to assess patients' problems comprehensively before selecting specific interventions, offering their Multimodal Therapy as one such approach (Lazarus, 1976, 1989).

The Possibilities of Single-Session Therapy. Permit single-session therapy to unfold. Rockwell and Pinkerton (1982) urge therapists to "be alert to the possibility [of single-session therapy], assess quickly when s/he has a [potential SST] case in hand, set the process in motion, and determine a satisfactory stopping point" (p. 39). It is helpful to assess the patient's motivation and expectations, as clinical experience and research (Pekarik & Wierzbicki, 1986) have shown the single best indicator of therapy duration is the patient's expectation of the likely number of sessions necessary. Determine solutions that have been attempted previously; often something that formerly proved helpful can be tried again.

It is often helpful to skip doing an extensive intake during your contact time. If you need a lot of detailed information about the client, obtain this in written form. Instead, take advantage of the heightened momentum for change that characterizes the initial session. Most change occurs early on in treatment. The patient's hopefulness that things are finally going to get better, thanks to his or her willingness to endure the difficult process of contacting a therapist and getting to the appointment, primes the patient to pay attention and deploy suggestions. This marvelous readiness to take chances and make changes coincides with the therapist's eagerness to make a difference in an as-of-yet unknown life. During this first meeting the therapist's alertness is high, because of the excitement that accompanies the challenge of discovering the best way to help a newly encountered individual. The anxiety both parties experience at this first meeting, if managed properly, can help both patient and therapist stay in the moderate zone of arousal that is associated with optimal learning and performance (some refer to this as the Yerkes-Dobson effect; others talk about it in terms of being in the "zone" of peak performance). The therapist's enthusiasm, confidence, and clarity can help mobilize anxiety constructively. If moderated properly, this mutual trepidation and vigilance can make this first meeting particularly electric and memorable.

The therapist's goal is to use the resource of this new, special encounter to create a mutual engagement that can propel the patient forward. In many respects the therapeutic relationship is most novel and attention-worthy at the outset. During the first encounter the experience most deviates from the usual way the patient spends time. This exceptionality in some ways increases the opportunity for the therapist to have an influence.

Many patients attend only one session of psychotherapy. Given clinicians' frequent reluctance to conduct a followup (variously because of the inconvenience, respect for the patient's privacy, desire to avoid rejection, etc.), it is often hard to distinguish between those single-session cases that represent premature termination and those signifying stunningly successful treatment. Talmon's (1990) data suggest that many patients find what they need in only one session. This implies that we should direct our energies to facilitating such effective single-session therapy whenever feasible. As far as the other cases of premature termination go, it still seems to behoove us to make optimal use of first sessions, because obviously the high rate of drop out after this initial contact means that the first session is frequently our only chance to make a difference.

It seems plausible that some patients give up on treatment after a single session because their eagerness for rapid change does not seem to be reciprocated by the therapists who approach the process envisioning a longer time frame and expecting a more leisurely pace. A "business-as-usual," thorough diagnostic workup and history-taking session may not suit the desires of a patient who feels primed for a fresh start or about to explode in pain.

Focus instead on the patients' presenting complaint and develop a clear understanding of how they are currently experiencing their symptoms. Their way of thinking about and experiencing their problem matters more than theoretical abstractions about what this reported symptom might mean diagnostically or what its etiological origin might be. The patients' way of experiencing the problem relates to how it must change in order for them to be satisfied with treatment. How patients want life to be different is key. Knowing this will help to align your motivation with theirs, and help you to articulate the treatment goals.

Community Support. An important step in therapy is to build natural sources of support in the community. Brief therapy attempts to replace the support function formerly provided by long-term treatment by allocating time to assist the client in developing a better natural support network. Creating a more varied, mutual, and elaborated social system upon which the client can draw following the end of formal therapy is a priority among many therapists focused on maintenance. Several studies indicate that long-term psychotherapy success is highly dependent upon the effectiveness with which the client's post-treatment social system functions. Long-term solutions therefore require attending to the client's need for ongoing social support. In long-term therapy this search for alternative means of addressing the client's support needs is sometimes postponed, because temporarily the therapist can adequately meet those needs.

At the beginning of treatment, solicit information about patients' informal support system (family, friends, and coworkers). Encourage development of these social resources. Try to get a clear sense of what others in the patients' life expect from them, in order to help the patients establish more satisfying mutual relationships outside of therapy.

Assist patients in maintaining family resources during times of high stress. For example, when a parent dies, the profound loss generally leaves all in the family feeling cheated. Paradoxically the loss of a frustrating, problem parent can often leave more intense feelings of despair than the death of a more gratifying parent. The death of an alcoholic parent who never kept promises and never seemed satisfied with a child's accomplishments puts an end to any hope of salvaging the relationship. Children who have worked hard to try to help a troubled parent can be left with a shocking sense of injustice; death guarantees their parent will never be able to repay their debt. To compensate for deep feelings of being cheated, many surviving children become greedily preoccupied with obtaining their share of the estate, often threatening relationships among remaining family members. Recognizing the potential for caring and mutual support that family members represent can help clients prevent destructive infighting. "Although it makes you mad that your sister's helping is limited to public, visible opportunities to offer assistance, isn't it helpful to you to have her trying to help at all, at least in some ways? The best she can do is quite limited, but it is a resource that may be of value to you in some way."

Terminating Treatment.   Stop before the end. Integrate outcome assessment and treatment by using goal attainment to define the session's focus and to trigger termination. Treatment goals should be expressed in clear, measurable terms. In assessing progress, enthusiastically emphasize the importance of even small steps in the desirable direction, rather than the negative exceptions. For instance, "Even though you felt like you were going to 'lose it' that afternoon and briefly considered hurting yourself, instead you started thinking about other options, and finally calmed yourself down by listening to some music." End therapy as soon as progress is being made in addressing the focal problem; communicate to the patient that you are confident the progress that has already been made will continue after treatment.

In brief therapy, change processes are frequently initiated without being completely worked through during the course of actual patient–therapist contact (Horowitz & Hoyt, 1979; Shectman, 1986). Brief therapy often ends before all aspects of the solution have been fine-tuned. Consolidation of treatment gains is expected to occur gradually over time. The possibility of patients' returning later for a "refresher" can be mentioned, but it is desirable to communicate optimism about patients' chances for future success all on their own. Managed care is expected by some to be associated with greater use of serial or intermittent short-term therapy, in which patients are more likely to seek future treatment because of an earlier satisfying experience with brief therapy (Cummings, 1977, 1990; Cummings & VandenBos, 1979; Budman & Gurman, 1983, 1988; Bennett, 1983, 1984).

Attacks on and Defense of Brief Therapy

Hoyt (1995) has found that some therapists find focused treatment frustrating and restrictive and view symptom relief and return to function as second-rate goals, even though these are the reasons most patients seek treatment and despite the fact that experience has shown that, in many cases, personality changes also occur in goal-oriented HMO therapy (Bennett & Wisneski, 1979). It is interesting to note that one survey of HMO therapists (Lange et al., 1988, p. 462) found "uniformly high ratings given HMOs by the providers who work for them," although, not surprisingly, some providers felt their clinical load was too great. A second survey (Austad, 1989) has confirmed the generally positive experience of therapists working within an HMO, who have found that quality and expediency are not mutually exclusive.

In some ways it is amusing that so many psychotherapists are feeling beleaguered and threatened by MCOs' recent application of Deming's "total quality management" concept of consumer-centered organizational conduct, when the whole notion of client-centered therapy has long been a cornerstone of much of what we do (Rogers, 1951). Didn't therapists more or less *invent* the client-centered concept? Managed care companies are very concerned with keeping customers satisfied, and traditionally, so are we.

While some schools of therapy maintain that clinicians should be mistrustful of clients' ability to assess what is truly in their best interest, other theoretical camps have long argued that we help most effectively by respecting the clients' internal capacity for development and potential for self-knowledge. Some of our field's difficulty in making peace with managed care is probably due to lingering suspicion about clients' desires for rapid cures. There are both selfless good and self-serving bad reasons for tempering a client's rush.

Part of why therapists have difficulty responding as a unified whole to managed care imperatives is undoubtedly due to some longstanding philosophical fractures within the psychotherapy field, especially those between the psychodynamic and person-centered perspectives. This division continues to run deep. A 1997 e-mail exchange among licensed clinical psychologists illustrated how quickly opinions on various matters still split along these lines. A discussion about the appropriateness of home offices led the dynamicists to rally against home offices on the grounds that these could easily contaminate transference, and the person-centered clinicians challenged the wisdom of therapists trying to be a "blank screen," rather than a "real person" with their clients. Tempers flared, attacks became personal, and it was clear to all readers that these professionals do not have a conceptual consensus. We probably should not let our response to MCOs be hampered by old divisions and the old debate over whether or not clients know best. Managed care's demand that we help people efficiently happens to dovetail with what clients have desired all along. "Help me quickly!" they have always implored.

Some psychotherapists have subtly been encouraged by their training to scoff at such pleas, even to pathologize them by seeing such insistence on urgency as symptomatic of deep-seated characterological flaws, immaturity, impulsivity, and egocentrism. The truth is that clients who are hurting and anxious are understandably eager for rapid resolution of their symptoms. For those of us who have been fairly consumer-centered all along, the MCO demand for the most efficient treatment possible is not new, unfamiliar, or ethically challenging. We've always struggled to work as expediently as possible; in this regard, we're natural allies of MCOs. The clinicians who might be expected to have the greatest difficulty with this transition are those whose experience tells them that clients who push for quick solutions are generally naive, simplistic, and problematically dependent on others for answers. These clinicians may construe reeducation as part of the therapeutic agenda: these clients need to learn patience and how to withstand the frustration arising from life's inevitable imperfections. Lengthy therapy can teach these lessons; however, one needs to ask whether individual outpatient therapy isn't a pretty expensive way to get this type of education.

Not all clients who push for rapid change do so pathologically. The most urgent clients are often most poised to make changes; those who patiently tolerate leisurely paced, cautious psychotherapy often seem to enjoy its lack of pressure for change. In some sense the latter group might be less serious about making progress.

One might even argue that sometimes traditional long-term treatment is attractive to clients precisely because it doesn't work. It expects little change from the client, while creating the appearance that efforts are being made to improve things. It can be used by someone who recognizes the impossibility of their current circumstances and/or behavior but isn't yet willing to change as a tool to procrastinate and stall taking active steps. Waiting is entirely legitimate; publicly subsidized collaborative delay in the guise of therapeutic activity is too expensive.

The reality may be that clients only move when they're ready. Paying clinicians to process and interpret clients' ambivalence while clients ready themselves to make changes may often be wasteful. The fact that eventually clients start moving to change their lives should not be accepted as proof of long-term therapy's efficacy. Time alone may have done the trick; the therapist's companionship is as likely to have deterred the client's desired initiation as to have facilitated it. The outcome research on long-term psychotherapy has generally failed to prove its advantages over short-term methods.

Hoyt argues that

> Doing brief therapy with most patients may help make longer-term treatment available for those patients who most require it, with innovative intermittent treatment, brief intensive treatment, and group therapies also being helpful. In addition to ethical and humanistic concerns, group- and staff-model HMO therapists know that the HMO is accountable (at risk) for the comprehensive health costs of its members and also know that there is a strong tendency for untreated psychological problems to result in excessive medical (including emergency room) services. As Shectman . . . has said, necessity sometimes proves to be the mother of intervention. (p. 325)

Brief therapy, like all therapy, can be done well or poorly, and abuses are possible. Because the incentive is toward efficiency (Bennett, 1988; Boaz, 1988; Kaplan, 1989; Kramon, 1989; Nelson, 1987), care must be taken to ensure that treatment is brief and effective, not just brief. Just as the fee-for-service practitioner must guard against the temptation to rationalize unnecessary prolongations of treatment, the HMO therapist must guard against the tendency to undertreat. Institutionalized forces that encourage UR and promote rapid turnover of patients need to be balanced against professional standards and values. Quality assurance is the watchword here, and good HMOs are well equipped to provide such assurances, through difficult-case seminars, continuing education presentations, and other training measures.

When Not to Use Brief Treatment

Contraindications for Brief Treatment with Adults

Many contend that treatment outcomes vary widely as a result of patient characteristics rather than elements of the treatment process (Blatt & Felsen, 1993). Optimizing treatment, then, requires us to ask the multivariate question "Which treatment, when offered to which type of client, by what type of therapist, is most effective?" This conceptualization was offered decades ago (Paul, 1966), yet few outcome studies since were sufficiently sophisticated to allow for this type of refined analysis.

Effects of Client Personality Characteristics on Brief Therapy. A reanalysis of the NIMH TDCRP data assessed whether the three treatment conditions differentially affected perfectionistic versus approval-seeking depressives (Blatt et al., 1995). Perfectionistic clients were found to do more poorly with all three forms of brief therapy provided in this study. Results of other studies suggest that these self-critical (introjective) clients respond better to long-term, intensive (four or five sessions weekly) psychodynamic treatment; they showed significantly greater improvement with this form of treatment than did their relationship-troubled (dependent or anaclitic) depressed counterparts (Blatt & Ford, 1994).

Perfectionism, or self-criticism, appears to be a consistent and significant disruptive factor that interferes with the capacity to enter effectively into and to benefit extensively from short-term treatment. Perfectionism is an integral aspect of the paranoia, obsessive-compulsive, and guilty depression disorders, described as the "introjective" configuration of psychopathology (Blatt & Shichman, 1983). Introjective clients are usually interpersonally and emotionally isolated, and they tend to use counteractive (e.g, intellectualization, projection, reaction formation, overcompensation) rather than avoidant defenses (denial and repression). These defenses may make it more difficult for introjective clients to establish an effective therapeutic alliance. However, once that relationship is established, in long-term treatment these clients can utilize their resources to fruitfully apply the insights gained in the treatment process.

Self-esteem is a function of achievement and perceived competence, but it is also a byproduct of expectations. Many clients feel inadequate because they demand the impossible from themselves. Challenging the inappropriateness of unreasonable personal expectations is another important function of therapy. Research suggests that for those who become depressed because of excessive self-critical and perfectionistic tendencies, traditional therapy is apt to be slow going.

Often the clients' underlying need to feel superior undermines the therapist's exhortations about the irrationality of perfectionism. Clients may in part expect these great things from themselves because on some level they enjoy the belief that one day they'll be able to deliver on these promises to themselves and others. While to an outsider it seems only punishing to employ unrealistically high standards, to such clients the pleasure associated with maintaining an idealized sense of their potential can offset the pain of repeated disappointment in actualizing this extraordinary latent self. Effective interventions must often simultaneously address the implicit grandiosity and the explicit inferiority feelings experienced by such clients. Doing only half the job frequently results in a therapeutic stalemate. Development of more effective, efficient means of helping these perfectionistic depressed clients is needed.

These findings demonstrate how variables other than diagnosis can mediate the impact of treatment. As we find the most relevant client dimensions, our ability to match particular brief treatment techniques with clients showing salient influential qualities will facilitate our ability to provide services that optimize clients' learning and progress. We need to inform MCOs about findings such as these. We are increasingly in a position to make empirically supported arguments about the inappropriateness of brief treatment in particular cases. Our ability to specify with greater precision when brief treatment is contraindicated will allow us to have a greater voice in shaping treatment decisions and consequently allow us to be more effective clinicians.

Lack of Predictors of Poor Response.   Although it is important to be aware of contraindications, it is also true that few predictors of poor response have emerged. According to Bloom:

> Except for the finding that lower social class patients have higher dropout rates, no other demographic variables (age, sex, level of intelligence) have been shown to be significantly related to therapeutic outcome . . . , although Chinen . . . has found that high levels of what he calls "self-contexting" (citing beliefs as opinions rather than as objective truths) are associated with improvement in brief psychotherapy among older patients but not among younger patients. Thus, contraindications to planned short-term psychotherapy are rarely found in demographic characteristics. Rather, the contraindications that have been suggested are mainly found in characterological and symptomatic domains.
>
> Malan and his group . . . have gone to considerable lengths to specify the criteria for rejection of applicants: (1) serious depression or gross destructive or self-destructive acting out, (2) drug addiction, (3) a history of long-term hospitalization or other signs of latent or actual psychosis, (4) more than one course of electroconvulsive therapy, (5) chronic alcoholism, (6) incapacitating chronic obsessional symptoms, and (7) incapacitating chronic phobic symptoms. (Bloom, 1992, p. 294)

Mann (1973) and Mann and Goldman (1982) proposed a number of exclusionary criteria: serious depression, acute psychosis, borderline personality organization, and the inability to identify a central issue. Patients who may have difficulty engaging and disengaging rapidly from treatment, including schizoid patients, certain obsessional and narcissistic patients; patients with strong dependency needs; depressive patients who are not able to form a rapid therapeutic alliance; and patients with psychosomatic disorders who do not tolerate loss well are not generally good candidates for brief therapy.

Three relative contraindications for planned short-term psychotherapy have been proposed by Reich and Neenan (1986). These include (1) psychosis or major thought disorder; (2) multiple severe psychiatric problems; and (3) character disorder, if patients lack a specific focus for treatment. MacKenzie (1988) identified the following commonly employed exclusion criteria: (1) patients who cannot attend to the process of active verbal interaction, (2) patients with diagnoses for which other treatment modalities take precedence, and (3) patients with a characterologic style that precludes the likelihood of enduring through the psychological work.

Preston, Varzos, and Liebert (1995) maintain that

> Even though brief therapy can be very helpful for many people, it is not always the appropriate course of action. Sometimes, brief psychotherapy is simply not enough. Some people have gone through tremendously difficult times and have very deep emotional wounds that require longer treatment. Their problems involve not just one major focus, but several. Serious difficulties may affect many aspects of life. Brief therapy can provide a starting point for such folks, and many are able to make some gains. But those who have a lot of healing or growth to do, while able to benefit from brief treatment, may subsequently enter with a support group or longer-term therapy.
>
> For two types of emotional problems, brief therapy is probably not a good idea at all. Those who have experienced *extreme* psychological traumas in childhood (physical, emotional or sexual abuse, or severe neglect) find that the intensity and depth of their emotional pain may not be adequately addressed in brief therapy. For them, there is the risk that a little therapy may open up emotional flood gates, without the opportunity to truly resolve and work through the pain. In such cases, brief therapy can be worse than ineffective; it can be harmful. People with severe, chronic mental illnesses (e.g., schizophrenia, manic-depressive or bi-polar illness, severe personality disorders) are [also] not likely to benefit much from brief therapy. These major emotional disorders almost always require long-term supportive treatment and/or psychiatric medication. (pp. 26–27)

Contraindications for Brief Treatment with Children

In treating children, L. Shapiro (1994) has found certain specific situations in which short-term therapy may do more harm than good:

> One example is the treatment of the traumatized child. I am not simply referring to children who have experienced a trauma, for often these children can be treated with time-limited techniques. I am referring rather to children who have been *traumatized*; those children who have been profoundly influenced by one or more traumatic events, to the extent that they have developed significant symptomatology or are otherwise dysfunctional. The traumatic event may range from experiencing a hurricane or flood, to the sudden loss of a parent or sibling, to the more common trauma of child abuse. In each of these events, the child may need an open-ended treatment, as opposed to a time-limited one, so that he or she will have the opportunity to work through the affective states associated with the trauma fully, as well as any potentially hidden memories. (p. 15)

Shapiro continues:

> Another category of children for whom long-term therapy is preferred is those children who have not completed the bonding process that normally takes place between the parent and child in the first two years of life. Typically, these children manifest severe personality disturbances such as autism, childhood schizophrenia, severe anxiety disorders, or chronic depression. What is most important for these children is to develop a relationship with an adult they can trust and care about,

one who will meet them with nurturance and empathy. While this can certainly happen in short-term therapy, these children deserve to know the full benefit of a complex and rich relationship with another human being without the limitations of time and expediency.

A third category of children for whom short-term therapy is contraindicated will have had at least a partially successful experience in bonding and will be proceeding along the road toward individuation. However, they remain vulnerable because they have had a substantial number of adult figures come in and out of their lives as a result of frequent moves, changes of teachers, and most commonly, divorce. These children will be best served by a therapist who can see them for an extended period of time if at all possible. . . . Certainly many therapists treat children for adjustment problems in a relatively short time with effective results. But other times, brief therapy for these children has only a palliative effect, and significant conflicts remain unresolved for many years, sometimes with irreversible psychic damage. . . . If children have not successfully completed many of the appropriate developmental tasks expected at their ages, or if they have had difficulty in meeting many of the demands and stresses of the maturational process, then long-term therapy might be indicated. (L. Shapiro, 1994, p. 16)

"Buying Time" for Those Who Need It

Despite the fact that short-term therapy is often what clients prefer (we can assess this from their behavior—they tend to leave treatment after five to eight sessions, independent of therapist's orientation) and often is highly effective (as previously discussed, a wealth of outcome studies, many of them meta-analytic summaries, testify to the efficacy of short-term therapies), brief therapy is not best in every single case. To provide for those cases in which additional sessions are necessary, we need to establish a reputation for being cost-conscious and accountable. We want insurers to believe us when we need to make a plea for continuation of treatment in a given case. We want the insurer to trust our evaluation and recognize that we are not dragging out an unproductive process. Managed care companies fear therapists who wish to endlessly extend sessions when treatment isn't working or treatment isn't absolutely necessary. But they respect therapists who recognize when more is truly necessary.

Partnering with MCOs for Optimum Patient Care

When Brief Treatment Fails: More May Not Always Be the Answer

Although various types of patients have been described as less likely to do well with brief treatment methods, it is important to keep in mind that for many of them, long-term approaches may be inadequate also. The assumption that longer therapy is the answer in such cases will often be questioned by reviewers.

When clients fail to improve, it is tempting to conclude that they need a higher dose of a given therapeutic technique. Many therapists have assumed that the best response to treatment-resistant clients is extended treatment. For example, clients with borderline personality disorder are notorious for being frustrating to treat: Their stubborn symptoms tend to recur, despite lengthy therapeutic contact. Many clinicians react by maintaining that these clients' failure to show improvement following brief interventions provides sufficient justification for continuing therapeutic contact indefinitely. It is assumed that eventually, if they just receive enough, therapy will do the trick. Yet it often doesn't. The record of treatment effectiveness with borderlines is abysmal (Kroll, 1995). An alternative possibility is that no amount of the standard interventions being offered to borderline clients in therapy will be helpful, and that, rather than extending this expensive, ineffective approach indefinitely, we need to develop more innovative strategies (Layden et al., 1995). It may be that the nature of borderlines' problems inherently precludes the effectiveness of once weekly conversational psychotherapy sessions. They may need support structured in different ways and more energy devoted to helping them develop and maintain a natural support system. Managing and maintaining their level of functioning may indeed be a long-term endeavor, but extended individual therapy may be an inappropriate priority for them. When less fails, more will not necessarily succeed.

Because most employers wish to allocate healthcare dollars for effective treatments that restore normal functioning, firms usually do not provide benefit coverage for therapies whose effectiveness is questionable for certain diagnostic procedures. For example: long-term treatment aimed at personality restructuring is generally not endorsed; rather, these clients are treated according to the goals of stabilization in times of crisis and restoration of baseline functioning.

When clients blossom in our care, it is tempting to want to extend contact. We feel helpful and effective. Clients enjoy their relationships with us and desire extended contact. The *Consumer Reports* (1995) survey showed that clients choosing longer-term treatment evaluate their therapists more favorably than those who opt for treatment of shorter duration. Some of this doubtless is due to the fact that those who were most satisfied with the therapeutic relationship stayed in therapy longer. Additionally, those receiving longer treatment had a stake in seeing it as more beneficial, or they would have been foolish to have persisted in making the sacrifices therapy required. But it is also probably the case that longer therapy allows us as clinicians to become more valuable to our clients and to have a more extended impact upon their lives. This makes doing long-term work extremely reinforcing. However, the fact that lengthier treatment may confer some additional benefits for some clients does not automatically justify extending treatment.

Using Healthcare Research to Mutual Advantage

While it may be financially untenable for insurers to provide intensive, long-term psychodynamic treatment, greater awareness of those clients for whom brief therapy is less likely to be effective can help us target those most likely to benefit from limited therapy resources. This knowledge can help us accurately inform clients early on about whether their insurance contract provides for coverage of the length of treatment they are likely to require. While it may be frustrating for them to learn that they may face out-of-pocket expenses, it may be more ethical to prepare them for this possibility as soon as possible in the treatment process.

Research detailing the types of clients less likely to profit from the brief treatment covered by managed care policies can also direct us to develop new approaches to these clients. By compelling the discovery of more efficient ways of addressing the particular problems confronting our more resistant clients (such as the perfectionistic depressed clients who respond poorly to brief therapy), managed care is actually fostering development of the discipline.

Summary of the Twelve Basic Steps of Brief Therapy

1. Cease the search for signs of psychopathology. Instead view patients as capable individuals who are eager to learn better ways of coping with their lives.
2. Focus on well-defined, specific, measurable outcomes that the patient values. Integrating outcome assessment in the treatment process keeps both the therapist and the patient more explicitly accountable.
3. Evaluate contraindications for brief therapy and attend to any immediate risk factors, such as danger to self or others.
4. Engage patients in constructive change from the very beginning; describe initiating treatment as their important first step. Try to be complimentary, enthusiastic, imaginative, and memorable as you work with the patient to generate the step-by-step strategy they will implement.
5. Foster optimistic ways of thinking. Reframe and temporize challenging situations. Reframing causes patients to react to the same situations differently, often making them less of a problem.
6. Provide specific, concrete, behavioral assignments to enhance the patient's sense of control. Have patients monitor relevant behaviors and internal reactions, and complete homework assignments. Address sleep and other self care issues. Remember: Most of the work of therapy occurs between your sessions.
7. Offer supplemental sources of information to facilitate learning between sessions: Internet sites, handouts, audiotapes, videotapes, and books.
8. Develop problem-solving skills, rather than solving all the problems.
9. Schedule therapeutic contacts on the basis of the patient's individual needs, rather than rigid expectations.
10. View each case as a potential example of single session therapy. Challenge yourself to make a meaningful difference in only one session. Realize that this first meeting may be your one chance to help.
11. Locate natural sources of social support for patients in the community and assist patients in making full use of these informal opportunities to receive attention and help.
12. Stop before the end. Integrate outcome assessment and treatment by using goal attainment to define the session's focus and to trigger termination.

Can Idealism Survive Constraints?

Insurers who are increasingly interested in providing "good enough" care define services above that satisfactory level as not medically necessary. Many clinicians are idealists and find it very frustrating to have their potential to do good constrained by financial limitations. But almost everyone must work within financial constraints. Car manufacturers would probably love to build the ultimate automobile with every conceivable engineering advantage. Yet they have always had to work within the limits of the consumer's ability to pay. Similarly, we must accept the reasonableness of insurers' asking us to distinguish between necessary and ideal care. They are not monstrous for drawing this distinction. Our capacity to serve is finite. If we can't deploy our talents fully in a given case because it isn't seen as absolutely necessary, we'll have more energy to devote elsewhere. The modal amount of subsidized treatment may be reduced, but a broader constituency may ultimately receive our help. With managed care, we may end up helping more people, even though on average each may be helped somewhat less. Perhaps this way of looking at our constrained partnership can partially satisfy our idealism.

SECTION SIX

Specialized Psychotherapy Strategies: Empirically Supported Treatment Approaches

Empirically supported treatments (ESTS), or evidence-based treatments, are based on studies recommended by Division 12 of the American Psychological Association in their report on empirically validated psychological treatments (Chambless et al., 1996; Task Force on Promotion and Dissemination of Psychological Procedure, 1995). The original listing was recently expanded to include fifty-seven treatments that had withstood the test of careful empirical scrutiny (Chambless & Hollon, 1998). Developing specific psychotherapeutic techniques for homogeneous populations is a current focus of psychotherapy research (Orlinsky & Howard, 1986).

To qualify for inclusion in the EST listing, research must have shown that the treatment leads to a reduction or remission of the disorder or problem at a rate higher than occurs with the passage of time (efficacious) or that it outperforms an alternative active treatment (efficacious and specific). Knowledge that a treatment has been shown to be efficacious should affect decisions according to many members of Division 12 and DeRubeis and Crits-Cristoph (1998).

The Pressure to Specialize

If just reviewing the summaries of the EST literature contained in this book leaves you feeling a bit overwhelmed, you'll understand why many people believe that future therapists will increasingly specialize. Staying abreast of the ever expanding treatment literature concerning just one disorder can keep a professional quite busy.

While some feel it is wise for new therapists to focus their professional talents on a particular problem and hone the appropriate diagnostic, treatment, and outcome evaluation skills related to that disorder, it may give you pause to consider that mental health professionals are increasingly valuing specialization just as the rest of medicine is moving away from it. There may be relevant lessons to be learned. Specialization has not always improved the quality of medical care; the current emphasis on more holistic, integrated primary care resulted from widespread disappointment with the fragmented care often provided by specialists.

Assuming that the number of psychotherapists in a region remains stable, specialization can make obtaining care less convenient for those unlucky enough to live across the county from the nearest specialist in what ails them. Making therapy less convenient can reduce continuation and compliance; the state-of-the-art services offered by the specialist may never be fully enjoyed as a result of these obstacles.

Using Treatment Guidelines

Clinical practice guidelines based on laboratory research, outcome data, and cost-containment needs are becoming increasingly common. Their use raises several serious practical and ethical questions. How can guidelines be customized to meet the specific needs of particular clients? How can we tailor treatments without compromising their established efficacy? How can clinicians preserve their own creativity and spontaneity while adhering to treatment guidelines? How can clinicians stay attuned to the idiosyncrasies of individual cases while employing treatment protocols? How can clinicians avoid becoming distracted and myopic in using treatment guidelines? How can clinicians accommodate the need to provide "partial" treatment?

While the guidance offered by these treatment literatures is invaluable, it is not enough simply to memorize a treatment protocol or manual and deliver it when we meet someone with the appropriate diagnosis. The need to customize ESTs in light of individual learning styles and preferences, the existence of codiagnoses, and other mediating variables will help to keep psychotherapy part "art" for some time to come!

Using ESTs in Making Managed Care Psychotherapy Work

Providers are expected to adhere to treatment guidelines described in manuals provided by individual MCOs. One of the frustrations associated with doing managed care work involves the lack of uniformity that exists across these guides. While all are derived from a common research literature on treatment efficacy, companies have worked independently to craft distinctive guidelines, which are considered proprietary. This restricts free and widespread access to this information and has stymied development of consensual "industry standard" guidelines.

Although initially you may feel baffled by the need to comply with disparate instructions about how to proceed with clients carrying a particular diagnosis, as you review the different manuals, you will notice considerable overlap. To simplify your clinical work, you may wish to focus on mastering the conclusions from the empirical treatment literature. This body of research forms the basis for all the separate clinical manuals MCOs have developed. If you can provide a case reviewer with the research basis for your treatment plan and process, minor deviations from the specific guidelines will generally be accommodated.

The chapters in this section organize the treatment efficacy literature according to diagnostic category. Dually diagnosed clients will require some creative merging of techniques, unless their particular combination of problems has been specifically addressed in the literature.

Studies selected for summary were taken from the national listing of ESTs developed by the American Psychological Association. The criteria for inclusion in the association's sample are described in detail elsewhere, but priority was given to carefully controlled, double-blind, randomized studies with adequate sample size and measures to ensure high treatment fidelity. Most of the controlled studies of psychological treatments have been conducted on behavioral or cognitive approaches, although recently there has been increased use of clinical trials methodologies in tests of other treatment approaches (DeRubeis & Crits-Cristoph, 1998).

The sections that follow describe current thinking about empirically supported treatments, based on extensive work conducted by Chambless & Hollon, 1998; Chambless et al., 1996; Compas et al., 1998; and DeRubeis & Crits-Cristoph, 1998. The efforts of these investigators have provided a very valuable comparative integration of decades of treatment outcome research. These researchers acknowledge that the incomplete sampling of different therapeutic approaches characterizing current outcome research precludes our excluding presently unevaluated methods from future consideration. Future experimental studies are expected to expand the therapeutic repertoire available to clinicians insisting on scientific validation of the methods they use.

Summaries of ESTs for Common Serious Mental Disorders

Anxiety Disorders

Some approaches seek to reduce anxiety problems generally. Saunders, Driskell, Johnston, et al. (1996) conducted a meta-analysis on thirty-seven studies investigating the effectiveness of stress inoculation training (SIT) in treating anxiety. SIT involves cognitive restructuring, behavioral anxiety management, and coping techniques. Their results showed that SIT decreased both performance anxiety and state anxiety and increased performance under stress. Type of population, training setting, and trainer experience level did not appear to hinder the overall effectiveness of SIT.

Preparing strategies for coping with stressors is also a feature of cognitive-behavioral therapy (CBT), which is also often quite helpful in addressing general anxiety problems, especially those accompanied by depressive symptoms. A general description of cognitive-behavioral group therapy methods follows.

A Description of Group CBT

Cognitive-behavioral therapy focuses on identifying and challenging unproductive thought patterns and distorted beliefs. One of the therapist's tasks is to help patients identify the dysfunctional thoughts that perpetuate symptoms. Once identified, the therapist helps group members learn to refute and challenge maladaptive thinking and generate alternative, more adaptive thoughts.

The therapist can begin with a general discussion of the importance of thinking patterns in contributing to behavior and mood patterns and how examining and changing thinking patterns will be critical to patients' success. Next, help patients learn to pay attention to their "internal dialogue" by asking: "What goes on in your head: Do you encourage, support, and praise yourself, or punish, fault, and criticize yourself?"

Emphasize that much of this self-talking goes on automatically, outside of one's awareness. This is dangerous because how we think about ourselves, others, and the world significantly affects our mood and behavior. Distorted, negative thinking often exacerbates depressed and anxious moods, poor self-esteem, compulsive behaviors, and relationship problems. One major goal of CBT is to increase awareness of automatic thought patterns, to identify those beliefs that are unhelpful, to challenge unrealistic thinking, and to develop alternative views that are more adaptive and that facilitate achievement of specific goals and enhance positive mood state. Gaining awareness and control of thinking can go a long way to improving mood and behavior.

The first step in dealing with distorted cognitions is to identify what patients say to themselves—how they instruct themselves in general and specifically related to their problem areas. For example, thinking patterns prior to symptomatic behavior should be identified and explored, and negative self-talk in general ("I can't handle this," "I'm no good") should be made conscious. The goal initially is for patients to pay closer attention to the content of their thoughts. Simply identifying the belief may result in their recognizing the distortions involved. To assist patients in developing an awareness of their cognitions, the therapist should review the following types of common distortions and provide examples.

One type of thinking pattern that leads to trouble for patients involves *cognitive imperatives*. In this style of thinking, many "rules" governing personal behavior are framed with the words "should" and "must," and reveal the critical, judgmental and perfectionistic attitudes so common in many patients. The rules often involve unrealistic standards that will inevitably be violated, leading to self-condemnation. Both the cognitive imperatives and negative self-evaluation that accompanies breaking the rules should be identified, challenged, and reframed.

Catastrophic and *all-or-nothing* thinking are common thinking styles that frequently get patients into trouble. Usually in catastrophic thinking the imagined negative consequences of a particular behavior are much exaggerated. For example, a belief might be "My boss passed me in the hall without talking to me so it must mean she's dissatisfied and will fire me." All-or-nothing thinking might involve beliefs such as "Disappointing my partner once means I'm a total failure; I give up. I will never be able to maintain a relationship." Patients should be taught to substitute more realistic and positive thinking such as "I probably shouldn't have eaten so much chocolate, but it's not the end of the world. I can allow myself occasional slips and not punish myself by giving up on my diet."

Patients can be asked to track their thoughts between sessions. The therapist should ask about any difficulties patients are experiencing in identifying the content of their automatic thinking and reassure them that with practice the task should become easier. In teaching patients to refute or challenge their distorted cognitions and substitute more realistic and constructive thoughts, it can be helpful to use role playing, especially when CBT is offered in a group. First, have a few participants share one or two of the thoughts that preceded a problem episode. The therapist should challenge these distorted cognitions and suggest several alternative, adaptive coping self-statements to substitute for the dysfunctional ones. Then have group members do the challenging and devising of coping statements in response to the dysfunctional thoughts of the participants.

Therapists should introduce the topic of maintenance and relapse prevention. Explain that occasional setbacks or lapses into old patterns will probably occur, but they do not invalidate progress made. What's important is that the lapse be temporary and not escalate into a long-term return to old maladaptive patterns.

A setback should be taken as an opportunity to learn and increase awareness. In order to prevent a setback from becoming a full-blown relapse, it is important to identify immediately any early warning signals. Therefore, the first goal is to prevent lapses into previous patterns by continuing to follow through on goals set and changes made. Second, it is important to recognize early warning signs of slipping back into old patterns. Third, lapses should be met immediately with a preplanned coping strategy for getting back on track.

Remind patients that lapses will probably involve a sequence including interpersonal events, mood, thinking, and behaviors. It is helpful to develop separate plans for coping with each element. Explore coping strategies that have helped in the past, and encourage patients to discuss new strategies they wish to try.

Instruct each member to recall a high-risk situation they handled well. Each member can describes the specific steps that enabled their success. Encourage patients to visualize and express in detail what they did, thought, and felt that helped them cope effectively. Patients can be urged to monitor warning signals for lapses using handouts and recording forms.

Generalized Anxiety Disorder

Generalized anxiety disorder (GAD) is quite common, with prevalence estimates ranging from 5.7% to 10%; however, only about half of those afflicted seek treatment. Commonly patients report diffuse, vaguely formed anxiety; pervasive worries lacking an exact source; and somatic signs of apprehension (muscle tension, fatigue, irritability). Clients often feel unhappy and uncomfortable and often hesitate and constantly express fears and worries to others.

Various anxiolytics (antianxiety) medications have been shown to be effective in reducing the anxiety of GAD clients, including diazepam (Valium), buspirone (BuSpar), clorazepate (Tranxene), and chlorprothixene (Taractan). Because it has no sedative or amnestic side effects and no risk of dependence, Buspirone is seen by some as the safest drug for chronic anxiety (Maxmen & Ward, 1995). Tricyclic antidepressants, including imipramine (Tofranil), have been found as effective as anxiolytics in reducing anxiety in many GAD clients (Preston & Johnson, 1995).

Cognitive-behavioral therapy is seen by many as the most efficacious psychological treatment (Borkovec & Costello, 1993; Durham & Allan, 1993). Cognitive therapy (CT) for GAD is usually based on Beck and Emery's (1985) model. The following steps can be useful:

1. Establish rapport and obtain focused history: Determine chronology of symptoms and situations that exacerbate symptoms.
2. Explain that CBT has been shown to treat GAD effectively, and that this therapy will require the client's direct participation. Discuss the rationale for CBT, including examination of the premise that negative thinking perpetuates anxiety and avoidance, but that with practice, negative thinking can be replaced with more positive, encouraging self-talk.

3. Help the patient list specific behavioral goals, translating general vague objectives (find someone to love and marry) into specific action steps that will lead to the general objective (go to three parties with friends, take a class to meet people, say hello to three people at work, etc.).
4. Troubleshoot specific presenting complaints. Discuss the plan for modifying specific behaviors, with an emphasis on reducing avoidance and increasing active, assertive involvement in various specific contexts. Present a behavioral assignment as an experiment. If the therapist encourages the patient to make more successful responses to immediate problem situations, the client's enthusiasm and hopefulness will increase. Therapeutic effectiveness is closely tied to the client's expectations of its effectiveness, so facilitating readily identifiable successes early on is very desirable.
5. Offer relaxation training to reduce physiological manifestations of anxiety.

Durham et al. (1994) found that CT for GAD led to greater improvement than analytic psychotherapy, especially at the 6-month followup; CT was somewhat better than anxiety management training, particularly in terms of proportion of GAD patients achieving clinically significant change by followup. On the other hand, Barlow, Rapee, and Brown (1992) found no significant differences across CT, relaxation, and combined relaxation and CT conditions, although all active treatment groups fared better than the wait-list control group, and gains were maintained during followup.

Chambless and Gillis (1993) summarized nine clinical trials of CT for GAD. All evaluated cognitive techniques described by Beck and Emery (1985) or a similar cognitive-behavioral package with some other behavioral techniques. Comparisons with pill-placebo, nondirective therapy, or wait-list control groups yielded an average effect size of 1.5. In two studies, CBT was found to be better than pill-placebo, in four studies it was superior to wait-list conditions, and in one study CBT produced greater symptom improvement than did nondirective therapy. In one study, CBT failed to outperform nondirective therapy with GAD, but Chambless and Gillis suggest that this study may have involved inadequate CBT trials (eight sessions versus the twelve employed by a comparable study). Applied relaxation for GAD was found to be significantly better than a wait-list control (Barlow et al., 1992), and significantly better than nondirective therapy at post-treatment (Borkovec & Costello, 1993).

Durham and Allen (1993) reviewed the clinical significance of psychosocial treatments for GAD. Using Jacobson, Follette, and Revenstorf's (1984) definition of clinical significance (the percent of patients who achieve a cut-off score set so that the patient is equally likely to be a member of either nondysfunctional or functional distributions) Durham and Allen report that 37% of patients in CT, 31% of patients who received anxiety management training, and only 10% of patients who received analytic psychotherapy achieved clinically significant change.

In comparing CBT and applied relaxation, studies have demonstrated a specific effect for CBT but not for applied relaxation. In direct comparisons of the two treatments, Borkovec and Costello (1993) demonstrated no difference at post-treatment but found CBT to be superior according to 12-month followup data (58% of CBT patients had clinically significant change on six to eight outcome indices; only 38% of the applied relaxation patients showed comparable change). In a similar study, Barlow, Rapee, and Brown (1992) reported no differences in a study with limited statistical power.

Social Phobia

Turner, Beidel, and Jacob (1994); Hope, Heimberg, and Bruch (1995); and Mattick, Peters, and Clark (1989) all found group exposure or flooding superior to controls (pill-placebo or wait-list conditions). In Hope, Heimberg, and Bruch, 70% of the exposure patients were classified as "responders," and none of the ten wait-list patients met the responder criteria. In Turner, Beidel, and Jacob, 56% of the exposure group showed significant improvement as compared to 6% of the placebo group. On raters' judgments of social phobia, 30% of the patients treated with exposure were judged to have "high end state functioning," as opposed to only 6% in the placebo group. Reports of maintenance have been variable. While the exposure group gains found by Turner, Beidel, and Jacob lasted over the 6-month followup period, Mattick, Peters, and Clark; Butler et al. (1984); and Hope, Heimberg, and Bruch all found that gains had eroded substantially by the followup.

Butler et al. (1984) compared exposure therapy alone and with added "anxiety management" procedures by assigning forty-five social phobia patients to one of these groups or a wait-list control. Anxiety management techniques included behavioral (relaxation and distraction) and cognitive (rational self-talk) procedures. Those receiving the exposure method improved more than the wait-list group, but less than those in the exposure plus anxiety management group. Gains were maintained during a 6-month followup.

Other tests of group exposure treatment combined with cognitive procedures (Mattick, Peters, & Clark, 1989; Hope, Heimberg, & Bruch, 1995; Heimberg et al., 1990) have found that exposure plus cognitive restructuring produces greater improvement than even highly credible placebo controls. Heimberg et al. found that 65% of the CBT patients experienced clinically significant improvement at the end of treatment, and 69% achieved this standard at the 6-month followup. In contrast, only 40% of the patients in their "educational supportive psychotherapy" placebo control group evidenced clinically significant change, and at followup this was down to 35%. Mattick, Peters, and Clark (1989) also found that CBT patients continued to improve during their 3-month followup. However, a meta-analytic review by Feske and Chambless (1995) concluded that the available evidence does not indicate superiority of the "combined" cognitive-behavioral treatment. This may be because their review excluded Butler et al. (1984), because their combined treatment included behavioral (relaxation and distraction) as well as cognitive procedures, and the Butler et al. "cognitive" component was very brief.

In a classic study, Paul (1967a) compared modified systematic desensitization, insight-oriented psychotherapy, attention-placebo treatment, and a no-treatment control in reassessing specific and general treatment effects. The battery of measures given initially and after 2 years were the IPAT Anxiety Scale, the Pittsburgh Social Extroversion-Introversion and Emotionality Scales, the Interpersonal Anxiety Scale of the S-R Inventory of Anxiousness (S-R), and a scale of specific anxiety. The return rate was superior than at any other assessment time, which indicated reduced interpersonal performance anxiety. Improvement was greatest for the systematic desensitization group (85%), with insight-oriented psychotherapy, attention placebo, and no-treatment following (50%, 50%, and 22%, respectively).

Woy and Efran (1972) compared a high-expectation systematic desensitization (HE-SD) with suggested improvement, neutral expectation systematic desensitization (NE-SD) with no suggestion, and a no-treatment group in the treatment of speaking anxiety. The HE-SD method entailed explaining systematic desensitization and suggesting that the treatment can be augmented by the intake of "Brevityl." This "drug" (actually nicotinic acid) was administered before each treatment session. The NE-SD method consisted of the same procedure as the HE-SD group except that they were not given the drug. The results indicated that systematic desensitization was effective in treating speaking anxiety and that there was a small expectancy effect; there was a significant difference between HE-SD and NE-SD on self-perception of improvement.

Paul and Shannon (1966) compared combined group desensitization, individual insight-oriented psychotherapy, individual systematic desensitization, and an individual attention-placebo treatment in the treatment of anxiety. The insight-oriented psychotherapy method employed an interview approach with the participant. The systematic desensitization method included deep muscle relaxation, development of an anxiety hierarchy, and counterconditioning hierarchy elements with the relaxation. The attention-placebo method entailed a therapeutic relationship with the therapist as well as a placebo of sodium bicarbonate. The combined group desensitization method consisted of constructing an anxiety hierarchy, relaxation, and group sharing and discussion. The results showed that the combined group desensitization method was superior to the other treatment categories on self-report measures and the public behavioral criterion of grades in a public speaking course.

Simple Phobia

Treatment of phobias involves exposing the client to the feared object or situation for an uninterrupted period of time. Flooding, graduated exposure, and systematic desensitization have all been shown to be effective in treating phobias. Assertiveness training involving role playing, modeling, and behavioral rehearsal has also been shown to be beneficial for some clients.

Bandura, Blanchard, and Ritter (1969) examined the treatment of snake phobia by comparing symbolic desensitization, symbolic modeling, live modeling combined with guided participation (contact desensitization), and no treatment. Symbolic desensitization entailed pairing deep relaxation with imagined representation of snakes in increasingly emotion-arousing order. Symbolic modeling consisted of viewing a film showing people interacting with snakes in gradually more threatening situations. Subjects were also taught relaxation during viewing. If a scene was too anxiety-provoking, subjects were allowed to stop the film, rewind it, induce relaxation, and attempt to view the scene again. This continued until the whole film could be viewed without emotional arousal. Live modeling with guided participation included the subject observing (through a one-way mirror) the experimenter interacting with a snake. The subject was then asked to join the experimenter in the room with the snake and the interaction was repeated in front of the subject. The next step involved the subject gradually being able to perform the interactions with the snake. No relaxation was taught in the contact desensitization method. The results indicated that modeling with guided participation was the most effective strategy (almost complete absence of phobia in subjects).

Ost (1978) compared fading, systematic desensitization and a wait-list control in the treatment of snake and spider phobia. The fading method consisted of slides of the phobic stimulus followed by slides of positive scenes, which allowed for calming feelings to work as anxiety antagonists. The systematic desensitization method included progressive relaxation and creation of a fear stimulus hierarchy (Wolpe, 1969). Ost's within-group comparison results indicated that fading and systematic desensitization produced significant improvement, while the control group did not. Furthermore, between-group comparisons showed that, on a third of the dependent measures used, the two treatment groups exhibited improvement.

Ost, Salkovskis, and Hellstrom (1991) compared therapist-directed exposure with self-directed exposure in treating spider phobia. The therapist-directed exposure consisted of prolonged exposure and modeling. The self-directed exposure entailed following a thirty-page manual about dealing with fear. Anxiety levels and a summary were recorded after each interaction with spiders. The results indicated that therapist-directed exposure was superior to self-directed exposure on self-report, behavioral, and clinician-rating measures.

Kirsch et al. (1983) compared systematic desensitization, expectancy modification procedure, and a wait-list control in the treatment of fear of snakes. The expectancy method consisted of a modified version of a systematic ventilation treatment, in which subjects relive encounters and free associate. The results showed no significant differences between the two treatment groups, although both treatment groups were significantly more improved than the control group.

Agoraphobia

Trull, Nietzel, and Main (1988) conducted a meta-analysis to evaluate the clinical significance of behavior therapy for agoraphobia. The meta-analysis revealed that the effects of behavior therapy for self-reported agoraphobic symptoms are clinically significant when an appropriate norm is used as the comparison. Treatment involving exposure was associated with a greater rate of improvement. Although levels of exposure were not related to the clinical improvement at the time of the post-test, there was a significant effect at the time of followup. Better outcomes were found among those receiving group as opposed to individual treatment for agoraphobia. The researchers also found doctoral-level providers to be superior to nondoctoral-level therapists. The study concluded that behavior therapy produces clinically significant outcomes that are well maintained at followup (Trull, Nietzel, & Main, 1988).

Several researchers have found exposure methods to be superior to attention control procedures in reducing agoraphobic avoidance. Chambless et al. (1979) compared imaginal flooding (with or without adjunctive pharmacological treatment) and an attention-placebo control (patients were given eight sessions of relaxation training and eight sessions of "supportive" psychotherapy). Patients who received flooding without adjunctive medication surpassed the control group on all of the fear and avoidance measures at the end of treatment. Gelder et al. (1973) assigned thirty-six patients (half agoraphobic and half with another phobic disorder) to three conditions: (1) exposure (flooding) therapy, (2) systematic desensitization therapy, or (3) a control condition called "associative psychotherapy" (patients were encouraged to free associate to phobic images provided by the therapist). Both the systematic desensitization condition and the flooding condition yielded effects approximately twice as large as what occurred in the control condition. There were no differences between flooding and desensitization, and at the 6-month followup the advantage of the active treatments was no longer significant.

Jannoun et al. (1980) compared an exposure method called "programmed practice" and an active placebo control group (patients focused on solving "stressful" problems that might lead to agoraphobic anxiety). Programmed practice produced significant reductions in agoraphobic symptoms; it appeared significantly better than the problem-solving procedure at the 3-month followup assessment, but not at the post-treatment or 6-month followup assessment.

McDonald, Sartory, and Grey (1979) compared a "discussion" control condition with a condition in which patients were given explicit exposure homework assignments. Exposure yielded a significant advantage on the target problem after treatment, as well as on a global phobia measure at the 1-month followup.

Arnow et al. (1985) compared partner-assisted exposure therapy with either couples relaxation training (CRT) or couples communication skills training (CCST) in the treatment of agoraphobia in women. The partner-assisted exposure therapy entailed discussion, homework, and partner-assisted in vivo training. The CRT method consisted of relaxation training, homework, discussion, and partner involvement, and the CCST method included training in listening, self-statements, constructive request-making, feedback delivery, and clarification as well as conflict resolution. The results showed that, in comparison to subjects in the CRT group, subjects in the CCST group had lower agoraphobia scores, more unaccompanied excursions outside the home, and better scores on a behavioral approach test.

Panic Disorder

Clients with panic disorder need to understand that their disorder typically has a fluctuating course and that they should not interpret symptom recurrence as a sign of individual or treatment failure. Improving the client's ability to function, despite the possibility of symptom recurrence, is the main objective of treatment.

Those with mild cases of panic disorder, involving intermittent attacks, should be educated about how even though their experiences are distressing, they are not life-threatening. Cognitive techniques aimed at reducing catastrophic thinking about episodic attacks have been shown to be quite effective (Barlow & Cerny, 1988). In cases of more severe panic attacks (occurring five or more times a week, with greater anxiety between attacks), medication in addition to cognitive techniques is usually recommended.

Several cognitive approaches to panic disorder have received empirical support (Beck, 1988a; D. Clark, 1986; Barlow & Cerny, 1988). These approaches assume that catastrophic misinterpretations of bodily sensations (including rapid respiration or heart rate) provoke the experience of panic. To avoid panic attacks, patients are taught to reinterpret bodily sensations as benign.

Beck, Stanley, and colleagues (1994) reported that 82% of patients (fourteen out of sixteen) responded to CT, compared to 36% of those completing a minimal-contact control condition. At the 6-month followup, all sixteen CT patients were classified as responders. In another study, post-treatment measures indicated that cognitive therapy surpassed applied relaxation, imipramine pharmacotherapy, and a control condition (D. Clark et al., 1994). "High end-state functioning" was achieved by 80% of the CT patients (after treatment they were panic-free and rated by an assessor as showing no more than "slight" panic distress/disability), compared to 25% of the applied relaxation, and 40% of the imipramine recipients. Very little change occurred in the control group's panic/anxiety scores. Treatment gains were largely maintained by the CT patients at the 6- and 15-month followup assessments, at which times 65% and 70% of the patients were classified as evidencing high end-state functioning.

Williams and Falbo (1996) found CT, exposure-based treatment, and a combination (CT with exposure) to be superior to a wait-list control. Fifty-seven percent of CT patients and 58% of exposure patients were judged panic-free at post-treatment, compared to 11% of the control patients. Gains were maintained at the followup assessments, with 69% and 67% of CT and exposure patients panic-free at 6 weeks post-treatment, and 50% and 80% still panic-free at a long-term assessment conducted 1 to 2 years after treatment. To assess generalizability Williams and Falbo included patients with differing levels of agoraphobic avoidance. They found that the three active treatments were extremely effective in reducing panic attacks in those patients who started treatment with relatively low levels of agoraphobic avoidance. Seventeen of eighteen subjects (94%) in this category were panic-free at post-treatment. However, only 52% (eleven of twenty-one) patients who were high on agoraphobic avoidance at pre-treatment finished treatment panic-free.

Arntz and van den Hout (1996) obtained greater changes (in panic frequency and on questionnaire scores) with CT than with applied relaxation group or a wait-list control; changes were largely maintained through the 6-month followup assessment, although the advantage of CT over applied relaxation disappeared, due to the relaxation group's continued improvement.

In a comparison between CT and a brief supportive psychotherapy control condition, Beck, Sokol, et al. (1992) found that after 8 weeks, 71% in the CT condition were panic-free, compared to 25% in the supportive psychotherapy condition. At the end of the 8-week comparison period, 94% of the patients in the brief supportive psychotherapy condition chose to change over to a 12-week course of CT; at the end of their 12-week trial, these patients exhibited substantial improvement. At 1-year followup, 83% of all the CT patients were panic-free.

In a comparison of CT, fluvoxamine pharmacotherapy, and placebo, Black et al. (1993) found CT significantly inferior to fluvoxamine on some of the key outcome measures, and not superior to placebo on most of the main measures. Roughly a third (36%) of the CT patients discontinued treatment, and the panic-free rate among completers was only 53%. The CT patients fared more poorly in this study than in several other investigations, perhaps because of design limitations (only one therapist provided the CT to all twenty-five patients, and raters were not blind to the treatment condition of the patient). Otto et al. (1993) and Spiegel et al. (1994) both found CT to be superior to no psychological treatment during discontinuation of alprazolam (an anti-anxiety medicine often used with anxiety disorders).

Shear et al. (1994) compared CBT with a "nonprescriptive" treatment intended as a nonspecific treatment control. Both groups responded well; roughly 75% of all the patients were panic-free at post-treatment and 6-month followup. Because even those in the nonprescriptive condition were given three sessions of pretreatment instruction about the role of physiological reactions in a panic attack, some might argue that the critical elements of CT were provided to all patients in this study.

Ost and Westling (1995) obtained similar effects from CT and applied relaxation (AR) on panic frequency. At post-treatment, 74% of CT patients and 47% of applied relaxation patients achieved high end-state functioning, but by 1-year followup, rates of high functioning were nearly identical (79% in CT and 82% in AR). Bouchard et al. (1996) found similar outcomes following group CT and group exposure treatments. While at post-treatment, 64% of CT and 86% of exposure patients were judged to have achieved high end-state functioning, 6 weeks later, only 57% and 64% of the patients were so rated.

Barlow and Cerny (1988) used panic control therapy (PCT), which incorporates elements similar to the Clark (1986) and Beck (1988) approaches, including methods encouraging patients to reappraise panic-inducing internal physiological cues. Barlow and colleagues tested PCT in two randomized trials. Barlow et al. (1989) found that PCT, relaxation, and a combination of PCT with relaxation surpassed a wait-list control. Roughly half of the patients in active treatment achieved high end-state functioning, while none of the wait-list patients did. Effects of all treatments were maintained until the 6-month followup.

Klosko et al. (1990) found PCT superior to both pill-placebo and wait-list controls. Eighty-seven percent of patients in the PCT condition were panic-free after treatment, compared to 36% for the pill-placebo group and 33% for those wait-listed.

Exposure-based treatments and Ost's (1988) applied relaxation have also performed fairly well: In a large-sample, two-site study, Marks et al. (1983) assigned patients with the diagnosis of Panic Disorder with Agoraphobia to a programmed exposure condition (plus a pill placebo) or to a relaxation condition (plus a pill placebo). Exposure yielded no advantage over relaxation on panic frequency (both groups improved), but exposure did produce greater change in fear and avoidance, and this advantage persisted through the 6-month followup.

Swinson et al. (1995) provided programmed exposure through eight sessions of phone contact only and found this method superior to a wait-list control. Post-treatment comparisons of patients' fear and avoidance ratings yielded effect sizes of 0.8 and 1.0; gains were maintained throughout the 6-month followup period.

Group and bibliotherapy exposure methods have been found to be superior to wait-list controls (Lidren et al., 1994); 83% of patients in both the group and bibliotherapy-based exposure conditions were panic-free at the post-treatment assessment, compared to 25% in the wait-list condition. Panic-free rates were maintained at 92% and 75% in the group and bibliotherapy conditions according to a 6-month followup.

There have been inconsistent findings pertaining to the relative efficacy of applied relaxation (AR) therapy. While Ost and Westling (1995), Beck, Stanley, et al. (1994), and Barlow et al. (1989) found AR and CT similarly effective, others have not. Beck, Stanley, et al. (1994) found relaxation training comparable to CT and superior to a minimal-contact control condition. Sixty-eight percent of the relaxation patients, 82% of the CT patients, and 36% of the control group responded; gains persisted during the 6-month followup. Barlow et al. (1989) found AR comparable to PCT and superior to a wait-list control; half the AR patients achieved high end-state functioning, compared to none who were wait-listed.

On the other hand, D. Clark et al. (1994) found AR inferior to CT; only 25% of the AR patients achieved high end-state functioning, compared to 80% in the CT condition. Gains persisted throughout a 15-month followup, but the AR patients continued to evidence more symptoms than did the CT patients. Arntz and van den Hout (1996) also found AR to be less effective than CT, although AR was more effective than the wait-list control. Here, the AR and CT difference disappeared during the 6-month followup, because the AR patients continued to improve while the CT patients remained stable.

Obsessive-Compulsive Disorder

The SSRI antidepressants have been found to be helpful in treating some cases of obsessive-compulsive disorder (OCD). However, although 70% of clients respond to some degree, most are left with residual symptoms. Only 10% to 15% of clients experience full remission with medication alone. Consequently, most cases of OCD are treated with a combination of approaches. Behavioral treatment involves graded exposure and response prevention of the compulsions.

Exposure and response prevention therapy (E&RP) (Foa, Steketee, et al., 1984) attempts to extinguish obsessive fears by exposing the patient to fear-provoking stimuli and to reduce avoidance behaviors by preventing compulsive responses to obsessive thoughts. Foa, Stecketee, et al. (1984) provided thirty-two

OCD patients either E&RP, exposure alone, or response prevention alone and found that E&RP patients improved significantly more than did the patients receiving either treatment element alone. After about a year, 80% of the E&RP patients remained improved, while only 27% of those in the other groups remained improved. Fals-Stewart, Marks, and Schafer (1993) found that both a group and an individual version of E&RP surpassed a relaxation training control group. Rachman et al. (1979) found that E&RP reduced OCD symptoms more than relaxation training when both were combined with either clomipramine or placebo. After only 3 weeks of behavioral treatment, patients on placebo combined with E&RP had improved substantially more than those on placebo combined with relaxation training.

While E&RP emphasizes breaking the avoidance cycle that characterizes OCD, CT focuses on challenging patients' maladaptive beliefs (e.g., "If I left the light on, my house will burn down"). Emmelkamp, Visser, and Hoekstra (1988) and Emmelkamp and Beens (1991) found no significant differences between E&RP and a cognitive therapy based on Ellis's (1962) rational emotive therapy. At the 6-month followup, eight of the nine CT patients were rated "improved" or "much improved," and all nine E&RP patients were rated this way. A larger study ($n = 57$) by Van Oppen et al. (1995) also found CT to be as effective as E&RP. Some results favored CT over E&RP; while 39% of the CT patients were judged to be "recovered" on all main outcome measures, only 17% in the E&RP condition were so judged.

Hiss, Foa, and Kozak (1994) examined E&RP paired with either relapse prevention or associative therapy in the treatment of OCD. In both treatment groups, participants received imaginal exposure, exposure in vivo, and response prevention. The response prevention method included stressors and risk situation identification, setback coping strategies, discussion with a significant other present, cognitive restructuring, and homework assignments. The associative method consisted of deep muscle relaxation, discussion of homework, vocalized associations, and significant other participation. The results indicated that, although both treatment groups showed initial improvement of symptoms, the response prevention group experienced fewer relapses.

Many evaluations of OCD treatments, including the van Balkom et al. (1994) meta-analytic review, have used within-group rather than RCT designs, focusing on change from pre- to post-treatment within single treatments, instead of comparisons between an active treatment and a control group. Exposure and response prevention (Foa, Steketee, et al., 1984) and CT (Beck, 1976; Salkovskis, 1985) have demonstrated impressive pre- to post-treatment comparison effect sizes (response rates).

Depression

Psychotherapy for affective disorders typically informs patients about their disorder, helps them feel less alone, provides suggestions for how to cope more effectively with their disorder, teaches how to identify triggering situations and develop alternative strategies for responding to these situations, teaches how to recognize symptoms early (to limit exacerbation), fosters more rational beliefs and cognitive strategies, and improves the interpersonal support network upon which the patient relies.

The choice of treatment is often based on the severity of the depressive episode. Severe depression is present when a person has nearly all of the symptoms of depression and the depression almost always keeps the person from doing regular day-to-day activities. Moderate depression is present when a person has many symptoms of depression that often keep the person from doing what needs to be done. Mild depression is present when a person has some of the symptoms of depression and it takes extra effort to do the things the person needs to do.

A significant number (roughly 50%) of patients with mild to moderate forms of depression obtain substantial symptom relief with psychotherapy. Many patients begin to feel the effects of psychotherapy in the first few weeks. If there is no symptom improvement at all within 6 weeks, the choice of treatment modality should be reevaluated. For patients who improve but who are still symptomatic after 12 weeks, treatment with medication is a strong consideration.

The evidence indicates that several forms of short-term psychotherapy (cognitive, interpersonal, or behavioral) are effective in treating most cases of mild or moderate depression. Other types of psychotherapy may also be helpful in the treatment of major depressive disorder, although their efficacy has not been evaluated fully, if at all. In individuals with mild to moderate depressions, time-limited psychotherapies appear equal in efficacy to antidepressant medications. Considerations for acute phase treatment with psychotherapy alone include:

- Patient preference
- Medication contraindicated or refused
- Less severe depression
- Less recurrent, chronic, or disabling depression
- Chronic psychosocial problems
- Absence of psychotic symptoms
- Prior positive response to psychotherapy

Comparative Treatment Studies

Cognitive therapy for depression is generally regarded as empirically validated (Beck, Rush, et al., 1979). A meta-analysis by Dobson (1989) concluded that CT is superior to many other forms of therapy for depression, including antidepressant medications. Unfortunately there are few studies of diagnosed depressed patients in which CT has outperformed a control condition or an alternative treatment. The best evidence for the efficacy of CT derives from studies in which the effects of CT were equal to those of well-conducted pharmacotherapy (Hollon et al., 1992; Murphy et al., 1984; Rush et al., 1977), but none of these studies included a control condition. With severely depressed patients, several studies indicate that CT and antidepressant medications are comparably effective (DeRubeis et al.,

1997; Hollon et al., 1992). Followup studies from some of these trials suggest that CT confers a relapse prevention benefit (Hollon et al., 1992).

A few studies have shown group CT to be superior to control and alternative treatment conditions for individuals with major depressive disorder. Shaw (1977) found that a group version of CT was superior to a "behavior modification" group, a "nondirective" control group, and a wait-list control group. Using an even larger sample, Covi and Lipman (1987) reported that group CT outperformed "traditional" (psychodynamic) group therapy. Using the Beck Depression Inventory (BDI), they found that only 5% of the patients in traditional group therapy achieved remission at the end of therapy (BDI scores under 10), while 52% achieved remission in CT. Neither Shaw nor Covi and Lipman reported followup data. Jamison and Scogin (1995) found that patients with mild or moderate major depressive disorder who were given bibliotherapy-based CT improved more than those assigned to a wait-list group. In the CT bibliotherapy condition, 59% of the patients met their improvement criteria (BDI score under 12 and BDI change of over 6 during the 4-week treatment period), whereas only 13% of the control group did.

The relative superiority of CT for depression has been recently challenged by the findings from three large-sample investigations in which CT was compared to other psychological treatments. In the NIMH study (Elkin, Shea, et al., 1989), "interpersonal therapy" (Klerman et al., 1984) produced effects that were at least equivalent to those of CT. In this ambitious, careful study, CT patients did not surpass those receiving placebo with clinical management; with more severely depressed patients, CT performed worse than medication (Elkin, Gibbons, et al., 1995).

In the second large-scale study (Shapiro et al., 1994), psychodynamic interpersonal psychotherapy was found to be equally or nearly equally as effective as a behavioral-cognitive therapy (a therapy similar to Beck, Rush, et al.'s [1979], although it gives greater emphasis to behavioral methods).

In the third study, Jacobson et al. (1996) found that neither of two versions of CT was more effective than behavior therapy. This large-scale (n = 150) study found no significant differences between behavior therapy and two cognitive therapy conditions. Improvement rates ranged from 58% to 68%; recovery rates (BDI under 8, no major depressive disorder) ranged from 46% (for behavior therapy) to 56% (for complete cognitive therapy). Treatment gains were maintained in the first 6 months of followup for all therapy groups.

Behavior therapy for depression is usually based on Lewinsohn's (1974) conceptualization; the central objective is to get the patient engaged in potentially rewarding activities. A large comparative study of behavior therapy (McLean & Hakstian, 1979) found significantly greater symptom change in the behavior therapy condition than in each of the other three conditions: (1) psychotherapy, based on Wolberg and Marmor; (2) relaxation therapy, used as an active placebo control; and (3) amitriptyline. Half of those in the behavior therapy group had BDI scores in the normal range at the end of treatment, whereas only 25% of those in the psychotherapy group achieved this outcome. However, at 3-month followup the mean difference (11.9 vs. 15.5) was no longer significant. Shaw (1977) found that patients in group behavior therapy performed better than those in a wait-list condition, although worse than those in CT. Treatment gains were maintained at the 1-month post-treatment followup, but followup data on the wait-list patients were not collected.

Problem-solving therapy (PST) for depression (Nezu, 1986; Nezu & Perri, 1989) has been associated with greater symptom reduction than has placement in a wait-list control group. In both studies the full PST outperformed incomplete versions. At the end of the 6-month followup period the full version was still outperforming the partial versions.

Arean et al. (1993) compared the effects of PST, reminiscence therapy, and a wait-list control on depression in later life. The PST consisted of labeling "emotions as cues for identifying the existence of a problem, inhibiting the tendency to respond automatically to problems, and engaging instead in the problem-solving process" (p. 1005). Also, this method taught participants "to better define and formulate the nature of problems, to generate a wide range of alternative solutions, to systematically evaluate the potential consequences of a solution and select the optimal ones to implement, and to monitor and evaluate the actual solution outcome after its implementation" (p. 1006). Reminiscence therapy entailed reviewing participants' life histories to gain a greater sense of perspective and satisfaction with what had not been accomplished during their lives. The objectives were "to facilitate acceptance of one's life with both successes and shortcomings, to enhance resolution of unresolved conflicts, and to encourage participants to pursue future goals that would enhance the meaning of their lives" (p. 1006). The results showed significant decreases in depression for both the PST and the reminiscence groups in comparison to the wait-list group, with the PST condition showing greater decreases than the reminiscence therapy condition.

C. Fuchs and Rehm (1977) compared a self-control behavior therapy program with a nonspecific group therapy method as well as a wait-list control in treatment for depression. The self-control method included training, self-monitoring, self-evaluation, and self-reinforcement skills and entailed homework. The nonspecific method consisted of therapists' encouraging discussion of past and current problems, interaction, and the reflection on and clarifications of feelings. Therapists did not, however, recommend out-of-therapy activities or behavioral principles. The results indicated that subjects in the self-control condition had reduced levels of depression on self-report and behavioral measures and greater improvement on the MMPI.

Rehm et al. (1979) compared assertion skills training with a self-control condition in the treatment of depression. The assertion skills method entailed role playing, daily records, instruction, rehearsal, group feedback, coaching, and modeling. The self-control method consisted of self-monitoring, self-evaluation, self-reinforcement skills training, and homework. The results indicated that self-control group members displayed more improvement on self-report and behavioral measures. The assertion skills group members improved more on assertion skills.

Interpersonal therapy (IPT) (Klerman et al., 1984) construes depression as a result of relationship conflicts or deficits. Treatment attempts to reduce these problems by enhancing awareness and interpersonal skills. DiMascio et al. (1979) found IPT to be superior to a minimal-contact control condition and equivalent to amitriptyline pharmacotherapy in reducing depressive symptoms, although symptom reduction was 1 to 2 weeks faster in the amitriptyline condition. Unfortunately this study did not provide information on the long-term effects of IPT.

In the NIMH study (Elkin et al., 1989), IPT and imipramine pharmacotherapy were comparably effective; IPT was slightly more effective than cognitive therapy. Among the more severely depressed patients, IPT was superior to placebo and clinical management. Followup results showed that one-third of the IPT patients who had recovered during the acute phase relapsed during the 18-month followup period (Shea et al., 1992). Given the acute phase recovery rate of 40%, only 26% of the IPT patients recovered and stayed well throughout followup, similar to the rates obtained for cognitive therapy (30%), pharmacotherapy (19%) and placebo (20%).

Psychodynamic interpersonal psychotherapy (Shapiro et al., 1994) is similar to IPT, but it relies more heavily on interpretations of the therapeutic relationship. Shapiro et al. found few differences between psychodynamic interpersonal psychotherapy and CBT in a large sample; the only measure on which the psychodynamic therapy was inferior to CBT was the BDI, and these differences were small.

Scogin and McElreath (1994) performed a meta-analysis on seventeen psychosocial treatment studies concerning depression in geriatric populations. Studies were chosen on the basis of containing a control condition or in comparison with another psychosocial treatment. The results revealed that, on both self-rated and clinician-rated measures, treatments were more effective than nontreatment in combatting depression.

Gallagher-Thompson and Steffen (1994) compared CBT and brief psychodynamic therapy on depressed family caregivers. This study demonstrated the general benefits of time-limited psychotherapy and found that those who had been caregivers for longer than 3.5 years benefitted more from CBT, while those who had been caregivers for less than that benefitted more from psychodynamic interpersonal therapy.

A Description of Group IPT

Interpersonal psychotherapy is a short-term, time-limited therapy that emphasizes the current interpersonal relations of the patient. This approach assumes that there is an interrelationship between negative mood, low self-esteem, traumatic life events, interpersonal functioning, and the patient's symptoms. Central to the treatment is the notion that symptomatic behaviors constitute a maladaptive solution for "underlying difficulties."

Major therapeutic tools are well-established techniques such as clarification of emotional states, improvement of interpersonal communication, reassurance, and testing of perceptions and performance through interpersonal contact. Interpersonal therapy concentrates on current disputes, frustrations, anxieties, and wishes defined in the interpersonal context. The influence of early childhood experiences is recognized as significant but is not emphasized in the therapy. Rather, the work focuses on the "here and now."

During the intake session the therapist and patient agree upon the interpersonal problem areas and goals. Treatment goals evolve from the four main interpersonal problem areas as specified by Klerman et al. (1984, p.88):

1. *Grief*
2. *Interpersonal disputes* with spouse, lover, children, other family members, friends, co-workers
3. *Role transitions*—a new job, leaving one's home, going away to school, relocation in a new home or area, divorce, economic or other family changes
4. *Interpersonal deficits*—loneliness and social isolation.

These identified problems and resultant goals serve as the basis for the patient's focus on interpersonal issues in group IPT.

When using a group format, therapists inform patients about how the process of understanding their relationship to other members of the group will provide them with valuable insight into how they create their own actual social life. The group is described as a place to work on identified problem areas. Patients are told that this "interpersonal laboratory" will provide a unique opportunity to: (1) work on the relationship difficulties they experience in their social life; (2) recognize and accept their feelings, opinions, and needs; and (3) transfer newly learned interpersonal skills to their outside social life.

The therapist helps patients translate their interpersonal goals into ways they can be manifested in the interpersonal milieu of the group. For instance, if a member struggles with interpersonal deficits, it is likely that she will have a difficult time connecting with group members, and she may assume that others do not like her. Predicting these difficulties is often the first step in helping a patient work toward change.

Members are informed about what they can do to facilitate their own therapy and recovery. Members are encouraged to practice giving and receiving feedback as well as to make personal disclosures related to content, process, and emotion. The patients are reassured that the therapist's role is to facilitate constructive communication, because communication that evaluates, blames, moralizes, or demands is not likely to be useful. Therefore, although the therapist's role is highly supportive, members will be challenged to identify feelings in the here and now and to communicate as effectively as possible. Initially the process of giving and receiving feedback and initiating self-disclosure will be difficult and anxiety-provoking. Group IPT teaches patients to begin translating what triggers their symptoms into underlying interpersonal problems (e.g., lack of intimacy in relationships, inability to express anger, social isolation, hypersensitivity to rejection).

Patients are forewarned about certain stumbling blocks of the group: confusion, discouragement, and frustration at not having the amount of personal attention they might like. The therapist predicts that after a couple of sessions they may want to drop out. Patients are instructed that this is a very common reaction and that, when these feelings come up, it is important to discuss them in the group. Patients are reassured that others will probably be having similar feelings.

Patients' conceptions and misconceptions about group therapy are elicited and discussed; the therapist attempts to augment the patients' confidence in group therapy by emphasizing that groups do not constitute an inexpensive, second-rate therapy. The therapist also emphasizes that, by providing a rich arena in which they can learn a great deal about how others perceive them and how they relate to others, group therapy represents a unique and particularly effective therapeutic modality. In fact, what group IPT does best is to help people understand more about their relationships with others. One of the ways that the group helps members to work on their relationships is by focusing on the relationships that develop among members. The rationale provided is that the better communication becomes with each of the members of the group, the better communication will become with people in their outside social life.

Post-Traumatic Stress Disorder

Debriefing immediately after trauma can reduce a victim's chances of developing post-traumatic stress disorder (PTSD). Debriefing typically includes disclosure of the events, exploration of troubling reactions, identification of practical coping strategies, exploration of feelings about leaving the disaster and future plans of action, and referrals to other source of help (Marmar & Freeman, 1988).

The PTSD treatment research has focused primarily on rape victims and combat veterans. Unfortunately there has been a lack of consensus concerning the target symptoms and primary measures for assessing PTSD treatment response, which makes it difficult to compare treatments. However, several studies have found that systematic exposure to traumatic stimuli, either alone or when added to usual treatment, is superior to control conditions.

Cooper and Clum (1989) found that patients who received imaginal flooding in addition to standard treatment improved more on all eleven of their measures compared to the standard treatment group; significant differences between the two groups were found on four of the measures. In a study using twenty-four Vietnam War veterans, Keane et al. (1989) compared implosive flooding therapy and a wait-list control. Flooding produced significantly greater decline in many symptoms, including depression (as measured by the BDI), trait anxiety (as measured by the State-Trait Anxiety Inventory), and therapist's rating of PTSD symptoms. Treatment gains were maintained through a 6-month followup.

Boudewyns and Hyer (1990) and Boudewyns et al. (1990) assigned Vietnam veterans to "direct therapeutic exposure" (DTE) or conventional therapy. The DTE patients showed fewer symptoms and better adjustment on the Veterans Adjustment Scale administered at a 3-month followup than did those receiving conventional therapy.

In a study using rape victims with PTSD, Foa et al. (1991) compared prolonged exposure, stress inoculation training (described subsequently), supportive counseling, and a wait-list control. The latter two groups improved negligibly, and significantly less so than those assigned to stress inoculation. Prolonged exposure did not initially yield superior results, although its effects exceeded those of the supportive counseling group by the 3-month followup, because of continuing improvement of the prolonged exposure patients. At followup, 56% of the prolonged exposure patients evidenced clinically significant improvement, compared to 33% of the supportive counseling group.

Stress inoculation therapy (SIT) for PTSD was adapted from Meichenbaum (1974) for rape victims by Veronen and Kilpatrick (1983) and was one of the active treatment conditions in the Foa et al.'s (1991) study. Stress inoculation therapy includes cognitive restructuring and behavioral anxiety management, and coping techniques (e.g., deep muscle relaxation and controlled breathing). At the end of treatment, SIT outperformed both the wait-list and the supportive counseling controls. While 71% of SIT patients met criteria for clinically significant change after treatment, only 19% of those in the control groups did. At 3-month followup, 67% of the SIT patients exhibited clinically significant improvement, while 33% of the supportive counseling patients did.

There has been growing interest in the efficacy and mode of action of *eye movement desensitization and reprocessing* (EMDR). This approach can be viewed as a special application of imaginal exposure (behavior therapy), because it involves repeated guided visual imagery of the traumatic event. It has also been considered a unique treatment by many, because the elicitation of rapid, saccadic eye movements during the imaginal exposure session is considered central by its practitioners. Francine Shapiro's (1989) EMDR treatment method for PTSD appears to facilitate "free association" in a manner similar to dreaming or REM sleep; it is sometimes accompanied by strong emotions, but this is highly variable across individuals and strong affect does not seem necessary for its efficacy. The treatment seems to facilitate increased insight and cognitive shifts allowing the traumatic experience(s) to remain "in the past" and reduces client reports of intrusive PTSD symptoms (sometimes dramatically).

Wilson, Becker, and Tinker (1995) compared EMDR to a wait-list control condition. Forty-six percent of the 80 patients met criteria for PTSD; all felt trauma was interfering with their lives. The EMDR process, administered in three 90-minute individual sessions, resulted in greater change than did the wait-list condition across a wide variety of measures. Comparable gains were observed in the initially wait-listed patients after they were given EMDR. Gains were maintained 90 days after treatment.

A dismantling study by Renfrey and Spates (1994) supports the view that EMDR may just be a variant of guided exposure treatment. In their study, PTSD patients were randomly assigned to EMDR or an imaginal exposure condition in which the patient was asked to focus on a fixed stimulus. The full EMDR condition produced no measurable advantage, although this may be attributable to limited sample size. Currently there is no published evidence that EMDR is either as effective as or superior to standard exposure treatments for PTSD.

Eating Disorders

Anorexia Nervosa

Few controlled studies of treatment of anorexia nervosa exist, and no one form of treatment has been empirically demonstrated to be superior to others (Compas et al., 1998). Hospitalization and behavior therapy have nonetheless been considered treatments of choice here. If the patient's weight is medically precarious, hospitalization is mandatory. Behavior therapy is used first to prevent starvation and then to restore nutritional balance and increase weight. In using behavioral methods, it is important to pick only battles that can be won. Treatment staff should tell the patient to notify them if the patient is tempted to overeat and reassure the patient that they will stop her from doing so. This is a powerful message: It shows they understand her dread of becoming fat, which allies them with her, rather than against her. This undercuts the rebellious aspect of overeating and circumvents the power struggles that occurred within the family.

Initially, parents should not have any responsibility for the patient's care. This reduces family tension and permits autonomy for the patient. Informal lunches including the whole family can help to assess family interactions at mealtime, to reduce intrafamily power struggles, and to promote more helpful behavior around the table.

Psychotherapy focuses on helping the patient learn to abandon self-destructive attempts at autonomy and to find more enduring self-control from within. Assertiveness training is helpful so patients can say "no" in family conflicts. Group therapy helps patients reestablish lost social skills, fashion appropriate expectations, and obtain support from peers.

Anorectics commonly suffer from depression; 40–60% benefit from antidepressant medication (Maxmen & Ward, 1995). Undernourished patients are unusually sensitive to drugs and are likely to have low blood pressure. Therefore SSRIs are often preferred because they have minimal effect on heart rhythms and don't cause orthostatic hypotension. Appetite enhancers (such as cyproheptadine, a serotonin antagonist) are also sometimes used.

Bulimia Nervosa

Clinical evidence suggests that bulimia nervosa often runs a chronic course, as most patients have exhibited many years of symptoms and often have made previous attempts at treatment (Russell, 1979; Herzog et al., 1991). Both antidepressant drugs and individual and group psychotherapy, using either CBT or psychodynamic (particularly interpersonal) approaches, are quite effective in treating bulimia.

The first stage of treatment typically focuses on breaking the binge-purge cycle; a behavioral approach can quickly reduce bingeing and purging. The patient keeps a careful record of food intake, vomiting, purging abuse, and the context of bingeing (time, place, mood, etc.). The abnormal pattern of eating is then shaped into a more normal pattern by avoiding precipitants of binges and substituting alternative pleasurable activities (showers, baths, walks, talking to a friend on the phone). Patients are also instructed to practice delaying (but not necessarily stopping) vomiting, especially if it happens after normal meals.

The second stage focuses on broad areas of behavior and attitudes. Cognitive-behavioral therapy is as effective as behavioral and interpersonal therapy at reducing bingeing and depression and more effective in modifying disturbed attitudes toward shape, weight, dieting, and the use of vomiting to control shape and weight (Wilfley et al., 1993). Patients who participate in CBT show greater overall improvement. One goal is eating for weight maintenance to break the binge-fast roller coaster.

Fairburn et al. (1993) compared CBT, IPT, and behavioral treatment. Few patients undergoing behavioral treatment alone ceased all forms of binge eating and purging, while patients in the CBT and IPT treatments made equivalent, substantial, and lasting changes across all areas. The IPT took longer to achieve success.

In bulimia nervosa, CBT uses both cognitive and behavioral procedures to change patients' behavior, their attitudes about shape and weight, and, when necessary, other cognitive distortions such as low self-esteem and extreme perfectionism. Cognitive-behavioral therapy assumes that eliminating dietary restriction, increasing the intake of a wider variety of foods, and decreasing the cognitive distortions are collectively sufficient for treatment effectiveness (Fairburn, 1985). Cognitive therapy does not focus on dysfunctional relationship patterns. Self-monitoring forms are used to elucidate dysfunctional eating patterns and to identify triggers to binge eating (eating, thinking, and mood patterns). Alternative eating patterns and coping strategies are emphasized, and unrealistic rules and fears associated with restricted eating patterns are confronted. Relapse prevention procedures consist of problem solving and identifying more effective methods of coping with high-risk situations, urges to binge, and lapses.

Bulimics' distorted thinking patterns may alternate between catastrophic predictions and rigid games of denial, rationalization, or justification. The latter type of thinking involves "fooling" oneself—for example, convincing oneself that because breakfast was skipped and lunch consisted of only an apple, "snacking" on a basket of chips at a Mexican restaurant before eating two large burritos really won't matter. Here, instead of the consequences being greatly exaggerated, they are minimized or denied. Both types of thinking can lead to problems and require consistent challenge and reframing.

Interpersonal therapy focuses on the patient's current relational functioning. It addresses the interpersonal context in which the disorder developed and has been maintained. In IPT there is no mention of the patient's eating problems or concerns about shape or weight other than during the initial assessment. Interpersonal therapy assumes that patients must develop greater control of their current social roles and adapt to interpersonal situations in order for treatment to be effective. Binge eating is believed to be triggered by negative mood, low self-esteem, and low interpersonal functioning frequently associated with obesity in a culture that values slimness (Fairburn et al., 1991).

Agras et al. (1989) compared a wait-list control with self-monitoring of caloric intake and purging behaviors, CBT, and CBT combined with response prevention of vomiting. The self-monitoring method entailed recording eating behaviors and then examining these records in detail with the therapist. The CBT consisted of self-monitoring, behavior change prescriptions (e.g., eating three adequate meals a day), critical examination of rules and fears associated with food and binge eating, challenging distorted thinking patterns, and relapse prevention. The response-prevention condition entailed CBT as well as consuming food enough to elicit an urge to vomit. This urge was allowed to dissipate over the remainder of the session, during which time distortions of bodily feeling and cognition were explored with the patient. All treatment groups experienced significant improvement, while the wait-list group did not. The CBT group showed the most improvement; inclusion of response prevention was not advantageous.

Thackwray et al. (1993) assessed the relative efficacy of CBT, behavioral therapy, and an attention-placebo for bulimia. At post-treatment, 92% of the CBT group, 100% of the behavioral therapy group, and 69% of the nonspecific monitoring placebo group were abstinent from bingeing/purging behavior. Cognitive and behavioral therapy were significantly more effective than the control. The followup rate of abstinence for CBT was impressive; the authors attributed this to CBT's use of homework and outside-of-treatment practice.

In Thackwray et al. (1993), the nonspecific self-monitoring placebo control group numerically indicated daily binge-purge episodes but did not address changes in eating habits. Behavior therapy group members were presented with a behavior eating habit control program that was modified to control bingeing and purging. In the first few sessions the subjects and therapist outlined behavior changes that would maintain their present weight while shaping a sensible food intake plan, including binge foods. In the later sessions, subjects, with the aid of a therapist, identified environmental factors believed to be antecedents of bingeing and purging and created strategies for dealing with environmental events. The CBT group received therapy resembling an abbreviated version of Fairburn's (1985) CBT program. The earlier therapy sessions were similar to those of the behavioral therapy group, but the latter session followed a cognitive-behavioral model with cognitive activity viewed as the mediator between environment, behavior, and consequences.

Nonpurging Bulimics

Binge eating among the obese has been recently recognized as an important clinical problem (Wilfley et al., 1993). Among obese individuals seeking treatment, 29% to 55% reported binge eating (Hudson et al., 1988; Loro & Orleans, 1981; Marcus, Wing & Lamparski, 1985; Spitzer et al., 1991, 1992). Some studies show that obese binge eaters experience levels of psychopathology comparable to those of anorectic and normal-weight people with bulimia (Hudson et al., 1988; Wilfrey, 1989).

Several studies and clinical reports show that overweight women with bulimic symptoms function less well than obese nonbingeing women (Marcus, Wing, & Hopkins, 1988; Wilson, 1976).

Telch et al. (1990) evaluated the initial effects of CBT in nonpurging bulimic subjects. This efficacy study compared the experimental group, those receiving CBT, with a wait-list control. At post-treatment, 79% of the CBT group reported abstinence from binge eating and 94% indicated a decrease in binge eating behavior; in the control group there was only a 9% decrease in binge eating behavior and a 0% abstinence rate. A 10-week followup assessment indicated a significant return of binge eating behavior, but these levels showed improvement in comparison to baseline levels.

Patients in the CBT group were informed that binge eating patterns had developed as a response to repeated restrictive dieting, and that binge eating behavior must be eradicated to restore healthy eating habits. Participants were taught to self-monitor their eating patterns, binge episodes, thoughts, moods, and the circumstances surrounding their eating. They did not monitor their weight.

Telch et al. (1990) argue that inclusion of relapse prevention training may enhance maintenance. Because CBT subjects did not lose weight during the study, many may have reverted to self-imposed restrictive dieting following treatment. To avoid this, Telch et al. suggest the subsequent use of behavioral therapy for weight loss following CBT for binge eating.

Wilfley et al. (1993) compared CBT, IPT, and a wait-list group. They found that CBT and IPT comparably reduced bingeing (64% and 68%, respectively); whereas the control group reduced bingeing by only 11%. These findings are similar to those of Fairburn et al. (1991). Despite the fact that IPT does not focus on eating behavior, it appears to be successful in treating nonpurging bulimia.

A study done by Agras et al. (1995) investigated the effectiveness of group IPT in treating overweight individuals suffering from binge eating disorder who did not respond well to 12 weeks of group CBT. The treatment group decreased the number of days on which binges occurred by 77%, whereas the control group only showed a 22% decrease. The individuals in the treatment group decreased their weight by 0.6 kg, while weight in the control group increased by 4.1 kg. IPT failed to add to the effects of CBT. Agras et al. emphasized the need to discover methods for helping those who do not respond to initial treatment.

Weight Loss

Bolocofsky, Spinler, and Coulthard-Morris (1985) compared behavioral treatment for weight change with and without hypnosis. The behavioral method consisted of collecting weight history, self-monitoring instruction, keeping a weight diary, progressive relaxation, and rule adherence. The hypnosis method entailed self-hypnosis and therapist-induced hypnosis. The results indicated that, at termination of treatment, both groups significantly improved. However, at 8 months and again at 2 years, clients in the hypnosis group showed additional significant weight loss.

Summaries of ESTs for Severe Mental Illnesses and Serious Refractory Problems

Schizophrenic Disorders

The goal of treatment in schizophrenic disorders is usually not cure, but improved quality of life, through minimization of symptoms, prevention of suicide, enhancement of self-esteem, improved social and occupational functioning, improved familial relationships, and prevention of relapse. The majority of schizophrenics benefit from antipsychotic medication. Atypical antipsychotics, such as clozapine and risperidone, block both dopamine and serotonin-2 receptors more effectively. These help in roughly one-third of the cases where traditional antipsychotics are ineffective (Maxmen & Ward, 1995). Acute care frequently requires hospitalization. Frequent contacts stressing reality testing and reassurance are most helpful. Transition care after discharge is most effective when stability is maximized. Noncompliance with medication is the single greatest factor responsible for relapse (Haywood et al., 1995; Sullivan et al., 1995). Chronic care should involve enhancement of social supports and education aimed at medication compliance. More psychotherapy is not always better with chronic schizophrenics; Hogarty et al. (1974) found that long-term intensive psychotherapy is ineffective in treating schizophrenia.

Most studies have compared different psychological treatments used in conjunction with antipsychotic medications, focusing on the possible relapse prevention effects of psychotherapy. Various attempts have been made to develop effective psychosocial interventions for schizophrenia, typically focusing on strengthening the coping capacities of the individual patient. Those approaches that have employed psychodynamic psychotherapy have been disappointing (Grinspoon, Ewalt, & Shader, 1972; May, 1968). Those involving social case work (Hogarty, Goldberg, et al., 1974; Hogarty, Schooler, et al., 1979) and behavioral psychology (Chambliss, 1988; Liberman, Wallace, et al., 1981) have shown limited efficacy.

Wallace and Liberman (1985) compared social skills training (SST) and a "holistic health" control group involving 200 hours of yoga, exercise, and stress management. Measures of social skills revealed a significant advantage for the SST condition. During the 2-year followup period, the SST group experienced fewer rehospitalizations (sixteen versus thirty in the holistic health group), but the relapse prevention advantage did not reach statistical significance. Hogarty, Anderson, et al. (1986) found that patients given SST exhibited a 20% relapse rate, compared to a 41% relapse rate in patients in a control group in which pharmacotherapy was provided in a supportive, didactic relationship context. A meta-analysis of SST studies by Benton and Schroeder (1990) found a significant effect size for SST on relapse prevention (0.5), despite inclusion of several studies with null results.

On the other hand, several studies have failed to find a significant relapse prevention advantage for SST groups when compared with controls (Bellack et al., 1984; Brown & Munford, 1983; Spencer, Gillespie, & Ekisa, 1983). Hayes, Halford, and Varghese (1995) failed to find an advantage of SST over a discussion group condition in alleviating schizophrenic symptoms or in improving community functioning.

In a review of the literature on behavior modification of schizophrenia, Liberman (1972) discusses the successful application of operant conditioning principles to this disorder. The high negative correlation between time spent in the hospital and chances for release is well known; the term "social breakdown syndrome" was coined by Zusman (1967) to refer to the process whereby the contingencies operating in public mental hospitals condition long-term patients to be compliant, passive, and socially and vocationally incompetent. Social and occupational skills that patients possess upon entering a hospital are frequently extinguished by the absence of any positive consequences to maintain them. Instead, quiet, docile, compliance is reinforced with staff attention and interest. However, the more effective patients are in adapting to the routines of the hospital, the more they are seen as requiring hospitalization and the more difficult their transition to the community following discharge becomes.

To reverse these patterns, token economies have been instituted to establish more therapeutic reinforcement contingencies within inpatient settings. The token economy is a systematic and consistent application of reinforcement principles to patients' behaviors in a ward milieu. It induces socially appropriate behavior through use of tokens, coupons, or points, which serve as a common currency making immediate reinforcement for adaptive behaviors possible. Patients' responses have clear-cut consequences. Failure to engage in socially appropriate behavior leads to absence of reinforcement (extinction of maladaptive behavior) or occasionally to punishment (i.e., fines), when tokens are taken away from the patient. In the token economy, patients assume responsibility for their behavior, much as they would do in the community outside the hospital (Ayllon & Azrin, 1968).

Multiple baseline designs have shown the efficacy of behavioral interventions with schizophrenics in reducing several different types of hallucinations, delusional speech, bizarre behavior, and apathy and in increasing social and recreational activities and improving release rates and long-term discharge success. Use of token economy treatment has been demonstrated to be highly cost effective, because it facilitates successful discharge (Foster, 1969).

Steps for Behavioral Rehabilitation

Steps for behavioral rehabilitation of schizophrenic patients are:

1. Precisely define the behavioral goals for each patient.
2. Measure the frequency of the desired behaviors.
3. Attach clear positive and negative consequences to adaptive and maladaptive behavior, respectively.
4. Use instructions and prompts to elicit desired behaviors.
5. Use shaping; reinforce patients for taking small steps in the desired direction.
6. Structure the inpatient setting to approximate the outside community.
7. Provide opportunities for patients to learn and practice vocational and housekeeping skills that have marketable value in the community or instrumental role value within the family.
8. Prepare patients and significant others to live in mutually supportive ways in the community through predischarge training and aftercare programs.
9. Teach significant others to use behavioral principles to maintain gains.
10. Coordinate community resources to reinforce and support discharged patients' coping efforts.

Enhancing Generalization

Liberman (1972) suggests several strategies for enhancing generalization:

1. Select target behaviors in the treatment setting that will continue to be reinforced in the natural milieu.
2. Pair praise, approval, and other social reinforcers with the more tangible reinforcers (tokens), so that naturally occurring social reinforcers will maintain the behavioral gains after discharge.
3. Gradually fade out the tangible reinforcers, relying solely on social reinforcers.
4. Gradually fade in the natural environment.
5. Simulate the natural environment with its stimulus characteristics in the treatment milieu, and reinforce behavior under these simulated conditions.
6. Train relatives and other caretakers in the community to carry out the reinforcement programs begun in the hospital.
7. Train patients to provide self-reinforcement for the behaviors under treatment.
8. Use intermittent and delayed schedules of reinforcement as the treatment proceeds.

Family Interventions

Family interventions have been studied by Falloon et al. (1985) and Randolph et al. (1994). In a 2-year longitudinal outcome study on schizophrenic treatments, Falloon et al. (1985) compared a family-based treatment approach to a patient-oriented approach of a similar intensity. Because environmental stress may contribute to the clinical morbidity of established cases of schizophrenia, the management of this disorder within the community should include efforts to reduce common stressors. This study was designed to assess whether family-based approaches are better than individual approaches in reducing the environmental stress associated with clinical exacerbations of schizophrenia.

The Falloon et al. family therapy enhances coping skills by increasing the efficiency of family problem-solving methods, by encouraging the family to employ a structured problem-solving method that involves discussing problems together, specifying a problem, considering a broad range of real solutions, and agreeing, together, on a detailed plan about how to carry out the solution. After 9 months, of those treated with family management, only 17% showed evidence of schizophrenia. Significantly fewer patients receiving family management were admitted to the hospital during the first 9 months. There were no differences between the two management therapies in terms of anxiety or depressive syndromes. The findings of this 2-year comparison offer support for a family-based approach in reducing the clinical morbidity of schizophrenia. The increased stability of the family-managed patients was evident both in terms of therapist observations over the length of the study and a tendency toward superior remission over the 2-year followup. Individual management was less effective in preventing major episodes of schizophrenia among initially stabilized patients who were living in stressful home environments. The major clinical effect of family management appeared to involve prevention of further escalation of the inevitable exacerbations that characterize this disorder (Falloon et al., 1985). Differential medication compliance did not account for the outcome differences.

Randolph et al. (1994) studied in-home behavioral family management and customary care for schizophrenics. The behavioral family management provided both the patient and their family with training on how to cope with stress, communication skills, and problem-solving training. They were given homework tasks to complete and social reinforcement for their completed tasks. The customary care patients received outpatient care including medication management, crisis intervention services, social skills such as living independently, and vocational skills. The behavioral family management combined with customary care experienced little or no exacerbations after treatment whereas over half of the patients with only customary care had exacerbations.

The Hogarty, Anderson, et al. (1986) study compared family and social skills training in an attempt to reduce the 41% first-year relapse rate among schizophrenic patients discharged with maintenance neuroleptic treatment. This 2-year–long aftercare study of 103 patients residing in high expressed emotion households examined the effects of four treatment approaches following discharge: family treatment and medication, SST and medication, combined (family treatment, social skills, and medication), and medication alone. Both family treatment and SST significantly reduced relapse rate, from the international relapse rate among medical controls of 41% (confirmed again here) to 19% and 20%, respectively. Combining these treatments had additive effects, resulting in a 0% relapse rate. During the first year of followup, relapse did not occur in any household that changed from high to low expressed emotion. In households remaining high in expressed emotion, only the combination of treatment was found to sustain remission. While their preliminary findings were very encouraging, longer-term findings suggest that, while these treatments are demonstrably effective in delaying relapse, they generally do not offer permanent protection.

The family approach was designed as an education and management strategy intended to lower the emotional climate of the home while maintaining reasonable expectations for patient performance (Hogarty et al., 1986). Traditional family therapy attempts to promote disclosure, insight, and resolution of intergenerational and marital issues were for the most part avoided.

Treatment sought to increase the stability and predictability of family life by decreasing the family's guilt and anxiety, increasing their self-confidence, and providing a sense of cognitive mastery through the provision of information about the nature and course of schizophrenia (Hogarty et al., 1986). The goal of this family treatment was to reduce both positive and negative symptoms of schizophrenia associated with extremes of stimulation encountered in either the therapeutic process or family life.

The SST component of the family intervention approach involved techniques previously explored by Liberman et al. (1975), Wallace et al. (1980), and Hersen and Bellack (1976). An individualized structured approach was used to guide performance of appropriate verbal and nonverbal social behaviors and develop accurate social perception skills. Instruction, modeling, role play, feedback, and assigned homework were used in conjunction with therapist support and empathy. Initially patients were encouraged to avoid conflict and actions believed to elicit high expressed emotion in family members. Early treatment efforts focused on teaching patients to express positive feelings, in order to reduce family dissatisfaction and elicit more favorable family responses. Social skills training indirectly attempted to "cool" the emotional climate of the household, in contrast to the more direct approach embodied in the family treatment method.

Other Treatments

Marder et al. (1996) compared behaviorally oriented SST with supportive group therapy in schizophrenic patients. These patients were stabilized with fluphenazine decanoate, which was supplemented with fluphenazine or a placebo. The social skills method entailed medication self-management and symptom self-management, social problem solving, and successful living skills (Liberman, DeRisi, & Mueser, 1989). The supportive group therapy method consisted of setting personal goals and working as a group to address problems and obstacles blocking goal achievement, cooperation, reflection, empathy, warmth, and encouragement (Rutan & Cohen, 1989; Liberman, 1994). The drug treatment condition entailed patients being randomly assigned to receive either oral fluphenazine (5 mg twice daily) or a placebo after experiencing a prodrome (Marder, Wirshing, Van Putten, et al., 1994). The results showed significant main effects for SST over group therapy on personal well-being and total on the Social Adjustment Scale II (SAS-II), and significant interactions between psychosocial treatment and drug treatment for external family, social and leisure activities, and SAS-II total. "Social skills training did not significantly decrease the risk of psychotic exacerbation in the full group, but an advantage was observed (post hoc) among patients who received placebo supplementation" (Marder, Wirshing, Van Putten, et al., 1994, p. 158).

Drake et al. (1996) compared group skills training and individual placement and support (IPS) models in the effectiveness of supported employment services for people with severe mental illness. The group skills training method consisted of individualized intake, group pre-employment training, individualized placement and on-site support, mental health provider contact, and continuous support. All of this was accomplished by the agency outside of the mental health center setting. The IPS method entailed immediate job placement and, if needed, training and support after employment. This method used the joint efforts of clinical and vocational services of the mental health center. The results showed that, during an 18-month period, more of those persons in the IPS group were competitively employed.

Borderline Personality Disorder and Suicide

Approximately 11% of all psychiatric outpatients meet criteria for borderline personality disorder (BPD). Of the personality disorders, BPD is the most commonly diagnosed, making up 33% of outpatients and 63% of inpatients with some form of personality disorder.

Parasuicidal behavior (any intentional, acute self-injurious behavior with or without suicidal intent, including both suicide attempts and self-mutilative behaviors) is particularly prevalent among individuals who meet criteria for BPD. The suicide rate for borderline patients who parasuicide is double that of non-parasuiciding patients with BPD. Both parasuicide and BPD are more prevalent among women.

Kroll (1993) discusses eight findings that he posits are useful in thinking about the treatment of borderline patients:

1. The effectiveness of psychotherapy with borderlines has not been demonstrated.
2. Fifty percent of borderlines quit therapy within 6 months.
3. Fifty percent of borderlines in successful therapy (successful as defined by their therapists) terminate therapy against the advice of their therapists.
4. Most borderlines improve around age 30.
5. About 8% to 15% of borderlines have committed suicide by the 10- or 15-year followup.
6. Suicide in borderlines is correlated with antisocial personality, ongoing alcohol abuse, and depressions of an angry-hostile nature.
7. Suicide is negatively correlated with wrist cutting.
8. About 70% to 80% of borderlines appear to have experienced some form of sexual and/or physical abuse in childhood.

Dialectical Behavior Therapy

Linehan et al. (1991) reported the results of a randomized, 1-year clinical study of parasuicidal borderline women, comparing dialectical behavior therapy (DBT), a program using individual and group therapy sessions, to a "treatment as usual" group. Dialectical therapy yielded a greater reduction in frequency and medical risk of parasuicidal behaviors, lower 1-year therapy dropout rates, and fewer inpatient hospital days. These effects occurred despite absence of significant changes on self-report measures.

Dialectical behavior therapy combines behavioral, cognitive, and supportive psychotherapies. Therapists apply directive, problem-oriented techniques (including behavioral skill training, contingency management, cognitive modification, and exposure to environmental cues) that are balanced with supportive techniques, such as reflection, empathy, and acceptance.

Both during and between sessions (telephone contact with the therapist between sessions is part of DBT), the therapist actively teaches and reinforces adaptive behaviors, especially as they occur within the therapeutic relationship. The therapist consistently withholds reinforcement of behaviors targeted for change. The emphasis is on teaching patients how to manage emotional trauma rather than on resolving crises.

An important objective in the treatment of BPD is to help patients achieve a greater level of emotional and behavioral stability and then to aid them in developing more effective coping skills. The weaker the ego functioning is, the more important it is to use stabilizing interventions (Preston, 1997).

Stabilizing interventions aim to decrease arousal, foster affective stability, and improve self-control. The following techniques can help to improve ego functioning (to enhance emotional control, improve thinking and problem solving, and increase reality testing) and to foster the development of more adaptive coping strategies:

- Avoid actions that promote regression or increase arousal.
- Help the patient to gain perspective: Reframe situations to help increase self-acceptance and self-compassion, and reduce the patient's affective intensity by countering the tendency to think in absolute, judgmental terms (e.g., "It shouldn't be that way!" or "I shouldn't feel this way!").
- Challenge the patient's cognitive distortions: Actively confront inaccurate, global, or arbitrary conclusions and encourage the client to "check it out" and "explore the facts." Counter overly negative, pessimistic predictions.

The following is a set of useful treatment goals:

- Reduce dangerous acting out and impulsive behaviors.
- Eliminate substance abuse.
- Use plans to prevent suicide and violence toward others.
- Develop strategies for containing and controlling emotions.

- Improve coping skills: Improve self-calming, problem solving, assertive interpersonal interactions, and structuring leisure time.
- Develop solutions for specific problems: Resolve a familial problem, address financial issues, resolve a troubled relationship, confront a work problem.

Linehan's (1993) hierarchy of targets in DBT is:

First-Stage Targets: Stability and Control
1. Decreasing suicidal behaviors
2. Decreasing therapy-interfering behavior
3. Decreasing quality-of-life-interfering behaviors
4. Increasing behavioral skills
   A. Core mindfulness skills
   B. Interpersonal effectiveness
   C. Emotion regulation
   D. Distress tolerance
   E. Self-management

Second-Stage Targets: Emotional Processing of the Past
5. Decreasing posttraumatic stress

Third-Stage Targets: Connection and Serenity
6. Increasing respect for self
7. Achieving individual goals

Many maintain that treatment of borderline patients is best done with supervision, even if all that is possible is peer group supervision. As it is hard to avoid mistakes in working with borderline patients, and as these mistakes seem to lead to more problems in therapy with borderlines, feedback from others is especially valuable. Because roughly 65% of BPD patients experience a diminution in emotional lability and impulsivity after age 40, if therapy can help them through their more tumultuous years and tide them over, there is real hope of a better, less chaotic life down the road. Helping to prevent suicide and self-mutilation, to avoid jail, and to not burn too many bridges (interpersonally and occupationally) are extremely worthwhile goals in the treatment of BPD (Preston, 1997).

Suicide Management

Therapists need to respond to the issue of suicide in a way that not only blocks patients from immediately killing or seriously harming themselves, but also reduces the probability of such future behavior. The goal of treatment is to help the patients develop safe means of managing personal crises, so they need not resort to self-harm.

Therapists can mention that they count on the patient to bring up any suicidal concerns during sessions, both to offer permission to explore these difficult issues and to emphasize the patient's ultimate responsibility for his or her own life.

According to Preston (1997), "The starting point when dealing with these behaviors is in uncovering, understanding, and acknowledging the client's legitimate feelings of loneliness, neediness, or fear of abandonment. The more these feelings can be expressed outwardly in words, the less likely they will be manifested in suicidal behavior. (p. 129)

In managing a suicidal patient, it can be useful to (1) Assess suicidal severity and conduct a behavioral analysis, (2) Discuss constructive alternatives, and (3) Help the patient commit to a non-suicidal behavioral plan.

First, assess suicidal severity and conduct a behavioral analysis by obtaining detailed information about the events, experiences, and actions that preceded the suicide-related behavior and the consequences of the behavior. This provides information about the sequence of events surrounding the target behavior to clarify its function. In addition, this process of analysis helps the patient see that suicidal or parasuicidal behavior was not a necessary response to what occurred.

Developing constructive alternatives is important because suicidal and parasuicidal individuals often think of their self-destructive behaviors as the only available solution to their problems. Help the patient to learn from a previous attempt by suggesting that rather than really wanting to be dead, possibly the patient felt overwhelmed and desperate, and engaged in the self-harming behavior in an effort to solve or avoid problems that seemed unendurable and unending. The therapist can then work with the patient to find other ways to cope. Challenging suicidal solutions by emphasizing their many negative consequences can also be helpful. Learning how to accept and tolerate the intense pain associated with certain situations is often important; remembering that these situations are almost always temporary can be extremely helpful.

Finally it is important to obtain commitment to a nonsuicidal behavioral plan and to reinforce use of more adaptive coping measures. Public commitments to maintain personal safety are especially helpful (Linehan, 1993).

Substance Abuse/Chemical Dependency

A major factor accounting for increasing mental health care costs has been the rise in inpatient treatment for alcohol and drug abuse. Some states passed laws mandating coverage of substance abuse, in some cases making it equal to other medical conditions. This additional coverage, coupled with an enormous need for substance abuse treatment, accelerated the growth of costs in this area.

Alcohol Abuse

A popular screening for alcoholism is the CAGE (Cut down, Annoyed, Guilty, and Eye Opener) questionnaire (Ewing, 1984). Positive answers to at least two questions is suggestive of alcohol dependence. This questionnaire accurately assesses alcoholism over 85% of the time.

1. Have you ever felt you should cut down your drinking?
2. Have other people annoyed you by criticizing your drinking?
3. Have you ever felt guilty about drinking?
4. Have you ever taken a drink in the morning to steady your nerves or get rid of a hangover?

The standard treatment of alcohol dependence is abstinence and AA (or similar recovery program). Abstinence should be urged, because clinicians cannot accurately predict the estimated 5% to 15% of alcoholics who can learn to drink moderately. The longer clients remain alcohol-free, the better their thinking, social, sexual, and occupational functioning becomes. Many clients deny they have a problem with alcohol, so getting clients to agree to a temporary period of abstinence, to experiment with what it feels like, is often useful.

Alcohol users with many previous treatment attempts are six times less likely to succeed in abstinence. However, alcohol patients with many previous treatment completions are four times more likely to be abstinent at 6 months (Opland, 1995). Polydrug patients who experienced depression in the past year are 2.3 times less likely to succeed in abstinence. It is helpful to provide a relapse prevention program for alcohol patients with a history of treatment completions, an alternative program to motivate treatment completion for those with a history of premature termination, and to offer depression treatment for polydrug users.

German (1994) cites a study of twenty-six controlled alcoholism treatment comparisons, which consistently found that results are more influenced by the content of interventions than by the settings in which treatment is offered. This has been used to support increasing reliance on outpatient treatment.

In outpatient settings, guidelines are needed to assist clinicians in determining when a patient's pattern of alcohol consumption warrants detoxification prior to outpatient treatment services. In particular, many clinicians have difficulty drawing distinctions regarding frequency of alcohol consumption (e.g., daily consumption vs. 1 or 2 days a week of use) and quantity (some patients arrive at our door drinking 1 quart of vodka daily; others arrive reporting daily consumption of 72 ounces of beer). At the Program for Addictions Consultation and Treatment (PACT) at St. Peter's Medical Center in New Brunswick, New Jersey, the following rules of thumb are used to refer people to inpatient detoxification programs (others are referred to outpatient therapy):

1. Drinking more than six standard drinks per day
2. Has never been able to establish even a short period of abstinence without significant withdrawal symptoms
3. Has clear history of withdrawal symptoms and has had either seizures or delirium tremens in the past when tried to self-detox

In their 1995 *Handbook of Alcoholism Treatment Approaches*, Miller and colleagues performed a meta-analysis ranking all current alcoholism treatments. They rated only studies that had randomly assigned alcoholics to at least one comparison group in addition to the treatment being evaluated. A total of 219 studies met their criteria. Forty-three treatments were ranked, although thirteen of them had too few studies to be definitively rated. Brief interventions had the highest score, followed by SST. At the bottom of the list in effectiveness were general alcoholism counseling and educational lectures and films about alcoholism. Alcoholics Anonymous received the lowest score among the thirteen treatments inadequately tested. Miller et al. noted that the treatments with the worst clinical record are almost universally the ones used by American alcoholism programs.

In a review of thirty-three different treatment modalities, Holder et al. (1991) concluded that there was good evidence for the efficacy of SST, self-control training, brief motivational counseling, behavioral marital therapy, community reinforcement, and stress management. They also felt that there is some evidence for the efficacy of covert sensitization and behavior contracting.

Eriksen, Bjornstad, and Gotestam (1986) found evidence for the efficacy of SST as part of inpatient treatment for patients with a diagnosis of alcohol dependence (*DSM-III*). Group-based SST yielded better outcomes than did a traditional discussion group. During the year after discharge, SST patients were abstinent 77% of the days, while control patients were abstinent 32% of the days.

Drummond and Glautier (1994) found cue exposure treatment superior to a relaxation control for inpatient alcohol-dependent subjects. During the 6 months after discharge, cue exposure therapy patients resumed heavy drinking later and consumed less total alcohol, compared to relaxation patients. Time until relatively heavy drinking among the cue exposure subjects averaged 110 days, versus 64 days for the relaxation condition.

Monti et al. (1993) found that alcohol-dependent (*DSM-III-R*) inpatients who had received cue exposure treatment combined with "urge coping skills" training were abstinent more days and reported fewer drinks per day during the 6 months after discharge than patients who received the standard inpatient treatment program.

Hunt and Azrin (1973) compared a "community reinforcement" procedure with a matched control group for the treatment of alcoholism in hospitalized alcoholics. The community reinforcement method entailed marital and family counseling; vocational, social, and reinforcer-access counseling; existing hospital programs; and community maintenance. The results indicated that subjects in the treatment group drank less, worked more, and experienced more family and out-of-hospital time.

Azrin (1976) compared the community reinforcement program with a modified community reinforcement program for treating alcoholics. The original community reinforcement program (Azrin, Flores, & Kaplan, 1975; Azrin, Naster, & Jones, 1973; Hunt & Azrin, 1973) entailed special job, family, social, and recreational procedures. The modified program included, in addition to these features, a "buddy system," daily report procedure, group counseling, and a special social motivation program to ensure the self-administration of Disulfiram (Antabuse). The results of this study showed that those in the modified community reinforcement program worked more, drank less, spent less time being institutionalized, and spent more time at home. Over all, the modified program took less time and was more effective than the original program.

O'Farrell, Cutter, & Floyd (1985) compared behavioral couples therapy, interactional couples therapy, and a no–marital treatment control for marital adjustment and communication in alcoholic males. The behavioral method entailed creating an Antabuse contract; planning shared activities; acknowledging caring behavior; learning to listen, express feelings, and use planned communication; and using positive requests, compromise, and written agreements. The interactional method consisted of mutual support, sharing of feelings, problem solving, discussion, verbal insight, homework assignments, written agreements, and Antabuse contracts. The results showed that the behavioral marital therapy group improved on desired relationship change, marital stability, and positiveness of communication measures. The interactional marital therapy group improved on desired relationship change and positive communication measures. The control group did not show any improvement on any of the measures. The behavioral therapy was superior to the interactional therapy on overall marital adjustment.

O'Farrell et al. (1992) compared behavioral marital therapy (BMT), an interactional couples therapy group, and a no–marital treatment control group in relation to the treatment of married male alcoholics. The BMT method included weekly homework assignments, behavioral rehearsal (Antabuse contract), encouragement of couple and family activities, and learning communication skills. The interactional couples therapy was that used in prior studies (Steinglass, 1976; Gallant et al., 1970). All subjects received alcohol counseling. The results showed that the BMT group experienced better marital outcomes (wives' positive marital adjustment and less time separated) than the no-treatment group, although the impact of these outcomes decreased with time after treatment. No advantage of BMT over alcohol counseling was observed after treatment.

Opiate Dependence

There have been many studies of psychotherapy for opiate dependence (Woody, Luborsky, McLellan, & O'Brien, 1989; Crits-Christoph & Siqueland, 1996). Neither opiate nor cocaine treatment studies have used traditional definitions of clinically significant change, probably because the focus is on abstinence initiation, rather than on achieving a score that is within a normative sample distribution. Abstinence rates in even the best of studies have not been impressive, especially given the common problem of high dropout rates.

Both supportive-expressive (SE) psychodynamic therapy and CT for opiate dependence (given in tandem with conventional drug counseling) have been supported empirically. Woody, Luborsky, McClellan, O'Brien, et al. (1983) and Woody, Luborsky, McLellan, and O'Brien (1990) compared drug counseling (DC), SE+DC, and CT+DC. Both SE and CT produced greater benefits than DC alone (in terms of opiate-positive urines, employment, legal problems, and psychiatric symptoms). Woody, McLellan, et al. (1995) reported a partial replication of this study comparing SE+DC to DC alone (using psychiatrically symptomatic opiate-dependent patients in community methadone programs). Their study also controlled for amount of professional contact through a comparison condition (DC+DC), in which two counselors were seen regularly by each patient. The SE+DC combination produced more benefit than did DC+DC. Opiate-positive urines increased for DC+DC patients during the final 12 weeks of treatment, while they decreased for SE+DC patients. The SE+DC patients also had fewer cocaine-positive urines and required lower doses of methadone. By a 6-month followup, DC+DC patients, while the SE+DC patients maintained or continued their improvement.

Carroll, Rounsaville, and Gawin (1991) compared a cognitive-behavioral–based relapse prevention treatment (RPT) to IPT. Fifty-seven percent of the RPT patients were abstinent for more than 3 weeks during the 12-week treatment, while only 33% of the IPT patients met this criterion (although this difference was not statistically significant). Among those with more psychiatric problems, RPT yielded significantly higher abstinence than did IPT. In a study of outpatients with cocaine dependence, Carroll et al. (1994) compared RPT plus desipramine, clinical management plus desipramine, RPT plus placebo, and clinical management plus placebo. All groups showed improvement during treatment, but there were no main nor interaction effects for medication and psychotherapy. However, at 1-year followup, RPT patients (either with desipramine or placebo) had significantly better outcomes than those who received supportive clinical management (either with desipramine or placebo).

Some behavioral treatments make reinforcement contingent on drug abstinence. Higgins et al. (1993) assessed the use of vouchers (exchangeable for goods and services) given for cocaine-free urines. This method was combined with drug counseling involving significant relationships; relapse prevention skills; establishment of alternative recreational activities; and employment, housing, financial, and legal guidance. The package was compared to standard drug counseling. Sixty-eight percent of patients in the reinforcement condition achieved 8 weeks of abstinence, compared to only 11% of the standard counseling patients.

Higgins et al. (1994) assigned patients to behavioral treatment with or without an added voucher incentive program. Retention was better in the voucher condition; 75% of the voucher group completed 24 weeks of treatment versus 40% in the behavioral treatment alone condition. Silverman et al. (1996) extended voucher-based reinforcement therapy to opiate-dependent patients who also abused cocaine. They found that providing contingent vouchers yielded better outcomes than noncontingent vouchers. In the contingent voucher condition, nearly half (47%) of patients achieved at least 7 weeks of continuous cocaine abstinence, while only 6% of those in the noncontingent treatment achieved more than 2 weeks of abstinence.

Smoking Cessation

Hill, Rigdon, and Johnson (1993) investigated four treatments: behavioral training, behavioral training and nicotine gum, behavioral training and physical exercise, and physical exercise for efficacy in smoking cessation. Behavioral training involved detailed information about the health risks related to smoking, removing smoking cues (ashtray, matches), and setting a definitive quitting date for which all participants signed a contract. They attended twelve 90-minute sessions in which they discussed hazards, temptations, and consequences of smoking. Nicotine gum was given to some with behavioral training on a weekly basis; the subjects were urged to chew the gum daily to avoid the urge to smoke. Some subjects with behavioral training also exercised. They spent 45 minutes, 3 days a week walking to increase their heart rate. A placebo group spent 45 minutes exercising without any additional behavioral training. The percentage of smokers quitting, respectively was 31.8, 36.4, 27.8, and 10.0. Behavioral training caused a greater cessation over the exercise-only program.

Stevens and Hollis (1989) compared relapse prevention coping strategies, a discussion control, and a no-treatment control condition for participants trained in behavioral and cognitive smoking cessation techniques. All participants went through smoking cessation. The coping strategies entailed positive behavioral, cognitive, and social alternatives to smoking, as well as rehearsal through role playing, use of props, and imagery techniques. The discussion condition included talking about problems and experiences and also provided social support. Results showed biochemically confirmed higher abstinence rates for the coping strategies group.

Cinciripini, Lapitsky, Wallfisch, et al. (1994) compared a scheduled smoking procedure with a minimal contact self-help treatment control in smoking cessation. The scheduled procedure method consisted of subjects using either scheduled smoking and relapse prevention or the American Cancer Society kit (1977). The self-help method included either no formal behavioral training or the "I Quit Kit". The results showed that after 6 and 12 months, 53% and 41%, respectively, of the scheduled smoking group experienced abstinence. Only an average of 6% of the control group experienced the same.

Cinciripini, Laptisky, Seay, et al. (1995) compared scheduled reduced smoking, nonscheduled reduced smoking, scheduled nonreduced smoking, and nonscheduled nonreduced smoking in the cessation of smoking behavior. The scheduled reduced method entailed smoking only at designated times of the day with the time between smoking gradually increasing. The nonscheduled reduced smoking method included gradually decreasing the consumption of cigarettes by using a weekly reduction quota. The scheduled nonreduced method consisted of the same smoking schedule as the first method; however, there were no reduced smoking markers. Participants in this group had to stop smoking abruptly on a target date. The final group (nonscheduled, nonreduced) were not set any guidelines besides the baseline level and were made aware that they would have to quit "cold turkey" at the target date. All participants also received CBT. The results indicated that, after a year, the scheduled reduced method showed the most effectiveness, while the nonscheduled reduced method exhibited the least. Methods containing schedules were more effective than those without schedules.

17 Summaries of ESTs for Problems in Living

Generally insurance covers only very brief treatment for problems in living, such as marital problems, sexual dysfunction, and parenting or childhood problems. However, there are relevant studies in these areas.

Marital Therapy

A large number of clients enter counseling in order to address relationship problems. Unlike most former indemnity plans, managed care benefits often permit inclusion of family members in care when this is expected to facilitate efficient achievement of therapy outcomes. This makes it all the more imperative for providers to stay current with shifting trends in the couples therapy literature. While couples therapy has been in widespread use for decades, recently some of its underlying assumptions have been called into question.

Behavioral treatments have been found to produce substantial, lasting improvement, as measured by self-reports of behavior (Goldiamond, 1965; Stuart, 1969), direct happiness ratings (Azrin, Naster, & Jones, 1973), or observation of interactions in the clinic and the Locke-Wallace (1959) questionnaire of marital adjustment (G. Patterson, Hops, & Weiss, 1975; Jacobson, 1977, 1978; Liberman et al., 1976).

Behavioral Marital Therapy

The technique of behavioral marital therapy focuses on identifying and correcting nonconstructive forms of communication, using behavior-shaping procedures and feedback from the therapist. The superiority of these behavioral methods has been demonstrated using a variety of comparison procedures, including a within-subject baseline (Stuart, 1969), a case study (Goldiamond, 1965), a discussion-type procedure in a within-groups design (Azrin, Naster, & Jones, 1973) or a between-groups design (Jacobson, 1977, 1978), or in a pre-test–post-test design (Paterson, 1988).

Goldiamond (1965) used contingency management and stimulus control techniques to resolve marital disorders, after applying an operant behavioral perspective to these problems. Stuart (1969) treated couples using a strict behavioral contracting method, in which tokens were used to mediate exchanges of specific reinforcers between partners. G. Patterson, Hops, and Weiss (1975) and Liberman et al. (1976) used quid pro quo contingency contracting and added problem solving and communication training.

Reciprocity Counseling

Reciprocity counseling (RC) has been associated with enhancements in happiness (Hunt & Azrin, 1973). Azrin et al. (1980) found that RC produced more improvement after four sessions than did discussion-type counseling. Furthermore, RC was associated with better maintenance during the 24 months of followup.

Couples in RC usually attend four weekly 90-minute sessions. Stimulus control, increased reinforcement exchange, and communication training are used to increase reinforcement exchange and control. Stimulus control helps couples reduce their preoccupation with unpleasant aspects of interaction. At the start of each session the counselor directs clients to number and describe the positive interactions that occurred since the last session. Next, partners list reinforcers that are being received and given. Each partner also comments on the other's list, to increase "reciprocity awareness."

Reinforcement exchange treatment was designed to multiply the number of reinforcements being offered by each partner, through behavioral contracting. Reinforcement requests are translated into written agreements between partners, including specification of how the request will be fulfilled. Communications training includes the "positive request rule," aimed at altering the way partners express the desire for reinforcement. The "annoyance procedure" teaches partners to communicate annoyance noncritically.

Behavior Exchange Therapy

Behavior exchange therapy is based upon the work of Jacobson and Margolin (1979). This behavioral method focuses on increasing the number of positive exchanges in the natural environment. Behavior exchange emphasizes immediate changes and uses clinical innovations aimed at producing beneficial cognitive and perceptual changes (Jacobson, 1983). Patients receiving this type of therapy first participate in a roundtable discussion with the therapist aimed at developing a consensual treatment plan and contract. Patients are required to complete homework assignments that contain progressively more demanding behavior change directives. The therapist conducts debriefing sessions that review each participant's performance of the homework assignments. Meetings initially occur weekly, but the interval between sessions increases to 2 weeks as treatment progresses. No explicit communication training is given.

Jacobson and Follette (1985) compared the effectiveness of behavior exchange therapy, communication/problem solving training, combined treatment, and a waiting-list control group. Behavior exchange, communication/problem solving training, and the combined therapy all proved to be equally effective in enhancing marital satisfaction and eliminating present problems. However, the combined treatment approach produced the most enduring and consistent changes. Obvious differences between the groups emerged at the 6-month followup. Behavior exchange couples deteriorated at a faster pace. Six months after treatment ended, 44% of the couples in the behavior exchange group reported lower marital satisfaction than had been reported on the post-test. This finding is consistent with the fact that behavior exchange emphasizes immediate change. Moreover, drops in overall improvement rate from the post-test to the followup were due largely to relapses among behavior exchange couples. Communication/problem solving training was found to be insufficient when used by itself. Couples focused exclusively on the skills being taught, which caused them to draw hasty conclusions about whether or not to remain together.

Problem Solving Therapy

Problem solving therapy (PST) focuses on teaching couples communication skills aimed at resolving conflicts more effectively. This method is also based upon the work of Jacobson and Margolin (1979) and uses behavior rehearsal and modeling. Problem solving therapy is based on the concept that couples may be taught to become more skilled at negotiation and positive control strategies, so that coercive tactics will be unnecessary and that couples can learn to control the negative communication practices that have become habits in their relationship. This approach is concerned with teaching behavior management, and it also focuses on enhancing positive exchanges. This treatment teaches the rules for effective communication, problem definition, and problem solution, including the making of contractual agreements. The problems between couples are defined in terms of specific manifest behaviors, and couples are taught communication skills such as paraphrasing.

Problem solving therapy emphasizes prevention and skills training and de-emphasizes immediate change. Therapy sessions focus on the practice and refinement of specific communication skills, helping couples become self-sufficient by teaching them to become their own therapists when problems arise after therapy has concluded.

Jacobson et al. (1993) compared the effectiveness of behavioral couples therapy versus CBT and an amalgamation of the two on depressed, married women 6 and 12 months after the conclusion of therapy. Individual CBT was as effective as couple-focused treatment.

Critics of behavioral couples therapy argue that the changes it produces are often perceived as mere compliance, rather than as motivated by genuine caring and concern on the part of the spouse. This may reduce the satisfaction these desired changes produce and foster complaints about why the partner did not change sooner. Alternative therapy methods, including those grounded in interpersonal and psychodynamic theory (Hendrix, 1988), have attracted considerable interest but have not yet been submitted to carefully controlled experimental assessment.

There has been relatively little research done on the use of dynamic approaches to marital therapy (Gurman, 1978). Snyder and Wills (1989) compared the effectiveness of behavioral and insight-oriented therapy in the enhancement of interspousal and interpersonal functioning and found both therapies comparably more effective than a control group. Snyder, Wills, and Grady-Fletcher (1991) conducted a 4-year followup study of fifty-nine couples in a controlled outcome study comparing couples randomly assigned to either behavioral or insight-oriented marital therapies. Although no significant differences between the two treatment conditions had been observed at termination or 6-month followup, 4 years following treatment a significantly higher percentage of behaviorally treated couples had experienced divorce. This difference was paralleled by greater deterioration among the behaviorally treated couples (these results persisted even when pre-treatment differences in level of distress were partialled out by using covariate procedures). There were no differences in couples' ratings of the helpfulness of the two treatments, although half of the ten divorced behaviorally treated couples refused to complete this measure at followup.

Insight-Oriented Therapy

The insight-oriented technique focuses on unconscious sources of conflict and attempts to teach the couple to interact more maturely and autonomously. It sometimes includes empathy training and instruction in listening.

Although Gurman, Kniskers, and Pinsof (1986) argue that insight alone is unlikely to produce lasting positive effects in marital therapy, problem-solving efforts resulting in premature or cursory resolution may promote short-term relationship satisfaction but longer-term deterioration. Hahlweg et al. (1984) presented data suggesting that traditional behavioral approaches may deal less well with the internal events affecting the emotional qualities of a relationship. Spouses' self-disclosure in more emotionally focused therapies may facilitate marital intimacy, which may promote cognitive changes accompanied by positive interpersonal change (Greenberg & Johnson, 1986). More recent behavioral approaches to marital therapy have been expanded to address cognitive components in relationship distress, including irrational relationship beliefs, faulty attributions, efficacy expectations, and values. The effects of these modifications in the behavioral approach may improve its effectiveness.

James (1991) compared communication skills training and emotionally focused therapy (EFT+CST), emotionally focused therapy only (EFT), and a wait-list control in the treatment of couples. The EFT method included therapist assessment, negative interactional cycle identification, unacknowledged feelings identification, problem reframing, encouragement, acceptance, "felt-needs" expression, exploration, and consolidation. The EFT+CST method included these as well as a communication element, which incorporated homework, didactic skill presentation, behavioral rehearsal, debriefing, and preparation through a manual. Results showed that couples in both treatment conditions improved on marital adjustment and target complaint measures; EFT+CST also indicated improvement on communication measures.

Johnson and Greenberg (1985) compared the relative effectiveness of two interventions in the treatment of marital discord: CBT that teaches problem-solving skills and an intervention focusing on emotional experiences underlying interaction patterns. Results indicated that both treatments were superior to a control group; however, the effects of the emotionally focused treatment were superior to those of the problem-solving treatment group, even upon followup. The study was limited by its reliance on self-report measures that may have been compromised by social desirability responding, but most other outcome research on marital therapy can be similarly criticized.

Emotionally Focused Treatment

Emotionally focused treatment represents an integrated affective systemic approach to marital therapy. This technique is based on the experiential tradition of psychotherapy, which emphasizes the role of affect and intrapsychic experience in change (Grendlin, 1974; Perls, Hefferline, & Goodman, 1951; Rogers, 1951). It also incorporates aspects of the systemic tradition, which emphasizes the role of communication and interactional cycles in the maintenance of problem states (Sluzki, 1978; Watzlawick, Beavin, & Jackson, 1967). This model views clients as active perceivers constructing meanings on the basis of their current emotional state and experiential organization. Clients are seen as having healthy needs and wants that can emerge in the safety of the therapeutic environment.

This approach maintains that it is the disowning or disallowing of experiences that leads to ineffective communication and escalating interactional cycles, not partners' feelings and wants. This model suggests that problems are maintained by self-sustaining, reciprocal, negative interaction patterns, the most basic of which appears to be a pursuer-distancer or attack-withdraw pattern that springs from and sustains each partner's distress and negative perceptions of the other. In this type of therapy the therapist identifies the negative interaction cycles and pays particular attention to the underlying vulnerabilities, fears, and unexpressed resentments held by the partners. Gestalt therapy is used in this method, along with innovations from client-centered therapy (Rice, 1974). The therapist reframes the problem for the couple in terms of emotional responses and encourages clients to identify with their disowned feelings and needs, as well as to accept and to respond to their partner's needs. There is a strong focus on the strengthening of trust and intimacy.

Gottman (1997) has studied the interactions of over 670 couples, some for as long as 14 years, some with intensive observation that monitors shifts in their heart rate and stress indicators in their blood and urine. Studying marriages in such minute detail, Gottman has even been able to chart the effects of small gestures; he discovered that when a spouse (particularly the wife) rolls her eyes while the other is talking, this predicts a high risk of divorce. Gottman found that contempt, indicated by eye rolling, criticism, defensiveness, and stonewalling are the four strongest divorce predictors; these behaviors identified those who would divorce with an accuracy of greater than 90%. Couples who stayed happily married scored higher in such categories as realistic expectations, communication, conflict resolution, and compatibility (Russo, 1997).

Gottman's findings suggest that extant interventions have not done an adequate job of helping couples. Knowing what is dysfunctional in a marriage apparently is insufficient; researchers must also study what works well in successful marriages. Gottman has found that what most distinguishes happy couples from unhappy couples is that they develop a "dialogue" about their perpetual problems, trying to effect what change they can with humor and affection while at the same time accepting their partners as they are.

Gottman's results indicate that couples argue about the same issues 69% of the time. They don't resolve their problems because many of them are actually insoluble. Should they change partners, they generally just get a different set of unresolvable issues. Gottman argues that therapists need to teach couples that they will never solve most of their problems. He maintains that the route to happiness is to "establish a dialogue" with the problems, learning to live with them much the way someone learns to live with a bad back. The trick is to acknowledge your partner's limitations, push for some improvement, while still communicating acceptance (Russo, 1997).

Gottman criticizes the current focus on empathy and active listening in resolving conflicts. This model "forms the basis of most complex multi-component marital treatments of all theoretical orientations, including behavior therapy, systems approaches, and object-relations theory." (p. 41) Gottman has found that happy couples do not employ active listening and empathy during conflict. The active listening model might work if people could really do it, but many find that it is just too hard to be an empathic, active listener when somebody is criticizing or attacking you (Russo, 1997).

Sexual Dysfunctions

The subject of sexual dysfunction is surrounded by much controversy, recurring methodological problems, and major gaps in knowledge. It is important to make sure that medical causes for symptoms have been ruled out before beginning to treat sexual problems with psychotherapy.

Modern sex therapies are short-term and experiential; aim for symptomatic relief; focus on the here-and-now sexual interactions of a couple; and combine treatments such as education, couples psychotherapy, use of vibrators, homework assignments, desensitizations, squeeze and start-stop techniques, and sensate focusing. Using modern sex therapies, Masters and Johnson (1970) report an 80% overall success rate, with 5% of patients having a recurrence of symptoms within a 5-year period.

According to a study of 365 married couples by Sarwer and Durlak (1997), published in the *Journal of Sex and Marital Therapy*, behavioral sex therapy is highly effective. Two-thirds of married couples reporting chronic sexual problems (from low sexual desire and inhibited female orgasm to male premature ejaculation) were helped through outpatient behavior therapy. Most couples showed improvement within 7 weeks, and 70% maintained the improvement after 3 months. The treatment may work because it requires couples to spend significant amounts of time together—often more than they had been spending on pleasurable activities.

In general, male dysfunctions respond best, with success rate highest for premature ejaculation. Efficacy is next best with retarded ejaculation, then with secondary impotence, and is lowest for primary impotence. Treatment is reputed to reverse vaginismus 100% of the time, with less success for generalized unresponsiveness and inhibited orgasm among women. Medications that have been reported, but not yet proved, to enhance responsiveness include testosterone (in men), yohimbine, and cyproheptadine.

LoPiccolo and Stock (1986) summarized the treatment literature by examining both male and female dysfunctions and how each of these dysfunctions are typically approached clinically.

Female Dysfunctions

For females there are three dominant sexual dysfunctions: primary orgasmic dysfunction, secondary orgasmic dysfunction, and vaginismus. In women the most common problem is arousal and orgasm problems, and low sexual desire is usually second to this. The diagnosis of primary orgasmic dysfunction is applied to women who have never experienced orgasm through any means. Secondary orgasmic dysfunction refers to women who are not orgasmic during sexual intercourse. Vaginismus refers to spastic contraction of the circum vaginal musculature, such that the penis or any other object cannot be admitted to the vagina without great difficulty and pain. Each dysfunction has varied treatments with different success rates.

Primary Orgasmic Dysfunction. The most effective treatment for primary orgasmic dysfunction is a program of directed masturbation. This has shown to be the most probable method of producing an orgasm as well as producing the most intense orgasm. It not only provides feedback to the woman, but also identifies sexually arousing stimulation techniques, and the intense orgasm can lead to increased vascularity in the vagina. Once orgasm has been achieved, it leads to psychological anticipation of pleasure in sex, and the increased vascularity helps to enable orgasms to be achieved with greater ease. The components of this program include education, self-exploration, and bodily awareness (Heimal, LoPiccolo, & LoPiccolo, 1976; LoPiccolo & Lobitz, 1972). There have been many criticisms of this technique, and it is not included in all the treatment programs for primary orgasmic dysfunction. Despite the criticisms the program has a 95% success rate in enabling women to have orgasms.

Secondary Orgasmic Dysfunction. In treating secondary orgasmic dysfunction, sexual technique training, systematic desensitization, communication techniques, and reeducation procedures are commonly used. Individual, couple, and group therapy methods are also frequently employed. One factor that seems to contribute to treatment success with this dysfunction is marital happiness prior to therapy. This has suggested that secondary inorgasmic women may respond better when traditional marital therapy is combined with sex treatment (McGovern, Stewart, & LoPiccolo, 1975). Systematic desensitization is also used to treat this dysfunction, especially when it is associated with high levels of sexual anxiety (Husted, 1975; Jones & Park, 1972; Obler, 1973).

Hurlbert et al. (1993) compared a women-only group, a couples-only group, and a wait-list group in the treatment of female hypoactive sexual desire. In both treatment groups the application of orgasm consistency training within the standard intervention model (LoPiccolo & Freidman, 1988) was identical. The results indicated that couples-only therapy was superior to women-only therapy on measures of sexual compatibility, sexual esteem, sexual desire, sexual fantasy, sexual assertiveness, and sexual satisfaction.

Zimmer (1987) compared relaxation and information prior to sex therapy, marital therapy prior to sex therapy, and a wait-list control in the treatment of women's complaints of secondary forms of sexual dysfunction. The relaxation and information method included relaxation training, partners' histories, and sex and sexuality information. The marital therapy consisted of communication training, conflict resolution, role playing, feedback, and homework. The sex therapy entailed anxiety reduction through in vivo exercises, developing positive body feelings, constructing behavioral skills, developing positive exchange, understanding of treatment rationale, attending to positive physical experiences, coping with negative cognitions, changing attribution style, and decreasing self-pressure and stress. The results showed that, at post-treatment and followup, both treatment groups significantly improved, although the group that received marital and sex therapy showed superior improvement.

Vaginismus. Vaginismus is often a situation-specific disorder. There is no physical reason for pain. To treat this disorder, relaxation training and progressive dilation of the vagina are used (Fuchs et al., 1978; LoPiccolo, 1984). The progressive dilation technique is highly effective if it is under the woman's control, but it is a slow process that cannot be rushed or it will confirm the fears of pain and make it harder to overcome.

Male Dysfunctions

Males have four main sexual dysfunctions: low sexual desire, erectile dysfunctions, premature ejaculation, and inhibited ejaculation. Low sexual desire is extremely rare for men; it is commonly attributed to hormonal problems, family of origin issues, or relationship problems. Although erectile dysfunctions have been seen as psychogenic (Masters & Johnson, 1970), recent studies have indicated that neurological, vascular, and hormonal abnormalities are often involved (Krauss, 1983). No cause has been identified for cases of premature ejaculation. Sociobiologists believe that it is to some evolutionary advantage (Hong, 1984), but it has also been theorized that men with premature ejaculation are unable to accurately perceive their own level of sexual arousal and thus do not engage in self-control (H. Kaplan, 1974). Inhibited ejaculation is a rare dysfunction that receives little attention; its etiology remains unclear and little is known about it (Masters & Johnson, 1970). Like the treatments for the female dysfunctions, the treatments for the male dysfunctions vary.

Low Sexual Desire.   The few available studies on treatment for low sexual desire have used complex CBT programs and have generally obtained good treatment results (Friedman, 1983; Schover & LoPiccolo, 1982). These studies indicate a need for a treatment focused specifically on low desire. Standard sex therapy often fails to raise sexual desire (H. Kaplan, 1979).

Premature Ejaculation.   Treatment of premature ejaculation involves using the pause and squeeze method developed by Semans (1956) and Masters and Johnson (1970). This approach has been found to be highly effective. The procedure works well in group as well as in individual treatment, and in self-help programs (it can be done in individual masturbation with relatively good generalization to sex with a partner). Success rates are between 90% and 98%.

Inhibited Ejaculation.   In the treatment of inhibited ejaculation, reducing performance anxiety and increasing physical stimulation are the major treatment elements. Other techniques such as the use of electric vibrators, behavioral orgasm triggers, and role play of exaggerated orgasm are also used.

Erectile Failure.   Erectile failure can be very disturbing. It entails a failure to achieve intromission in 25% or more of the individual's coital encounters (Auerbach & Kilmann, 1977; Masters & Johnson, 1970). Researchers distinguish between two types: primary and secondary (H. Kaplan, 1974; Masters & Johnson, 1970). A male with primary erectile failure has never accomplished successful intromission in either heterosexual or homosexual relations. In secondary erectile failure a male has, in at least one instance, achieved successful intromission. It is suspected that this latter type of erectile failure is primarily caused by performance anxiety (H. Kaplan, 1974; Masters & Johnson, 1970). Systematic desensitization as a treatment for erectile failure holds promise because it reduces anxiety (Masters & Johnson, 1970).

Some cases may involve both organic and psychogenic problems. In these cases the therapist must decide which cause is more influential in order to find the best treatment. If it is more organic, then regular sex therapy will be ineffective. For organic cases the use of pharmacotherapy or a prosthesis implant is recommended. In some cases, vascular surgery can help. Over all, there is a lower success rate in this type of sexual dysfunction.

Auerbach and Kilmann (1977) compared systematic desensitization with a relaxation placebo control. Both groups were informed that problems with sexual relations were a result of nervousness or anxiety and that treatment would consist of deep muscle relaxation. The systematic desensitization group members were told they would have to imagine sexual situations that made them anxious.

During the first session of systemic desensitization, group members develop rapport, allay mutual anxieties, and grow acquainted. Training in accelerated relaxation (Wolpe & Lazarus, 1966) is the next step in this treatment. Patients are asked to practice the relaxation exercises at home for 15 minutes in the morning and evening for the first 3 days, and 10 minutes at each time for the remainder of the week.

During the third session, patients create a hierarchy of anxiety-laden situations. They are then asked to imagine the situations associated with anxiety in a state of deep relaxation. When patients feel anxiety, they indicate this by raising a finger. After this indication the threatening scene is terminated, and ideas of relaxation again become the focus of the session. This procedure is repeated for the remaining sessions (Auerbach and Kilmann used fifteen meetings). The criterion for successful completion of the hierarchy was the ability to imagine the most anxiety-laden situation for 10 seconds without the presence of signaled anxiety.

Auerbach and Kilmann (1977) found that members of the desensitization group experienced significantly more improvement in erectile and nonsexual functioning than those assigned to the control condition. Partner perceptions also favored the desensitization treatment method, offering some validation of the self-report measure used. The fact that the control group shared expectancy of improvement and experienced deep muscle relaxation suggests that the inclusion of the hierarchy component was critical to the success of the systemic desensitization.

Treating Dysfunctional Couples

Everaerd and Dekker (1981) compared sex therapy with communication therapy in the treatment of orgasmic dysfunction in couples. The sex therapy method included sensate focus, sexual stimulation exercises, prohibition of intercourse (Masters & Johnson, 1970), discussion, and relaxation. The communication therapy entailed active and passive listening, verbalization and reflection of feelings, productive conflict management, and assertive behavior, with some discussion. The results indicated an increase in female sexual satisfaction in both therapies; however, the increase evolved more quickly with sex therapy. Male sexual satisfaction rose with sex therapy but decreased with communication therapy. Sex therapy provided greater experience of sexual interaction and orgasmic experience in both males and females; in females, communication therapy heightened experience. Satisfaction with the total relationship increased in the males in communication therapy and in the females in sex therapy.

Parenting/Childhood Problems

Attention Deficit Hyperactivity Disorder

The main features of attention deficit hyperactivity disorder (ADHD) are hyperactivity, short attention span, and impulsivity that is developmentally inappropriate and endures at least 6 months. Distinguishing ADHD from conduct disorder can be difficult. Most ADHD children exhibit all behaviors at high rates, including positive ones such as petting animals and helping out strangers. In contrast, children with conduct disorders flaunt their meanness to people and animals. Because other conditions frequently co-occur with ADHD, referral for IQ, psychological, speech, language, and learning disabilities should be made if clinically indicated.

Medications are frequently helpful. A child given trials of dextroamphetamine and methylphenidate has a greater than 90% chance of responding to one or the other (Maxmen & Ward, 1995). Stimulants diminish overactivity, impulsiveness, irritability, and emotional fluctuations; they increase vigilance, attention span, and general sociability. These medications do not facilitate learning directly, but when attention span lengthens and reduced criticism enhances self-esteem, learning improves. These pharmacological agents can work in 2 days but often require 1 to 2 weeks. As alternatives to stimulants, antidepressants (e.g., imipramine, desipramine) help some ADHD children, particularly those with depression, anxiety, or tics. Individual tutoring, family counseling, and behavior therapy can be very useful. These children do best with a consistent, supportive, moderately structured environment.

Maxmen and Ward (1995) offer the following recommendations: (1) family therapy if there is family dysfunction; (2) individual and/or group therapy for poor self-esteem and peer problems; (3) SST (including empathy training) and cognitive therapies for attention/impulsivity symptoms (one goal is to have them verbalize/think before acting); and (4) parent behavior training to develop appropriate, consistent, limit-setting abilities and behavior modification programs for behavior problems. Parents can become very discouraged; books like *Raising Your Spirited Child* by Mary Sheedy Kurcinka (1991) can help them harness their children's energy and "spiritedness" for positive purposes (p. 444).

Aggressiveness and Conduct Disorder

Walter and Gilmore (1973) evaluated behavior modification techniques by comparing them with an attention placebo control. The procedures for the treatment group parents were those routinely employed with families of conduct-disordered boys (Patterson et al., 1972). After six baseline observation sessions the parents in the treatment condition were given the programmed text *Living with Children* (Patterson & Gullion, 1968). Group therapists used role playing, modeling, and didactic instruction to teach the principles of behavior management. To duplicate the time and attention of the book reading period, placebo group parents were given tape recorders and invited to practice making recordings about their problems for the upcoming meetings. As in the treatment condition, placebo families were telephoned regularly to stimulate cooperation and to answer questions. The treatment group showed a 61% decrease in targeted deviant behavior (comparable to the decrease in the Wiltz, 1969 study; Walter, 1971), while the placebo group showed a 37% increase.

Childhood Oppositional Disorder

Children who are oppositional, stubborn, noncompliant, and aggressive are frequently referred for treatment. Of all 2- to 5-year-olds referred to a child mental health facility, 47% were found to display oppositional and aggressive behavior; at ages 5 to 12, 74% displayed these problems (S. Wolff, 1961, 1967; Wells & Forehand, 1985).

Wells and Egan (1988) evaluated the comparative treatment efficacy of two treatments for childhood oppositional disorder. This carefully conducted assessment made use of multiple dependent measures, including a reliable and valid system for coding noncompliant child behavior and other parent–child interactions (Forehand, Peed, & Roberts, 1978), and parent self-report inventories. Their results favored social learning–based parent training over a systems family therapy approach based on the work of Minuchin (1974) and Haley (1976).

Social learning–based parent training, the approach found favorable by Wells and Egan (1988), has been widely researched. This treatment is based on the assumption that oppositional child behavior is acquired and maintained in the context of family behavior exchanges and that treatment must therefore focus on direct modification of maladaptive parent–child interaction patterns (G. Patterson, 1982). Numerous studies have documented the efficacy of this treatment, in terms of direct observations of parent and child behavior, parent-completed child behavior checklists, parents' satisfaction with treatment, and parents' perceptions of their own adjustment (Forehand, Wells, & Griest, 1980; Karoly & Rosenthal, 1977; Patterson, Chamberlain, & Reid, 1982; Peed, Roberts, & Forehand, 1977; Wells & Egan, 1988; Wells, Griest, & Forehand, 1980; Wiltz & Patterson, 1974).

Social learning parent training focuses on reducing child noncompliance. In the first phase, parents learn to be more effective reinforcing agents by increasing the frequency and range of social rewards and by reducing the frequency of competing verbal behavior such as commands, questions, and criticisms. Parents learn to use social attention and rewards contingent upon appropriate child behavior, particularly compliance with parental commands. In the second phase of treatment, parents learn to give direct, concise, age-appropriate commands and expectations to their children and to allow them sufficient time to comply. If compliance is not forthcoming, parents learn to implement a time-out procedure, involving placing the child in a secluded chair for 5 to 10 minutes. Role playing by the therapist and parent and modeling of desired behaviors by the therapist help parents to learn these skills. Parents are given homework assignments to practice daily skills learned in the therapy sessions (Wells & Egan, 1988).

Thumbsucking

Thumbsucking is often considered offensive aesthetically, and it has been shown to be associated with dental problems, particularly for children older than 3 years of age (Wright, Schaefer, Solomons, 1979). Thumbsucking is found in 46% of 3-year-olds and 37% of 4-year-olds (Honzik & McKee, 1962). A survey found 22% of children to still suck their thumbs at age 12 (Baalack & Frisk, 1971).

The operant habit reversal method of treatment consists of teaching competing responses, identifying the habit-prone situation(s), arranging social support by the family, providing a response contingent period of competing reactions, and identification of response precursors. This method was compared with the commonly used method of painting the thumb and fingers with a bitter-tasting substance in a study by Azrin, Nunn, and Frantz-Renshaw (1980). Children receiving habit reversal treatment had a mean reduction of 88% on the first day, 95% thereafter until the twentieth month when the reduction was 89%. This was far better than children in the bitter-tasting substance control group, who showed only a 34% to 44% reduction during the 3 months of followup.

Habit reversal children had a mean of 1.8 episodes per day, whereas control group children had a mean of 21.2 episodes per day. At the 3-month followup, 47% of the habit reversal treatment children had stopped thumbsucking completely and all of the others had a reduction of at least 50%. Of the control children, only 10% had stopped sucking entirely, and 60% showed little or no change (less than a 50% reduction).

The habit reversal method has been found to be nearly as effective as the palatal or crib with spurs (Haryett, Hansen, & Davidson, 1970), without causing the emotional, eating, and speaking problems frequently associated with the crib method of treatment. The magnitude of the reduction associated with the habit reversal method is substantial and immediate.

Azrin, Nunn, and Frantz-Renshaw (1980) reported a first-day mean reduction of sucking of 88%, which progressed to a 98% reduction at their 5-month followup. Given the absence of the problematic side effects linked to other professional methods of treatment, the demonstrated efficacy of the habit reversal method, which is described in detail in the following paragraphs, seems to make it the general treatment of choice for this problem.

In the first component of habit reversal, counseling occurs in a single session of 1–2 hours' duration, the first portion of which is spent teaching the child what to do. In the second part of the session the child describes the program to the parent and requests the parent's assistance.

During an "annoyance review" the child lists all the problems created by the thumbsucking. In the "heightened awareness" procedure the child acts out the usual response sequence, especially the precursors of the thumbsucking so as to identify the stimulus antecedents of the behavior (Azrin, Nunn, & Frantz-Renshaw, 1980).

The treatment steps are presented as a game involving clenching and gripping exercises that are the responsibility of the child. Parents are asked to provide helpful reminders and encouragement. The child is taught competing reactions, such as making a fist in which the thumb grips the fingers if the child is a fingersucker or the fingers grip the thumb if the child is a thumbsucker, or the child grasps some convenient object. The competing responses are rehearsed until performed correctly. The gripping-clenching response is to be maintained for about 1–3 minutes. The child times the duration by counting aloud slowly to 100 (younger children can count to 10 several times). The competing response serves as a preventive measure in the identified habit-prone situations and as a corrective measure when thumbsucking or face touching occurs.

Social support is encouraged by asking parents to praise their child when sucking is absent and by providing pleasant surprises, visits, etcetera when sucking is absent for an extended time period. Parents are instructed to turn off the television or interrupt the suggested bedtime story when sucking occurs. Children identify a concerned person (e.g., neighbor or grandparent) to call to report on their progress.

Nailbiting

Nailbiting is a common nervous habit. The disorder, which includes both nailbiting and nailpicking, produces several types of deformations, including cuticle damage, roughness of the nail edge, shortened nails, and skin damage. People often want to stop biting their nails for a variety of reasons (Coleman & McCalley, 1948; Billig, 1941). For instance, some people want to improve the appearance of their nails. Others may want to stop the embarrassment associated with their habit.

Previous treatments for nailbiting have included shock aversion (Bucher, 1968), negative practice (Smith, 1957), the use of a bitter substance (Billig, 1941), covert sensitization (Paquin, 1977), self-recording (Horan, Hoffman, & Marci, 1974), and habit reversal (Azrin & Nunn, 1973). Comparative studies have failed to show differential treatment effectiveness, generally concluding that expectation of treatment benefits and heightened awareness are sufficient in reducing nailbiting. Efficacy evaluations have made use of different measures, such as the clinical rating of appearance of nails, cuticles, and skin, length of nails (Malone & Massler, 1952; Billig, 1941), and the number of nailbiting episodes (Delparto et al., 1977; Bucher, 1968).

Azrin, Nunn, and Frantz (1980) attempted to evaluate whether the habit reversal method reduced nailbiting more than negative practice when self-recording, heightened awareness, and expectation of benefits were assessed. Habit reversal includes awareness training as well as practice periods. The evaluators found the habit reversal method to be more effective than the negative practice method in reducing the frequency of nailbiting. Forty percent of habit reversal subjects stopped biting their nails entirely, whereas only 15% of the negative practice subjects stopped biting their nails. Negative practice was found to reduce nailbiting episodes by up to 60%. On the other hand, habit reversal was found to reduce nailbiting and/or nailpicking episodes by 99% percent.

Habit Reversal. The first session of the Azrin, Nunn, and Frantz (1980) habit reversal treatment was 2 hours long and involved two groups of people who bit their nails. The second session was devoted exclusively to nail inspection and discussion. Clients were paired and practiced alternative behaviors with one another under the counselor's supervision. The nailbiters learned to engage in a competing hand grasping reaction for 3 minutes whenever the nailbiting occurred. Positive nail care, including nail filing and the use of hand lotion, was emphasized. All nailbiting episodes and hand-to-face movements were followed by the grasping reaction and positive nail care activities. Subjects were made to practice biting their nails in front of their therapist or partner to facilitate identification of the response. Subjects were taught to identify situational, social, and postural precursors in order to be able to anticipate the behavior. During the first 2 weeks after the sessions, followup calls were made every few days. Following that, calls were made every 2 weeks for several months.

Negative Practice.   Negative practice was administered in a 2-hour session, in which subjects met in groups. During the session, patients simulated nailbiting in front of one another while telling themselves how ridiculous they looked. The counselor described the rationale of the treatment, answered questions, and supervised the patients' practice. Patients were given written instructions, which were originally written by Smith (1957). In addition to these instructions, patients were given recording charts. Patients had to practice the exercises for 30 seconds every hour following the treatment session. Once the nailbiting and/or nailpicking had been eliminated, patients had to continue the exercise for 4 days. Over a period of 2 weeks the exercise was gradually decreased.

Encopresis

Wright and Walker (1978) conducted a controlled outcome study of a simple behavioral treatment program for psychogenic encopresis and found the approach to be 100% effective when adhered to carefully. Encopresis, or fecal soiling of the clothes, is a frequent complaint of parents. Because organic factors account for many cases, it is important to rule these out before initiating psychological treatment. The principles of operant conditioning are extremely effective in eliminating this problem. The systematic approach employed by Wright and Walker at the University of Oklahoma Medical School in over a hundred cases usually takes 4 months to complete, but typically requires the treating psychologist or physician to have only minimal involvement after the first session. The parents carry out the steps of the treatment program.

After organic factors and serious psychopathology are ruled out, the parents are given details about the program. The parents are usually the ones responsible for explaining the program to their child.

To begin the program, the child should go to the bathroom immediately upon awakening in the morning. The parents supervise this and offer praise and a reward (agreed upon in advance) as an incentive for the child's trying.

If the child does not produce a reasonable amount of feces on his own, the parent inserts a glycerine suppository and permits the child to dress, have breakfast, and prepare to leave for school. After breakfast the suppository generally will have had its effect; the parent returns the child to the bathroom to defecate before school. The child receives a smaller reward for succeeding this second time.

If shortly before it is time to leave the child has not yet defecated, the parent then administers an enema. The enema used should be a method safe for repeated administration and side effects should be watched and controlled for. In most cases the child will be able to evacuate on his own, making repeated administrations of suppositories and enemas unnecessary. When prolonged use is required, the schedule of administration is lengthened to one every other day or one every third day.

Essentially defecation must occur every morning during the program. While it is not physically necessary for a person to defecate daily, during this training the child is learning how to regularize bowel habits, and daily practice is helpful.

At the end of the day the child's clothing is examined at a specified time, usually shortly before bedtime. If there is no soiling, the child receives a small reward. If there is soiling, the child receives a mild punishment.

Choice of both rewards and punishments should occur prior to initiating the program and requires considerable individualization. Among the rewards that have been found to be effective are such things as money, candy, small toys, praise, extra privileges, tickets to recreational events, and movie rentals. One effective reward is "child time": allotting children a certain period of time (20 minutes or so) in which their parents will do anything they ask, such as playing games, reading a book, talking, or giving a piggy-back ride. This gives children a socially acceptable way of controlling their environment, which can help to supplant the previous maladaptive strategy. Restriction of television viewing, loss of privileges, monetary fines, and extra chores (especially chores of siblings) have proved to be effective punishments. Having the child sit in a chair for a set period of time is also an effective punishment.

This regime is continued without interruption. Parents must be encouraged to be entirely consistent in carrying out this program, even when visitors or vacations threaten to disrupt the daily routine. The parents are asked to keep a daily notebook, treating the experience the way they would an experiment in the lab, recording events, times, and outcomes. It is often helpful to inform parents that, when properly conducted, this treatment virtually never fails (Wright & Walker, 1978). These notes, along with information about how the child seems to be feeling and doing on the program, are mailed to the therapist's office at the end of each week. The therapist makes a phone contact with the parents each week, generally after receipt of the notes, to give encouragement, support, and any necessary advice.

After 2 consecutive weeks without soiling, phase out begins. Cathartics are eliminated one day of the week. The remainder of the program continues as before. If no soiling occurs for another week, a second "no cathartic" day is added. This continues until the child is free of soiling and no longer makes use of cathartics. At this point the reward and punishment system is terminated. If soiling recurs, the procedure is to retreat one step and start over again.

Most children spontaneously begin to show improvement in other areas of their lives, seeming happier, more self-confident, more competent at school, and showing better response to discipline. This treatment takes approximately 30 minutes of the therapist's time at the initial parent-training session and a few minutes each week to supervise the family's conduct of the program.

O'Brien, Ross, and Christophersen (1986) found that cathartics and child time increased the rate of appropriate bowel movements (in 8–11 weeks), although only half of the children ceased experiencing soiling accidents. For these children, appropriate bowel movements were achieved after 32–39 weeks of punishment with suppository fading.

Enuresis

Reaching a consensus about the treatment of children's bed wetting has proved to be difficult. Research shows that 7% of all 8-year-old children wet their beds (Fergusson, Horwood, & Shannon, 1986). Studies indicate that 90% of enuretic children are of the nocturnal variety (Copeland, Baucom-Copeland, & Perry, 1982). It is a common belief that children will simply outgrow bed wetting, but this is not always true.

Kupfersmid (1989) conducted a study examining several different treatments for nocturnal enuresis. When organic factors have been ruled out, the pad and buzzer system has proved to be the most effective treatment of nocturnal enuresis. The success of this treatment is one of the most well-documented techniques in psychology.

A variety of medications have been used to treat enuresis, with equivocal results (Blackwell, & Currah, 1973; Freeman, 1975; Lovibond & Coote, 1970). Many studies comparing imipramine and placebos have reported statistically significant results; however, the reported cure rates are typically only 10% to 20%. Usually the effects of imipramine occur within the first week of administration; however, subjects tend to relapse immediately after drug withdrawal (Blackwell & Currah, 1973; S. Johnson, 1983). Results of followup studies have shown that improvement with imipramine is no higher than the spontaneous remission rate. Research has generally not supported the effectiveness of stimulants, MAO-inhibitors, sedative-hypnotics, major tranquilizers, anticonvulsants, diuretics, or anticholinergics (Blackwell & Currah, 1973; Pierce, 1975).

There are several different behavioral conditioning approaches used for the treatment of enuresis. The most popular is the pad and buzzer. This technique was first reported by Mower and Mower (1938). The commercially available apparatus is designed so urine acts as an electrical conductor between two electrodes, activating an alarm. There are sometimes problems with the apparatus, such as false alarms due to perspiration or pad slipping, and failure of the alarm to rouse the child.

Literature reviews have consistently reported that 80% to 90% of subjects reach an initial criterion of 7 to 14 consecutive dry days within 6 weeks of treatment (Dische, 1973; Doleys, 1977; Lovibond & Coote, 1970; R. Turner, 1973). Relapses have been reported to occur in 25% to 40% of those successfully treated; however, of those who relapse, two-thirds have successfully been reconditioned (Doleys, 1977; R. Turner, 1973). Two behavioral techniques have been developed to reduce relapse: retention control training and overlearning. Retention control training was designed to increase a child's bladder capacity to reduce the need for night urination. The child gradually increases intake of liquids and withholds voiding as long as possible. Overlearning involves having a child drink a specified amount of liquid prior to bedtime to compel practice with night awakenings.

Another behavioral treatment is dry bed training. This is an intensive procedure involving the use of an alarm, the parent awakening the child at set times, and positive reinforcements for dry nights.

The role of parents in the treatment of enuresis is important to consider. Studies have found that 18% of enuretic children's parents have failed to follow through when referred for treatment (Young & Morgan, 1972b) and that 27% of parents terminate treatment prematurely (Young & Morgan, 1972a). Doleys (1977) has maintained that the one most common reason for treatment failure is lack of parental cooperation.

Houts, Berman, and Abramson (1994) reviewed 112 treatment groups and 53 no-treatment or placebo groups. Of the treatment groups, 66 (59%) involved psychological treatment and 46 (41%) involved pharmacological treatment. Psychological treatment consisted of 47 groups using a urine alarm, 5 groups using verbal psychotherapy, and 14 groups using other forms of behavioral therapy. Pharmacological treatment consisted of 20 groups using imipramine, 9 groups using other tricyclic antidepressants, 4 groups using desmopressin, 6 groups using sedatives, and 7 groups using stimulant medication.

The reviewers found that children who underwent any type of treatment (psychological or pharmacological) were more likely to cease bed wetting than those in the no-treatment or placebo control group. Children receiving psychological treatments surpassed those receiving pharmacological treatments, and those using the alarm showed the highest cessation. The longer the treatment with the alarm, the greater the improvement.

Psychosomatic Illnesses in Children

Although systems family therapy was not found to be the preferred treatment modality in helping oppositional children (Wells & Egan, 1988), research has supported its effectiveness in treating psychosomatic disorders in children (Lask & Matthew, 1979; Liebman, Minuchin, & Baker, 1974; Minuchin, Baker, & Rosman, 1975). Systems family therapy begins with the therapist observing the family process, looking for evidence of enmeshed or disengaged subsystems, covert coalitions, imbalanced hierarchies, repetitive maladaptive behavior sequence, and/or use of conflict avoidance tactics. When dysfunctional family processes or structures are identified, direct and/or paradoxical strategies are implemented to alter the process and to relabel and reframe ongoing patterns.

Childhood Anxiety Disorders

Kendall (1994) compared a psychosocial treatment approach with a wait-list control in the treatment of anxiety disorders in children. This method consists of recognizing anxious feelings and physical reactions, understanding cognitions during anxiety, developing a coping strategy, examining performance, and self-reinforcement (Kendall et al., 1990; Kendall, 1990). The results showed that more treated children, at a 1-year followup, no longer fit the diagnostic criteria for anxiety disorders.

Menzies and Clarke (1993) compared in vivo exposure (IVE), vicarious exposure (VE), a combination (IVVE), and an assessment-only control in treating children's phobic anxiety and avoidance of water. The VE method entails observing a model in a pool engaging in progressively challenging water-related activities. The IVVE method includes observing the model and then actually practicing activities in the water. The IVE method has children enter the water gradually, praising them for practicing water activities. The results favored IVE, although adding VE may enhance maintenance.

Barrett, Dadds, and Rapee (1996) compared treatment of anxiety in children through CBT, CBT plus family management, and a wait-list group. The CBT involves recognizing anxious feelings and somatic reactions to anxiety, cognitive restructuring in anxiety-provoking situations, coping self-talk, exposure to feared stimuli, evaluating performance, and administering self-reinforcement. Family management focuses on process methods for empowering parents and children by forming an expert team with them. It includes open sharing of information, joint determination of the content and processes of therapy, and reinforcement of family members for any existing areas of expertise they have (Sanders & Dadds, 1993). The results indicated that children in both treatment groups no longer fulfilled diagnostic criteria for anxiety (69.8%). One year after treatment, 70.3% of the CBT group and 95.6% of the combined group no longer met diagnostic criteria.

SECTION SEVEN

Summary

As one assimilates the spreading public condemnation of managed care and the undeniable imperfections in the way it is currently administered, it is easy to feel discouraged and pessimistic. Yet times of transition demand informed action, and taking action requires some degree of hopefulness. The multiplying criticisms can be taken as signals that all has been lost and evil has triumphed. Or the very attention being paid to the criticisms can be interpreted as a cause for optimism: The system works! Errors are being detected and discussed. We are possibly learning from our mistakes. (Reframing is truly a godsend, no?)

This section attempts to consolidate your understanding of the issues associated with providing psychotherapy in the managed care era. It will help you to approach the imposing task of balancing the competing interests of consumers, providers, care reviewers, insurers, and payors. Calm, deliberate, conscientious reflection will usually facilitate your finding ways to negotiate the fairest solutions. A prediction: Developing the workable compromises that the changing marketplace demands will provide you with challenges for a very long time to come.

18 Conclusions: Meeting the Demands of the Future

Thinking about Therapy from a Managed Care Perspective

Managed care companies demand that psychotherapists demonstrate both the need for their services and the efficacy of their interventions. They expect timely provision of services, measured outcomes, and relatively rapid client change. This means that many psychotherapists must make major adaptations. The frustration currently being expressed by many clinicians stems from the fact that, in the absence of accountability, many may not have learned how to justify their services appropriately. Today's psychotherapists have no choice but to learn how to market their professional talents more competently.

Although many people are predicting the demise of managed care in a few years, no one is seriously predicting a return of the former indemnity plan/fee-for-service system. Most accept that the shift to greater accountability and insistence on high-quality, efficient service is here to stay. While the present incarnation of managing behavioral healthcare costs is not going to last forever, its cost-consciousness is likely to be permanent. The autonomy previously enjoyed by psychotherapists receiving third-party reimbursement is a relic of the past.

As the sands keep shifting, it might be tempting to just stand back and wait it out, rather than invest a lot of energy trying to develop the skills that today's MCOs are looking for. The problem is that change will continue; if you're set on waiting for the next permanent, timeless program, settle in . . . it could be a while.

Instead, it is probably more constructive to learn how to manage the new demands of managed care. The new goals of mental health providers include: (1) becoming adept at delivering appropriate, empirically supported, brief treatments (state-of-the-art technical eclecticism); (2) using group service delivery methods whenever appropriate; (3) striving to develop new ways to help more people, more lastingly, with fewer resources; and (4) communicating more effectively with utilization reviewers. Even though all of your clients will not be managed care subscribers, the expectations of all clients will reflect the profession's growing systematicism being compelled by managed care.

Empiricism

Some practicing therapists seem to have no interest in the empirical research support for what they do. Managed care has confronted such practitioners with the perhaps intimidating demand to demonstrate the efficacy of their interventions. Practitioners need to be familiar with therapy outcome research. They must also be able and willing to change their behavior if the data so warrant.

The bottom line is that psychotherapy must demonstrate its effectiveness, at least as compared to no treatment. If it's not effective, then why do it? This is not to say that each therapist must follow a manualized approach or that each intervention must be successful with each client. However, one ought to be able to use statistics to demonstrate that significant positive change is associated with the treatment methods being used. Each mode of treatment must be able to operationalize its objectives to permit empirical validation.

The scientific method entails the systematic pursuit of knowledge through the recognition and formulation of a problem, the collection of data through observation and experiment, and the formulation and testing of hypotheses. Clinicians must demonstrate their effectiveness through use of this scientific method.

How do you and the client know what has been accomplished and when this expensive process of therapy is complete? What is it the client wants to do or not do? How will the client and therapist know when this has been accomplished? How can this be measured reliably and objectively? Who else might have access to signs that the therapeutic objective has been achieved?

By approaching therapy in this manner, the therapist creates a simple experiment in which the therapist and the client can assess if the therapy has been successful. Clients often say that they want to feel better. We need to help them translate their goal into a measurable form, so that the outcomes of the experiments we will conduct with them can be assessed. In therapy we need to help clients move from the abstract and global to the specific and well-defined. When, where, and with whom do they wish to feel differently? When do they not feel good? How do they assess that now? How do they know when they do feel good? In this way, clients can evaluate the impact of our help more meaningfully. Simultaneously this process leaves clients better prepared to conduct future experiments in living on their own, once therapy has been concluded.

Survival Prerequisites

Surviving the managed behavioral healthcare revolution requires practitioners to make both attitudinal and behavioral changes. We need to shift away from regressive nostalgia for the freedom and autonomy that psychotherapists formerly enjoyed and focus instead on the opportunities of the present and future. An understanding of the indictments leveled against some clinicians of the past who may have exploited the old third-party payment indemnity plan system may help us appreciate why radical change was needed.

Developing your therapeutic practice in light of the new accountability and efficiency imperatives involves becoming outcome-focused and streamlined in your work. Many traditional treatment models were premised on the idea that the best psychotherapy proceeds slowly and cautiously. This assumption (that more therapy sessions produce more client improvement) has increasingly been challenged from within the field. Research findings questioning the positive correlation between treatment length and outcome have been slowly accumulating since the 1950s. We've been working to tailor and trim our clinical contacts with clients for decades.

In principle, our disciplines' values have long paralleled those of the MCOs; we all have been looking for ways to help clients improve their lives as rapidly as possible. Those who continue to insist on the general value of an exceedingly gradual therapeutic process are hard pressed to substantiate their claims that more is better.

Considering the potential risks associated with long-term psychotherapy can help us view the pressure to speed up treatment in more benign terms. If lengthy treatment sometimes creates harms that can outweigh the advantages of such longer treatment, then MCOs' insistence on timely turnaround can seem more appropriate. If less therapy can create more benefits over all, then our goal of helping clients most effectively can be compatible with the managed care goal of helping clients rapidly.

Such rethinking can move us to the next important steps: addressing the details of this shift in orientation. How can we systematically do more with less? What techniques allow us to make the best use of limited time with clients? How can we engineer homework assignments for maximum effect? At what point does "less" become a problem? With whom is cutting corners too costly? How can we offset the costs associated with the greater demands of these more taxing clients?

Importance of Evidence-Based Treatment Methods

Staying current with the burgeoning clinical literature is more of a priority than it was in the past. As we seek to cut corners in treatment in order to effect cost savings, we will become increasingly dependent upon empirical evaluations of the impact of these efficiencies on the quality of outcome for our clients. A rigorous experimental mindset is vital.

Various professional groups are responding to this increasing need for current information about empirically supported treatment methods. The American Psychological Association has developed one of the most sophisticated, nonproprietary listing of ESTs, and plans to continue to update this information regularly (many of these research-supported methods were summarized in the preceding chapters). Similarly, the American Psychiatric Association has developed detailed treatment protocols for many disorders.

Accessing the latest research findings is easier than ever, thanks to the evolving information highway. Learning how to subscribe to relevant e-mail lists and access web sites containing state-of-the-art information on diagnosis and treatment can help clinicians make prudent decisions about how to pare treatment and thereby improve their effectiveness.

Improved communication between providers and MCOs can also facilitate collaboration. Exaggerated notions about the "evils" of MCO procedures and criteria can be tempered with accurate information about these rapidly changing businesses. As competition increases, MCOs are becoming more values-focused. They need the help of well-informed providers to forge better clinical answers. It is in their best interest to work as allies with providers. To facilitate this alliance, providers must keep their defensiveness in check and stay focused on the mutual objectives that guide their work with MCOs.

Limitations of ESTs

While part of our clinical arsenal includes empirically substantiated techniques of demonstrated clinical utility, currently many of our best techniques often only work with relatively rare problems. For instance, systematic desensitization is terrific in modifying simple phobias, but only a minority of clients present with this delimited type of problem. Evidence of its effectiveness with other problems, such as general anxiety reactions and strong emotional responses, is slowly accumulating but is limited at present. F. Shapiro's (1995b) EMDR technique shows promise, but only a minority of clients are plagued with the intrusive traumatic memories it was designed to ameliorate.

Cognitive therapy's demonstrated effectiveness with depression and anxiety is a bit more relevant to highly prevalent psychological problems, but here, while improvement is reported by the majority of clients, few experience total relief and cessation of symptoms. Many clients present with mixed disorders that can complicate response to treatment; thus, techniques known to work with "pure" diagnosis cases may not always be sufficient. In addition, we certainly have no proven methods for addressing the common existential questions clients frequently present us with in outpatient treatment, such as "How do I decide what to do with my life?" and "Isn't there more?" Much of the unfocused, supportive, "self-esteem building" talk therapy of the past four decades has not proved superior to informal, inexpensive counseling provided in nonprofessional venues (Dawes, 1994).

The demand for accountability compels us to differentiate more carefully between the techniques that are uniquely ours and less specific forms of helping available in a wide variety of less expensive contexts. This demand also necessitates streamlining treatment and challenging many assumptions about the change process that hold us back from working most efficiently.

Defining Optimal Treatment Techniques

As we work to contribute our ideas to the development of appropriate criteria for reimbursement, we may not be able to defend taxpayer or insurance company subsidies for certain types of "therapy." Psychotherapists need to participate in the detailing of clear criteria and guidelines for reimbursement of mental healthcare. We must acknowledge the past abuses of our profession, rather than asserting that managed care is all in the wrong.

We need to distinguish between psychological services that should be reimbursed and those that shouldn't be reimbursed. We as professionals must lead the way in responsibly informing the policies that increasingly shape delivery of mental healthcare services. We are in some respects the best judges of what can be defended as effective, necessary care. Lines need to be drawn; we must help draw them.

Brief, problem-focused and specialized, empirically validated approaches must be distinguished from open-ended psychotherapy. Short-term, solution-focused, nonspecific treatment and evidence-based, specific forms of treatment known to be generally effective with particular identifiable diagnosed disorders are very different from long-term, open-ended, rambling, nonspecific treatment without empirical grounding. The former two types of therapy are fair candidates for reimbursement. Short-term, focused, nonspecific treatment is justified in terms of the general outcome research showing its measurable, desirable impact on a client's productivity (at work and at home) and immunological competence (thereby yielding savings of future healthcare dollars). Specialized procedures of demonstrated efficacy are justifiable on the grounds that they are scientifically established standards of care, deemed appropriate when certain diagnostic criteria are met. In contrast, the latter type of psychotherapy, nonspecific and open-ended, is generally not reimbursed by managed care policies, nor perhaps should it be.

Health-Focused Psychotherapy

With integrated healthcare delivery systems, MCOs will seek the least expensive means of keeping people healthy. As physical health is extremely dependent on behavioral choices people make (involving how they eat, exercise, drink, smoke, sleep, attend to early warning signs of serious illness, etc.), helping professionals who are skilled at educating and motivating people to make healthier choices are obviously working on the same team as the MCOs. As allies in their efforts to get customers to avail themselves of preventive techniques, psychotherapists will have an important role in the overall managed care game plan. Use of this type of service should increase. Similarly, it is well documented that physical health is significantly influenced by how individuals respond to life stressors.

Psychotherapists who orient their work to helping clients maximize their health will be valued because in the long run their clients will stay healthier. Because they create savings for MCOs, these therapists will be highly regarded and given continuing referrals. The outpatient role of psychotherapists will shift as a result of the steerage of MCOs; rather than being seen as professionals devoted primarily to helping people feel better, psychotherapists will be seen as professionals who help people function more effectively in order to maintain their health.

To do this, therapists will teach more optimal ways of coping with stress and will help clients learn how to use problem-solving and decision-making strategies that help efficiently resolve the external struggles giving rise to stress. They will also work with clients to formulate perspectives on events that mitigate destructive immunological responses to uncontrollable stressful circumstances.

Not all traditional approaches to psychotherapy can claim to foster physical health; empirical demonstration of beneficial health impact varies somewhat across different methods. As these differences are delineated, it may be determined that some unfocused, long-term therapeutic approaches are actually counterproductive, because they increase chronic sympathetic nervous system arousal in ways that can actually compromise physical health. As techniques are submitted to this new practical acid test (what impact does this particular psychotherapy approach have on the physical well-being of the client?), MCOs will understandably favor approaches with outcomes more consonant with their own goals (maintaining healthy bodies that rarely require professional intervention). To the extent that psychotherapists can convincingly demonstrate that their short-term, relatively inexpensive interventions yield long-term medical care savings, our profession will experience expansion as a result of the shift to managed care. If brief contact with a psychotherapist (perhaps three or four meetings) can redirect a person to make different health-related choices or to use more effective stress-reducing coping strategies, the relative inexpensiveness of our expertise will help psychotherapy to become a treatment of choice in the eyes of cost-conscious MCOs. We must identify with greater precision these types of helping, in order to help MCOs understand why they should be so attractive to them.

We need improved ways of discerning these different types of helping and articulating the relevant distinctions to those outside our disciplines. We should help insurers and managed care providers develop and use fair, consistent standards for evaluating services, in order to preserve optimal quality care for the majority. Wasteful spending on unfocused, open-ended treatment detracts from the resources available for more efficacious and truly necessary interventions. The pot has limits, and we must be judicious.

We must also establish mechanisms for adding new reimbursable treatment procedures as they are developed and experimental evidence of efficacy accumulates. In the future, reimbursement policies will guide not only clinical practice but also clinical research. Favored will be research assessing the impact of innovative interventions that can clearly be distinguished from nonspecific factors present across formal and informal helping settings. We need to consider carefully how reimbursement guidelines, in shaping research, will drive clinical science. We need to shape its influence, so that it will be a constructive rather than a distorting influence on the discipline.

Responding to Managed Care's Demand for Efficiency: Making Less More

Managed care's insistence on efficiency means that we must streamline the treatment process. Admittedly, taking the time to get to know patients thoroughly is an incredible pleasure. Most psychotherapists entered the field because of an affinity for people. Our clients are fascinating individuals, each with a unique story to tell. Their willingness to share the intimate details of their lives with us allows us as therapists to enjoy a greatly expanded sense of life's possibilities. Through our clients we come to experience vicariously countless paths not taken. All this is immeasurably enriching for the therapist. But it is not what we're being paid to do. Perhaps it is a luxury our society can no longer afford to subsidize.

The new therapeutic era demands increased impatience with ourselves as professionals. We should keep in mind that, while it is rewarding for us to feel we have developed an in-depth understanding of our clients, their childhoods, their family members, their community (past and present) and their current work environment, it may not be necessary for the attainment of the therapeutic objectives selected by the clients. And it is their priorities that matter most. Our leisurely pursuit of detailed historical information is not only costly in financial terms; it also often stalls the clients' relief.

We must take a critical look at all that we do, sorting the habitual from the intended. In conducting psychotherapy, perhaps our starting point should be the desired end-point. After therapy, what does the client hope to have changed? Clients can seek therapy to change their mind, their decisions, their feelings, or their behavior. Distinguishing among these different therapeutic agendas is important in streamlining the helping process.

It is vital to pin point the client's desired objective early on, because this not only provides a yardstick for evaluating treatment efficacy, but also should shape the selection of therapeutic interventions. Clarity about what the client desires allows therapists to circumvent much resistance. It can guide how every minute of the session is used and how therapists allocate their attention. It can shape how therapists phrase their comments, in order to make them maximally influential. The client's objectives should shape the process and outcome measures used to evaluate treatment efficacy.

Instead, diagnosis often leads the way. It guides the choice of treatment strategy and sometimes dictates much of the client's therapy experience. This can be a problem, because similarly diagnosed individuals frequently seek very different things from treatment. Therapists who adopt a paternalistic stance and rationalize that they know best what the client needs from therapy generally encounter frustrating resistance and premature termination. While the field has frequently chosen to cast such uncompleted therapy as signifying a failure on the client's part, it is probably fairer to consider early attrition a sign that the therapy wasn't appropriately directed or that the client had gained all that was desired.

It is interesting to consider that some of our one session "failures" may really have been our most striking successes: Whether or not we understood what was happening in the one session, it may have been just right for the client. This isn't just wishful thinking: Therapists have often been surprised to receive referrals from clients whose cases they had labeled as unsuccessful, one-session "therapy rejections." These clients apparently gained exactly what they wanted from their consultations with us and went on to commend our work to others. These episodes are reminders of the frequent incongruence between what clients may be experiencing during a meeting and our own experience of the session. It also illustrates the need for accurate followup information to guide clinicians in assessing the relative effectiveness of different therapeutic courses of action.

Programmatic, specialized diagnoses-based forms of treatment offered impersonally, according to "standard protocol" may at first blush seem to be more "state-of-the-art," scientific, and efficient. In fact, if delivered improperly, they are often inefficient, because, while they may elicit the clients' begrudging compliance within the session, they rarely affect clients on a deep subjective level. Without this, these treatments rarely produce lasting change. We should be careful to learn from medicine: Too much of a specialized, technical approach has proved undesirable. Healing is facilitated by individualized partnerships with clients, which can accommodate the enormous variability that exists among people. Clients learn differently, even when they carry the same diagnosis. Generally more customized, individualized approaches to psychotherapy are far more effective for clients long term. However, customized treatment can still be focused and efficient and can still be based on empirically validated methods.

Streamlining requires reducing the helping process to its most basic elements and then refining those basics to maximize efficiency without sacrificing quality. Cutting out unnecessary practices requires a clear sense of our objectives. It requires that theoretical biases and blinders be removed. It requires that we distinguish between what we enjoy doing with clients and what they really want and need from us. We need to apply available information in order to help each of our clients learn how to use their brains to adapt most expediently. Accomplishing more with less per patient is quite a challenge. But think how many more lives we'll be able to influence as a result of our commitment to optimizing the treatment process.

Future Therapy

Managed care will not stabilize in its present form. Many expect the rate of change to accelerate and new trends to emerge. Technology is self-creating or autocatalytic. For example, faster computers enable the creation of even faster ones. Every change increases the rate of change.

Never again will therapists practice interminably without any care for what it costs. There is a growing recognition that ethical therapy must be cost-accountable. It also seems clear that the era of autonomy and cloistered privacy is gone for good. In order to continue practicing, the majority of therapists will belong to some sort of network or organization, and they will probably become much more active politically to ensure that their professional interests are protected at the state and federal level. They will make better use of community resources as adjuncts to therapy, including self-help groups, school and church programs, and public classes and workshops. Therapy of the future will probably be more eclectic and integrative, more tied to measurable outcomes, and more democratic. Therapists will provide briefer, less costly treatments to a wider range of individuals.

Some predict that, in the next decade, treatment guidelines will be revolutionized by a more expansive conceptualization of the therapeutic process. Although cognitive and behavioral interventions were most emphasized initially because they were the easiest to validate, as research progresses, many expect the dynamic and person-centered techniques to be empirically endorsed (Cummings, 1997). This may create a resurgence of interest in these methods and pave the way for more sophisticated, integrative, empirically validated strategies.

In the coming decade innovative practitioners are also expected to contribute to an era of greater integration of psychotherapy services and primary healthcare. Clinicians will employ evidence-based methods to target specific physical conditions, using psychological methods to improve lives and limit the need for overall healthcare spending.

I hope you will enjoy being part of some interesting times!

GLOSSARY

A Primer of Managed Care Terminology

Capitation: In a capitated system a provider or a group of providers agrees to deliver all of the mental healthcare required by a given population for a fixed cost (per member per month). Providers thereby assume financial risk for a given population because payment to the provider is the same regardless of the amount of service rendered.

Fixed "per head" (hence "capitation") payment discourages providers from ordering tests and treatment beyond a certain spending level. Capitation rewards providers who offer efficient, effective treatment and those whose emphasis on prevention obviates the need for expensive procedures and hospitalization. Some contracts include incentive plans that provide a bonus to physicians who keep costs down.

Mental health capitation rates range widely, from $.22 per member per month for chemical dependency treatment services only in a commercial HMO (the lowest behavioral health capitation rate that I've seen) to $2.00–2.50 per member per month (typical mental health and chemical dependency benefit capitation in a commercial HMO) to $30 per member per month (for a blended rate capitation in a state-financed capitated benefit).

Care (or case) managers: These managed care company employees or independent subcontractors make referrals to appropriate providers after determining the necessity of treatment. Care managers function as the gatekeepers for the managed care system, because their decisions about medical necessity, rather than the provider's or the client's, determine whether reimbursable treatment will be initiated.

The title "case manager" is now primarily used in treatment settings (often at the county level) to refer to paraprofessional service providers who assume responsibility for overseeing the care of severely and persistently mentally ill clients. These case managers assist in coordinating the various community resources these clients need and help to streamline the transition from inpatient to outpatient treatment settings.

Carve outs: Particular categories of coverage (e.g., mental or behavioral healthcare) are often managed outside an HMO. Often this managerial function is performed by an MCO; however, provider groups with capitation contracts can assume responsibility for both providing and doing utilization review for the contracted services.

Co-payment: This is the portion of the service fee the client is expected to pay.

Fee-for-service: This is the traditional means of paying healthcare providers proportional to the services they rendered. This system of payment created a financial incentive for healthcare providers to do more with a given client in order to earn more. In the traditional fee-for-service model the provider bills the consumer for a specified amount, typically on the basis of the amount of time spent delivering the service.

Gag clauses: These contractual clauses prohibit managed care providers from disclosing information about the details of their relationship with the managed care company.

Some gag clauses also enjoin providers to avoid public criticism of the HMO or MCO. A number of states have moved to make gag clauses in providers' contracts illegal.

Health Maintenance Organizations (HMOs): These companies entrusted primary care physicians with the responsibility for making appropriate professional determinations about the need for referral to a more expensive specialist's care. Primary care physicians were increasingly motivated to act responsibly in avoiding unnecessary referrals by being placed at financial risk through contracts that gave incentives for few specialist referrals or capitation arrangements. These contracts gave the primary care physicians a fixed amount of money with which they were expected to provide all needed services to the enrollees covered. If enrollees' health could be maintained (hence the name "HMO") while fewer expensive services were provided, the primary care physicians reaped the "profit." The financial risk associated with this capitation counterbalances the tradition of practicing defensive medicine in order to reduce risks of potential litigation.

When HMOs initially approached mental health providers, they met with little cooperation. Consequently many HMOs turned to MCOs to provide the utilization review for "carved out" mental health services that primary care physicians were often professionally ill equipped to do.

Impairment: This refers to behavior-based description of patient dysfunction.

Independent Practice Associations (IPAs): These are associations of providers working in group practices, usually compensated on a per capita, fee-for-service basis.

Managed Care Organizations (MCOs) or Managed Behavioral Healthcare Organizations (MBHOs): These organizations were designed to provide independent utilization review of behavioral healthcare services. They developed strict proprietary guidelines that constrained reimbursement for services and effected substantial savings in mental healthcare dollar outlays. The term "MCO" is being replaced in some contexts by its more descriptive counterpart "MBHO" (managed behavioral healthcare organization).

Medical necessity: Insurance carriers frequently limit coverage to tests and services satisfying the following conditions:

1. It is reasonable to apply the test, service, or treatment to the condition.

2. The relevant medical community (e.g., family practitioners, urologists, psychologists) would consider the treatment to be indicated for the condition and not experimental.

3. It is necessary—that is, there is a good clinical reason for doing the test, service, or treatment (not just "Well, let's see what it might show").

4. It is legal to do (e.g., if it's a drug, it must be approved by the FDA).

5. It is not considered experimental, unproved, or investigational. Most contracts spell out how the payor will in general determine this: If subject to approval by a government agency, it must have received such approval, must be supported by a reasonable quantity and quality of evidence in peer-reviewed medical literature, must not be the subject of a formal investigation or clinical trial, and so forth.

In addition, a payor has the right to select among treatments or tests when they are equally efficacious but one costs less (either the item actually costs less or, while it may cost more, it lowers the overall cost of treatment or diagnosis); this is part of the essence of "managed" care.

Point of Service (POS):   Point-of-service plans combine a health maintenance organization policy with the freedom of an indemnity policy. Consumers get the HMO benefits
at their discounted rates or pay more out of pocket to go to the provider of their choice.
Statistics show this to be the product with the most growth potential in the near future.
   Very often three "tiers" of choice are offered at the point of service (i.e., when the
consumer decides to access service). Tier one is the HMO, which offers the most restrictive network but the lowest prices and greatest opportunity for quality control by the
payor. The second tier is a preferred provider organization, which offers a network of
hospitals and providers that are under contract to take a certain amount of reimbursement and agree to abide by utilization review determinations; the provider network is
usually much bigger than an HMO's, but the consumer has to pay greater co-insurance.
With tier three the consumer may go to any doctor or hospital, but of course has a much
larger co-insurance payment for which the patient assumes financial responsibility.
Here there is still some basic utilization review done and typically no quality control.
   A problem with POS programs is that HMOs may sway patients to go outside
the HMO network for more expensive procedures they need by dragging their feet
in making authorizations or specialty appointments.

Preferred Provider Organizations (PPOs):   PPOs are based on contracts between providers and insurers stipulating that providers will discount their fees in exchange for
guaranteed referrals.

Preferred providers (or panel providers):   These are selected clinicians whose professional services are available to participants in a given MCO. Clients with behavioral
healthcare coverage through an MCO usually have restricted choice of clinicians,
which some criticize on the grounds that it is undemocratic to deny clients' freedom
to choose the therapist they deem best suited to meet their needs.

Proprietary information: This is restricted, copywritten information that managed care
companies do not routinely disclose, which is used to make determinations about
medical necessity, appropriate care, and provider effectiveness. Managed care companies defend this secrecy on the grounds that this information, which is used to
make utilization decisions, is the "product" they are selling. This expertise permits
them to regulate use of healthcare money while theoretically continuing to provide
quality care. This information is the basis for their rational allocation of resources.
Dissemination of this information could destroy its utility, because there is concern
that clients and providers might use the criteria information to manipulate the system to pay for unneeded care (see "Gaming the System," Morreim [1991]).

Prospective payment and DRGs: As part of the effort to control spiraling healthcare
costs, Health Care Financing Administration (HCFA) payors, dissatisfied with the
fee-for-service models, developed a prospective payment system for the costs of services to Medicare clients. The HCFA pays fixed prices for treatment of each of 468
diagnosis-related groups (DRGs) to hospitals on the basis of a client's diagnoses
coded at discharge, regardless of the amount of service actually provided.

Provider contracts: The participating provider agreement stipulates the risks and
rewards that define your work with the managed care company. These are rather
technical legal documents; to avoid unpleasant surprises, it is generally recommended
that prospective providers have an attorney review their contract before signing it.
   For example, in the insurance and indemnification section of a contract, many
think it is valuable to check to make sure the contract includes the following protec-
tive clause: The MCO agrees to indemnify and hold the provider harmless against

any claims or liabilities arising by reason of responsibilities and duties of the MCO. Such a clause offers the provider some protection against suits based on inadequate provision of care, if the MCO's utilization review prevented you from providing additional care. Without such a clause the MCO is free to restrict care unduly while the provider bears all responsibility for the client's potentially negative outcome. When this occurs, most providers feel ethically obligated to provide free or drastically reduced-fee services when treatment authorization is denied, which can rapidly become economically unviable.

Provider profiling: Managed care companies develop criteria to evaluate the effectiveness of providers in delivering prompt, appropriate, efficacious treatment. Making appointments quickly, having prompt contact with clients, and having clients provide favorable responses on the MCO's satisfaction surveys are central to many companies' profiling systems. Performance information broken down by specialization or diagnosis can help the managed care company make optimal referrals in specific cases. Managed care companies may also use data from utilization reviews to gauge the professionalism and efficiency of a provider.

Provider profiling with severity adjustment: Several outcome management systems do provider profiling with severity/case mix adjustment, so that clinicians working with a higher proportion of patients with severe disorders are not penalized for poorer outcomes.

Severity rating: This rating describes the degree of (1) danger or risk to self or others or (2) compromised function due to an impairment (for mental health impairments).

Subcapitation: This refers to instances when a provider or group of providers takes a portion of the capitation to provide to a "carved out" portion of the services covered by the insurance.

Utilization Review (UR):   This process of care review assesses whether healthcare services are being used appropriately. Service provision is reviewed independently of the client and provider, using information they provide to assess how well treatment is conforming to the MCO's expectations, based on standard protocols and normative data. Utilization review is intended to ensure quality service delivery and avoid unnecessary, wasteful overtreatment. The careful, unbiased review of each case's treatment and progress provides information used to make decisions about discontinuing or extending care.

Utilization review is viewed by many as the heart of managed care; it involves careful evaluation of the medical necessity of treatment, selection of the optimal form(s) of intervention, monitoring of the delivery and outcomes of this treatment, and appropriate termination of completed treatment. Historically these tasks, and especially the task of deciding when psychotherapy was complete, rested solely with the client and the therapist. The utilization reviewer's job is now to perform these tasks from an objective perspective. The general result has been significantly briefer courses of psychotherapy treatment than was the case prior to utilization review.

Utilization review appeals: When utilization reviews are contested, MCOs frequently use paid professional consultants from the provider's specialty to assess the reasonableness of care. These consultants evaluate whether the treatment is appropriate to the presenting problem, whether treatment is meeting objectives, and whether treatment is appropriately tied to the initial referral problem (requests for treatment for unrelated problems that surface during therapy are often denied).

LISTING OF EMPIRICALLY SUPPORTED PSYCHOLOGICAL TREATMENTS

Well-Established Treatments	Citation for Efficacy
Anxiety and Stress:	
Cognitive behavioral therapy for panic disorder with and without agoraphobia	Barlow et al. (1989) Clark et al. (1994)
Cognitive behavioral therapy for generalized anxiety disorder	Butler, Fennell, et al. (1991) Borkovec et al. (1987)
Exposure treatment for agoraphobia	Trull, Nietzel, & Main (1988)
Exposure/guided mastery for specific phobia	Bandura, Blanchard, & Ritter (1969) Ost, Salkovskis, & Hellstrom (1991)
Exposure and response prevention for OCD	van Balkom et al. (1994)
Stress inoculation training for coping with stressors	Saunders et al. (1996)
Depression:	
Behavioral therapy	Jacobson et al. (1996) McLean & Hakstian (1979)
Cognitive therapy	Dobson (1989)
Interpersonal therapy	DiMascio, Weissman, et al. (1979) Elkin et al. (1989)
Marital Discord:	
Behavioral marital therapy	Azrin et al. (1980) Jacobson & Follette (1985)
Health Problems:	
Behavioral therapy for headache	Blanchard et al. (1980) Holroyd & Penzien (1990)
Cognitive-behavioral therapy for bulimia	Agras, Schneider, et al. (1989) Thackwray et al. (1993)
Multicomponent cognitive-behavioral therapy for pain associated with rheumatic disease	Keefe et al. (1990a) Keefe et al. (1990b) Parker et al. (1988)

Multicomponent cognitive-behavioral therapy with relapse prevention for smoking cessation	Hill, Rigdon, & Johnson (1993) Stevens & Hollis (1989)

Problems of Childhood:

Behavior modification for enuresis	Houts, Berman, & Abramson (1994)
Parent training programs for children with oppositional behavior	Walter & Gilmore (1973) Wells & Egan (1988)

Probably Efficacious Treatments Evidence	**Citation for Efficacy**

Depression:

Brief dynamic therapy	Gallagher-Thompson & Steffen (1994)
Cognitive therapy for geriatric patients	Scogin & McElreath (1994)
Reminiscence therapy for geriatric patients	Arean et al. (1993) Scogin & McElreath (1994)
Self-control therapy	C. Fuchs & Rehm (1977) Rehm et al. (1979)
Social problem-solving therapy	Nezu (1986) Nezu & Perri (1989)

Anxiety:

Applied relaxation for panic disorder	Ost (1988)
Applied relaxation for generalized anxiety disorder	Barlow, Rapee, & Brown (1992) Borkovec & Costello (1993)
Cognitive-behavioral therapy for social phobia	Heimberg et al. (1990) Feske & Chambless (1995)
Cognitive therapy for OCD	van Oppen et al. (1995)
Couples communication training adjunctive to exposure for agoraphobia	Arnow et al. (1985)
EMDR for civilian PTSD	Rothbaum (in press) S. Wilson, Becker, & Tinker (1995)
Exposure treatment for social phobia	Feske & Chambless (1995)
Stress inoculation training for PTSD	Foa et al. (1991)
Relapse prevention program for OCD	Hiss, Foa, & Kozak (1994)
Systematic desensitization for animal phobia	Kirsch et al. (1983) Ost (1978)

2

Systematic desensitization for public speaking anxiety	Paul (1967a) Woy & Efran (1972)
Systematic desensitization for social anxiety	Paul & Shannon (1966)

Substance/Chemical Abuse and Dependence:

Behavior therapy for cocaine abuse	Higgins et al. (1993)
Brief dynamic therapy for opiate dependence	Woody et al. (1990)
Cognitive-behavioral relapse prevention therapy for cocaine dependence	Carroll et al. (1994)
Cognitive therapy for opiate dependence	Woody et al. (1990)
Cognitive-behavioral therapy for benzodiazepine withdrawal in panic disorder patients	Otto et al. (1993) Spiegel et al. (1994)
Community reinforcement approach for alcohol dependence	Azrin (1976) Hunt & Azrin (1973)
Cue exposure adjunctive to inpatient treatment for alcohol dependence	Drummond & Glautier (1994)
Project CALM for mixed alcohol abuse and dependence (behavioral marital therapy plus disulfiram)	O'Farrell, Cutter, & Floyd (1985) O'Farrell et al. (1992)
Social skills training adjunctive to inpatient treatment for alcohol dependence	Eriksen, Bjornstad, & Gotestam (1986)

Health Problems:

Behavior therapy for childhood obesity	Epstein et al. (1994) Wheeler & Hess (1976)
Cognitive-behavioral therapy for binge eating disorder	Telch et al. (1990) Wilfley et al. (1993)
Cognitive-behavioral therapy adjunctive to physical therapy for chronic pain	Nicholas, Wilson, & Goyen (1991)
Cognitive-behavioral therapy for chronic low back pain	J. Turner & Clancy (1988)
EMG biofeedback for chronic pain	Flor & Birbaumer (1993) Newton-John et al. (1995)
Hypnosis as an adjunct to cognitive-behavioral therapy for obesity	Bolocofsky, Spinler, & Coulthard-Morris (1985)

Interpersonal therapy for binge eating disorder	Wilfley et al. (1993)
Interpersonal therapy for bulimia	Fairburn et al. (1993)
Multicomponent cognitive therapy for irritable bowel syndrome	Lynch & Zamble (1989) Payne & Blanchard (1995)
Multicomponent cognitive-behavioral therapy for pain of sickle cell disease	Gil et al. (1996)
Multicomponent operant-behavioral therapy for chronic pain	J. Turner & Clancy (1988) Turner et al. (1990)
Scheduled, reduced smoking adjunctive to multicomponent behavioral therapy for smoking cessation	Cinciriprini et al. (1994) Cinciriprini et al. (1995)
Thermal biofeedback for Raynaud's syndrome	Freedman, Ianni, & Wenig (1983)
Thermal biofeedback plus autogenic relaxation training for migraine	Blanchard et al. (1978) Sargent et al. (1986)

Marital Discord:

Emotionally focused couples therapy for moderately distressed couples	James (1991) Johnson & Greenberg (1985)
Insight-oriented marital therapy	Snyder & Wills (1989) Snyder, Wills, & Grady-Fletcher (1991)

Sexual Dysfunction:

Hurlbert's combined treatment approach for female hypoactive sexual desire	Hurlbert et al. (1993)
Masters and Johnson's sex therapy for female orgasmic dysfunction	Everaerd & Dekker (1981)
Zimmer's combined sex and marital therapy for female hypoactive sexual desire	Zimmer (1987)

Problems of Childhood:

Behavior modification of encopresis	O'Brien, Ross, & Christophersen (1986)
Cognitive-behavioral therapy for anxious children (overanxious, separation anxiety, and avoidant disorders)	Kendall (1994) Kendall et al. (1997)
Exposure to simple phobia	Menzies & Clarke (1993)

Family anxiety management training for anxiety disorders	Barrett, Dadds, & Rapee (1996)
Habit reversal and control techniques	Azrin et al. (1980b) Azrin et al. (1980c)

Schizophrenia:
Family intervention	Falloon et al. (1985) Randolph et al. (1994)
Social skills training for improving social adjustment of schizophrenic patients	Marder at al. (1996)
Supported employment for severely mentally ill clients	Drake et al. (1996)

Borderline Personality Disorder:
Dialectical behavior therapy	Linehan et al. (1991)

Sex Offenders:
Behavior modification	Marshall et al. (1991)

Note: Studies cited for efficacy evidence are linked to specific treatment manuals or to procedures well described in the study's report. The operational definition of the treatment is to be found in those manuals; the labels used here do not suffice to identify the particular treatment judged to be efficacious.

Reprinted from Chambless et al. (1998), "Update on Empirically Validated Treatments, II." *The Clinical Psychologist, 51*(1), 3–16, by permission of Division 12 (Clinical Psychology) of the American Psychological Association.

LISTING OF PHARMACOTHERAPIES FOR DIFFERENT DISORDERS

Disorder	Generic Medications	Brand Medications	Dosage
Anti Anxiety Medications:			
1. G.A.D.	busiprone	BuSpar	5–40 mg
2. Stress-related Anxiety	diazepam	Valium	5–40 mg
	chlordiazepoxide	Librium	15–100 mg
	oazepam	Serax	30–120 mg
	clorazepate	Tranxene	15–60 mg
	lorazepam	Ativan	2–6 mg
	prazepam	Centrax	20–60 mg
	alprazolam	Xanax	.25–4 mg
	clonazepam	Klonopin	.5–4 mg
3. Panic Disorder	alprazolam	Xanax	.25–8 mg
	clonazepam	Klonopin	.5–4 mg
	tricyclic antidepressants		
	MAO Inhibitors		
4. Social Phobia	propranolol	Inderal	20–80 mg
	MAO Inhibitors		
5. Stress-related Initial Insomnia	flurazepam	Dalmane	15–30 mg
	temazepam	Restoril	15–30 mg
	triazolam	Halcion	.25–.5 mg
	quazepam	Doral	7.5–15 mg
	zolpidem	Ambien	5–10 mg
	estazolam	Prosom	2–4 mg
Obsessive-Compulsive Disorder:			
	clomipramine	Anafranil	150–300 mg
	fluoxetine	Prozac	20–80 mg
	sertraline	Zoloft	50–200 mg
	paroxetine	Paxil	20–50 mg
	fluvoxamine	Luvox	50–300 mg

Depression:
The evidence indicates that over 50 percent of depressed outpatients who begin treatment with anti-depressant medication experience marked improvement or complete remission of their depressive symptoms. Considerations for acute phase treatment with medication are:
    More severe symptoms.
    Chronicity.

Recurrent episodes. (Two prior episodes indicate treatment with medication.)
Presence of psychotic features (hallucinations or delusions).
Presence of melancholic symptoms.
Family history of depression.
Prior response to medication treatment.
Incomplete response to psychotherapy alone.
Patient preference.

Combined treatment: Combined treatment (medication plus psychotherapy) should be considered in various situations, including:
More severe depression.
Recurrent depression with poor interepisode recovery.
Incomplete therapeutic response.
Evidence of a significant personality disorder.
Patient preference.

Generic Medications	Brand Medications	Dosage
Heterocyclics:		
imipramine	Tofranil	150–300 mg
desipramine	Norpramin	150–300 mg
amitriptyline	Elavil	150–300 mg
nortriptyline	Aventyl, Pamelor	75–125 mg
protriptyline	Vivactil	15–40 mg
trimipramine	Surmontil	100–300 mg
doxepin	Sinequan, Adapin	150–300 mg
maprotiline	Ludiomil	150–225 mg
amoxapine	Asendin	150–400 mg
trazodone	Desyrel	150–400 mg
fluoxetine	Prozac	20–80 mg
bupropion	Wellbutrin	200–450 mg
sertraline	Zoloft	50–200 mg
paroxetine	Paxil	20–50 mg
venlafaxine	Effexor	75–375 mg
nefazodone	Serzone	100–500 mg
fluvoxamine	Luvox	50–300 mg
MAO Inhibitors:		
phenelzine	Nardil	30–90 mg
tranylcypromine	Parnate	20–60 mg
isocarboxazid	Marplan	20–40 mg

Special Problems and Medications of Choice

The Problem:

1. High suicide risk

2. Concurrent depression and panic attacks
3. Chronic pain with or without depression

Drugs of Choice:

1. trazodone, fluoxetine sertraline, paroxetine bupropion, venlafaxine

2. phenelzine, imipramine fluoxetine
3. amitriptyline, doxepin

4. Weight gain on other antidepressants	4. fluoxetine, bupropion, sertraline, paroxetine
5. Sensitivity to anticholinergic side effects	5. trazodone, fluoxetine, phenelzine, bupropion, sertraline, paroxetine, tranylcypromine
6. Orthostatic hypotension	6. nortriptyline, bupropion, sertraline

Anorexia

Many anorectics also have major depression, which sometimes improves with weight restoration. Between 40–60% of patients benefit from antidepressants. Because their blood pressure is already low, these medications should be employed with caution, since malnourished patients are especially sensitive to drugs. Orthostatic hypotension is the biggest risk with tricyclic antidepressants. The SSRIs don't cause orthostatic hypotension and have minimal effect on heart rhythms.

Bulimia

Bulimia, or at least bingeing, is moderately responsive to antidepressants (TCAs, SSRIs, and MAOIs). On average, antidepressants decrease bulimics' binge frequencies by 50%, with 20% achieving complete recovery. Both depressed and nondepressed bulimics show equally effective responses. The highest dose (60 mg) of fluoxetine, usually reserved for obsessive-compulsive disorder, works better than the usual antidepressant dose (20 mg). However, when bulimic patients are treated with antidepressants alone, by 12 months, antidepressants do no better than placebo. When antidepressants are combined with therapy, there are fewer dropouts and possibly an additive effect of the therapy.

Psychosis	Generic Medications	Brand Medications	Dosage
		Low Potency:	
	chlorpromazine	Thorazine	50–1500 mg
	thioridazine	Mellaril	150–800 mg
	clozapine	Clozaril	300–900 mg
	mesoridazine	Serentil	50–500 mg
		High Potency:	
	molindone	Moban	20–225 mg
	perphenazine	Trilafon	8–60 mg
	loxapine	Loxitane	50–250 mg
	trifluoperazine	Stelazine	10–40 mg
	fluphenazine	Prolixin	3–45 mg
	thiothixene	Navane	10–60 mg
	haloperidol	Haldol	2–40 mg
	pimozide	Orap	1–10 mg
	risperidone	Risperdal	4–16 mg
Bipolar Disorder	Lithium carbonate		
	Divalproex sodium	Depakote	

Medication Alternatives for Subtypes:

Bipolar II   MAO inhibitors

Rapid Cyclers   Carbamazepine   Tegretol

Borderline Personality Disorder

Sub-Groups:	*Drugs of Choice:*
1. Impulsivity/Anger Control Problems	Sertogenic antidepressants, e.g. fluoxetine, sertraline
2. Schizotypal (peculiar thinking, transient psychosis)	Low doses of anti-psychotic medications e.g. 1 mg. haloperidol 25–50 mg. thioridazine 1 mg. risperidone
3. Extreme sensitivity to rejection/being alone	MAO inhibitors; serotonergic anti-depressants

Attention Deficit Disorder

	Generic Medications	Brand Medications	Dosage
		Stimulants:	
	methylphenidate	Ritalin	5–40 mg
	dextroamphetamine	Dexedrine	5–40 mg
	pemoline	Cyclert	37.5–112.5 mg
		Antidepressants:	
	fluoxetine	Prozac	20–80 mg
	desipramine	Norpramin	75–300 mg
	imipramine	Tofranil	75–300 mg
	buproprion	Wellbutrin	200–400 mg

Excerpted and included with permission from John Preston, *Clinical Psychopharmacology Made Ridiculously Simple,* MedMaster Inc., 1995.

REFERENCES

Achenbach, T., & Edelbrock, C. (1991). *Manual for the Child Behavior Checklist/4–18 and 1991 Profile*. Burlington: University of Vermont, Department of Psychiatry.

Acosta, F. (1984). Psychotherapy with Mexican Americans: Clinical and empirical gains. In J. L. Martinez & R. H. Mendoza (Eds.), *Chicano Psychology* (2d ed.) (pp. 163–189). New York: Academic Press.

Acosta, F., & Sheehan, J. (1976). Preferences toward Mexican American and Anglo American psychotherapists. *Journal of Consulting and Clinical Psychology, 44*, 272–279.

Agras, W., Schneider, J., Arnow, B., Raeburn, S., & Telch, C. (1989). Cognitive-behavioral and response-prevention treatments for bulimia nervosa. *Journal of Consulting and Clinical Psychology, 57*, 215–221.

Agras, W. S., Telch, C. F., Arnow, B., Eldredge, K., Detzer, M. J., Henderson, J., & Marnell, M. (1995). Does interpersonal therapy help patients with binge eating disorder who fail to respond to cognitive-behavioral therapy? *Journal of Consulting and Clinical Psychology, 63*, 356–360.

Allen, M., Hunter, J., & Donohue, W. (1989). Meta-analysis of self-report data on the effectiveness of public speaking anxiety treatment techniques. *Communication Education, 38*(3), 54–76.

Allgeyer, J. (1973). Using groups in a crisis-oriented outpatient setting. *International Journal of Group Psychotherapy, 23*, 217–222.

Altman, L., & Frisman, L. (1987). Preferred provider organizations and mental health care. *Hospital and Community Psychiatry, 38*, 359–362.

Altman, L., & Goldstein, J. (1988). Impact of HMO model type on mental health service delivery: Variation in treatment and approaches. *Administration in Mental Health, 15*, 246–261.

American Medical Association (1995). *American Medical News 1994 Data Survey summary*. Chicago: Author.

American Psychiatric Association (1989a). *Guidelines for psychiatric practice in staff model health maintenance organizations*. Washington, DC: Task Force on Professional Practice Issues in Organized/Managed Care Settings.

American Psychiatric Association (1989b). *Treatments of psychiatric disorders*. Washington, DC: Author.

American Psychiatric Association (1994). *Diagnostic and statistical manual of mental disorders* (4th ed.). Washington, DC: Author.

Anderson, M., & Fox, P. (1987). Lessons learned from Medicaid managed care approaches. *Health Affairs* (Spring), 72–86.

Andrade, S., & Burstein, A. (1973). Social congruence and empathy in paraprofessional and professional mental health workers. *Community Mental Health Journal, 9*, 388–397.

Andrews, D., Zinger, I., Hoge, R., Bonta, J., Gendreau, P., & Cullen, F. (1990). Does correctional treatment work—a clinically relevant and psychologically informed metaanalysis. *Criminology, 28*, 369–404.

Andrews, G., Guitar, B., & Howie, P. (1980). Meta-analysis of the effect of stuttering treatment. *Journal of Speech and Hearing Disorders, 45*, 287–307.

Andrews, G., & Harvey, R. (1981). Does psychotherapy benefit neurotic patients? A reanalysis of the Smith, Glass, and Miller data. *Archives of General Psychiatry, 38*, 1203–1208.

Anonymous (1995). Hidden benefits of managed care. *Professional Psychology: Research and Practice, 3*, 235–237.

Appelbaum, S. (1975). Parkinson's law in psychotherapy. *International Journal of Psychoanalytic Psychotherapy, 4*, 426–436.

Arean, P., Perri, M., Nezu, A., Schein, R., Christopher, F., & Joseph, T. (1993). Comparative effectiveness of social problem-solving therapy and reminiscence therapy as treatments for depression in older adults. *Journal of Consulting and Clinical Psychology, 61*, 1003–1010.

Arnow, B., Taylor, C., Agras, W., & Telsch, M. (1985). Enhancing agoraphobia treatment outcome by changing couple communication patterns. *Behavior Therapy, 16*, 452–467.

Arntz, A., & van den Hout, M. A. (1996). Psychological treatment of panic disorder without agoraphobia: Cognitive therapy versus applied relaxation. *Behaviour Research and Therapy, 34*, 113–121.

Astrachan, J., & Astrachan, B. (1989). Medical practice in organized settings: Redefining medical autonomy. *Archives of Internal Medicine, 149*, 1509–1513.

Atkinson, D. (1985). A meta-review of research on cross-cultural counseling and psychotherapy. *Journal of Multicultural Counseling and Development, 1*, 138–153.

Attkisson, C., & Zwick, R. (1982). The Client Satisfaction Questionnaire. Psychometric properties and correlations with service utilization. *Evaluation and Program Planning, 5*, 233–237.

Attneave, C. (1985). Practical counseling with American Indian and Alaska Native clients. In P. Pedersen (Ed.), *Handbook of cross-cultural counseling and therapy* (pp. 135–140). Westport, CT: Greenwood.

Auerbach, R., & Kilmann, P. (1977). The effects of group systematic desensitization on secondary erectile failure. *Behavior Therapy, 8*, 330–339.

Austad, C. (1989). *A comparison: Psychotherapists in independent practice and managed health care.* Symposium presented at the annual convention of the American Psychological Association, New Orleans, LA.

Austad, C. (1996). *Is long-term psychotherapy unethical?* San Francisco: Jossey-Bass.

Austad, C., & Hoyt, M. (1992). The managed care movement and the future of psychotherapy. *Psychotherapy, 29*, 109–118.

Austad, C., Sherman, W., & Holstein, L. (1993). Psychotherapists in the HMO. *HMO Practice, 7*(3), 122–126.

Ayllon, T., & Azrin, N. (1968). *The token economy: A motivational system for therapy and rehabilitation.* New York: Appleton-Century-Crofts.

Azrin, H., Nunn, R., Frantz, S. (1980a). Habit reversal versus negative practice treatment of nailbiting. *Behavioral Resources and Therapy, 18*, 281–285.

Azrin, H., Nunn, R., Frantz-Renshaw, S. (1980b). Habit reversal treatment of thumbsucking. *Behavior Resources and Therapy, 18*, 395–399.

Azrin, N. (1976). Improvements in the CR approach to alcoholism. *Behaviour Research and Therapy, 14*, 339–348.

Azrin, N., Bersalel, A., Bechtel, R., Michalicek, A., Mancera, M., Carroll, D., Shuford, D., & Cox, J. (1980). Comparison of reciprocity and discussion-type counseling for marital problems. *American Journal of Family Therapy, 8*, 21–28.

Azrin, N., Flores, T., & Kaplan, S. (1975). Job-finding club: A group-assisted program for obtaining employment. *Behaviour Research and Therapy, 13*, 17–27.

Azrin, N., Naster, B., & Jones, R. (1973). Reciprocity counseling: A rapid learning based procedure for marital counseling. *Behaviour Research and Therapy, 11*, 365–382.

Azrin, N., & Nunn, R. (1973). Habit reversal: A method of eliminating nervous habits and tics. *Behaviour Research and Therapy, 1*, 619–628.

Azrin, N., Nunn, R., & Frantz, S. (1980). Habit reversal vs. negative practice treatment of nailbiting. *Behaviour Research and Therapy, 18*, 281–285.

Azrin, N., Nunn, R., & Frantz-Renshaw, S. (1980). Habit reversal treatment of thumbsucking. *Behaviour Research and Therapy, 18*, 395–399.

Baalack, I., & Frisk, A. (1971). Finger-sucking in children: A study of incidence and occlusal conditions. *Acta Orthodontia Scandinavia, 29*, 499–512.

Bakwin, H. (1945). Pseudodoxia Pediatrica. *New England Journal of Medicine, 232*, 691–697.

Balaban, B., & Melchionda, R. (1979). Outreach redefined: The impact of staff attitudes on a family education project. *International Journal of Addictions, 14*(6), 833–846.

Balestrieri, M., Williams, P., & Wilkinson, G. (1988). Specialist mental health treatment in general practice: A meta-analysis. *Psychological Medicine, 18*, 711–717.

Bandler, R., & Grinder, J. (1975). *Patterns of the hypnotic techniques of Milton H. Erickson, M.D.* (vol. 1). Cupertino, CA: Meta Publications.

Bandler, R., & Grinder, J. (1979). *Frogs into princes.* Moab, UT: Real People Press.

Bandura, A., Blanchard, E., & Ritter, B. (1969). Relative efficacy of desensitization and modeling approaches for inducing behavioral, affective, and attitudinal changes. *Journal of Personality and Social Psychology, 13*, 173–199.

Barber, J. (1994). Efficacy of short-term dynamic psychotherapy: Past, present, and future. *Journal of Psychotherapy Practice and Research, 3*, 108–121.

Barker, S., Funk, S., & Houston, B. (1988). Psychological treatment versus nonspecific factors: A meta-analysis of conditions that engender comparable expectations for improvement. *Clinical Psychology Review, 8*, 579–594.

Barlett, D., & Steele, J. (1992). *America: What went wrong.* Kansas City, MO: Andrews & McMeel.

Barlow, D., & Cerny, J. (1988). *Psychological treatment of panic.* New York: Guilford Press.

Barlow, D., Craske, M., Cerny, J., & Klosko, J. (1989). Behavioral treatment of panic disorder. *Behavior Therapy, 20*, 261–282.

Barlow, D., Rapee, R., & Brown, T. (1992). Behavioral treatment of generalized anxiety disorder. *Behavior Therapy, 23*, 551–570.

Barrett, P., Dadds, M., & Rapee, R. (1996). Family-based treatment of anxious children. *Journal of Consulting and Clinical Psychology, 64*, 333–342.

Barten, H. (1971). *The expanding spectrum of the brief therapies.* In H. H. Barten (Ed.), Brief Therapies (pp. 3–23). New York: Behavioral Publications.

Bartsch, D., Shern, D., Cohen, A., et al. (1995). *Service needs, receipt, and outcomes for types of clients with serious persistent illness.* Denver: Colorado Mental Health Division.

Bateson, G. (1972). *Steps to an ecology of mind.* New York: Ballantine.

Battagliola, M. (1994). Breaking with tradition. *Business and Health, June 6, 1994,* 53–56.

Baumcom, D., Sayers, S., & Sher, T. (1990). Supplementing behavioral marital therapy with cognitive restructuring and emotional expressiveness training: An outcome investigation. *Journal of Consulting and Clinical Psychology, 58,* 636–645.

Baxter, L., Schwartz, J., Bergman, K., Szuba, M., Guze, B., Mazziotta, J., Alazraki, A., Selin, C., Ferng, H., Munford, P., & Phelps, M. (1992). Caudate glucose metabolic rate changes with both drug and behavior therapy for obsessive-compulsive disorder. *Archives of General Psychiatry, 49,* 681–689.

Baxter, L., Schwartz, J., Guze, B., Bergman, K., et al. (1990). PET imaging in obsessive compulsive disorder with and without depression. Symposium: Serotonin and its effects on human behavior (1989, Atlanta, GA). *Journal of Clinical Psychiatry, 51*(suppl.), 61–69.

Beck, A. (1976). *Cognitive therapy and the emotional disorders.* New York: International Universities Press.

Beck, A. (1988a). Cognitive approaches to panic disorder: Theory and therapy. In S. Rachman & J. Maser (Eds.), *Panic: Psychological perspectives.* Hillsdale, NJ: Erlbaum.

Beck, A. (1988b). *Love is never enough.* New York: Harper Collins.

Beck, A., Emerson, N., Brown, G., et al. (1988). An inventory for measuring clinical anxiety: Psychometric properties. *Journal of Consulting and Clinical Psychology, 56,* 893–897.

Beck, A., & Emery, G. (1985). *Anxiety disorders and phobias: A cognitive perspective.* New York: Basic Books.

Beck, A., Rush, A., Shaw, B., & Emery, G. (1979). *Cognitive therapy of depression.* New York: Guilford Press.

Beck, A., Sokol, L., Clark, D., Berchick, R., & Wright, F. (1992). A crossover study of focused cognitive therapy for panic disorder. *American Journal of Psychiatry, 149,* 778–783.

Beck, A., Stanley, M., Baldwin, L., Deagle, E., III, & Averill, P. (1994). Comparison of cognitive

therapy and relaxation training for panic disorder. *Journal of Consulting and Clinical Psychology, 62,* 818–826.

Beecher, H. (1959a). Placebos and the evaluation of the subjective response. In S. O. Waife and A. Shapiro, eds., *The Clinical Evaluation of New Drugs.* New York: Haeber-Harper. pp. 61–75.

Beecher, H. (1959b). *Measurement of Subjective Responses: Quantitative Effects of Drugs.* New York: Oxford University Press.

Bellack, A., Turner, S., Hersen, M., & Luber, R. (1984). An examination of the efficacy of social skills training for chronic schizophrenic patients. *Hospital and Community Psychiatry, 35,* 1023–1028.

Bennett, M. (1983). Focal psychotherapy—terminable and interminable. *American Journal of Psychotherapy, 37,* 365–375.

Bennett, M. (1984). Brief psychotherapy and adult development. *Psychotherapy, 21,* 171–177.

Bennett, M. (1988). The greening of the HMO: Implications for prepaid psychiatry. *Behavioral Healthcare Tomorrow, 2*(3), 28–32.

Bennett, M., & Wisneski, M. (1979). Continuous psychotherapy within an HMO. *American Journal of Psychiatry, 136,* 1283–1287.

Benton, M., & Schroeder, H. (1990). Social skills training with schizophrenics: A meta-analytic evaluation. *Journal of Consulting and Clinical Psychology, 58,* 741–747.

Bergin, A., & Lambert, M. (1978). The evaluation of therapeutic outcomes. In S. L. Garfield & A. E. Bergin (Eds.), *Handbook of psychotherapy and behavior change: An empirical analysis* (2d ed.) (pp. 139–189). New York: Wiley.

Bergman, J. (1985). *Fishing for barracuda: Pragmatics of brief systemic therapy.* New York: Norton.

Berman, J., Miller, R., & Massman, P. (1985). Cognitive therapy versus systematic desensitization: Is one treatment superior? *Psychological Bulletin, 97,* 451–461.

Berman, J., & Norton, N. (1985). Does professional training make a therapist more effective? *Psychological Bulletin, 98,* 401–406.

Berman, M. (1997). *Practice Builder Association* promotional brochure, 18351 Jamboree Road, Irvine, California.

Beutler, L. (1991). Have all won and must all have prizes? Revisiting Luborsky et al.'s verdict. *Journal of Consulting and Clinical Psychology, 59,* 226–232.

Beutler, L. (1998). Identifying empirically supported treatments: What if we didn't? *Journal of Consulting and Clinical Psychology, 66,* 113–120.

Beutler, L., Engle, D., Mohr, D., Daldrup, R., Bergan, J., Meredith, K., & Merry, W. (1991). Predictors of differential response to cognitive, experiential, and self-directed psychotherapeutic procedures. *Journal of Consulting and Clinical Psychology, 59*, 333–340.

Billig, A. (1941). Fingernail biting: The incipiency, incidence, and amelioration. *Genetic Psychology Monographs, 24*, 123–218.

Birmaher, B., Holder, D., Johnson, B., & Kolko, D. (1996). Cognitive therapy in the treatment of adolescent depression. *Star Center Link*, University of Pittsburgh Medical Center, October, 1–2.

Bittker, T. (1985). The industrialization of American psychiatry. *American Journal of Psychiatry, 21*, 171–177.

Black, D., Gleser, L., & Kooyers, K. (1990). A meta-analytic evaluation of couples weight-loss programs. *Health Psychology, 9*, 330–347.

Black, D., Wesner, R., Bowers, W., & Gabel, J. (1993). A comparison of fluvoxamine, cognitive therapy, and placebo in the treatment of panic disorder. *Archives of General Psychiatry, 50*, 44–50.

Blackwell, B., & Currah, J. (1973). The psychopharmacology of nocturnal enuresis. In I. Kolvin, R. MacKeith, & S. Meadow (Eds.), *Bladder control and enuresis* (pp. 231–256). Philadelphia: Lippincott.

Blackwell, B., Gutmann, M., & Gutmann, L. (1988). Case review and quantity of outpatient care. *American Journal of Psychiatry, 145*, 1003–1006.

Blanchard, E., Andrasik, F., Ahles, T., Teders, S., & O'Keefe, D. (1980). Migraine and tension headache: A meta-analytic review. *Behavior Therapy, 11*, 613–631.

Blanchard, E. B., Theobold, D. E., Williamson, D. A., Silver, B. V., & Brown, D. A. (1978). Temperature biofeedback in the treatment of migraine headaches. *Archives of General Psychiatry, 35*, 581–588.

Blatt, S., & Felsen, I. (1993). "Different kinds of folks may need different kinds of strokes": The effect of patients' characteristics on therapeutic process and outcome. *Psychotherapy Research, 3*, 245–259.

Blatt, S., & Ford, R. (1994). *Therapeutic change: An object relations perspective.* New York: Plenum.

Blatt, S., Quinlan, D., Pilkonis, P., & Shea, M. (1995). Impact of perfectionism and need for approval on the brief treatment of depression: The National Institute of Mental Health treatment of depression collaborative research program revisited. *Journal of Consulting and Clinical Psychology, 63*, 125–132.

Blatt, S., & Shichman, S. (1983). Two primary configurations of psychopathology. *Psychoanalysis and Contemporary Thought, 6*, 187–254.

Block, J., & Block, J. (1980). The role of ego-control and ego-resiliency in the organization of behavior. In W. A. Collins (Ed.), *Minnesota symposia on child psychology* (vol. 13) (pp. 39–101). Hillsdale, NJ: Erlbaum.

Block, J., & Kremen, A., (1996). IQ and ego-resiliency: Conceptual and empirical connections and separateness. *Journal of Personality and Social Psychology, 70*, 349–361.

Bloom, B. (1975). *Changing patterns of psychiatric care.* New York: Human Sciences Press.

Bloom, B. (1992). *Planned short-term psychotherapy.* Boston: Allyn & Bacon.

Boaz, J. (1988). *Delivering mental healthcare: A guide for HMOs.* Chicago: Pluribus Press.

Bolocofsky, D., Spinler, D., & Coulthard-Morris, L. (1985). Effectiveness of hypnosis as an adjunct to behavioral weight management. *Journal of Clinical Psychology, 41*, 35–41.

Borkovec, T., & Costello, E. (1993). Efficacy of applied relaxation and cognitive-behavioral therapy in the treatment of generalized anxiety disorder. *Journal of Consulting and Clinical Psychology, 61*, 611–619.

Borkovec, T., Mathews, A., Chambers, A., Ebrahimi, S., Lytle, R., & Nelson, R. (1987). The effects of relaxation training with cognitive or nondirective therapy and the role of relaxation-induced anxiety in the treatment of generalized anxiety. *Journal of Consulting and Clinical Psychology, 55*, 883–888.

Borus, J., Olendzke, M., Kessler, L., et al. (1985). The "offset effect" of mental health treatment on ambulatory medical care utilization and changes. *Archives of General Psychiatry, 42*, 573–580.

Boszormenyi-Nagy, I., & Krasner, B. (1986). *Between give and take.* New York: Brunner/Mazel.

Bouchard, S., Gauthier, J., LaBerge, B., French, D., Pelletier, M., & Godbout, C. (1996). Exposure versus cognitive restructuring in the treatment of panic disorder with agoraphobia. *Behaviour Research and Therapy, 34*, 213–224.

Boudewyns, P., & Hyer, L. (1990). Physiological response to combat memories and preliminary treatment outcomes in Vietnam veteran PTSD patients treated with direct therapeutic exposure. *Behavior Therapy, 21*, 63–87.

Boudewyns, P., Hyer, L., Woods, M., Harrison, W., & McCranie, E. (1990). PTSD among Vietnam veterans: An early look at treatment outcome using direct therapeutic exposure. *Journal of Traumatic Stress, 3,* 359–368.

Bowers, T., & Clum, G. (1988). Relative contribution of specific and nonspecific treatment effects: Meta-analysis of placebo controlled behavior therapy research. *Psychological Bulletin, 103,* 315–323.

Brammer, L., Abrego, P., & Shostrom, E. (1993). *Therapeutic counseling and psychotherapy.* Englewood Cliff, NJ: Prentice-Hall.

Brink, S. (1998). I'll say I'm suicidal. *U. S. News & World Report, 124,* 63–64.

Brodie, J. (1998). Media depictions of managed care. *Health Affairs, 3,* 45–51.

Broome, M., Lillis, P., & Smithe, M. (1989). Pain interventions with children—a meta-analysis of research. *Nursing Research, 38,* 154–158.

Brown, C., & Myers, R. (1975). Student vs. faculty curriculum advising. *Journal of College Student Personnel, 16,* 226–231.

Brown, J. (1995). *The quality management professional's study guide.* Pasadena, CA: Managed Care Consultants.

Brown, M., & Munford, A. (1983). Lifeskills training for chronic schizophrenics. *Journal of Nervous and Mental Disease, 171,* 466–470.

Brown, R., & Lewinsohn, P. (1984). A psychoeducational approach to the treatment of depression: Comparison of group, individual, and minimal contact procedures. *Journal of Consulting and Clinical Psychology, 52,* 774–783.

Brown, S. (1990). Studies of educational interventions and outcomes in diabetic adults—a meta-analysis revisited. *Patient Education and Counseling, 16,* 189–215.

Brown, W. (1974). Effectiveness of paraprofessionals: The evidence. *Personal & Guidance Journal, 53,* 257–263.

Brown, W. (1997). Placebos. *Psychology Today, 30,* 5, 57–60, 80, 82.

Browning, C., Browning, B., & Duncliffs, B. (1995). *Surviving and prospering in the managed mental health care marketplace.*

Bryan, D. (1989). Psychological and psychopharmacological treatment of bulimia: A meta-analytic review. Doctoral dissertation, Kent State University. *Dissertation Abstracts International, 50,* 2615B.

Bucher, B. (1968). A pocket-portable shock device with application to nailbiting. *Behavior, Research, and Therapy, 6,* 389–392.

Budman, S. (1989, August). *Training experienced clinicians to do brief treatment—silk purses into sow's ears.* Paper presented at the 97th annual convention of the American Psychological Association, New Orleans, LA.

Budman, S. (1992). Models of brief individual and group therapy. In J. L. Feldman, & R. J. Fitzpatrick (Eds.), *Managed mental health care: Administrative and clinical issues.* Washington, DC: American Psychiatric Press.

Budman, S., et al. (1981). Experiential pre-group preparation and screening. *Group, 5,* 19–26.

Budman, S., & Bennett, M. (1983). Short-term group psychotherapy. In H. I. Kaplan & B. J. Sadock (Eds.), *Comprehensive group psychotherapy* (2d ed.). Baltimore, MD: Williams & Wilkins.

Budman, S., Bennett, M., & Wisneski, M. (1981). An adult developmental model of short-term group psychotherapy. In S. H. Budman (Ed.), *Forms of brief therapy.* New York: Guilford Press.

Budman, S., & Gurman, A. (1983). The practice of brief therapy. *Professional Psychology, 14,* 277–292.

Budman, S., & Gurman, A. (1988). *Theory and practice of brief therapy.* New York: Guilford Press.

Burk, J., Summit, P., & Yager, J. (1992). Outpatient management teams: Integrated educational and administrative tasks. *Academic Psychiatry, 16,* 24–28.

Burnett, K., Taylor, C., & Agras, W. (1985). Ambulatory computer-assisted therapy for obesity: A new frontier for behavior therapy. *Journal of Consulting and Clinical Psychology, 5,* 698–703.

Burns, B., Smith, J., Goldman, H., et al. (1989). The CHAMPUS Tidewater demonstration project. *New Directions for Mental Health Services, 43,* 97–116.

Butcher, J., & Koss, M. (1978). Research on brief and crisis-oriented psychotherapies. In S. L. Garfield & A. E. Bergin (Eds.), *Handbook of psychotherapy and behavior change: An empirical analysis* (2d ed.). New York: Wiley.

Butler, G., Cullington, A., Munby, M., Amies, P., & Gelder, M. (1984). Exposure and anxiety management in the treatment of social phobia. *Journal of Consulting and Clinical Psychology, 52,* 642–650.

Butler, G., Fennell, M., Robson, P., & Gelder, M. (1991). Comparison of behavior therapy and cognitive behavior therapy in the treatment of generalized anxiety disorder. *Journal of Consulting and Clinical Psychology, 59,* 167–175.

Butler, S., & Strupp, H. (1986). Specific and nonspecific factors in psychotherapy: A problematic paradigm for psychotherapy research. *Psychotherapy, 23,* 30–40.

Caffey, E., Galbrecht, C., & Klett, C. (1971). Brief hospitalization and aftercare in the treatment of schizophrenia. *Archives of General Psychiatry, 24,* 81–86.

Campbell, T. (1992). Therapeutic relationships and iatrogenic outcomes: The blame-and-change maneuver in psychotherapy. *Psychotherapy, 29*(3), 474–480.

Cannella, K. (1988). The effectiveness of stress coping interventions: A meta-analysis with methodological implications. Doctoral dissertation, Georgia State University, College of Education, 1987. *Dissertation Abstracts International, 48,* 1705A.

Carkhuff, R. (1969). *Helping and human relations.* New York: Holt, Rinehart & Winston.

Carkhuff, R., & Truax, C. (1966). Toward explaining success and failure in interpersonal learning experiences. *Personality and Guidance Journal, 44,* 723–728.

Carpi, J. (1996). Stress . . . it's worse than you think. *Psychology Today, 29,* 35–41.

Carr-Kaffashan, L. (1989, August). Psychologists: Many roles within managed care systems. Paper presented at the 97th annual convention of the American Psychological Association, New Orleans, LA.

Carroll, K., Rounsaville, B., & Gawin, F. (1991). A comparative trial of psychotherapies for ambulatory cocaine abusers: Relapse prevention and interpersonal psychotherapy. *American Journal of Drug and Alcohol Abuse, 17,* 229–247.

Carroll, K., Rounsaville, B., Gordon, L., Nich, C., Jatlow, P., Bisighini, R., & Gawin, F. (1994). Psychotherapy and pharmacology for ambulatory cocaine abusers. *Archives of General Psychiatry, 51,* 177–187.

Carroll, L. (1962[1865]). *Alice's adventures in wonderland.* Harmondsworth, Middlesex, England: Penguin Books.

Casas, J. (1985). The status of racial- and ethnic-minority counseling: A training perspective. In P. Pedersen (Ed.), *Handbook of cross-cultural counseling and therapy* (pp. 267–274). Westport, CT: Greenwood.

Casey, R., & Berman, J. (1985). The outcome of psychotherapy with children. *Psychological Bulletin, 98,* 388–400.

Castillo, A. (1998). *Meanings of madness.* Pacific Grove, CA: Brooks/Cole.

Cedar, B., & Levant, R. (1990). A metaanalysis of the effects of parent effectiveness training. *American Journal of Family Therapy, 18,* 373–384.

Cedar, R. (1986). A meta-analysis of the parent effectiveness training outcome research literature. Doctoral dissertation, Boston University, 1985. *Dissertation Abstracts International, 47,* 420A. (University Microfilm International No. 86-09263.)

Chambless, D., Babich, K., Crits-Christoph, P., Frank, E., Gilson, M., Montgomery, R., Rich, R., Steinberg, J., & Weinberger, J. (1993). Task force on promotions and dissemination of psychological procedures. *Report adopted by the APA Division 12 Board,* 1–17.

Chambless, D., Foa, E., Groves, G., & Goldstein, A. (1979). Flooding with brevital in the treatment of agoraphobia: Countereffective? *Behaviour Research and Therapy, 17,* 243–251.

Chambless, D., & Gillis, M. (1993). Cognitive therapy of anxiety disorders. *Journal of Consulting and Clinical Psychology, 61,* 248–260.

Chambless, D., & Hollon, S. (1998). Defining empirically supported therapies. *Journal of Consulting and Clinical Psychology, 66,* 7–18.

Chambless, D., Sanderson, W., Shoham, V., Bennett Johnson, S., Pope, K., Crits-Cristoph, P., Baker, M., Johnson, B., Woody, S., Sue, S., Beutler, L., Williams, D., & McCurry, S. (1996). An update on empirically validated therapies. *The Clinical Psychologist, 49*(2), 5–18.

Chambliss, C. (1988). Sex and aging: Getting B.R.A.C.E.D. for changes. *Social and Behavioral Sciences Documents, 18*(1).

Chambliss, C. (1996). How managed care is dividing the helping professions. *Perspectives: A Mental Health Magazine, 1,* 4.

Chambliss, C., & Murray, E. (1979a). Cognitive procedures for smoking reduction: Symptom attribution versus efficacy attribution. *Cognitive Therapy and Research, 3*(1), 91–95.

Chambliss, C., & Murray, E. (1979b). Efficacy attribution, locus of control and weight loss. *Cognitive Therapy and Research, 11*(1).

Chambliss, C., Pinto, D., McGuigan, J., Murgia, C., Luscian, C., Garner, C., & Loveland, T. (1996). Psychotherapy provider attitudes toward managed care. *Resources in Education,* ERIC/CASS, ED396231.

Champney, T., & Schultz, E. (1983). *A reassessment of the effects of psychotherapy.* Midwestern Psychological Association, ERIC Document Reproduction Service No. ED 237 895.

Chapman, P., & Huygens, I. (1988). An evaluation of three treatment programmes for alcoholism: An experimental study with 6- and 18-

month follow-ups. *British Journal of Addiction, 83,* 67–81.

Chevalier, A. (1995). *On the client's path: A manual for the practice of solution-focused therapy.* Oakland, CA: New Harbinger.

Chick, J., Ritson, B., Connaughton, J., Steward, A., & Chick, J. (1988). Advice versus extended treatment for alcoholism: A controlled study. *British Journal of Addiction, 83,* 159–170.

Christensen, A., & Jacobson, N. (1994). Who (or what) can do psychotherapy: The status and challenge of nonprofessional therapies. *Psychological Science, 5,* 8–14.

Christensen, H., Hadzi-Pavlovic, D., Andrews, G., & Mattick, R. (1987). Behavior therapy and tricyclic medication in the treatment of obsessive-compulsive disorder: A quantitative review. *Journal of Consulting and Clinical Psychology, 55,* 701–711.

Christensen, K. (1995). Ethically important distinctions among managed care organizations. *Journal of Law, Medicine, and Ethics, 23,* 223–229.

Cinciripini, P., Lapitsky, G., Wallfisch, A., Mace, R., Nezami, & VanVunakis (1994). An evaluation of a multicomponent treatment program involving scheduled smoking and relapse prevention procedures: Initial findings. *Addictive Behaviors, 19,* 13–22.

Cinciripini, P., Lapitsky, L., Seay, S., Wallfisch, A., Kitchens, K., & van Vunakis, H. (1995). The effects of smoking schedules on cessation outcome: Can we improve on common methods of gradual and abrupt nicotine withdrawal? *Journal of Consulting and Clinical Psychology, 63,* 388–399.

Cinciripini, P., Lapitsky, L., Wallfisch, A., Mace, R., Nezami, E., & van Vunakis, H. (1994). An evaluation of a multicomponent treatment program involving scheduled smoking and relapse prevention procedures: Initial findings. *Addictive Behaviors, 19,* 13–22.

Clark, D. (1986). A cognitive approach to panic. *Behaviour Research and Therapy, 24,* 461–470.

Clark, D., Salkovskis, P., Hackman, A., Middleton, H., Anastasiades, P., & Gelder, M. (1994). A comparison of cognitive therapy, applied relaxation, and imipramine in the treatment of panic disorder. *British Journal of Psychiatry, 164,* 759–769.

Clark, K. (1972). Foreword. In A. Thomas & S. Sillen (Eds.), *Racism and psychiatry.* New York: Brunner/Mazel.

Clement, P. (1996). Evaluation in private practice. *Clinical Psychology: Science and Practice, 3,* 146–159.

Cohen, S., Tyrrell, D., & Smith, P. (1991). Psychological stress and susceptibility to the common cold. *New England Journal of Medicine, 325,* 606–612.

Coleman, J., & McCalley, J. (1948). Nail-biting among college students. *Journal of Abnormal and Social Psychology, 43,* 517–525.

Compas, B., Haaga, D., Keefe, F., Leitenberg, H., & Williams, D. (1998). Sampling of empirically supported psychological treatments from health psychology: Smoking, chronic pain, cancer, and bulimia nervosa. *Journal of Consulting and Clinical Psychology, 66,* 89–112.

Compass Information Services (1995). *Scientific foundation of the COMPASS System.* Philadelphia: Compass Information Services.

Consumer Reports (1995, November). Mental health: Does therapy help? pp. 734–739.

Cook, P. (1988). Meta-analysis of studies on self-concept between the years of 1976 and 1986. Doctoral dissertation, North Texas State University. *Dissertation Abstracts International, 48,* 1984A.

Cook, T., Cooper, H., Cordray, D., Hartmann, H., Hedges, L., Light, R., Louis, T., & Mosteller, R. (Eds.) (1992). *Meta-analysis for explanation: A casebook.* New York: Russell Sage Foundation.

Cooper, G. (1997a). Chasing dollars. *The Family Therapy Networker, 21*(4), 15.

Cooper, G. (1997b). Misusing research. *The Family Therapy Networker, 21*(4), 14.

Cooper, G. (1997c). Panicked is as panicked does. *The Family Therapy Networker, 21*(4).

Cooper, G. (1997d). Prozac's world conquest. *The Family Therapy Networker, 21*(4), 16.

Cooper, G. (1997e). Warming the therapy bench. *The Family Therapy Networker, 21*(4), 18.

Cooper, N., & Clum, G. (1989). Imaginal flooding as a supplementary treatment for PTSD in combat veterans: A controlled study. *Behavior Therapy, 20,* 381–391.

Copeland, E., Baucom-Copeland, S., & Perry, L. (1982). A behavioral approach to enuresis for the family physician. *Journal of the National Medical Association, 74,* 1035–1040.

Covi, L., & Lipman, R. S. (1987). Cognitive behavioral group psychotherapy combined with imipramine in major depresssion. *Psychopharmacology Bulletin, 23,* 173–177.

Craig, T., & Patterson, D. (1981). Productivity of mental health professionals in a prepaid health plan. *American Journal of Psychiatry, 138,* 498–501.

Crits-Christoph, P. (1992). The efficacy of brief dynamic psychotherapy: A meta-analysis. *American Journal of Psychiatry, 149*, 151–158.

Crits-Christoph, P. (1997). Limitations of the Dodo Bird Verdict and the role of clinical trials in psychotherapy research: Comment on Wampold et al. (1997). *Psychological Bulletin, 122*, 216–220.

Crits-Christoph, P., Baranackie, K., Kurcias, J., Carroll, K., Luborsky, L., McLellan, T., Woody, G., Thompson, L., Gallager, D., & Zitrin, C. (1991). Meta-analysis of therapist effects in psychotherapy outcome studies. *Psychotherapy Research, 1*, 81–91.

Crits-Christoph, P., & Mintz, J. (1991). Implications of therapist effects for the design and analysis of comparative studies of psychotherapies. *Journal of Consulting and Clinical Psychology, 59*, 20–26.

Crits-Christoph, P., & Siqueland, L. (1996). Psychosocial treatment for drug abuse: Selected review and recommendations for national health care. *Archives of General Psychiatry, 53*, 749–756.

Cross, D., Sheehan, P., & Kahn, J. (1982). Short and long term follow-up of clients receiving insight-oriented therapy and behavior therapy. *Journal of Consulting and Clinical Psychology, 50*, 103–112.

Cryer, B. (1998). *Chaos and Coherence: Leveraging Human Intelligence Through Inner Quality Management*. New York: Butterworth-Heinemann.

Cummings, N. (1977). Prolonged (ideal) versus short-term (realistic) psychotherapy. *Professional Psychology, 4*, 491–501.

Cummings, N. (1986). The dismantling of the American health system. *American Psychologist, 41*, 426–431.

Cummings, N. (1988). Emergence of the mental health complex: Adaptive and maladaptive responses. *Professional Psychology: Research and Practice, 19*, 308–315.

Cummings, N. (1998). Postgraduate training in behavioral healthcare delivery. Paper presented at The Institute for the Advancement of Human Behavior, Scottsdale, Arizona, April 1998.

Cummings, N. (1995). Impact of managed care on employment training: A primer for survival. *Professional Psychology: Research and Practice, 26*, 10–15.

Cummings, N. (1996). Does managed mental health care offset costs related to medical treatment? In J. A. Lazarus (Ed.), *Controversies in managed mental health care*. Washington, DC: American Psychiatric Press.

Cummings, N. (1997, September). *Beyond managed care: Visions of a behavioral healthcare futurist.* Paper presented at Beyond Managed Care: The Evolution of Psychotherapy in the Next Millennium, The Institute for the Advancement of Human Behavior, Washington, DC.

Cummings, N., & Duhl, L. (1987). The new delivery system. In L. J. Duhl & N. A. Cummings (Eds.), *The future of mental health services: Coping with crisis* (pp. 87–98). New York: Springer.

Cummings, N., & VandenBos, G. (1979). The general practice of psychology. *Professional Psychology: Research and Practice, 10*, 430–440.

Cunningham, R. (1995). Assessing cost and quality in behavioral managed care. *Medicine and Health Perspectives*, June 5, 1–4.

Darko, D., Wilson, N., Gillin, J., et al. (1991). A critical appraisal of nitrogeninduced lymphocyte proliferation in depressed patients. *American Journal of Psychiatry, 148*, 337–344.

Davanloo, H. (1978). *Basic principles and techniques in short-term dynamic psychotherapy.* New York: Spectrum.

Dawes, R. (1994). *House of cards: Psychology and psychotherapy built on myth.* New York: Free Press.

DeLissovoy, G., Rice, T., Gabel, J., & Gelzer, H. (1987). Preferred provider organizations one year later. *Inquiry, 24*, 127–135.

Delparto, D., Aleh, E., Bambush, J., & Barclay, L. (1977). Treatment of fingernail biting by habit reversal. *Journal of Behavior Therapy and Experimental Psychiatry, 8*, 319.

Depression Guideline Panel (1993, April). *Depression in primary care: Vol. 2. Treatment of major depression.* Clinical Practice Guideline, No. 5. (AHCPR Publication No. 93-0551.) Rockville, MD: U.S. Department of Health and Human Services, Public Health Service, Agency for Health Care Policy and Research.

DeRubeis, R., & Crits-Christoph, P. (1998). Psychological treatments for adult mental disorders. *Journal of Consulting and Clinical Psychology, 66*, 37–52.

DeRubeis, R., Gelfand, L., Tang, T., & Simons, A. (1997). *A meta-analysis of cognitive therapy versus pharmacotherapy for severely depressed patients.* Unpublished manuscript.

de Shazer, S. (1982). *Patterns of brief family therapy.* New York: Guilford Press.

de Shazer, S. (1988a). *Clues: Investigating solutions in brief therapy.* New York: Norton.

de Shazer, S. (1988b). *Keys to solutions in brief therapy.* New York: Norton.

de Shazer, S., Berg, I., Lipchik, E., Nunnally, E., Gingerich, W., & Weiner-Davis, M. (1986). Brief therapy: Focused solution development. *Family Process, 25,* 207–222.

de Shazer, S., & Molnar, A. (1984). Four useful interventions in brief family therapy. *Journal of Marital and Family Therapy, 10,* 297–304.

Devine, E. C. (1984). Effects of psychoeducational interventions: A meta-analytic review of studies with surgical patients. Doctoral dissertation, University of Illinois at Chicago, 1983. *Dissertation Abstracts International, 44,* 3356B. (University Microfilms International No. 84-04400.)

Devine, E., & Cook, T. (1983). A meta-analytic analysis of effects of psychoeducational interventions on length of postsurgical hospital stay. *Nursing Research, 32,* 267–274.

Dewey, D., & Hunsley, J. (1990). The effects of marital adjustment and spouse involvement on the behavioral treatment of agoraphobia: A meta-analytic review. *Anxiety Research, 2*(2), 69–83.

Diener, E., & Larsen, R. (1993). The experience of emotional well-being. In M. Lewis & J. M. Haviland (Eds.), *Handbook of emotions* (pp. 404–415). New York: Guilford Press.

Diener, E., Sandvik, E., Seidlitz, L., & Diener, M. (1993). The relationship between income and subjective well-being: Relative or absolute? *Social Indicators Research, 28,* 195–223.

DiMascio, A., Klerman, G., Weissman, M., Prusoff, B., Neu, C., & Moore, P. (1979). A control group for psychotherapy research in acute depression: One solution to ethical and methodologic issues. *Journal of Psychiatric Research, 15,* 189–197.

DiMascio, A., Weissman, M., Prusoff, B., Neu, C., Zwilling, M., & Klerman, G. (1979). Differential symptom reduction by drugs and psychotherapy in acute depression. *Archives of General Psychiatry, 36,* 1450–1456.

Dische, S. (1973). Treatment of enuresis with an enuresis alarm. In I. Kovin, R. MacKeith, & S. Meadows (Eds.), *Bladder control and enuresis* (pp. 211–230). Philadelphia: Lippincott.

Dobson, K. (1989). A meta-analysis of the efficacy of cognitive therapy for depression. *Journal of Consulting and Clinical Psychology, 57,* 414–419.

Doheny, K. (1988, October 2). Self-help. *Los Angeles Times,* p. **VI**1.

Dole, A., Rockey, P., & DiTomasso, R. (1983, April). Meta-analysis of outcome research in reducing test anxiety: Interventions, rigor and inertia. Paper presented at the annual meeting of the American Educational Research Association, Montreal, Quebec, Canada.

Doleys, D. (1977). Behavioral treatments for nocturnal enuresis in children: A review of the recent literature. *Psychological Bulletin, 84,* 30–54.

Donovan, J., Bennett, M., & McElroy, C. (1981). The crisis group: Its rationale, format and outcome. In S. Budman (Ed.), *Forms of brief therapy.* New York: Guilford Press.

Doran, M., Simonin, D., Morse, L., Smith, A., Maloney, C., Wright, C., Underwood, M., Hoppel, A., O'Donnell, S., & Chambliss, C. (1998). The asymmetrical quality of psychological internet resources for addressing common versus rare problems. *Resources in Education* (RIE). ERIC/CASS. CG028277.

Dorosin, D., Gibbs, J., & Kaplan, L. (1976). Very brief interventions: A pilot evaluation. *Journal of the American College Health Association, 24,* 191–194.

Dorwart, R. (1990). Managed mental health care: Myths and realities in the 1990s. *Hospital and Community Psychiatry, 41,* 1087–1091.

Dotson, J. (1990). Physician-delivered smoking cessation interventions: An information synthesis of the literature. Doctoral dissertation, University of Maryland, 1989. *Dissertation Abstracts International, 50,* 1953A.

Drake, R., McHugo, G., Becker, D., Anthony, W., & Clark, R. (1996). The New Hampshire supported employment study. *Journal of Consulting and Clinical Psychology, 64,* 391–399.

Drummond, D. C., & Glautier, S. (1994). A controlled trial of cue exposure treatment in alcohol dependence. *Journal of Consulting and Clinical Psychology, 62,* 809–817.

Duncan, B. (1997). Stepping off the throne. *The Family Therapy Networker, 21,* 4, 22–33.

Duncan, B., & Moynihan, D. (1994). Applying outcome research: Intentional utilization of the client's frame of reference. *Psychotherapy, 31*(2), 294–302.

Duncan, B., Solovey, A., & Rusk, G. (1992). *Changing the rules: A client-directed approach to therapy.* New York: Guilford Press.

Durham, R., Murphy, T., Allan, T., Richard, K., Treliving, L., & Fenton, G. (1994). Cognitive therapy, analytic pyschotherapy, and anxiety managment training for generalized anxiety disorder. *British Journal of Psychiatry, 165,* 315–323.

Durham, R. C., & Allen, T. (1993). Psychological treatment of generalized anxiety disorder: A review of clinical significance of results in outcome studies since 1980. *British Journal of Psychiatry, 163,* 19–26.

Durlak, J. (1979). Comparative effectiveness of paraprofessional and professional helpers. *Psychological Bulletin, 86,* 80–92.

Durlak, J., Fuhrman, T., & Lampman, C. (1991). *Effectiveness of cognitive behavior therapy for maladapting children: A meta-analysis.* Unpublished manuscript, Loyola University, Chicago.

Durlak, J., & Lipsey, M. (1991). A practitioner's guide to meta-analysis. *American Journal of Community Psychology, 19,* 291–332.

Durlak, J., & Riesenberg, L. (1991). The impact of death education. *Death Studies, 15*(1), 39–58.

Dush, D., Hirt, M., & Schroeder, H. (1983). Self-statement modification with adults: A meta-analysis. *Psychological Bulletin, 94,* 408–422.

Dush, D., Hirt, M., & Schroeder, H. (1989). Self-statement modification in the treatment of child behavior disorders: A meta-analysis. *Psychological Bulletin, 106,* 97–106.

Duzinski, G. (1987). The educational utility of cognitive behavior modification strategies with children. Doctoral dissertation, University of Illinois at Chicago. *Dissertation Abstracts International, 48,* 339A.

Edwards, G., Orford, J., Egert, S., Guthrie, S., Hawker, A., Hensman, C., Mitcheson, M., Oppenheimer, E., & Taylor, C. (1977). Alcoholism: A controlled trial of "treatment" and "advice." *Journal of Studies on Alcohol, 38,* 1004–1031.

Efforts to rein in managed care worry blues plans (1998). *Best News,* February 18, 1998.

Eifert, G., & Craill, L. (1989). The relationship between affect, behaviour, and cognition in behavioural and cognitive treatments of depression and phobic anxiety. *Behaviour Change, 6* [Special issue—Depression: Treatment and Theory], 96–103.

Eli, K., Nishimoto, R., Mediansky, L., et al. (1992). Social relations, social support, and survival among patients with cancer. *Journal of Psychosomatic Research, 36,* 531–541.

Elkin, I., Gibbons, R., Shea, M., & Shaw, B. (1996). Science is not a trial (but it can sometimes be a tribulation). *Journal of Consulting and Clinical Psychology, 64,* 92–103.

Elkin, I., Shea, M., Watkins, J., Imber, S., Sotsky, S., Collins, J., Glass, D., Pilkonis, P., Leber, W., Dockerty, J., Fiester, S., & Parloff, M. (1989). NIMH Treatment of Depression Collaborative Research Program: General effectiveness of treatments. *Archives of General Psychiatry, 46,* 971–983.

Elliott, C., & Denney, D. (1975). Weight control through covert sensitization and false feedback. *Journal of Consulting and Clinical Psychology, 43,* 842–850.

Elliott, R., Stiles, W., & Shapiro, D. (1993). Are some psychotherapies more equivalent than others? In T. Giles (Ed.), *Handbook of effective psychotherapy.* New York: Plenum.

Ellis, A. (1962). *Reason and emotion in psychotherapy.* New York: Stuart.

Ellwood, P. (1988). Shattuck Lecture: Outcomes management: A technology of patient experience. *New England Journal of Medicine, 318,* 1549–1556.

Emmelkamp, P., & Beens, H. (1991). Cognitive therapy with obsessive-compulsive disorder: A comparative evaluation. *Behaviour Research and Therapy, 29,* 293–300.

Emmelkamp, P., de Haan, E., & Hoodguin, C. (1990). Marital adjustment and obsessive-compulsive disorder. *British Journal of Psychiatry, 156,* 55–60.

Emmelkamp, P., Visser, S., & Hoekstra, R. (1988). Cognitive therapy vs. exposure in vivo in the treatment of obsessive-compulsives. *Cognitive Therapy and Research, 12,* 103–114.

Emmons, R. (1986). Personal strivings: An approach to personality and subjective well-being. *Journal of Personality and Social Psychology, 51,* 1058–1068.

Engelkes, J., & Roberts, R. (1970). Rehabilitation counselor's level of training and job performance. *Journal of Counseling Psychology, 17,* 522–526.

Engels, G., Garnefski, N., & Diekstra, R. (1993). Efficacy of rational-emotive therapy: A quantitative analysis. *Journal of Consulting and Clinical Psychology, 61,* 1083–1090.

Epstein, L., Valoski, A., Wing, R., & McCurley, J. (1994). Ten-year outcomes of behavioral family-based treatment for childhood obesity. *Health Psychology, 13,* 373–383.

Eriksen, L., Bjornstad, S., & Gotestam, K. (1986). Social skills training in groups for alcoholics: One-year treatment outcome for groups and individuals. *Addictive Behaviors, 11,* 309–329.

Erickson, M. (1954). Pseudo-orientation in time as a hypnotic procedure. *Journal of Clinical and Experimental Hypnosis, 2,* 261–283.

Evans, D., Leserman, J., Pedersen, C., et al. (1989). Immune correlates of stress and depression. *Psychopharmacology Bulletin, 25,* 319–324.

Everaerd, W., & Dekker, J. (1981). A comparison of sex therapy and communication therapy: Couples complaining of orgasmic dysfunction. *Journal of Sex and Marital Therapy, 7,* 278–289.

Ewalt, P. (1973). The crisis-treatment approach in a child guidance clinic. *Social Casework, 54,* 406–411.

Ewing, J. (1984). Electric aversion and individualized imagery therapy in alcoholism: A controlled experiment. *Alcohol, 1,* 101–104.

Eysenck, H. (1952). The effects of psychotherapy: An evaluation. *Journal of Consulting Psychology, 16,* 319–324.

Eysenck, H. (1978). An exercise in mega-silliness. *American Psychologist, 33,* 517.

Eysenck, H. (1993). Forty years on: The outcome problem in psychotherapy revisited. In T. Giles (Ed.), *Handbook of effective psychotherapy.* New York: Plenum.

Eysenck, H. (1994). The outcome problem in psychotherapy: What have we learned? *Behavior Research and Therapy, 32*(5), 477–495.

Fabrega, H. (1998). Cultural relativism and psychiatric illness. In H. Castillo (Ed.), *Meanings of madness* (pp. 7–17). Pacific Grove, CA: Brooks/Cole.

Fairburn, C. (1985). Cognitive-behavioral treatment for bulimia. In D. M. Garner & P. E. Garfinkel (Eds.), *Handbook of psychotherapy for anorexia nervosa and bulimia.* New York: Plenum.

Fairburn, C., Jones, R., Peveler, R., Hope, R., & O'Conner, M. (1993). Psychotherapy and bulimia nervosa: Longer-term effects of interpersonal psychotherapy, behavior therapy, and cognitive behavior therapy. *Archives of General Psychiatry, 50,* 419–428.

Falloon, I., Boyd, J., McGill, C., Williamson, M., Razani, J., Moss, H., Gilderman, A., & Simpson, G. (1985). Family management in the prevention of morbidity of schizophrenia: Clinical outcome of a two-year longitudinal study. *Archives of General Psychiatry, 42,* 887–896.

Fals-Stewart, W., Marks, A., & Schafer, B. (1993). A comparison of behavioral group therapy and individual behavior therapy in treating obsessive-compulsive disorder. *Journal of Nervous and Mental Disease, 181,* 189–193.

Farberman, R. (1997). What's leading America astray? *APA Monitor, 28*(9), 1–15.

Fawsy, F., Fawsy, N., Hyun, C., et al. (1993). Malignant melanoma: Effects of an early structured psychiatric intervention, coping, and affective state on recurrence and survival six years later. *Archives of General Psychiatry, 50,* 681–689.

Feehan, G. (1984). A meta-analysis of psychotherapeutic interventions for the cessation and reduction of smoking. Doctoral dissertation, University of Manitoba. *Dissertation Abstracts International, 45,* 1583B.

Feldman, S. (1986). Mental health in health maintenance organizations: A report. *Administration in Mental Health, 13,* 165–179.

Feldman, S. (1992). Managed mental health services: Ideas and issues. *Managed Mental Health Services,* 3–26.

Fensterheim, H., & Raw, S. (1996). Psychotherapy research is not psychotherapy practice. *Clinical Psychology: Science and Practice, 3,* 168–171.

Fergusson, D., Horwood, L., & Shannon, F. (1986). Factors related to the age of attainment of nocturnal bladder control: An 8 year longitudinal study. *Pediatrics, 78,* 884–890.

Fernandez, E., & Turk, D. (1989). The utility of cognitive coping strategies for altering pain perception: A meta-analysis. *Pain, 38,* 123–135.

Feske, U., & Chambless, D. (1995). Cognitive behavioral versus exposure only treatment for social phobia: A meta-analysis. *Behavior Therapy, 26,* 695–720.

Fiester, A., & Rudestam, K. (1975). A multivariate analysis of the early dropout process. *Journal of Consulting and Clinical Psychology, 43,* 528–535.

Fisch, R. (1982). Erickson's impact on brief psychotherapy. In J. K. Zeig (Ed.), *Ericksonian approaches to hypnosis and psychotherapy* (pp. 155–162). New York: Brunner/Mazel.

Fisch, R., Weakland, J., & Segal, L. (1982). *The tactics of change: Doing therapy briefly.* San Francisco: Jossey-Bass.

Fisher, K. (1990). Worksite smoking cessation: A meta-analysis of controlled studies. Doctoral dissertation, University of Oregon, 1989. *Dissertation Abstracts International, 50,* 5007B.

Fisher, S., & Greenberg, R. (1997). *From placebo to panacea: Putting psychiatric drugs to the test.* New York: Wiley.

Flexner, J. (1984). *Washington: The indispensable man.* New York: Signet.

Flinn, D., McMahon, T., & Collins, M. (1987). Health maintenance organizations and their implications for psychiatry. *Hospital and Community Psychiatry, 38,* 255–263.

Flor, H., & Birbaumer, N. (1993). Comparison of the efficacy of electromyographic biofeedback, cognitive-behavioral therapy, and conservative medical interventions in the treatment of chronic musculoskeletal pain. *Journal of Consulting and Clinical Psychology, 61,* 653–658.

Flor, H., Fydrich, T., & Turk, D. (1992). Efficacy of multidisciplinary pain treatment centers: A meta-analytic review. *Pain, 49,* 221–230.

Foa, E., Rothbaum, B., Riggs, D., & Murdock, T. (1991). Treatment of posttraumatic stress disorder in rape victims: A comparison between cognitive-behavioral procedures and counseling. *Journal of Consulting and Clinical Psychology, 59,* 715–723.

Foa, E., Steketee, G., Grayson, J., Turner, R., & Latimer, P. (1984). Deliberate exposure and blocking of obsessive-compulsive rituals: Immediate and long-term effects. *Behavior Therapy, 15,* 450–472.

Folkers, C., & Steefel, N. (1991). Group psychotherapy in HMO settings. In C. S. Austad & W. H. Berman (Eds.), *Psychotherapy in managed health care: The optimal use of time and resources.* Washington, DC: American Psychological Association.

Forehand, R., Peed, S., & Roberts, M. (1978). *Coding manual for scoring mother–child interactions* (3d ed.). Unpublished manuscript, University of Georgia, Athens.

Forehand, R., Wells, K., & Griest, D. (1980). An examination of the social validity of a parent training program. *Behavior Therapy, 11,* 488–502.

Foster, J. (1969, September). The economies of behavior modification programs. Paper presented at the annual meeting of the American Psychological Association, Washington, DC.

Frances, A., Clarkin, J., & Perry, S. (1984). *Differential therapeutics in psychiatry: The art and science of treatment selection.* New York: Brunner/Mazel.

Frank, J. (1961). *Persuasion and healing.* Baltimore, MD: Johns Hopkins University Press.

Frank, J. (1973). *Persuasion and healing* (2d ed.). Baltimore, MD: Johns Hopkins University Press.

Frank, J. (1978). Expectation and therapeutic outcome—the placebo effect and the role induction interview. In J. D. Frank, R. Hoehn-Saris, S. D. Imber, B. L. Liberman, & A. R. Ston (Eds), *Effective ingredients of successful psychotherapy* (pp. 1–34). New York: Brunner/Mazel.

Frank, J., & Frank, J. (1991). *Persuasion and healing* (3d ed.). Baltimore, MD: Johns Hopkins University Press.

Frank, J., & Frank, J. (1993). *Persuasion and healing: A comparative study of psychotherapy.* Baltimore, MD: Johns Hopkins University Press.

Frank, J., Gliedman, L., Imber, S., et al. (1959). Patients' expectancies and relearning as factors determining improvement in psychotherapy. *American Journal of Psychiatry, 115,* 961–968.

Frasure-Smith, N., Lesperance, F., & Talajic, M. (1993). Depression following myocardial infarction. *JAMA, 270,* 1819–1825.

Freedman, R., Ianni, P., & Wenig, P. (1983). Behavioral treatment of Raynaud's disease. *Journal of Consulting and Clinical Psychology, 51,* 539–549.

Freeman, E. (1975). The treatment of enuresis: An overview. *International Journal of Psychiatry in Medicine, 6,* 403–412.

Fremouw, W., & Harmatz, M. (1975). A helper model for behavioral treatment of speech anxiety. *Journal of Consulting and Clinical Psychology, 43,* 652–660.

Freud, S. (1955[1921]). Group psychology and the analysis of the ego. In J. Strachey (Ed.), *The standard edition of the complete psychological works of Sigmund Freud* (vol. 18). London: Hogarth Press.

Friedman, J. (1983). Treatment program for low sexual desire. Unpublished doctoral dissertation. State University of New York at Stony Brook.

Frisch, M., Cornell, J., Villanueva, M., & Retzlaff, P. (1992). Clinical validation of the quality of life inventory: A measure of life satisfaction for use in treatment planning and outcome assessment. *Psychological Assessment, 4,* 92–101.

Fuchs, C., & Rehm, L. (1977). A self-control behavior therapy program for depression. *Journal of Consulting and Clinical Psychology, 45,* 206–215.

Fuchs, K., Hoch, Z., Paidi, E., Abramoviel, H., Brandes, J., Timor-Tritach, I., & Kleinhaus, M. (1978). Hypnodesensitization therapy of vaginismus: In vitro and in vivo methods. In J. LoPiccolo & L. LoPiccolo (Eds.), *Handbook of sex therapy* (pp. 261–270). New York: Plenum.

Galanter, M. (1988). Zealous self-help groups as adjuncts to psychiatric treatment: A study of Recovery, Inc. *American Journal of Psychiatry, 145,* 1248–1253.

Gallagher-Thompson, D., & Steffen, A. (1994). Comparative effects of cognitive-behavioral and brief psychodynamic psychotherapies for depressed caregivers. *Journal of Consulting and Clinical Psychology, 62,* 543–549.

Gallant, D., Rich, A., Bey, E., & Terranova, L. (1970). Group psychotherapy with married couples: A successful technique in New Orleans alcoholism clinic patients. *Journal of the Louisiana Medical Society, 122,* 41–44.

Garb, H. (1989). Clinical judgment, clinical training, and professional experience. *Psychological Bulletin, 105,* 387–392.

Garfield, S. (1981). Psychotherapy: A 40-year appraisal. *American Psychologist, 36,* 174–183.

Garfield, S. (1986a). Problems in diagnostic classification. In T. Millon & G. Klerman (Eds.), *Contemporary directions in psychopathology: Toward the DSM-IV.* New York: Guilford Press.

Garfield, S. (1986b). Research on client variables in psychotherapy. In S. L. Garfield & A. E. Bergin (Eds.), *Handbook of psychotherapy and behavior change: An empirical analysis* (3d ed.). New York: Wiley.

Garfield, S. (1995). *Psychotherapy. An eclectic-integrative approach.* New York: Wiley.

Garfield, S. (1998). Some comments on empirically supported treatments. *Journal of Consulting and Clinical Psychology, 66,* 121–125.

Garfield, S., & Kurtz, R. (1977). A study of eclectic views. *Journal of Consulting and Clinical Psychology, 45,* 78–83.

Garrett, C. (1985a). Effects of residential treatment on adjudicated delinquents: A meta-analysis. *Journal of Research in Crime and Delinquency, 22,* 287–308.

Garrett, C. (1985b). Meta-analysis of the effects of institutional and community residential treatment on adjudicated delinquents. Doctoral dissertation, University of Colorado, 1984. *Dissertation Abstracts International, 45,* 2264A. (University Microfilms International No. 84-22608.)

Gelder, M., Bancroft, J., Gath, D., Johnston, D., Mathews, A., & Shaw, P. (1973). Specific and nonspecific factors in behavior therapy. *British Journal of Psychiatry, 123,* 445–462.

Gellert, G., Maxwell, R., & Siegel, B. (1993). Breast cancer patients receiving adjunctive psychosocial support therapy: A ten-year follow-up study. *Journal of Clinical Oncology, 2,* 66–69.

Gelso, C., & Carter, J. (1985). The relationship in counseling and psychotherapy—components, consequences and theoretical antecedents. *The Counseling Psychologist, 13,* 155–243.

Gensheimer, L., Mayer, J., Gottschalk, R., & Davidson, W., II (1986). Diverting youth from the juvenile justice system—a meta-analysis of intervention efficacy. In S. J. Apter & A. P. Goldstein (Eds.), *Youth violence* (pp. 39–57). New York: Pergamon Press.

German, M. (1994). Effective case management in managed mental health care: Conditions, methods and outcomes. *HMO Practice, 8*(1), 34–40.

Getz, W., Fujita, B., & Allen, D. (1975). The use of paraprofessionals in crisis intervention: Evaluation of an innovative program. *American Journal of Community Psychology, 3,* 135–144.

Giblin, P., Sprenkle, D., & Sheehan, R. (1985). Enrichment outcome research: A meta-analysis of premarital, marital, and family interventions. *Journal of Marital and Family Therapy, 11,* 257–271.

Gil, K. M., Wilson, J. J., Edens, J. L., Webster, D. A., Abrams, M. A., Orringer, E., Grant, M., Clark, W. C., & Janal, M. N. (1996). The effects of cognitive coping skills training on coping strategies and experimental pain sensitivity in African Amercian adults with sickle cell disease. *Health Psychology, 15,* 3–10.

Glass, G. (1976). Primary, secondary, and meta-analysis of research. *Education Research, 5,* 3–8.

Glass, G., & Kliegl, R. (1983). An apology for research integration in the study of psychotherapy. *Journal of Consulting and Clinical Psychology, 51,* 28–41.

Glass, G., McGaw, B., & Smith, M. (1981). *Meta-analysis in social research.* Thousand Oaks, CA: Sage.

Glasscote, R., & Fishman, M. (1973). *Mental health on the campus: A field study.* Washington, DC: American Psychiatric Association.

Gleick, E. (1996). Picking a health plan. *Time, 147*(5), 60–61.

Glick, I., Hargreaves, W., & Goldfield, M. (1974). Short vs. long hospitalization: A prospective controlled study: The preliminary results of a one-year follow-up of schizophrenics. *Archives of General Psychiatry, 30,* 363–369.

Goldiamond, I. (1965). Self-control procedures in personal behavior problems. *Psychological Reports, 17,* 851–868.

Goldfield, N. (1991). Measurement and management of quality in managed care organizations: Alive and improving. *Quality Review Bulletin, 17,* 343–348.

Goldfried, M., & Wolfe, B. (1996). Psychotherapy practice and research: Repairing a strained alliance. *American Psychologist, 51,* 1007–1016.

Goldman, W. (1988). Mental health and substance abuse services in HMOs. *Administration in Mental Health, 15,* 189–200.

Goodman, M., Brown, J., & Deitz, P. (1996). *Managing managed care: A mental health practitioner's survival guide.* Washington, DC: American Psychiatric Press.

Goodstein, L. (1986, December 12). Letter to the editor. *The Wall Street Journal,* p. 35.

Gormally, J., Black, S., Daston, S., & Rardin, D. (1982). The assessment of binge-eating severity among obese subjects. *Addictive Behaviors, 7,* 47–53.

Gottman, J. (1997). A Scientifically-based Marital Therapy, workshop presented by the Seattle Marital and Family Institute, Inc. and the University of Washington, November 14, 1997, Philadelphia, PA.

Gottschalk, R., Davidson, W., II, Gensheimer, L., & Mayer, J. (1987). Community-based interventions. In H. C. Quay (Ed.), *Handbook of juvenile delinquency* (pp. 266–289). New York: Wiley.

Gould, R., & Clum, G. (1993). A meta-analysis of self-help treatment approaches. *Clinical Psychology Review, 13,* 169–186.

Grant, D. (1994). America's economic outlaw: The U.S. health care system. *Bulletin of the New York Academy of Medicine, 55,* 20–24.

Greenberg, R., Bernstein, R., Greenberg, M., & Fisher, S. (1992). A meta-analysis of antidepressant outcome under "blinder" conditions. *Journal of Consulting and Clinical Psychology, 60*(5), 664–669.

Greenberg, L., & Johnson, S. (1986). Affect in marital therapy. *Journal of Marital and Family Therapy, 12,* 1–10.

Greenburg, L., & Johnson, S. (1988). *Emotionally focused couples therapy.* New York: Guilford Press.

Greist, J., & Jefferson, J. (1992). *Obsessive-compulsive disorder: A guide.* Madison, WI: Information Systems, Dean Foundation.

Grendlin, E. (1974). Client-centered and experiential psychotherapy. In D. A. Wesler & L. North Rice (Eds.), *Innovations in client centered therapy* (pp. 211–246). New York: Wiley.

Griffith, M., & Jones, E. (1978). Race and psychotherapy: Changing perspectives. In J. H. Masserman (Ed.), *Current psychiatric therapies* (vol. 18) (pp. 225–235). New York: Grune & Stratton.

Grimsmo, A., Helgesen, G., & Borchgrevink, C. (1981). Short-term and long-term effects of lay groups on weight reduction. *British Medical Journal, 283,* 1093–1095.

Grinspoon, L., Ewalt, J., & Shader, R. (1972). *Schizophrenia, pharmacotherapy and psychotherapy.* Baltimore, MD: Williams & Wilkins.

Grissom, R. (1996). The magical number .7 + .2: Meta-meta-analysis of the probability of superior outcome in comparisons involving therapy, placebo, and control. *Journal of Consulting and Clinical Psychology, 64,* 92–103.

Groth-Marnat, G., & Edkins, G. (1996). Professional psychologists in general healthcare settings: A review of the financial efficacy of direct treatment interventions. *Professional Psychology: Research and Practice, 27,* 161–174.

Gurevitz, H. (1984). Psychiatry and preferred provider organizations. *Psychiatric Annals, 14,* 342–349.

Gurman, A. (1978). Contemporary marital therapies: A critique and comparative analysis of psychoanalytic behavioral and systems theory approaches. In T. J. Paolino & B. S. McCrady (Eds.), *Marriage and marital therapy* (pp. 445–566). New York: Brunner/Mazel.

Gurman, A., Kniskers, D., & Pinsof, W. (1986). Research on the process and outcome of marital and family therapy. In S. L. Garfield & A. S. Bergin (Eds.), *Handbook of psychotherapy and behavior change: An empirical analysis* (2d ed.) (pp. 817–901). New York: Wiley.

Gustafson, P. (1984). An integration of brief dynamic psychotherapy. *American Journal of Psychiatry, 141,* 935–944.

Hahlweg, K., & Markman, H. (1988). Effectiveness of behavioral marital therapy: Empirical status of behavioral techniques in preventing and alleviating marital distress. *Journal of Consulting and Clinical Psychology, 56,* 440–447.

Hahlweg, K., Schindler, L., Revenstorf, D., & Brengelmann, J. (1984). The Munich Marital Therapy Study. In K. Hahlweg & N. S. Jacobson (Eds.), *Marital interaction: Analysis and modification* (pp. 3–26). New York: Guilford Press.

Haley, J. (1973). *Uncommon therapy: The psychiatric techniques of Milton H. Erickson, M.D.* New York: Norton.

Haley, J. (1976). *Problem solving therapy.* New York: Harper & Row.

Hamilton, S., Rothbart, M., & Dawes, R. (1986). Sex bias, diagnosis, and DSM-III. *Sex Roles, 15,* 279–284.

Hampton, B. (1988). The efficacy of paradoxical interventions: A quantitative review of the research evidence. Doctoral dissertation, University of Texas at Austin. *Dissertation Abstracts International, 49,* 2378B.

Hargreaves, W., Glick, I., Drues, J., Shaustack, J., & Feigenbaum, E. (1977). Short vs. long hospitalization: A prospective controlled study: VI: Two-year follow-up results for schizophrenics. *Archives of General Psychiatry, 34,* 305–311.

Haryett, R., Hansen, F., & Davidson, P. (1970). Chronic thumbsucking. A second report on treatment and its psychological effects. *American Journal of Orthodontics, 57,* 164–178.

Hathaway, D. (1985). Meta-analysis of studies which examine the effect preoperative instruction of adults has on postoperative outcomes. Doctoral dissertation, University of Texas, Austin, 1984. *Dissertation Abstracts International, 46,* 475B. (University Microfilms International No. 85-08277.)

Hattie, J., Sharpley, C., & Rogers, H. (1984). Comparative effectiveness of paraprofessional and professional helpers. *Psychological Bulletin, 95,* 534–541.

Hayes, R., Halford, W., & Varghese, F. (1995). Social skills training with chronic schizophrenic patients: Effects on negative symptoms and community functioning. *Behavior Therapy, 26,* 433–449.

Haywood, T., Kravitz, H., Grossman, L., Cavanaugh, J., Davis, J., & Lewis, D. (1995). Predicting the "revolving door" phenomenon among patients with schizophrenic, schizoaffective, and affective disorder. *American Journal of Psychiatry, 152,* 856–861.

Hazelrigg, M., Cooper, H., & Borduin, C. (1987). Evaluating the effectiveness of family therapies: An integrative review and analysis. *Psychological Bulletin, 101,* 428–442.

Heard, H., & Linehan, M. (1994). Dialectical behavior therapy: An integrative approach to the treatment of the borderline personality disorder. *Journal of Psychotherapy Integration, 4,* 55–82.

Hedges, L., & Olkin, I. (1985). *Statistical methods for meta-analysis.* San Diego, CA: Academic Press.

Heimal, J., LoPiccolo, L., & LoPiccolo, J. (1976). *Becoming orgasmic: A sexual growth program for women.* Englewood Cliffs, NJ: Prentice-Hall.

Heimberg, R., Dodge, C., Hope, D., Kennedy, C., & Zollo, L. (1990). Cognitive behavioral group treatment for social phobia: Comparison with a credible placebo control. *Cognitive Therapy and Research, 14,* 1–23.

Hendrix, H. (1988). *Getting the love you want.* New York: Harper Perennial.

Herink, R. (1980). *The psychotherapy handbook.* New York: New American Library.

Hersen, M., & Bellack, A. (1976). Social skills training for chronic psychiatric patients. *Comprehensive Psychiatry, 17,* 559–580.

Herzog, D., Keller, M., Lavori, P., & Sacks, N. (1991). The course and outcome of bulimia nervosa. *Journal of Clinical Psychiatry, 52*(10), 4–8.

Hester, R., Miller, R., Delaney, H., & Meyers, R. (1990, November). Effectiveness of the community reinforcement approach. Paper presented at the 24th annual meeting of the Association for the Advancement of Behavior Therapy, San Francisco.

Higgins, F. (1994). Quality and access in the managed behavioral healthcare industry. *Behavioral Healthcare Tomorrow* (September/October).

Higgins, S., Budney, A., Bickel, W., Hughes, J., Foeg, F., & Badger, G. (1993). Achieving cocaine abstinence with a behavioral approach. *American Journal of Psychiatry, 150,* 763–769.

Hill, K. (1987). Meta-analysis of paradoxical interventions. *Psychotherapy, 24,* 266–270.

Hill, R., Rigdon, M., & Johnson, S. (1993). Behavioral smoking cessation treatment for older chronic smokers. *Behavior Therapy, 24,* 321–329.

Hiss, H., Foa, E., & Kozak, M. (1994). Relapse prevention program for treatment of obsessive-compulsive disorder. *Journal of Consulting and Clinical Psychology, 62,* 801–808.

Hoffman, D., & Remmel, M. (1975). Uncovering the precipitant in crisis intervention. *Social Casework, 56,* 259–267.

Hogarty, G., Anderson, C., Reiss, D., Kornblith, S., Greenwald, D., Javna, C., & Madonia, M. (1986). Family psychoeducation, social skills training, and maintenance chemotherapy in the aftercare treatment of schizophrenia: I. One-year effects of a controlled study on relapse and expressed emotion. *Archives of General Psychiatry, 43,* 633–642.

Hogarty, G., Goldberg, S., Schooler, N., & Ulrich, R. (1974). Drug and sociotherapy in the aftercare of schizophrenic patients: II. Two year relapse rates. *Archives of General Psychiatry, 31,* 603–608.

Hogarty, G., Schooler, N., Ulrich, R., Musssare, F., Ferro, P., & Herron, E. (1979). Fluphenazine and social therapy in the aftercare of schizophrenic patients: Relapse analysis of a two-year controlled trial. *Archives of General Psychiatry, 36,* 1283–1294.

Holder, H., Longabaugh, R., Miller, R., & Rubonis, A. V. (1991). The cost effectiveness of treatment for alcoholism: A first approximation. *Journal of Studies on Alcohol, 52,* 517–540.

Hollon, S., DeRubeis, R., Evans, M., Wiemer, M., Garvey, M., Grove, W., & Tuason, V. (1992). Cognitive therapy and pharmacotherapy for depression: Singly and in combination. *Archives of General Psychiatry, 49,* 774–781.

Holroyd, K. A., & Penzien, D. B. (1990). Pharmacological versus nonpharmacological prophylaxis of recurrent migraine headache: A meta-analytic review of clinical trials. *Pain, 42,* 1–13.

Hong, L. (1984). Survival of the fastest. *Journal of Sex Research, 20,* 109–122.

Honzik, M., & McKee, J. (1962). The sex difference in thumb-sucking. *Journal of Pediatrics, 61,* 726–732.

Hope, D., Heimberg, R., & Bruch, M. (1995). Dismantling cognitive-behavioral group therapy for social phobia. *Behaviour Research and Therapy, 33,* 637–650.

Horan, J., Hoffman, A., & Marci, M. (1974). Self-control of chronic fingernail biting. *Journal of Behavioral Therapy and Experimental Psychiatry, 5,* 307–309.

Horowitz, M., & Hoyt, M. (1979). Book notice of Malan's "The Frontier of Brief Psychotherapy." *Journal of the American Psychoanalytic Association, 27,* 279–285.

Horvath, A., & Symonds, B. (1991). Relation between working alliance and outcome in psychotherapy:

A meta-analysis. *Journal of Counseling Psychology, 38*, 139–149.

Horwitz, R., & Horwitz, S. (1993). Adherence to treatment and health outcomes. *Archives of Internal Medicine, 153*, 1863–1868.

House, J., Landis, K., & Umberson, D. (1988). Social relationships and health. *Science, 241*, 540–545.

Houts, A., Berman, J., & Abramson, H. (1994). Effectiveness of psychological and pharmacological treatments for nocturnal enuresis. *Journal of Consulting and Clinical Psychology, 62*, 737–745.

Howard, K., Kopta, S., Krause, M., & Orlinsky, D. (1986). The dose–effect relationship in psychotherapy. *American Psychologist, 41*, 159–164.

Howard, K., Krause, M., & Orlinsky, D. (1986). The attrition dilemma: Toward a new strategy for psychotherapy research. *Journal of Consulting and Clinical Psychology, 54*, 106–110.

Howard, K., Krause, M., Saunders, S., & Kopta, S. (1997). Trials and tribulations in the meta-analysis of treatment differences: Comment on Wampold et al. (1997). *Psychological Bulletin, 122*, 221–225.

Howell, J. (1985). Effects of preoperative preparation of children having minor surgery: A literary synthesis with meta-analysis. Doctoral dissertation, University of Texas, Austin, 1984. *Dissertation Abstracts International, 46*, 1116B. (University Microfilms International No. 85-13231.)

Hoy, E., Curtis, R., & Rice, T. (1991). Change and growth in managed care. *Health Affairs* (Winter), 18–35.

Hoyt, M. (1995a). *Brief therapy and managed care.* San Francisco: Jossey-Bass.

Hoyt, M. (1995b). *Partnering with managed care.* San Francisco: Jossey-Bass.

Hudson, J., Pope, H., Wurtman, J., Yurgelun-Todd, D., Mark, N., & Rosenthal, N. (1988). Bulimia in obese individuals: Relation to normal weight bulimia. *Journal of Neurons and Mental Power, 176*, 144–152.

Huey, S., & Weisz, J. (1997). Ego control, ego resiliency, and the five-factor model as predictors of behavioral and emotional problems in clinic-referred children and adolescents. *Journal of Abnormal Psychology, 106*(3), 404–415.

Huey, W., & Rank, R. (1984). Effects of counselor and peer-led group assertive training on black adolescent aggression. *Journal of Counseling Psychology, 31*, 95–98.

Hunt, G., & Azrin, N. (1973). A community reinforcement approach to alcoholism. *Behaviour Research and Therapy, 11*, 91–104.

Hunter, J., & Schmidt, F. (1990). *Methods of meta-analysis: Correcting error and bias in research findings.* Thousand Oaks, CA: Sage.

Hurlbert, D., White, C., Powell, R., & Apt, C. (1993). Orgasm consistency training in the treatment of women reporting hypoactive sexual desire: An outcome comparison of women-only groups and couple-only groups. *Journal of Behavior Therapy and Experimental Psychiatry, 24*, 3–13.

Husted, J. (1975). Desensitization procedures in dealing with female sexual dysfunction. In J. LoPiccolo & L. LoPiccolo (Eds.), *Handbook of sex therapy* (pp. 195–208). New York: Plenum.

Hyman, R., Feldman, H., Harris, R., Levin, R., & Malloy, G. (1989). The effects of relaxation training on clinical symptoms—a meta-analysis. *Nursing Research, 38*, 216–220.

Iglehart, J. (1996). Managed care and mental health. *New England Journal of Medicine, 334*, 131–135.

Imber, S., & Evanczuk, K. (1990). Brief crisis therapy groups. In R. A. Wells & V. J. Giannetti (Eds.), *Handbook of the brief psychotherapies.* New York: Plenum.

Imber, S., Pilkonis, P., Sotsky, S., Elkin, I., Watkins, J., Collins, J., Shea, M., Leber, W., & Glass, D. (1990). Mode-specific effects among three treatments for depression. *Journal of Consulting and Clinical Psychology, 58*, 352–359.

Institute of Medicine (1989). *Controlling cost and changing patient care? The role of utilization management.* Washington, DC: National Academy Press.

Iverson, B., & Levy, S. (1982). Using meta-analysis in health education research. *Journal of School Health, 52*, 234–239.

Jacobs, M., & Goodman, G. (1989). Psychology and self-help groups: Predictions on a partnership. *American Psychologist, 23*, 536–545.

Jacobson, E. (1929). *Progressive relaxation.* Chicago: University of Chicago Press.

Jacobson, G., Wilner, D., Morley, W., Schneider, S., Strickler, M., & Sommer, G. (1965). The scope and practice of an early-access brief treatment psychiatric center. *American Journal of Psychiatry, 121*, 1176–1182.

Jacobson, N. (1977). Problem solving and contingency contracting in the treatment of marital discord. *Journal of Consulting and Clinical Psychology, 45*, 92–100.

Jacobson, N. (1978). Specific and nonspecific factors in the effectiveness of a behavioral approach to the treatment of marital discord. *Journal of Consulting and Clinical Psychology, 46*, 442–452.

Jacobson, N. (1983). Clinical innovations in behavioral marital therapy. In K. Craig & R. J. McMahon (Eds.), *Advances in clinical behavior therapy.* New York: Brunner/Mazel.

Jacobson, N. (1991). Behavioral versus insight-oriented marital therapy: Labels can be misleading. *Journal of Consulting and Clinical Psychology, 59,* 142–145.

Jacobson, N. (1995). The overselling of therapy. *The Family Therapy Networker, 19,* 40–41.

Jacobson, N., Dobson, K., Truax, P., Addis, M., Koerner, K., Gollan, J., Gortner, E., & Prince, S. (1996). A component analysis of cognitive-behavioral treatment for depression. *Journal of Consulting and Clinical Psychology, 64,* 295–304.

Jacobson, N., & Follette, W. (1985). Clinical significance of improvement resulting from two behavioral marital therapy components. *Behavior Therapy, 16,* 249–262.

Jacobson, N., Follette, W., & Revenstorf, D. (1984). Psychotherapy outcome research: Methods for reporting variability and evaluating clinical significance. *Behavior Therapy, 15,* 336–352.

Jacobson, N., Fuzzetti, A., Dobson, K., Whisman, M., & Hops, H. (1993). Couple therapy as a treatment on depression II: The effects of relationship quality and therapy on depressive relapse. *Journal of Consulting and Clinical Psychology, 61,* 516–519.

Jacobson, N., & Hollon, S. (1996a). Cognitive-behavioral therapy versus pharmacotherapy: Now that the jury's returned its verdict, it's time to present the rest of the evidence. *Journal of Consulting and Clinical Psychology, 64,* 74–80.

Jacobson, N., & Hollon, S. (1996b). Prospects for future comparisons between drugs and psychotherapy: Lessons from the CBT-versus-pharmacotherapy exchange. *Journal of Consulting and Clinical Psychology, 64,* 104–108.

Jacobson, N., & Margolin, G. (1979). *Marital therapy: Strategies based on social learning and behavior exchange principles.* New York: Brunner/Mazel.

James, P. (1991). Effects of a communication training component added to an emotionally focused couples therapy. *Journal of Marital and Family Therapy, 17,* 263–275.

Jamison, C., & Scogin, F. (1995). The outcome of cognitive bibliotherapy with depressed adults. *Journal of Consulting and Clinical Psychology, 63,* 644–650.

Janickott, P., Davis, J., Gibbons, R., Ericksen, S., Chang, S., & Gallagher, P. (1985). Efficacy of ECT: A meta-analysis. *American Journal of Psychiatry, 142,* 297–302.

Janis, I. (1983). *Short-term counseling: Guidelines based on recent research.* New Haven, CT: Yale University Press.

Jannoun, L., Munby, M., Catalan, J., & Gelder, M. (1980). A home-based treatment program for agoraphobia: Replication and controlled evaluation. *Behavior Therapy, 11,* 294–305.

Jason, L., Gruder, C., Martino, S., Flay, B., Warnecke, R., & Thomas, N. (1987). Work site group meetings and the effectiveness of a televised smoking cessation intervention. *American Journal of Community Psychology, 15,* 57–72.

Jencks, S., Horgan, C., & Taube, C. (1987). Evidence of provider response to prospective payment. *Medical Care, 25,* S37–S41.

Jenkins, A. (1985). Attending to self-activity in the Afro-American client. *Psychotherapy, 22,* 335–341.

Jerrel, J., & Rightmyer, J. (1982). Evaluation of employee assistance programs: A review of methods, outcomes, and future directions. *Evaluation and Program Planning, 5,* 255–267.

Johnson, L. (1995). *Psychotherapy in the age of accountability.* New York: Norton.

Johnson, S. (1983). The treatment of enuresis. In M. P. Keller & L. Ritt (Eds.), *Innovations in clinical practice: A source book* (vol. 2) (pp. 86–100). Sarasota, FL: Professional Resource Exchange.

Johnson, S., & Greenberg, L. (1985). Differential effects of experiential and problem-solving interventions in resolving marital conflict. *Journal of Consulting and Clinical Psychology, 53,* 175–184.

Joint Commission on Accreditation of Healthcare Organizations (1994). *Accreditation manual for mental health, chemical dependency, and mental retardation/developmental disabilities services (1995 MHM), vol 1: Standards.* Oakbrook Terrace, IL: Author.

Jones, L. (1983). A meta-analytic study of effects of childbirth education research from 1960 to 1981. Doctoral dissertation, Texas A & M University. *Dissertation Abstracts International, 44,* 1663A. (University Microfilms International No. 83-23680.)

Jones, W., & Park, P. (1972, March). Treatment of single-partner sexual dysfunction by systematic desensitization. *Obstetrics and Gynecology, 39,* 411–417.

Jorm, A. (1989). Modifiability of trait anxiety and neuroticism—a meta-analysis of the literature. *Australian and New Zealand Journal of Psychiatry, 23,* 21–29.

Kandel, E., & Hawkins, R. (1992). The biological basis of learning and individuality. *Scientific American, 262*(3), 78–86.

Kaplan, H. (1974). *The new sex therapy.* New York: Brunner/Mazel.

Kaplan, H. (1979). *Disorders of desire.* New York: Brunner/Mazel.

Kaplan, J. (1989). Efficacy: The real bottom line in health care. *HMO Practice, 3,* 108–110.

Karg-Bray, R., Norcross, J., & Prochaska, J. (1996). Clinical psychologists and managed care in the 1990s. Paper presented at the 1996 Eastern Psychological Association convention, Philadelphia.

Karlsruher, A. (1976). The influence of supervision and facilitative conditions on the psychotherapeutic effectiveness of nonprofessional and professional therapists. *American Journal of Community Psychology, 4,* 145–154.

Karoly, P. (1981). Self-management problems in children. In E. J. Mash & L. G. Terdal (Eds.), *Behavioral assessment of childhood disorders* (pp. 79–126). New York: Guilford Press.

Karoly, P., & Rosenthal, M. (1977). Training parents in behavior modification: Effects on perceptions of family interaction and deviant child behavior. *Behavior Therapy, 8,* 406–410.

Karon, B. (1995). Provision of psychotherapy under managed health care: A growing crisis and national nightmare. *Professional Psychology: Research and Practice, 26,* 5–9.

Kaufman, P. (1985). *Meta-analysis of juvenile delinquency prevention programs.* Unpublished manuscript, Claremont Graduate School.

Kavale, K. (1982). The efficacy of stimulant drug treatment for hyperactivity: A meta-analysis. *Journal of Learning Disabilities, 15,* 280–289.

Kavale, K., & Forness, S. (1983). Hyperactivity and diet treatment: A meta-analysis of the Feingold hypothesis. *Journal of Learning Disabilities, 16,* 324–330.

Kavale, K., & Nye, C. (1984). The effectiveness of drug treatment for severe behavior disorders: A meta-analysis. *Behavioral Disorders, 9,* 117–130.

Kazdin, A. (1982). Single-case experimental designs. In P. C. Kendall & J. N. Butcher (Eds.), *Handbook of research methods in clinical psychology* (pp. 461–490). New York: Wiley.

Kazdin, A. (1991). Effectiveness of psychotherapy with children and adolescents. *Journal of Consulting and Clinical Psychology, 59,* 785–798.

Kazdin, A. (1992). *Research design in clinical psychology* (2d ed.). Boston: Allyn & Bacon.

Kazdin, A., & Wilcoxon, L. (1976). Systematic desensitization and nonspecific treatment effects: A methodological evaluation. *Psychological Bulletin, 83*(5), 729–758.

Keane, T., Fairbank, J., Caddell, J., & Zimering, R. (1989). Implosive (flooding) therapy reduces symptoms of PTSD in Vietnam combat veterans. *Behavior Therapy, 20,* 245–260.

Keefe, F. J., Caldwell, D. S., Williams, D. A., Gil, K. M., Mitchell, D., Robertson, C., Martinez, S., Nunley, J., Beckham, J. C., & Helms, M. (1990a). Pain coping skills training in the management of osteoarthritic knee pain: A comparative study. *Behavior Therapy, 21,* 49–62.

Keefe, F., Caldwell, D., Williams, D., Gil, K., Mitchell, D., Robertson, C., Martinez, S., Nunley, J., Beckham, J., Crisson, J., Helms, M. (1990a). Pain coping skills training in the management of osteoarthritic knee pain: A comparative study. *Behavior Therapy, 21,* 49–62.

Keefe, F., Caldwell, D., Williams, D., Gil, K., Mitchell, D., Robertson, C., Martinez, S., Nunley, J., Beckham, J., Crisson, J., Helms, M. (1990b). Pain coping skills training in the management of osteoarthritic knee pain-II: Follow-up results. *Behavior Therapy, 21,* 435–447.

Kendall, P. (1994). Treatment of anxiety disorders in children: A randomized clinical trial. *Journal of Consulting and Clinical Psychology,* 100–110.

Kendall, P. (1998). Empirically supported psychological therapies. *Journal of Consulting and Clinical Psychology, 66,* 3–6.

Kendall, P., & Braswell, L. (1993). *Cognitive behavior therapy for impulsive children* (2d ed.). New York: Guilford Press.

Kendall, P., Flannery-Schroeder, E., Panichelli-Mindel, S., Southam-Gerow, M., Henin, A., & Warman, M. (1997). Treatment of anxiety disorders in youths: A second randomized clinical trial. *Journal of Consulting and Clinical Psychology, 65,* 366–380.

Kendall, P., Kane, M., Howard, B., & Siqueland, L. (1990). *Cognitive-behavioral therapy for anxious children: Treatment manual.* (Available from Philip C. Kendall, Department of Psychology, Temple University, Philidelphia, PA 19122).

Kessler, K. (1978). Tricyclic anti-depressants: Mode of action and clinical use. In M. A. Lipton, A. DiMascio, & K. F. Killam (Eds.), *Psychopharmacology: A generation of progress.* New York: Raven Press.

Kiesler, C. (1982). Mental hospitals and alternative care: Noninstitutionalization as potential public policy for mental patients. *American Psychologist, 37*, 1051–1057.

Kirsch, I., Tennen, H., Wickless, C., Saccone, A., & Cody, S. (1983). The role of expectancy in fear reduction. *Behavior Therapy, 14*, 520–533.

Klein, D. (1996). Preventing hung juries about therapy studies. *Journal of Consulting and Clinical Psychology, 64*, 81–87.

Klein, R. (1985). Some principles of short-term group therapy. International *Journal of Group Psychotherapy, 35*, 309–321.

Kleinman, A. (1998). How do professional values influence the work of psychiatrists? In R. Castillo (Ed.), *Meanings of madness* (pp. 21–29). Pacific Grove, CA: Brooks/Cole. Reprinted from A. Kleinman (1988), *Rethinking psychiatry* (pp. 77–94). (New York: The Free Press).

Klerman, G., Weissman, M., Rounsaville, B., & Chevron, E. (1984). *Interpersonal psychotherapy of depression*. New York: Basic Books.

Klosko, J., Barlow, D., Tassinari, R., & Cerny, J. (1990). A comparison of alazopram and behavior therapy in the treatment of panic disorder. *Journal of Consulting and Clinical Psychology, 58*, 77–84.

Kobasa, S. C. (1979a). Personality and resistance to illness. *American Journal of Community Psychology, 7*, 413–423.

Kobasa, S. C. (1979b). Stressful life events, personality, and health: An inquiry into hardiness. *Journal of Personality and Social Psychology, 37*, 1–11.

Kogan, L. (1957a). The short-term case in a family agency Part I: The study plan. *Social Casework, 38*, 231–238.

Kogan, L. (1957b). The short-term case in a family agency Part II: Results of study. *Social Casework, 38*, 296–302.

Kogan, L. (1957c). The short-term case in a family agency Part III: Further results and conclusion. *Social Casework, 38*, 366–374.

Kopta, S., Howard, K., Lowry, J., & Beutler, L. (1994). Patterns of symptomatic recovery in time-unlimited psychotherapy. *Journal of Clinical and Consulting Psychology, 62*, 1009–1016.

Koss, M., & Butcher. (1986). Research on brief therapy. In S. Garfield, & A. E. Bergin (Eds.), *Handbook of psychotherapy and behavior change* (3d ed.). New York: Wiley.

Koss, M., Butcher, J., & Strupp, H. (1986). Brief psychotherapy methods in clinical research. *Journal of Consulting and Clinical Pscyhology, 54*, 60–67.

Koyanagi, C., Manes, J., Surles, R., et al. (1992). On being very smart: The mental health commu-nity's response in the health care reform debate. *Hospital and Community Psychiatry, 44*, 537–542.

Kraft, R., Clairborn, C., & Dowd, E. (1985). Effects of positive reframing and paradoxical directives in counseling for negative emotions. *Journal of Counseling Psychology, 32*, 617–621.

Kramon, G. (1989, July 2). Why Kaiser is still the king. *New York Times*, Business Section, p. 1.

Krauss, D. (1983). The physiologic basis of male sexual dysfunction. *Hospital Practice, 2*, 193–222.

Kreilkamp, T. (1989). *Time-limited, intermittent therapy with children and families*. New York: Guilford Press.

Kristel, O., Fielding, S., & Chambliss, C. (1997). An outcome assessment of a high school peer helpers program. *Resources in Education*, ERIC/CASS, CG027875.

Kristel, O., Young, J., & Chambliss, C. (1997). High school students' perceptions of adolescent problems. *Resources in Education*, ERIC/CASS, CG027710.

Kroll, J. (1993). *PTST/Borderlines in therapy: Finding the balance*. New York: Norton.

Krupnick, J., & Pincus, H. (1992). The cost-effectiveness of psychotherapy: A plan for research. *American Journal of Psychiatry, 149*, 1295–1305.

Kuchera, M. (1987). The effectiveness of meditation techniques to reduce blood pressure levels: A meta-analysis. Doctoral dissertation, Loyola University of Chicago. *Dissertation Abstracts International, 47*, 4639B.

Kuder, A., & Kuntz, M. (1996). Who decides what is medically necessary? In J. A. Lazarus (Ed.), *Controversies in managed mental health care*. Washington, DC: American Psychiatric Press.

Kupfersmid, J. (1989). Treatment of nocturnal enuresis: A status report. *The Psychiatric Forum, 14*, 37–46.

Kurcinka, M. S. (1991). *Raising your spirited child*. New York: Harper Collins.

Laessle, R., Zoettl, C., & Pride, K. (1987). Metaanalysis of treatment studies for bulimia. *International Journal of Eating Disorders, 6*, 647–653.

Lamb, D., & Clack, R. (1974). Professional versus paraprofessional approaches to orientation and subsequent counseling contacts. *Journal of Counseling Psychology, 21*, 61–65.

Lambert, M. (1992a). Implications of outcome research for psychotherapy integration. In J. C. Norcross & M. R. Goldfried (Eds.), *Handbook of psychotherapy integration*. New York: Basic Books.

Lambert, M. (1992b). Psychotherapy outcome research: Implications for integrative and eclectic therapists. In J. C. Norcross & M. R. Goldfried (Eds.), *Handbook of psychotherapy integration.* New York: Basic Books.

Lambert, M., & Bergin, A. (1994). The effectiveness of psychotherapy. In A. E. Bergin & S. L. Garfield (Eds.), *Handbook of psychotherapy and behavior change* (4th ed). New York: Wiley.

Lambert, M., Shapiro, D., & Bergin, A. (1986). The effectiveness of psychotherapy. In S. Garfield & A. E. Bergin (Eds.), *Handbook of psychotherapy and behavior change* (3d ed.). New York: Wiley.

Land, S. (1998). Why do organizations choose an HMO? *Drug Benefit Trends, 3,* 8–10.

Landman, J., & Dawes, R. (1982). Psychotherapy outcome: Smith and Glass's conclusions stand up under scrutiny. *American Psychologist, 37,* 504–516.

Lange M., Chandler-Guy, C., Forti, R., Foster-Moore, P., & Rohman, M. (1988). Providers' views of HMO mental health services. *Psychotherapy: Theory, Research, and Practice, 25,* 455–462.

Langs, R. (1973). *The technique of psychoanalytic psychotherapy.* New York: Aronson.

Lask, K., & Matthew, D. (1979). Childhood asthma: A controlled trial of family psychotherapy. *Archives of Diseases in Children, 54,* 116–119.

Law, M., & Tang, J. (1995). An analysis of the effectiveness of interventions intended to help people stop smoking. *Archives of Internal Medicine, 155,* 1933–1941.

Layden, M., Newman, C., Freeman, A., & Morse, S. (1995). *Cognitive therapy of borderline personality disorder.* Boston: Allyn & Bacon.

Lazarus, A. (1976). *Multimodal behavior therapy.* New York: Springer.

Lazarus, A. (1989). *The practice of multimodal therapy.* Baltimore, MD: Johns Hopkins University Press.

Lazarus, A. (1995). Managed care Practice and psychiatric deaths: Must we assign blame? *Administration and Policy in Mental Health, 22,* 457–461.

Lazarus, A. (1997). Technical eclecticism revisited: Old answers to new challenges. Paper presented at Beyond Managed Care: The Evolution of Psychotherapy in the Next Millennium, The Institute for the Advancement of Human Behavior, September, Washington, DC.

Lazarus, A., & Fay, A. (1990). Brief psychotherapy: Tautology or oxymoron? In J. K. Zeig & S. G. Gilligan (Eds.), *Brief therapy: Myths, methods, and metaphors.* New York: Brunner/Mazel.

Lee, M., Love, S., Mitchell, J., et al. (1992). Mastectomy or conservation for early breast cancer: Psychological morbidity. *European Journal of Cancer, 28,* 1340–1344.

Leong, F. (1986). Counseling and psychotherapy with Asian-Americans: Review of the literature. *Journal of Counseling Psychology, 33,* 196–206.

Levin, B., Glasser, J., & Jaffee, C. (1988). National trends in coverage and utilization of mental health, alcohol, and substance abuse services within managed health care systems. *American Journal of Public Health, 78,* 1222–1223.

Levit, K., Lazenby, H., & Braden, B. (1998). National Health Spending Trends. *Health Affairs, 17*(1), 35–51.

Levitz, L., & Stunkard, A. (1974). A therapeutic coalition for obesity: Behavior modification and patient self-help. *American Journal of Psychiatry, 131,* 423–427.

Lewinsohn, P. (1974). A behavioral approach to depression. In R. Friedman & M. Katz (Eds.), *The psychology of depression: Contemporary theory of research* (pp. 157–176). New York: Wiley.

Liberman, R. (1972). Behavioral modification of schizophrenia: A review. *Schizophrenia Bulletin, 1*(6), 37–48.

Liberman, R. (1994). Psychosocial treatments for schizophrenia. *Psychiatry, 57,* 104–114.

Liberman, R. (1996). Two-year outcome of social skills training and group psychotherapy for outpatients with schizophrenia. *American Journal of Psychiatry, 153,* 1585–1592.

Liberman, R., DeRisi, W., & Mueser, K. (1989). *Social Skills Training for Psychiatric Patients.* New York: Pergamon Press, Inc.

Liberman, R., King, D., DeRisi, W., & McCann, M. (1975). *Personal effectiveness.* Champaign, IL: Research Press.

Liberman, R., Levine, J., Wheeler, M., Sanders, N., & Wallace, C. (1976). Marital therapy in groups. A comparative evaluation of behavioral and interactional formats. *Acta Psychiatrica Scandinavica, 266,* 1–34.

Liberman, R., Wallace, C., Falloon, I., & Vaughn, C. (1981). Interpersonal problem-solving therapy for schizophrenics and their families. *Comprehensive Psychiatry, 22,* 627–629.

Lichtenstein, E., & Glasgow, R. (1992). Smoking cessation: What have we learned over the past decade? *Journal of Consulting and Clinical Psychology, 60,* 518–527.

Lidren, D. M., Watkins, P. L., Gould, R. A., Clum, G. A., Asterino, M., & Tulloch, H. L. (1994). A comparison of bibliotherapy and group therapy in the treatment of panic disorder. *Journal of Consulting and Clinical Psychology, 62,* 865–869.

Lieberman, M. (1986). Self-help groups and psychiatry. In A. J. Frances & R. E. Hales (Eds.), *American*

Psychiatric Association annual review (vol. 5) (pp. 744–759). Washington, DC: American Psychiatric Press.

Liebman, R., Minuchin, S., & Baker, L. (1974). The role of the family in the treatment of anorexia nervosa. *Journal of Child Psychiatry, 13,* 264–274.

Lindstrom, L., Balch, P., & Reese, S. (1976). In person versus telephone treatment for obesity. *Journal of Behavior Therapy and Experimental Psychiatry, 7,* 367–369.

Linehan, M. (1993). *Skills Training Manual for Treating Borderline Personality Disorder.* New York: Guilford Press.

Linehan, M., Armstrong, H., Suarez, A., Allmon, D., & Heard, H. (1991). Cognitive-behavioral treatment of chronically parasuicidal borderline patients. *Archives of General Psychiatry, 48,* 1060–1064.

Linehan, M., Heard, H., & Armstrong, H. (1993). Naturalistic follow-up of a behavioral treatment for chronically parasuicidal borderline patients. *Archives of General Psychiatry, 50,* 971–974.

Lipsey, M. (1988). Practice and malpractice in evaluation research. *Evaluation Practice, 9*(4), 5–24.

Lipsey, M. (1992). Juvenile delinquency treatment: A meta-analytic inquiry into the variability of effects. In T. D. Cook, H. Cooper, D. S. Cordray, H. Hartmann, L. V. Hedge, R. J. Light, T. A. Louis, & F. Mosteller (Eds.), *Meta-analysis for explanation,* (pp. 83–127). New York: Russell Sage Foundation.

Lipsey, M., Crosse, S., Dunkle, J., Pollard, J., & Stobart, G. (1985). Evaluation: The state of the art and the sorry state of the science. *New Directions for Program Evaluation, 27,* 7–28.

Lipsey, M., & Wilson, D. (1993). The efficacy of psychological, educational, and behavioral treatment: Confirmation from meta-analysis. *American Psychologist, 48*(12), 1181–1209.

Littlepage, G., Kosloski, K., Schnelle, J., McNees, M., & Gendrich, J. (1976). The problems of early outpatient terminations from community mental health centers: A problem for whom? *Journal of Community Psychology, 4,* 164–167.

Locke, H., & Wallace, K. (1959). Short marital-adjustment and prediction tests: Their reliability and validity. *Journal of Marriage and Family Living, 21,* 251–255.

Lonergan, E. (1981). *Group intervention: How to begin and maintain groups in medical and psychiatric settings.* New York: Aronson.

LoPiccolo, J. (1984). *Treating vaginismus* [Film]. New York: Multi-Focus.

LoPiccolo, J., & Lobitz, W. (1972). The role of masturbation in the treatment of orgasmic dysfunction. *Archives of Sexual Behavior, 2,* 163.

LoPiccolo, J., & Stock, W. (1986). Treatment of sexual dysfunction. *Journal of Consulting and Clinical Psychology, 54,* 158–167.

Loro, A., & Orleans, C. (1981). Binge eating in obesity: Preliminary findings and guidelines for behavioral analysis and treatment. *Addictive Behavior, 6,* 155–166.

Losel, F., & Koferl, P. (1989). Evaluation research on correctional treatment in West Germany: A meta-analysis. In H. Wegener, F. Losel, & J. Haisch (Eds.), *Criminal behavior and the justice system: Psychological perspectives* (pp. 334–355). New York: Springer.

Lovibond, S., & Coote, M. (1970). Enuresis. In L. Costello (Ed.), *Symptoms of psychopathology* (pp. 373–396). New York: Wiley.

Luborsky, L., Crits-Cristoph, P., Mintz, J., & Auerbach R. (1988). *Who will benefit from psychotherapy?* New York: Basic Books.

Luborsky, L., McClellan, A., Woody, G., O'Brian, C., & Auerbach, A. (1985). Therapist success and its determinants. *Archives of General Psychiatry, 42,* 602–611.

Luborsky, L., Singer, B., & Luborsky, L. (1975). Comparative studies of psychotherapies: Is it true that "Everyone has won and all must have prizes"? *Archives of General Psychiatry, 32,* 995–1008.

Luft, H. (1978). How do health-maintenance organizations achieve their "savings"? Rhetoric and evidence. *New England Journal of Medicine, 298,* 1336–1343.

Lurie, N., Moscovice, I., Finch, M., & Christianson, J. (1992). Does capitation affect the health of the chronically mentally ill? *Journal of the American Medical Association, 267,* 3300–3304.

Lynch, P. M., & Zamble, E. (1989). A controlled behavioral treatment study of irritable bowel syndrome. *Behavior Therapy, 20,* 509–523.

Lynn, D., & Donovan, J. (1980). Medical versus surgical treatment of coronary artery disease. *Evaluation in Education, 4,* 98–99.

MacKenzie, K. (1988). Recent developments in brief psychotherapy. *Hospital and Community Psychiatry, 39,* 742–752.

MacKenzie, K. (Ed.) (1995). *Effective use of group therapy in managed care.* Washington, DC: American Psychiatric Press.

MacKenzie, K. (1997). The increasing importance of group psychotherapy: A powerful cost-effective treatment alternative. Paper presented at Beyond Managed Care: The Evolution of Psychotherapy in the Next Millennium, The Institute for the Advancement of Human Behavior, September, Washington, DC.

Magakis, G., & Chambliss, C. (1997a). Lessons for incisive psychotherapy: Why less is often more. *Resources in Education,* ERIC/CASS, CG027953.

Magakis, G., & Chambliss, C. (1997b). Therapeutic realities: A guide to doing brief Ericksonian therapy. *Resources in Education,* ERIC/CASS, CG027948.

Malan, D. (1976). *Toward a validation of a dynamic psychotherapy.* New York: Plenum.

Malan, D., Heath, E., Bacal, H., & Balfour, F. (1975). Psychodynamic changes in untreated neurotic patients. II. Apparently genuine improvements. *Archives of General Psychiatry, 32,* 110–126.

Malone, A., & Massler, M. (1952). Index of nailbiting in children. *Journal of Abnormal and Social Psychology, 47,* 193–202.

Malone, M., Strube, M., & Scogin, F. (1989). Meta-analysis of non-medical treatments for chronic pain: Corrigendum. *Pain, 37*(1), 128.

Mann, J. (1973). *Time-limited psychotherapy.* Cambridge, MA: Harvard University Press.

Mann, J., & Goldman, R. (1982). *A casebook in time-limited psychotherapy.* New York: McGraw-Hill.

Manning, R. (1986). Use of outpatient mental health care: Trial of prepaid group practice versus fee for service. RAND Study, Santa Monica, CA.

Manning, W., et al. (1989). *Effects of mental health insurance: Evidence from the health insurance experiment.* Santa Monica, CA: RAND.

Marcus, M., Wing, R., & Hopkins, J. (1988). Obese binge eaters. *International Journal of Eating Disorders, 9,* 69–77.

Marcus, M., Wing, R., & Lamparski, D. (1985). Binge eating and dietary restraint in obese patients. *Addictive Behaviors, 10,* 163–168.

Marder, S., Wirshing, W., Mintz, J., McKenzie, J., Johnston, K., Eckman, T., Lebell, M., Zimmerman, K., & Liberman, R. (1996). Two-year outcome of social skills training and group psychotherapy for outpatients with schizophrenia. *American Journal of Psychiatry, 153,* 1585–1592.

Markowitz, J. (1996). Psychotherapy for dysthymic disorder. *The Psychiatric Clinics of North America, 19,* 133–150.

Markowitz, J., Moran, M., Kocsis, J., & Frances, A. (1992). Prevalence and comorbidity of dysthymic disorder among psychiatric outpatients. *Journal of Affective Disorders, 24,* 63–71.

Marks, I. (1983). Are there anticompulsive or antiphobic drugs? Review of the evidence. *British Journal of Psychiatry, 143,* 338–347.

Markus, E., Lange, A., & Pettigrew, T. (1990). Effectiveness of family therapy—a metaanalysis. *Journal of Family Therapy, 12,* 205–221.

Marmar, C. & Freeman, M. (1988). Brief dynamic psychotherapy of post-traumatic stress disorders: Management of narcissistic regression. *Journal of Traumatic Stress, 1,* 323–337.

Marmor, J. (1973). *Psychiatry in transition.* New York: Brunner/Mazel.

Marshall, W., Jones, R., Ward, T., Johnson, P., & Barbaree, H. (1991). Treatment outcome with sex offenders. *Clinical Psychology Review, 11,* 465–485.

Masi, D., & Caplan, R. (1992). *Employee assistance programs in managed mental health care: Administrative and clinical issues.* Washington, DC: American Psychiatric Press.

Masson, J. (1988). *Against therapy: Emotional tyranny and the myth of psychological healing.* New York: Atheneum.

Masters, W., & Johnson, V. (1970). *Human sexual inadequacy.* Boston: Little, Brown.

Mattick, R., Peters, L., & Clarke, J. (1989). Exposure and cognitive restructuring for social phobia: A controlled study. *Behavior Therapy, 20,* 3–23.

Mavissakalian, M., Michelson, L., Greenwald, D., Kornblith, S., & Greenwald, M. (1983). Cognitive-behavioral treatment of agoraphobia: Paradoxical intention vs. self-statement training. *Behaviour Research and Therapy, 21,* 75–86.

Maxmen, J., & Ward, N. (1995). *Essential Psychopathology and Its Treatment,* W. W. Norton & Co.: New York.

May, P. (1968). *Treatment of Schizophrenia.* New York: Science House.

Mayer, J., Gensheimer, L., Davidson, W., II, & Gottschalk, R. (1986). Social learning treatment within juvenile justice—a meta-analysis of impact in the natural environment. In S. J. Apter & A. P. Goldstein (Eds.), *Youth violence* (pp. 24–39). New York: Pergamon Press.

Mazzuca, S. (1982). Does patient education in chronic disease have therapeutic value? *Journal of Chronic Disease, 35,* 521–529.

McCullough, L., Winston, A., Farber, B., Porter, F., Pollack, J., Laikin, M., Vingiano, W., & Trujillo, M. (1991). The relationship of patient–therapist interaction to outcome in brief psychotherapy. *Psychotherapy: Theory, Research, Practice, Training, 28,* 525–533.

McDonald, R., Sartory, G., & Grey, S. (1979). The effects of self-exposure instructions on agoraphobic outpatients. *Behaviour Research and Therapy, 17,* 83–85.

McGovern, K., Stewart, R., & LoPiccolo, J. (1975). Secondary orgasmic dysfunction: Analysis and strategies for treatment. *Archives of Sexual Behavior, 4,* 265.

McLean, P., & Hakstian, A. (1979). Clinical depression: Comparative efficacy of outpatient treatments. *Journal of Consulting and Clinical Psychology, 47,* 818–836.

Mechanic, D., et al. (1995). Management of mental health and substance abuse services: State of the art and early results. *Milbank Quarterly, 73*(1), 19–55.

Medicare program: Prospective payment for Medicare final rule (1984). *Federal Register, 23,* 234–340.

Meichenbaum, D. (1979). Teaching children self-control. In B. B. Lahey & A. E. Kazdin (Eds.), *Advances in clinical child psychology* (vol. 2) (pp. 1–33). New York: Plenum.

Meichenbaum, D., & Turk, D. (1987). *Facilitating treatment adherence: A practitioner's guidebook.* New York: Plenum.

Meltzoff, J., & Kornreich, M. (1970). *Research in psychotherapy.* New York: Atherton Press.

Menzies, R., & Clarke, J. (1993). A comparison of in vivo and vicarious exposure in the treatment of childhood water phobia. *Behavior Research and Therapy, 31,* 9–15.

Miller, G. (1969). Psychology as a means of promoting human welfare. *American Psychologist, 24,* 1063–1075.

Miller, I. (1995). Managed care is harmful to outpatient mental health services. *Professional Psychologist,* Fall.

Miller, I. (1996). Time-limited brief therapy has gone too far: The result is invisible rationing. *Professional Psychology Research and Practice, 27,* 567–576.

Miller, R., & Berman, J. (1983). The efficacy of cognitive behavior therapies: A quantitative review of the research evidence. *Psychological Bulletin, 94,* 39–53.

Miller, W., Brown, J., Simpson, T., Handmaker, N., Bien, T., Luckie, L., Montogomery, H., Hester, R., & Tonigan, J. (1995). What works? A methodological analysis of the alcohol treatment outcome literature. In R. K. Hester & W. R. Miller (Eds.), *Handbook of alcoholism treatment approaches: Effective alternatives* (pp. 12–44). Boston: Allyn & Bacon.

Miller, W. & Hester, R. (1986). Inpatient alcoholism treatment: Who benefits? *American Psychologist, 41,* 794–805.

Minuchin, S. (1974). *Families and family therapy.* Cambridge, MA: Harvard University.

Minuchin, S., Baker, L., & Rosman, B. (1975). A conceptual model of psychosomatic illness in children. *Archives of General Psychiatry, 32,* 1031–1038.

Montgomery, L. (1991). The effects of family therapy for treatment of child identified problems: A meta-analysis. Doctoral dissertation, Memphis State University, 1990. *Dissertation Abstracts International, 51,* 6115B.

Monti, P., Rohsenow, D., Rubonis, A., Niaura, R., Sirota, A., Colby, S., Goddard, P., & Abrams, D. (1993). Cue exposure with coping skills treatment for male alcoholics: A preliminary investigation. *Journal of Consulting and Clinical Psychology, 61,* 1011–1019.

Montross, J. (1990). Meta-analysis of treatment efficacy in Raynaud's phenomenon. Doctoral dissertation, Texas A & M University, 1989. *Dissertation Abstracts International, 50,* 4811B.

Morreim, E. (1991). Gaming the system: Dodging the rules, ruling the dodgers. *Archives of Internal Medicine, 151,* 443–447.

Morse, L., Doran, M., Simonin, D., Smith, A., Maloney, C., Wright, C., Underwood, M., Hoppel, A., O'Donnell, S., & Chambliss, C. (1998). Preferred psychological internet resources for addressing anxiety disorders, parenting problems, eating disorders, and chemical dependency. *Resources in Education,* ERIC/CASS, CG028198.

Mower, O., & Mower, W. (1938). Enuresis—a method for its study and treatment. *American Journal of Orthopsychiatry, 8,* 436–459.

Mumford, E., Schlesinger, H., & Glass, G. (1982). The effects of psychological intervention on recovery from surgery and heart attacks: An analysis of the literature. *American Journal of Public Health, 72,* 141–151.

Munoz, R. (1982). The Spanish-speaking consumer and the community mental health center. In E. E. Jones & S. J. Korchin (Eds.), *Minority mental health* (pp. 362–398). New York: Praeger.

Murphy, G., Simons, A., Wetzel, R., & Lustman, P. (1984). Cognitive therapy and pharmacotherapy: Singly and together in the treatment of depression. *Archives of General Psychiatry, 41,* 33–41.

Murry, J. (1972). The comparative effectiveness of student-to-student and faculty advising programs. *Journal of College Student Personnel, 13,* 562–566.

Nagel, J., Cimbolic, P., & Newlin, M. (1988). Efficacy of elderly and adolescent volunteer counselors in a nursing home setting. *Journal of Counseling Psychology, 36,* 81–86.

Najavits, L., & Strupp, H. (1994). Differences in the effectiveness of psychodynamic therapists: A process-outcome study. *Psychotherapy: Theory, Research, Practice, Training, 31,* 114–123.

NAMI Advocate (1998). The facts about mental illness and work, a brochure from the Research and Training Center on Mental Illness and Work at Matrix Research Institute (MRI) and the University of Pennsylvania.

Nathan, P. (1998). Practice guidelines: Not yet ideal. *American Psychologist, 53,* 290–299.

Nelson, J. (1987). The history and spirit of the HMO movement. *HMO Practice, 1,* 75–85.

Newman, F., & Tejeda, M. (1996). The need for research that is designed to support decisions in the delivery of mental health services. *American Psychologist, 51,* 1040–1049.

Newton-John, T. R. O., Spence, S. H., & Schotte, D. (1995). Cognitive-behavioral therapy versus EMG biofeedback in the treatment of chronic low back pain. *Behaviour Research and Therapy, 33,* 691–697.

Nezu, A. (1986). Efficacy of a social problem-solving therapy approach for unipolar depression. *Journal of Consulting and Clinical Psychology, 54,* 196–202.

Nezu, A. (1996). What are we doing to our patients and should we care if anyone else knows? *Clinical Psychology: Science and Practice, 3,* 160–163.

Nezu, A., & Perri, M. (1989). Social problem-solving therapy for unipolar depression: An initial dismantling investigation. *Journal of Consulting and Clinical Psychology, 57,* 408–413.

Nicholas, M., Wilson, P., & Goyen, J. (1991). Comparison of operant-behavioural and cognitive-behavioural group treatment, with and without relaxation training, for chronic low back pain. *Behaviour Research and Therapy, 29,* 225–238.

Nicholson, R., & Berman, J. (1983). Is follow-up necessary in evaluating psychotherapy? *Psychological Bulletin, 93,* 261–278.

Nicholson, T., Duncan, D., Hawkins, W., Belcastro, P., & Gold, R. (1988). Stress treatment: Two aspirins, fluids, and one more workshop. *Professional Psychology: Research and Practice, 19,* 637–641.

Norcross, J. (1995). Dispelling the Dodo bird verdict and the exclusivity myth. *Psychotherapy: Theory, Research, Practice, Training, 32,* 500–504.

North, T. (1989). The effect of exercise on depression: A meta-analysis. Doctoral dissertation, University of Colorado at Boulder, 1988. *Dissertation Abstracts International, 49,* 5027B.

Novack, D., et al. (1989). Physicians' attitudes towards using deception to resolve difficult ethical problems. *JAMA, 261,* 2980–2985.

Nowak, R. (1994). Problems in clinical trials go far beyond misconduct. *Science, 264,* 1538–1541.

Nunes, E., Frank, K., & Kornfeld, D. (1987). Psychological treatment for the Type A behavior pattern and for coronary heart disease: A meta-analysis of the literature. *Psychosomatic Medicine, 49,* 159–173.

Obler, M. (1973). Systematic desensitization in sexual disorders. *Journal of Behavior Therapy and Experimental Psychiatry, 4,* 93–101.

O'Brien, S., Ross, L., & Christophersen, E. (1986). Primary encopresis: Evaluation and treatment. *Journal of Applied Behavior Analysis, 19,* 137–145.

O'Connor, K., Helverson, J., & Chambliss, C. (1995). The effects of peer mediation training on third party facilitated conflict resolution. *Resources in Education,* ERIC/CASS, CG026159.

O'Farrell, T., Cutter, H., Choquette, K., Floyd, F., & Bayog, R. (1992). Behavioral marital therapy for male alcoholics: Marital and drinking adjustment during the two years after treatment. *Behavior Therapy, 23,* 529–549.

O'Farrell, T., Cutter, H., & Floyd, F. (1985). Evaluating behavioral marital therapy for male alcoholics: Effects on marital adjustment and communication from before to after treatment. *Behavior Therapy, 16,* 147–167.

Office of Technology Assessment (1982). Technology transfer at the National Institutes of Health, a technical memorandum (Library of Congress Catalog Card Number 82-600529). Washington, DC: U.S. Government Printing Office.

Office of Technology Assessment (1994, September). *Identifying health technologies that work: Searching for evidence* (Publication no. OTA-H-608). Washington, DC: U.S. Government Printing Office.

O'Flynn, A. (1983). Meta-analysis of behavioral intervention effects on weight loss in the obese. Doctoral dissertation, University of Connecticut, 1982. *Dissertation Abstracts International, 43,* 2502B. (University Microfilms International No. 83-02083.)

Ogles, B., Lambert, M., & Sawyer, J. (1995). Clinical significance of the National Institute of Mental Health Treatment of Depression Collaborative Research Program data. *Journal of Consulting and Clinical Psychology, 63,* 321–326.

O'Hanlon, W. (1993). *Solution-oriented therapy.* New York: Norton.

O'Hanlon, W., & Weiner-Davis, M. (1989). *In search of solutions: A new direction in psychotherapy.* New York: Norton.

Okun, M. A., Olding, R., & Cohn, C. (1990). A meta-analysis of subjective well-being interventions among elders. *Psychological Bulletin, 108,* 257–266.

Opland, E. (1995). *Clinical quality information systems.* MCC Behavioral Care, Eden Prairie, Minnesota.

Orlinsky, D., & Howard, K. (1986). The relation of process and outcome in psychotherapy. In S. Garfield & A. Bergin (Eds.), *Handbook of psychotherapy and behavior change.* New York: Wiley.

Oss, M. (1998). What are "Best practices," anyway? *Behavioral Health Management, 18,* 3.

Ost, L. (1978). Fading vs systematic desensitization in the treatment of snake and spider phobia. *Behaviour Research and Therapy, 16,* 379–389.

Ost, L. (1988). Applied relaxation vs progressive relaxation in the treatment of panic disorder. *Behaviour Research and Therapy, 26,* 13–22.

Ost, L., Salkovskis, P., & Hellstrom, K. (1991). One-session therapist-directed exposure vs. self-exposure in the treatment of spider phobia. *Behavior Therapy, 22,* 407–422.

Ost, L., & Westling, B. (1995). Applied relaxation vs. cognitive behavior therapy in the treatment of panic disorder. *Behaviour Research and Therapy, 33,* 145–158.

Otto, M., Pollack, M., Sachs, G., Reiter, S., Meltzer-Brody, S., & Rosenbaum, J. (1993). Discontinuation of benzodiazepine treatment: Efficacy of cognitive behavioral therapy for patients with panic disorder. *American Journal of Psychiatry, 150,* 1485–1490.

Oxman, E., & Chambliss, C. (1998). *Reducing psychiatric inpatient violence through solution-focused group therapy.* Annual American Psychological Association convention, San Francisco.

Pallak, M. (1987, August). *Psychotherapy and public policy (or Daniel enters the lion's den).* Invited address presented at the 95th annual convention of the American Psychological Association, New York.

Paquin, M. (1977). The treatment of a nail-biting compulsion by covert sensitization in a poorly motivated client. *Journal of Behavior Therapy and Experimental Psychiatry, 8,* 181–183.

Parker, J. C., Frank, R. G., Beck, N. C., Smarr, K. L., Buescher, K. L., Phillips, L. R., Smith E. I., Anderson, S. K., & Walker, S. E. (1988). Pain management in rheumatoid arthritis patients: A cognitive-behavioral approach. *Arthritis and Rheumatism, 31,* 593–601.

Parloff, M. (1980). Psychotherapy research: An anaclitic depression. *Psychiatry, 43,* 279–293.

Paterson, C. (1988). Progressive relaxation: A meta-analysis. Doctoral dissertation, Ohio State University, 1987. *Dissertation Abstracts International, 48,* 2790B.

Patterson, D. (1994). Outpatient services, the managed care view. In R. K. Schreter, S. S. Sharfstein, & C. A. Schreter (Eds.), *Allies and adversaries: The impact of managed care on mental health services.* Washington, DC: American Psychiatric Press.

Patterson, G. (1982). *Coercive family process.* Eugene, OR: Castalia.

Patterson, G., & Chamberlain, P. (1992). A functional analysis of resistance (A neobehavioral perspective). In H. Arkowitz (Ed.), *Why don't people change: New perspectives on resistance and noncompliance.* New York: Guilford Press.

Patterson, G., Chamberlain, P., & Reid, J. (1982). A comparative evaluation of a parent-training program. *Behavior Therapy, 13,* 638–650.

Patterson, G., & Gullion, M. (1968). *Living with children: New methods for parents and teachers.* Champaign, IL: Research Press.

Patterson, G., Hops, H., & Weiss, R. (1975). Interpersonal skills training for couples in early stages of conflict. *Journal of Marriage and the Family, 37,* 295–303.

Paul, G. (1967a). Insight vs. desensitization in psychotherapy two years after termination. *Journal of Consulting Psychology, 31,* 333–348.

Paul, G. (1967b). Outcome research in psychotherapy. *Journal of Consulting Psychology, 31,* 109–188.

Paul, G. (1967c). The strategy of outcome research in psychotherapy. *Journal of Consulting Psychology, 31,* 109–118.

Paul, G., & Shannon, D. (1966). Treatment of anxiety through systematic desensitization in therapy groups. *Journal of Abnormal Psychology, 71,* 124–135.

Payne, A., & Blanchard, E. B. (1995). A controlled comparison of cognitive therapy and self-help support groups in the treatment of irritable bowel syndrome. *Journal of Consulting and Clinical Psychology, 63,* 779–786.

Peck, R. (1997). Report card woes: NAMI vs. behavioral MCOs. *Behavioral Health Management, 17,* 31.

Peed, S. Roberts, M., & Forehand, R. (1977). Evaluation of the effectiveness of a standardized parent training program in altering the interactions of mothers and their non-compliant children. *Behavior Modification, 1,* 323–350.

Pekarik, G., & Wierzbicki, M. (1986). The relationship between clients' expected and actual treatment duration. *Psychotherapy, 23,* 532–534.

Pennebaker, J. W., Kiecolt-Glaser, J. K., & Glaser, R. (1988). Disclosure of trauma and immune function: Health implications for psychotherapy. *Journal of Consulting and Clinical Psychology, 56*(2), 239–245.

Perls, F., Hefferline, R., & Goodman, P. (1951). *Gestalt therapy.* New York: Julian Press.

Perry, J. (1992). Problems and considerations in the valid assessment of personality disorders. *American Journal of Psychiatry, 149,* 1645–1653.

Perry, S. (1994). In reply [letter to the editor]. *Archives of General Psychiatry, 51,* 247–248.

Perry, S., & Fishman, B. (1993). Depression and HIV: How does one affect the other. *JAMA, 270,* 2609–2610.

Perry, S., Fishman, B., Jacobsberg, I., et al. (1992). Relationships over one year between lymphocyte subsets and psychosocial variables among adults with infection by human immunodeficiency virus. *Archives of General Psychiatry, 49,* 396–401.

Phelps, R., Eisman, E., & Kohout, J. (1998). Psychological practice and managed care: Results of the CAPP Practitioner Survey. *Professional Psychology: Research and Practice, 29,* 31–36.

Phillips, E. (1985). *A guide for therapists and patients to short-term psychotherapy.* Springfield, IL: Thomas.

Phillips, E. (1988). Length of psychotherapy and outcome: Observations stimulated by Howard, Kopta, Krause, and Orlinsky. *American Psychologist, 43,* 669–670.

Pierce, C. (1975). Enuresis and encopresis. In A. Freeman, H. Kaplan, & B. Sadock (Eds.), *Comprehensive textbook of psychiatry* (vol. 2) (2d ed.) (pp. 2116–2125). Baltimore, MD: Williams & Wilkins.

Pinto, D., McGuigan, J., Scholl, A., & Chambliss, C. (1996). *Psychologists' and psychiatrists' attitudes toward managed care.* Annual Pennsylvania Psychological Association convention, Philadelphia, June.

Piper, W., & Perrault, E. (1989). Pretherapy preparation for group members. *International Journal of Group Psychotherapy, 39,* 17–34.

Pipher, M. (1996). *Reviving Ophelia.* Grosset Books.

Polder, S. (1986). A meta-analysis of cognitive behavior therapy. Doctoral dissertation, University of Wisconsin-Madison. *Dissertation Abstracts International, 47,* 1736B.

Posavac, E. (1980). Evaluations of patient education programs: A meta-analysis. *Evaluation and the Health Professions, 3,* 47–62.

Posavac, E., Sinacore, J., Brotherton, S., Helford, M., & Turpin, R. (1985). Increasing compliance to medical treatment regimens: A meta-analysis of program evaluation. *Evaluation and the Health Professions, 8,* 7–22.

Poynter, W. (1994). *The preferred provider's handbook.* New York: Brunner/Mazel.

Preston, J. (1997). *Shorter term treatments for borderline personality disorders.* Oakland, CA: New Harbinger.

Preston, J. & Johnson, J. (1995). *Clinical psychopharmacology made ridiculously simple,* MedMaster: Miami, Florida.

Preston, J., Varzos, N., & Liebert, D. (1995). *Every session counts: Making the most of your brief therapy.* San Luis Obispo, CA: Impact.

Prince Henry Hospital (1983). A treatment outline for depressive disorders: The quality assurance project. *Australian and New Zealand Journal of Psychiatry, 17,* 129–146.

Prioleau, L., Murdock, M., & Brody, N. (1983). An analysis of psychotherapy versus placebo studies. *The Behavioral and Brain Sciences, 6,* 275–310.

Prochaska, J., & Norcross, J. (1983). Contemporary psychotherapists: A national survey of characteristics, practices, orientations, and attitudes. *Psychotherapy: Theory, Research and Practice, 20,* 161–173.

Prochaska, J., & Norcross, J. (1994). *Systems of psychotherapy: A transtheoretical analysis* (3d ed.). Pacific Grove, CA: Brooks/Cole.

Quirk, M., Strosahl, K., Erdberg, P., & Kreilkamp, T. (1995). Personality feedback consultation to families in a managed mental health care practice. *Professional Psychology: Research and Practice, 26,* 27–32.

Rachman, S., Cobb, J., Grey, S., McDonald, B., Mawson, D., Sartory, G., & Stern, R. (1979). The behavioural treatment of obsessional-compulsive disorders, with and without clomipramine. *Behaviour Research and Therapy, 17,* 467–478.

Rachman, S., & Wilson, G. (1980). *The effects of psychological therapy* (2d ed.). New York: Pergamon Press.

Randolph, E., Eth, S., Glynn, S., Paz, G., Leong, G., Shaner, A., Strachan, A., Van Vort, W., Escobar, J., & Liberman, R. (1994). Behavioural family management in schizophrenia: Outcome from a clinic-based intervention. *British Journal of Psychiatry, 144,* 501–506.

Reed, L., Myers, E., & Scheidemandel, P. (1972). *Health insurance and psychiatric care: Utilization and cost.* Washington, DC: American Psychiatric Association.

Rehm, L., Fuchs, C., Roth, D., Kornblith, S., & Romano, J. (1979). A comparison of self-control and assertion skills treatments of depression. *Behavior Therapy, 10,* 429–442.

Reich, J., & Neenan, P. (1986). Principles common to different short-term psychotherapies. *American Journal of Psychotherapy, 40,* 62–69.

Renfrey, G., & Spates, C. R. (1994). Eye movement desensitization: A partial dismantling study. *Journal of Behavior Therapy and Experimental Psychiatry, 25,* 231–239.

Reynolds, K., Ogiba, S. & Chambliss, C. (1998). *Client and therapist expectations of psychotherapy.* ERIC Counseling and Personnel Services.

Rice, L. (1974). The evocative function of the therapist. In D. Wexler & L. Rice (Eds.), *Innovations in client centered therapy* (pp. 289–312). New York: Wiley Interscience.

Richardson, L., & Austad, C. (1991). Realities of mental health practice in managed-care settings. *Professional Psychology: Research and Practice, 22,* 52–59.

Roberts, A., Kewman, D., Mercier, L. et al. (1993). The power of nonspecific effects in healing: Implications for psychosocial and biological treatment. *Clinical Psychology Review, 13,* 375–391.

Robins, L., & Regier, D. (Eds.) (1991). *Psychiatric disorders in America.* New York: Free Press.

Robinson, L., Berman, J., & Neimeyer, R. (1990). Psychotherapy for the treatment of depression: A comprehensive review of controlled outcome research. *Psychological Bulletin, 108,* 30–49.

Rockwell, W., & Pinkerton, R. (1982). Single-session psychotherapy. *American Journal of Psychotherapy, 36,* 32–40.

Rodin, J., & Langer, E. (1976). Health effects of control on nursing home residents, *Journal of Personality and Social Psychology, 34,* 191–199.

Rodwin, A. (1995). Conflicts in managed care. *New England Journal of Medicine, 332*(9), 604–607.

Rogers, C. (1951). *Client centered therapy.* Boston: Houghton Mifflin.

Rogers, C. (1970). *Carl Rogers on encounter groups.* New York: Harper & Row.

Roller, B., Schnell, C., & Welsch, M. (1982). Organization and development of group psychotherapy programs in health maintenance organizations. (Mimeographed.) In *Proceedings.* Detroit, MI: Group Health Institute.

Rosenbaum, R. (1983, August). Life-cycle psychotherapies and health maintenance organizations. Paper presented at the American Psychological Association convention, Anaheim, CA.

Rosenthal, R. (1991a). Meta-analysis: A review. *Psychosomatic Medicine, 53,* 247–271.

Rosenthal, R. (1991b). *Meta-analytic procedures for social research* (rev. ed.). Thousand Oaks, CA: Sage.

Rosenzweig, S. (1936). Some implicit common factors in diverse methods in psychotherapy. *American Journal of Orthopsychiatry, 6,* 412–415.

Rothbaum, B. (in press). A controlled study of eye movement desensitization and reprocessing in the treatment of posttraumatic stress disordered sexual assault victims. *Bulletin of the Menninger Clinic.*

Rudd, T. (1998). Firm targets major depression treatment with pilot disease management effort. *Managed Behavioral Health News, 4,* 1.

Rush, A., Beck, A., Kovacs, M., & Hollon, S. (1977). Comparative efficacy of cognitive therapy and pharmacotherapy in the treatment of depressed patients. *Cognitive Therapy Research, 1,* 17–37.

Rush, D., & Hollon, S. (1991). Depression. In B. Beitman & G. Klerman (Eds.). *Integrating pharmacotherapy and psychotherapy* (pp. 121–142). Washington, DC: American Psychiatric Press.

Russell, G. (1979). Bulimia nervosa: An ominous variant of anorexia nervosa. *Psychological Medicine, 9,* 429–448.

Russell, R., & Wise, F. (1976). Treatment of speech anxiety by cue-controlled relaxation and desensitization with professional and paraprofessional counselors. *Journal of Counseling Psychology, 23,* 583–586.

Russo, F. (1997). Can the government prevent divorce? *Atlantic Monthly, 280,* 28–42.

Rutan, J., & Cohen, A. (1989). Group psychotherapy. In A. Lazare (Ed.), *Outpatient psychiatry: Diagnosis and treatment.* Baltimore, MD: Williams & Wilkins.

Rutkin, A., & Garay, E. (1997). ERISA preempts many HMO claims. *The National Law Journal,* February 14, 1997, p. 4.

Ryan, V., Krall, C., & Hodges, W. (1976). Self-concept change in behavior modification. *Journal of Consulting and Clinical Psychology, 44,* 638–645.

Sabin, J. (1998). Public-sector managed behavioral health care: I. Developing an effective case management program. *Psychiatric Services, 49,* 31–33.

Sabin, J., & Daniels, N. (1994). Determining "medical necessity" in mental health practice. *Hastings Center Report, 24*(6), 5–13.

Saeman, H. (1996). Psychologists frustrated with managed care, economic issues, but plan to hang tough. *The National Psychologist, 5,* 1–2.

Saeman, H. (1998). Psychologists' incomes plummet. *The National Psychologist, 7,* 1–2.

Safren, S., Heimberg, R., & Juster, H. (1997). Clients' expectancies and their relationship to pretreatment symptomatology and outcome of cognitive-behavioral group treatment for social phobia. *Journal of Consulting and Clinical Psychology, 65,* 694–698.

Saile, H., Burgmeier, R., & Schmidt, L. (1988). A meta-analysis of studies on psychological preparation of children facing medical procedures. *Psychology and Health, 2,* 107–132.

Salkovskis, P. (1985). Obsessional-compulsive problems: A cognitive-behavioural analysis. *Behaviour Research and Therapy, 23,* 571–583.

Sanders, M., & Dadds, M. (1993). *Behavioral family intervention.* Boston: Allyn & Bacon.

Sargent, J., Solbach, P., Coyne, L., Spohn, H., & Segerson, J. (1986). Results of a controlled experimental outcome study of non-drug treatment for the control of migraine headache. *Journal of Behavioral Medicine, 9,* 291–323.

Sarvis, M., Dewees, S., & Johnson, R. (1959). A concept of ego-oriented psychotherapy. *Psychiatry, 22,* 277–287.

Sarwer, D., & Durlak, J. (1997). A field trial of the effectiveness of behavioral treatment for sexual dysfunctions. *Journal of Sex and Marital Therapy, 23,* 87–97.

Saunders, S., Howard, K., & Orlinsky, D. (1989). The Therapeutic Bond Scales: Psychometric characteristics and relationship to treatment effectiveness. *Psychological Assessment, 4,* 323–330.

Saunders, T., Driskell, J., Hall, J., & Salas, E. (1996). The effect of stress inoculation training on anxiety and performance. *Journal of Occupational Health Psychology, 1,* 170–186.

Saunders, T., Driskell, J., Johnston, J., & Salas, E. (1996). The effect of stress inoculation training on anxiety and performance. *Journal of Occupational Health Psychology, 1,* 170–186.

Schade, C., Jones, E., & Wittlin, B. (1998). A ten-year review of the validity and clinical utility of depression screening. *Psychiatric Services, 49,* 55–61.

Scheff, T. (1975). *Labelling madness.* Englewood Cliffs, NJ: Prentice-Hall.

Schilling, B. (1993). Integrated care: An applied model with lessons for reform. *Practitioner Focus,* August, 4–5.

Schlesinger, M. (1989). Striking a balance: Capitation, the mentally ill, and public policy. *New Directions for Mental Health Services, 43,* 97–116.

Schmidt, F. (1992). What do data really mean? Research findings, meta-analysis, and cumulative knowledge in psychology. *American Psychologist, 47,* 1173–1181.

Scholl, A., Pinto, D., McGuigan, J., Murgia, C., Luscian, C., Garner, C., & Chambliss, C. (1996). Psychiatrists' and psychologists' attitudes toward managed care. *Resources in Education,* ERIC/CASS.

Schover, L., & LoPiccolo, J. (1982). Treatment effectiveness for dysfunctions of sexual desire. *Journal of Sex and Marital Therapy, 8,* 179–197.

Schreter, R. (1997). Essential skills for managed behavioral health care. *Psychiatric Services, 48*(5), 653–658.

Schreter, R., & Budman, S. (1997). Office-based services. In R. K. Schreter, S. S. Sharfstein, & C. A. Schreter (Eds.), *Managing care, not dollars: The continuum of mental health services.* Washington, DC: American Psychiatric Press.

Schreter, R., Sharfstein, S., & Schreter, C. (1994). *Allies and adversaries: The impact of managed care on mental health services.* Washington, DC: American Psychiatric Press.

Scogin, F., Bynum, J., Stephens, G., & Calhoon, S. (1990). Efficacy of self-administered treatment programs: Meta-analytic review. *Professional Psychology: Research and Practice, 21,* 42–47.

Scogin, F., & McElreath, L. (1994). Efficacy of psychosocial treatments for geriatric depression: A quantitative review. *Journal of Consulting and Clinical Psychology, 62,* 69–74.

Scotti, J., Evans, I., Meyer, L., & Walker, P. (1991). A meta-analysis of intervention research with problem behavior: Treatment validity and standards of practice. *American Journal on Mental Retardation, 96,* 233–256.

Sederer, L., & St. Clair, R. (1989). Managed health care and the Massachusetts experience. *American Journal of Psychiatry, 146,* 1142–1148.

Segal, P., et al. (1995). The quality of psychiatric emergency evaluations and patient outcomes in county hospitals. *American Journal of Public Health, 85,* 1429–1431.

Seligman, M. (1995). The effectiveness of psychotherapy: The Consumer Reports study. *American Psychologist, 50,* 965–974.

Seligman, M., & Levant, R. (1998). Managed care policies rely on inadequate science. *Professional Psychology: Research and Practice, 29,* 211–212.

Selmi, P., Klein, M., Greist, J., Sorrell, S., & Erdman, H. (1990). Computer-administered cognitive-behavioral therapy for depression. *American Journal of Psychiatry, 147,* 51–56.

Semans, J. (1956). Premature ejaculation: A new approach. *Southern Medical Journal, 49,* 353–357.

Shadish, W. (1995). The logic of generalization: Five principles common to experiments and ethnographies. *American Journal of Community Psychology, 23,* 419–428.

Shadish, W., Montgomery, L., Wilson, P., Wilson, M., Bright, I., & Okwumabua, T. (1993). Effects of family and marital psychotherapies: A meta-analysis. *Journal of Consulting and Clinical Psychology, 61*, 992–1002.

Shadish, W., Navarro, A., Crits-Christoph, P., Jorm, A., Nietzel, M., Robinson, L., Svartberg, M., Matt, G., Siegle, G., Hazelrigg, M., Lyons, L., Prout, H., Smith, M., & Weiss, B. (1997). Evidence that therapy works in clinically representative conditions. *Journal of Consulting and Clinical Psychology, 65*(3), 355–365.

Shadish, W., & Ragsdale, K. (1996). Random versus nonrandom assignment in psychotherapy experiments: Do you get the same answer? *Journal of Consulting and Clinical Psychology, 64*, 1290–1305.

Shadish, W., Jr. (1992). Do family and marital psychotherapies change what people do? A meta-analysis of behavioral outcomes. In T. D. Cook, H. Cooper, D. S. Cordray, H. Hartmann, L. V. Hedges, R. J. Light, T. A. Louis, & F. Mosteller (Eds.), *Meta-analysis for explanation* (pp. 129–208). New York: Russell Sage Foundation.

Shadish, W., Jr., & Sweeney, R. (1991). Mediators and moderators in meta-analysis: There's a reason we don't let dodo birds tell us which psychotherapies should have prizes. *Journal of Consulting and Clinical Psychology, 59*, 883–893.

Shadle, M., & Christianson, J. (1988). The organization of mental health care delivery in HMOs. *Administration in Mental Health, 15*, 201–225.

Shapiro, D., Barkham, M., Rees, A., Hardy, G., Reynolds, S., & Startup, M. (1994). Effects of treatment duration and severity of depression on the effectiveness of cognitive-behavioral and psychodynamic-interpersonal psychotherapy. *Journal of Consulting and Clinical Psychology, 62*, 522–534.

Shapiro, A., Frick, R., Morris, L., et al. (1974). Placebo induced side effects. *Journal of Operational Psychiatry, 6*, 43–46.

Shapiro, A., & Shapiro, E. (1984a). Controlled study of pimozide vs. placebo in Tourette syndrome. *Journal of the American Academy of Child Psychiatry, 23*, 161–173.

Shapiro, A., & Shapiro, E. (1984b). Patient–provider relationships and the placebo effect. In J. D. Matarazzo, S. M. Weiss, J. A. Herd, et al. (Eds.), *Behavioral health: A handbook of health enhancement and disease prevention*. New York: Wiley.

Shapiro, A., & Shapiro, E. (1997). *The powerful placebo: From ancient priest to modern physician*. Baltimore, MD: Johns Hopkins University Press.

Shapiro, D., & Shapiro, D. (1982). Meta-analysis of comparative therapy outcome studies: A replication and refinement. *Psychological Bulletin, 92*, 581–604.

Shapiro, D., & Shapiro, D. (1983). Comparative therapy outcome research: Methodological implications of meta-analysis. *Journal of Consulting and Clinical Psychology, 51*, 42–53.

Shapiro, F. (1989). Efficacy of the eye movement desensitization procedure in the treatment of traumatic memories. *Journal of Traumatic Stress, 62*, 199–223.

Shapiro, F. (1995a). Doing our homework. *Family Therapist Networker, 19*, 49–50.

Shapiro, F. (1995b). *Eye movement desensitization and reprocessing: Basic principles, protocols, and procedures*. New York: Guilford Press.

Shapiro, L. (1994). *Short-term therapy with children*. King of Prussia, PA: Center for Applied Psychology.

Shaw, B. (1977). Comparison of cognitive therapy and behavior therapy in the treatment of depression. *Journal of Consulting and Clinical Psychology, 45*, 543–551.

Shea, M., Elkin, I., Imber, S., Sotsky, S., Watkins, J., Collins, J., Pilkonis, P., Beckham, E., Glass, D., Dolan, R., & Parloff, M. (1992). Course of depressive symptoms over follow-up: Findings from the National Institute of Mental Health Treatment of Depression Collaborative Research Program. *Archives of General Psychiatry, 49*, 782–787.

Shear, M., Pilkonis, P., Cloitre, M., & Leon, A. (1994). Cognitive behavioral treatment compared with nonprescriptive treatment of panic disorder. *Archives of General Psychiatry, 51*, 395–401.

Shectman, F. (1986). Time and the practice of psychotherapy. *Psychotherapy, 23*, 521–525.

Shlien, J., Nosak, H. & Dreikurs, R. (1962). Effect on time limits: A comparison of two psychotherapies. *Journal of Counseling Psychology, 9*, 31–34.

Shoham, V., & Rohrbaugh, M. (1997). Interrupting ironic processes. *Psychological Science, 8*, 151–153.

Shoham-Salomon, V., & Rosenthal, R. (1987). Paradoxical interventions: A meta-analysis. *Journal of Consulting and Clinical Psychology, 55*, 22–28.

Shore, K. (1995). Psychotherapists' Catch-22. *The Wall Street Journal*, February 3.

Shore, K. (1996). Coalition of Mental Health Providers presidential address. The Nurses' Managed Care March on Washington, DC, May 10.

Sifneos, P. (1979). *Short-term dynamic psychotherapy: Evaluation and technique*. New York: Plenum.

Silverman, K., Higgins, S., Brooner, R., Montoya, I., Cone, E., Schuster, C., & Preston, K. (1996). Sustained cocaine abstinence in methadone maintenance patients through voucher-based reinforcement therapy. *Archives of General Psychiatry, 53,* 409–415.

Silverman, W. (1996). Cookbooks, manuals, and paint-by-numbers: Psychotherapy in the '90s. *Psychotherapy, 33,* 207–215.

Silverman, W., & Beech, R. (1979). Are dropouts, dropouts? *Journal of Community Psychology, 7,* 236–242.

Skinner, B. (1971). *About behaviorism.* New York: Random House.

Sleek, S. (1995). Battling breast cancer through group therapy. *APA Monitor,* December, 1–2.

Sloane, R., & Staples, F. (1984). Psychotherapy versus behavior therapy: Implications for future psychotherapy research. In J. B. W. Williams & R. L. Spitzer (Eds.), *Psychotherapy research: Where are we and where should we go?* New York: Guilford Press.

Sloane, R., Staples, F., Cristol, A., Yorkston, N., & Whipple, K. (1975). *Psychotherapy versus behavior therapy.* Cambridge, MA: Harvard University Press.

Sluzki, C. (1978). Marital therapy from a systems theory perspective. In T. J. Paolino & B. S. McCrady (Eds.), *Marriage and marital therapy* (pp. 366–394). New York: Brunner/Mazel.

Smith, M. (1957). Effectiveness of symptomatic treatment of nailbiting in college students. *Psychology Newsletter, 8,* 219–231.

Smith, M., & Glass, G. (1977). Meta-analysis of psychotherapy outcome studies. *American Psychologist, 32,* 752–760.

Smith, M., Glass, G., & Miller, T. (1980). *The benefits of psychotherapy.* Baltimore, MD: Johns Hopkins University Press.

Snowden, L. (Ed.) (1982). *Reaching the underserved: Mental health needs of neglected populations.* Thousand Oaks, CA: Sage.

Snyder, D., & Wills, R. (1989). Behavioral versus insight-oriented marital therapy: Effects on individual and interspousal functioning. *Journal of Consulting and Clinical Psychology, 57,* 39–46.

Snyder, D., Wills, R., & Grady-Fletcher, A. (1991). Long-term effectiveness of behavioral versus insight-oriented marital therapy: A four-year follow up study. *Journal of Consulting and Clinical Psychology, 59,* 138–141.

Speers, R. (1962). Brief psychotherapy with college women: Technique and criteria for selection. *American Journal of Orthopsychiatry, 32,* 434–444.

Spencer, P., Gillespie, C., & Ekisa, E. (1983). A controlled comparison of the effects of social skills training and remedial drama on the conversational skills of chronic schizophrenic inpatients. *British Journal of Psychiatry, 143,* 165–172.

Sperry, L., Brill, P., Howard, K., & Grissom, G. (1996). *Treatment outcomes in psychotherapy and psychiatric interventions.* New York: Brunner/Mazel.

Spiegel, D. (1993). Psychosocial intervention in cancer. *Journal of the National Cancer Institute, 85,* 1198–1205.

Spiegel, D., Bruce, T., Gregg, S., & Nuzzarello, A. (1994). Does cognitive behavior therapy assist slow-taper alprazolam discontinuation in panic disorder? *American Journal of Psychiatry, 151,* 876–881.

Spitzer, R., Devlin, M., Walsh, B., Hassin, D., Wing, R., Marcus, M., Stunkard, A., Wadden, T., Yanovski, S., Agras, W., Mitchell, J., & Nonas, C. (1991). Binge eating disorder: To be or not to be in DSM-IV. *International Journal of Eating Disorders, 10,* 627–629.

Spitzer, R., Devlin, M., Walsh, B., Hassin, D., Wing, R., Marcus, M., Stunkard, A., Wadden, T., Yanovski, S., Agras, W., Mitchell, J., & Nonas, C. (1992). Binge eating disorder: A multisite field trial of the diagnostic criteria. *International Journal of Eating Disorders, 11,* 191–203.

Spitzer, R., & Endicott, J. (1978). Medical and mental disorder: Proposed definition and criteria. In R. L. Spitzer & D. F. Klein (Eds.), *Critical issues in psychiatric diagnosis.* New York: Raven Press.

Spoerl, O. (1975). Single-session psychotherapy. *Diseases of the Nervous System, 36,* 283–285.

Srebnik, D., Uehara, E., & Smukler, M. (1998). Field test of a tool for level-of-care decisions in community mental health systems. *Psychiatric Services, 49,* 91–97.

Standley, J. (1986). Music research in medical-dental treatment—meta-analysis and clinical applications. *Journal of Music Therapy, 23*(2), 56–122.

Stanton, M., & Shadish, W. (1997). Outcome, attrition, and family-couples treatment for drug abuse: A meta-analysis and review of the controlled, comparative studies. *Psychological Bulletin, 122,* 170–191.

Starker, S. (1988). Self-help treatment books: The rest of the story. *American Psychologist, 43,* 599–600.

Starr, P. (1982). *The social transformation of American medicine.* New York: Basic Books.

Steenbarger, B. (1994). Duration and outcome in psychotherapy: An integrative review. *Professional Psychology, 25,* 111–119.

Stein, D., & Lambert, M. (1984). On the relationship between therapist experience and psychotherapy outcome. *Clinical Psychology Review, 4*, 127–142.

Stein, D., & Lambert, M. (1995). Graduate training in psychotherapy: Are therapy outcomes enhanced? *Journal of Consulting and Clinical Psychology, 63*, 182–196.

Stein, M. (1992). Future directions for brain, behavior, and the immune system. *Bulletin of the New York Academy of Medicine, 68*, 390–410.

Stein, M., Miller, A., & Trestman, R. (1991). Depression, the immune system, and health and illness: Findings in search of meaning. *Archives of General Psychiatry, 48*, 171–178.

Stein, S., Hermanson, K., & Spiegel, D. (1993). New directions in psycho-oncology. *Current Opinion in Psychiatry, 6*, 838–846.

Steinbrueck, S., Maxwell, S., & Howard, G. (1983). A meta-analysis of psychotherapy and drug therapy in the treatment of unipolar depression with adults. *Journal of Consulting and Clinical Psychology, 51*, 856–863.

Steinglass, P. (1976). Experimenting with family treatment approaches to alcoholism, 1950–1975: A review. *Family Process, 15*, 97–123.

Stevens, V., & Hollis, J. (1989). Preventing smoking relapse, using an individually tailored skills-training technique. *Journal of Consulting and Clinical Psychology, 57*, 420–424.

Stubbs, J., & Bozarth, J. (1994). The dodo bird revisited: A qualitative study of psychotherapy efficacy research. *Applied and Preventive Psychology, 3*, 109–120.

Stiles, W., Shapiro, D., & Elliott, R. (1986). Are all psychotherapies equivalent? *American Psychologist, 41*, 165–180.

Stiles, W., Shapiro, D., & Firth-Cozens, J. (1988). Do sessions of different treatments have different impacts? *Journal of Counseling Psychology, 35*(4), 391–396.

Stock, W., Okun, M., Haring, M., & Witter, R. (1985). Race and subjective well-being in adulthood. *Human Development, 28*, 192–197.

Stone, M. (1993). *Abnormalities of personality: Within and beyond the realm of treatment*. New York: Norton.

Storms, M., & Nisbett, R. (1970). Insomnia and the attribution process. *Journal of Personality and Social Psychology, 16*, 319–328.

Strupp, H. (1989). Psychotherapy: Can the practitioner learn from the researcher? *American Psychologist, 44*, 717–724.

Strupp, H. (1995). The psychotherapist's skills revisited. *Clinical Psychology: Science and Practice, 2*, 70–74.

Strupp, H., & Binder, J. (1984). *Psychotherapy in a new key: A guide to time-limited dynamic psychotherapy*. New York: Basic Books.

Strupp, H., & Hadley, S. (1979). Specific vs nonspecific factors in psychotherapy: A controlled study of outcome. *Archives of General Psychiatry, 36*, 1125–1136.

Stuart, R. (1969). Operant-interpersonal treatment for marital discord. *Journal of Consulting and Clinical Psychology, 33*, 675–682.

Stuart, R. (1981). *Helping couples change: A social learning approach to marital therapy*. New York: Guilford Press.

Stubbs, J., & Bozarth, J. (1994). The dodo bird revisited: A qualitative study of psychotherapy efficacy research. *Applied and Preventive Psychology, 3*, 109–120.

Sue, D., & Sue, D. (1985). Asian-American and Pacific Islanders. In P. Pedersen (Ed.), *Handbook of cross-cultural counseling and therapy* (pp. 141–146). Westport, CT: Greenwood.

Sue, S. (1995). Psychotherapeutic services for ethnic minorities: Two decades of research findings. *American Psychologist, 43*, 301–308.

Sue, S., Allen, D., & Conway, L. (1978). The responsiveness and egality of mental health care to Chicanos and Native Americans. *American Journal of Community Psychology, 6*, 137–146.

Sue, S., Wagner, N., Ja, D., Margullis, C., & Lew, L. (1976). Conceptions of mental illness among Asian and Caucasian American students. *Psychological Reports, 38*, 703–708.

Sullivan, G., Wells, K., Morganstern, H., & Leake, B. (1995). Identifying modifiable risk factors for rehospitalization: A case-control study of seriously mentally ill persons in Mississippi. *American Journal of Psychiatry, 152*, 1749–1756.

Swinson, R. P., Fergus, K., Cox, B. J., & Wickwire, K. (1995). Efficacy of telephone-administered behavioral therapy for panic disorder with agoraphobia. *Behaviour Research and Therapy, 33*, 465–469.

Szapocznik, J., Kurtines, W., Santisteban, D., & Rio, A. (1990). Interplay of advances between theory, research, and application in treatment interventions aimed at behavior problem children and adolescents. *Journal of Consulting and Clinical Psychology, 58*, 696–703.

Szapocznik, J., Rio, A., Murray, E., Cohen, R., Scopetta, M., Rivas-Vasquez, A., Hervis, O., Posada, V., & Kurtines, W. (1989). Structural family versus psychodynamic child therapy for problematic Hispanic boys. *Journal of Consulting and Clinical Psychology, 57*, 571–578.

Szasz, T. (1974). *The myth of mental illness*. New York: Harper & Row.

Talbott, J. (1981). Commentary: The emerging crisis in chronic care. *Hospital and Community Psychiatry, 32*, 447–454.

Talmon, M. (1990). *Single session therapy: Maximizing the effect of the first (and often only) therapeutic encounter*. San Francisco: Jossey-Bass.

Tarlov, A., Ware, J., Greenfield, S., Nelson, E., Perrin, E., & Zubkoff, M. (1989). The medical outcomes study: An application of methods for monitoring the results of medical care. *Journal of the American Medical Association, 262*, 928–943.

Task Force on Promotion and Dissemination of Psychological Procedures (1995, Winter). Training in and dissemination of empirically validated psychological treatments: Report and recommendations. *The Clinical Psychologist, 48*, 3–24.

Task Force on Psychological Intervention Guidelines (1995). *Template for developing guidelines: Interventions for mental disorders and psychosocial aspects of physical disorders*. Washington DC: American Psychological Association.

Telch, C., Agras, W., Rossitier, E., Wilfrey, D., & Kenardy, J. (1990). Group cognitive-behavioral treatment for the no-purging bulimic: An initial evaluation. *Journal of Consulting and Clinical Psychology, 58*, 629–635.

Telles, C., Karno, M., Mintz, J., Paz, G., Arias, M., Tucker, D., & Lopez, S. (1995). Immigrant families coping with schizophrenia: Behavioral family intervention v. case management with a low-income Spanish-speaking population. *British Journal of Psychiatry, 167*, 473–479.

Temoshok, L., Heller, B., & Saveviel, R. (1985). The relationship of psychological factors of prognostic indicators in cutaneous malignant melanoma. *Journal of Psychosomatic Research, 28*, 139–153.

Thackwray, D., Smith, M., Bodfish, J., & Meyers, A. (1993). A comparison of behavioral and cognitive-behavioral interventions for bulimia nervosa. *Journal of Consulting and Clinical Psychology, 61*, 639–645.

Tillitski, C. (1990). A meta-analysis of estimated effect sizes for group versus individual versus control treatments. *International Journal of Group Psychotherapy, 40*, 215–224.

Tischler, G. (1990). Utilization management of mental health services by private third parties. *American Journal of Psychiatry, 147*, 967–973.

Trimble, J., & La Fromboise, T. (1955). American Indians and the counseling proces: Culture, adaptation, and style. In P. Pedersen (Ed.), *Handbook of cross-cultural counseling and therapy* (pp. 127–134). Westport, CT: Greenwood.

Truax, C., & Carkhuff, R. (1962). *Toward effective counseling and psychotherapy*. Chicago: Aldine.

Truax, C., & Carkhuff, R. (1964). The old and the new: Theory and research in counseling and psychotherapy. *Personality and Guidance Journal, 42*, 860–866.

Truax, C., & Carkhuff, R. (1965). Client and therapist transparency in the psychotherapeutic encounter. *Journal of Counseling Psychology, 12*, 3–9.

Truax, C., & Carkhuff, R. (1967). *Toward effective counseling and psychotherapy*. Chicago: Aldine.

Truax, C., & Mitchell, K. (1971). Research on certain therapist interpersonal skills in relation to process and outcome. In A. E. Bergin & S. L. Garfield (Eds.), *Handbook of psychotherapy and behavior change*. New York: Wiley.

Trull, T., Nietzel, M., & Main, A. (1988). The use of meta-analysis to assess the clinical significance of behavior therapy for agoraphobia. *Behavior Therapy, 19*, 527–538.

Turley, M. (1984). A meta-analysis of informing mothers concerning the sensory and perceptual capabilities of their infants. Doctoral dissertation, University of Texas, Austin, 1983. *Dissertation Abstracts International, 45*, 1B. (University Microfilms International No. 84-14461.)

Turnbull, H. (Ed.) (1981). *The least restrictive alternative: Principles and practices*. Washington, DC: American Association on Mental Deficiency.

Turner, J., & Clancy, S. (1988). Comparison of operant-behavioral and cognitive behavioral group treatment for chronic low back pain. *Journal of Consulting and Clinical Psychology, 56*, 261–266.

Turner, J. A., Clancy, S., McQuade, K. J., Cardenas, D. D. (1990). Effectiveness of behavioral therapy for chronic low back pain. *Journal of Consulting and Clinical Psychology, 58*, 573–579.

Turner, R. (1973). Conditioning treatment of nocturnal enuresis: Present status. In I. Kolvin, R. MacKeith, & S. Meadow (Eds.), *Bladder control and enuresis* (pp. 195–210). Philadelphia: Lippincott.

Turner, S., Beider, D., & Jacob, R. (1994). Social phobia: A comparison of behavior therapy and atenolol. *Journal of Consulting and Clinical Psychology, 62*, 350–358.

Uehara, H., Smukler, M., & Newman, F. (1994). Linking resource use to consumer level of need: Field test of the Level of Need-Care Assessment (LONCA) method. *Journal of Consulting and Clinical Psychology, 62*, 695–709.

van Balkom, A., van Oppen, P., Vermeulen, A., Nauta, N., Vorst, H., & van Dyck, R. (1994). A meta-analysis on the treatment of obsessive compulsive disorder: A comparison of anti-depressants, behaviour and cognitive therapy. *Clinical Psychology Review, 14*, 359–381.

van Oppen, P., de Haan, E., van Balkom, A., Spin-hoven, P., Hoogduin, K., & van Dyck, R. (1995). Cognitive therapy and exposure in vivo in the treatment of obsessive compulsive disorder. *Behaviour Research and Therapy, 33*, 379–390.

Veronen, L., & Kilpatrick, D. (1983). Stress management for rape victims. In D. Meichenbaum & M. B. Jaremko (Eds.), *Stress reduction and prevention* (pp. 341–374). Plenum: New York.

Voelker, R. (1997). Quality standards intend to bring psychiatry, primary care into closer collaboration. *Journal of the American Medical Association, 277*, 366.

Vuori, H. (1987). Patient satisfaction—an attribute or indicator of the quality of care? *Quality Review Bulletin, 13*.

Wachtel, P. (1993). *Therapeutic communication: Principles and effective practice*. New York: Guilford Press.

Wallace, C., & Liberman, R. (1985). Social skills training for patients with schizophrenia: A controlled clinical trial. *Psychiatry Research, 15*, 239–247.

Wallace, C., Nelson, C., Liberman, R., Aitchison, R., Lukoff, D., Elder, J., & Ferris, C. (1980). A review and critique of social skills training with schizophrenic patients. *Schizophrenia Bulletin, 6*, 42–63.

Walter, H. (1971). Placebo versus social learning effects in parent training procedures designed to alter the behaviors of aggressive boys. Unpublished doctoral dissertation, University of Oregon.

Walter, H., & Gilmore, S. (1973). Placebo versus social learning effects in parent training procedures designed to alter the behavior of aggressive boys. *Behavior Therapy, 4*, 361–377.

Walter, J., & Peller, J. (1994). *Becoming solution-focused in brief therapy*. New York: Brunner/Mazel.

Walworth, J., O'Donnell, P., Pearson, J., & Solem, E. (1987). Quality assurance I—what are employers demanding? Paper presented at the meeting of the Group Health Association of America, Washington, DC.

Wampler, K. (1983). Bringing the review of literature into the age of quantification: Meta-analysis as a strategy for integrating research findings in family studies. *Journal of Marriage and the Family, 44*, 1009–1023.

Wampold, B., Mondin, G., Moody, M., & Ahn, H. (1997). The flat earth as a metaphor for the evidence for uniform efficacy of bona fide psychotherapies: Reply to Crits-Christoph (1997) and Howard et al. (1997). *Psychological Bulletin, 122*, 226–230.

Wampold, B., Mondin, G., Moody, M., Stich, F., Benson, K., & Ahn, H. (1997). A meta-analysis of outcome studies comparing bona fide psychotherapies: Empirically, "All must have prizes." *Psychological Bulletin, 122*, 203–215.

Wardle, J., Hayward, P., Higgitt, A., Stabl, M., Blizard, R., & Gray, J. (1994). Effects of concurrent diazepam treatment on the outcome of exposure therapy in agoraphobia. *Behaviour Research and Therapy, 32*, 203–215.

Ware, J., Jr., Brook, R., Rogers, W., Keeler, E., Davies-Ross, A., Sherbourne, C., Goldberg, G., Camp, P., & Newhouse, J. (1986). Comparison of health outcomes at a health maintenance organization with those of fee-for-service care. *Lancet, 1*, 1017–1022.

Ware, N., Lachicotte, W., Kirschner, S., Cortes, D., & Good, B. (1998). *Clinician experiences of managed mental health care: A re-reading of the threat*. Medical Anthropology Quarterly, in press.

Watzlawick, P., Beavin, J., & Jackson, D. (1967). *Pragmatics of human communication: A study of interactional patterns, pathologies, and paradoxes*. New York: Norton.

Watzlawick, P., Weakland, J., & Fisch, R. (1974). *Change: Principles of problem formation and problem resolution*. New York: Norton.

Waxler-Morrison, N., Hislop, T., & Mears, B. (1992). Effects of social relationships on survival for women with breast cancer: A prospective study. *Social Science and Medicine, 33*, 177–183.

Weed, L. (1991). *Knowledge coupling: New premises and new tools for medical care and education*. New York: Springer-Verlag.

Wegner, D., & Smart, L. (1997). Deep cognitive activation: A new approach to the unconscious. *Journal of Consulting and Clinical Psychology, 65*, 984–995.

Weinberger, J. (1995). Common factors aren't so common: The common factors dilemma. *Clinical Psychology: Science and Practice, 2*, 45–68.

Weiner-Davis, M. (1990, November). *Brief solution-oriented therapy with couples* [Workshop]. Sponsored by Group Health Cooperative Mental Health Services, Seattle, WA.

Weisz, J., Weiss, B., Alicke, M., & Klotz, M. (1987a). Effectiveness of psychotherapy with children and adolescents: A meta-analysis for clinicians.

Journal of Consulting and Clinical Psychology, 55, 542–549.

Weisz, J., Weiss, B., Alicke, M., & Klotz, M. (1987b). Effects of psychotherapy with children and adolescents revisited: A meta-analysis of treatment outcome studies. *Psychological Bulletin, 117,* 450–468.

Weisz, J., Weiss, B., & Donenberg, G. (1992). The lab versus the clinic. *American Psychologist, 47,* 1575–1585.

Wells, K., & Egan, J. (1988). Social learning and systems family therapy for childhood oppositional disorder: Comparative treatment outcome. *Comprehensive Psychiatry, 29,* 138–146.

Wells, K., & Forehand, R. (1985). Conduct and oppositional disorder. In P. Bornstein & A. Kazdin (Eds.), *Handbook of clinical behavior therapy with children,* New York: Dorsey.

Wells, K., Griest, D., & Forehand, R. (1980). The use of a self-control package to enhance temporal generality of a parent training program. *Behavior Research Therapy, 18,* 347–353.

Wells, K. B., Hosek, S., & Marquis, S. (1992). Effects of preferred provider options on use of outpatient mental health services by three employee groups. *Medical Care, 30,* 412–427.

Wells, K., Rogers, W., Davis, J., et al. (1993). Quality of care for hospitalized depressed elderly before and after prospective payment system. *American Journal of Psychiatry, 150,* 1799–1805.

Wheeler, M., & Hess, K. (1976). Treatment of juvenile obesity by successive approximation control of eating. *Journal of Behavior Therapy and Experimental Psychiatry, 7,* 235–241.

Whitehead, J., & Lab, S. (1989). A meta-analysis of juvenile correctional treatment. *Journal of Research in Crime and Delinquency, 26,* 276–295.

Wilfley, D. (1989). Interpersonal analyses of bulimia : Normal weight and obese. Unpublished doctoral dissertation, University of Missouri, Columbia.

Wilfley, D., Agras, W., Telch, C., Rossiter, E., Schneider, J., Cole, A., Sifford, L., & Raeburn, S. (1993). Group cognitive-behavioral therapy and group interpersonal psychotherapy for the nonpurging bulimic: A controlled comparison. *Journal of Consulting and Clinical Psychology, 61,* 296–305.

Wilkins, W. (1986). Placebo problems in psychotherapy research: Social psychological alternatives to chemotherapy concepts. *American Psychologist, 41,* 551–556.

Williams, J., Rabkin, J., Remien, R., et al. (1991). Multidisciplinary baseline assessment of homosexual men with and without human immuno-deficiency virus infection. *Archives of General Psychiatry, 48,* 124–130.

Williams, S., & Falbo, J. (1996). Cognitive and performance-based treatments for panic attack in people with varying degrees of agoraphobic disability. *Behaviour Research and Therapy, 34,* 253–264.

Wilson, G. (1976). Obesity, binge eating and behavior therapy: Some clinical observations. *Behavioral Therapy, 7,* 700–701.

Wilson, L., Simson, S., & McCaughey, K. (1983). The status of preventive care for the aged: A meta-analysis. *Prevention in Human Services, 3,* 38.

Wilson, S., Becker, L., & Tinker, R. (1995). Eye movement desensitization and reprocessing (EMDR) treatment for psychologically traumatized individuals. *Journal of Consulting and Clinical Psychology, 63,* 928–937.

Wiltz, N., Jr. (1969). *Modifications of behaviors of deviant boys through parent participation in a group technique.* Unpublished doctoral dissertation, University of Oregon.

Wiltz, N., & Patterson, G. (1974). An evaluation of parent training procedures designed to alter inappropriate aggressive behavior in boys. *Behavior Research Therapy, 5,* 215–221.

Winegar, N. (1992). *The Clinician's Guide to Managed Health Care,* Binghamton, New York: Haworth Press.

Wittman, W., & Matt, G. (1986). Meta-Analyse als Integration von Forschungsergebnissen am Beispiel deutschsprachliger Arbeiten zur Effektivitaet von Psychotherapie [Meta-analysis as a method for integrating psychotherapy studies in German-speaking countries]. *Psychologische Rundschau, 37,* 20–40.

Wolberg, L. (1967). *Short-term psychotherapy.* New York: Grune & Stratton.

Wolberg, L. (1977). *The technique of psychotherapy* (3d ed.). New York: Grune & Stratton.

Wolff, S. (1961). Symptomatology and outcome of pre-school children with behavior disorders attending a child guidance clinic. *Journal of Child Psychology and Psychiatry, 2,* 269–276.

Wolff, S. (1967). Behavioral characteristics of primary school children referred to a psychiatric department. *British Journal of Psychiatry, 113,* 885–893.

Wolff, T. (1969). Undergraduates as campus mental health workers. *Personnel and Guidance Journal, 48,* 294–304.

Wolpe, J. (1969). *The practice of behavior therapy.* New York: Pergamon Press.

Wolpe, J., & Lazarus A. (1966). *Behavior therapy techniques*. New York: Pergamon Press.

Woody, G., Luborsky, L., McLellan, A., & O'Brien, C. (1990). Corrections and revised analyses for psychotherapy in methadone maintenance patients. *Archives of General Psychiatry, 47*, 788–789.

Woody, G., Luborsky, L., McLellan, A., O'Brien, C., Beck, A., Blaine, J., Herman, I., & Hole, A. (1983). Psychotherapy for opiate addicts: Does it help? *Archives of General Psychiatry, 40*, 639–645.

Woody, G., McLellan, A., Luborsky, L., & O'Brien, C. (1995). Psychotherapy in community methadone programs: A validation study. *American Journal of Psychiatry, 192*, 1302–1308.

Woy, R., & Efran, J. (1972). Systematic desensitization and expectancy in the treatment of speaking anxiety. *Behaviour Research and Therapy, 10*, 43–49.

Wright, L., Schaefer, A., & Solomons, G. (1979). *Encyclopedia of pediatric psychology*. Baltimore, MD: University Park Press.

Wright, L., & Walker, C. (1978). A simple behavioral treatment program for psychogenic encopresis. *Behaviour Research and Therapy, 16*, 209–212.

Wroten, D. (1997). The Impact of ERISA. *Business Insurance*, February 10, 1997, Crain Communications; Chicago, Illinois.

Wylie, M. (1994). Endangered species. *The Family Therapy Networker*, March–April, 20–27, 30–33.

Wyman, R. (1990). Involving children as active agents of their own treatment: A meta-analysis of self-management training. Doctoral dissertation, Fuller Theological Seminary, School of Psychology. *Dissertation Abstracts International, 51*, 0B.

Young, G., & Morgan, R. (1972a). Childhood enuresis: Termination of treatments by patients. *Community Medicine, 127*, 247–250.

Young, G., & Morgan, R. (1972b). Non-attending enuretic children. *Community Medicine, 127*, 158–159.

Young, J., Kristel, O., & Chambliss, C. (1997). The effectiveness of high school peer helper training. *Resources in Education*, ERIC/CASS, CG027711.

Zach, J., & Cohen, M. (1993). Managing mental health costs is a balancing act. *Personnel Journal, 72*(3), 107–111.

Zimet, C. (1979). Developmental task and crisis groups: The application of group psychotherapy to maturational processes. *Psychotherapy: Theory, Research and Practice, 16*, 2–8.

Zimet, C. (1989). The mental health care revolution: Will psychology survive? *American Psychologist, 44*, 703–708.

Zimmer, D. (1987). Does marital therapy enhance the effectiveness of treatment for sexual dysfunction? *Journal of Sex and Marital Therapy, 13*, 193–209.

Zultowski, W., & Catron, D. (1976). Students as curriculum advisers: Reinterpreted. *Journal of Community Psychology, 4*, 89–95.

Zunker, V., & Brown, W. (1966). Comparative effectiveness of student and professional counselors. *Personnel and Guidance Journal, 44*, 738–743.

Zusman, J. (1967). Some explanations of the changing appearance of psychotic patients: Antecedents of the social breakdown syndrome concept. *International Journal of Psychiatry, 3*, 216–237.

Zwanziger, J., & Auerbach, R. (1991). Evaluating PPO performance using prior expenditure data. *Medical Care, 29*, 142–151.

Zweben, A., Pearlman, S., & Li, S. (1988). A comparison of brief advice and conjoint therapy in the treatment of alcohol abuse: The results of the marital systems study. *British Journal of Addiction, 83*, 899–916.

INDEX